SINOPHONE STUDIES

Global Chinese Culture

GLOBAL CHINESE CULTURE

David Der-wei Wang, Editor

Michael Berry, *Speaking in Images:*
Interviews with Contemporary Chinese Filmmakers

Sylvia Li-chun Lin, *Representing Atrocity in Taiwan:*
The 2/28 Incident and White Terror in Fiction and Film

Michael Berry, *A History of Pain:*
Literary and Cinematic Mappings of Violence in Modern China

Alexa Huang, *Chinese Shakespeares:*
A Century of Cultural Exchange

SINO PHONE STUDIES

A Critical Reader

EDITED BY

SHU-MEI SHIH,

CHIEN-HSIN TSAI,

AND BRIAN BERNARDS

Columbia University Press

New York

Columbia University Press wishes to express its appreciation for assistance given by the Chiang Ching-kuo Foundation for International Scholarly Exchange and Council for Cultural Affairs in the publication of this book.

Columbia University Press
Publishers Since 1893
New York   Chichester, West Sussex
cup.columbia.edu
Copyright © 2013 Columbia University Press
All rights reserved

Library of Congress Cataloging-in-Publication Data
  Sinophone studies : a critical reader / edited by Shu-mei Shih, Chien-hsin Tsai, and Brian Bernards.
    p. cm.—(Global Chinese culture)
  Includes bibliographical references and index.
  ISBN 978-0-231-15750-6 (cloth : alk. paper)—ISBN 978-0-231-15751-3 (pbk.)—
  ISBN 978-0-231-52710-1 (electronic)
 1. Chinese diaspora. 2. Chinese–Foreign countries–Ethnic identity. 3. Chinese–Foreign countries–Intellectual life. 4. National characteristics, Chinese. I. Shi, Shumei, 1961–II. Tsai, Chien-hsin, 1975–III. Bernards, Brian.

  DS732.S57 2013
  305.800951–dc23

2012011978

∞

Columbia University Press books are printed on permanent and durable acid-free paper.
This book was printed on paper with recycled content.

Printed in the United States of America

COVER IMAGE: *Untitled* by Hung Chang (c. 1959). Oil on canvas. By permission of the estate of Hung Chang.

References to Internet Web sites (URLs) were accurate at the time of writing. Neither the author nor Columbia University Press is responsible for URLs that may have expired or changed since the manuscript was prepared.

Contents

Acknowledgments

Before the term *Sinophone* was coined with critical valence and historical specificity, many scholars, thinkers, and writers had expressed ideas and sentiments akin to what are now more critically and historically envisioned as Sinophone studies. The definitional and historical considerations of the Sinophone owe much to the insights of these scholars and writers from various parts of the world, some of whose works are anthologized here. The editors would like to thank all those who came before and helped us frame Sinophone studies, ranging from those who debated on "South Seas color" in colonial Malaya to those who critiqued Chineseness in different parts of the world (including China), and to also thank those scholars who have in recent years joined the adventure in the emergent field of Sinophone studies with great gusto and sophistication.

This volume would not have been possible without the support of the series editor, David Der-wei Wang; the executive editor, Jennifer Crewe at the Columbia University Press; and the supportive and constructive reviews by two anonymous readers.

Shu-mei Shih would like to personally thank fellow travelers of Sinophone studies in Malaysia (Fah Hing Chong and Choon Bee Lim), Taiwan (Kim Tong Tee, Hsinya Huang, and Chien-chung Chen), the United Kingdom (Margaret Hillenbrand), Italy (Claudia Pozzana), Hong Kong (Mirana May Szeto, P. K. Leung, Kam Louie, Sze Wei Ang, and K. C. Lo), and those in different parts of the United States (David Der-wei Wang, Rey Chow, Ping-hui

Liao, David Eng, Shuang Shen, Eric Hayot, E. K. Tan, and Jing Tsu, among others). Over the years, she has presented her work on Sinophone studies in various institutions across the United States, Asia, and Europe, and she is grateful for all those who patiently listened to and responded to her presentations. Almost always the discussions and debates exceeded allotted times, and this expressed passion has sustained her work in this area through the years. Finally, she would like to acknowledge the important contribution of both of the coeditors (Chien-hsin Tsai and Brian Bernards), but her greatest gratitude is to Brian Bernards, who shouldered the heaviest task of putting together the manuscript in the final stages of work.

Chien-hsin Tsai first thanks his coeditors, Shu-mei and Brian, for their professionalism and enthusiasm that have seen the project through its different stages. Shu-mei's critical vision and tireless devotion are instructive in bringing together constructive dialogues from varied fields and making this a most stimulating and rewarding collaboration. Brian's acumen and conscientiousness are sources of valuable inspiration. Chien-hsin also wishes to thank Andrea Bachner, Yvonne Sung-sheng Chang, Lingchei Letty Chen, Eileen Cheng-yin Chow, Benjamin Frederick, Carlos Rojas, Jing Tsu, Michelle Yeh, and especially David Der-wei Wang for their unwavering support.

Brian Bernards wishes to thank the Department of East Asian Languages and Cultures at the University of Southern California, the UCLA Asia Institute, the University of California Pacific Rim Research Program, Fulbright-Hays, the National University of Singapore's Asia Research Institute, and Professor Quah Sy Ren of Nanyang Technological University for providing critical logistical and/or financial support that benefitted this project. Brian would also like to acknowledge the support and assistance of his coeditors, Shu-mei and Chien-hsin, and all of his cocontributors, especially Tee Kim Tong, David Wang, and E. K. Tan, for their comments, feedback, and expertise.

The editors would also like to collectively acknowledge the following authors and publishers for granting permission to abridge and reprint their work:

Ien Ang, "Can One Say No to Chineseness?" first appeared in *boundary 2* 25, no. 3 (Autumn 1998): 223–242. Abridged and reprinted with the permission of Duke University Press.
Rey Chow, "On Chineseness as a Theoretical Problem" first appeared in *boundary 2* 25, no. 3 (Autumn 1998): 1–24. Abridged and reprinted with the permission of Duke University Press.
Rey Chow, "Things, Common/Places, Passages of the Port City: On Hong Kong and Hong Kong Author Leung Ping-kwan" first appeared in

differences 5, no. 3 (Fall 1993): 179–204. Abridged and reprinted with the permission of Duke University Press.

Leo Ou-fan Lee, "On the Margins of the Chinese Discourse" first appeared in *Daedalus* 120, no. 2 (Spring 1991): 207–226. Abridged and reprinted with the permission of MIT Press Journals.

Shu-mei Shih, "Against Diaspora: The Sinophone as Places of Cultural Production" is adapted and updated from *Visuality and Identity: Sinophone Articulations Across the Pacific* (Berkeley: University of California Press, 2007), 1–39. Revised and reprinted with the permission of the University of California Press.

Wei-ming Tu, "Cultural China: The Periphery as Center" first appeared in *Daedalus* 120, no. 2 (Spring 1991): 1–32. Abridged and reprinted with the permission of MIT Press Journals.

Gungwu Wang, "Chineseness: The Dilemmas of Place and Practice" first appeared in *Cosmopolitan Capitalists: Hong Kong and the Chinese Diaspora at the End of the Twentieth Century*, ed. Gary G. Hamilton (Seattle: University of Washington Press, 1999), 118–134. Abridged and reprinted with the permission of the University of Washington Press.

Ling-chi Wang, "The Structure of Dual Domination: Toward a Paradigm for the Study of the Chinese Diaspora in the United States" first appeared in *Amerasia Journal* 21, no. 1 (1995): 149–169. Abridged and reprinted with the permission of the UCLA Asian American Studies Center Press.

Introduction

What Is Sinophone Studies?

SHU-MEI SHIH

Sinophone studies situates itself at the intersection of a variety of academic discourses and fields that have either not been linked with each other or placed into productive relationships and comparisons in the past. Without implying any hierarchy in sequence, the first is the study of colonial language cultures in previous or current colonies led by Anglophone and Francophone studies that examine the legacies of British and French imperialism in Asia, the Caribbean, and Africa. Other competitive empires from about the same historical period such as those of the United States, Germany, and, later, Japan, as well as those empires that had reached their height in earlier periods such as those of Spain and Portugal, have received much less attention in postcolonial studies, not to mention those that were not recognized as such at all, especially that of China. Only in the last ten years or so have American historians of China led the way to document, analyze, and theorize the history and nature of Qing China (1644–1911) as an Inner Asian empire to produce what has been called a "New Qing history." Their meticulous research on Qing military conquest and political colonization of vast areas beyond "China proper"—Mongolia, Xinjiang, and Tibet—has generated a new conception of China's role in world history of the last two hundred years from that of victim to that of empire.

This belated identification of China as empire compels one to query the reasons for its previous misrecognition, which leads one to question the very criteria for the definition of empire prior to this turn in the historiography of China. The obvious answer is that the models of modern empires have largely been European and oceanic, whereas Qing expansion was non-European and occurred largely on the continental land mass. "European" not merely as geographical designation but as connoting values of superiority, rationality, and enlightenment, which Europe supposedly embodied and spread through its colonial enterprises, did not apply to China, hence Qing imperialism was conveniently left out. German philosopher of history G. W. F. Hegel ingeniously linked the sea with Europeanness: "The European state is truly European only in so far as it has links with the sea."[1] He went on to emphasize that Europe's maritime principle is the means and reason for European dominance and superiority, whereas Asia is limited by its landlocked status, for which "the sea is without significance."[2] The maritime principle—the embracing of the elements of "flux, danger, and destruction"—brings to fulfillment the European drive to "found" colonies and is therefore the basis of European colonialism. Lacking this principle, and therefore lacking the "outlet" for "life to step beyond itself," the Asiatic by definition could not found colonies and be empires.[3] One may answer Hegel's provocation in at least two ways: by emphasizing the long maritime history of China, as many scholars have done, to prove that China was not landlocked as presumed,[4] and by recognizing a different mode of colonialism for China, of what may be called "continental colonialism," and thus challenging the inevitable coupling of modern imperial dominance with the oceanic mode of expansion.

Historians of China have explained the belated recognition with an entirely different rationale, as the fault of hegemonic Chinese historiography, which constructed a retrospective, uninterrupted narrative of China as victim, even though most of that narrative was based on events after the mid-nineteenth century. In this narrative of victimhood, the seeds of China's weakness were found to have been germinating throughout the Qing Dynasty, and therefore eighteenth-century Qing expansionism was "without significance," to borrow Hegel's phrase. It was a convenient way to commit Qing imperialism to oblivion so that a coherent narrative of victimhood could be retrospectively constructed and solidified. This victim narrative was crucial in legitimizing the rising tide of Chinese nationalism from the Republican revolution through the present day, even though China is emerging as one of the most powerful countries in the contemporary world. Should Qing imperialism be brought up to counter the victim narrative, however, Han nationalists can also conveniently qualify it as Manchu and assert that Republican revolution was an event against Manchu degradation of the Han Chinese nation. Han nationalists, in other words, can choose to claim late-Qing victimhood and deny mid-Qing imperialism, using either the discourse of pan-Chinese nationalism or Han nationalism. All the while, the fact of the matter is that present-day China has inherited all the colonial spoils from the Qing empire, with the exception of Outer Mongolia.

The continental colonialism of Qing expanded the territory of "China proper" by more than twofold, and this super-enlarged territorial "integrity" was largely inherited by the Republic of China (1911–1949) and People's Republic of China (established in 1949). Continental colonialism then is a Qing legacy that continues up to the present, and it underscores the contours of a major area for Sinophone studies as the study of colonized peoples and their cultures—now national minority peoples or, in the official lingo, "minority nationalities"—within the nation-state of China. By virtue of its continental nature, colonized territories not able to attain independence from China have been systematically incorporated into the nation-state. While Francophone studies has as its object ex-colonies that are independent or colonies that remain dependent but are geographically located outside of France proper, the colonial legacies of Qing China continue to be played out largely *within* the nation-state of China due to the continental nature of China's colonialism. Sinophone studies has as one of its objects the culture, history, and society of minority peoples who have acquired or are forced to acquire the standard Sinitic language of Mandarin, often at the expense of their native languages. The Chinese government abolished bilingual education in Xinjiang in 2009, for instance. This is the colonial context of Sinophone studies.

The second area with which Sinophone studies is engaged in dialogue is the study of the dispersal of imperial language cultures around the world in the so-called diaspora studies. From the outset, it should be made clear that Sinophone studies is alert to the limits of the diasporic paradigm. The term *diaspora*, when applied to those with power, is largely a euphemism that covers up the systematic and widespread violence against native peoples that accompanied the settlement of imperial subjects, such as the French in Quebec, the British in the United States and Australia, and the Spanish and Portuguese in the Americas. This form of settlement falls clearly under the category of settler colonization, not diaspora. Settler colonialism is, in this sense, the dark historical underside of the so-called diaspora of imperial subjects. The violence of settler colonialism was more often forgotten than otherwise, because the settlement had happened a long time ago, which supposedly renders ambiguous as to who has priority to claim the nation, the "nation" being the settlers' creation to begin with. This is the first psychosocial dynamic of the dominant, colonial settler or otherwise, that can be described as a willful amnesia exercised on the past. Additionally, the violent condition of settler colonialism has not ended in most of these places, now in combination with internal colonialism against not only indigenous peoples but also ethnic minorities in contemporary nation-states. This is the second psychosocial dynamic of the dominant that can be described as a disavowal of the present. The two psychosocial procedures of amnesia and disavowal are two sides of the same coin, mutually justifying each other to maintain the status quo of settler colonial (Hispanic, Anglo-Saxon, Han, or otherwise) supremacy in various settler colonies.

In China, the continuous, large-scale, state-sponsored migration and settlement of the dominant Han Chinese to the territories of Tibet, Xinjiang (literally meaning the "new dominion"), and Inner Mongolia, as well as to the southwestern regions inhabited by various indigenous peoples, can be viewed as a comparable case, again through a process of continental colonialism that takes the form of settler-cum-internal colonialism. The land-based, state-sponsored settlement makes diaspora an improbable category here, not only because the colonies are contiguous in geography with the metropole, but also because this Han "diaspora" is not occurring in the context of duress as with the Jewish diaspora. These Han settlers are largely motivated to migrate to these "frontier" regions for economic reasons, not unlike most settler colonizers throughout history in different parts of the world. In many parts of these large "frontier" regions, the Hans are gradually becoming—if not already have become—the majority over the native peoples. This massive Han migration and settlement has spawned a process of Hanification, as well as Han-centric development, and has profoundly altered the cultural, linguistic, political, economic, and religious landscapes of these areas, not to mention increased volatility in ethnic relations, as witnessed by the uprisings and riots in Tibet and Xinjiang in 2008 and 2009.

Prior to the Qing, the migration of the Hans in large numbers had mainly been through the sea routes to Taiwan and Southeast Asia, which had also produced situations of settler colonialism, albeit in layered colonial conditions due to European presence. When the Ming loyalists arrived in Taiwan in the seventeenth century, Taiwan was a Dutch colony. From the occupation by the Dutch to the present, there has been a systematic and widespread oppression of the Austronesian indigenous peoples in Taiwan by what can be called a *serial* colonialism where the Dutch, Japanese, and Han colonizers in turn took up the job of colonial control and oppression via what Italian Marxist Antonio Gramsci has called both wars of maneuver (military conquest and domination through violence) and wars of position (ideological and cultural inculcation and control).[5] Indigenous communities in Taiwan continue to be stricken with alcoholism, out-migration, economic hardship, and cultural threat even as indigenous consciousness and multicultural awareness are on the rise.

The Han settlers in parts of Southeast Asia, locally called the Hua or the Hoa, prior to the arrival of European colonizers could also be considered settler colonies. Southeast Asia, or "Nanyang" in the Chinese imaginary, has historically been the place where the Han Chinese went to acquire a livelihood, and most desirably, a fortune. Philip Kuhn's study *Chinese Among Others* shows the extensive and continuous emigration of Chinese peoples from the southern coastal areas of China to the region, after Zheng He's successful expeditions there in the early fifteenth century and roughly since around the time Columbus reached America, underscoring how Chinese emigration constitutes an important factor for the global maritime trade connecting Asia to the Americas and Europe. Qing emperor Kangxi's 1684 edict explains why it was important to lift the maritime ban, intermittently imposed and abolished through the centuries, and promote maritime trade and associated migration not only for the sake of "popular livelihood" and the "economic prosperity of Fujian and Guangdong provinces," but also "to enhance state revenue from merchant profits."[6] With or without the imperial court's sanctions, Chinese emigrants left for Southeast Asia to become port managers, customs collectors, city builders, tax farmers, and trading middlemen, becoming, after the arrival of European colonialism, the "essential coadjutors" of Western colonialism.[7] They were so successful that their financial power sometimes exceeded that of the European colonizers or the native elites.[8]

Before the competition and suppression by European colonialism, however, some Chinese emigrants actually set up self-governing, territorial regimes with armed militia forces in Malaya and West Borneo.[9] "Lan Fang Republic," established by Hakkas from Canton in today's Western Kalimantan, was supposed to have been in existence for more than a hundred years, until the Dutch destroyed it. Such collective effect of emigration by merchants, laborers, as well as outlaws, is akin to settler colonialism until the arrival of the Europeans, and maybe even through the European colonial period, because it was during the European period that the migration from China reached its peak. The practice was so widespread and the situation was so well known that it led to none other than the prominent late Qing reformer and a doyen of modern Chinese thought, Liang Qichao, to declare in 1906: "In the hundred or more kingdoms of the Nanyang, the majority of the population are descended from the Yellow Emperor. Whether from the standpoint of geography or history, they are natural colonies of our people."[10] After all, Nanyang consisted of "barbarian islands" inhabited by "barbarians,"[11] and whoever got there should be able to take "natural colonies." The occasion was Liang's hagiography of eight Chinese colonizers in Southeast Asia in an essay entitled "Biographies of Eight Great Men in Chinese Colonialism," where he celebrated the lives of eight Chinese sultans and monarchs across Southeast Asia. The experience of Chinese emigration to Southeast Asia, in sum, is decidedly different from that to the Western world, even though there were also contract laborers and coolies involved.[12] Kuhn concludes that we can consider this history of emigration as "China's own form of overseas expansion."[13] Considering the middleman identity of many Chinese emigrants there under European colonialism, we might also consider this a kind of "middlemen settler colonialism" that exerts power over the local populations under putative control by the Europeans.

"Chinese diaspora" as a universal category is therefore problematic in many ways.[14] First, "diaspora" is a euphemism that diverts attention from the violence of settler colonialism and thus standardizes amnesia and disavowal as the necessary condition of settler colonizer's hegemony. The situations in Taiwan and Southeast Asia are different to the extent that Taiwan, like Singapore, continues to be a Han-dominant society, whereas the Hua are now minorities in most Southeast Asian countries with the exception of some periods of Malayan history prior to the independence of Malaysia. Second, the idea of the "Chinese diaspora" also ties the Hans in Taiwan and Southeast Asia to the Chinese "homeland" even after centuries have passed, and presumes cultural dependence on, if not political loyalty to, China. But the Han peoples in Taiwan and Southeast Asia are not *Zhongguoren* (Chinese nationals), a term usually mistranslated as "the Chinese." The Chinese Malaysians call themselves the "Ma Hua" and their Hokkien rendering of Chineseness is Tionghoa, not the version from China, Zhonghua.[15] Unless we equate "being Chinese" with being "Han" (though China has at least 55 other officially recognized ethnic groups) and confuse it again with being a "Chinese national" (though there are many different kinds of Chinese peoples in different parts of the world with all different nationalities), we need to use the term *Zhongguoren/the Chinese* with much greater caution and specificity and be aware of the variety of ways of being Hua and Sinophone, Taiwanese, Malaysian, or otherwise.

The third field with which Sinophone studies will have productive dialogue is ethnic studies or minority studies. Wherever the Hans have migrated over the centuries (as coolies, indentured or contract laborers, merchants, students, immigrants, or multinational capitalists) and become an ethnicized and racialized Hua minority, their maintenance and creolization of their various Sinitic languages and cultures—predominantly Teochiu, Fukienese, and Cantonese in earlier periods, and more pervasively Mandarin today—constitutes the basis for a particular aspect of Sinophone studies as the study of Sinitic-language cultures outside China and across the world. Places such as the United States, Britain, Germany, Australia, and Canada have seen Sinophone cultures to be either vibrant or vanishing, with earlier immigrants having localized more and more thoroughly over generations and with new immigrants continuously replenishing the coffers of Sinophone cultural productions.[16] The change of political fortunes for the Hua people after the independence of the Southeast Asian nation-states also renders them a minority in these countries in so far as their political and cultural power is not commensurate with their economic power, and they are perniciously subjected to state-sponsored ethnocentrism. But Sinophone culture was and is not only produced by the Hua people but also by people of various ethnicities, and thus it is defined not by ethnicity (though ethnicity and language sometimes correspond) but by language. With the rise of China, one can anticipate the rise of an official version of the Sinophonie, similar to the French official version of the Francophonie, where the officially sanctioned standard Mandarin—ironically and appropriately called Hanyu, the language of the Hans—acquires absolute value in and of itself.[17] The complexities and challenges facing Sinitic-language cultures and communities in terms of their location, definition, production, and dissemination are inevitably manifold, such that one needs always to particularize a given cultural practice and explore its meanings in relation to a given place at a given historical moment.

The emphasis here on the resonances with ethnic studies has at least two implications. It foregrounds the non-diasporic, local nature of Sinophone culture in a given nation-state as an integral part of that nation-state's multiculturalism and multilingualism. For instance, Sinophone American culture is American culture, and Sinitic languages spoken in the United States should be considered as minority American languages. It understands that, even in its strongest nostalgia for the mythical or actual "China," Sinophone culture is place-based and belongs to the place where it is produced. Nostalgia for China in Sinophone American culture is nostalgia produced from the experience of living in the United States, hence it is a form of American nostalgia. Sinophone culture is a transnational phenomenon as one can find it everywhere in the world, but in its specific expression and practice, it is different from place to place. Sinophone culture is therefore transnational in constitution and formation but local in practice and articulation.

Sinophone Multilingualism

In the past few years, scholars have used the term *Sinophone* for largely denotative purposes to literally mean "Chinese-speaking" or "written in Chinese." Sau-ling Wong used it to designate Chinese American literature written in Chinese as opposed to English;[18] Qing historians Pamela Kyle Crossley, Evelyn S. Rawski, and Jonathan Lipman described "Chinese-speaking" Muslims in China as Sinophone Muslims (also known as the Hui) as opposed to Uyghurs Muslims who speak Turkic languages;[19] and Patricia Schiaffini and Lara Maconi distinguished between Tibetan writers who write in the Tibetan script and Sinophone Tibetan writers.[20] Even though the main purpose of these scholars' use of the term is denotative, their underlying intent is to clarify contrast by the act of naming: Wong exposes the Anglophone bias of Asian Americanist scholars and shows that Asian American literature is multilingual; Crossley, Rawski, and Lipman emphasize that Muslims in China have divergent languages, histories, and experiences; Schiaffini and Maconi suggest the predicament of Tibetan writers who write in the "language of the colonizer" and whose identity is bound up with linguistic differences.[21] In my earlier use of the term, I wished to emphasize, with specific reference to Sinophone Malaysian and Indonesian literature, the necessity of differentiating Sinophone literature as minor literature as opposed to Chinese literature as major literature. I attempted, by the term *Sinophone*, to give a name to those bodies of texts that have been given the torturous and confusing nomenclature "literature in Chinese" (*huayu wenxue*, written outside China) as opposed to "Chinese literature" (*Zhongguo wenxue*, written inside China). The semantic ambiguity of the two terms arises out of the use of "Chinese" in both cases, which is too homogenizing to make any critical work possible.[22] My model at the time was what had been known as Mahua literature—literally, Malaysian literature written by the Hua or written in Huayu or Huawen—which belongs to Malaysian national literature, but is marginalized in Malaysia and everywhere else. Sinophone Malaysian literature is a minor literature not in the sense that it is a minor literature written in the major language (à la Deleuze and Guattari), but a minor literature written in a minority language within a given nation state, bidding for linguistic and cultural heterogeneity within the presumed monolingual, Malay-dominant, national literature of Malaysia.

The confluence of these different, denotative uses of the term *Sinophone* has allowed me to consider the Sinophone as the product of discrepant but interrelated historical processes involving different colonial formations (continental, internal, settler), the movements of Hua people, and the dissemination of Sinitic languages by will or by force, producing minor and minority cultures on the margins of China and Chineseness within the geopolitical boundary of China as well as without, in various locations across the world. The Sinophone spaces are scattered around the world and Sinophone culture is produced in different locations, but in each site the Sinophone is a place-based, local culture, in dialogue with other cultures of that location. This multi-local Sinophone needs also to be examined from many different disciplinary perspectives—such as literature, film, anthropology, and history—thus Sinophone studies is inherently a multidisciplinary and inter-disciplinary inquiry. This current volume has chosen to focus more on lit-erature because literature has been a privileged genre in Sinophone cultures across the world, but the study of Sinophone cinema, music, performance, newspaper publishing, and so forth needs to be promoted as well.

One main difference in this conception of the Sinophone from its previ-ous uses as "Chinese-speaking" resides in the assertion that, just as the Sinitic languages are multi-tongued, Sinophone is not monophonic but polyphonic. Sinitic languages belong to the so-called Sino-Tibetan language family (Han-zang yuxi), which is one of the largest in the world. The Tibetan part of the family refers to "Tibeto-Burman" languages that include almost four hun-dred languages in total spoken across China, Tibet, South Asia, and parts of Southeast Asia. The "Sino" part of the language family refers to the Sinitic languages, where the so-called dialects are actually different languages or topolects, as Victor Mair has shown.[23] Sinitic language communities there-fore refer to all the communities that speak Mandarin, Cantonese, Fukienese, Hakka, Teochiu, and so forth, and hence Sinophone studies is a study involv-ing many languages and Sinophone literature is itself a multilingual literature. It is not easy for the Sinophone to be monolingual or monological, and it inevitably registers the multiple tongues spoken in constant interaction and creolization with indigenous and other local languages in a given place. Sino-phone Malaysian writers, for instance, often incorporate English, Malay, and Tamil into their work, not to mention often crossing between different Sinitic languages such as Mandarin, Hokkien, and Cantonese. In this sense, Sino-phone literature should be translated in Mandarin as *Huayu yuxi wenxue*, lit-eratures of the Sinitic language family, to denote the multiplicity of languages within the family, not *Huayu wenxue* or *Huawen wenxue*, literature written in standard Mandarin.

The production of a standard language is the inevitable consequence of the process of nation formation, as it was and continues to be in China where the standard language was called the "national language" (*guoyu*) dur-ing the Republican period and then the "common language" (*putonghua*) since. Equally, Malay became the national language of Malaysia only after its independence, and it is continuously promoted in place of English, Mandarin, and Tamil. This is to say that the actual linguistic cartography of the world, though filled with nations that assert linguistic homogeneity in the form of the standard "national language," is much messier. The predominant language of nineteenth-century Han immigrants to the United States was, for instance, Cantonese, and they did not call themselves *Zhongguoren* but "Tang persons" (*tongyin*). They became "Chinese" or "Chinamen" only by racialized assigna-tion after their arrival in a hostile United States. The predominant languages of Chinese Malaysians are Teochiu, Hokkien, and Cantonese, with all the local inflections and hybridizations, and they call themselves Hua, not "Chinese," and call the standard Mandarin the Huayu (the language of the Hua), not Hanyu (the language of the Han). The predominant Sinitic language of Taiwan is Minnan, while that of Chinese Koreans is Shandongese and Chinese Italians Wenzhouhua, and so forth. Between and among the forty or so varieties, Sinitic languages are so diverse that their speakers are often mutually incomprehensible to each other, not to mention the inevitable creolization and localization of these languages that has occurred and continues to occur in various localities outside China. Languages are, after all, living entities. The Sinophone, in short, is polyphonic and multilingual.

When the spoken Sinitic languages are rendered in written form, the standard script is most often used, and this standard script is shared by all Sinophone communities. This situation is similar to Arabic, spoken as many mutually intelligible or unintelligible languages but written in one standard, classical script. However, Cantonese, Taiwanese, Hokkien, and other Sinitic languages offer a wide range of different characters from the standard script, with new characters added each day to register the varieties of Sinitic languages, not to mention that the standard Sinitic script was never immune to the pressures of localization and hybridization. In Sinophone Taiwan literature, for instance, newly invented characters register Minnan, Hakka, and aboriginal sounds; in Sinophone Malaysian literature, Malay, English, and Tamil words and expressions pressure the "purity" of the Sinitic script desired by such writers as Li Yong-ping; and in Sinophone French literature, French syntax and expression ineluctably find their way into the standard script. In the case of Sinophone minority literature in China, words from various minority languages such as Tibetan, Mongolian, Thai, or Arabic appear frequently either transliterated or translated, heterogenizing the standard script to a significant extent. Sinitic languages in their localized uses in sound and in script therefore pose important challenges to the fictive construction of Han ethnolinguistic homogeneity on the one hand, and the arbitrary valuation of what is the standard language or the national language, on the other. The Sinophone is therefore not only of many sounds (polyphonic) but also of multiple orthographies (polyscriptic).

Monolingualism of the national language shares with nationalism the three paradoxes that Benedict Anderson has attributed to the latter: it is supposed to be modern, but it retroactively creates a genealogy of antiquity to justify itself and is thus atavistic; it is supposed to be universal, but its concrete manifestations are particular; it has political power but is poor and incoherent as a philosophy.[24] Monolingualism of the national language is, in short, deterministic, atavistic, and philosophically weak, foreclosing present and future potentialities of linguistic diversity and richness. In contrast, linguistic communities are open and changing communities where memberships fluctuate, languages mutate or even disappear, and dynamics among languages and their usages constantly transform each language. French philosopher Etienne Balibar makes an important point when he notes that the "language community is a community *in the present*, which produces the feeling that it has always existed, but which lays down no destiny for the successive generations." The linguistic community, furthermore, has a "strange plasticity," and "it is always possible to appropriate several languages and to turn oneself into a different kind of bearer of discourse and of the transformations of language."[25] Sinophone studies takes as its premise the plasticity of Sinitic languages to no predetermined destinies, even to the extent that the field of Sinophone studies might reach its demise at the limit. Hence it is important to recognize that Sinophone cultures can be vibrant or vanishing, and neither is a phenomenon to either celebrate or lament. Sinophone cultures and communities exist, period, and they deserve to be studied.

Historical Processes

To sum up, Sinophone studies takes as its objects of study *the Sinitic-language communities and cultures outside China as well as ethnic minority communities and cultures within China where Mandarin is adopted or imposed.* These linguistic communities, as can be gleaned from the previous discussion, are largely formed through three interrelated historical processes of continental colonialism, settler colonialism, and (im)migration, with these processes sometimes intersecting or overlapping with each other. To elaborate further:

Continental Colonialism: Unlike Spanish, Portuguese, British, French, and British colonialisms that established colonies mainly overseas via an oceanic trajectory, China's colonies or internal colonies are products of continental colonialism.

The territories of Mongolia, Tibet, and Xinjiang (which was previously called Zungharia in the north and the Tarim Basin in the south) were incorporated and annexed by the Qing Empire in the eighteenth century through a series of colonial wars leading to an extensive and well-run colonial administration. For its expressed interest in interethnic relationships within the empire, recent Qing historiography has been dubbed the "ethnic turn in Chinese Studies." Sinophone studies situates itself within this ethnic turn as the study of Sinitic language, especially the standard Hanyu, cultures by ethnic minorities in China. Mongols, Manchus, Tibetans, and many other ethnic peoples speak multiple languages. They are Sinophone to the extent that they speak and write in Mandarin, a willingly acquired or forcefully imposed language. Other minority communities such as those in the Southwestern border areas also form multilingual communities that resist or adapt to pressures of Han Chinese assimilation in different ways and to different degrees.

The closest parallel to these minority Sinophone communities within China might be found in post-Soviet states such as Georgia, Ukraine, and Kazakhstan that are Russophone through a process of continental colonialism during the Czarist and Soviet periods. They share in common, for instance, the more recent legacy of a particular socialist version of multiculturalism and its eventual demise. In the case of Inner Mongolia, Tibet, and Xinjiang, however, they are not yet postcolonial, hence their cultural and political projects tend to be centered on anticolonial or decolonial efforts, similar to those of the indigenous peoples in the United States. In this sense, Sinophone aboriginal literature from Taiwan might offer the best parallel example with Sinophone Tibetan literature or Sinophone Uyghur literature. An analysis of the particular nature of continuously existing continental colonial conditions is therefore very much in order whenever we analyze Sinophone cultural materials from these so-called "frontier" regions, bearing in mind that these areas are designated "frontiers" from the Han-centric perspective comfortably ensconced in a centuries-old "central plain-ism" (zhongyuan zhongxin zhuyi). This book includes several chapters on minority literature from China, which show how ethnic minority writers painfully negotiate between languages and cultures to write in the dominant language of the Han. The paradigm of "minor literature," as set up by Deleuze and Guattari, works well with this body of works, in that this minor literature is written in the majority language, it is political in nature, and it often takes on a collective value.[26]

Settler Colonialism: The category of settler colonialism applies to countries where the settlers continue to be holders of major forms of institutional, political, economic, and cultural power. The large influx of Han Chinese today to Xinjiang and Tibet that is tilting the balance of demographics to Han favor may be considered a new form of settler colonialism that operates seamlessly with continental colonialism. Immigrants from China arrived on the island of Taiwan beginning in the seventeenth century and proceeded to colonize the aboriginal Austronesian peoples, even though Taiwan had previously been subjected to Dutch colonialism, and later to Japanese colonialism, followed by a new regime from China after World War II. The Han Taiwanese in Taiwan speak Mandarin, Hakka, and Hoklo, while the indigenous peoples speak a variety of Austronesian languages as well as the language of the colonizer, Mandarin. It is a situation of a layered colonialism, but the power of the Han Taiwanese over the aborigines remains uncontested. Furthermore, Taiwan is increasingly marginalized internationally and subject to the rising power of China, which some may consider a new form of colonial relationship. Francophone Quebec, a settler colony later subjected to British imperialism, is in a certain sense similar to Taiwan's serial and layered colonial condition—both settler colonial and subjected or beholden to another power. Since Taiwan is a major site of Sinophone literature, several chapters on Taiwan literature are included in this volume, including one on aboriginal writers' negotiation with Han Taiwanese hegemony.

Han Chinese immigrants speaking different Sinitic languages settled in British colonial Malaya, and, as mentioned earlier, wielded immense economic and cultural power before and after the British arrival. In Sinophone Malaysian literature, most notably in the rainforest trilogy by Taiwan-based writer Chang Kuei-hsing, we see a powerful critique of Han immigrants' settler colonial practices on the land and people of Malaya. After Malaysia's independence, Singapore was eventually established as a separate nation-state, where the Hua hold major political and economic power, but Sinophone culture is not the dominant culture. It is perhaps a historical irony that compared to Sinophone Malaysian literature, which can boast of an unbroken and vibrant genealogy of writing from the colonial period to the present, Sinophone Singaporean writing appears to have lost some of its sense of urgency. The fact that postcolonial Singapore adopted English as the national language, even though each citizen is allowed free expression in his or her "mother tongue," appears to have led to Sinophone Singaporean literature's not being the most desired language of expression. Sinophone literature in Singapore therefore must always be examined in conjunction with Anglophone literature in the context of the official policy of multlingualism on the one hand and the globalizing impulses of the city-state on the other.

(Im)migration: Emigration, migration, and immigration from China have occurred over centuries, and there are old and new Sinophone communities where they settled all across the world. Philip Kuhn's *Chinese Among Others* documents this history quite thoroughly. This historical process affects not only those countries where there is a significant settlement of immigrants from China such as Malaysia (about 26 percent of the population), but also where the immigrants clearly constitute a minority, such as the United States and elsewhere. In these receiving countries, Chinese immigrants are usually not holders of major institutionalized forms of power, wherein lies its distinction from settler colonialism. In the cases of Malaysia and the Philippines, however, Chinese Malaysians and Chinese Filipinos wield considerable economic power, though not political power. These conditions of relative power will need to be calibrated in detail when one studies Sinophone Malaysian and Sinophone Filipino cultures. This body of Sinophone literature in a given

nation-state constitutes minority literature written in minority languages, hence it is not the Deleuzean "minor literature," such as the minor literature written in the majority's language by Sinophone aboriginal writers of Taiwan.

Overview of This Book

These three historical processes can overlap and intersect, and the distinctions are useful but not absolute. Overall, the delineation of the contours of Sinophone studies here is a historical and place-based one, showing that the Sinophone is not a unifying category but a heterogeneous formation calibrated by the time and place specificities of each practice and articulation.

These three historical determinations also largely guide the selection of objects and topics of research for Sinophone studies in this volume. Prior to a more concrete delineation of Sinophone studies as a field, scholars had explored, from different locations and intellectual viewpoints, the meanings and implications of being on the margins of China and Chineseness. Their frameworks included "the wandering Chinese," "diaspora," "the structure of dual domination," "cultural China," and so on, and we include excerpts of some of these widely read essays in the section entitled "Discrepant Perspectives" to register their efforts to describe this marginality that did not seem to fit neatly into any existing area of study. In the opening section entitled "Issues and Controversies," we include excerpts from another set of widely read essays that have been particularly provocative in challenging existing paradigms and offering unorthodox ways of articulating or resisting "Chineseness" across Australia, Hong Kong, Malaysia, Taiwan, and the United States. Two new chapters written for this volume join the aforementioned ones in this section. Together, the chapters in these two sections show the contentious interpretations of what it means to be on the margins of China and Chineseness or Malaysia and Malaysianness, and so forth, and they exemplify the unnamed but shared desires to name a field that is now emerging as Sinophone studies.

In the third, longest section of this volume, entitled "Sites and Articulations," short chapters on major Sinophone writers and literary texts are considered in their geohistorical contexts. We chose literature as the cultural genre of focus because, historically, the writing of literature has been the quintessential endeavor for many Sinophone communities that are either trying to maintain their ancestral languages or are forced to do so due to colonial impositions. Sinophone literature is the space where we can find the most concentrated exploration of what it means to be Sinophone, in all its multifarious, contentious, and paradoxical ways. These shorter chapters are meant to complement the more conceptual ones in the first two parts of the book by offering substantive introductions to and critical reflections on some of the major Sinophone writers and their works from different parts of the world. Together, the three parts hope to offer an adequate view of the possible domains of Sinophone studies. The largely humanistic orientation of this book anticipates further dialogues with social science work in Sinophone studies, such as sociological, historical, and other approaches to migration, citizenship, and colonialism.

Notes

Portions of the Introduction are drawn from "The Concept of the Sinophone," *PMLA* 126.3 (May 2011) and "Theory, Asia, and the Sinophone," *Postcolonial Studies* 12, no. 4 (2010): 465–484.

1. *Lectures on the Philosophy of World History*, trans. T. H. B. Nisbet (Cambridge: Cambridge University Press, 1980), 196.

2. Ibid.

3. *The Philosophy of Right*, trans. T. M. Knox (Oxford: Oxford University Press, 1967), 247–249.

4. See, for instance, *Maritime Asia*, edited by Karl Anton Sprengard and Roderich Ptak and *Maritime China in Transition, 1750–1850*, edited by Wang Gungwu and Ng Chin-Keong, two volumes published in the series entitled "South China and Maritime Asia" published by Harrassowitz in Wiesbaden, Germany.

5. Antonio Gramsci, *Prison Notebooks* (New York: Columbia University Press, 1992).

6. Philip Kuhn, *Chinese Among Others: Emigration in Modern Times* (Lanham and New York: Roman and Littlefield, 2008), 21.

7. Ibid., 12.

8. Kuhn notes, for instance, that by the late eighteenth century, Chinese wealth in the Dutch East Indies overshadowed that of the Dutch and the Indonesians and eventually led to Dutch crackdown (154).

9. Kuhn, *Chinese Among Others*, 56.

10. Quoted in Kuhn, *Chinese Among Others*, 246.

11. From a 1724 document written by Lan Dingyuan to the Qing court, Ibid., 88.

12. Many contract laborers and coolies were actually brought over to Southeast Asia by Chinese merchants and managers. For a history of Chinese immigration to the United States, see Ronald Takaki, *Strangers from a Different Shore: A History of Asian Americans*, updated and revised edition (Boston, New York, London: Little, Brown, and Company, 1998), and Iris Chang, *The Chinese in America: A Narrative History* (New York: Penguin Books, 2003).

13. Kuhn, *Chinese Among Others*, 12.

14. See Shih and Ang in this volume for a more detailed critique of the diaspora paradigm.

15. Many thanks to Chong Fah Hing who has given me a precise gloss on these terms as they are used in Malaysia.

16. On the vanishing of the Sinophone, see Shih in this volume.

17. The Hanban, a state organization that promulgates and promotes Hanyu-study all across the world, has aggressively moved, with its newly acquired financial power, to establish Confucius Institutes in major universities in the United States and Europe. Hanban's full name in English is the Office of the Chinese Language Council International.

18. "The Yellow and the Black: The African American Presence in Sinophone Chinese American Literature," *Chung Wai Literary Monthly* 34, no. 4 (September 2005), 15–54. Also see Wong in this volume.

19. See the work of Pamela Kyle Crossley, Evelyn S. Rawski, and Jonathan Lipman, especially Lipman's essay in *Empire at the Margins: Culture, Ethnicity, and Frontier in Early Modern China* (Berkeley: University of California Press, 2005), 86.

20. Patricia Schiaffini, "The Language Divide: Identity and Literary Choices in Modern Tibet," *Journal of International Affairs* 57, no. 2 (Spring 2004): 94; Lara Maconi, "Lion of the Snowy Mountains The Tibetan Poet Yi Dam Tshering and His Chinese Poetry: Reconstructing Tibetan Cultural Identity in Chinese" in *Tibet, Self, and the Tibetan Diaspora*, ed. Christiaan Klieger (London: Brill, 2002), 165–194.

21. Schiaffini, "The Language Divide," 89.

22. See Shih, "Against Diaspora," in this volume.

23. Victor Mair, "What is a Chinese 'Dialect/Topolet'? Reflections on Some Key Sino-English Linguistic Terms," *Sino-Platonic Papers* 29 (September 1991): 1–31.

24. Benedict Anderson, *Imagined Communities: Reflections on the Origin and Spread of Nationalism* (London: Verso, 1991), 5.

25. Etienne Balibar, "The Nation Form," in *Race, Nation, Class: Ambiguous Identities*, eds. Etienne Balibar and Immanuel Wallterstein (London and New York: Verso, 1991), 98–99.

26. *Kafka: Towards a Minor Literature*, trans. Dana Polan (Minneapolis: University of Minnesota Press, 1986).

ISSUES AND CONTROVERSIES

Sinophone studies underscores issues and controversies pertaining to multiple identities, ethnicities, languages, and cultures in contrast to the singular and all-consuming "obsession with China."[1] The Sinophone departs and distinguishes itself from such an obsession, as well as the dominant discourse of Chineseness, and maintains its own subjectivity with an emphasis on heterogeneous practices of language and culture of Sinophone communities in a variety of locales. As Shu-mei Shih explains:

> The Sinophone peoples . . . are closer or farther from China, Taiwan, or Hong Kong, or the other Sinophone sites in Asia where they have emigrated from, depending on their perceptions of both geographical and psychic space. In their rootedness in the local place, the Sinophone peoples across different oceans and territories negotiate the relationship between space and place creatively.[2]

While some may continue to have both cultural and political allegiances to China, others may hold an opposite view, especially in the context of ethnic, linguistic, and cultural heterogeneity of the place where they reside. For the second generation, their birth country is more likely considered by them as their home country, and their attachment to a faraway country called China is at best tenuous, if not altogether a form of imaginary nostalgia. An immigrant mother's and her locally born daughter's geographical distance to China may be the same, but their relationships to the "psychic space" of China—a space closely associated with memory and imagination—are bound to be different. In other words, the Sinophone—as lived cultures as well as living languages and peoples—is spatially and temporally specific to different generations and in different locations. The Sinophone can be and is in fact many things depending on place (site of settlement) and time (history of migration). The Sinophone therefore cannot be contained by the China-centric and uniform definitions of Chineseness, as it is constantly engaged with local revisions and reinventions of Chineseness in relation to local languages and cultures. Ien Ang puts it slightly differently in her 1998 essay "Can One Say No to Chineseness?", which remains fitting even now:

> Chineseness is not a category with a fixed content—be it racial, cultural or geographical—but operates as an open and indeterminate signifier whose meanings are constantly renegotiated and rearticulated in different sections of the Chinese diaspora.

In part I, we have included chapters that reverberate with the critics' call to rethink—if not necessarily undo—Chineseness, which frequently appears as an identificatory category not so much to designate one's ancestral origin but to establish and reinforce certain political affiliations. Each of these chapters serves as a unique entrance to further inquiries of issues such as immigration, identity, as well as multilingualism that have become inextricably linked to Sinophone communities and central to Sinophone studies. In her provocative chapter, Ang takes issue with the notion of "Cultural China" coined by Wei-ming Tu (see part II). While Ang acknowledges the importance of Tu's pioneering attempt to interrogate the cultural ties of the "overseas Chinese" (*Huaqiao* or *Huaren*) to China, she also notes that Tu's notion of Cultural China risks repeating the logics of Chinese ethnocentrism. In a culturally and economically deterritorialized space such as the world today, the title of Ang's chapter exemplifies a certain ambiguity and ambivalence. It is both a rhetorical question and a categorical imperative, indicating that one *can* say no to Chineseness (but is one willing to?) on the one hand, and one *must* say no to Chineseness on the other simply because the definition of Chineseness (as that of all other identities) varies in different places and times. Saying no to Chineseness does not deny any ancestral or cultural ties to China; on the contrary, it is to reject the problematic assumption that Chinese studies is (limited to) the study of China or that there is a more authentic or the best definition of Chineseness. Saying no to Chineseness offers Sinophone communities in different parts of the world an opportunity to reflect on, to comment on, and to question the totalizing forces of genealogy, consanguinity, as well as the so-called "Chinese culture," to foreground how such forces are being negotiated in different locations. And by way of extension, saying no to Chineseness further illuminates how Sinophone peoples may construct their own identity relationally. Simply put, to answer "yes" to Ang's seemingly alarming call is not to deny the very existence of a political entity, or a civilization-state called China; rather, it is to begin thinking more theoretically about an overdetermined series of historical, cultural, or political factors behind any identity (and allegiance), as Rey Chow also does in her chapter.

In her compelling 1998 essay "On Chineseness as a Theoretical Problem," Chow unpacks the relational construction of the Chinese and the non-Chinese. Chow's chapter is not so much an anthropological and sociological discussion of ethnogensis as an acute critical reflection on Chinese/Chineseness that many indiscriminately use to support a "homogeneously unified, univocal China." In response to drastic changes accompanying contacts with Western powers especially between the mid-nineteenth and the early twentieth centuries, Chinese/Chineseness surfaces as a problematic ethnic supplement that simultaneously stresses China as an underdeveloped "other" that awaits education and improvement, and China as a particular entity whose presence complicates and enriches existing values of universality. Chow advocates a dissociation among ethnicity, race, nation, and the state by expounding on the various clashes between the "discriminatory practices of the old Western hegemony" and China's vehement riposte to them. Chow's reminder of how an ethnic category called "the Chinese" is operative on the levels of literary and cultural production as well as linguistic enunciation is well taken. Indeed, by the turn of the twenty-first century, Chineseness as a monolithic given linked to China has come under much interrogation and critique, but more refined critical interventions into the politics of Chineseness still await.

Shu-mei Shih's coinage of the term *Sinophone* is the most recent engagement with Chineseness from the perspective of literary and cultural production. The Sinophone does more than repackage what we may call the polyphony and heteroglossia in literature and cinema from modern China that have already inspired several academic monographs. The Sinophone may be understood as a critical response to Chow's urge to "theorize the controversial connections among language possession, ethnicity, and cultural value." To borrow James Clifford's famous saying, the Sinophone highlights the complex dynamics between "roots," the invisible and at times the imaginary pulling forces of the homeland, and "routes," the process of traveling to and settling down (planting new "roots") in a "foreign" land.[3] As Shih aptly puts in her chapter "Against Diaspora: The Sinophone as Places of Cultural Production," the Sinophone is a "study of Sinitic-language cultures and communities on the margins of China and Chineseness." On the surface, the

Sinophone may appear as an exclusionary approach to China and Chinese studies—exclusionary because Shih strategically draws critical attention to cultural productions *outside and beyond* the geopolitical boundary of China proper. The Sinophone disengagement with China is a postcolonial splitting of a monolithic identity that is Chineseness, a move that echoes and supplements existing critical discussions as seen in the works of Ien Ang, Rey Chow, Stuart Hall, and others. In short, the Sinophone decouples Chineseness and China, bringing to the fore a critical perspectivalism and an interpretive positionality that are essential in our reconceptualization of "diaspora" (Chinese or otherwise) in the twenty-first century. Rather than arguing that the precarious center cannot hold and will one day become a new margin, the Sinophone makes clear that the center is always already the margin, thereby providing a nuanced new look at the taxonomy that old area studies employ to label "them" and "us," enemies and allies.

The fact that the Sinophone does not engage with Han Chinese writers, intellectuals, artists, and filmmakers from China may appear puzzling to many. We may understand the Sinophone's disengagement with mainstream cultural brokers in China in light of what Ien Ang calls "an inclusion by virtue of othering." Insofar as the Sinophone proclaims to be focusing on the particularity of the local, it never intends a negligence of the center. Critics have already written much about the imbrications of the center and the periphery, which the Sinophone does more than repeating. Including China by virtue of othering, the Sinophone promises a refinement of existing understanding of ethnic and linguistic politics in the field of Chinese studies. And by refining the dynamics and dialectics between presence and absence, as well as writers inside and outside of China, the Sinophone further theorizes the study of China, its constituting cultures, its many peoples, and their multiplying tongues with critical perspectives.

Following the chapters by Ang, Chow, and Shih, Kim Chew Ng's chapter focuses on the language issue. Born in Malaysia, Ng is both a noted literary critic in Taiwan and a superb fiction writer in his own right. Ng's chapter "Sinophone/Chinese: 'The South Where Language Is Lost' and Reinvented" reminds the reader that in Malaysia, the standard Sinitic language (called *huayu* throughout Southeast Asia) is not the lingua franca of immigrants from China. Hailam, Hakka, Hokkien, Teochiu, and other languages all have a longer history in Malaysia than *huayu* or the *putonghua* (Beijing standard). Communication between people whose ancestors come from different regions and speak different topolects becomes a practice of creolization, that is, a process that mingles varied linguistic expressions, inflections, and intonations. The existing standard Sinitic characters, phrases, and idioms are simply ineffective in visualizing such vital and vibrant cross-pollination of topolects and the cultures and histories behind them. One of the many challenges a Sinophone Malaysian writer like Kim Chew Ng faces may be the difficulty to adequately express herself/himself in written words, but never a "loss of language," as charged by Chinese writer Wang Anyi.

And the issue becomes even more complex if we are to take into account the history of "national language" and "Sinitic language" education in relation to cultural politics and anti-Chinese sentiment in Malaysia, Indonesia, and Singapore. Descendants of settlers from China who speak varied Sinitic languages at home must deal with policies that are hostile to their cultural and linguistic heritages. In addition to politics related to anti-Chinese/Sinophone sentiments in their birth countries, they are also faced with the violent wrestling between opposing ideological views, namely that of the Republic of China (Taiwan) and the People's Republic of China. Both China and Taiwan attempt to advance their own political agenda and exert influence on Sinophone communities abroad by linking cultural heritage unabashedly to Mandarin (*putonghua, guoyu*), the official language of both sides of the Taiwan Strait, which many settlers and their descendants do not necessarily read, write, and speak.

It needs to be remarked here that the linguistic challenge of which Ng urges readers of the vernacular Sinitic script to take note is a challenge that remains prevalent well into the twenty-first century after its initial emergence during the May Fourth Movement of 1919. Premodern Chinese scholars and officials were not concerned with the split between spoken and written language. It was at this important historical juncture of the May Fourth Movement that the Chinese intellectuals began to radically revamp the existing way of thinking and writing. For them, the unification of spoken and written languages marks the first step toward the reinvigoration of China and its culture in the face of pressing imperial forces from the West and Japan. At one point, progressive scholars such as Qian Xuantong and Wu Zhihui even proposed to abolish the Sinitic script and adopt the Roman alphabet. Needless to say, their proposal was dismissed. We could only imagine how it would have altered the landscape of modern Chinese literature.

To be certain, there are writers whose experience of emigration predates the May Fourth Movement. Their struggle to eke out a living in a new land was their first priority, not the use of language for nationalist causes. There is the crisis of which Ng speaks, but there are also émigré writers who strip their Sinophone writings of local influences and insist on using the classical language (*wenyan wen*) and poetry to document their expatriation and demonstrate their loyalty to their homeland. David Der-wei Wang's chapter offers a historical overview of Chinese émigré writings in Taiwan from the perspective of loyalism and loyalist discourse. In this seminal chapter, Wang explains how loyalism (which is always already post-loyalism)—an age-old notion, as well as an entrenched way of life—helps to shape various structures of feeling in the contested relationship among emigrants, émigré writers, and their homeland. The writers from seventeenth-century China and Taiwan that Wang discusses continue to exert their influence on contemporary Sinophone writers much in the same way that the specters of homeland continue to haunt Chinese emigrants and their descendants. Thus studies of Sinophone Taiwan may begin from an earlier time, as David Wang's mention of Shen Guangwen and Koxinga (Zheng Chenggong) shows, to avoid suppressing the unique cultural hybridity resultant from Taiwan's colonial pasts (from Dutch to Ming and Qing China to Japan) and, some might argue, the colonial present (under the KMT).

The issue of loyalty and loyalism is even more complex in the case of Ha Jin, an Anglophone Chinese American writer who has given up writing in his mother tongue. Jin, who teaches at Boston University, chose to write and publish stories in American English. He won his first award—the Flannery O'Connor Award for short fiction—in the United States in 1996 with his "Under the Red Flag." Since then, he has continued to receive critical acclaim with captivating stories and novels. In "Exiled to English," Ha Jin tactfully responds to Ien Ang's call on *not* speaking Chinese by opening language onto a broader sociocultural terrain. Ordinarily, a person in exile tends to write in the language of the homeland from which he is banished. In Ha Jin's case, however, as he is banished from his homeland, he has banished the language of his homeland. The title of his chapter, "Exile to English," thus posit(ion)s a more nuanced understanding of exile as self-exile. Choosing not to write in his mother tongue amounts to self-exile, exile not only from the country but also from the language; and choosing not to write in his mother tongue is choosing not to be Sinophone. In fact, Ha Jin is well aware of the creolization within the Sinophone, in which different practices of cultural and linguistic articulations crisscross.

Jin's voluntary banishment of Mandarin in his stories has an unlikely but complementary echo to the language crisis in Sinophone Malaysian writings as Ng observes in his chapter. His conscious decision to turn away from Mandarin in favor of American English is an apt illustration of how diaspora has an expiration date, and the vanishing of the Sinophone in various communities is part of the historical process of localization.[4] Jin's Anglophone writing problematizes the linkage between identity and consanguinity, between language and nationality, between loyalty and betrayal, between voluntary and involuntary exiles, and between politics and geography. And on an even larger scale, Jin's writing is what David Damrosch would call an engaging example of "world literature," which, while being attentive to certain national and geopolitical boundaries, engages with different localities, and "circulate[s] beyond their culture or origin, either in translation or in their original language."[5] Curiously enough, if for an intellectual in exile like Ha Jin homeland is to be found in the English language and Chineseness is mediated through English, then the boundaries of the English language—that is, the Anglophone—are also being vigorously redrawn by Jin and his literary forebears and contemporaries such as Joseph Conrad, Vladimir Nabokov, Milan Kundera, and Andreï Makine.

The attachment to China-centrism has traversed many phases. After losing the two Opium Wars, Qing China was forced to seriously reflect on its position in a new world map of military powers and divergent cultures where the Qing was no longer the center of the universe. Moving from seclusion and exclusion to inclusion, the Chinese began to incorporate into the existing body of knowledge foreign concepts and ideas for self-strengthening. One may call it the traveling of knowledge and the Sinicization of new ideas. The bottom line is: "Chinese culture" as such is already hybrid with other non-Chinese elements since at least the late-Qing, if not earlier.

The same process has since repeated itself after 1919, which is known as the start of the Chinese Enlightenment, or the May Fourth Movement. Chinese intellectuals, politicians, and writers alike rushed to experiment on all fronts—from language (debates on abolishing the Sinitic script for Esperanto) to literature, from social sciences to law, from health sciences to statecraft. Marxism, after all, is also a foreign import; "socialism with Chinese characteristics" marks as much about its Chineseness as its un-Chineseness. It is not the inherent heterogeneity of China that is being critiqued by Sinophone studies but the disavowal of this heterogeneity by Hancentrism (its oppression of ethnic minorities) and China-centrism (hypernationalist defense of China). As China strengthens economically, the heterogeneity of what ethnically as well as culturally constitutes China as a political entity risks overgeneralization. Under the totalizing effect of late capitalism in an increasingly globalized world, it is all the more important to *not* think of China (or any other nation-states for that matter) as a monolithic system in terms of ethnicity, culture, language, and nationality. Sinophone studies disaggregates these categories of identity and attends to their multifarious combinations.

The Sinophone will eventually lose its raison d'être when Sinophone peoples' "local concerns voiced in local language gradually supersede pre-immigration concerns for immigrants and their descendents through generations."[6] China and Chineseness as such gradually ceases to be a matter of concern for these people when they adopt the local language and become more and more localized, as has been the historical experience of many who have emigrated from China over the centuries. The increased emigration of people from China today, for now, is creating new Sinophone communities across the world, especially in Europe and Africa. The way these new communities negotiate their identity through their language choice, cultural mixing, and political (dis)engagement will provide rich grounds for future work in Sinophone studies. The chapters in this part of the book show the various phases and faces of the Sinophone. Together, they remind us to ponder a crucial paradox in the usage of Chinese/Chineseness as an example of strategic essentialism: where visibility increases, reality vanishes. From varied engagements with imperial legacy, ethnic prejudice, linguistic conundrum, and postcolonial discourse, these chapters stand as initial critical inquiries into our constant reassessment of China and Chineseness in the twenty-first century from Sinophone perspectives. Finally, it is worth repeating that in Sinophone studies, China is the present absence. As Shu-mei Shih convincingly argues: "The Sinophone may articulate a China-centrism if it is the nostalgic kind that forever looks back at China as its cultural motherland or the source of value, nationalist or otherwise; but the Sinophone is often the site where powerful articulations against China-centrism can be heard."[7]

Notes

1. This is a term coined by C. T. Hsia who uses it to refer to Chinese scholars and intellectuals' heavy concerns with national issues. See C. T. Hsia, *A History of Modern Chinese Fiction* (New Haven: Yale University Press, 1961), 533–554.

2. Shu-mei Shih, *Visuality and Identity: Sinophone Articulations Across the Pacific* (Berkeley: University of California Press, 2007), 37.

3. James Clifford, *Routes: Travel and Translation in the Late Twentieth Century* (Cambridge, Mass: Harvard University Press, 1997).

4. Shih, chapter 1, this volume.

5. David Damrosch. *What is World Literature* (Princeton: Princeton University Press, 2003), 4.

6. Ibid., 32.

7. Shih, *Visuality and Identity*, 31.

Against Diaspora

The Sinophone as Places of Cultural Production

SHU-MEI SHIH

This chapter is a broad, programmatic piece to parse out a space for Sinophone studies (*huayu yuxi yanjiu*), situated at the intersection of postcolonial studies, transnational studies, global studies, Chinese studies, and ethnic studies, as the study of Sinitic-language cultures and communities on the margins of China and Chineseness. Here, "the margins of China and Chineseness" is understood not only specifically but also generally to locate those Sinophone cultures situated outside the geopolitical China proper and in many parts of the world through historical processes of (im)migration and settlement spanning several centuries; it is also understood as those non-Han cultures within China where the imposition of the dominant Han culture has elicited numerous responses, from assimilation to anticolonial resistance in the dominant language, Hanyu. Sinophone studies as a whole is therefore inherently comparative and transnational, but it is everywhere attentive to the specificity of time and place of its different objects of study. In this spirit, this chapter does not focus explicitly on literature, but lays out the broad contours of Sinophone studies through an analysis and critique of what I consider to be the misconceived category of "the Chinese diaspora."

"The Chinese Diaspora"

The scattering of peoples from China across the globe over a millennium has long been an object of study as a subfield in Chinese studies, Southeast Asian

Studies, and Asian American Studies and has a small presence in European Studies, African Studies, and Latin American Studies in the United States. This subfield, whose parameters are set by wherever the peoples from China have gone, has been called the study of the Chinese diaspora. The Chinese diaspora, understood as the dispersion of "ethnic Chinese" people around the globe, stands as a universalizing category founded on a unified ethnicity, culture, language, and place of origin or homeland. A Uigur from Xinjiang province, a Tibetan from Tibet and surrounding regions, or a Mongolian from Inner Mongolia who has emigrated out of China is not normally considered part of the Chinese diaspora, for instance, whereas the Manchus may or may not be included. The measure of inclusion appears to be the degree of sinicization of these ethnicities, because what often gets completely elided is the fact that the Chinese diaspora refers mainly to the diaspora of the Han people. "Chinese," in other words, is a national marker passing as an ethnic, cultural, and linguistic marker, a largely Han-centric designation, since, in fact, there are altogether fifty-six official ethnicities in China and far more diverse languages and topolects spoken across the nation. The Chinese language, as it is generally assumed and understood, is nothing but the standardized language imposed by the state, that is, the language of the Han, the *Hanyu*, also known as *putonghua* (literally, the common language); the Chinese, as is generally assumed, are largely limited to the Han people; and Chinese culture refers mainly to the culture of the Han. "Chinese" functions as a category of ethnicity, language, and culture only to the extent that it designates the Han, excluding all the other ethnicities, languages, and cultures. The term "ethnic Chinese" is therefore a serious misnomer. In short, there is no such group called "ethnic Chinese." There can be ethnic Tibetan Chinese or Uigur Chinese, but not "ethnic Chinese" as such. The reduction of Chineseness to Han ethnicity in places outside China is the inverse of the hegemonic claims on Chineseness by the Han majority within China. Historically, various ethnic peoples have contributed significantly to what "China" has become today, such as the important legacies of the Manchu dynasty of the Qing (1644–1912). Hence, this procedure of ethnicized reductionism of the Chinese as the Han is not unlike the racist misrecognition of authentic Americans to be white Anglo-Saxons. In each case, a different but similar form of ethnocentrism is in operation.

To elaborate further on how the uniform idea of "the Chinese" was coproduced by agents inside and outside China, we may trace it back to a racialized ideology of the Western powers since the nineteenth century that presented Chineseness along the color line, disregarding the many diversities and differences within China. This was when the Chinese became "yellow" and reduced to one ethnicity, when in fact there were historically people of many different phenotypes in changing geopolitical boundaries of China. The external production of Chinese uniformity paradoxically worked well with the unifying intent of the Chinese state, especially since the end of Manchu rule in 1912, which eagerly presented a unified China and Chineseness to emphasize its cultural and political autonomy from the West. Only in this context can we understand why since the turn of the nineteenth century the notion of "Chinese national characteristics" that had been propounded by Western missionaries became popular among Westerners and the Han Chinese alike, inside and outside China, and why it would continue to be a compelling idea for the Han majority in China in the present.[1] On the one hand, there is no better way to understand this desire to universalize Chineseness as a racialized boundary marker than that, for the Western powers, it legitimated the semicolonization of the Chinese up until 1949 and the management of their Chinese immigrants and minorities within their own nation-states from the late nineteenth century to the present, for both of which the discourse of "the Yellow Peril" served distinctly useful purposes. On the other hand, for China and the Han Chinese, the racialized concept of "the Chinese" correlates at least with three different purposes: the unified nation's resistance against imperialism and semicolonialism in the early twentieth century; a practice of self-examination that internalized Western categories of the self; and, finally and most importantly, the suppression of its ethnic minorities for their claims on and contributions to the nation and the dispelling of some of the sovereignty claims of these minority groups.

What is abundantly clear from this very short and broad exposition of the problems of such umbrella terms as "Chinese" and "Chineseness" is that the terms were activated through contacts with other peoples outside China as well as confrontations with their internal others. These terms dwell not only on the most general level for their signification but also on the most exclusive; thus, they are universal and particular at the same time. More precisely, they are hegemonic particulars passing themselves off as the universal, which is complicit with the crude generalizations imposed on China, the Chinese, and Chineseness by the West and to a certain extent other Asian countries such as Japan and Korea, where resistances to the Chinese sphere of cultural and political influence have been prominent since the nineteenth century, if not earlier. Both Japan and Korea had explicitly engaged in "de-Hanification" campaigns in their movements to define their national languages against Chinese cultural hegemony, for instance, undermining the importance of Kanji (Japanese for the Han script) and Hanja (Korean for the Han script) in their respective languages.

As much as the study of the Chinese diaspora has tried to broaden the question of the Chinese and Chineseness by emphasizing the localizing tendencies of those peoples migrated out of China in their countries of sojourn and sometimes colonial settlement, such as in various countries in Southeast Asia (especially Indonesia, Malaysia, Thailand, the Philippines, and Singapore), Chineseness continues to be the major category within this field. It is important to interrogate, however, the unifying category of the Chinese diaspora in the present moment, not only because it is complicit with China's nationalist calling to the "overseas Chinese" who are supposed to long to return to China as their homeland and whose ultimate purpose is to serve China, but also because it unwittingly correlates with and reinforces the Western and other non-Western (such as American and Malaysian) racialized construction of Chineseness as perpetually foreign ("diasporic") and hence Chinese immigrants as not qualified to be authentic locals. In postcolonial nation-states across Southeast Asia, Africa, and South America, it is not far-fetched to argue that the Sinophone peoples have been historically constitutive of the local. After all, some of them have been in Southeast Asia since as early as the sixth century, long before nation-states ever existed and surely long enough to outlast many identity labels tied to nationality.[2] The question, then, is who is preventing them from being just a Thai, a Filipino, a Malaysian, an Indonesian, or a Singaporean who happens to have ancestors from China and who can be recognized as simply multilingual and multicultural like their fellow citizens.[3] Similarly, who is preventing the immigrants from China in the United States (whose ancestors came as early as the mid-nineteenth century) from simply being or becoming Chinese Americans with an emphasis on the latter of the compound term, American? We can consider the various racialized acts of exclusion—such as the Chinese exclusion acts in the United States, the expulsion of the Hoa (local construction of the Chinese) by the Vietnamese government, ethnic riots against the Chinese in Indonesia, the massacre of the Chinese by the Spanish in the Philippines and by the Dutch in Java, the kidnapping of Chinese children in the Philippines, and many other such examples—to see how the reified category of "the Chinese" as a racial and ethnic marker readily serves such purposes of exclusion, scapegoating, and persecution. While Italian, Jewish, and Irish immigrants have gradually become "white," merging into the mainstream white American society, the yellowness of "the Chinese" has continued to plague Chinese Americans' struggles for recognition.

Paradoxically, scholarship on the Chinese diaspora provides ample evidence of the desire of these immigrants to localize within their lands of settlement. In Singapore, even before it became an independent city-state, intellectuals who had migrated from China saw that their culture was centered in the land of their settlement. They coined the category "Nanyang" (the South Seas) for themselves, and many rejected the claim that their culture was an overseas Chinese culture.[4] The locally born peranakans in Indonesia and mixed-race babas in Malaysia—the so-called "Straits Chinese"—developed their own particular cultures of hybridity and resisted the "resinicization" pressures from China.[5] Many Chinese Americans have long considered themselves to be the children of the civil rights movements and refuted the "dual domination" and manipulation by both the Chinese state and the U.S. state.[6] The Sino-Thais have localized their surnames and have more or less completely integrated into the fabric of Thai society. The Malaysian Communist Party, established in 1930, was one of the most active anticolonial units against the British and the Japanese, and its membership was mainly Chinese Malaysians of Han ethnicity.[7] The racially or ethnically mixed populations with some traceable ancestry in China, such as the Lukjins of Siam, the Metis of Cambodia and Indochina, the Injerto and Chinocholos of Peru, the Creoles in Trinidad and Mauritius, and the Mestizos of the Philippines, present us with the question of whether it makes any sense to continue to register these categories at all and what purposes and for whose benefit such registration serves.[8] We continue to see a certain ideology of racial and ethnic purity that mandates the tracing of origins even after centuries have passed. Whether racialized pressure from the outside or internalized racialization, the basis of such an ideology is not unlike the one-drop-of-blood rule for African Americans in the United States.

The sentiments of Sinophone settlers in different parts of the world of course are various, and there was a strong sojourner mentality in the earlier phases of the dispersion since many were traders and coolies. Their different intentions for staying or leaving provide different measuring mechanisms for their desire to integrate or not integrate. But the fact of the Sinophone peoples' dispersion through all continents and over such a long historical span calls into question the viability of the umbrella concept of the Chinese diaspora, where the criteria of determination is Chineseness, or, to put it more precisely, different degrees of Chineseness. In this scheme, for instance, one can be *more* Chinese and another can be *less* Chinese, and Chineseness effectively becomes evaluatable, measurable, and quantifiable. Wang Gungwu, the renowned scholar of the Chinese diaspora, therefore posited the idea of the "cultural spectrum of Chineseness." As an illustration, he notes that the Chinese in Hong Kong are "historically" more Chinese, although they are "not as yet fully Chinese as their compatriots in Shanghai," but the Chinese in San Francisco and Singapore have more "complex non-Chinese variables."[9] Another renowned scholar of the Chinese diaspora, Lynn Pan, states that the Chinese in the United States have lost their cultural grounding and are therefore "lost to Chineseness." Pan further charges that the Chinese Americans' involvement in the civil rights movement was nothing short of "opportunism."[10] Here, we hear echoes of the accusation by immigrant parents, in the early twentieth-century San Francisco Chinatown, that their American children were less than satisfactorily Chinese by calling them empty bamboo hearts (*juksing*), or the nationalistic Chinese from China who claim that their Chineseness was the most authentic compared with those living outside China. If one Chinese American can be complimented for speaking good English in the United States due to the racist equation of whiteness and authenticity, he or she can be equally complimented for speaking good Hanyu in China, as someone who is not authentically Chinese enough.

Two major points of blindness in the study of the Chinese diaspora are its inability to see beyond Chineseness as an organizing principle and the lack of communication with the other scholarly paradigms such as ethnic studies in the United States (where ethnic identities and nationality of origin can be disaggregated), Southeast Asian studies (where the Sinophone peoples are inevitably seen more and more as Southeast Asians), and various language-based postcolonial studies such as Francophone studies (where the French-speaking Chinese are French per the ideology of French republicanism).[11] Furthermore, in most of the scholarship on the Chinese diaspora, the "Chinese American" is a missing person, and even the Hongkonger or Taiwanese are missing persons who are only recognized as Hong Kong Chinese or Chinese in Taiwan.[12] The overinvestment in the notion of the homeland in the study of the Chinese diaspora cannot account for either the global dispersion of Sinophone peoples or the increasing heterogenization of ethnicities and cultures within any given nation. From the perspective of the *longue durée* of globalization, Samir Amin tells us, heterogenization and hybridization have been the norm rather than the exception since time immemorial.[13]

The Sinophone, as Such

I coin the notion of the Sinophone to designate Sinitic-language cultures and communities outside China as well as those ethnic communities within China, where Sinitic languages are either forcefully imposed or willingly adopted. The Sinophone, like the history of other nonmetropolitan peoples who speak metropolitan and/or colonial languages, has a colonial history. When China was a cultural empire, the literary, classical Han script was the lingua franca of the East Asian world where scholars could converse by conducting so-called "pen conversations" (*bitan*) through writing. Studies of Qing imperialism of the eighteenth and nineteenth centuries have, in the past two decades, also shown the continuous effects of this imperialism on those internal colonies within China today: Tibet, Inner Mongolia, and Xinjiang, for instance. This is similar to the official Francophonie whose existence owes largely to the expansion of the French empire and its cultural and linguistic colonization of parts of Africa and the Caribbean, as was the Spanish empire in Hispanophone America, British Empire in India and Africa, the Portuguese empire in Brazil and Africa, and so forth. It goes without saying that not all empires acted the same way, and linguistic colonization and influence did occur through varying degrees of coercion and cooperation and to different degrees of success. What these empires uniformly left behind, however, are the linguistic consequences of their cultural dominance. In standard Japanese and Korean languages, for instance, there is a lasting, clearly recognizable presence of the classical Han script in localized forms. In today's China, the imposition of the Hanyu and the Han script on its non-Han others— Tibetans, Uigurs, Mongolians, and so forth—is akin to a colonial relationship, a relationship that most dare not criticize for fear of China's ire.

Contemporary Sinophone communities outside China, however, are not strictly colonial or postcolonial in relation to China except in a few cases. This is the major difference between the Sinophone and the other postcolonial language-based communities such as the Francophone, the Hispanophone, and so forth. Singapore as a settler colony with the majority of the population being Han is akin to the United States as a settler Anglophone country. By historical developments in the twentieth century, Singapore's postcolonial language is Anglophone, not Sinophone. Taiwan, whose majority population is Han who settled there during the seventeenth century and later, is also similar to the colonial United States in its intention to become formally independent from the country of immigration. Furthermore, Taiwan's situation is akin to Francophone Quebec. In Quebec, roughly 82 percent of the population is Francophone, and a similar percentage of the Taiwanese speak the standard Mandarin. The French-Canadian identity in Quebec has increasingly given way to a localized, modern Quebecois identity through what has been known as a process of "révolution tranquille,"[14] just as the imposed uniform Chinese identity by the Guomindang regime in Taiwan has gradually given way to a localized New Taiwanese identity in today's Taiwan. Mandarin is now only one of the official languages in Taiwan's multilingual society, where the majority of the people actually speak Hoklo and the rest speak Hakka and various aboriginal languages. As settler colonies, however, Han peoples of Singapore and Taiwan, no matter which Sinitic language they speak (Hoklo/ Taiwanese, Hakka, Cantonese, Teochiu, or others), are colonial vis-à-vis the indigenous peoples there. From the indigenous perspective, the history of Taiwan is a history of serial colonialism (Dutch, French, Chinese, Japanese, etc.) that has never ended. Taiwan has never been postcolonial.

For those who settled in various parts of Southeast Asia, they also rarely speak the standard language defined by the Chinese state but various old forms of topolects from the time and place from which they had emigrated.[15] "The time" in this context is important because the topolects would have evolved differently inside and outside China. The Han people living in South Korea, for instance, speak a mixture of Shandongnese and Korean, often creolized to the extent that the semantics, syntax, and grammar of the two languages are intermingled to a very high degree such that the two seem to be organically interdependent. This is especially true for second- and third-generation Shandongnese in South Korea, although the standard Hanyu was taught in the educational system set up by the locals originally supported by the Taiwan government and now by the Chinese government after the reestablishment of diplomatic ties between South Korea and China. Like elsewhere, Hanyu there is standard only to the extent that it is a written language; when spoken, it is sounded out in Shandongnese. The Shandongnese they speak is also different from the Shandongnese spoken in the Shandong province of China, where there are in fact many topolects that all call themselves Shandongnese. The same can be said about the speakers of Teochiu, Hokkien, Hakka, and Cantonese and Hailam in Southeast Asia, Cantonese in Hong Kong, and all the different topolect speakers and Chinglish or pidgin speakers in the United States. The Straits Chinese (who settled in the British Straits settlements), such as the babas, speak English as well as patois Malay.[16] It goes without saying that there are various degrees of creolization of the Sinitic languages as well as outright abandonment of any ancestral linguistic links to China. Increasingly, for instance, the main linguistic influence on Sinophone Chinese Malaysians is Hong Kong television shows and movies, a Hong Kong-style Cantonese with distinct divergences from the Cantonese spoken in the Guangdong province in China. Essentially, creolized to different degrees, these Sinitic languages comprise a multilingual Sinophone world across national borders.

The Sinophone recognizes that speaking fractions of different Sinitic languages associated with China is a matter of choice and other historical determinations, and hence the Sinophone exists only to the extent that these languages are somehow maintained. The Sinophone recedes or disappears as soon as these languages in question are abandoned, but this recession or disappearance should not be seen as a cause for lament or nostalgia. Francophone African nations have, to varying degrees, sought to maintain or abandon the colonial language and to devise their own linguistic futures. Hence, unlike the conception of the Chinese diaspora, the Sinophone foregrounds not the ethnicity or race of the person but the languages he or she speaks in either vibrant or vanishing communities of those languages. Instead of the perpetual bind to nationality, the Sinophone may be inherently transnational and global and includes wherever various Sinitic languages are spoken on the margins of China and Chineseness. By virtue of its residual nature, the Sinophone is largely confined to immigrant communities across all of the continents as well as those settler societies where the Han are the majority. As such, the Sinophone can only be a notion in the process of disappearance as soon as it undergoes the process of becoming, when local concerns voiced in local languages gradually supersede preimmigration concerns for immigrants and their descendents through generations, with the Sinophone eventually losing its raison d'être. The Sinophone as an analytical and cognitive category is therefore both geographically and temporally specific.

From the perspectives of Democratic Party members in Hong Kong or independentists in today's Taiwan, Sinophone articulations, furthermore, may contain an anticolonial intent against Chinese hegemony. The Sinophone is a place-based, everyday practice and experience, and thus it is a historical formation that constantly undergoes transformation that reflects local needs and conditions. It can be a site of both a longing for and rejection of various constructions of Chineseness; it can be a site of both nationalism of the long-distance kind, anti-China politics, or even nonrelation with China, whether real or imaginary. Speaking Sinitic languages with certain historical affinity to China does not necessarily need to be tied to contemporary China, just as speaking English does not tie oneself to England per se. In other words, Sinophone articulations can take as many different positions as possible within the realm of human expression, whose axiological determinations are not necessarily dictated by China but by local, regional, or global contingencies and desires. Rather than a dialectics of rejection, incorporation, and sublimation, there is at least a trialectics, since mediation is exercised by more agents than one, the so-called perennial other. The Sinophone, therefore, maintains a precarious and problematic relation to China—similar to the Francophone to France, the Hispanophone to Spain, and the Anglophone to England—in its ambiguity and complexity. The dominant Sinophone language may be standard Hanyu, but it can be implicated in a dynamic of linguistic power struggles. As a major language, standard Hanyu is the object against which various minor articulations are launched, resulting in its destandardization, creolization, fragmentation, or sometimes outright rejection.

The Sinophone may articulate a China-centrism if it is the nostalgic kind that forever looks back at China as its cultural motherland or the source of value—nationalist or otherwise; however, the Sinophone is often the site where the most powerful articulations against China-centrism are heard. The Sinophone Taiwan, for instance, is only an aspect of Taiwan's multilingual community where aboriginal languages are also spoken, and postmartial law

Taiwan cultural discourse is very much about articulating symbolic "farewells to China."[17] The Sinophone pre-1997 Hong Kong also saw the emergence of a nativist fetishization of Cantonese against the looming hegemony of Beijing standard Hanyu.

It goes without saying that the Sinophone is a very important, critical category for literature. In the past, the distinction between literature written in the standard Sinitic language from inside and outside China has been rather blurry, and this blurriness has had the effect of throwing literature written in Sinitic languages, standard or otherwise, outside China into neglect and marginalization, if not total oblivion. What used to be categorized in English as "Chinese literature" (*Zhongguo wenxue*, literature from China) and "literature in Chinese" (*huawen wenxue*, literature from outside China) added to the confusion. The singularity of the word "Chinese" in both terms shows the "Chinese" as the hegemonic sign and easily slips into or becomes complicit with China-centrism. In effect, the notion of "literature in Chinese" or "world literature in Chinese" places Chinese literature as the hegemonic model in relation to which the various different kinds of "Chinese literature" are categorized and organized. There is a bourgeoning industry of studies of "world literature in Chinese" (*shijie huawen wenxue*) with established scholarly associations and academic programs in China, the political intensions of which are probably not very dissimilar to the official notion of the Francophonie of the French state. Much like the model of categorization where European and American literatures are deemed normative, universal, and hence generic whereas the rest of the world produced literature of "the world at large," "world literature" as such was therefore often a code word for all of those literatures that are non-European and non-American. "World literature in Chinese" exercises a similar function where "Chinese literature" is its unnamed but hegemonic, generic, and empty signifier, with the rest of the world producing "world literature in Chinese." In this construction, the "world" is the gathering of particular places beyond the universe of China proper but everywhere connected to China in their insistence to write in the Sinitic script. The historical coincidence of the expansion of studies of "world literature in Chinese" in China with China's global ambitions presents itself for a critical analysis of political economy.

The Sinophone therefore usefully designates Sinitic-language literatures in various parts of the world without the assumed centrality of Chinese literature. It is multilingual in and of itself by virtue of the simple fact that the Sinitic language family consists of many different languages, and different communities tend to speak a particular Sinitic language in addition to its non-Sinitic inflections. Sinophone Malaysian literature, for instance, vividly captures Cantonese and other Sinitic languages alongside the standard

Hanyu, not to mention their sometimes occasional and sometimes extensive creolizations by Malay, English, and Tamil. Similarly, in Sinophone Taiwanese literature, the body of works written by indigenous Austronesian peoples often mixes their various indigenous languages with the imposed Hanyu by the Han settler colonizers in a dialectical confrontation and negotiation. To a different extent, one sees the drive toward writing explicitly in a newly invented script of Hoklo in Taiwan literature, just as Hong Kong writers have tried to invent a Cantonese script to register the distinctness of Sinophone Hong Kong literature in contradiction to Chinese literature.

In the different context of American literature, there had been no clear way to designate Chinese American literature written in a given Sinitic language, hence Sau-ling Wong's recent, important distinction between "Anglophone Chinese American literature" and "Sinophone Chinese American literature."[18] In the case of Chinese American literary history and criticism, literature written in the Sinitic languages has been systematically marginalized, if not considered politically suspect for its presumed "un-Americanness" that can arouse fears of charges of unassimilability. Dismissed in both the canons of "Chinese literature" and "Chinese American literature," which are both based on models of nationality and ethnicity with standard Hanyu and standard English as their languages of choice, the Sinophone literally had been crying for a name for itself. Early Sinophone American literature had largely been written in Cantonese or with Cantonese inflections, whereas the post-1965 body of literature is largely in standard Hanyu, refracting the particular geographical contours of immigration from China, Taiwan, and elsewhere in different historical periods. The English-centrism of American literature is clearly refuted by the prolific production of Sinophone American literature by generations of immigrants from various other Sinophone communities. American literature, like all national literatures, is a multilingual literature. This is a simple and obvious fact that is often occluded by linguistic and literary politics exercised by the dominant.

If both Sinophone Taiwanese literature written by the indigenous peoples and Sinophone American literature written by Chinese American minorities register their discontent against the respective dominant cultures in Taiwan and the United States and express anticolonial or decolonial intent (the former does so more than the latter), we must consider Sinophone Tibetan or Sinophone Mongolian literature in a similar vein. Many Sinophone Tibetan writers, for instance, are themselves subjects living under a colonial condition, external (if their desire is sovereignty) or internal (if they feel oppressed). They may write in the standard Hanyu, but their sensibilities are ambiguously positioned vis-à-vis politico-cultural China and a uniform construction of Chineseness as Han-centered and Han-dominant. As historians tell us, it is the expansion of the Qing Empire that brought the far-flung regions such as Tibet, present-day Xinjiang, and Inner Mongolia into the fold of China with effective military conquests and cultural managements in a typical colonial fashion.[19] A case must be made, therefore, about internal colonialism in China where Han hegemony over its linguistic, cultural, and ethnic others needs to be thoroughly investigated. Ethnic writers such as Tibetans and Uigurs who choose to write in the standard Hanyu do so with a distinctively bicultural, if not bilingual, sensibility, where "cross-epistemological conversations"[20] take place in antagonistic, dialectical, or any other number of ways. The Sinophone, like the category of the "Third World" that can also exist within the First World, then also exists on the margins within China.

Similar to its complex relationship to China and Chineseness, the Sinophone also evinces a complex relationship with the sites of its settlement and lived experience. For first-generation Chinese Americans who have emigrated from various other Sinophone sites or China, for example, their relationship to the cultures and languages of the United States is, although equally ambivalent and complex, of a qualitatively different kind. As the Sinophone distinguishes itself from the dominant construction of Chineseness, it also distinguishes itself from the dominant construction of Americanness in a way that is borne out by the exigencies of lived experience in the United States. Through heterogenizing both the dominant constructions of Chineseness and Americanness it maintains its own subjectivity. Some might flaunt this as the postmodernist in-between-ness; others see this as the existential condition of the Sinophone as a local practice. Place matters as the grounding where Sinophone acquires its valance and relevance.

The definition of the Sinophone must therefore be place-based and sensitive to time to attend to the process of its formation and disappearance. For recent immigrant communities in the United States that speak Cantonese, Hoklo, and various other Sinitic languages, their political allegiances often run the gamut of extreme positions at odds with each other, while their psychosocial investment in the land of settlement may increasingly outweigh older attachments. The Sinophone is kept alive by successive waves of new immigrants while earlier immigrants may move further toward the mainstream to heterogenize the mainstream culture in a bid for pluralism and equality. The history of the official Francophonie cautions us that the notion of the Sinophone also bears the risk of being appropriated by the Chinese state. In the case of the Francophonie as an institutional concept, the French state can willfully neglect the anticolonial character of the Francophone and instead highlight the state's potential as the champion of pluralism in order to refute the overpowering pressure of American cultural hegemony.[21] The Francophonie can be partly seen as spectral remains of the

French empire under whose shadow contemporary France's waning cultural influence in the globe can be temporarily displaced. Unfortunately, it can be turned into a new fantasy of French global influence, if not a point of mobilization for imperial nostalgia. The notion of the Chinese diaspora has led to similar consequences—it centered China as the place of origin and implicitly demonstrated China's global influence. Rather than a testament to the classical Chinese empire, such as the premodern Sinophone worlds of Vietnam, Japan, and Korea, or an emerging Chinese empire that claims the sole right to Chineseness, contemporary Sinophone articulations may determine whether to respond to such claims or to ignore them altogether. In the last two centuries, Japan tried to "overcome" China militarily by instigating the two Sino-Japanese Wars and symbolically through a vernacular movement that displaced the Han written script. For Korea, the resistance was more circuitous. Denouncing the ideology of "serving the great" (*sadae chuui*) in the seventeenth century was simultaneously producing its authenticity as preserver of Chinese culture against the Manchus,[22] but twentieth-century history saw a gradual move away from Chinese influence until the rise of China in the global scene in the early twenty-first century.

Sinophone Studies, Literary or Otherwise

To sum up then, the conceptualization of the Sinophone here emphasizes two major points:

1. *Diaspora has an end date.* When the (im)migrants settle and become localized, many choose to end their state of diaspora by the second or third generation. The so-called "nostalgia" for the ancestral land is often an indication or displacement of difficulties of localization, voluntary or involuntary. Racism and other hostile conditions can force immigrants to find escape and solace in the past, while cultural or other superiority complexes can estrange immigrants from the locals. Emphasizing that diaspora has an end date is therefore to insist that cultural and political practice is always place-based. Everyone should be given a chance to become a local.

2. *The linguistic community is a community of change and an open community.* When the descendants of immigrants no longer speak their ancestors' languages, they are no longer part of the Sinophone community. The Sinophone community is therefore a community of change, occupying a transitional moment (however long in duration) that inevitably integrates further with local communities and becomes constitutive of

the local. Furthermore, it is an open community because it is defined not by race or nationality of the speaker but by the languages one speaks. Just as Anglophone speakers are not necessarily British or American, Sinophone speakers need not be Chinese by nationality. To the extent that communities are most often multilingual, linguistically determined communities necessarily trace porous and contingent boundaries.

What does Sinophone studies do, then? Or rather, what can Sinophone studies do? To these questions, I offer several tentative answers by way of the following proposals:

1. By debunking "the Chinese diaspora" as the organizing concept for the study of various immigrant peoples who left China from centuries ago up to the present, it is possible to propose organizing concepts other than such essentialist notions as "Chineseness" and "the Chinese." Instead, rigorously rearticulated concepts such as multiplicity, difference, creolization, hybridity, *métissage/mestisaje*, and others can be deployed for more complex understandings of histories, cultures, and literatures. Ethnic studies, other "phone" studies such as Francophone studies and Anglophone studies, postcolonial studies, transnational studies, and additional relevant modes of inquiry may all be drawn from for Sinophone studies in a comparative vein.

2. Sinophone studies allows us to rethink the relationship between roots and routes by considering the conceptions of roots as place-based rather than ancestral or routes as a more mobile conception of home-ness rather than wandering and homelessness.[23] To decouple home-ness and origin is to recognize the imperative of living as a political subject within a particular geopolitical place in a specific time with deep local commitments. To link home-ness with the place of residence therefore becomes an ethical act that chooses concrete political engagement in the local. The claim of rootlessness by some nostalgia-driven, middle-class, first-generation immigrants is, for example, oftentimes narcissistic to the extent that it is not aware of its own trenchant conservatism and even racism.[24] The place of residence can change—some people migrate more than once—but to consider that place as home may thus be the highest form of rootedness. Routes, then, can become roots. This is not a theory of mobile citizens who disidentify from the local nation-state and disengage from local politics but the politicization of that mobility.

3. When routes can be roots, multidirectional critiques are not only possible but also imperative. Transcending national borders, Sinophone

communities can maintain a critical position toward both the country of origin and the country of settlement. It is no longer an either/or choice between the ancestral land and the local place, which has been shown to jeopardize the well-being of the immigrants and their descendants. A Chinese American can be critical of China and the United States at the same time. In the case of Taiwan, this double critique allows for the emergence of a critical, articulatory position beyond the conventional association of Taiwan with the American right so that Taiwan can be critical of Chinese and U.S. policies of containment as well as their collusion and complicity without being forced to choose one over the other. The Sinophone as a concept, then, allows for the emergence of a critical position that does not succumb to nationalist and imperialist pressures and allows for a multiply-mediated and multiply-angulated critique. In this way, Sinophone can be considered a method. Starting from being a historical and empirical category of communities, cultures, and languages, the Sinophone can also be rearticulated as an epistemology.

By way of conclusion, Malaysian writer Ho Sok Fong's intriguing short story "Never Mention It Again" offers a refreshingly sharp and critical look at the world from Sinophone perspectives.[25] In this story, a married Chinese Malaysian man has secretly converted to Islam in order to take advantage of tax breaks and other economic benefits provided by the government. In Malaysia, a policy of "positive discrimination" has been practiced for approximately the past forty years as a way to guarantee Malay success in economy and government while restricting Chinese Malaysian and Indian Malaysian access to success. This man has also apparently married a couple of Muslim women without his Chinese Malaysian wife's knowledge. Things were going really well until he dies. At his funeral planned as a Daoist ritual by his Chinese Malaysian wife and children, government officials storm the funeral and announce that only Muslims can bury a Muslim. What ensues is a physical struggle over the corpse of the man, with two sides grabbing and holding onto one-half of the corpse in a tug-of-war. At the height of this tug-of-war, the corpse defecates. Small, hard, broken pieces of his feces land on everyone, as the violent motion of the tug-of-war creates a large radius for their spread. In the end, the Muslims take his corpse, the Chinese Malaysians are reduced to gathering the feces and burying them in a family grave, and the Chinese Malaysian wife is, by Malaysian law, disinherited of all her husband's property because she cannot inherit a Muslim's property. This theater of the absurd may serve as a perfect allegory for a double critique of state racism (of the Malaysian state) and Chinese cultural essentialism (of the Chinese family), both as flipsides of each other that reinforce and enhance each other, while no one is immune from the feces of the corpse, which contaminate everyone equally. This is the ugly and smelly picture of hybridity, not the hybridity that is celebrated by some scholars of postcolonial theory—ugly and smelly precisely because hybridity is not acknowledged by state racism and Chinese cultural essentialism and is not an easy condition. The Sinophone articulates itself into being through such difficulty and complexity.

Notes

This chapter is based on excerpts from *Visuality and Identity: Sinophone Articulations Across the Pacific* (Berkeley and Los Angeles: University of California Press, 2007) but has gone through extensive revision for this volume.

1. The early twentieth-century version of national characteristics is evinced in the work of none other than the reputed "father" of modern Chinese literature, Lu Xun, who saw his mission to be curing the diseased Chinese people inflicted with a host of recognizable, negative characteristics as a literary doctor. The contemporary version of the idea of national characteristics is the hot topic of the "quality" (*suzhi*) of the Chinese people. The argument goes that the quality of the Chinese needs to be improved in order for China to advance quickly on the path of modernization.

2. Trade routes between China and Southeast Asia were opened as early as the second century, and by the sixth century, communities of people from China could already be found in port cities throughout the region. See C. F. FitzGerald, *The Third China* (Melbourne: F. W. Cheshire, 1965).

3. Instructive comparisons can be made between Sinophone societies and those European countries where nationality and ethnicity are clearly not equated. We can think of Latvia, for instance, where only about 56 percent of its population is Latvian, and the rest are Russians and others.

4. David L. Kenley, *New Culture in a New World: The May Fourth Movement and the Chinese Diaspora in Singapore, 1919–1932* (New York and London: Routledge, 2003), 163–185.

5. Wang Gungwu, *The Chinese Overseas: From Earthbound China to the Quest for Autonomy* (Cambridge, MA: Harvard University Press, 2000), 79–97.

6. "Dual domination" is Lingchi Wang's descriptive term for this condition. See Wang, L., "The Structure of Dual Domination: Toward a Paradigm for the Study of the Chinese Diaspora in the United States," *Amerasia Journal* 21, nos. 1 & 2 (1995): 149–169.

7. Carolyn Cartier, "Diaspora and Social Restructuring in Postcolonial Malaysia," in *The Chinese Diaspora*, ed. Lawrence J. C. Ma and Carolyn Cartier (Lanham, Boulder, New York, Oxford: Roman & Littlefield, 2003), 69–96.

8. Lynn Pan lists these peoples under the category "hybrids," which is also a chapter title in Pan's book *Sons of the Yellow Emperor: A History of the Chinese Diaspora* (Boston, Toronto, London: Little, Brown, 1990), 156–158.

9. See Wang Gungwu, "Chineseness: The Dilemmas of Place and Practice," in *Cosmopolitan Capitalists*, ed. Gary Hamilton (Seattle: University of Washington Press, 1999), 188–234.

10. Lynn Pan, *Sons of the Yellow Emperor: A History of the Chinese Diaspora*, 289–295.

11. See Leo Suryadinata, ed., *Ethnic Chinese as Southeast Asians* (Singapore: Institute of Southeast Asian Studies, 1997).

12. Both Wang Gungwu's and Lynn Pan's books referred to earlier exemplify this.

13. See, for instance, Emanuel Wallerstein's three-volume *The Modern World-System* (San Diego: Academic Press, 1974, 1980, 1989) and Samir Amin, *Capitalism in the Age of Globalization* (London and New York: Zed Books, 1997).

14. Margaret A. Majumdar, *Francophone Studies* (London: Arnold, 2002), 210, 217.

15. Victor Mair's important work shows that what we know to be standard Chinese belongs to the Sinitic language group, where the mistakenly named "dialects" are not variations of standard Chinese but actually different languages. Hoklo and Cantonese are thus different languages from Mandarin (Taiwan standard) and *putonghua* (China standard). See Victor Mair, "What Is a Chinese 'Dialect/Topolect'? Reflections on Some Key Sino-English Linguistic Terms," *Sino-Platonic Papers* 29 (September 1991): 1–31. See also Mair, V., "Introduction," in *Hawai'i Reader in Traditional Chinese Culture*, ed. Victor Mair, Nancy Shatzman Steinhardt, and Paul Rakita Goldin (Honolulu: University of Hawai'i Press, 2005), 1–7.

16. Carolyn Cartier, "Diaspora and Social Restructuring in Postcolonial Malaysia," in *The Chinese Diaspora: Space, Place, Mobility, and Identity*, ed. Laurence J. C. Ma and Carolyn Cartier (Lanham, MD: Rowman & Littlefield, 2003), 69–96.

17. *Farewell China* is the title of a film made by then Hong Kong-based, British-trained filmmaker Clara Law. Taiwanese cultural critic Yang Zhao's famous book *Farewell China* (*Gaobie Zhongguo*) captures this sentiment vividly.

18. "Sinophone Asian American literature" may simply be changed to "Sinophone American literature," as this literature is categorized by language. Similarly, one can make a distinction between Chinese America and Sinophone America, the latter referring to Sinitic-language-speaking American communities. Again, linguistic designation allows the possibility of overcoming distinctions made solely based on ethnicity or race. See Sau-ling Cynthia Wong, "The Yellow and the Black: The African-American Presence in Sinophone Chinese American Literature," *Chung-Wai Literary Monthly* 34, no. 4 (September 2005): 15–53.

19. See, for instance, Pamela Kyle Crossley, Helen F. Siu, and Donald S. Sutton, eds., *Empire at the Margins: Culture, Ethnicity, and Frontier in Early Modern China* (Berkeley and Los Angeles: University of California Press, 2006) and Joanna Waley-Cohen, *The Culture of War in China: Empire and the Military Under the Qing Dynasty* (London, New York: I. B. Tauris, 2006).

20. The phrase "cross-epistemological conversations" is from Walter Mignolo, *Local Histories/Global Designs* (Princeton: Princeton University Press, 2000), 85.

21. Margaret Majumdar, "The Francophone World Moves into the Twenty-First Century," in *Francophone Post-Colonial Cultures*, Kamal Salhi, ed. (Lanham, Boulder, New York, Oxford: Lexington Books, 2003), 4–5.

22. Choson Korea considered itself the *"sojunghwa"* (literally, small China), which was more authentically Chinese than the Manchu Qing Dynasty.

23. The term "wandering Chinese" had enjoyed much currency. See, for instance, the now classic group of essays under the special issue title "The Living Tree: The Changing Meaning of Being Chinese Today," *Daedalus* 120, no. 2 (Spring 1991).

24. Sau-ling Wong analyzed racism against African Americans prevalent in overseas Chinese literature or Sinophone Chinese American literature written by first-generation immigrant students in the United States. While wallowing in self-pity over a sense of rootlessness, some of these writers had the most conservative tendencies toward questions of race, gender, and class. See Wong, S., "The Yellow and the Black: The African-American Presence in Sinophone Chinese American Literature," *Chung Wai Literary Monthly* 34, no. 4 (September 2005): 15–54. See this volume for the shorter English version.

25. Ho Sok Fong, "Never Mention It Again" (*Biezai tiqi*), in *Yuanxiang ren* [The man who longed for a far away home], David Der-wei Wang and Kim Chew Ng, eds. (Taipei: Maitian, 2004), 228–234.

On Chineseness as a Theoretical Problem

REY CHOW

The Ethnic Supplement and the Logic of the Wound

The parallel between academic and political economies does not stop at the level of what works, be it in the form of cultural or financial capital. Both are marked, as well, by a recurrent symptom, the habitually adamant insistence on *Chineseness* as the distinguishing trait in what otherwise purport to be mobile, international practices. Just as socialism, modernization, or nationalism at the level of realpolitik has been regularly supplemented by the word *Chinese*, so, in the much smaller sphere of the academic study of China, is the word *Chinese* frequently used to modify general, theoretical issues such as modernity, modernism, feminism, poetic tradition, novels, gay and lesbian issues, film theory, cultural studies, and so forth. One can almost be certain that, once a new type of discourse gains currency among academics at large, academics working on China-related topics will sooner or later produce a "Chinese" response to it that would both make use of the opportunity for attention made available by the generality of the theoretical issue at hand and deflect it by way of historical and cultural characteristics that are specific to China.

This collective habit of supplementing every major world trend with the notion of "Chinese" is the result of an overdetermined series of historical factors, the most crucial of which is the lingering, pervasive hegemony of Western culture. Against the systematic exclusivism of many hegemonic Western practices, the ethnic supplement occurs first and foremost as a struggle for access to representation while at the same time contesting the conventional simplification and stereotyping of ethnic subjects as such.[1] Nevertheless, even when such access is achieved, the mainstream recognition of non-Western representations is not necessarily, often not at all, free of prejudice. As I have pointed out in my discussion of contemporary Chinese cinema, there remains in the West, against the current facade of welcoming non-Western "others" into putatively interdisciplinary and cross-cultural exchanges, a continual tendency to stigmatize and ghettoize non-Western cultures precisely by way of ethnic, national labels.[2] Hence, whereas it would be acceptable for authors dealing with specific cultures, such as those of Britain, France, the United States, or the ancient Greco-Roman world, to use generic titles such as *Women Writers and the Problem of Aesthetics, Gender Trouble, Otherness and Literary Language, The Force of Law, The Logic of Sense, This Sex Which Is Not One, Tales of Love,* and so on, authors dealing with non-Western cultures are often expected to mark their subject matter with words such as *Chinese, Japanese, Indian, Korean, Vietnamese,* and their like. While the former are thought to deal with intellectual or theoretical issues, the latter, even when they are dealing with intellectual or theoretical issues, are compulsorily required to characterize such issues with *geopolitical realism,* to stabilize and fix their intellectual and theoretical content by way of a national, ethnic, or cultural location. Once such a location is named, however, the work associated with it is usually considered too narrow or specialized to warrant general interest. That this vicious circle of discriminatory practice has gone largely uncontested even by those who are supposedly sensitive to cultural difference is something that bespeaks the insidious hypocrisy of what purports, in North America at least, to be an enlightened academy. To this extent, authors who feel obliged to comply with this convention (of categorizing intellectual subject matter by way of ethnic labeling, which is deemed unnecessary in the case of whites and imperative in the case of nonwhites) are not personally responsible for the situation even as they perpetuate the problem by adhering to the convention. Such authors often have no choice.

In the case of China, the problematic of the ethnic supplement predates the current trends in North American academe. For a continuous period between the mid-nineteenth and the early twentieth centuries, China was targeted for territorial and military invasions by numerous Western powers as well as Japan, invasions that led to the signing of a series of what were known as unequal treaties between the Chinese government and various foreign nations, which were granted major monetary indemnities, territorial concessions, trading privileges, and legal exemptions (known as extraterritoriality) on Chinese soil. The unspoken rule of the scramble for China at the turn of the twentieth century was simple: attack China, then proclaim you're being attacked and demand heavy compensation; if China fails to pay up, attack it some more, demand more compensation, and so forth. The recent historic return of the British Crown Colony of Hong Kong to the People's Republic was, for Chinese populations all over the world, regardless of their political loyalties, a major watershed that put an end to this 150-year history of aggression and violence against China. And yet, even as the history of humiliation that officially began with the Treaty of Nanking (signed as the result of the First Opium War, which led to the ceding of Hong Kong Island to Britain in 1842) formally closed on July 1, 1997—without violence or bloodshed— the media in the West, led by Britain and the United States, continued their well-worn practice of broadcasting all news about China as a *crisis*, picking on the smallest details in a militant goading on of so-called democracy in order to demonize China and thus affirm Western moral supremacy.[3]

While this is not exactly the place to recapitulate modern Chinese history in detail—interested readers will be able to find volumes devoted to the topic easily—I highlight it for the purpose of underscoring the historicity behind the issue of ethnic supplementarity. Chinese intellectuals' obsession with China and their compulsion to emphasize the Chinese dimension to all universal questions are very much an outgrowth of this relatively recent world history.[4] In the face of a preemptive Western hegemony, which expressed itself militarily and territorially in the past, and expresses itself discursively in the present, Chinese intellectuals in the twentieth century have found themselves occupying a more or less reactive, rather than active, position. The subsequent paranoid tendency to cast doubt on everything Western and to insist on qualifying it with the word *Chinese* thus becomes typical of what I would call *the logic of the wound*. Beginning as a justified reaction to aggression, and gathering and nurturing means of establishing cultural integrity in defense, the logic of the wound is not unique to China. Nonetheless, it is something modern and contemporary Chinese culture seems enduringly reluctant to give up.

In the habitual obsession with Chineseness, what we often encounter is a kind of cultural essentialism—in this case, Sinocentrism—that draws an imaginary boundary between China and the rest of the world. Everything Chinese, it follows, is fantasized as somehow better—longer in existence, more intelligent, more scientific, more valuable, and ultimately beyond comparison. The historically conditioned paranoid reaction to the West, then, easily flips over and turns into a narcissistic, megalomanic affirmation of China; past victimization under Western imperialism and the need for national "self-strengthening" in an earlier era, likewise, flip over and turn into fascistic arrogance and self-aggrandizement. Among the young generations of Chinese intellectuals in the People's Republic, the mobilization of an unabashedly chauvinistic Sinocentrism—or what I would call, simply, Sino-chauvinism—has already taken sensationally propagandist forms, typified by the slogan "China Can Say No."[5]

This paradoxical situation in which what begins as resistance to the discriminatory practices of the older Western hegemony becomes ethnicist aggression is part and parcel of what Etienne Balibar describes as the general displacement of the problematic of racism in the post–World War II period. From the older racism based on biology and genetics, Balibar writes, the decolonized world has steadily shifted into a new, "differentialist racism," which finds its justification no longer in the absoluteness of blood but in the insurmountability of cultural difference. Ironically, this new, second-order racism has been encouraged in part by the ideologically humanistic, indeed antiracist, arguments of the postwar phenomenon of anthropological culturalism, which is "entirely oriented towards the recognition of the diversity and equality of cultures." Such an emphasis on cultural differentials has led to a situation in which "culture" itself and the aggressive racist conduct that is adopted to fortify cultural boundaries have become naturalized: "What we see here," Balibar argues, "is that biological or genetic naturalism is not the only means of naturalizing human behaviour and social affinities. . . . *culture can also function like a nature*, and it can in particular function as a way of locking individuals and groups a priori into a genealogy, into a determination that is immutable and intangible in origin."[6]

As China emerged as a world power at the end of the twentieth century, these volatile realities of ethnicity inevitably became a central part of modern Chinese studies. It is in this context that we should rethink the use of the label "Chinese," which occurs as frequently as its status remains untheorized and taken for granted. In recent years, as various alternative forces have been gathering momentum, we have begun to see a gradual epistemic shift that seeks to modify the claim of a homogeneously unified, univocal China. Among such alternative forces are studies of China's minority populations (e.g., the Huis, or Chinese Moslems), continual demands for the liberation of Tibet, intermittent protests from Xinjiang and Inner Mongolia, repeated assertions of political and national autonomy by Taiwan, and concerted efforts for democratic government and the rule of law in post-British Hong Kong. As well, in the relatively new area of cultural studies, the notion of Chineseness as a monolithic given bound ultimately to mainland China has been interrogated and critiqued by scholars attentive to issues of the Chinese diaspora such as David Yen-ho Wu, Ien Ang, and Allen Chun.[7] However flawed and unsatisfactory, the modes of inquiries made under the rubric of identity politics have indisputably opened up new avenues of engaging with ethnicity, which is, strictly speaking, an unfinished process. As Stuart Hall writes, "We still have a great deal of work to do to *decouple* ethnicity, as it functions in the dominant discourse, from its equivalence with nationalism, imperialism, racism and the state. . . . What is involved is the splitting of the notion of ethnicity between, on the one hand the dominant notion which connects it to nation and 'race' and on the other hand what I think is the beginning of a positive conception of the ethnicity of the margins, of the periphery."[8]

It is such "splitting" of the notion of ethnicity that will, I believe, be instrumental to the reimagining of a field such as modern Chinese studies. Insofar as it deals with the politics of literary culture and representation, modern Chinese studies has, all along, we may say, been constructed precisely on the very ambiguity of the ethnic supplement—of the victim-cum-empire status of the term *Chinese*. Once ethnicity is introduced consciously as a theoretical problem, the conventions of understanding practices that are not explicitly about ethnicity as such take on new and provocative implications. For instance, what is Chinese about the Chinese language and Chinese literature? If language and literature in the narrow sense have been fundamentally dislocated in poststructuralist theory by way of the "differences" inherent to signification, *Chinese* language and literature must now be seen as a further dislocation of this fundamental dislocation, requiring us to reassess "ethnicity" (as a site of difference) not only in terms of a struggle against the West but also, increasingly, in terms of the permanently evolving mutations internal to the invocation of ethnicity itself, in particular as such mutations bear upon the practices of writing.

Having raised these general issues of ethnicity that pertain to the field of China studies as a whole, I will now move on to a brief analysis of the more specific aspects of the relation between Chineseness and the study of Chinese language and literature.

The Language Issue

One assumption that binds the discipline of Chinese studies is that of a so-called standard language, by which is meant the language spoken in Beijing, Mandarin, which has been adopted as the official "national language" since the early twentieth century. Known in the People's Republic by its egalitarian-sounding appellation Putonghua (common speech), the hegemony of Mandarin has been made possible through its identification more or less with the written script, an identification that lends it a kind of permanence and authority not enjoyed by other Chinese speeches. Even in the instrumental uses of language, though, Chineseness—just what is Chinese about "standard Chinese"—inevitably surfaces as a problem. As John DeFrancis writes, "the 'Chinese' spoken by close to a billion Han Chinese is an abstraction that covers a number of mutually unintelligible forms of speech."[9] The multiple other languages—often known subordinately as "dialects"—that are spoken by Chinese populations in China and elsewhere in the world clearly render the monolithic nature of such a standard untenable.[10]

In the West, meanwhile, this untenable standard is precisely what continues to be affirmed in the pedagogical dissemination of Chinese. When there are job openings in the area of Chinese language and literature in North American universities, for instance, the only candidates who will receive serious consideration are those who have verbal fluency in Mandarin. A candidate who can write perfect standard Chinese, who may have more experience writing and speaking Chinese than all the Caucasian members of a particular East Asian language and literature department combined, but whose mother tongue happens to be (let's say) Cantonese, would be discriminated against and disqualified simply because knowledge of Chinese in such cases really does not mean knowledge of *any* kind of Chinese speech or even command of the standardized Chinese written language but, specifically, competence in Mandarin, the "standard" speech that most white Sinologists learn when they learn to speak Chinese at all.

Such, then, is the fraught, paradoxical identity of a non-Western language in the postcolonial era: Mandarin is, properly speaking, also *the white man's Chinese*, the Chinese that receives its international authentication as "standard Chinese" in part because, among the many forms of Chinese speeches, it is the one inflected with the largest number of foreign, especially Western, accents. Yet, despite its currency among nonnative speakers, Mandarin is not a straightforward parallel to a language such as English. Whereas the adoption of English in non-Western countries is a sign of Britain's colonial legacy, the enforcement of Mandarin in China and the West is rather a sign of the systematic *codification and management of ethnicity* that is typical of modernity, in this case through language implementation. Once we understand this, we see that the acquisition of the Chinese language as such, whether by environment or by choice, is never merely the acquisition of an instrument of communication; it is, rather, a participation in the system of value production that arises with the postcolonized ascriptions of cultural and ethnic identities.

In a context such as British Hong Kong, for instance, it was common for Chinese people in Hong Kong to grow up with a reasonable command of the Chinese language even as they were required to learn English. Nonetheless, with the systematically imposed supremacy of English in the colony, the knowledge of Chinese possessed by the majority of Chinese people, however sophisticated it might be, was generally disregarded as having any great value.[11] But the same was not true of Westerners: the rare instance of a Westerner knowing a few phrases of Chinese, let alone those who had actually learned to speak and read it, was instead usually hailed with wonderment as something of a miracle, as if it were a favor bestowed on the colonized natives. Similarly, in the West, knowledge of Chinese among non-Chinese Sinologists is often deemed a mark of scholarly distinction (in the form of "Wow, they actually know this difficult and exotic language!"), whereas the Chinese at the command of Chinese scholars is used instead as a criterion to judge not only their ethnic authenticity but also their academic credibility. For the white person, in other words, competence in Chinese is viewed as a status symbol, an additional professional asset; for the Chinese person, competence in Chinese is viewed as an index to existential value, of which one must supply a demonstration if one is not a native of Beijing. And, of course, if one is not a native of Beijing and thus not bona fide by definition, this attempt to prove oneself would be a doomed process from the beginning. Those who are ethnically Chinese but for historical reasons have become linguistically distant or dispossessed are, without exception, deemed inauthentic and lacking.[12]

There are, in sum, at least two sets of urgent questions around the language issue. The first has to do with the "other" Chinese languages that have so far remained incidental realities both in terms of state policy and in terms of pedagogy. As the polyphony of these other speeches and their respective ethnicities is likely to become louder in the decades to come, it will be increasingly impossible to continue to treat them simply as the negligible aspects of a canonized discipline. Officials and scholars alike will undoubtedly need to respond to the plurality that has hitherto been suppressed under the myth of "standard Chinese." But such a response cannot simply take the form of adding more voices to the existing canon. The second set of questions, therefore, has to do with a much needed effort not only to multiply the number of languages recognized but also to theorize the controversial connections among language possession, ethnicity, and cultural value.

"Chinese" Literature: A Literary or Ethnic Difference?

Another major assumption that binds the discipline of Chinese studies is that of an unproblematic linkage between Chineseness as such and Chinese literary writing. In such a linkage, what is Chinese is often imagined and argued as completely distinct from its counterparts in the West, even as such counterparts are accepted in an a priori manner as models or criteria for comparison.

To use a classic example in this *systematically reactive construction of a fictive ethnicity in literary studies*,[13] let us take the prevalent belief among some Sinologists that ancient Chinese writing is distinguished by a nonmimetic and nonallegorical (as opposed to a mimetic and allegorical) tradition. This belief, I should emphasize, is fundamentally akin to the premise of postwar anthropological culturalism, namely, that there is a need to recognize cultural difference in a world still run by the erasure of such difference. At the same time, the assertion of the Chinese difference tends often to operate from a set of binary oppositions in which the Western literary tradition is understood to be metaphorical, figurative, thematically concerned with transcendence, and referring to a realm that is beyond this world, whereas the Chinese literary tradition is said to be metonymic, literal, immanentist, and self-referential (with literary signs referring not to an otherworldly realm above but back to the cosmic order of which the literary universe is part). The effort to promote China, in other words, is made through an a priori surrender to Western perspectives and categories.[14] Accordingly, if mimesis has been the chief characteristic of Western writing since time immemorial, then nonmimesis is the principle of Chinese writing.[15] Haun Saussy captures the drift and implications of these arguments in the following. According to the Sinologists, he writes,

> Without "another world" to refer to, no Chinese writer can possibly produce allegories. There are only contextualizations. . . .
>
> The secret of Chinese rhetoric is that there is no rhetoric. The seeming allegories, metaphors, and tropes of Chinese poets do no more than report on features of the Chinese universe. . . .
>
> Metaphor and fiction, instead of being dismissed or bracketed as constructs of Western ontology, have now been promoted (as categories) to the status of realities. It is an astonishing conclusion.[16]

Such arguments about the Chinese difference, as Saussy points out, have been made with great erudition. In referring to them, my point is not to challenge the technical mastery and historical knowledge that unquestionably accompany their formulation. Rather, it is to foreground the fact that, in the insistent invocation of a Chinese tradition—and with it Chinese readers with Chinese habits, sensibilities, perspectives, points of view, and so forth—seldom, if ever, has the question been asked as to what exactly is meant by *Chinese*. Why is it necessary at all to reiterate what is Chinese in Chinese poetry by way of so-called Western attributes of poetic writing? What does it mean to supply this particular *copula*—to graft a term that is, strictly speaking, one of ethnicity onto discourses about literary matters such as allegory?

If such erudite and authoritative accounts have succeeded in explaining the formal details of texts (by expounding on literary and historical commentaries that deal with the various uses of poetic conventions, for instance), little, if anything, has been done about the nonliterary term *Chinese* even as it is repeatedly affixed to such studies. The (rhetorical) status of the term remains external to the formal issues involved, and the question of cultural difference, which such discussions of literary matters are supposedly addressing, simply refuses to disappear because it has, in fact, not yet been dealt with.

What happens as a result of latching the investigation of literary specificities to this unproblematized, because assumed, notion of Chineseness is that an entire theory of ethnicity becomes embedded (without ever being articulated as such) in the putative claims about Chinese poetics and literary studies. For instance, when it is assumed that poets, literati, commentators, and readers engage in literary practices in the Chinese way, the discourse of literary criticism, regardless of the intentions of the individual critic, tacitly takes on a cross-disciplinary significance to resemble that of classical anthropology. And, once classical anthropology is brought in, it becomes possible to see that the practitioners of Chinese writing—or the Chinese practitioners of writing—are, in effect, read as ethnics, or natives, who are endowed with a certain *primitive logic*. As the paradigm of anthropological information retrieval would have it, such treasures of primitive thought, however incomprehensible to the contemporary mind (and precisely because they are so incomprehensible), must be rescued. The Western Sinologist thus joins the ranks of enlightened progressives engaged in the task of salvaging the remains of great ancient civilizations. Since it is no longer possible to interview the natives of ancient China—the writers of classical Chinese narratives and poems, and their contemporary readers—the texts left behind by them will need to be upheld as evidence of their essential ethnic difference.

But what is this essential ethnic difference? As I already indicated, it is, according to these Sinologists, nonmimeticism, a way of writing and reading that is said to be natural, spontaneous, immanentist—and, most important, lacking in (the bad Western attributes of) allegorical, metaphorical, and fictive transformation. While ostensibly discussing literary matters, then, these Sinologists have, de facto, been engaged in the (retroactive) construction of a certain ethnic identity. The Chinese that is being constructed is, accordingly, a nonmimetic, literal-minded, and therefore virtuous primitive—a noble savage.

The implications of this are serious and go well beyond the study of an esoteric literary tradition. The characterization, however well intended, of an entire group of people (the Chinese of ancient China) in such cognitive, psychological, or behavioral terms as a disposition toward literalness, is, in the terms of our ongoing discussion, racist. Even though it takes the benevolent form of valorizing and idealizing a projected collective "difference,"[17] such racism is, to use the words of Ang, "reinforced precisely by pinning down people to their ethnic identity, by marking them as ethnic."[18] To use the words of Balibar, this is a racism "whose dominant theme is not biological heredity but the insurmountability of cultural differences." Culture here functions as "a way of locking individuals and groups a priori into a genealogy, into a determination that is immutable and intangible in origin."[19]

From this it follows that it is antiquity that remains privileged as the site of the essence of Chineseness, which appears to be more bona fide when it is found among the dead, when it is apprehended as part of an irretrievable past. Within the field of Chinese, then, the dead and the living are separated by what amounts to *an entangled class and race boundary*: high culture, that which is presumed to be ethnically pure, belongs with the inscrutable dead; low culture, that which is left over from the contaminating contacts with the foreign, belongs with those who happen to be alive and can still, unfortunately, speak and write. It is not an accident that one of the most memorable studies of the ancient Chinese is R. H. Van Gulik's *Sexual Life in Ancient China*, a fascinating account in which, at the crucial moments, highly metaphorical passages about sexual activities, written in classical Chinese—already a challenge to the imagination with their allusions to dragons, phoenixes, cicadas, jades, pearls, clouds, and rain—are translated into Latin.[20] If the trends of modern and contemporary society move in the direction of fluidity and translatability between cultures, the Sinologist, on the contrary, finds his vocation rather in the painstaking preservation of savage thought. He does this by rendering such thought indecipherable except to the learned few, West and East. Primitive logic, here in the form of the art of the bedchamber, is thus museumized and dignified, gaining its exotic value and authority at once through a punctilious process of fossilization.

Ridden with the contradictions of a modernist, rationalist attempt to redeem the past, Western Sinology seems ultimately unable to extricate itself from a condition of captivity in which the only kind of specialty it can claim is, by logic, "hypotheses inimical to [its own] conclusions."[21] With the passage of time, Sinology has hardened into an obstinate elitist practice with the presumption that Chineseness—that very notion it uses to anchor its intended articulation of cultural difference—is essentially incomparable and hence beyond history. One could only surmise that, if Sinology had been a little more willing to subject the belief in Chineseness to the same fastidious scrutiny it lavishes on arcane textual nuances, the intellectual results produced would perhaps have been less ephemeral.

Reimagining a Field

Although the abstract notion of the field of modern Chinese literary studies has hitherto been harnessed to the fantasy of an essentialized ethnicity, a standardized language, and a coercive equivalence between literary writing and Chineseness per se, even the most reactionary of the field's practitioners cannot be blind to the fact that, in the past decade or so, there has been an increasing noncoincidence between Chinese literary studies as such and what is actually taking place under its rubric. More and more scholars are turning to texts and media that are, strictly speaking, nonliterary (including film, television dramas, radio programs, art exhibits, and pop music), while non-China-related publications dealing with modernism, modernity, feminism, gay and lesbian studies, postcoloniality, philosophy, history, and so forth regularly fill China scholars' bibliographical lists. Against the rigidity of the norm of Chinese studies, then, a considerable range of discourses that are not Chinese by tradition, language, or discipline is making a substantial impact on the study of Chinese literature and culture. With the invasion of these foreign elements, how can the legitimating disciplinary boundary of Chinese versus non-Chinese be maintained? And, if we should attempt to redefine the field from Chinese language and literature to Chinese literary studies or Chinese cultural studies, what is the precise relation among these words—*Chinese, literary, cultural, studies*? Do Chinese literary studies and Chinese cultural studies mean the literary studies and cultural studies that are Chinese—in which case we would be confronted once again with the essentially external status of *Chinese* as an ethnic qualifier—or do these designations mean the studies of Chinese literature and Chinese culture—in which case we would face the same problem, which was in the past circumvented by a grounding in language and ethnicity, a grounding that must nonetheless no longer be taken for granted? (The same pair of questions can probably be asked of similar claims about British, French, or American literary and cultural studies.) In either configuration, what remains to be articulated is what, after the formulations of literature, culture, and literary or cultural studies, constitutes the ethnic label itself.

Notes

This chapter was modified and reprinted with permission from Rey Chow, "On Chineseness as a Theoretical Problem," *boundary 2* 25, no. 3 (Autumn 1998): 1–24.

1. A discussion that has been helpful to my formulation of ethnicity here is Stuart Hall, "New Ethnicities," in *Black Film, British Cinema* (London: ICA Documents, 1988), 27–31.

Referring to the black experience in Britain, Hall writes: "The struggle to come into representation was predicated on a critique of the degree of fetishization, objectification and negative figuration which are so much a feature of the representation of the black subject. . . . The cultural politics and strategies which developed around this critique had many facets, but its two principal objects were: first the question of access to the rights to representation by black artists and black cultural workers themselves. Secondly the contestation of the marginality, the stereotypical quality and the fetishised nature of images of blacks, by the counter-position of a 'positive' black imagery" (27; Hall's emphasis).

2. See the section "Chinese Film in the Age of Interdisciplinarity" in my *Primitive Passions: Visuality, Sexuality, Ethnography, and Contemporary Chinese Cinema* (New York: Columbia University Press, 1995), 26–28.

3. For a more sustained discussion of this point, see Rey Chow, "King Kong in Hong Kong: Watching the 'Handover' from the USA," *Social Text* 55 (summer 1998): 93–108.

4. As Naoki Sakai reminds us, this tendency toward self-referentiality on the part of the modern non-Western culture should be understood as always already operating in a comparative framework in what he refers to alternately as a "schema of cofiguration" or "regime of translation." See, in particular, Chapter 2 of *Translation and Subjectivity: On "Japan" and Cultural Nationalism, foreword by Meaghan Morris* (Minneapolis: University of Minnesota Press, 1997), "The Problem of 'Japanese Thought': The Formation of 'Japan' and the Schema of Cofiguration," 40–71.

5. See Song Qiang et al., *Zhongguo keyi shuo bu* (China can say no) (Hong Kong: Ming Pao, 1996); and *Zhongguo haishi neng shuo bu* (China can still say no) (Hong Kong: Ming Pao, 1996). For a discussion of the ramifications of such Sinochauvinism, especially as it has surfaced in theoretical debates among contemporary PRC scholars, see the essay by Michelle Yeh in this volume. See also the essay by Chris Berry on the related problem of theorizing collective agency in the case of contemporary Chinese cinema.

6. Etienne Balibar, "Is There a 'Neo-Racism'?" trans. Chris Turner, in *Race, Nation, Class: Ambiguous Identities* by Etienne Balibar and Immanuel Wallerstein (New York: Verso, 1991), 21–22; Balibar's emphasis. Balibar is making his arguments primarily from the perspective of a culturally hegemonic postwar France, but they are also applicable to the attitudes typical of Sinochauvinism. For another major discussion of the "new racism" (this time in contemporary Britain) that is based less on biological essentialism than on the notion of a pure and homogeneous cultural and national identity, see Paul Gilroy, *There Ain't No Black in the Union Jack* (London: Routledge, 1991). For an example of a collective attempt, prior to the introduction of poststructuralism, to rethink anthropology as a Western, in particular a post–World War II phenomenon, see some of the essays in Dell Hymes, ed., *Reinventing Anthropology* (New York: Pantheon, 1969).

7. David Yen-ho Wu, "The Construction of Chinese and Non-Chinese Identities," *Daedalus* 120, no. 2 (spring 1991): 159–79; Ien Ang, "On Not Speaking Chinese," *New Formations* 24 (winter 1994): 1–18; Allen Chun, "Fuck Chineseness: On the Ambiguities of Ethnicity as Culture as Identity," *boundary 2* 23, no. 2 (summer 1996): 111–138. For a related discussion of the way the governments in mainland China and the Chinese overseas have interacted during alternating periods of strength and weakness in the Chinese polity, see Wang Gungwu, "Greater China and the Chinese Overseas," in *Greater China: The Next Superpower?* ed. David Shambaugh (Oxford: Oxford University Press, 1995), 274–296.

8. Hall, "New Ethnicities," 29; Hall's emphasis.

9. John DeFrancis, *The Chinese Language: Fact and Fantasy* (Honolulu: University of Hawai'i Press, 1984), 39.

10. See DeFrancis, *The Chinese Language*, 54–57, for a discussion of the controversy over the classification of different varieties of spoken Chinese, a controversy that constitutes part of the global problem of the relationship between dialect and language.

11. The devaluing of Chinese in Hong Kong continues in the post-British period. An ongoing controversy since July 1, 1997, for instance, has to do with the Hong Kong government's attempt to implement the use of Cantonese (the mother tongue of the overwhelming majority of the population) as the medium of instruction in the local education system. This has been met with severe criticism and opposition from large sectors of Hong Kong's Chinese population, who prefer to retain English as that medium. For a discussion of the inferior cultural position occupied by colonial Hong Kong vis-à-vis both mainland China and Britain, especially as this position is negotiated in fictional writing and literary criticism, see the essay by Leung Ping-kwan in this volume.

12. It should be pointed out that those who are considered "inauthentic" Chinese are often discriminated against in other major ways as well. For instance, in Southeast Asian countries such as Indonesia and Malaysia, where anti-Chinese sentiments are traditionally strong, Chinese people are discriminated against by not being allowed to *forget* that they are Chinese, even when their families have lived in those countries for generations and they do not speak Chinese languages at all. For a moving discussion of this vast historical scenario relating to what are known as the Peranakan Chinese, see Ien Ang, "On Not Speaking Chinese"; see also Ang's chapter in this volume for a critique of the recent discourse of "cultural China," which, despite its seeming openness, is in the end still deeply China rooted and hence unable to address such issues of Chineseness as those constitutive of the diasporic experiences of the Peranakan Chinese populations.

13. I borrow the term *fictive ethnicity* from Balibar, "The Nation Form: History and Ideology," in Balibar and Wallerstein, *Race, Nation, Class*, 86–106; see, in particular, the discussion on page 96.

14. In his study of Japan, Naoki Sakai perceptively calls this kind of effort to promote an ethnic culture mimetic: "The desire to identify either with Japan or the West is . . . invariably a mimetic one, so that the insistence on Japan's originality, for instance, would have to be mediated by the mimetic desire for the West" (*Translation and Subjectivity*, 52). As my arguments show, this mimeticism fundamental to modern East-West relations is further complicated in the China situation by Sinologists' (ideological) insistence that classical Chinese writings are, in and of themselves, nonmimetic in nature.

15. For an informative discussion of the intellectual problems generated by such arguments in the field of ancient Chinese poetry and poetics, see Yong Ren, "Cosmogony, Fictionality, Poetic Creativity: Western and Traditional Chinese Cultural Perspectives," *Comparative Literature* 50, no.2 (Spring 1998): 98–119. In his well-known essay "White Mythology," Jacques Derrida, explaining the classical Western philosophical tradition, has suggested that, for a major philosopher such as Aristotle, mimesis "belongs to *logos*" itself and is "tied to the possibility of meaning and truth in discourse" in general. Accordingly, mimesis is "proper to man. Only man imitates properly. Man alone takes pleasure in imitating, man alone learns to

imitate, man alone learns by imitation. The power of truth, as the unveiling of nature (*physis*) by *mimesis*, congenitally belongs to the physics of man, to anthropophysics. Such is the natural origin of poetry, and such is the natural origin of metaphor" (*Margins of Philosophy*, trans., with additional notes, by Alan Bass [Chicago: University of Chicago Press, 1982], 237). Because my purpose here is to foreground the problem of ethnicity as it relates to literature (rather than the generality of mimesis [in writing] per se), a full-fledged discussion of the implications of Derrida's reading of Aristotle will have to be taken up on a different occasion.

16. Haun Saussy, *The Problem of a Chinese Aesthetic* (Stanford, Calif.: Stanford University Press, 1993), 27, 31. Saussy offers an informed discussion of the views that Sinologists doing "comparative poetics" typically advance to support the claim that Chinese literature is nonmimetic and nonallegorical. See, in particular, Chapter 1, "The Question of Chinese Allegory."

17. A good analogy here is Julia Kristeva's "positive" and laudatory reading of Chinese women by way of the psychoanalytic notions of pre-oedipality, motherhood, the semiotic, and so forth, in *About Chinese Women*, trans. Anita Barrows (London: Marion Boyars, 1977). For an incisive recent critique of this kind of essentialist reading of "ethnic" cultures by critics following theorists such as Kristeva, see Tomo Hattori, "Psycholinguistic Orientalism in Criticism of *The Woman Warrior* and *Obasan*," in *Other Sisterhoods: Literary Theory and U.S. Women of Color*, ed. Sandra Kumamoto Stanley (Urbana: University of Illinois Press, 1997), 119–138.

18. Ien Ang, "The Differential Politics of Chineseness," *Communal/Plural* (Research Centre in Intercommunal Studies, University of Western Sydney, Nepean) 1 (1993): 25.

19. Balibar, "Is There a 'Neo-Racism'?" 21–22.

20. R. H. Van Gulik, *Sexual Life in Ancient China* (1961; reprint, Leiden: Brill, 1974).

21. "The juxtaposition of Eastern and Western poetics outlined by these critics seems to involve hypotheses inimical to their conclusions" (Saussy, *The Problem of a Chinese Aesthetic*, 34).

3

Can One Say No to Chineseness?

Pushing the Limits of the Diasporic Paradigm

IEN ANG

William Yang was born in 1943 and grew up in Dimbulah, a small mining town in northern Queensland, Australia. Today a celebrated photographer working and living in Sydney, he is presented—classified—as "a third-generation Australian-Chinese." In an autobiographical account of his life, he recounts:

> One day, when I was about six years old, one of the kids at school called at me "Ching Chong Chinaman, Born in a jar, Christened in a teapot, Ha ha ha." I had no idea what he meant although I knew from his expression that he was being horrible.
>
> I went home to my mother and I said to her, "Mum, I'm not Chinese, am I?" My mother looked at me very sternly and said, "Yes you are."
>
> Her tone was hard and I knew in that moment that being Chinese was some terrible curse and I could not rely on my mother for help. Or my brother, who was four years older than me, and much more experienced in the world. He said, "And you'd better get used to it."[1]

This is a classic tale of revelation that can undoubtedly be told in countless variations and versions by many people throughout the world, articulating the all-too-familiar experience of a subject's harsh coming into awareness of his own, unchosen, minority status. "Chineseness" here is the marker of that status, imparting an externally imposed identity given meaning, literally, by a practice of discrimination. It is the dominant culture's classificatory prac-tice, operating as a territorializing power highly effective in marginalizing the other, that shapes the meaning of Chineseness here as a curse, as something to "get used to." Yang reveals that for most of his life, he has had negative feel-ings about "being Chinese." But what does his Chineseness consist of? "We were brought up in the western way," explains Yang. "None of us learned to speak Chinese. This was partly because my father, a Hukka [sic], spoke Man-darin, whereas my mother, a See Yup [sic], spoke Cantonese, and they spoke English at home. My mother could have taught us Cantonese but she never did—frankly she couldn't see the point."[2]

This glimpse into one ordinary family's history indicates the apparent lack of interest Yang's parents had in transmitting their Chinese roots and cultural traditions to their children. This would have been a difficult thing to do in Australia in the forties and fifties, when the official ideology was still one of "white Australia" and required the few nonwhite people in the country to assimilate. But at the same time, Yang's family obviously never lost a sense of certainty about the self-declared fact of their Chineseness. But are they indeed Chinese? What makes them so? And how do they know?

Scholars have always been bewildered by China. The intricate empirical multifariousness and historical complexity of the country is hardly con-tainable in the sophisticated (inter)disciplinary apparatus and theoreti-cal armory of Western researchers. Language, culture, civilization, people, nation, polity—how does one describe, interpret, and understand China, that awesome, other space that has never ceased to both fascinate and infuri-ate its dedicated scholar? The difficulty has grown exponentially, however, with the emergence of a so-called diasporic paradigm in the study of Chine-seness. The booming interest in what is loosely termed the Chinese diaspora has unsettled the very demarcation of China as an immensely complex yet ontologically stable object of study. The view from the diaspora has shat-tered the convenient certainty with which Chinese studies has been equated, quite simply, with the study of China. "China" can no longer be limited to the more or less fixed area of its official spatial and cultural boundaries nor can it be held up as providing the authentic, authoritative, and uncontested standard for all things Chinese. Instead, how to determine what is and what is not Chinese has become the necessary preliminary question to ask, and an increasingly urgent one at that. This, at least, is one of the key outcomes of the emergent view from the diaspora.

Central to the diasporic paradigm is the theoretical axiom that Chi-neseness is not a category with a fixed content—be it racial, cultural, or geographical—but operates as an open and indeterminate signifier whose meanings are constantly renegotiated and rearticulated in different sections of the Chinese diaspora. Being Chinese outside China cannot possibly mean the same thing as inside. It varies from place to place, molded by the local circumstances in different parts of the world where people of Chinese ancestry have settled and constructed new ways of living. There are, in this paradigm, many different Chinese identities, not one. This proposition entails a criticism of Chinese essentialism, a departure from the mode of demarcating Chineseness through an absolutist oppositioning of authentic and inauthentic, pure and impure, real and fake. The anti-essentialism of the diasporic paradigm opens up a symbolic space for people such as Yang, a distant member of the diaspora, to be Chinese in his own way, living a decentered Chineseness that does not have to live up to the norm of "the essential Chinese subject."[3]

Chineseness is not the innocent reflection of a natural reality that is passively waiting to be discovered; rather, the very quest for knowledge actively brings into being, in the knower's experience and understanding of the world, slices of reality he or she then calls and classifies as Chinese. Furthermore, there are stakes involved in the ongoing ontological confirmation of Chineseness, just as nineteenth-century Western science had a stake, beyond the noble one of scientific progress, in producing the existence of distinct, and hierarchically ordered, human "races." This analogy should provoke us to interrogate the political and ideological significance of the ongoing currency, as well as shifting currents, of discourses, claims, and disclaims to Chineseness in the modern world. How Chineseness is made to mean in different contexts, and who gets to decide what it means or should mean, is the object of intense contestation, a struggle over meaning with wide-ranging cultural and political implications.

I also have a personal investment in this interrogation of Chineseness. Like Yang, though along a rather different historical trajectory, I am intimately familiar with the injunction to "get used to being Chinese." I was born into a so-called Peranakan Chinese family in Indonesia, a country that has always had a problem with its long-standing and economically significant Chinese minority (as, of course, is the case throughout Southeast Asia, except Singapore).[4] In Indonesia, from the sixties to the present, I have found being Chinese a profoundly ambivalent experience, fraught with feelings of rejection by the majority of Indonesians) and alienation (from an identity that was first and foremost an imposed one). The need to come to terms with the fact of my Chineseness remained a constant after I relocated—in a peculiar diasporic itinerary informed by the historical connections established by European colonialism—to the Netherlands, where I spent my teenage and young adult years, and later, after I transferred to Australia (where I live now). In these different geocultural spaces, the meaning of being Chinese was both the same and different, shaped by changing specific contexts, yet enduringly framed by the fact that I could not take my Chineseness (or lack of it) for granted. In short, the status of Chineseness as a discursive construct—rather than as something natural—is a matter of subjective experience to me, not just a question of theory.[5]

Conceiving Chineseness as a discursive construct entails a disruption of the ontological stability and certainty of Chinese identity; it does not, however, negate its operative power as a cultural principle in the social constitution of identities as Chinese. In other words, the point is not to dispute the fact that Chineseness exists (which, in any case, would be a futile assertion in a world where more than a billion people would, to all intents and purposes, identify themselves as Chinese in one way or another, either voluntarily or by force), but to investigate how this category operates in practice, in different historical, geographical, political, and cultural contexts. As Stuart Hall remarks, the fact that race is not a valid scientific category does not undermine its symbolic and social effectuality. The same could be said about Chineseness. What highlighting the constructed nature of categories and classificatory systems does, however, is shift "the focus of theoretical attention from the categories 'in themselves' as repositories of cultural [meaning] to the process of cultural classification itself."[6] In other words, how and why is it that the category of Chineseness acquires its persistence and solidity? And with what political and cultural effects?

What I call the view from the diaspora, which will be my starting point, is necessarily unstable. After all, the spirit of diasporic thought, motivated as it is by notions of dispersal, mobility, and disappearance, works against its consolidation as a paradigm proper. Contained in the diasporic perspective itself, therefore, are the seeds of its own deconstruction, which provides us with the opportunity to interrogate not just the different meanings Chineseness takes on in different local contexts, but, more fundamentally, the very significance and validity of Chineseness as a category of identification and analysis.

The process of decentering the center, which is so pivotal to diasporic theory, has been forcefully articulated in the recent influential collection *The Living Tree: The Changing Meaning of Being Chinese Today*, edited by Tu Wei-ming, professor of Chinese history and philosophy at Harvard.[7] In this collection, Tu elaborates on the contours of a symbolic universe he calls "cultural China,"[8] a newly constructed cultural space "that both encompasses and transcends the ethnic, territorial, linguistic, and religious boundaries that normally define Chineseness."[9] For Tu, the project of cultural China is one designed to decenter the cultural authority of geopolitical China, an intellectual effort to redefine "the periphery as the center" in current engagements with what it means to be Chinese.[10] This project is critical insofar as it aims to break with static and rigid, stereotypical and conventional definitions of

Chinese as "belonging to the Han race, being born in China proper, speaking Mandarin, and observing the 'patriotic' code of ethics" (preface, vii). Instead, Tu wants to "explore the fluidity of Chineseness as a layered and contested discourse, to open new possibilities and avenues of inquiry, and to challenge the claims of political leadership (in Beijing, Taipei, Hong Kong or Singapore) to be the ultimate authority in a matter as significant as 'Chineseness'" (preface, viii). The impetus for this intervention is a certain disillusion, if not despair, about the political reality of mainland China, the People's Republic of China. As Tu observes, "Although realistically those who are on the periphery . . . are seemingly helpless to affect any fundamental transformation of China proper, the center no longer has the ability, insight, or legitimate authority to dictate the agenda for cultural China. On the contrary, the transformative potential of the periphery is so great that it seems inevitable that it will significantly shape the intellectual discourse on cultural China for years to come" ("Cultural China," 33–34).[11]

It is important to note the political implications of Tu's project. His position is known to be explicitly neo-Confucianist and largely anticommunist, which we need to keep in mind when assessing his critiques of "the center." Placed in the context of Chinese cultural history, however, the assertion of the periphery as the center is a radical one. The notion of a single center, or cultural core, from which Chinese civilization has emanated—the so-called Central Country complex—has been so deeply entrenched in the Chinese historical imagination that it is difficult to disentangle our understandings of Chineseness from it. Yet the very emergence of a powerful discourse of cultural China enunciated from the periphery and formulated to assert the periphery's influence at the expense of the center is a clear indication of the increasingly self-confident voice of some Chinese intellectuals in diaspora, such as Tu Wei-ming himself. This growing self-confidence has much to do with the historical and economic state of affairs in global modernity at the end of the twentieth century. As Tu puts it, "While the periphery of the Sinic world was proudly marching toward an Asian-Pacific century, the homeland seemed mired in perpetual underdevelopment" ("Cultural China," 12). Indeed, it is precisely the homeland's seeming inability to transform itself according to the ideal image of a truly modern society—an image still hegemonically determined by the West—that has led to the perceived crisis of Chineseness, which the project of cultural China aims to address.

Central to the intellectual problematic of cultural China is what one sees as the urgent need to reconcile Chineseness and modernity. There are two interrelated sides to this challenge. On the one hand, the question is how to modernize Chineseness itself in a way that will correct and overcome the arguably abject course taken by the existing political regime in China, a course almost universally perceived as wrong and, provocatively, as somehow having a debilitating effect on the fate of Chineseness. According to Tu, the Chinese diaspora will have to take the lead in the modernization of Chineseness. "While the overseas Chinese may seem forever peripheral to the meaning of being Chinese," he writes, in an implicit attack on the center, "they [can] assume an effective role in creatively constructing a new vision of Chineseness that is more in tune with Chinese history and in sympathetic resonance with Chinese culture" ("Cultural China," 34).

On the other hand, there is also the reverse question of how to Sinicize modernity—how, that is, to create a modern world that is truly Chinese and not simply an imitation of the West. The radical iconoclasm of the May Fourth Movement—which was based on the assumption that China's modernization could only be realized through a wholesale process of Westernization and a simultaneous renunciation of Chinese culture—is now regarded as completely outdated. Instead, inspiration is drawn from the economic rise of East Asia to look for models of modernity—Chinese modernity—which pose challenging cultural alternatives to the Western model. Tu refers specifically to Taiwan, Hong Kong, Singapore, and the Chinese communities in Southeast Asia. The experiences of these countries suggest for Tu that "active participation in the economic, political, social, and cultural life of a thoroughly modernized community does not necessarily conflict with being authentically Chinese," signaling the possibility that "modernization may enhance rather than weaken Chineseness" ("Cultural China," 8).

The privileging of the periphery—the diaspora—as the new cultural center of Chineseness in Tu's discourse is an important challenge to traditional, centrist, and essentialist conceptions of Chinese culture and identity. Yet I want to suggest that the very postulation of a cultural China as the name for a transnational intellectual community held together not just by a "common awareness" but also by "a common ancestry and a shared cultural background, . . . a transnational network to explore the meaning of being Chinese in a global context" ("Cultural China," 25), is a move that is driven, and motivated, by another kind of centrism, this time along notionally cultural lines.

An important element here is the continued orientation of, if not obsession with, the self-declared periphery-as-center in the discourse of cultural China in relation to the old center, even if this center is so passionately denied its traditional authority and legitimacy. "What mainland China eventually will become remains an overriding concern for all intellectuals in cultural China" ("Cultural China," 33), writes Tu, and in this ongoing preoccupation with the center, the periphery not only reproduces unintentionally its own profound entanglement with the former; it also, by this very preoccupation, effects its own unwarranted internal homogenization and limits the much more radical potential that a diasporic perspective allows. In other words, while the aim would seem to be to rescue Chineseness from China, to de-hegemonize geopolitical China, which is found wanting in its own, heavy-handed politics of modernizing Chineseness/Sinicizing modernity, the rescue operation implies the projection of a new, alternative center, a decentered center, whose name is *cultural* China, but China nevertheless. It is clear, then, that the all-too-familiar "obsession with China," which has been a key disposition in the work of Chinese intellectuals in the twentieth century, remains at work here with undiminished intensity.[12] This obsession, which is so profoundly inscribed in the psychic structure of a wounded Chinese civilizationalism, "privileges China's problems as uniquely Chinese, which lays absolute claim to the loyalty of Chinese in all parts of the world."[13]

According to Leo Ou-fan Lee, who came from Taiwan to the United States as a graduate student more than thirty years ago and who describes himself as "a voluntary exile situated forever on the fringes of China," the "excessive obsession with their homeland has deprived Chinese writers abroad of their rare privilege of being truly on the periphery." For Lee, it is only by being truly on the periphery that one can create a distance "sufficiently removed from the center of the obsession," allowing one to "subject the obsession itself to artistic treatment."[14] From this point of view, cultural China definitely does not occupy a truly peripheral position at all. On the contrary. An overwhelming desire—bordering indeed, on obsession to somehow maintain, redeem, and revitalize the notion of Chineseness as a marker of common culture and identity in a rapidly postmodernizing world—is the driving force behind Tu's conception of cultural China. While the meaning of Chineseness is defined explicitly as fluid and changeable, the category of Chineseness itself is emphatically not in question here: Indeed, the notion of cultural China seems to be devised precisely to exalt and enlarge the global significance of Chineseness, raising its importance by imbuing it with new, modernized meanings and heightening its relevance by expanding its field of application far beyond the given spatial boundaries of geopolitical China.

The Chinese diaspora, as we have seen, is posited as one of the key pillars of the imagined community of cultural China. It is noteworthy that Tu persistently accentuates the quest for Chineseness as a central motif in his wide-ranging discussion of variant diaspora narratives. In the case of Southeast Asian families of Chinese descent remigrating from Malaysia or Vietnam to North America, Western Europe, or Australia, he sees the "irony of their not returning to their ancestral homeland but moving farther away from China with the explicit intention of preserving their cultural identity" ("Cultural China," 24). In mainland Chinese intellectuals' decision not to return to China after the Tiananmen event in 1989, he reads a "conscious and, for some, impulsive choice to realize one's Chineseness by moving far away from one's homeland" ("Cultural China," 24). But isn't Tu being too insistent in foregrounding the salience of Chineseness in the configuration of these diasporic flows and movements? Doesn't this emphasis unduly confine diverse strands of the diaspora to the narrow and claustrophobic shaft of a projected, if highly abstract, "obsession with Chineseness"?

The organic metaphor of "the living tree" to describe cultural China provides us with a clear insight into the problem I am hinting at here. A living tree grows and changes over time; it constantly develops new branches and stems that shoot outward, in different directions, from the solid core of the tree trunk, which in turn feeds itself on an invisible but life-sustaining set of roots. Without roots, there would be no life, no new leaves. The metaphor of the living tree dramatically imparts the ultimate existential dependence of the periphery on the center, the diaspora on the homeland. Furthermore, what this metaphor emphasizes is continuity over discontinuity: In the end, it all flows back to the roots.

In thus imputing an essential continuity and constancy in the diaspora's quest for Chineseness, the discourse of cultural China risks homogenizing what is otherwise a complex range of dispersed, heterogeneous, and not necessarily commensurable diaspora narratives—a homogeneity for which the sign of Chineseness provides the a priori and taken-for-granted guarantee. But in this way, the hegemony of "China" (cultural, if not geopolitical, China) is surreptitiously reinforced, not undercut. As Tu rightly notes, "Hegemonic discourse, charged with an air of arrogance, discriminates not only by excluding but also by including. Often it is in the act of inclusion that the art of symbolic control is more insidiously exercised" (preface, vii). Tu refers here to the coercive manner in which the People's Republic includes a variety of others (such as the non-Han minorities inside the borders of China) within the orbit of its official political control. But a wholesale incorporation of the diaspora under the inclusive rubric of "cultural China" can be an equally hegemonic move, which works to truncate and suppress complex realities and experiences that cannot possibly be fully and meaningfully contained within the singular category of "Chinese."

Ironically, Tu recognizes the fact that not all members of the diaspora would feel comfortable with their inclusion in the grand design of cultural China. Indeed, he writes, "learning to be truly Chinese may prove to be too heavy a psychological burden for minorities, foreign-born, non-Mandarin speakers, or nonconformists; for such people, remaining outside or on the periphery may seem preferable" (preface, vii–viii). Let's ignore the surprising return to cultural essentialism—the ghost of the "truly Chinese"—here.

What we must start to question is the very validity and usefulness of the spatial matrix of center and periphery that is so constitutive of the conventional thinking about the Chinese diaspora; we must give the living tree a good shake.

The condition of diaspora—literally, "the scattering of seeds"—produces subjects for whom notions of identity and belonging are radically unsettled. As James Clifford puts it in his very useful discussion of contemporary theorizing on diasporas, "Diasporic subjects are distinct versions of modern, transnational, intercultural experience." In this sense, diasporic subjects are exemplary cases of the multiple and hybrid subjectivities so favored by postmodern and poststructuralist theory. Interestingly, however, as I have discussed earlier, a dominant tendency in thinking about the Chinese diaspora is to suppress what Clifford calls "the lateral axes of diaspora," the ways in which diasporic identities are produced through creolization and hybridization, through both conflictive and collaborative coexistence and intermixture with other cultures, in favor of a hierarchical centering and a linear rerouting back to the imagined ancestral home. Such a conceptual focus on the center, Clifford notes, inhibits an understanding of the significance of diaspora cultures in the late twentieth century. As he puts it, "The centering of diasporas around an axis of origin and return overrides the specific local interactions (identifications and ruptures, both constructive and defensive) necessary for the maintenance of diasporic social forms. The empowering paradox of diaspora is that dwelling *here* assumes solidarity and connection *there*. But *there* is not necessarily a single place or an exclusivist nation."[15]

Indeed, for Clifford, the most important aspect of diasporic formations is the multiplicity of "here's" and "there's," which together make up "decentered, partially overlapping networks of communication, travel, trade, and kinship [that] connect the several communities of a transnational 'people.'"[16] The metaphor of the living tree is not at all suited to capture the features of such dispersed, discontinuous, fractal cultural formations.

Leo Lee, with his claimed desire to be "truly on the periphery," comes close to embodying the diasporic Chinese subject who has renounced the debilitating obsession with the center. "By virtue of my self-chosen marginality I can never fully identify myself with any center," he writes. He defines his marginality in relation to two centers, China and America: "On the peripheries of both countries, I feel compelled to engage actively in a dialogue with both cultures." Freed from the usual obsession with China, Lee declares himself "unbounded" by his homeland. Instead, he advocates what he calls a "Chinese cosmopolitanism," a cosmopolitanism "that embraces both a fundamental intellectual commitment to Chinese culture and a multicultural receptivity, which effectively cuts across all conventional national boundaries."[17] Cosmopolitanism, of course, is an idea warranting a discussion of its own (which I cannot provide here), but what is the surplus gained in the addition of the word *Chinese* to *cosmopolitanism* here? And what does Lee mean by a fundamental (that is to say, a priori, fundamentalist) intellectual commitment to Chinese culture? What makes Lee's vantage point so interestingly contradictory is that while he places himself on the margins of both "China" and "America," he does this from a position of unquestioned certainty about his own ontological Chineseness and his (inherited?) proprietorship of "Chinese culture." Once a Chinese, always a Chinese?

Ouyang Yu, a poet and a specialist in English and Chinese literature, who moved from mainland China to Australia many years ago, actively resists such ethnic determinism. "Where is the way out for people such as me?" he asks. "Is our future predetermined to be Chinese no matter how long we reside overseas?" Ouyang expresses a desire to contribute to his present culture—Australian culture—"more than as just a Chinese." But, he tells us, he has been prevented from doing so: "My effort to 'English' myself has met with strong resistance from all sorts of people ever since I came here. Even if I wanted to be English, they wouldn't let me be. I would find my frequent criticism of China was not appreciated. On many occasions, I found people preaching that I should be proud of being a Chinese. . . . I was made to feel uneasy with my disloyalty."[18]

This story highlights how difficult it can be for people like Ouyang to embrace a truly diasporized, hybrid identity, because the dominant Western culture is just as prone to the rigid assumptions and attitudes of cultural essentialism as is Chinese culture. In other words, there seems to be a cultural prohibition of de-Sinicization, at least for intellectuals from mainland China or Taiwan, such as Ouyang Yu and Leo Lee, who have moved to the West. It would be interesting to speculate why this should be so. It would be easy—and perhaps too simplistic—to suggest the antagonizing work of racism or Orientalism here; their capacity as forces that perpetuate and reinforce essentialist notions of the Chinese other should not be underestimated. However, the important point to make here is that Lee's ideal of "being truly on the periphery" is inherently contradictory if, not a virtual impossibility, because his notion of the periphery is still grounded in the recognition of a center of sorts, the deterritorialized center of Chinese culture or, perhaps, of Chineseness itself.

Without wanting to devalue the decentering discourses articulated by intellectuals such as Lee and Ouyang, I would nevertheless argue that there are other narratives that tell of much more radical, complicated, and checkered routes of diasporic dispersal. In these narratives, the very validity of the category of Chineseness is in question, its status as a signifier of identity thrown into radical doubt. It is in these narratives that the diasporic paradigm is pushed to its limits, to the extent that any residual attachment to the center tends to fade.

The Peranakan Chinese in Southeast Asia are often mentioned as one distinct group of Chinese people who have lost their Chinese cultural heritage and have gone "native." The Peranakans are an old diaspora. From the tenth century onward, traders, mostly men from South China, visited various Southeast Asian ports. At first they remained temporarily and rarely established permanent Chinese communities, but between the sixteenth and nineteenth centuries, Chinese trading quarters in cities such as Bangkok, Manila, and Batavia became large and permanent, aided by the ascendancy of European colonialism in the region. Over the course of centuries, they intermarried with local women, began to speak the local languages, and adapted to local lifestyle (while selectively holding on to some Chinese traditions). This is not the place to enter into a detailed historical discussion of this important diaspora; the question to ask here is, Why are they still called Chinese? As David Yen-ho Wu observes, "While the 'pure' Chinese may question the legitimacy of the peranakans' claim to being authentic Chinese, the peranakans themselves are quite confident about the authenticity of their Chineseness. They are often heard referring to themselves as 'we Chinese.'"[19] Having been born into a Peranakan family myself, I can testify to the correctness of this observation: There is an instinctiveness to our (sometimes reluctant) identification as Chinese that eludes any rationalization and defies any doubt.[20] Yet it is a fraught and ambivalent Chineseness, one that is to all intents and purposes completely severed from the nominal center, China. In contemporary Indonesia, for example, where the state deploys a strict assimilation policy to eradicate Chinese difference within the national culture (for example, by banning the use of Chinese characters from public display), Peranakan Chinese are said to "see themselves as Indonesian rather than Chinese, [but] recognize their Chinese origin, albeit knowing very little of Chinese culture and tradition."[21] And for many Peranakans, "China" has no relevance at all in their lives, so what meaning does the notion of "Chinese origin" still carry?[22]

Wu argues that two sentiments identify those who see themselves as Chinese. The first, a culturalist sentiment, is a feeling of connectedness with the fate of China as a nation, a patriotism associated with "a sense of fulfillment, a sense of being the bearers of a cultural heritage handed down from their ancestors, of being essentially separate from non-Chinese."[23] But it is clear that this sentiment does not apply to those in the diaspora who not only have lost most of their cultural heritage, language being chief among them, but also do not have a great attachment to the ancestral homeland at all, while still identifying themselves (and being identified) as Chinese. The Peranakans in Indonesia are a case in point, but so, for that matter, is William Yang, the "Australian-Chinese" photographer, with whose story I began this chapter.

Yang's story illuminates the precarious meaning of Chineseness at the outer edge of the diaspora. If Yang, brought up the Western way in small-town Australia, can be described as Chinese at all, then his is a Chineseness that is stripped of any substantial cultural content. This, of course, is the case with millions of "ethnic Chinese" throughout the West, those who have settled in all corners of the world in a checkered history of several centuries of dispersal from the original "homeland." To understand Yang's Chineseness in terms of his imaginary and subjective relationship to this imputed homeland, which can only be an extremely tenuous relationship anyway, would be missing the point altogether. As his own account of the formative event shows, he came to know about his Chinese identity only because someone else, arguably a non-Chinese, labeled him as such, to Yang's own initial surprise and to his later chagrin, when his mother confirmed that he was, indeed, Chinese. In other words, Yang's identification as Chinese took place in a context of coexistence and copresence with others, others who were *different* from him. Yang's Chineseness, then, is fundamentally relational and externally defined, as much as it is partial. Its boundaries are fuzzy. Its meaning, uncertain. Yang both is and is not Chinese, depending on how he is perceived by himself and by others. But what is it, we might ask, that still ultimately determines the possibility of Yang's categorization as Chinese in the first place?

This brings us to the second sentiment, which, according to Wu, is common to those identifying themselves as Chinese. This is the sentiment that Chinese share of seeing themselves as members of "the Chinese race" or "the Chinese people."[24] We are returned here to a concept that, as I remarked earlier, refuses to go away from social discourse despite its repudiation as a "scientific" concept in the West: race. So when Yang's mother affirmed sternly that he *was* Chinese, his brother adding insult to injury by informing him that he'd "better get used to it," the only tangible markers of distinction could only have been those associated with "race." The glee with which the schoolkid, most probably white, could yell "Ching Chong Chinaman" at Yang was based on the former's dominant positioning within the prevailing social network, which gave him the *power* to offend in this way, but it also depended on the availability of some clues that enabled him to single out the guileless William as an appropriate object of such an attack: What else could it have been but his "yellow skin" and "slanty eyes," the key "racial" markers for Chineseness in the West?

While scientific racism has long been discarded, then, it is in situations like these that the notion of race continues to thrive in everyday life, where race theories operate in practice as popular epistemologies of ethnic distinction, discrimination, and identification—which are often matched by more or less passionate modes of self-identification. The idea of being part of a race produces a sense of belonging based on naturalized and fictive notions of kinship and heredity; in Chinese discourse, of course, this is eminently represented by the enduring myth of the unity of the Chinese people as children of the Yellow Emperor.[25] What Rey Chow calls the "myth of consanguinity"[26] has very real effects on the self-conception of diasporic subjects, as it provides them with a magical solution to the sense of dislocation and rootlessness that many of them experience in their lives. Yang describes it this way: "I've been back to China and I've had the experience that the ex-patriot [sic] American writer Amy Tan describes; when she first set foot in China, she immediately became Chinese. Although it didn't quite happen like that for me I know what Amy's talking about. The experience is very powerful and specific, it has to do with land, with standing on the soil of the ancestors and feeling the blood of China run through your veins."[27]

In this extraordinary narrative of return to the imposing center, Yang constructs himself as a prodigal son who had lost his way, a fallen leaf that has blown back to the soil where the living tree has its roots. In this narrative, race—blood—operates as the degree zero of Chineseness to which the diasporic subject can resort to recover his imaginary connectedness with China and to substantiate, through the fiction of race, what otherwise would be a culturally empty identity.

But, as Chow has rightly pointed out, "the submission to consanguinity means the surrender of agency"[28]: The fiction of racial belonging would imply a reductionist interpellation (in the Althusserian sense of the term) that constructs the subject as passively and lineally (pre)determined by blood, not as an active historical agent whose subjectivity is continuously shaped through his or her engagements within multiple, complex, and contradictory social relations that are overdetermined by political, economic, and cultural circumstances in highly particular spatiotemporal contexts. Race, in other words, provides a reductionist, essentializing discursive shortcut, in which, to paraphrase Stuart Hall, the signifier *Chinese* is "torn from its historical, cultural and political embedding and lodged in a biologically constituted racial category."[29] In the imagining of "the Chinese race," differences that have been constructed by heterogeneous diasporic conditions and experiences are suppressed in favor of illusory modes of bonding and belonging. Recently, I had a taxi ride in Sydney with a driver who was from mainland China. We mutually recognized each other as Chinese, but I had to tell him that, unfortunately, I couldn't speak Chinese. "Well," he said, "it will be easy for you to learn. After all, you have Chinese blood." As if my imputed racial identity would automatically and naturally give me access to some enormous reservoir of cultural capital!

If we are to work on the multiple, complex, overdetermined politics of "being Chinese" in today's complicated and mixed-up world, and if we are to seize on the radical theoretical promise of the diasporic perspective, we must not only resist the convenient and comforting reduction of Chineseness as a seemingly natural and certain racial essence; we must also be prepared to interrogate the very significance of the category of Chineseness per se as a predominant marker of identification and distinction. Not only does the moment of pure Chineseness never strike; there are also moments—occurring regularly in the lives of those "truly on the periphery," in Leo Lee's words—in which the attribution of Chineseness does not make sense in the first place. The liberating productivity of the diasporic perspective lies, according to Rey Chow, in the means it provides "to *unlearn* that submission to one's ethnicity such as 'Chineseness' as the ultimate signified."[30] This will allow diasporic subjects to break out of the prison house of Chineseness and embrace lives—personal, social, political—"more than as just a Chinese" (Ouyang), to construct open-ended and plural "post-Chinese" identities through investments in continuing cross-influences of diverse, lateral, unanticipated intercultural encounters in the world at large. As it happens, Yang, who now calls himself "bicultural," does occupy such a position in his public life. His celebrated photographs of friends suffering from AIDS testify to his identification with Western gay culture, which he represents as entangled with, but also distinct from, the cultural identifications derived from his ethnicity, and articulate a hybrid, disaggregated, multiple identity that is uncontainable, in any meaningful sense, by the category of "Chinese."[31]

As I have put it elsewhere, "If I am inescapably Chinese by *descent*, I am only sometimes Chinese by *consent*. When and how is a matter of politics."[32] The politics involved here reaches far beyond the identity politics of individual subjects, in diaspora or otherwise. What is at stake are the possibilities and responsibilities of these subjects to participate, as citizens of the world, in the ongoing political construction of world futures: We face ever greater challenges in light of growing global economic disparity, continuing environmental degradation, rapid technological change, increasingly massive transnational migrations, and shifting geopolitical (im)balances of power. There is no necessary advantage in a Chinese identification here; indeed, depending on context and necessity, it may be politically mandatory to refuse the primordial interpellation of belonging to the largest race of the world, the "family" of "the Chinese people." In such situations, the significant question is not only, Can one say no to China? but also, Can one, when called for, say no to Chineseness?[33]

Notes

This chapter was modified and reprinted with permission from "Can One Say No to Chineseness? Pushing the Limits of the Diasporic Paradigm," *boundary 2* 25, no. 3 (Autumn 1998): 223–242.

1. William Yang, *Sadness* (St. Leonards, Australia: Allen and Unwin, 1996), 65.

2. Ibid., 63–64.

3. See Stuart Hall's similar critique of the notion of the essential black subject, for example, in his essays "New Ethnicities" and "What Is This 'Black' in Black Popular Culture?" reprinted in *Stuart Hall: Critical Dialogues in Cultural Studies*, ed. David Morley and Kuan-Hsing Chen (London: Routledge, 1997), 441–449 and 465–475.

4. For a discussion on the position of Chinese in Southeast Asia, see, for example, *Ethnic Chinese as Southeast Asians*, ed. Leo Suryadinata (Singapore: Institute of Southeast Asian Studies, 1997).

5. See my "On Not Speaking Chinese."

6. Stuart Hall, "For Allon White: Metaphors of Transformation" in *Stuart Hall: Critical Dialogues in Cultural Studies*, 302.

7. *The Living Tree: The Changing Meaning of Being Chinese Today*, ed. Tu Wei-ming (Stanford, Calif.: Stanford University Press, 1994). This book is a reprint (with some additions) of a special issue of *Daedalus* 120.2 (Spring 1991).

8. The emergence of a discourse on cultural China, as launched by Tu, is closely related to the growing prominence of the discourse of "Greater China." The latter is the most commonly used term, in English at least, for "the system of interactions among mainland China, Hong Kong, Taiwan and people of Chinese descent around the world" (Harry Harding, "The Concept of 'Greater China': Themes, Variations and Reservations," *China Quarterly* 136 (1993): 683. Harding distinguishes three key themes in the contemporary discourse of Greater China: the rise of a transnational Chinese economy; the (prospect of a) reunification of a Chinese state; and the emergence of a global Chinese culture, to which Tu's discussion of cultural China is an important contribution.

9. Tu Wei-ming, preface to *The Living Tree*, v. Subsequent references to the preface are cited parenthetically.

10. Tu Wei-ming, "Cultural China: The Periphery as the Center," in *The Living Tree*, 1–34. Subsequent references to this essay are cited parenthetically.

11. It should be noted that Tu's paper first appeared in 1991, only two years after the crushing of prodemocracy demonstrators at Tiananmen Square in June 1989 by the People's Liberation Army. This event has arguably had a massive impact on the fate of representations of Chineseness in the contemporary world and has been of major significance in the emergence of the dissident discourse of cultural China.

12. C. T. Hsia, "Obsession with China: The Moral Burden of Modern Chinese Literature," in *A History of Modern Chinese Fiction*, 2nd ed. (New Haven, Conn.: Yale University Press, 1971), 533–554.

13. Leo Ou-fan Lee, "On the Margins of Chinese Discourse: Some Personal Thoughts on the Cultural Meaning of the Periphery," in Tu Wei-ming, *The Living Tree*, 232.

14. Leo Ou-fan Lee, "On the Margins of Chinese Discourse," 226, 232.

15. James Clifford, "Diasporas," in *Routes: Travel and Translation in the Late Twentieth Century* (Cambridge: Harvard University Press, 1997), 266, 269, Clifford's emphases.

16. Clifford, "Diasporas," 269.

17. Leo Ou-fan Lee, "On the Margins," 231, 229.

18. Ouyang Yu, "Lost in the Translation," *Australian Review of Books* 2, no. 9 (October 1997): 10, 35.

19. David Yen-ho Wu, "The Construction of Chinese and Non-Chinese Identities," in Tu Wei-ming, *The Living Tree*, 161.

20. See my "On Not Speaking Chinese."

21. Mely G. Tan, "The Ethnic Chinese in Indonesia: Issues of Identity," in *Ethnic Chinese as Southeast Asians*, ed. Leo Suryadinata (Singapore: Institute of Southeast Asian Studies, 1997), 51.

22. Suryadinata mentions a survey that reveals that most Southeast Asian Chinese capitalists who have invested in mainland China are those who are "culturally Chinese." Peranakan Chinese have, by and large, been prevented from this "return" for economic purposes because "having lost their command of Chinese, [they] are unable to communicate with the mainland Chinese" (Suryadinata, "Ethnic Chinese in Southeast Asia," in *Ethnic Chinese as Southeast Asians*, 16). Sadly, as has been made all too clear by the recent anti-Chinese mass violence that erupted throughout Indonesia in early 1998 as a consequence of a severe economic downturn, which saw massive price increases, a rise in unemployment, and social chaos in the country, the meaning of being of Chinese origin in this context can all too easily become related to fear and scapegoatism. I partly address the complex and ambivalent positioning of Indonesian Chinese in the Chinese diaspora in a forthcoming paper entitled "Indonesia on My Mind: Diasporic Intellectualism and the Politics of Hybridity."

23. David Yen-ho Wu, "Construction of Chinese and Non-Chinese Identities," 149.

24. David Yen-ho Wu, "Construction of Chinese and Non-Chinese Identities," 150.

25. See Etienne Balibar, "The Nation Form: History and Ideology," in, *Race, Nation, Class, Ambiguous Identities*, ed. Etienne Balibar and Immanuel Wallerstein (London: Verso, 1991), 99. For a discussion of Chinese conceptions of race, see Frank Dikötter, *The Discourse of Race in Modern China* (Stanford, Calif.: Stanford University Press, 1992).

26. Rey Chow, *Writing Diaspora*, 24.

27. William Yang, *Sadness*, 23.

28. Rey Chow, *Writing Diaspora*, 24.

29. Hall, "What Is This 'Black' in Black Popular Culture?" 472.

30. Rey Chow, *Writing Diaspora*, 25; Chow's emphasis.

31. Yang's book *Sadness* (originally presented as a one-man slide show) alternately traces two stories of his life—one about his Chinese family and the other about his gay community in Sydney.

32. Ien Ang, "On Not Speaking Chinese," 18.

33. The first question is posed by Rey Chow, "Can One Say No to China?" *New Literary History* 28, no. 1 (Winter 1997): 147–151. On the second question, I am thinking of, for example, the ideological role Chinese essentialisms and chauvinisms have played in the rising power of ethnic Chinese business networks throughout the Asia-Pacific region and its exclusionary and potentially oppressive implications for non-Chinese Asians. See *Ungrounded Empires: The Cultural Politics of Modern Chinese Transnationalism*, eds. Aihwa Ong and Donald M. Nonini, (New York: Routledge, 1996); and Arif Dirlik, "Critical Reflections on 'Chinese Capitalism' as a Paradigm," *Identities: Global Studies in Culture and Power* 3, no. 3 (1997): 303–330.

4

Sinophone/Chinese

"The South Where Language Is Lost" and Reinvented

KIM CHEW NG

Analyzing the Sinophone

Standard Mandarin, as the collective language of the ethnic Han people, has both its "Sinophone" and "Chinese" variants. In the latter case, it is either the "Common Language" (*Putonghua*) of mainland China or the "National Language" (*Guoyu*) of Taiwan. In Malaysia and Singapore, Mandarin (*Huayu*) corresponds to the self-denotation of the "Hua people" (*Huaren*). Unlike "Chinese" (*Zhongguohua*), a term whose connotations are even more ambiguous and confusing, *Huayu* does not account for regional dialects. A Chinese person (*Zhongguoren*) transforms into an "Overseas Chinese" (*Huaqiao*) and subsequently a Hua person through a historically determined process of "purification" in which one's "Chinese essence" is removed, especially as it refers to political loyalties to "China." In other words, this so-called "purification process" returns to using race, in the anthropological sense of the word, to mark the individual. In a similar vein, the Sinophone and Chinese variants (both written and spoken) of Standard Mandarin can be recognized as separable entities, forming a binary in the following manner:

1. The standard Sinitic script (*Huawen*)/the standard Sinitic language (*Huayu*)/Hua people (*Huaren*)
2. The Chinese script (*Zhongwen*)/spoken Chinese (*Zhongguohua*, including both *Putonghua* and *Guoyu*)/Chinese people (*Zhongguoren*)

Of course, this sort of separation is not a definitive split—the similarities between the two variants are greater and more obvious than their differences. The main thrust of this chapter is to foreground that supposed "infinitesimal" difference between the Sinophone and Chinese and to problematize an issue that has perhaps never been considered an issue at all. Here I uncover the language quandary of Sinophone Malaysian literature in search of a critical vocabulary suitable to discuss this issue.

I begin with the subject of Mandarin (*Huayu*), the lingua franca of the Hua peoples of Malaysia and Singapore, and then move on to its written form— the vernacular Sinitic script (*Huawen*)—as it is used in Sinophone Malaysian literature (*Ma Hua wenxue*). The language of Sinophone Malaysian literature follows *Huayu* precisely as it is spoken in daily life, and in this case, it is the same as the *Huawen* in newspapers, magazines, letters, and other documents. This relates to another issue, which is the basic level of education in Sinophone Malaysian society as it is reflected in language, especially the language of literature. The language of literature is generally regarded as the richest, purest, and most refined language of a society or ethnic group. Therefore, the issue of language is at the same time an issue of culture and education. Here, "literature" is not considered a product that conveys morality, an aesthetic object, a symbol of identification, or an ethnocultural artifact, but is understood as a form of knowledge production that possesses total significance. It symbolizes society and culture in a specific place. Through the study of literature, one can further diagnose the issues of Sinophone Malaysian culture.

In the subsections that follow I discuss a few aspects of the language quandary in Sinophone Malaysian literature.

Linguistic Realism

From the perspective of intellectual history, the vernacular Sinitic script, as a language of literature, has been dominated by the language philosophy of dogmatic, leftist "realism." This kind of language philosophy only emphasizes the most basic function of language: to communicate function is the function of transmitting information. The literature guided by this concept is similar to propaganda deprived of subjectivity—it simply serves as an ideological or referential vehicle. Yet this ideology overlooks the fact that the function of language is not limited to this, especially in literature, where language ideally manifests its possibilities rather than its limits. The type of ideology that regards language as a transparent tool fundamentally denies the other significations of language beyond its ability to transmit and be referential. The manipulators of language who employ this ideology lack an intuitive feel for language. They regard it as a simple and crude object because their grasp of it is so elementary.

Sinophone Malaysian realism, inherited from the dogmatic, leftist Chinese Marxists of the 1930s and 1940s, makes three basic appeals to writers. The first is for the writing to be accessible to popular audiences. This appeal is on all grounds made superficial by the need to conform to an abstract and impoverished "masses" of the imagination. Accessibility to a mass readership is the central theme as well as the moral haven of Sinophone Malaysian realism. This appeal provides a rationale and legitimacy for the mediocrity of the works themselves.[1] The second appeal is for the works to represent reality. This is also the moral obligation of realism and its proponents. "Reality" is the unique literary foundation of Sinophone Malayan literature.[2] However, the problem has never been whether the literature is able to represent reality but rather that the reality represented has always been nothing more than an intellectual's dull impression of it. The third appeal is for the literature to enlighten or awaken of the masses. This is the moral reasoning explaining why the prose essay is generally the preferred literary form. However, all of the literary forms make this latent appeal, as it is even given ample space in poetry and fiction.[3]

These three appeals form the basic literary characteristics of Sinophone Malaysian realism. They also represent the latent restrictions on the vernacular Sinitic script and its potential forms as the language is forcibly constrained by the appeal to literary function.

A Multilingual Environment

In its attempt to replicate reality, the basic problem that the vernacular Sinitic script encounters is the multilingual environment of Malaysian society. Besides the Chinese dialects that are difficult to render in writing such as Cantonese, Hokkien, Teochiu, and Hailam, there are also Malay, English, and Indian languages, all of which seep into the spoken Mandarin or *Huayu*. Indeed, it is not an easy task to transform the materiality of pronunciation into the materiality of the written script, which is the transformation of an aural sense into a visual one. The superiority of the vernacular script is challenged when faced with so many sounds that lack corresponding characters to depict them. One can only hollow out the original shape of the written character, turning it into a purely phonetic script,[4] and use form to "translate" sound. Naturally, this kind of Sinophone writing is heterogeneous. In Malaysia, the heterogeneity of Sinophone writing has already developed its own structure. First is Malay, which, as the only official language, is responsible for many place names, such as the names of Malaysian states, towns, and streets as well as all of the names associated with politics and government. Second are English borrowings, mostly related to ideas and tools associated with modernization, such as *motor* and *service*. Third are borrowings from Hokkien and other dialects. When heard publically in spoken Mandarin and accompanied with body language, these borrowings do not present problems. Once they are rendered in written form, the reader is likely to have a difficult time locating their origins. The anticipation of this struggle compels authors to borrow characters as phonetic transcriptions. If an author chooses to ignore other languages in his works and instead "paraphrase," then although his vernacular script reads smoothly, the replication of the linguistic environment loses its authenticity. Scholars have consistently read such markers of place as symbolic of the "unique features of Sinophone Malaysian literature."

Form of Literary Genre

Newspapers are the most common site for the exhibition of the vernacular Sinitic script. The function of newspaper reporting predetermines the writing. The writing is entirely utilitarian regardless of the section in which it appears. In fact, news reports ironically adhere most closely to the demands of the "realists" because they best capture the "nature of society." As far as "reflecting reality" is concerned, Sinophone Malaysian fiction is nowhere near as comprehensive and meticulous as news reports. Likewise, prose essays lack the "substance" of newspaper editorials.[5] The "principle" spoken of in free verse and prose does not reach loftier heights than newspaper speech. Literary language, because it shares the same ideology of language, only attains the same degree of quality as the language of newspapers. This kind of collectivity is the underlying condition that highlights the problem with the vernacular Sinitic script (as the language of both journalism and literature): the reason literature is literature should be because it contains something that only belongs to it. *Literariness* is often exhibited in the *form* of a given work, especially in its application of the basic material component of literature—language. Literary genres are distinct based on their form, not their function.[6] The cultivation of form is treated seriously in Sinophone Malaysian modernism, yet it is a pity that its major authors do not fully engage their environment.[7]

Cultural Literacy

The existential condition of the vernacular Sinitic script, to borrow the rhetoric of a scholar in Taiwan who addresses a similar issue, is that it bears a nature that is far more "social" than "cultural."[8] We may even go so far as to suggest that the inflated social nature of the vernacular script is in fact its cultural nature, even though this cultural nature appears deprived. In the case of newspapers, the vernacular script tends to employ no more than 3,000 characters. Its vocabulary, sentence patterns, and forms of expression are extremely limited. In that secret word bank of the Sinitic script, there are by conservative estimates at least 30 or 40 thousand characters. Among them are of course many that are now obsolete. Among my generation, there are few writers and scholars who can master all of the available vocabulary. This is due to a general decline in cultural literacy and reflects the dulling of writers' senses toward the written script. Innumerable ways to express observation have been reduced to the verbs "to watch" (*kan*) and "look at" (*qiao*), just as ways to express grasping an object are simplified into the more abstract senses of "holding" (*na*) or "taking" (*ti*). More serious than the loss of words and phrases is the loss of the subtle perceptiveness, understanding, and feeling toward objects and reality that they contain.

In Malaysia, where Mandarin is not given the priority of being an official language and Sinology is crippled, the words *cultural literacy* are bound to make many people feel uneasy. Yet this feeling, whether it leaves people sympathetic or upset, will not solve the problem. My intentions here are simply to recognize that the issue of cultural literacy is a problem, as this recognition is the first step toward resolution. Not recognizing it as such is what has allowed the problem to persist for ages.

Linguistic Intuition

It is not easy to use daily language for the expression of subtle perception, deep and complex analysis, or new ideas and things. At its most sophisticated, daily language is only the beginning of a specialized language. This is reflected in all of the specialized disciplines, including not only the sciences but philosophy, literature, and literary criticism as well. Revolutions in academic disciplines accord to revolutions in language, because old language is always constrained by old worldviews.[9] The May Fourth New Literature Movement, which began its "revolution" with the classical literary language, is a very good example of this. Furthermore, every writer must launch his own individual language revolution with respect to the generation that precedes him and the tradition into which he is thrust. In other words, all writers must possess their own linguistic intuition, especially composers of literature whose language and script is their art. In Malaysia, linguistic intuition is predominantly exhibited in a modernist framework that typically emphasizes a return to ancient Chinese cultural traditions. Nearly everyone has followed this trend, from the poets of the Sirius (Tianlangxing) and Divine Land (Shenzhou) poet societies, including Wen Rui'an and his brother Renping, to more contemporary authors such as Lim Chin Chown, Sen Kim Soon, Chan Tah Wei, and Li Tian Poh.[10] In other words, these works follow a trajectory from the "Sinophone" back to "Chinese." The linguistic intuition involved in this process is, in terms of both cause and effect, one's cultural intuition.

From Sinophone to Chinese: Written Script and Cultural Identity

A writer in China or Taiwan is perhaps preordained to write in the Sinitic script. Abroad, especially in a country where Hua people are oppressed and regarded as a minority, a writer's choice of the Sinitic script involves a serious value judgment and has significance in terms of cultural identity. Therefore, his choice becomes fully imbued with emotion. The difference between this decision, made at one's own initiative, and that for writers within the Chinese cultural sphere, is that the latter are chosen by language. The former decision, on the other hand, requires an exertion of effort, as the language is something that must be "acquired." Because it is an "acquisition" that one must strive to attain (as opposed to a "natural endowment"), the writer is likely to develop especially strong attachments to this gift. The significance of this "attachment" is the sense of psychological compensation it carries, causing one to care deeply for and reiterate the "Chineseness" (the cultural essence) of the written language to a greater degree than writers within the Chinese cultural sphere. Until recently, the Sinophone Malaysian writer Li Yung-p'ing has demonstrated the strongest such "attachment," as his following statement indicates:

> I studied foreign languages for many years, so naturally I recognize the value in acquiring them. Foreign language education trained me to distinguish between the capacities of different languages. What is Chinese? What is English? I refuse to accept a "despicably Westernized" Chinese, as the "comprador style" of culture and language is the most profane. In our society, there are too many compradors. I envy French writers. What painstaking efforts they make to protect the purity and dignity of French! France is indeed a great nation of culture. I remember one time in a Mandarin course I took in college when the professor, Yue Hengjun, analyzed the succinctness and robustness of Chinese for the students. I was stunned and stirred by his moving, heartfelt, and flowery speech. I would go on

to write *The Jiling Chronicles*, which took eight years of intermittent but painstaking writing. What I sought was to refine a kind of pure Chinese literary form.[11]

Here, Li derives his ability to authenticate Chinese from his foreign language education. The process transforming a foreign language into Chinese parallels that transforming a Hua descendant into a Chinese person. It is worth noting that the Chinese he defines is "Chinese" and not "Sinophone," as "Chinese" indicates China. The authors he criticizes are those who have been influenced by modernist writers from Taiwan and who are part of the "Chinese cultural sphere"—the "despicably Westernized" such as Wang Wen-hsing, Qideng Sheng, and the "Japanese stylists" such as Lei Hsiang. His accusations of "comprador style" are extremely serious: the comprador is the running dog of the Westerner, and the running dog is not human. The greatest sin of the "comprador" is that he has lost his pride in his own ethnic group. While this accusation is extremely "nationalist," it is also very "traditional," referencing the age-old difference between the Barbarians and the descendants of the Xia dynasty—the Chinese. The "difference between the Barbarians and the Xia" is measured by the superiority of culture to blood or race. One who is close to China is thus Chinese, while one who comes from the Barbarian lands is thus Barbarian. Although Li Yung-p'ing is a Hua descendant from foreign lands, he nonetheless recognizes himself as a more "pure" Chinese than Wang Wen-hsing because of his cultural identity, his ethnic pride, and his literary endeavor "to refine a kind of pure Chinese literary form." He writes: "By doing this, I will reveal the noble tradition of the Chinese language, bringing comfort and consolation to my literature and my ethnic conscience."[12]

Li's movement from being "stunned and stirred" to "comforted and consoled" is the movement from a "discovery" (discovering "Chinese") to a "fulfillment" (completing the transformation of a Westernized Chinese language through the creation of an idealized Chinese). In the process, Li Yung-p'ing's ethnic sentiments allow for his "self-fulfillment" as he becomes culturally more purely Chinese than the Hua peoples of Taiwan.

Li Yung-p'ing, by attaining unity between cultural and national identity, is an extreme example. His linguistic experimentation also reaches another unprecedented "limit"—the "resurrection" of written characters that have been pronounced dead in the last hundred years. It is crucial to note that his linguistic experiment is not that of a "Chinese person" from Chinese territory, but rather of a "Hua person" or a "Hua descendant" (*Huayi*, the more formal term) from beyond China's borders. This sentiment is exactly like that expressed in the Taiwan author Ping Lu's statement that "writers abroad can only experience homecoming through their use of the written script." The so-called "writers abroad" Ping Lu mentions indicate the Taiwanese authors who traveled and wrote in the United States, such as Liu Daren (fiction), Cheng Chou-yu (poetry), and Yang Mu (prose), who all say that "the more time they spent in the U.S., the more precise their Chinese became."[13] Citing the foundational modernist James Joyce as their precedent, they emphasize their generation's "years spent abroad." From Li Yung-p'ing to the younger generation of authors, there seem to be three factors involved on the path of transformation from Hua to Chinese: first, the authors are all modernists; second, they are all drifters (either internally or externally, beyond China, as some even become naturalized citizens abroad); and third, they are all intellectuals.

For the modernist writer, language and script are the final homeland, as well as the final fortress of self-consciousness: "it is because the writer cannot modify in any way the objective data which govern the consumption of literature . . . that he voluntarily places the need for a free language at the sources of this language and not in its eventual consumption."[14] Resisting consumption and resisting various demands made of him (such as the demand that his writing have a "social nature"), the writer is compelled to return to "the instruments of creation"—that is, language itself. A fervent Chinese consciousness (and the psychological scars from the severance with the cultural mother) has led Li Yung-p'ing and those who have followed the same psychological path to extend the thesis of modernist language all the way to the lexicon of the ancient Chinese cultural imaginary. They follow the path allowing them the freedom to choose both exile and homecoming. The inflexible ego created by the rupture with tradition that is at the center of the modernist psychology gives Li Yung-p'ing's writing a kind of dogmatism reminiscent of Wang Wen-hsing. Li's idealized Chinese is restructured according to a modernist formulation, yet this modernism does not utterly wallow in the collective psychological detachment of the classics typical of old-fashioned instructors in Chinese academics. Li Yung-p'ing's pure and orthodox Chinese is not the traditional literary language of classical prose and poetry. Rather, he reveres the vernacular novel, a literary form that was deemed "unrefined" by classical Chinese aesthetics. He strives to put to expression all the advantages of the literary language—its succinctness, its conciseness, its high level of density, and its depth of a geological sort.[15] Using an ancient style, Li does not however write in the traditional literary language. His language still operates in the same mode that most Sinophone writing does: the written vernacular. The difference is that while Sinophone writings have been severely shackled by the vernacular, Chinese has by and large strengthened its written form, as its oral patterns have been transformed into writing. Li Yung-p'ing bravely claims to safeguard the purity and dignity of Chinese because his Chinese follows a route that Professor Kung Peng-cheng calls a poetics or cultural logic insisting upon the "superiority of written script."[16]

When the Chinese language takes this route, it comes to the entrance of an ancient labyrinth—a cultural totality of ancient Chinese symbols, values, and canonical works that is the collective construct of several thousands of years of cultural intellectuals. Kung argues that this totality has produced its own logical and historical rationale for literary production: "the superiority of written script." He argues that script (*wen*) and speech (*yan*), existing in distinction for many ages, unite in the phenomenon of written language. Throughout "Chinese literary history," the classical literary language, because of its literariness, has always occupied a position of superiority. Since the mid-Tang, the speech form of written language has gradually risen to prominence. The literati gradually appropriated this vernacular writing as it continued to develop in the Ming and Qing dynasties and attempted to remove it from popular spheres. As it "united with script," this vernacular writing became another form of "literary language," but it did not achieve quite the same level of sophistication as the original literary language.

During the May Fourth era, proponents of the New Culture Movement naively assumed that the "vernacular script" had finally freed itself and could in one fell swoop cast off the literary language, bringing about the true unity of the oral and written languages. This kind of muddled fantasy was shattered quickly, because the "vernacular script" is indeed a "script" and not a "spoken language." In the process of being written down, the language gradually shifted toward the delineation of rules, becoming a kind of newly revived "literary language."[17]

According to this type of cultural logic, the "vernacular script" has little space to exist when it is almost entirely drowned out by the scholarly logic of the "written script." This logic oversimplifies the interactions, conflicts, and tensions between the "vernacular" and the "written script." It has concealed its own rules of valuation, long denying that the value of the "vernacular" is determined by the literati's own aesthetic judgment and sense of superiority. The cultural logic of the "written script" is that of the victors, and it reflects the values that the traditional literati of China, as a cultural totality, have chosen to reject or accept. The rationale of this logic is a form of collective violence, yet it has produced a widespread (cultural) faith. Once one chooses to believe in it, the essence of "Chineseness" becomes a gift that is traditionally bestowed either silently or in words. As a weapon, it cannot be grasped physically. It must undergo continuous subjectification and reproduction so that the existence of the faith is always verifiable. The verification process includes not only writing, but a repetitious reading of and commentary on cultural tradition, forming a classical system of annotation and circulation that is exclusive.

Powered by the light of faith, the "essence" is regarded as eternal, transcending history and geographical boundaries, just like the blood ties of the Han people. Since the written characters of the Sinitic script are the most basic unit of Chinese heritage, they are regarded as the genes of cultural blood ties. Within a more than 2,000-year-old tradition of studying the literary classics, the Sinitic script has come to form the basic link of cultural genealogy. The form and pronunciation of every Sinitic character and the meaning of words have successively congealed, forming the miniature segments of Chinese cultural history. The endless supply of written characters, words, and canonical works also composes a boundless network of signification. The essence, ensured by faith, is silent and hidden—it is an abyss. One cannot enter this abyss if they do not possess the requisite faith and educational background. Those who are denied entrance lack the "cultural essence," while those who enter will not necessarily exit. Those who do not exit become proponents, as well as imitators and duplicators, of classical aesthetics and aesthetic sentiments—they become bodies possessed by ancient spirits. Thus, they allow "culture" to drown out the concreteness and historicity of existence. Since culture offers them too many readily available motifs, and since a motif might take the form of a giant beast, one's lived experience gets swallowed up by it.

When writers outside China who write in the vernacular Sinitic script refine their craft, they must, at the insistence of this faith through the "superiority of written script," seek the aid of traditional Chinese culture. Pan Yutong, Li Yung-p'ing, Chang Kuei-hsing, Shang Wanjun, and Wen Rui'an are obvious examples. In reaching their goal of linguistic refinement, they arrive at a deep understanding of Chinese culture, classical aesthetics, and the uniqueness of the written Chinese script. They inevitably fall deep into tradition and take one step closer to becoming "one who is close to China." As they refine their script, their cultural emotions swell. In their hearts and between lines of their writing, an exquisitely refined and classically elegant "internal China" develops. These writers therefore create "Chinese" and not the "Sinophone." As soon as they choose the Sinitic script, it is almost as if they are at the same time choosing a cultural identity, as the "internal China" is also encoded in the Sinitic script. The logic expressed by "Chinese" is not really the same as what Lim Kien Ket cites as typical semiotic logic,[18] but rather adheres more closely to Kung Peng-cheng's so-called "logic of cultural semiotics."[19]

The South Where Language Is Lost: From Chinese to Sinophone

As languages of literature, the Sinophone and Chinese form a highly complex binary. This complexity can be explained through a comparison of the language of Sinophone literature with the reinvention of language in the avant-garde, experimental fiction of mainland China, en vogue since the 1980s. Since a detailed comparison of the two is beyond the scope of this essay, we may conveniently refer to the mainland novelist Wang Anyi's thoughts on the matter, since she came to Singapore and Malaysia on a lecture tour in 1991 and made extensive contacts with local writers and social spheres. Following the tour, she published a long investigative report ripe with implication for this study. In another related essay, she offers a probing comparison of language in mainland versus Taiwan fiction. The observations she makes in both articles relate directly to the logic of Chinese and the Sinophone analyzed here.

In "The Fate of Language," Wang Anyi reflects upon the state of language in the Malaysian and Singaporean linguistic environments. As an outsider from China, and because Standard Mandarin in China does not exist in the state of crisis that it does in Singapore and Malaysia, Wang Anyi is allowed a rather detached view and straightforwardly points out: "In Singapore, the issue is really not whether one should speak Mandarin, but that the nation is in need of its own complete language."[20]

Wang Anyi explains that a so-called "complete language" (she also calls it a "thoroughly pure language") should not simply be instrumental and functional but must also be cultural and emotional. Wang proceeds to accurately point out that the "expense" of Singapore's "integration into the international community and economy is the sacrifice of its memories of ethnic origins." This is simply a historical fact: it is not really the expense but rather the condition for Singapore's speedy entrance into the international community and its rapid pace of modernization. The consequence is that "Hua people must endure speaking the language of another ethnic group." As for those Hua people who have no use for the burden of culture, "Mandarin no longer has any relationship to their lived reality. At most it simply triggers a sentimental connection." In a linguistic environment such as this, the study of Mandarin is actually the study of a foreign language.

The linguistic environment in Malaysia is quite different. At one point, Wang Anyi vividly describes her impressions of Johor Bahru: "Some of those narrow streets, with their shops crowded together, resemble streets in Hong Kong or Guangzhou. The signboards of shops flaunt big Chinese and small Malay text."[21] She describes the members of the *Sin Chew Daily* newspaper branch that invited her as speaking with "the thick flavor of the countryside, almost as if they had just come from the mountainous regions of South China. They were like new arrivals who had just laid down their plows and harrows. . . . Like real farmers, they are clumsy with language and they treat people with simple honesty." She depicts Chinese Malaysians as "simple and honest, speaking a sing-song Mandarin." It is worth noting two aspects of Mandarin that Wang exposes: first, it possesses sentimental value for Hua people; second, it possesses value symbolic of the status of Chinese Malaysians. Wang indicates the possibility that a structural dialectics of race oppression in Malaysia has given the Chinese Malaysians a sentimental space devoted to linguistic survival. This quality ascribed to Mandarin is different from Singapore and has not yet fully been challenged: if the Hua were the national "hosts" in Malaysia, like the Malays, "would they still care so much about language as a marker of race?" Wang Anyi's analysis raises two key questions: First, beyond its sentimental value, is language simply a strategy for Chinese Malaysians to gain political standing? Second, is the success of Chinese Singaporeans a foreboding of the future direction of the Chinese Malaysians and their language?

Wang Anyi's analogy between the existential position of Chinese Malaysians and the richness of South China's rural villages only emphasizes that Hua people of Malaysia "are clumsy with language" and that they "treat people with simple honesty." Beyond that, Wang mentions nothing of her impressions of the vernacular script in Sinophone Malaysian literature and newspapers. The focus of the article is entirely on the spoken language. What is Wang Anyi holding back in her silent treatment of the written language? Underneath the surface sentiments of the narrative, Wang Anyi interprets the "fate of language" for the Hua people of both Singapore and Malaysia as following the same logical standard (sentimental value/existential condition/modernization). She thus appears to rely on the same criteria to assess the Sinophone writings of both places. In her comments on a theatrical language game in Singapore, she expresses her opinions freely: "In all fairness, the sentences they string together are unimpressive and strained. I sense that the vocabulary of their Mandarin is lacking, as they are constrained by grammatical rules."[22]

She qualifies her aforementioned argument as a response to a generation "that is predominantly educated in English instead of Mandarin." It is unfortunate that in her observations of the Sinophone environment in Malaysia she does not address the writing there. How do the written expressions of Chinese Malaysians, of whom a majority can speak Mandarin, measure up? "Clumsy with language"? Noam Chomsky informs us that as soon as the study of language must first pass through grammar, it can already be considered a foreign language, even if it is a national language with special significance for a particular ethnic group.[23] Singapore's situation is extremely serious, and given the common emphasis on grammar in recent years in Sinophone Malaysian education, how could it be any different there? The origins of a language's vocabulary are the canonical literary texts of the past. The richness of its vocabulary thus necessitates a profound, expansive literary and cultural repertoire, and neither Singapore nor Malaysia meets this condition. Since Wang Anyi refrains from discussing the language of the literature of those two locales, we can borrow her distinctions between the language in mainland versus Taiwan fiction in order to make broader comparisons between the vernacular Sinitic script as written outside mainland China and written Chinese from within its national borders.

In her article "A Comparison of the Language in Mainland versus Taiwan Fiction,"[24] Wang Anyi compares her own works, along with those of Li Rui (one of the most important authors of the 1980s avant-garde and roots-seeking movements), to the works of Taiwan's Sung Tze-lai.[25] To facilitate discussion, I have drawn several important points from Wang's text in the following, interspersing them with my own comments.

Emphasis on Colloquial Speech/Emphasis on Technique

From the beginning of her essay, Wang Anyi makes this point very clear: "The language of mainland fiction emphasizes colloquial speech: this oral nature brings to the literature an extremely strong sense of place. It therefore demonstrates a greater grasp of dialect and popular language. On the other hand, the language of Taiwan fiction emphasizes the technique of Mandarin, which can be called an emphasis on grammaticality and literariness." In particular, the emphasis on colloquial speech indicates the peasant speech of North China. Wang offers several examples as iconic representations of this speech. The rest of the article adheres to and builds on this basic premise.

Technique versus Culture

With Taiwan's Sung Tze-lai as her example, Wang Anyi argues that an emphasis on language technique (its grammaticality and literariness) involves the use of many rhetorical devices, such as the strange use of familiar words, the novel use of old words, and the frequent display of language's elasticity. Wang claims that "in fact this technique simply extends and exaggerates the content and form of lexical definition, activating the content of Mandarin itself." In contrast, the colloquial speech of the Mandarin in mainland fiction "adopts the language strategies of regional dialect and popular speech. It actually acquires the cultural content of language in its concrete usage, emphasizing language's cultural background." As an example, Wang cites that "in some villages in North China, breasts and breast milk are called 'mommy.'" This type of usage demonstrates the unique and rich stuff of culture.

Duality/Metafictionality

Wang claims that "fiction by mainland authors frequently transcends language in its direct exhibition of setting, story, and character, whereas fiction by Taiwan authors creates meaning through actual language itself. These authors offer readers words telling them what kind of setting, what kind of story, and what kind of characters are being portrayed." She adds that the mainland authors possess a "sense for writing" while the Taiwanese authors demonstrate a "sense for reading." With respect to the relationship between language and reality, the mainland writers portray reality directly, and therefore reality and its portrayal exist as a duality. Taiwan fiction, however, is a recoding of reality: it possesses a metafictional and explanatory quality.

The Grammar of Spoken Dialogue

Wang Anyi goes on to argue that in Taiwan fiction, "even though there is spoken dialogue, it still exhibits itself as being narrated. Even colloquial speech has been rendered literary and grammatical." Offering an example, she explains that those colloquialisms "have all been grammatically arranged, replete with predicates, objects, and proper sentence beginnings and endings. This is proper Mandarin that is regulated, clear, and concise."

This fourth aspect cuts right to the heart of the matter, as Wang remarks that even when portraying dialogue (let alone in other areas of the narrative), Taiwan fiction closely observes grammatical rules. In contrast, the language of mainland fiction is depictive of colloquial speech even when there is no dialogue. As opposed to the stark nakedness of technical language, its grammar is concealed, and therefore it is "intimately natural."[26]

From Wang Anyi's analysis we can see that mainland fiction represents the "unity of speech and writing," while Taiwan fiction represents their "separation." Wang Anyi opines that when reading the Taiwan fiction that produces such a linguistic effect, the presence of an observing intellectual and his "intellectual tone" are always detectable, because the author uses a "language and linguistic method" that are both his own (and not really a duality). Thus, the writing produces "the tone of a scholarly essay," as it "expresses the conditions of peasant life with a scholar's perspective and language." This kind of language manipulation exhibits a "mastery, knowledge, and refinement of the linguistic aspects of writing." It reveals the expertise of one who specializes in language. Why is this the case? How is it that the language in the fiction of the two places could be so different? How is it that Taiwan writings could be so "intellectual"?

The answer is in fact very simple. It is because Taiwan, Singapore, Malaysia, and South China share a commonality: historically, they are all regions whose spoken dialects have never been fully transformed into written language, forever banished from the writing system. On the other hand, the dialects of North China, from the outset, belonged to the same system as "Standard Mandarin." The dialectal varieties that Wang Anyi describes are in fact the foundation upon which this written language was built throughout its long historical development. Those "wonderful colloquialisms" correspond comfortably with written characters. Even their syntax is readily available and easily rendered natural in written form. The history of rendering the dialects of the South (Hokkien, Cantonese, Teochiu, Hailam) in writing is by contrast extremely short. For this brief history they can thank the May Fourth New Culture Movement, which "freed" the vernacular script. The spread of support for China's national independence movements to Taiwan, Singapore, and Malaysia necessitated the writing of books in the vernacular script there. Yet even in those locales, the so-called "vernacular and colloquial" spoken Mandarin followed the system that belonged to North China's dialects, as that massive territory readily claimed ownership of the written language's most convenient and abundant resources. As for the South beyond China's borders, Sinophone writing must confront a vernacular script that appears dull, impoverished, and strained, as well as dialects that are difficult to tame in this script (not to mention the languages of other ethnic groups). The writing environment there is one of translation. For Wang Anyi, as an author and reader of the North, those unavoidably awkward and stiff phrasings evoke distress, so she claims: "When our writers of the South want to express the culture and life of the South using the written language of the North, they lose their language."

Regardless of whether we call the written language of the South Sinophone or Chinese, the true issue is that lacking a script in which dialect can be directly mimicked and recorded, as in the North, writers have no choice but to rely heavily on linguistic technique. Chinese within the national border, endowed with an innate sense of superiority, can rely on the geographical isolation and enclosed self-sufficiency of the mainland countryside. This language, rendered natural with ease, is at the same time far from the natural landscape of modern civilization. Throughout its historical development it appears to be isolated from time, as its lexical and expressive modes, as well as its scope and world-view, all seem to belong to a distant, long-departed era. This language naturally possesses an aura of simple, common folk. Wang Anyi emphasizes these "retained" components of the peasant's language as well as her anxiety over its struggle to express the urban condition. As for the "South where language is lost," everything is modernized and avant-garde—nowhere does there exist a countryside or hinterland sealed off from the world for ages.

As for their reliance on technique, the Sinophone and Chinese are equals. The emphasis on linguistic technique is inevitable for both and has already become a condition for their survival. The problem of Sinophone Malaysian literature is not that it overemphasizes technique, but that it has not in fact developed its technique sufficiently. The movement toward rendering a language in script and developing its technique is not simply mono-directional: "Chinese" is only one direction among many. The South where language is lost has needed to invent language because it has always been the frontier to the Central Plains of China. It is inevitable that in the written works of the South, language itself invents meaning. At the same time, because of modernization and the multilingual environment in the South, the grammar of foreign languages and sentence patterns also become referential objects for the written language. As opposed to the "Chinese" of Mainland fiction or the "Chinese" of the variety espoused by Li Yung-p'ing, we must fashion new linguistic possibilities and develop a new linguistic culture on a new social foundation. Since the Chineseness of this language should not be emphasized (as in the term "Overseas Chinese"), we may as well call it the "Sinitic language." The uniqueness of this language is that it is in fact highly specialized—even to the point of being thoroughly intellectualized—because Mandarin/the vernacular script are born into a collective loss of language. The main characteristics of Sinophone writing expounded upon by Wang Anyi (first, that it operates on an easily intelligible level and develops its meaning out of words and phrases from the classical literary language; second, that it tends toward Europeanization of sentence grammar—for example, inverted word order, the passive voice, long subordinate clauses, etc.) accurately depicts its mode of existence. Outside the visual field of Chinese writers within China's borders, grammar is stripped naked. This symbolizes the materiality of language, as the meanings of words are deepened, extended, stretched, or twisted.

Thus concludes my supplement to the deep, long, and significant silence that Wang Anyi maintains in regard to local Sinophone writings in Malaysia—one spot in the South that lost its language. For my generation, language does not possess a so-called fate; it only has "encounters" that extend it, defer it, and direct it toward limitless possibilities.

— *Translated by Brian Bernards*

Notes

This chapter was modified and reprinted with permission from Kim Chew Ng (Huang Jinshu), "Huawen/Zhongwen: 'shiyu de nanfang' yu yuyan zaizao," in *Ma Hua wenxue yu Zhongguo xing* [Sinophone Malaysian literature and Chineseness] (Taipei: Yuanzun wenhua, 1998), 53–92.

1. Since most readers have likely forgotten the origins of such thinking, I will offer an example here. In "The Local Characteristics of Sinophone Malayan Literature" (*Ma Hua wenyi de defang xing*), Tie Kang mentions that Sinophone Malayan literature "should skillfully absorb the colloquialisms of the Hua masses to give its works a sense of popular appeal, vivaciousness, and vitality" (*Tie Kang zuopin xuan* [Selected works of Tie Kang], ed. Fang Xiu [Singapore: Shanghai shuju, 1979], 110). His argument that "the theme should be Malayan, relating directly to real life, and its subject should bear the burdens of the overseas Hua masses" (ibid.) has an extremely obvious political ambition. In fact, after the economy began to prosper, popular literature was the only type the "masses" could produce or accept. Local Sinophone literature was absolutely no match for the huge market in Malaysia and Singapore for romantic, erotic, and martial arts literature from Hong Kong and Taiwan.

2. Malaya refers to Peninsular Malaysia prior to 1963, at which time Singapore and the British Borneo territories were incorporated into the new Federated States of Malaysia. Singapore was expelled from the Federation in 1965 (*trans.*).

3. The verbose poems of You Chuan, Xiao Man, and Fu Chengde are all examples of this.

4. The most extreme example is Ye Hong's "Freedom and Roti" (*Ziyou yu mianbao*), which is full of English and Malay. One only needs to examine a single sentence: "Pergi, Pergi, nanti saya panggil mata!" (qtd. in Su Fei, *Zhanhou ershinian xin Ma Hua wen xiaoshuo yanjiu* [Study of twenty years of post-war Malaysian fiction] [Puli: Jinan daxue chubanshe, 1991], 147). Also, Tie Kang in *The Orality of Sinophone Malaysian Literature* [*Ma Hua wenxue zuopin zhong de kouyu*] (ed. Fang Xiu) draws attention to the linguistic mixture in Sinophone Malaysian writing. He recognizes "linguistic hybridity" as a phenomenon that the realist writers must face squarely in order to bring to completion the "authenticity" of their works. Tie Kang's own work "The Western Toy" [*Yang wanju*] (in Fang Xiu's *Compendium of Sinophone Malayan Literature* [*Ma Hua wenxue daxi*], Vol. 2: Fiction) is an outstanding example of the attempt at "linguistic hybridity."

5. Roland Barthes writes: "[T]he writing of realism can never be convincing; it is condemned to mere description by virtue of this dualistic dogma which ordains that there shall only ever be one optimum form to 'express' a reality as inert as an object, on which the writer can have no power except through his art of arranging the signs" (*Writing Degree Zero*, trans. Annette Lavers and Colin Smith [London: Jonathan Cape, 1967], 74). In other words, realism is a kind of stylized writing and is very close to newspaper reporting, as it partakes of the same philosophy.

6. True "formalists" (this is the conventional satirical label ascribed to modernist writers by "proponents of realism") are craftsmen of linguistic stylization: writings "without a style" are their specialty. Just as Barthes states, after becoming modernists, writers often transform into "craftsmen of style" (see Barthes, *Writing Degree Zero*, 68–79). Language becomes the material condition of literature, just like color for painting.

7. Around the time he wrote *Black* (*Hei*), Xiao Hei was very modernist, and his fiction also emphasized the minor details of minor characters. When he emerged again at the end of the 1980s, his language became as dull as water. He put greater emphasis on the larger message, and his depiction of reality lost its depth and became superficial. Time is still needed to assess the practice of the newer generation of Sinophone Malaysian writers, but the early prospects look promising.

8. In "The Root of the Vernacular Problem," Lu Cheng-hui discusses the "real" versus the cultural nature of language. His notion of "realism" bears the clear influence of Lukacs. The connotations of linguistic "realism" are similar to the idea of the "social nature" of language. See Lu Cheng-hui, *Zhanhou Taiwan wenxue jingyan* [The post-war experience of Taiwanese literature] (Taipei: Xindi, 1992), 124.

9. For more details, refer to Thomas Kuhn, *The Structure of Scientific Revolutions* (University of Chicago Press, 1970).

10. Generally speaking, Chen Dawei's *Taming the Flood: A Prelude* is, in its use of language, similar to Wong Yoon Wah's *Beyond Ideograms* series, except that it has wilder ambitions and a broader scope, covering everything from the great thinkers of the Pre-Qin to myths and legends. Xin Yinsong's China sentiments follow in the vein of Yu Guangzhong and betray the influence of the Sirius Poet Society. Lim Chin Chown's exile complex is similar, except that, in addition to cultural origins, it emphasizes blood origins in the manner of Yang Mu (i.e., the "upstream-swimming salmon complex"). From tone, imagery, and narration to subject matter, Li Tianbao's novels are clearly influenced by Pai Hsien-yung and Eileen Chang. Except for a few phrases of local dialect and some local Malaysian place names, there is nothing to shake this "Chinese" totality. These writers and their manipulation of language produces a "local reality" that is thoroughly and unavoidably exoticized. This exotic tone is actually a reflection of the individual author's interiority and is clearly related to the modernist psyche's emphasis on interiority or writing of the inner world.

11. "Li Yung-p'ing Responds to Five Questions from the Editor," *Wen xun* [Literary transmission] 29 (1987): 125.

12. Li Yung-p'ing, "Preface to the Second Printing," *Jiling chunqiu* [The Jiling chronicles] (Taipei: Hongfan, 1986).

13. Ping Lu, "Abroad, Composing in Chinese," *Lianhe bao – Lianhe fukan* [United Daily News – United Supplement] (January 27, 1994).

14. Barthes, *Writing Degree Zero*, 21–22.

15. Barthes writes: "Thus under each Word in modern poetry there lies a sort of existential geology, in which is gathered the total content of the Name. . . . The Word, here, is encyclopedic" (*Writing Degree Zero*, p. 54).

16. See Kung Peng-cheng, "*Shuo 'wen' jie 'zi'*: The Structure Developed by Chinese Literary Technique," in his book *Wenxue piping de shiye* [The visual field of literary criticism] (Taipei: Da'an, 1990).

17. Ibid. Also see Chen Pingyuan, *Transformations in the Narrative Model of Chinese Fiction* (Jiuda, 1990), especially Chapters 5–7, and Appendix 1.

18. Lim Kien Ket, "Why Sinophone Malaysian Literature?" *Zhongwai wenxue* [Chung Wai literary monthly] 21.10 (1993): 97.

19. Kung Peng-cheng, *Wenhua fuhaoxue* [Cultural semiotics] (Xuesheng shuju, 1992).

20. Wang Anyi, "The Fate of Language (Part 1)," *Xingzhou ribao, xingyun ban* [Sin Chew daily starcloud supplement] (December 7, 1993).

21. Wang Anyi, "The Fate of Language (Part 2)," *Xingzhou ribao, xingyun ban* [Sin Chew daily starcloud supplement] (July 13, 1993).

22. Wang Anyi, "The Fate of Language (Part 1)," *Sin Chew Daily Starcloud Supplement*, December 7, 1993.

23. In constructing his theory of grammar, Noam Chomsky's basis is the "native speaker" (see *Chomsky*, trans. Fang Li, Zhang Jingzhi [Guigan chuban, 1992], 22). In other words, a language can be considered foreign when the study of that language begins with its grammar. In this case, Wang Anyi stands in the position of the "native speaker," relying on her instinct for the language to make judgments.

24. Published in *Shanghai wenxue* [Shanghai literature] (March 1990).

25. One of the most important contemporary authors in Taiwan, Sung Tze-lai has written both modernist as well as nativist fiction. Baptized into the modernist trend, his work composes portraits of the psyche of middle and lower class characters in a changing rural society. He is a suitable example here.

26. *Shanghai wenxue* [Shanghai literature] (March 1990). Here, Wang Anyi borrows from a term used by Chen Ying-chen.

5

Post-Loyalism

DAVID DER-WEI WANG

Writings about the historical experiences of immigration and colonialism have drawn much attention in Taiwanese literary scholarship in recent years. By contrast, few studies have been done of loyalist writings and the loyalist consciousness. The emigrant, as the name implies, turns his back on his homeland to set out for a foreign country. The colonized person suffers under a foreign nation's imposed system of rule, losing his cultural and political autonomy. The loyalist, however, goes against the mandate of heaven, remaining ardently attached to the former country even in extraordinary circumstances. There are, however, similarities among the three terms. For a civilization that places great emphasis on attachments to the native land and the importance of historical inheritance, all of the terms—the emigrant, the colonized, and the loyalist—signify a collective sense of abandonment on both physical and psychological levels.

Within the discourse of Taiwanese nationalism, full play has been given to the melancholia of the emigrant and the colonized person, whereas the loyalist consciousness is merely regarded as the dregs of old-fashioned conservatism. For the serious scholar of Taiwan's literature and history, however, the loyalist depiction of scars left by dynastic transition and the entanglements of history are indispensable components of the formation of Taiwanese subjectivity. The term *loyalist* (*yi-min*) originally meant "one who remains loyal to a former dynasty and is ashamed to serve a new dynasty when a change in state power occurs."[1] As a political identity, the loyalist tradition goes back ages. When King Wu of Zhou conquered the Shang, he moved all of its peoples to the various states of Song, Wei, and Lu to consolidate Zhou control of the Central Plains. This created the first mass migration of people in China's recorded history. Pining for the former dynasty, the Shang people were unable to control themselves and strove to retain the attire and rituals of the bygone era. This marked the beginning of the loyalist consciousness. At the time, Boyi and his brother Shuqi of the Shang surrendered to Zhou. However, upset over King Wu's destruction of the Shang, they refused to eat the rice of Zhou and thus starved to death at the foot of Mount Shouyang.[2] This is still regarded as the paradigmatic example of the loyalist character.

Loyalist discourse peaked in the late Ming and early Qing periods. In 1644, when the Manchus stormed the capital, Emperor Chongzhen hanged himself and the empire changed hands. In an era of dynastic change, the righteous few who refused to capitulate to the Qing formed a loyalist stronghold. Only decades later did their stronghold finally dissolve. The routes taken by these adherents to a lost cause can be categorized according to a few distinct trends. In some cases they aspired to recover their former positions of rule (such as Koxinga [Zheng Chenggong] and Zhang Huangyan). In other cases they retreated into the mountains and forests, where they pined for the past (such as Zhang Dai) or found refuge from the times in religion and the arts (such as Shi Tao and Zhu Da [aka Bada Shanren]). Still others abandoned themselves to utter hopelessness and indulged in wine and women (such as Mao Xiang), while some wrote scholarly or philosophical treatises on the prospects of civilization's survival (such as Gu Yanwu and Huang Zongxi). Also among the loyalists were those who sought refuge overseas such as Zhu Shunshui and Shen Guangwen. They may have originally intended to only temporarily reside abroad while formulating plans for a large-scale recovery, but they eventually discovered that the road leading back to the Central Plains was too far to travel. As time ran its course, they settled down and planted their roots in the new land, becoming involuntary immigrants.

Upon its historical twists and turns, Taiwan has welcomed both immigrants and loyalists. While the immigrant embodies spatial transformation, the loyalist exposes fissures in time. While the homeland awaits one's return, the new land awaits cultivation. Anxiety pervades this period of unrealized return. The sense of melancholy over fading memories of home and the sense of expectation at taking root in the new land—precisely the two hardships of the Taiwan experience—are evident even in ancient times. They have only intensified over time.

Although the loyalists of the late Ming and early Qing indulged their grief over loss of country, the perceptive officials of the time recognized an inevitable outcome to this period of transformation. For example, Huang Zongxi said: "Loyalism is not hereditary," meaning that a father's debt need not be passed on to his son. This sentiment echoes the emigrant/immigrant's condition. The former dynasty or country is only a memorial for a single generation. After a certain amount of time passes, the descendants of immigrants and loyalists become natives of the new land. Yet memories, aspirations, and even ideologies do not recede silently into the night. They can become the capital used to construct a national imaginary or formulate political struggle. Of course, they can also become sources for literary composition.

Koxinga (Zheng Chenggong, 1624–1662) was twenty-one years old when the Ming dynasty fell. The family of this young man from Fujian had no background in the pedagogy of loyalty and filial piety. Yet for Koxinga, in a time of great change, these virtues embodied a different kind of heroic cause. At the imperial college, Koxinga studied the history of the classics and received instruction under the renowned scholar-official Qian Qianyi. Following the Ming's defeat, he wept at the Confucius Temple and burned his scholar's clothes. In addition to mourning, however, he led soldiers in revolt and was willing to even break ties with his father, who had surrendered to the Qing. He set sail across the sea to Taiwan and drove out the Dutch. This was far beyond the ordinary capacities of scholar-officials.

In 1659, two years prior to capturing Taiwan, Koxinga led his army in an unsuccessful attack of the North. He retreated to defend Quemoy and Amoy in what was the largest anti-Qing military operation since the defeat of the Ming. This last stand marked the end of a historical stage but also another beginning to Taiwanese history. In 1661, when Koxinga drove out the Dutch colonizers and moved his troops onto the island, he brought about great changes that would become the focal point of a national dispute three hundred years later. It is in light of future events that the historical image cast by Koxinga has such grand significance. By driving out the Dutch colonizers, he became Taiwan's earliest example of an anticolonial hero. Overseas, he made a living observing the rites of the Ming until his death. Few Ming loyalists can be mentioned in his category of loyalty. More importantly, however, Koxinga led a horde of soldiers and civilians to Taiwan, where he organized and trained them. He was thus the first one to take up the cause of immigrants to Taiwan. Many years later, stories of Koxinga's family background, the sense of transnationalism and diaspora embedded in his mission, the pioneer spirit undergirding his lofty ideals and aspirations, and his anxiety and angst over the fate of history have all become important resources for Taiwanese subjectivity.

On the subject of literature, the loyalist genre is best represented by the writers who came to Taiwan at the end of the Ming, especially Shen Guangwen (1612–1688). Originally from Zhejiang, Shen continued to follow the

Southern Ming kings after the fall of the dynasty. None of these kings seemed fit to rule, yet Shen Guangwen bore no complaints or resentments and remained faithfully at their service. It was in writing that Shen unloaded his heavy emotional burden and found temporary solace: "Year after year, I endlessly long to return, weeping that no divergent road appears before me and that there is no one to accompany me."[3] Thus begins Shen's poem "Longing to Return" (*Si gui*). Forced to forget the northern homeland to which he cannot return, the mournful words can barely describe the heart of a wandering exile. However, while longing to return year after year, Shen eventually had to open his eyes to the environment around him. He needed the things of Taiwan for daily survival. His poems record many tropical flowers, plants, fruits, and vegetables: he mused on the coconut, the tangerine, the custard apple, and so on.[4] Did the transformation in dietary habits symbolize the beginning of another change? However much one remains loyal to his previous homeland, he needs to put food on the table, and thereby he begins cultivating the foreign land into a new homeland. When Zheng Keshuang, the grandson of Koxinga, surrendered to the Qing in 1683, Shen Guangwen refused overtures by the Qing court and decided instead to live out the remainder of his life in Taiwan. In addition to receiving students, he started a literary salon in 1685 called the Eastern Recital Poets Society (*Dongyin shishe*), the earliest Taiwanese literary association. Shen spent his entire life drifting on the political margins, yet he is remembered for planting the seeds of culture on the island of Taiwan. Quan Zuwang called him "the forebear who begins the literary tradition of the Eastern Seas." Ji Qiguang also said, "When Taiwan had no literature, this great man came and from then on, it had one."[5]

Loyalist discourse, passed down from the age of Koxinga in Taiwan, underwent a complex transformation in the late Qing. The catalyst for the change was the Qing cessation of Taiwan in 1895, inducing the shock that brought about the cry of "All is Lost." On the Mainland, every political misstep made by the late Qing government resulted in a rallying cry around the issue of race and the need to reinstate Han rule. Nationalism, on the rise in the late nineteenth century, began to challenge the loyalist's ideological authority of loyalty to one reign. Combined with this, the introduction of the concept of the "modern" and the tremendous changes in temporal perception implied by the term composed the "disconcerting threats" of the era.

In Taiwan, the mutual agitation of these issues created the conditions for the *simultaneous* appearance of several types of loyalist discourse within a few decades: these were discourses based on dynastic, racial, national, cultural, and regional loyalties. These discourses form a complex dialogue, urging us to reconsider the questions: What kind of identity consciousness did twentieth-century interactions bring about for the loyalist? How did the loyalist tradition multiply, contradict, or critique itself? Perhaps in looking to the "past" we might find that the loyalist consciousness, by continuing to place in high esteem loyalty to one's lord, bears some trace of modernity. This is where my notion of the "post-loyalist" begins to surface.

On April 27, 1895, Li Hongzhang signed the Treaty of Shimonoseki in Japan, "ceding forever to Japan" Taiwan and the Penghu islands. The news sent tremors through the government and the public. The shock was a source of utter anguish for Taiwanese officials in particular. This trauma symbolized the beginning of the "modern" experience for Taiwan and even China. Liang Qichao addressed the situation thusly: "The loss of the Sino-Japanese War, the cessation of Taiwan, and the indemnity in the amount of two hundred billion *yuan* has just awakened my country from a 4,000 year-long dream."[6]

The historical effects of the 1895 cessation of Taiwan can still be seen clearly even now. Yet the loyalist discourse touched off by this event seems to have not drawn much attention.[7] The literal meaning of "loyalist" or *yi-min* always indicates a political subject out of touch with the times. The loyalist consciousness is therefore a kind of political and cultural stance one takes to mourn a loss when situations and scenes change. It derives its meaning from the margins where its legitimacy and subjectivity have already vanished. As stated before, Taiwan inherited the loyalist tradition of Koxinga. The island always maintained lukewarm relations with the Qing government. The Japanese occupation of Taiwan only intensified the island's entrance into the politics of colonial geography and the phenomenon of its inability to regain suzerainty. Naturally, issues of abandonment and separation became topics of fixation for an entire generation of Taiwanese writers.

The loyalist consciousness is further complicated when added to the discussion of modernity. The "modern" is only such because of the term's indication of a violent temporal rupture between past and present, tradition and reform. Critics have long pointed out that the irony of modernity is both its emphasis on a temporal rupture that creates a distinct "experience of the past" and its exposure of a sense of nostalgia. In one respect, modernity exaggerates the necessity of meanings and values that have no precedent, while in another it cannot feign indifference to radical reforms or ulterior motives.[8] Faced with omens of civilizational rupture, intellectuals of the late Qing expressed shock at the magnitude of "an unprecedented crisis." They were aware that the shock of the "modern" was even more assaulting than the aftermath of another dynastic transition. This indirectly explains the sense of loss following the founding of the republic. Perceptive scholars, despite recognizing the inevitable trend of the times, found it difficult to conceal their strong sense of loss. After democratic reforms, they only saw before them a giant ruin of culture and spirit. Their "mourning" defines the zeitgeist of an entire era.[9]

It is startling to find that the crisis of modernity did not bring about the disappearance of the loyalist consciousness. Instead, the loyalist consciousness was given a unique angle to expose the ideological and temporal paradoxes of modernity. *We can never go back*: standing before the ruin of history, the modern subject only feels a sense of limitless desolation. Alone in the great void, he inevitably looks to the past to ascertain his current position. In this sense, the modern condition has made us all the loyalists or *yi-min* of time.

The Mandarin term *yi-min* literally means the "abandoned people." The word *yi* has several connotations: it can mean "lost" or "abandoned," but also "incomplete," "deficient," or "remaining." It can also mean "bequeathed," indicating that although something has been passed on to a recipient, the recipient is at the same time left behind. In retrospect, these three connotations of *yi* were all at play in the loyalist discourse of the Ming and Qing. However, it was only in the late Qing and early Republican era—the time of a "crisis of unprecedented magnitude"—that the overturning of history no longer simply meant a change in dynasty but had an entirely new significance. This forced a qualitative change upon the loyalist consciousness, which now represented not the dregs of feudal thinking but an *ethical burden* shouldered by the subject entering modernity and facing the collapse of time.[10] This ethical burden, of course, has psychological origins. The loyalist's sense of bereavement is more than mere mourning in which one bids farewell to the past. Bereavement can be a posture the loyalist takes, or even the substance of his life. Bereavement causes the sentimental subject to lose himself in reverie, unable to find peace. To borrow from Freud, the subject, faced with the loss of a desired object, cannot divert his suffering through mourning. Rather, his bereavement intensifies as he internalizes the lost object. This is the subject's continuous cycle of melancholia. I must stress here that bereavement, as a loyalist posture, is chosen. Even though bereavement is not conventionally understood as an optional condition, it is clear that, when faced with the loss of the desired object to the orbit of time, it is chosen. The dead remains of history are not easy to shirk. Likewise, the loyalist influence does not simply vanish. The dilemma of modernity appears subdued in memory or forgotten, abandoned yet passed on, in between the disenchantment with a modern state and the specters of summoned pasts.[11]

In the late Qing, vociferous debates on race inundated the public. The Qing imperial family was of course the product of a Manchu invasion of the Central Plains. The legitimacy of its clansmen steadily declined and was being challenged after more than two hundred years of rule. The campaign to "overthrow the Manchus and restore the Han" became, especially after the failure of the Hundred Days Reform, the novel cause of revolutionaries.

In the context of Taiwan's history, however, the concept of Han revival had a different source. Although the loyalist overseas ambitions embodied by Koxinga had long vanished, they had always been important resources for the Taiwanese popular consciousness. Therefore, following the cessation of Taiwan, loyalist discourse did not take aim at the Qing imperial family or the democratic state that replaced it, but leapt over the great chasm of time to become the Ming loyalist's counterpart, or in even broader terms, the loyalist of Han civilization.

Since the 1920s, the generation of writers from the era of Taiwan's cessation has receded from view. Gradually, the scars from the early period of Taiwanese cessation were submerged beneath the surface. Over time, Japanese cultural and educational policies, both soft and hard in nature, were implemented, thus creating the conditions for the newly imagined Taiwanese subject. Yet the loyalist consciousness continued to be passed on among those who bore strong attachments to the past, increasing in its level of complexity.

Wu Zhuoliu (1900–1976) is one example. In December 1941, when the Pacific War erupted, the question of Taiwan's collective and national identity became increasingly urgent. The "Japanization Movement" that began in 1937 entered a new phase. Meanwhile, there appeared a young group of intellectuals that were oriented toward the Chinese Central Plains. Some of them took off for the Mainland while others went into hiding on the island. During the time of their absence or seclusion, they came to realize the drifting and uncertain political status of the Taiwanese people. Wu Zhuoliu is but one among this group who has happened to draw the most critical attention. In 1946, Wu Zhuoliu published *Orphan of Asia* (Jap. *Ajia no koji*, Chin. *Yaxiya de gu'er*) in Japanese. The novel narrates the life of the young Hu Taiming, who, in order to pursue his cultural and national ideals, travels from Taiwan to Japan to Mainland China and finally back to Taiwan. "No matter where he went, he found no place to commit his identity. He was simply a man born in the wrong era."[12] In the end, Hu Taiming goes insane. In a state of delusion, he writes:

I aspired to be a scholar,
But bowed to thugs—
Where is the hammer to beat violence?
As the hero ever dreams,
The Han spirit lives—
I will lose this life of mine.[13]

Only after the onset of insanity does Hu Taiming write these fervent poetic phrases. As in Lu Xun's "A Madman's Diary," Hu Taiming's fortitude arrives circuitously and only by way of a weakened psychological state, thus making it difficult for the reader to take his posturing seriously. Upon his loyalist image, Taiming further projects himself as the "orphan of Asia." While the loyalist is still able to reflect upon the distant past—a past to which he commits his identity—the orphan is left all alone in the world, bereft of his parents. For him, the past can never be known in any detail whatsoever.

In 1949, the Nationalist (KMT) regime lost the Mainland and retreated to Taiwan. By conservative estimates, 1.5 million people made the journey. The majority came to Taiwan as commoners, military personnel of both lower and middle classes, or government employees and teachers. Their Mainland backgrounds differed, as did their reasons for coming to Taiwan, but as soon as they arrived on the island, they were lumped into the category of "Mainlanders" (*waishengren*). They offered mutual assistance, formed regional associations based on their province of origin, and began to discover the possibility of settling down once more. When the Mainlanders first reached Taiwan, they were extremely nostalgic for home. During times of hardship linking both sides of the Straits (as well as past and present), many found solace in writing. The Mainland Chinese scholar Li Xiangping describes the narrative and ideological imaginary of the Taiwanese intellectuals of this period as a "new loyalist complex." Li feels that the literary culture of Taiwan has consistently demonstrated a loyalist quality, and that the Chinese who came to Taiwan after 1949 or went abroad reinterpreted this loyalist tradition. They "all maintained an intimate psychological connection to Chinese culture in its itinerant form from the late-imperial era on. Maybe this is due to their belief in the rejuvenation of Chinese culture, or it may be an affinity passed along in the tradition of writing in the Sinitic script." Their writing is unique for its demonstration of "an emigrant mobility as well as an analysis and memory of language and spiritual culture that borders on obsession." These writers "search for a way to settle down and carry on with life" through "aesthetic structure and literary theory."[14] The ideological explorations of Xu Fuguan, the aesthetic theories of Wang Meng'ou, the poetry of Yu Kwang-chung (Yu Guangzhong), and the fiction of Pai Hsien-yung (Bai Xiangyong) can all be viewed as examples of this new loyalist complex.

Li Xiangping's questioning of form is insightful because it cuts into a historical phenomenon. However, his observations of the early modern Taiwanese loyalist discourse probably risk oversimplification. Since 1895, the loyalist stance and loyalist utterances of Taiwanese writers exhibit great ambiguity, making it difficult to summarize them in conventional terms. Even though those who came to Taiwan from the Mainland in the post-1949 era started afresh, they still had to engage in dialogue with the established loyalist discourse of their new locale. The aesthetic structures and literary theories of the "new loyalist" authors were indeed new. However, if we want to emphasize the historical uniqueness of these aesthetic tendencies, we must shatter the conceptualization of writing in its narrow meaning to inquire not only how intellectuals at the time wrote history, but also how history "wrote" literature. In this sense, a new loyalist aesthetic can also be perceived in simplistic works such as anticommunist literature and melancholic works such as nostalgic fiction and prose.

It is worth noting that "new loyalist" literature began to undergo qualitative change after the 1970s. As time relegated the Mainlanders' migration to Taiwan further into the past and the numbers of those who made the migration steadily declined, writings of the past became unable to recover the heart-wrenching pain of the early years after their arrival. Yet the literature changed also because the island's political structure changed, calling a new territorial consciousness into being. The previous "new loyalist" writings no longer bore the stamp of political orthodoxy. Nativist literature's transplantation of attachments from the opposite side of the Straits to the Taiwanese side and the metamorphosis of anti-Communist literature into the literature of military veterans or those visiting estranged relatives signaled the complete transformation of an era.

We should not overlook one irony, however: the loyalist consciousness did not disintegrate simply because a local identity became the new political phenomenon but rather because the local identity became the vehicle that carried Taiwanese literature from the modern to the contemporary. The urgent shirking of every situation designated as colonial (whether Chinese, Japanese, Qing, KMT, and Chinese Communist Party [CCP]) marked a moment of wholehearted devotion to sovereignty: to discuss the loyalist consciousness at such a time would thus spoil the party. Yet it only requires a careful reading of contemporary literature to become aware of the still-haunting presence of the loyalist specter. This specter is in fact one of the main tenets of nationalist discourse. It is at this moment that we endeavor to understand the "post-loyalist." To reiterate, the loyalist originally indicated a political subject out of touch with his times. As a mourner of a past polity and culture, the term loyalist derives meaning from the crumbling margins of legitimacy and subjectivity. The *post* in *post-loyalist* therefore suggests liberation from existing confinements of loyalist discourse. The truth, however, is not so. The loyalist consciousness perpetually hints at a vanished space in time, fixating on a political orthodoxy that may have never been orthodox.

The loyalist pines deeply for a home now destroyed. Although its inhabitants are long dead, they still haunt his consciousness. The discourse of the post-loyalist thrusts these specters onstage. The loss of the ontology of Confucian subservience to one's lord and father is the burden of original sin shouldered by the loyalist. The incessant sobbing of the post-loyalist recalls this collective dance of departed souls. In the loyalist's historical imaginary, perhaps the father and lord for whom he pines still commands his ministers, or perhaps this figure is essentially an absent idol, a phantasm of phantasms. Here, Derrida's notion of "hauntology" finds its complex Eastern parallel.[15] With "hauntology," Derrida intended to draw attention to the haunting influence of the "specters of Marx" after the decline of Marxist thought in the West. He criticizes the ontological style of dialectics perpetuated by theorists and philosophers who evade discussion of the shadowy origins of these theories. He writes that "haunting is historical, to be sure, but it is not dated, it is never docilely given a date in the chain of presents, day after day, according to the instituted order of a calendar."[16] In other words, the specter not only comes from the past, but also foretells its continuous, lingering presence in the future.

Based on Derrida's argument, we can speak of the post-loyalist's "refusal to comprehend the mandate." The post-loyalist opens a Pandora's box, releasing all types of historical demons. On the one hand, this act ultimately dislodges the loyalist memory from the neat order of time, while on the other hand it extends and exaggerates the post-loyalist ego's a priori attachments to the loyalist consciousness. Time's continuum becomes disjointed and forms of remembering become unrestricted. The post-loyalist's sense of loss and his inability to let go of his love and resentment are no longer bound by systematic thinking. These feelings rather become endlessly evolving burdens and quagmires—or ghostly seductions.

When pushed to their logical limit, post-loyalist discourse gives birth to a reverse dialectic. Whereas the loyalist's management of the "loss" of a previous dynasty or orthodoxy becomes his condition for living the rest of his life, the post-loyalist takes it one step further, forcing "absence" into "presence." For him, the existence of a previous reign or orthodoxy may no longer be essential in inducing feelings of grief for the former state. If a previous dynasty or polity did not exist, the logic of the post-loyalist is still able to fabricate one, creating an affinity to a historical—nay, desired—object that he seeks to recover or restore.

It is easy to imagine that a genealogy of post-loyalist writings would include military compound literature (*juancun wenxue*). The fathers and brothers of the authors who write in this genre gave their lives to defend Taiwan, but the majority of the writers themselves never experienced the chaos of war. It is perhaps for this very reason that their experiences growing up offered ironic proof to the saying that "old soldiers never die." As the crusades of yesteryear are slowly tamed, stubborn doctrines are shaken. When tracing one's bloodline to the island became the new intellectual practice and "Defend Taiwan to the death!" became the trendy slogan, the writers of military compound literature must have been shocked: everything that their fathers and brothers sacrificed to defend Taiwan instead became their original sin. From stories such as "In Remembrance of My Buddies from the Military Compound" (*Xiang wo juancun de xiongdimen*) by Chu T'ien-hsin (Zhu Tianxin) to "Tale of Two Strangers" (*Yixiang ren*) by Yuan Jen (Yuan Ren), these authors depict the sense of loss and helplessness of the children of military families. Reflecting on the old "doctrine" and "nation," their fathers and older brothers may feel neither resentment nor regret, yet the authors themselves betray a profound sense of unease.

This sense of unease is but a point from which the post-loyalist narrative begins. Carrying this notion forward, we must ask how someone who settles and resides abroad can become the very one who passes on the loyalist tradition. How should we look at Taiwan's aborigines who have been repeatedly dislocated and marginalized over centuries? Are they, too, loyalists by way of the definitions of ethnicity and civilization? Could there still be someone hidden away from the scars of history who, in order to cope with the changing objectives of national identity, discovers or invents his own loyalist identity? More importantly, post-loyalist writings are concerned with more than the shattering of nation and faith—those are still components of history's "grand narrative." In confronting the "disconcerting threats" of "modernity," post-loyalist writings are more concerned with varied understandings of temporality, the disintegration of the cultural imaginary, and minor acts of disobedience in routine daily life.

As diasporic theory seemed to gain popularity in the 1990s, post-loyalist writings fittingly tended to the unique situation in Taiwan. In post-loyalist writings, the diasporic condition does not conclude with death. Rather, it can never be put to rest. The most profoundly felt sense of diaspora emerges from the scattered entanglements of memory, forgetting, and vain fears. The turmoil of time and the withering of the body lead one to forget things that should be remembered and remember things that should be forgotten. While death should be the period at the end of the diasporic sentence, it is here merely a comma.

It is at this juncture that diaspora and writing (or the narrative of memory) perform a balancing act. The writer cannot explain with clarity scars that have broken open, nor can he finish writing about them. Moreover, writing only evinces the clarity of hindsight—it is doomed to be a posture of eternal mourning. Yet without writing, diaspora would be unable to leave behind any traces for future generations to forget. Before, I discussed the rhetorical art of the term *yi*. *Yi* describes loss, yet even without anyone to carry a particular tradition forward, what is lost is still passed on. Thus, the term indicates both survival and peril. Desires presumably severed spontaneously emerge and an imaginary nostalgia spreads. It is almost as if we can hear the authors mumbling that the project of writing these sentiments "can never be completed." However, at their most radical (or conservative), post-loyalist writings work directly against the (political) organization of time. Mainland critics like to emphasize that Taiwan's literary history has been dominated by an overseas loyalist trend whose sentiments are oriented toward the motherland, even though the definition of "motherland" is extremely vague. Opposed to this characterization, Taiwan's independence-oriented authors and critics regard the inheritance of the Mainland loyalist tradition as an enemy to cast off entirely. The fact that the establishment of an independent state has yet to succeed has not prevented these ambitious men and women from taking a lead by writing histories of the future nation. They see future peace and stability as dependent on their embellishment of the nation's previous historical narrative.[17] Many of the various master narratives of Taiwan and studies of Taiwanese literary history in recent years are based on the motivation to instate a new political orthodoxy and literary canon. In retracing national history from its beginning, the discourse of the nation relies on a consistent imaginative source to stay above criticism.[18] Yet when writers or critics endeavor to construct an argument boasting of righteous legitimacy, they unconsciously revert back to a historical perspective of the pre-democratic era.

This is a bizarre moment of haunting by the post-loyalist specter. At the moment when "a new state is founded upon a beautiful land," the most effective nationalist discourse is not necessarily based on its potential for foresight but on its repetitious cycle of recollecting the loss of the "mandate of heaven." The so-called Taiwanese subjects, in their uniformity, become bright rays of light transcending their historical existence to await the day the country is rebuilt. They are both prefigured and postscripted subjects. Whether the subject is a "Han loyalist" (Lai He) or an "orphan of Asia" (Wu Zhuoliu), they may all stand in the lineup of nation-founding narratives. Writers such as Lai He and Wu Zhuoliu have followed different itineraries, but in the discourse of the nation they are universally regarded as having reached the same destination. As they rove about the "prehistory" before the birth of the current reign and act as if this reign were something lost in the past, they appear as accidental loyalists—recluses waiting for their talents to be discovered. They are loyalists in disguise that the future (predicts) will disclose and summon. When the postscript is prefigured, post-loyalist discourse in fact constructs a "pre-loyalist" identity according to its own whims.

The new century represents a period of intense inventory taking in Taiwanese politics and culture. In the process, several strands of post-loyalist discourse are unfolding. Of the literary achievements already made, the following four examples—Chu T'ien-hsin (1958–), Wu He (1948–), Li Yung-p'ing (Li Yongping, 1947–), and Lo Yi-chin (Luo Yijun, 1967–)—are starting points to carry the discussion forward. These writers come from very different backgrounds but they reflect similarly on their personal life experiences upon the shifting grounds of the island's politics, situating their identities both outside and post-mainstream. Through metaphor or memoir, they depict a feeling of incompatibility with their era. More significantly, their works demonstrate a broad field of vision and make profound observations by rethinking the origins of their personal historical position.

Traces of Chu T'ien-hsin's sense of loyalist anxiety are evident in her early works of the 1980s, such as *Unfinished* (*Wei liao*), but this anxiety first receives ceremonial treatment in "In Remembrance of My Buddies from the Military Compound." From a contemporary perspective, Chu succeeded at the time in transcending the political confines of ethnicity, gender, and locality. By *The Old Capital* (*Gudu*), her concerns begin to break away from the constraints of a single place and time, giving way to a multitude of reveries on questions about the nature of life and existence. In *The Old Capital*, the middle-aged female author, who seems a portrait of Chu herself, returns from Japan and discovers that if she reexamines Taipei from the perspective of a Japanese tourist, the city where she grew up suddenly seems extremely unfamiliar and even terrifying. Relying on a map from the era of Japanese Occupation, she wanders the main streets and narrow alleys of fin-de-siècle Taipei, where sights appear wretched and dilapidated like ruins. Taipei is a city that has forgotten its history and abandoned its memory to the extent that even wandering spirits and lost ghosts find no place to stay. Chu's journey home is, for one generation of Taipei's citizens, a journey into the "heart of darkness."

In recent years, Chu T'ien-hsin has been known for writing a series of "old soul" roles. The old souls she depicts can see through the façade of the world at too early an age, leading them to harbor long-lasting sorrows. They drift through previous incarnations in this life and can no longer live with carefree innocence. Chu herself is an old soul, but her anxiety is predestined by history. As an author among the second generation of Mainlanders, Chu witnessed the rise of passionate nativism and felt compelled to voice her sense of despondence and estrangement. She is also saddened by the passing of former greats, in whom she believed, and the debunking of their doctrine. She seeks a moment of repose in Taipei, but is actually a wandering spirit, migrating along the margins of amnesia and vain hopes in search of the dregs of history. In *The Flâneuse* (*Manyou zhe*), she transcends the setting of the military compound and the old capital, allowing herself to traverse life and death, dream and reality, foreign lands and homelands, lingering about so that the reader cannot know where it will end.

The post-loyalists find a permanent home in the limitless exaggeration of loss, deficiency, and death as metaphysical topics. Centuries later, those endlessly weeping adherents to a lost cause who still miss those lords and fathers of the ancient past finally find happiness. In Chu T'ien-hsin's case, she suddenly awakens to find (or dreams!) that, after having been banished or gone willingly into self-exile outside the march of history, she has become a primordial visitor passing through the universe—a loyalist of time.

When time is no longer teleological, narrative order is destined to disintegrate. The vast spatial imagery of Chu's *The Flâneuse* spots the traces of remnants. The post-loyalist no longer seeks reclusion: Chu Tien-hsin's second-person narrator explores everywhere—the caves of New Zealand, the canals of Venice, the bustling streets of Tokyo, and the windswept sands of Mediterranean shores—in search for a place to live out her days and rest in peace. Unaware if she is dead or alive, she writes to contradict the orderliness of life and morality. She also inevitably confuses the roles of author and reader. Whether on the ground or on the page, her *flâneuse* spins on the margins of illusion and nihilism. One could say she is like the antiromantic Don Quixote, but she would prefer the life of the lower-class Nemadi (a nomadic society of Moors in North Africa), walking along the ageless periphery of the Sahara Desert: "I am the true owner of this land, whisked away by the Moors."[19]

Wu He, who is from Tainan, began his writing career in the mid 1970s. His early writings describe familial disintegration, dismal hometowns, and defeated lives, continuing in the style of Taiwanese decadent writings initiated by writers of the 1930s such as Weng Nao and Lung Ying-tsung (Long Yingzong).[20] In 1980s Taiwan, when different social movements were in full force, Wu He went into reclusion and did not publish anything for thirteen years. After his second emergence, he garnered attention for stories such as "Sadness" (*Beishang*), "Collecting Bones" (*Shi gu*), and "My Brother, A Runaway Soldier" (*Taobing erge*). He depicts lives ravaged by the nation and political mechanisms, able-bodied youth with no prospects, men and women indulging in perverse love affairs, dejected aborigines living out a destitute existence, and people ridden with anxiety and bipolar disorders. These characters typically come from the middle and lower classes—their vain and irrational hopes and roller-coaster emotional states offer unique slices of Taiwanese life.

Elsewhere, I gave Wu He the nickname "Bone Collector" based on his story "Collecting Bones."[21] Exploring the scars of history, he dissects humanity's collusions as if he were unearthing shattered remnants in the blind spots of time and space, trying to open a dialogue with them. By way of his archaeology of knowledge, things already forgotten and that should not be remembered float effortlessly onstage: the sublime and the trivial, the public and the private, the erotic and the bleak—all matter of human affairs. This is the beginning of Wu He's post-loyalist narrative, or, borrowing the title of his novel *Remains of Life* (*Yu sheng*), his style of memory and writing "life-remains." This type of writing takes death as a prelude. One must live out his fate as the major catastrophe has already occurred. Situated within this fate, Wu He and his characters inhabit a fools' paradise. The biggest challenge they face is not the limited nature of their future but that they have too much time. Death and decline are an endless waiting period, as it takes another lifetime to put back in order the so-called aftermath of life.

Yet Wu He has not vocalized all his thoughts on the matter. In 1997 he went to the Atayal tribal settlement in Musha (Wushe) in Nantou County in central Taiwan, where he once again discovered the meaning of "life-remains" in the aftermath of the Musha Incident. Beginning in 1930, the Atayal aborigines in Musha waged large-scale anti-Japanese resistance activities, in which they decapitated hundreds of Japanese. This marked one of the biggest incidences of resistance in the Taiwanese history of Japanese colonialism. Wu He offered three reasons for his visit to Musha: to investigate the "timeliness and opportune nature" of the incident, to analyze what he called the "second Musha Incident," and to pursue a young woman in the tribe. Wu He sought to repetitiously write the three projects as one to demonstrate not the novel's aesthetics of time but rather the "simultaneity" of the three occurrences.[22] This statement demonstrates the sincerity of his project. Wu He explored the tribal settlement, visiting the descendants of those who lost their lives in the Musha Incident. In addition to paying homage to the official memorial, he also saw the dilapidated, unofficial monument: the "life-remains" of the families. His writings display the synchronicity of the catastrophe and memories of it. A linear narrative would be unable to articulate clearly the appearance and aftermath of scars.

Wu He asks the reader to consider whether Musha was purely an incidence of anti-Japanese resistance or if it was the reenactment of an inherited and primitive *mgaya* ("out of the bush") headhunting ritual. Could the catastrophe's survivors be the loyalists spoken of by the Han, or are they the "remains of life" in the eyes of the Atayal? The aborigines could not endure the oppression of the colonizer and they rose up against his tyranny. This fact is no doubt recorded by history, but overemphasizing their spirit of martyrdom covers up their preexisting sense of tribal righteousness calling them to rally around the enemy. Following Wu He's line of questioning, we may ask if perhaps the Atayal warriors' sudden attack on the Japanese and their flaunting of decapitation actually reenact the "timeliness" of the *mgaya* tradition.

More importantly, Wu He is aware that the life-remains story of the Musha Incident is also the story of the remains of his "own life." Wu He admits that he was first moved by stories of the Musha Incident back in the 1960s. Thirty years later, during the time between martial law and parliamentary government when non-KMT political movements were being organized, Wu He, withdrawn and drifting, thought long and hard about his own historical position. "I did not come to Kawanakajima [a tribal area in Musha] by chance. It was due purely to the words 'life-remains' that I decided to stay. I wanted to understand what 'post-catastrophic life-remains' truly meant. The 'Incident' itself was merely a secondary effect I would have to feel."[23] Wu He's account is an eyewitness report, forcing us to rethink his emphasis on the "simultaneity" of life-remains. Happenstance and karma, history and the immediate moment, and the lives of self and others are mutually illuminated as Wu He douses his own depression with the trauma of others. Here, we are reminded of Theodor Adorno's description of Walter Benjamin: "He is driven not merely to awaken congealed life in petrified objects—as in allegory—but also to scrutinize living things so that they present themselves as being ancient, 'ur-historical' and abruptly release their significance."[24]

Li Yung-p'ing was born and raised in Malaysian Borneo and went to Taiwan to pursue his studies in 1967. Since the 1970s, he has garnered a great deal of attention for "A La-tzu Woman" (*Lazi fu*) and *The Jiling Chronicles* (*Jiling chunqiu*). Yet it was during the 1990s that Li truly became a kind of phenomenon. In 1992, he published the first volume of *Haidong Blues* (*Haidong qing*), a prolific work of more than 500,000 words. This novel describes the bustling degeneration of the Haidong (Taipei?) metropolis. The novel almost has no plot to speak of, and the level of obscurity and difficulty of its vocabulary is enough to cause most readers to retreat at one glance. Even more incredible is that Li committed a major offense by writing China-based, anti-communist plots in marked contrast to the nativist movement that was already generating quite a following.

Li Yung-p'ing's holistic trinity is composed of his ancestral Chinese homeland, his Chinese mother, and his Chinese script. The interactive and substitutive referencing between the three symbolizes Li's literary consciousness. This trinity also gives birth to a boundless sense of emptiness and listlessness. His writing, which occupies a position of lonely drifting "without mother tongue," predicts all sorts of impossibilities.[25] There are very few authors of contemporary Taiwanese literature who possess Li's sense of extraordinary ambition and contradiction. Li's own description of *Haidong Blues* as "a giant failure" is not out of aesthetic frustration but merely representative of his full retreat from history and desire.[26]

Haidong Blues is the story of Jin, a returned student from the United States. On a day spent drifting about on the streets of Haidong City (Taipei?), Jin has a chance meeting with Zhu Ling, a young girl between five and seven. There is nothing special about the plot, but in Li Yung-p'ing's depiction of the city's debauchery and chaos, linguistic wonders appear one after the other. His feats of language are matched by his sensitivity to the KMT regime, as he likens records of the government's movement to Taiwan to the Bible's emergence from Egypt. On the one hand, *Haidong Blues* is a pedophilic, *Lolita*-inspired narrative, while on the other it is an obsolete anti-Communist prophecy. So far behind the times, it is no wonder that *Haidong Blues* raised some eyebrows.

Only by contrasting the novel with Li's earlier works can we understand his outrageous sense of ambition. Taiwan—Haidong—eventually floats to the surface, becoming the meeting grounds for his imagination of the ancestral homeland. Taiwan is a miniature projection of ethnic Han culture and the starting point for the return to the motherland. Taiwan is the second homeland—Li accepts it even though he is not content with it. However, Taiwan has already entered a process of degeneration: the countdown to its destruction has already begun. Li's extravagant script is enshrouded in the anxiety over this fate. The mere fact that 500,000 words were not enough to complete the story should be food for thought. Li Yung-p'ing exerted an incredible amount of energy to perfect a literary homeland, but the story he told works against this image. I believe this does not reflect a self-imposed aesthetic challenge that Li undertook, but rather the ironies of consciousness beyond the text. His narrative form and desire are entangled, making it difficult to find a reasonable means of resolving them. The type of modernism in which Li is steeped can never reconcile its form with its content. Looking deeper, however, it should be stressed that if Li Yung-p'ing's ultimate goal in writing is to summon the China/mother that was originally lost, his words can only record the hollow echoes of his own voice. That he is left with nothing in the end determines the failure not of his narrative but rather of his desire (or belief system).

My study of post-loyalism concludes with Lo Yi-chin. Lo Yi-chin is younger than the three authors discussed before. When Lo arrived on the scene, Taiwan had already entered the postmodernist wave. Perhaps because of this, his early works understandably flirt with the metafictional style. Yet Lo had other literary designs. He displays an uncontainable curiosity for the excruciatingly ambiguous scenes in life, but the price he pays for this curiosity is self-exposure. His writing takes his very own body as a point of convergence for the unrestrained release of desire and the ubiquity of the threat of violence and death. The uncanny and the eccentric, as well as anxiety and sorrow, pervade his writing.

Lo Yi-chin comes from a second generation Mainlander family of government workers. His works such as *The Moon Clan* (*Yueqiu xingshi*) and *Far
Away* (*Yuanfang*) deal with the subjects of Mainlander communities and
cross-Straits families, and therefore it is easy to attach labels to them. Lo Yi-
chin is intent on depicting the feelings and experiences, both real and prepos-
terous, of these generations. In *Far Away*, he writes the role of a Taiwanese
son who rushes to the Mainland to look after his father. There, he and his
"long lost brother" tend to the needs of their father, who can no longer control his bodily functions. In the end, they transport his large, sickly body to
Taiwan. In *The Moon Clan*, Lo writes the role of a lost child on the streets who
cannot find his home despite walking all over Taipei. In the end he reaches
a place that resembles a ruin. On a windy, moonless night, the boy examines
the ruin closely only to discover that he is standing on the construction site
of the Chiang Kai-shek Memorial Hall.

Lo Yi-chin's writing clearly shows the indirect influence of Chu T'ien-hsin.
In terms of post-loyalist discourse, however, the two are quite different. Chu
T'ien-hsin is forlorn and resentful toward the inevitability of the changing
times and the relegation of certain events to the past. Despite shuttling back
and forth between past and current lives, she is frequently troubled by the
irreversibility of time and the dissolution of values that accompanies it. Lo
Yi-chin's works do not put the sequence of time's advance or retreat in such
a simple chronological order. He is certainly aware of the ruthlessness of the
tricks that time plays, which causes him anxiety, but unlike Chu T'ien-hsin,
he does not devote much energy to voicing this anxiety and he does not
assume that he is on the side of justice. Lo Yi-chin writes precisely because of
the destruction of time and meaning.

This is where Lo Yi-chin's post-loyalist narrative begins. Ng Kim Chew
(Huang Jinshu) has used the term *abject stories* to summarize Lo's aesthetics
of narrative and temporality.[27] As opposed to the *yi* (abandoned) in *yi-min*
(loyalist), the term Lo feels strongly about is *qi* (discarded or abject), a nearly
indescribable act of expungement. Time becomes evidence of the abjection,
whether active or passive, while writing bears the traces of this act. By this
act, trauma becomes the *innate* existential condition of life.

Ng Kim Chew believes that Lo Yi-chin's writings come from a psychological complex due to an "originary abjection." In looking for a way to break
out of this complex, Lo casually treats this "originary abjection" as the "abandonment of history" through deferral of the uncanny and mimicry of the
ancients. In *The Moon Clan*, he exaggerates the position of second-generation
Mainlanders as adherents to a lost cause, but, unable to touch upon the most
painful areas, he adopts a strategy of taking the easy way out. It is in *Banished Sorrow*, when Lo Yi-chin's imagination engages in a dialogue with Chiu

Miao-chin (Qiu Miaojin), the lesbian author who committed suicide, that Luo finally unveils the psychological disorder in its entirety. *Banished Sorrow* states its intentions from the outset, reflecting on the conditions of death and the limits of its narration.

If Chiu Miao-chin regards death as the finale to the "endless night" of life's narrative, then Lo Yi-chin begins from there. The written word is no longer that talisman that renders reality transparent, but is itself a kind of transparent medium, something similar to remnants. In the second half of his life, the survivor must learn how to find antecedents to the "endless night" while fumbling about in the dark as well as learn how to find diversion from a type of sorrow that crashes in and recedes like the tide.

Lo Yi-chin's narrative of death is also notable for its continual reveries on love and desire. He discards this object of love/desire without truly letting go, perhaps because he secretly feels the complicity between love and death. Lo Yi-chin is not necessarily a believer in Freudian psychoanalysis, but the progression of his writings verifies that the ultimate aim of love and desire is to return to the womb/the original source. In a dream scene from *Banished Sorrow*, the narrator sees his mother sleeping naked. Unable to control himself, he puts his finger inside her. The deeper he goes, the greater his delight, until he has put his entire hand insider her. What is frightening, however, is that in the end, he is unable to pull his hand back out. The mother's womb as well as the ultimate pleasure of returning to the mother—the *chora*, the original source—bring about a repetitious circulation between (r)ejection and abjection. No contemporary writer develops the internalization and spectacle of the abject quite like Lo Yi-chin. In this way, writing is like that taboo dream of desire prohibiting entrance into the mother's body as well as the "irresistibility of using his five fingers to open it up."

Lo Yi-chin's writing of dream, the game of the flesh, absurd familial relations, and conflicted ethnic identity does not necessarily possess the abstruseness of realism. He covers up the illegitimate with the legitimate, utilizing universally approved materials to discover nullified meaning in rhetoric and story. The playful collage, mimicry, and transformation of metafiction are for him tools to expose the "materiality" of script. His words are continually lifelike: they do not promise foresightedness but repeatedly perform mourning and bereavement. He changes form and position from story to story, traversing strained interpretation. To borrow the most shocking image from *Banished Sorrow*, this is the work of "transporting corpses." In the opening scene of *Banished Sorrow*, the narrator's mother has just died, and he hurriedly pushes her corpse to catch the last train so he can donate her organs before it is too late. In what becomes a frantic journey, he embarks and disembarks at various stations. He does not know when he will arrive at his destination, but the significant action has already been set in motion. What has been keeping him company all along is the corpse of his mother, an ultimate symbol of love.

Taiwanese discourse at the turn of the twenty-first century is replete with ambitions for change. The more it draws a distinct boundary to demarcate the "former emperor and dynasty," however, the more it demonstrates that the distant past has not yet been left far behind. Since the "orphan of Asia" has discovered he is a "child of Taiwan," ghosts of the old-fashioned discourses of consanguinity and identity have staged a comeback. As the "Republic of China" is emptied of meaning, the new leaders surprisingly borrow the lens of a former dynasty to interpret affairs. At this moment, they become the dubious inheritors of the loyalist government of the bygone era. It is hard to take them seriously when they carry on the same old tune. In Eileen Chang's words, "a strange feeling toward surrounding reality emerges, a suspicion that this is an absurd, ancient world."[28]

As the entire country diligently learns how to be a New Taiwanese, we should reflect on the challenges that a post-loyalist consciousness poses. Does it dismiss the previous form of ideological orthodoxy, or does it make superficial changes as it anxiously supervises past—and future—history? If the myth of "national restoration" has been deconstructed, then why should we not subject the myth of "the nation's founding" to the same treatment? By the same reasoning, does not the birth of a standard canon always foretell the abandonment and discarding of a previous one? The cacophonous political discourses of the era share the goal of simplifying history. This is a paradigmatic example of how language and power make use of each other. At the moment when politicians do not know what they are talking about, literary historians should perhaps appeal to problematization, remembering what we have forgotten and reminding us of things we were told not to think about. All post-loyalist writings share but one thing in common, that is the politics of time and the politics of memory.

To illustrate one last example of post-loyalist discourse, I conclude with an excerpt from Lo Yi-chin's poem, "The Story of Qi" (*Qi de gushi*)[29]:

If abandonment is a kind of posture,
Then it is certainly the image of me,
Curled up in my mother's womb,
It is me, cast out on the road,
Proof that I once walked,
Or am still walking,
Forever abandoned,

Yet it is the greediest image of all,
The vain attempt to tiptoe upon memory,
Expanding poetic territory.[30]

— Translated by Brian Bernards

Notes

This chapter was modified and reprinted with permission from David Der-wei Wang (Wang Dewei), *Hou yimin xiezuo* [Post-loyalist writings] (Taipei: Maitian chuban, 2007), 23–70.

1. Xie Zhengguang, *Qingchu shiwen yu shiren jiaoyou kao* [A study of the language of official occasional poetry in the early Qing] (Nanjing: Nanjing University, 2001), 6. For the definition of a Ming-Qing loyalist, see Lynn Struve, "Ambivalence and Action: Some Frustrated Scholars of the K'ang-hsi Period," in *From Ming to Ch'ing: Conquest, Region, and Continuity in Seventeenth-Century China* (New Haven: Yale University Press, 1979), 327. On the definition of a Song loyalist, see Jennifer W. Jay, *A Change in Dynasties: Loyalism in Thirteenth-Century China* (Bellingham: Western Washington University Press, 1991), 6. For research on the loyalist, I gratefully express my debt to professors Yang Chin-lung (Yang Jinlong) and Lawrence Yim at Academia Sinica for providing materials and criticism.

2. A poem in the "Biography of Boyi and Shuqi" in Sima Qian's *Records of the Grand Historian (Shiji)* recounts: "We climbed West Hill / we picked its bracken. / Brute force for brute force– / he knew not it was wrong. / Shen-nong, Yu, and Xia / gone in a flash, / where can we turn? / Ah, let us depart now, / our lifespans are done." [Translation from *An Anthology of Chinese Literature*, ed. and trans. Stephen Owen (New York: W. W. Norton, 1996), 143].

3. Shen Guangwen, "Longing to Return" (*Si gui*), in *Quan Tai shi* [The complete poetry of Taiwan], Vol. 1 (Taipei: Yuanliu, 2004), 59. Also see Shih Yi-lin's (Shi Yilin) discussion in *Cong Shen Guangwen dao Lai He: Taiwan gudian wenxue de fazhan yu tese* [From Shen Guangwen to Lai He: The characteristics and development of Taiwan's classical literature] (Kaohsiung: Chunhui, 2000), 20–27.

4. See Shen Guangwen, "The Custard Apple," "The Tangerine," and "The Coconut" in *Quan Tai shi* [The complete poetry of Taiwan], Vol. 1, 42–43.

5. Qtd. in Shih Yi-lin, *Cong Shen Guangwen dao Lai He* [From Shen Guangwen to Lai He], 25.

6. Liang Qichao, "Excerpt of the Beginning and End of My Response to Kang Youwei," in *Wuxu zhengbian ji* [On the Hundred Days Reform] (Taipei: Zhong Hua shuju, 1969), 1.

7. For a record of anti-Japanese resistance on Taiwan, including tales of death and destruction, see Hsu Chun-ya (Xu Junya), *Taiwan xieshi shizuo zhi kangri jingshen yanjiu* [A study of the spirit of anti-Japanese resistance in Taiwanese realist poetry] (Taipei: Guoli bianyiguan, 1998), Chap. 3.

8. As an immigrant Jewish writer, Walter Benjamin came from an ethnic group demonstrating a strong loyalist consciousness. Caught between Western capitalist culture, leftist revolutionary ideology, and the mystical beliefs of Judaism, Benjamin's writings reflect his senses of contradiction. In an era when the foundations of civilization were disintegrating, Benjamin

attempted to offer a dialectical historical perspective as a response. He believed that we could no longer formulate cut and dry explanations of the relationship between past and future, but that it was rather like scavenging in a darkened ruin, in other words a painstaking affair. In an era emphasizing progress and efficiency, Benjamin's scavenger appears useless: he rummages through dead dreams and failed promises in the rubbish bin of history. Walking alone, he hauls the "dregs of history." Yet is this scavenger identity possible? The revolutionary's homesickness is hidden amongst these castaway objects. Perhaps this vision of the stragglers exposed the game of playing with the "future" long ago. See Walter Benjamin, *Charles Baudelaire: A Lyric Poet in the Era of High Capitalism*, trans. Harry Zohn (New York: Verso, 1997).

9. See for example Liu Na's discussion in Chapter 3 of *Shanbian: Xinhai geming shiqi zhi wusi shiqi de Zhongguo wenxue* [Evolutions: Chinese literature from the Republican Revolution to the May Fourth] (Beijing: Zhongguo shehui kexue chubanshe, 1998).

10. Sigmund Freud, "Mourning and Melancholia," in *A Freud Reader*, ed. Peter Gay (London: Penguin, 1988), 213. Also see Jacques Derrida, *Writing and Difference*, trans. Alan Bass (Chicago: University of Chicago Press, 1978), 201: "Memory, thus, is not a psychical quality among others; it is the very essence of the psyche: resistance, and precisely, thereby, an opening to the effraction of the trace."

11. In the history of modern China, the case of Wang Guowei (1877–1927) illustrates this point. In 1927, Wang Guowei drowned himself at the Summer Palace. His death gave rise to much debate and even prompted the appearance of a conservative political faction in his name that equated Wang's suicide to an act of sacrifice to the defeated Qing. Yet there might be a deeper reason for Wang's suicide. It may be more accurate to assume that his desire to die was due not to his inability to grapple with national transformation, but to his melancholic despair at what he perceived as a moment of peril for an ancient civilization. We may even venture to argue that Wang Guowei's suicide was not only the belated gesture of a loyalist but also a kind of excruciating foresight of the decline of culture, whether traditional or modern. Compared to those incisive writers and politicians who collided with their era, Wang Guowei's call to "not progress" is probably more complex and carefully constructed. At the dawn of a new era, he was already aware that revolutionary enlightenment would bring about more than so-called "modernity"—it would also bring about its brutal price. Confronting various challenges to both the public and private sphere, he decided to erase his own existence. By way of negation, he solemnly bore witness to the complicated meanings modernity could imply—this involved a resistance to modernity itself. Thus, with his suicide, there ironically appeared a kind of untraditional (but not anti-traditional) "modern" subjectivity. Only in light of this can we comprehend Chen Yinke's eulogy of Wang Guowei: "Men of lofty ideals, both ancient and contemporary, in China and abroad, always appear full of grief and melancholia . . . the cause of his suffering and death was nothing more than a given place and a given time. There is certainly a rationale for his decision to transcend time and place, yet this rationale must be one that the majority belonging to his time and place cannot explain."

12. Wu Zhuoliu, Postscript, *Orphan of Asia*, trans. Fu En-rung (Fu Enrong) (Taipei: Nan Hua, 1962), 302. For a discussion of Hu Taiming's orphaned consciousness, see Chen Wan-yi (Chen Wanyi), "Hu Taiming and His Orphaned Consciousness: Discrepancies Between the Coasts in *The Orphan of Asia*," in *Yu wusheng chu ting jinglei* [Sudden thunder in a silent place] (Tainan: Tainan shili wenhua zhongxin), 71–89.

13. Ibid., 294 [English translation of poem based on Ioannis Mentzas (New York: Columbia University Press, 2006), 244. However, I have retained the term "Han" in the original poem rather than following Mentzas's translation as "Chinese" (*trans.*)]. See also Huang Mei-e's (Huang Mei'e) paper, "Blood-and-Iron and Beyond: Reading the Poet Wu Zhuoliu," given at the International Conference on the Works of Wu Zhuoliu (2000).

14. Li Xiangping, *Wenxue Taiwan: Taiwan zhishizhe de wenxue xushi yu lilun xiangxiang* [Literary Taiwan: The literary narrative and theoretical imagination of Taiwanese intellectuals] (Beijing: Renmin wenxue chubanshe, 2003), 292–293.

15. See Peggy Kamuf, "Violence, Identity, Self-Determination and the Question of Justice: On Specters of Marx," in *Violence, Identity, and Self-Determination*, eds. Hent DeVries and Samuel Weber (Stanford, Calif.: Stanford University Press, 1997), 271–283, and Nigel Mapp, "Specter and Impurity: History and the Transcendental in Derrida and Adorno," in *Ghosts: Deconstruction, Psychoanalysis, History*, eds. Peter Buse and Andrew Stott (Houndmills, U.K.: Palgrave Macmillan, 1999), 92–124. For criticism of Derrida, see *Ghostly Demarcations: A Symposium on Jacques Derrida's* Specters of Marx, ed. Michael Sprinker (London: Verso, 1999).

16. Jacques Derrida, *Specters of Marx: The State of the Debt, the Work of Mourning, and the New International*, trans. Peggy Kamuf (New York: Routledge, 1994), 4.

17. See, for example, Hsiao A-chin's (Xiao Aqin) analysis, "The Development of Taiwanese Nationalism Since 1980: An Analysis of 'Taiwanese' (National) Literature,'" *Taiwan shehui yanjiu* [Taiwan social studies] 3 (July 1999): 1–51, especially pages 9 and 35–38.

18. Eric Hobsbawm, "Introduction: Inventing Traditions," in *The Invention of Tradition*, eds. Eric Hobsbawm and Terence Ranger (Cambridge: Cambridge University Press, 1983), 13, 271–273. There have been many writings in recent years that use the theory of narratology to discuss the structure and deconstruction of nationalism. The most recent examples include Sun Longji, "Nationalism in the Late Qing and the Invention of Yellow Emperor Worship," in *Lishi xuejia de jingxian* [Historians meridian] (Guilin: Guangxi shifan daxue chubanshe, 2004), 1–22, Takashi Fujitani, "Inventing, Forgetting, Remembering: Toward a Historical Ethnography of the Nation-State," *Cultural Nationalism in East Asia: Representation and Identity*, ed. Harumi Befu (Berkeley: Institute of East Asian Studies, University of California, 1993), 85–91, and Lan Shi-chi (Lan Shiqi), "Beyond the National Imagination: China's Taiwan Discourse and Discourse of the Nation," in *Kuajie de Taiwan shi yanjiu: yu Dongya shi de jiaocuo* [Cross-border studies of Taiwanese history: Intersections with East Asian history], eds. Wakabayashi Masatake and Wu Mi-cha (Wu Micha) (Taipei: Bozhongzhe, 2004), 313–348. Also refer to Benedict Anderson, *Imagined Communities: Reflections on the Origin and Spread of Nationalism* (New York: Verso, 1991), and Prasenjit Duara, *Rescuing History from the Nation: Questioning Narratives of Modern China* (Chicago: University of Chicago Press, 1995).

19. Chu T'ien-hsin, "Milky Way Railroad," in *Manyou zhe* [The flâneuse] (Taipei: Lianhe wenxue, 2000), 122.

20. Shih Shu (Shi Shu), "The Origins of the Decadent Consciousness in Taiwanese Fiction from the Era of Japanese Occupation," in *Liang an wenxue lunji* [Cross-Straits literary criticism] (Taipei: Xindi wenxue, 1997), 102–120.

21. David Der-wei Wang, "The Bone Collector Wu He: Thoughts on Wu He," in *Kua shiji fenghua: dangdai xiaoshuo ershi jia* [Into the New Millennium: Twenty Chinese Fiction Writers] (Taipei: Maitian chuban, 2002), 299–326.

22. Wu He, Afterword, *Yu sheng* [Remains of life] (Taipei: Maitian chuban, 2000), 251.

23. Ibid., 185.

24. Theodor W. Adorno, "A Portrait of Walter Benjamin," in *Prisms*, trans. Samuel Weber and Sierry Weber (Cambridge, MA: MIT Press, 1981), 233.

25. See Chen Chiung-ju (Chen Qiongru), "Li Yung-p'ing: From One Island to Another," in *Zhitu: Li Yongping zixuan ji, 1968–2002* [On the sly: Self-selected fiction of Li Yung-p'ing, 1968–2002], by Li Yung-p'ing (Taipei: Maitian, 2003), 402.

26. Ibid., 400.

27. Ng Kim Chew, "Abject Stories: Cracks in the Room Next Door—On Lo Yi-chin," in *Qian beihuai* [Banished sorrow], by Lo Yi-chin (Taipei: Maitian chuban, 2001), 339–357. Also see my article entitled "My Magnificent Sadness and Perversity" in Lo Yi-chin's *Qian beihuai* [Banished sorrow], 7–30.

28. Zhang Ailing, "My Writing," trans. Wendy Larson, in *Modern Chinese Literary Thought: Writings on Literature, 1893–1945*, ed. Kirk A. Denton (Stanford, Calif.: Stanford University Press, 1996), 438.

29. The title is a pun on the mythical emperor named Qi and the term for "abjection." The emperor is named "Qi" because he was allegedly an illegitimate child and was abandoned soon after his birth [*trans.*].

30. Lo Yi-chin, "The Story of Qi," in *Qi de gushi* [Abject stories] (Taipei: Self-published, no date), 16.

6

Exiled to English

HA JIN

In February 2005, ten months before he died of cancer, I again met Mr. Binyan Liu, one of the top Chinese dissidents in North America. I went to Princeton to give a talk, and we had dinner at Perry Link and Tong Yi's home in the evening. Over tea Mr. Liu complained about how empty of soul current Chinese literature was. He sighed and said to me, "Nobody is interested in exploring the Chinese soul anymore." He paused, then added, "If I were fifteen years younger, I would return to literature." His tone of voice was so sincere that I didn't know how to respond, as I remembered how certain he had once been about his political role.

The first time I'd met him was in the spring of 1989, when I was finishing my dissertation at Brandeis University so that I could return to my teaching position at Shandong University that fall. I was anxious, unsure if China would continue keeping its door open. I had known of several scholars who had earned graduate degrees in the West forty years before, but whose knowledge of our field, English and American literature, had grown obsolete over the decades because they'd never had opportunities to communicate with scholars outside China. One evening in mid-April, together with a friend I called on Mr. Binyan Liu, who was at Harvard that spring. During our conversation I told him my concern, and he assured me that things were improving in China. "Look," he said, "Su Xiaokang is about to become a vice president of a drama school. Your fear is groundless." At the time Su Xiaokang was a controversial figure, attacked by the hard-liners, because he had made the

TV series *River Elegy*, so his promotion was heartening news to most reform-minded people.

I respected Mr. Liu but couldn't share his optimism. He was a well-known political figure and an eminent reportage writer, whereas I was just a graduate student, so my concern might not have made much sense to him. Indeed, I myself felt it was rather trivial at the time.

Six weeks later, when the tanks rolled into Beijing and gun shots rang out in Tiananmen Square, Mr. Liu was still optimistic. Even three days after the June 4 massacre, at our demonstration in front of Boston City Hall, Mr. Liu gave a short speech and announced that the Li Peng regime would step down in a matter of days. Some of the demonstrators, mostly Chinese students, scholars, and people from Chinatown, seemed to be similarly hopeful.

Few of us could see what such a tragedy meant to many of us personally— it would change our lives for good. For weeks I was in a daze and in pain as though something had shattered deep inside. I had served in the People's Liberation Army for more than five years in the early 1970s, and we soldiers had always been instructed that our principle was to serve and protect the people. That was why we were called the people's army. Now the gunfire, the carnage, and the bald-faced lies afterward had blown that principle to pieces. As a result, a part of my reference frame had collapsed. For the first time I was tormented by the monstrous apparition of my native country.

By then I'd had my first volume of poems accepted for publication, but I took this English book only as an excursion because I believed I would write in Chinese eventually. I'd kept in touch with a few friends, poets, in China, and we thought that the Chinese language, polluted by revolutionary movements and political jargon, had reached the stage where changes must be made, and that we could work to improve the poetic language. As a possibility, we might attempt to create a new kind of language for poetry. The immediate effect of the Tiananmen massacre on me was that I would have to revise my personal plan if I couldn't go back to China soon. I began looking for a job, ideally something related to Chinese, such as teaching it or writing and translating for a Chinese-language newspaper. It turned out that for every opening there were hundreds of applicants, who mostly had degrees in Chinese, which I didn't have. The only diplomas in my hands were in English, on which I would have to depend when seeking employment. How I envied some of my friends who could make a living by using our mother tongue.

To make matters worse, my dissertation was in comparative poetics, aimed at China's academia, and had no use for most English departments in the United States. As a result, I couldn't find an academic job. On paper my application looked strong and could get me some interviews, yet when people saw me in person and heard my accent, they would change their minds.

I dreamed of going to California, but no school on the West Coast gave me an interview.

Despite displacement and adversity, one had to survive and figure out how to make the best use of one's life. I felt I must not just wait for a historical change, the course of which doesn't take the individual's fate into account. Like many Chinese students, I considered changing my field, and even my parents urged me to go to law or business school, or into computer science, but I knew I wouldn't be good at any of those. So I started thinking about shifting my field a bit—to write in English. I believed that after publishing three or four books, I might be able to land a job teaching creative writing as some of my American friends were doing, usually with one book under their belts. There were several reasons for taking this step. First, we—my wife and I—decided to immigrate so that our child could get out of the vicious cycle in Chinese history where violence had been gratuitous, serving no purpose. Second, I was unpublished in my mother tongue, and if I wrote in Chinese, I might have to publish in mainland China eventually and be at the mercy of its censorship. Third, I wouldn't let the Chinese state power shape my existence anymore—in other words, I wanted to get out of its field of force. To preserve the integrity of my work and to separate my existence from the powers that be, I could not but write in English.

However, it was easy to lay out those rationalities but hard to actually take the leap. For months I felt as though running a fever, overwhelmed by the odds. I was uncertain if I could write in English and how far I could go. But gradually I realized that certainty was not human condition. I had to ask myself whether I could accept failure as the final outcome. After a long soul searching, I concluded that I could face failure, which meant having wasted my life without getting anywhere. I was sure that even if I failed, my family would still love me and stay with me.

At the time I'd been reading Chekhov, both his stories and his correspondence. In his early years Chekhov didn't take his talent seriously, writing stories under pseudonyms only for bread. In his own confession, prior to 1886, when he was twenty-six, he had never worked on a story for longer than a day. In February 1886, D. V. Grigorovich, a reputable novelist, wrote Chekhov a letter, which "caused an emotional explosion" in the young writer. The older man said: "I am convinced that you are destined to create some admirable and truly artistic works. And you will be guilty of a great moral sin if you do not live up to these hopes. . . . I do not know what your financial situation is. If it is poor, it would be better for you to go hungry, as we did in our day . . ."[1] From that point on, Chekhov began writing longer stories with a clear artistic vision and eventually left us his best works, those small classics of his last decade. As I was reading his letters, it dawned on me that in America, as long as you were healthy and did some work, you wouldn't go hungry. Artists here could be poor, wretched, and paranoid, but they didn't starve. Compared to Chekhov's time and the czarist Russia, we were in a much better situation. Speaking about hunger, I was also deeply affected by Kafka's story "The Hunger Artist." The protagonist cannot find normal food that can satisfy his hunger, so he has to fast and take fasting as his art, an art that makes no sense to others. Eventually he breaks the fasting record and dies from enacting the art, yet even his best performance and highest achievement turn out to be meaningless to others and to himself. This character is a quintessential figure of artistic failure and success. In other words, neither success nor failure means anything to him. I realized that I wanted to write also because I couldn't find another way to appease the hunger within. Success or failure would be less relevant as long as I could write.

In English there were two models I could follow. One was exemplified by Yutang Lin, who served as a "cultural ambassador" and who spoke to the West about China and to the Chinese about the West. He functioned as a bridge—a link between two countries, two languages, and two cultures. In essence he viewed himself as a cultural spokesman of China. For some time such a grand role was very attractive to me, but I soon began to be aware of my inadequacy and to feel uneasy about Lin's dependency on China for his literary existence. The other model was embodied by Conrad and Nabokov, who didn't represent their native countries and instead found their places in English. In fact, Conrad and Nabokov have established a great tradition in English prose, in which some nonnative speakers have become essential writers. This is a unique phenomenon, one of the glories English has.

It took me more than a year to decide on the convention of Conrad and Nabokov. They both depended on nothing but their individual talent and found their destinies in their adopted language. What I attempted to do was just follow the path they had opened. There was no originality in my choice— all would depend on whether I had the courage, the ability, and the luck.

At the time, China was my only subject matter, and I assumed I would spend the rest of my life translating Chinese historical experiences into literature. I didn't pay much attention to a fissure in my conception—the contradiction between my subject matter and the language I used, a language by nature alien to my subject matter. As I continued writing in English, I began to feel this alienation widening and taking place inside myself as well, and gradually I grew less and less interested in China. I realized that I wanted to write about something else, especially the American immigrant experience, which was closer to my heart.

This desire to enter a new territory—to arrive somewhere—is in part related to my choice of writing in English. Writers of my situation exist in a margin between two languages and two cultures, so we have to become our own monuments—if we do not produce a body of significant works, we cannot claim our existence in either language. We can easily be diminished and even crushed by the forces projected from the centers. Just the isolation alone is potent enough to erase most of us. Therefore, the pressure of survival is a constant presence to us. This high-strung condition makes us restless to produce new works and treat every book as a beginning and departure. We have no permanent turf under our feet and have to move on. In some cases, our desperation and even our anger can fuel our ambitions, spur creativity, and clarify our visions. With few references around us and without any reliance on the collective, we have to seek, imagine, and set up landmarks for ourselves, and ultimately, have to figure out how to go further than our predecessors and thus enrich the tradition we work in.

Even within this English tradition, writers each have an individual way of existence. It is commonly known that Nabokov disliked Conrad. When people compared him to Conrad, Nabokov would insist that he was different because he had written poetry and fiction in Russian whereas Conrad had never published in Polish. What Nabokov implied was that he had a place in both languages while Conrad existed only in English. Nabokov is a paragon of dual linguistic identity, which few writers can claim. However, we should keep in mind that similar to Nabokov's dual literary citizenship, Conrad is also part of Polish literature, embraced by the Poles as their own—even school pupils in Poland read him. In other words, the literary citizenship is not always determined by language alone. It is also decided by the subject matter, the quality of the author's works, the experiences they present, and the writer's origin. In the end, everything will depend on the quality of the works and on whether they can enrich and bring honor to a literature. If they are valuable enough, they might be embraced by more than one language and culture. In this sense, a writer's first responsibility is to write well and produce significant works. That is all we can aspire to do.

Yet there is a good deal of pride in the way Nabokov differentiated himself from Conrad. I greatly admire his kind of contribution to both his mother tongue and his adopted tongue. He demonstrated how a writer can contribute to his native language and literature while working in another language and living away from his motherland. But we should bear in mind that Nabokov's unique linguistic identity was shaped by the circumstances of exile. In fact, he wrote all his fiction in English after he had immigrated to America in 1940, and in his later years he lost the excitement in composing in Russian.[2] Even he himself divided his writing career into the Russian period and the English period. Every nonnative writer has his or her own unique problems and situation and has to figure out a personal way of survival. As beginners, it might be insane for us to seek a place in multiple languages, because the task of surviving in one language is already Herculean. Sometimes we have to make great sacrifice in order to proceed, including giving up a country or a language.

The novelist Dai Sijie, who writes in French, once said in an interview that I was too high-minded about the possibility of creating genuine literature in an adopted tongue and of bringing something new to "the mainstream literature in the West." He claims that the Western readers accept our works merely as some kind of novelty. "Like Chinese food," in his words.[3] I was appalled by such self-denigration. If we don't try to write literature, why should we endure all the painful struggles in another tongue? If we don't attempt to produce serious art, we will reduce ourselves to cultural peddlers and will not deserve all the anxiety, despair, and loneliness that we have to suffer in our pursuit. In brief, if we don't take our adoption of another language as an earnest artistic choice, how can we expect readers to take us seriously? Mr. Dai must have been unaware that many of those in power in China couldn't wait to see us fail or become mediocre, because that would bring us closer to them and vindicate their mediocrity. Worse, that would set a frightening example for those artists who dare escape from the dominance of the Chinese state power.

Up to now, the bulk of my fiction is set in China. I have been accused of betraying my native country and uglifying the Chinese to please the Western audience. All those accusations will be proved groundless eventually, as I have always held translatability and similarity as my literary principle. I can say with certainty that most of my fiction means much more to the Chinese than to the readers in the West. That is why all my books except for *Waiting* have been banned in mainland China. In fact, audience shouldn't be a literary writer's concern. In American poetry, we all know that a poet should start by speaking to "vacuum," as Joseph Brodsky stressed, or "to emptiness," as Robert Creeley asserted as the needed courage. For whom do we write? "For the dead you love," as John Berryman declared. We write to please the dead masters, who are also our rivals, and we all know it is the isolation and loneliness that refines one's work and hones one's art. All the talk about the book market and selling points is sheer nonsense, which I have felt too ashamed to heed.

Accusations against me are largely based on the conviction that one must be loyal to one's native country. But loyalty is a two-way street, especially when the individual doesn't rely on China for his or her existence. Why don't we speak about how a country betrays an individual? Has a country ever been loyal to an individual? Why should a country always demand service and sacrifice from the individual? Indeed for a country, the individual is only to be used and consumed. This is okay if the individual is a willing party. Yet if a country has abused and oppressed its people, isn't it tyrannical to demand their loyalty? And what is loyalty? It's easy to talk and point the finger, but it is difficult to do something meaningful and valuable for your country. If a Chinese writer moves into a foreign language and produces significant works in it, the ultimate upshot, from the country's viewpoint, will be that the effort might expand China's cultural map. Is that not a higher order of service? At least, it will mean much more to China than patriotic platitudes and empty talk of loyalty.

I am often revolted by the litany that one must love one's country unconditionally. Even some intellectuals and artists have joined the fanatic chorus.[4] They believe that the country's holiness must never be questioned. But creeds not backed by reason are likely to be deceiving and self-serving. What if your country has become a fascist state? What if your country invades another country or commits genocide? What if your country bullies its own people and robs them of their voices? What if your country makes your life miserable and insufferable? Let us face it—in human history most atrocities have been committed in the name of the country. It is simpleminded, if not hypocritical, to propagate that kind of blind patriotism. An intellectual's basic task is to speak truth to power, and if necessary, speak against power.

When I began writing in English, I didn't expect to draw so much flak. Let me be candid about the controversy over me. To my mind, it mainly has two origins. The first is that publicly I have always been vocal about the Tiananmen massacre, which still rankles, and thus I have become a persona non grata to the Chinese government. Because of my feud with the Communist Party, its propaganda officials have orchestrated most of the personal attacks, including character assassination. The second cause is that my existence as a writer exemplifies that an individual doesn't have to depend on a country to survive. In other words, my existence outside China's political and literary apparatuses has become an eyesore to the authorities and to some writers and critics who are also state officials, who have to justify their inadequacy to their superiors and inferiors.

After my last meeting with Mr. Binyan Liu in February 2005, I have often thought about his words, his claim that he would have returned to literature if he had been fifteen years younger. He might have been disappointed by continuing to play his political role, passively and hopelessly waiting for the historical change in China that might bring him back to our motherland.

Fifteen years before our last meeting would be the beginning of 1990, just months after the Tiananmen massacre and when many of us had been scrambling to figure out how to exist in America. Since then he had never returned to China and must eventually have been disillusioned by the long wait. His last claim seemed to have revealed some self-doubts and many other implications.

Did he mean he might have endeavored to write significant literature? Did he aspire to cure the disease in the Chinese soul as Lu Xun had attempted to eight decades before? Like Lu Xun's, his conception of literature must have been quite utilitarian. Did he regret having spent his later years gleaning information on China from newspapers and magazines and writing political articles? He might have preferred to live differently in America by having a literary life, although I couldn't see how he would have been able to define his existence without the political context of China. A celebrated exile like him could not conceive his independence from our native country. In that resided his tragedy and honor.

I am sure that Mr. Binyan Liu was aware of the difference between a literary life and a political life—the latter is predicated on power and the collective, without which no political figure can achieve anything significant. By contrast, a literary life doesn't need those, and it mainly relies on the individual's talent and effort—through the private endeavor some writers might also achieve greatness if they have created works of lasting value. Of course, in Mr. Liu's situation, even though he had returned to literature, he wouldn't have needed to make any drastic change. For him, to continue writing in Chinese would make more sense because he was also an established semi-literary figure in China and his voice would be more resonant in our mother tongue. But for a beginner and an immigrant like me, the only choice was English, in which I would have to make my solitary journey and turn my back to our menacing native land whenever it becomes too exacting and too overpowering. This alienating stance is essential for artistic survival, because one cannot afford to let politics overwhelm one's art. As a writer, I must not be responsible for a country or a group, and I can be responsible only for my characters and for the words I use.

Notes

1. Ernest J. Simmons, *Chekhov: A Biography* (Boston: Little Brown, 1962), 96.

2. Nabokov confessed in an interview: "Of the two instruments in my possession, one—my native tongue—I can no longer use, and this not only because I lack a Russian Audience, but also because the excitement of verbal adventure in the Russian medium has faded away gradually after I turned to English in 1940." See Vladimir Nabokov, *Strong Opinions* (New York: McGraw-Hill, 1973), 106.

3. Dai Sijie, *Xin Jing Bao*, July 22, 2007.

4. Even Ji Xianlin, the late Beijing University professor and "a master of Chinese national culture," was known for saying, "You must love your country unconditionally" (*ai guo mei shangliang*).

II

DISCREPANT PERSPECTIVES

While the chapters in part I address the major issues and types of critical controversies that the concept of the Sinophone and the field of Sinophone studies address, the chapters in part II, all of which were originally published during the 1990s, have been reprinted here because they in many ways lay the groundwork for the emergence of Sinophone studies in the twenty-first century. By drawing attention to issues of the relationship between place and practice as well as culture and historical context, the chapters in this part register the critical impulses to locate, define, and specify the multiple and heterogeneous sites of difference delineated by the Sinophone.

The chapters in part II and their influence on Sinophone studies can be contextualized according to two historical contingencies of the last two decades of the twentieth century. Firstly, the emergence and popularity of discourses of postcolonialism, diaspora, and ethnic studies generated new critical vocabularies for scholars in the disciplines of history, literature, and area studies. Increased interest in topics such as transnationalism, immigration, exile, ethnic/national minoritization, center/periphery dynamics, and colonial legacy lent immediate critical relevancy to the types of issues raised in the following chapters. Secondly, China's globalization in the post-Mao and post-Tiananmen eras forced the authors of these chapters to grapple with questions of how the reality of China's modern evolution as a geopolitical entity concerns individuals and communities who maintain or evoke Chinese cultural affiliations outside China. Despite their diverse methodological approaches ranging from historical or sociological to literary criticism, the authors represented in part II are driven by an intuitive or historical necessity to locate and offer theoretical paradigms for understanding different kinds of Chineseness outside mainland China, from Taiwan and Hong Kong to Southeast Asia and the United States. These paradigms include the "Chinese diaspora" (Gungwu Wang), "cultural China" (Wei-ming Tu), the "Wandering Chinese" exile (Leo Ou-fan Lee), and the "structure of dual domination" (Ling-chi Wang).

In his article on "Chineseness" (1999), the Singaporean historian Gungwu Wang rejects a racialized definition of Chineseness that equates the term with "descent and blood" and that ignores "the significance of social and cultural attributes." Perhaps the foremost scholar of the field known as Chinese diaspora studies, Gungwu Wang is apprehensive of the liberal and unqualified use of the term *overseas Chinese*, feeling it is misapplied to communities that happen to trace ancestral origins to China but do not necessarily retain certain sociocultural attributes that Wang identifies as "Chinese." For Wang, the notion of the "ethnic Chinese" is distinct from Chineseness, as the latter is a question of cultural identity. However, he struggles with the possibility that "the Chineseness of China will always be considered the only authentic kind, and those outside must choose to return or forever confront their dilemmas of place and practice." These are the dilemmas implicit in the categories of the "overseas Chinese," which indicates temporary residence outside China, and the "diaspora," which remains bound by the notion of a shared ancestral homeland. For both of these identitarian categories, the practice of Chineseness must reconcile its historical relationship with its particular "place" outside China. Wang's articulation of the dilemma of place and practice is a critical step for Sinophone studies, which asserts the historical situatedness of the practice of Chineseness in its various locales of articulation. However, Gungwu Wang conceptualizes Chineseness along a spectrum that ranges from sites in or along the Chinese mainland (Shanghai and Hong Kong) to farther flung sites of Han immigrant majority (Singapore) or significant minority (San Francisco). Therefore, Chineseness in Wang's model prioritizes relations in terms of degrees and measures of a cultural center (China) to its peripheries, which in the case of Singapore and San Francisco he describes as "foreign territories."

In "Cultural China" (1991), Wei-ming Tu addresses the cultural and territorial ambiguities of the term *Chinese*, noting that its meaning is entangled with "China as a geopolitical concept and Chinese culture as a lived reality." According to Tu, the diasporic Chinese imaginary conceives of China as a "civilization-state." The idea of a Chinese civilization is similar to that of a European civilization but distinct in that throughout history, the former has been pressured to unify into a single political state. Inheriting control of the necessary "symbolic resources" for the diasporic cultural imaginary, the modern Chinese state feels it can legitimately demand the political loyalties of the diaspora. In order to assert the diaspora's right to claim the symbolic cultural resources as their own, Tu elicits the notion of a "cultural China" as distinct from the territorial Chinese state. Arguing for the existence of variegated "symbolic universes" of cultural China, Wei-ming Tu attempts to destabilize the Chinese political center's hegemony of signification over those whom based on cultural orientation maintain an interest in Chinese civilization of past, present, and/or future. Thus, in addition to drawing attention to the ambiguous valences of the term "Chinese," Tu's ambition to decenter the Chinese state's political monopoly on culture by locating other distinct sites and spheres of cultural signification registers one of the key critical impulses of Sinophone studies. However, Wei-ming Tu's assumptions that the "diaspora Chinese cherish the hope of returning to and being recognized by the homeland" and "lack a sense of permanence in their adopted country" reveal affinities to the degrees and measures of "Chineseness" in Gungwu Wang's model.

In "On the Margins of the Chinese Discourse" (1991), Leo Ou-fan Lee, a leading U.S. scholar of modern Chinese literature, analyzes the literary figure of the "Wandering Chinese" outside China as reflecting a condition of psychological exile that stems from the inability to anchor one's identity "on the margins" of the adopted homeland. Examining the discourse of the "Wandering Chinese" exile in the literature of Nieh Hua-ling, Yuh Li-hua, and Pai Hsien-yung, Lee argues that the protagonists suffer because they are unable to embrace the sense of intellectual freedom that the exile's position on the margins of both Chineseness and American society offers. In a manner reminiscent of the foundational postcolonial critic Edward Said's seminal essay "Reflections on Exile,"[1] Lee embraces the voluntary exile's "true peripheral perspective" because it offers writers "a distance sufficiently removed from the center" of their psychological obsession—in this case China—with which they can "subject the obsession itself to artistic treatment." Lee's critique of the psychology of exile provides a valuable model of literary interpretation for Sinophone studies because he examines how the site of exile (place) endows the expression and performance of culture (practice) with new aesthetic possibilities or limitations. The Sinophone model carries Lee's line of critique forward by asking how the "literature of Chinese students abroad" in which "both author and subject are in America but the language remains Chinese" also claims a place on and gives meaning to the margins of *American* literature and culture as "Sinophone American literature."[2] Lee's definition of his own exilic stance as a form of "Chinese cosmopolitanism" that retains a "fundamental commitment to Chinese culture" suggests that locating "Chinese margins," rather than American ones, remains his discursive priority. Lee's meditations on the margins of Chinese discourse are influenced by the cultural and literary activities, particularly the *xungen* ("search for roots") movement, of a new generation of exiled intellectuals in the post-Tiananmen era. These writers and cultural critics explore the political and ethnic margins of China and Chineseness in order to reshape and hybridize the center (Beijing), thus destabilizing its monopoly on the geopolitical imaginary. Despite expressing that his ultimate concern lies with the state of the Chinese cultural "motherland," Lee's analogy between different evocations of the margins—the literary discourse in China on peripheral, non-Han ethnic minorities and that of the "Wandering Chinese" figure among immigrant minority communities in the United States—points to potential comparative analyses and strategic affiliations for Sinophone studies.

In Ling-chi Wang's essay (1995), the author takes a critical approach to Chinese diaspora studies and moves it into Chinese American studies in deriving his concept of the "structure of dual domination," which refers to the geopolitical discursive hegemonies of the United States and China that the author argues dominate "all aspects of Chinese American life." According to Wang, American discourse (in English) on Chinese Americans has historically perpetuated an "assimilationist" model that measures the degree to which Chinese immigrants and subsequent generations conform to a "Euro-American" normative standard. Wang redefines the assimilationist model as a pillar of domestic "racial exclusion and oppression" propping up the structure of dual domination. The second pillar, which is "extraterritorial and racial," refers to the enactment of policies in twentieth-century China (both in the People's Republic of China [PRC] and the Republic of China [ROC]) meant to enforce loyalty by exerting "extraterritorial rule over the Chinese diaspora," which the nation views as "external colonies" on the basis of ethnicity. According to Wang, both the domestic (U.S.) and extraterritorial (China) discourses tend to be "chauvinistic and ethnocentric," manipulating Chinese Americans for their own political and economic advantage. Wang sharply points to the glaring lack of interaction between ethnic studies research in Chinese and English that has prevented inquiries into the historical formation of resistance tactics against dual domination among Chinese Americans. He argues that the new generation of Chinese Americans rejects dual domination while positing their "Chinese racial and cultural origin to be in China," insisting their "identity and destiny to be exclusively rooted in and derived from the Chinese experience in the U.S." Wang's attention to the ways in which different linguistic discourses (Sinophone and Anglophone) shape and confine the scope of research as well as his call for more interaction between ethnic studies and Chinese diaspora studies to generate a broader and fuller picture of local realities articulate precisely some of the goals of Sinophone studies. Furthermore, Wang's analysis diverges from previous models (those of Gungwu Wang, Wei-ming Tu, and Leo Lee) by locating *two* geopolitical centers that exert hegemony over the resources of cultural and racial signification. Yet Wang's model assumes that the structure of dual domination exerts an inevitable impact on Chinese Americans, whereas the Sinophone model offers an alternative formation of identity as a complex dialectic between language and ethnicity that gives potentiality to the deconstruction of the racialized and territorialized "pillars" of that very structure.

From one geopolitical center and one theoretical paradigm to another, the chapters in part II engage in a dialogue on the issue of Chineseness and the meaning of the margins. Despite these differences, all of the chapters continue to invoke the term *Chinese* as a kind of cultural identity or ethnic assignation outside China. Further discussion of these chapters might elaborate on the historical consequences of the usage of *Chinese* and how the introduction of the term *Sinophone* intervenes or offers a different paradigm for understanding some of the issues these authors present. Finally, given the various historical realities and the weight of identitarian terms presented in these articles, we might also consider how these chapters serve as discrepant interlocutors with or against whom other thinkers formulated their ideas in Sinophone studies.

Notes

1. Anthologized in Edward Said, *Reflections on Exile and Other Essays* (Cambridge, Mass.: Harvard University Press, 2000), 173–186.

2. For more on Sinophone American literature, see the chapters by Sau-ling Wong, Te-hsing Shan, and Shuang Shen in part III of this volume.

A

7

Chineseness

The Dilemmas of Place and Practice

GUNGWU WANG

Identifying Chinese

Chineseness in people is hard to pin down. It calls for judgments about identity and meaning. Being part of the Chinese diaspora myself, the outsider in me remains intrigued by it. How have the different communities of the diaspora changed in response to the demands of their adopted countries? What kinds of ethnic identities are being constructed to deal with other people's sense of nationhood? Does Chinese nationalism still mean anything for ethnic minorities outside China?

I shall approach this difficult subject by looking at the differences produced by place and practice. By place, I refer to the locality and environment in which people live. Each place obviously has its own set of practices. I shall focus on changes in practice over time and the ways in which each ethnic community coped with those changes. In the context of place and practice, does being Chinese always mean the same thing, or does it change from time to time and place to place? Do we begin with variations and adaptations of the "Great Chinese Tradition" that has always been associated with the power and intellectual centers of North China in the past? Do we assume that modern urban Chinese today have moved away from all that? Could we still say that numerous small traditions of rural China, with their distinctive sets of local practices, may each be more directly and quintessentially Chinese? Or is Chineseness something more abstract, a collection of cultural traits that can be isolated and used to measure each person's willingness to acknowledge them whether they live inside Chinese territory or not?

These questions bring out the relationship between the concrete experience of being Chinese and the abstract qualities of Chineseness. They imply that being Chinese is not absolute. One could be more or less Chinese at any one point in time. One could remain stationary, true and unwavering in maintaining what one believes to be vitally rooted in tradition. That suggests an act of will, without which one could become less Chinese. This also means that if found to be inadequately Chinese, one could correct that by acquiring cultural attributes that would intensify the qualities that make one Chinese. This implies a "scientific" approach that tries to determine, however inexactly, the attributes that make someone Chinese and to measure the degrees of change that could either diminish or enhance one's Chineseness.

Who Are "Overseas Chinese"?

This leads me to make a correction to recent writings that define the "overseas Chinese" as all Chinese outside the People's Republic of China (PRC), including those of Taiwan and Hong Kong.[1] This would immediately separate Hong Kong from Shanghai and place Hong Kong together with Singapore and San Francisco. This makes no sense where Chineseness is concerned. Also, many of the writings that take this approach show carelessness and ignorance. Others have had an economic, or an ideological, agenda for separating "capitalist" Chinese from "communist" Chinese. The most striking example of this usage was the espousal by *The Economist* in 1992 of this distinction as a hard economic fact. According to that counting, the populations of Taiwan and Hong Kong-Macau were added to the estimated 25 million people of Chinese descent around the world, which led to the author's total of over 50 million "overseas Chinese."

There are several problems with this definition and with the figures for Chinese. Firstly, although isolating all other Chinese from the PRC may serve the interests of Taiwan as the Republic of China, the Taipei government totally rejects the inclusion of the people of Taiwan as "overseas Chinese." Their own use of the term *huaqiao* (that is, overseas Chinese) has a long history going back to the decade before the Republic was founded in 1912. It referred to Chinese citizens who were temporarily living outside Chinese territories and under foreign governments, or who were so regarded by a series of Chinese governments.[2] Adding to the confusion, the Taipei authorities have always treated Hong Kong Chinese as their *huaqiao*, for these same historical reasons, since Hong Kong was ruled by the British. However, the

Hong Kong people do not consider themselves overseas Chinese, although many had once been overseas Chinese or still have family ties overseas. Some of them have, however, accepted the Taiwan usage because *huaqiao* status confers certain benefits in Taiwan, especially for entry into Taiwan's more prestigious universities. In contrast, where the PRC is concerned, the greater advantage for Hong Kong and Macau people comes from being called *tongbao* (compatriots). Indeed, in the PRC, the Taiwanese are also consistently called *tongbao*. In no way could Taiwanese be considered overseas Chinese, which would imply that they lived in foreign territory.

Secondly, even the lower figure of 25 million Chinese who live outside the PRC, Taiwan, and Hong Kong-Macau assumes an accurate definition about who is and who is not Chinese. For Southeast Asia alone, the 1992 figure is 23 million. Of this, only the census figures for Malaysia and Singapore define ethnic Chinese more or less consistently, but none of the other estimates can be considered reliable. What is remarkable is that Chineseness is equated with descent and blood, and ignores all questions of identity and the significance of cultural and social attributes. It fails to note the high percentage of mixed marriages in Thailand, the Philippines, Vietnam, and Myanmar that produced progeny who considered themselves local and only incidentally Chinese. Nor does it take into account the effectiveness of the national education that was introduced after the independence of each of the new nation-states. Thus, if this misleading figure is linked with political loyalties and the potential for subversion, as it was during the period of the Cold War, it could be more alarming to China's neighbors. Strategic and diplomatic considerations aside, this way of counting heads is dangerously close to a kind of racism that resembles anti-Semitism. I refer to the prejudice that, in modern times, turned into a systematic discrimination and political persecution that began by identifying every Jew in pseudoscentific ways, in the name of social biology, breeding, even eugenics.

As far as the Chinese themselves are concerned, only those who live outside Chinese territories, especially those who have settled in foreign countries and become their citizens, might be included in the idea of a Chinese diaspora. More accurately, in order to avoid calling them *huaqiao*, or sojourners, these citizens of Chinese descent are referred to as "Chinese overseas" or are described as hyphenated Chinese—Malaysian Chinese, Sino-Thai, and Chinese Americans, for example. But clearly, for them, the term *huaqiao* (conventionally translated as "overseas Chinese") is a misnomer, for it implies that such "overseas Chinese" are really citizens of China temporarily residing outside China. In the PRC, Taiwan, and Hong Kong today, these Chinese tend now to be called *haiwai huaren*, or *huaren* for short. This has been rendered as "ethnic Chinese" in more recent scholarly writings—and is strongly preferred by L. Suryadinata[3]—but it must be said that the term *haiwai huaren* still causes confusion because it is the literal translation of "overseas Chinese." Allow me to simplify the matter: the diaspora or Chinese overseas do not include the people of Taiwan and Hong Kong-Macau, nor those, whatever their descent, who deny that they are Chinese and have nothing to do with the rituals, practices, and institutions associated with the Chinese.

Places and Practices

I shall compare the diaspora with some communities in China and concentrate on four cities. Two of them, Shanghai and Hong Kong, are clearly Chinese; their Chineseness is entwined with problems of modernization. The other two, Singapore and San Francisco, have large Chinese communities for whom Chineseness means cultural identity, and this subject has divided each community as to how Chinese they are and ought to be. Before I proceed with these large cities, it is important to remember the dilemmas of place and practice can be just as complex where Chinese communities are small as where they are large. I shall use three examples to illustrate that point.

In Tahiti in French Polynesia, the Chinese number about 10,000, almost 10 percent of the population.[4] More than a hundred years ago, they had come as laborers and small businessmen from the villages and townships of the Pearl River delta just north of Hong Kong. They became well-off, and in some cases immensely wealthy, during World War II when the United States took over from the Vichy French and gave the Chinese some exclusive agencies and contracts. Since the end of the war when the French returned, the leading families have been true to their Chinese past and remained successful by positioning themselves in the middle, politically with the French and economically with the American companies that helped them get started. Among the young, however, there is intermarriage and conversion to Christianity, even sympathy for Tahitian independence, but also immigration to Europe and North America. Inevitably, this has caused a loosening of their ties with the community. This tight and small community consists mainly of Hakkas, who are particularly proud of the way they have carried their Chineseness with them wherever they have gone. There is concern that the younger generation should maintain their Chineseness. The generational struggle over being Chinese is no less intense, partly because the elders have tried hard to make up for their isolation in one corner of the South Pacific.

At the other end of the world, in mobile and cosmopolitan Britain, the Chinese are but one of many minorities and they do not have economic dominance over the native population as they do in Tahiti. Also, the Chinese have not clustered there as much as they have in some other parts of Europe.[5] The links with Hong Kong, from which most of them have come, are strong and maintaining their cultural identity is much easier. The bulk of the Chinese are first-generation immigrants. Among them are many whose educational backgrounds ensured upward social mobility for their children. Chinese language skills, including the ability to write Chinese, have been kept up, and global ties with other Chinese communities have been encouraged. The serious test will come when another generation grows up. Stable politics and a sound economy in Britain will guarantee a high degree of tolerance toward the Chinese, which should increase the opportunities to assimilate.

The story is somewhat different in Japan, another native but non-colonial setting on a group of islands where the Chinese community is small and dispersed. It is also a stable and economically prosperous country, albeit in Asia. The major difference is that the Chinese in Japan moved into a country whose people once acknowledged a great cultural debt to China. But modern Japan has always been more restrictive about immigration than Britain, and much more reluctant to assimilate their immigrant workforce. In contrast to their harsh policies toward Korean residents, however, the Japanese have shown great ambiguity in their treatment of the Chinese. The unique mixture of respect and contempt that the Chinese experience there aggravates the dilemmas of place and practice: a place that is proximate and even culturally familiar, and a practice that is hierarchical, discriminatory, and highly controlled. The diaspora experience there is not only totally different from that in the other two territories, but also markedly different from that in Southeast Asia.[6] All of them remind us that, even for the smallest communities, being Chinese is not simple.

Four Cities

The people of the four cities can be distinguished as the Hongkongers and Shanghainese who live on the edge of the China coast, and as Singaporeans and the Bay Area Chinese Americans who live far away. As people living in different environments, with different political and cultural systems, they are obviously not the same. What kind of Chineseness then can be identified in all of them? The difference in place determines a great deal of what people do and think, how they live, and what loyalties they owe. But the fact that all four are great cities, and the regional centers of urban, commercial, and cultural activity, brings out much that is common to all global cities. In an increasingly large number of areas, notably in business, technology, and academia, similar goals prevail and it hardly matters whether or not one is Chinese. Wealth, work, education, and certain levels of cultural pursuits bring the cities and their successful people together, making Chineseness far from essential for their respective successes.

Nevertheless, two factors remain important in challenging this prototype of Chinese who are urban, and middle class, and who may also be described as capitalistic, or people servicing a capitalist economic system. The first is that in a spectrum ranging from those who are obviously Chinese to those who are only barely recognizable as Chinese, the Shanghai Chinese, who are the pioneers of modern Chineseness, would be closest to what may be seen as historically Chinese. Along such a spectrum, Hong Kong Chinese today, despite having been ruled by the British for so long, would not be all that distant from those of Shanghai. Those who have settled in Singapore and the Bay Area are further along the spectrum because they have many more complex non-Chinese variables in their lives with which to contend.

The second factor is that political identities and practices still count for a great deal and will be more evident as an increasingly nationalistic China makes more specific demands on Shanghai and Hong Kong Chinese. Such demands may also influence the thought and behavior patterns of Chinese outside China, but there are good reasons why the Chinese in Singapore and San Francisco would be able to resist them. Of particular importance is the more general question, how will regional and global responses to a resurgent China impact ethnic Chinese residents in Southeast Asia and North America?

Shanghai

I begin with Shanghai because, by any criterion, its people are Chinese and have always been seen as Chinese.[7] Chineseness for them simply means leading the way toward becoming modern Chinese. Shanghai became the model of a modern Chinese city for all Chinese inside and outside China. Its people were also considered the very models of modern Chinese. If there are dilemmas there, they stem from the question of how far modernization should go for its people. As an integral part of China, there were constraints on how much faster they could go without leaving their compatriots behind. Shanghai began by welcoming a wide range of Chinese from all over China, especially those from the wealthiest and best-educated peoples of the Yangzi delta. The city thus attracted a galaxy of creative and innovative talent who were drawn by its openness and a miscellany of practices that allowed far more leeway to challenge convention with innovation.

The Chinese who want to identify themselves as Shanghainese may be described as those who mastered the earliest challenges of the West's impact on China and indubitably became the first examples of modern Chinese. Their city was the first truly international city in Asia. Their success in learning and adapting from the West without losing their Chinese identity was greatly admired throughout China. But there was more, much more, that was contradictory and perplexing to the Chinese in the interior. Shanghai was home to both nationalism and revolution; it also produced some of the keenest minds, who proceeded to instruct the rest of China about the most advanced ideas in science and the arts from all parts of the world. Paradoxically, it was also the first city in China to symbolize the negative images of what had been borrowed from the West. It stood for extravagance and waste, glitter and shallowness, cosmopolitan rootlessness and disloyalty, betrayal of Chinese values, even treachery toward China itself. In short, identity of a modern Chinese in all its manifestations can be said to have evolved in Shanghai.

After the Communist victory in 1949, cosmopolitan Shanghai came to an end, although it remained the most modern city in the PRC for the next forty years. Four decades of re-Sinification followed for the people of Shanghai. They were not asked to return to being Chinese in the Great Tradition, but to make their contribution to that curious mix of peasant simplicity and socialist experimentation that Mao Zedong imposed on all of China. In Shanghai, there was a conscious effort to eliminate all the dross of foreign capitalist practice and residual feudal values, while retaining the skills necessary for a basic industrialization modeled on another foreign example, that of the Soviet Union. When this experiment was declared a failure in the 1970s, an older Shanghai tried to be reborn. Interestingly, this recrudescence did not seek to restore traditional Chinese culture but to rejuvenate something of the amalgam that Shanghai had created earlier in the twentieth century. That had been the peak of modern Chineseness, which was seen as the hallmark of the Shanghainese. And they are well on their way to succeeding in the opinion of most people who have been to Shanghai recently.

Hong Kong

In comparison, Hong Kong was marked by its beginnings as the colonial backwater of a single power, the British. Its small Chinese villages remained remarkably parochial and stubbornly impervious to modern influences. Thus, Chineseness in early Hong Kong was not associated with modernization. It remained traditional and provincial up to the 1940s. Whatever modernity the place could produce was either Anglo-Chinese or largely an imitation of the new Chinese practices that were emerging in Shanghai.[8]

Hong Kong's translation to a global meeting place of goods and services, peoples, and cultures came about only after the 1950s. Since then, radical changes have given the place a multidimensional appearance. Certainly, what is Chinese there today is no longer easy to describe or understand because several processes took place at the same time. Although many modern Chinese from Shanghai brought their dynamism and creativity to Hong Kong, the place was also flooded by people who came out of traditional villages of the Pearl River delta in search of work in the newly developed industries. People voted with their feet against the Maoist revolution in the PRC. For the first time, there was a consensus in Hong Kong that modernization was to be found in the open, international, market economy. It was another beginning of an alternative Chineseness anchored in modern entrepreneurship and new standards of material and technological success.[9]

Given this new inspiration, the heart of this modernity came less from place than from practice. By practice, I refer to the Anglo-Chinese system of authority and management, marked in particular by efficient administration and the rule of law.[10] This modern system enabled rapid changes to occur without disorder and instability, and the Hong Kong people came to admire and depend on it. Although the system had begun with a foreign overarching authority, most Hong Kong people today accept it as a vital part of their modern heritage, a valuable accretion to what Hongkongers may eventually bring to another kind of Chineseness.

After the 1950s, British colonial policies were modified in response to the closure of Shanghai and the new opportunities thus provided. The new practices offered a unique experience of openness to restless and dynamic people who could readily come and go. But events in China after 1949 continued to bring uncertainty to Hong Kong. A series of campaigns and disturbances followed, which came to a climax during the Cultural Revolution. Although most of the subsequent surprises were more benign, they did not cease, not even after the tragedy at Tiananmen Square in 1989.

When a place and its practices are subject to external pressures for change as Hong Kong has been, its people face the dilemmas involved in having to choose what kind of modern Chinese they wish to become.[11] This may mean asking whether to stay or leave, whether to change with the times or stand firm, whether to be passive and receptive, or whether to actively seek to identify with China or not. The standards and qualities in the modern values to which people aspire must be placed in the context of trying to be both modern and Chinese on the periphery of China. The Hong Kong Chinese can claim to have developed their own version of a new Chineseness during the past four decades. The question is, will they be rewarded for that contribution? Or will they have to pay a price for having gone their own way?

Singapore

Let me now turn to Singapore, another city with a Chinese majority that has gone its own way, but, unlike Hong Kong, has been fortunate enough to become an independent state. The Singapore Chinese formed a commercial community that was the freest and most active in Southeast Asia.[12] Interactions with the neighboring areas of Java, Sumatra, Borneo, the Malay Peninsula, and Thailand laid the foundations for the role the island was to play thereafter—the provider of trading services. The first Chinese leaders of the Straits Settlements came from the small Baba (local-born) communities that had left China generations earlier. Most of them had lost the use of the Chinese language, but, together with those of the Malay Peninsula, they retained close links with traditional Chinese organizations. Despite their ties to the British administration, they showed a willingness to support Chinese causes when there was occasion to do so. We might mention examples of loyal supporters of Sun Yat-sen who readily sacrificed their lives for China, and others later on who did likewise in the service of the Communist Revolution. Indeed, this phenomenon continued beyond World War II[13] and was even truer of those first-generation Chinese who knew little or no English, as well as the thousands of others who were educated in local Chinese schools up to the 1950s. The latter were adept at using modern methods of organization and communication to bring much needed help to China. During the first 150 years of Singapore history, most of these Chinese considered themselves Chinese, and the question of Chineseness posed no problems for them.[14]

This was true not only in territories of the British Empire. What distinguished local British practice in the Straits Settlements were the legal and administrative measures, the relative media freedom, and the mix of public and private education systems that produced many of the modern skills that China wanted. The links with another British colony, Hong Kong, brought the two cities close together and enabled a degree of coordination that facilitated common action. They thus shared Anglo-Chinese features in the way their peoples responded to modernization. Also, the advanced business methods they imbibed from the capitalist world gave them distinct advantages when they returned more recently to be active on the China coasts.

During periods of grave uncertainty, traditional values provided some solace and sanity. The motley clutch of ideas that promoted modernization but was derived from multiple sources was more difficult to handle. In fact, in colonies open to many forces, new people came and went who had little expectation of permanence. They were migratory and pragmatic.[15] For such Chinese, the institutional features of the Great Tradition had largely been left behind, and their personal cultural baggage was light and adaptable. This is the source of their strength, the willingness to adjust to any place and any practice if necessary.

After World War II, we see this strong adaptability among the growing number of Chinese who settled in Singapore. They had preserved what they could of Chinese culture without much difficulty. But in the 1960s, they were forced to surrender parts of that heritage in order to take up the unexpected opportunity to become the political majority of a small Southeast Asian city-state.[16] As Singaporeans, those of Chinese descent now face a different destiny. Their loyalties are to their new nation, whose survival has depended on looking outward. Apart from the immediate region, they have looked for their economic development in the international market economy. No less than the commercial and industrial cities of Shanghai and Hong Kong, they have turned to global business networks in which the Chinese connections have become important.[17] Thus, when modernity is secure, it is in this direction that the new Chineseness has turned.

San Francisco

In comparison with the other three cities, San Francisco's Chinese population is not dominant but forms a significant minority. Although it is on another continent, it has also attracted clusters of different kinds of Chinese, especially during the second half of this century. The Chinese of San Francisco began by meeting the harshest tests of Chineseness. They had to endure hostile conditions for three generations before the United States' revision of its Chinese immigration policies brought new life to the Bay Area.[18] Thus, a century after the Chinese first arrived in California, Chineseness became legitimized for a strong and distinct minority in an immigrant country of European cultural origins. The story is one of many paradoxes.

On the one hand, there was the near disappearance of Chinese community life. Despite the strenuous efforts of small numbers of the local born and educated to find acceptance as Americans through assimilation and to fight for the rights of other Chinese, the exclusion policies persisted. They affected social attitudes toward Chinese at all levels, which led to the truncation or division of many families. This brought isolation for many, especially for the old who rejected Western ways yet did not wish to return to China. Nevertheless, tenacious links with relatives in China and Hong Kong managed to heighten certain kinds of Chinese loyalty. On the other hand, new arrivals after the 1950s enriched the new communities, reminiscent of the way the cities of Shanghai and Hong Kong became great amalgams of all kinds of Chinese. In addition to newcomers from cities of mainland China such as Shanghai, or from elite families of Taiwan, the population was also augmented by the relatives of earlier immigrants from Hong Kong and the Pearl River delta.

Will this new mix bring a unique brand of Chineseness peculiar to Chinese Americans.? The new community has continued to grow, and more and more of its members are participating fully in the modern political and social practices of the country.[19] If this process continues, it could eventually offer new elements of modernity from which the Chinese elsewhere in Shanghai, Hong Kong, or even Singapore might be willing to learn. But it may also be that the Chineseness of China will always be considered the only authentic kind, and those outside must choose to return or forever confront their dilemmas of place and practice.

Toward Modern Chineseness

I have not tried to cover all four cities and their groups of Chinese equally. Each group in each city faces its own unique set of practices. In the cultural spectrum of Chineseness, the Shanghai Chinese would be at one end and the Singapore and San Francisco Chinese at the other, with the Hong Kong Chinese somewhere in between. The cultural gaps between Shanghai and Hong Kong, and those between them and the Singapore–San Francisco variety, are uneven and difficult to measure. But all Chinese faced modern transformations in this century, and the idea of Chineseness was exposed to the modern forces of international capitalism.

Events inside and outside of China will develop beyond the control of any of these groups, and much within their own respective localities will undergo change. Many will ask, what matters if they were more Chinese or less? Or whether they were rich or poor in tradition? Or, in some cases, even if they were Chinese at all? But if, after all that, others still treat them as Chinese and they still consider themselves Chinese, then they can well stand up and say that a resilient modern Chineseness has been reinforced. Each group could claim that theirs is the start of new traditions.

The four cities are now key nodes in the extensive business and professional networks established during the past two decades. But Hong Kong, whose people are not yet as fully Chinese as their compatriots in Shanghai, and also clearly not "overseas" as are those in Singapore and San Francisco, provides a valuable test of the politics of identity. Differences in practice will pull the cities in different directions. Hong Kong's dilemmas at the handover remind us that Hong Kong people will have to face issues of being Chinese that are quite different from those confronting people in Singapore or San Francisco. Despite the capitalistic intercourse that might bring Chinese peoples together, location and the distance in political practice alone preclude the sharing of a common Chinese identity. Instead, being Chinese in Hong Kong hereafter may be compared with what Shanghai people had to face in the past.[20] Shanghai's role as an international city that led the way in creating a modern Chinese identity may be the nearest example for Hong Kong to emulate. Most Hong Kong people will choose to stay and turn toward that former Shanghai model.

Finally, for a variety of reasons that we cannot predict, there will be Hongkongers who will choose not to follow the Chineseness of new Shanghai but to leave China altogether.[21] If and when they do, they will be choosing to become ethnic Chinese in foreign countries, setting out to eventually lose themselves among non-Chinese or looking for a vision of universal Chineseness among the millions spread around the world.[22] If they truly want to pursue that quest, it is not obvious that such Hongkongers would find their way to Singapore, even though the city-state has a Chinese majority and is geographically closer to Hong Kong and China. Singapore's place in the Malay Archipelago is ultimately alien to people accustomed to a vast Chinese hinterland. Hong Kong people would tend to feel confined in space and limited in opportunity without a continental backdrop. Although it has far fewer Chinese, San Francisco, together with other similar cities in North America and Australia, may be more attractive to Hongkongers, not only because these cities promise more of the freedoms they have learned to enjoy but also because the Chinese there are more recent immigrants. As such, they display a familiar kind of modern Chineseness that makes them people with whom Hongkongers could more easily relate and, ultimately, the kind of Chinese overseas they themselves would like to become.

Notes

This chapter was modified and reprinted from Gungwu Wang, "Chineseness: The Dilemmas of Place and Practice," in *Cosmopolitan Capitalists: Hong Kong and the Chinese Diaspora at the End of the Twentieth Century*, ed. Gary G. Hamilton (Seattle: University of Washington Press, 1999), 118–134.

1. There are many journalistic essays that take this view, notably *The Economist* (November 21, 1992). It is less comprehensible when serious studies follow this usage (Gordon S. Redding, *The Spirit of Chinese Capitalism* [Berlin: Walter de Gruyter, 1990], 23–24; East Asia

Analytical Unit, *Overseas Chinese Business Networks in Asia* [Canberra: Department of Foreign Affairs and Trade, 1995]; and Constance Lever-Tracy, David Ip, and Noel Tracy, *The Chinese Diaspora and Mainland China: An Emerging Economic Synergy* [New York: St. Martin's Press, 1996]).

2. Wang Gungwu, *Community and Nation: Essays on Southeast Asia and the Chinese* (Singapore and Sydney: Heinemann Educational Books and George Allen & Unwin Australia, 1981), 124–126.

3. Leo Suryadinata (ed.), *Southeast Asian Chinese and China, 2 Volumes. Vol. 1: The Politico-Economic Dimension. Vol. 2: The Social-Cultural Dimension* (Singapore: Times Academic Press, 1995), *and Ethnic Chinese as Southeast Asians* (Singapore: Institute of Southeast Asian Studies, 1997).

4. Richard Ulmer Munch, *Economic Relations of the Chinese in the Society Islands* (Harvard University: Unpublished PhD dissertation, 1963).

5. David Parker, "Emerging British Chinese Identities: Issues and Problems," in *The Last Century of Chinese Overseas*, ed. Elizabeth Sinn (Hong Kong: Hong Kong University Press, 1988), 91–114, and "Chinese People in Britain: Histories, Futures and Identities," in *The Chinese in Europe*, ed. Gregor Benton and Frank N. Pieke (New York: St. Martin's Press, 1988), 67–95.

6. Yoshinobu Shiba, *Kakyo* [The overseas Chinese] (Tokyo: Iwanami Shoten, 1995), and Tai Kuo Hui, *Kakyo: "rakuyo kikon" kara "rakuchi seikon" e no kumon to mujun* [Overseas Chinese: The agonies and contradictions, from sojourning to settlement] (Tokyo: Yamamoto Shoten, 1980).

7. Betty Peh-t'i Wei, *Shanghai: Crucible of Modern China* (Hong Kong: Oxford University Press, 1987), and Marie-Claire Bergere, "'The Other China': Shanghai from 1919 to 1949," in *Shanghai: Revolution and Development in an Asian Metropolis*, ed. Christopher Howe (Cambridge: Cambridge University Press, 1981), 1–34.

8. Wong Siu-lun, *Emigrant Entrepreneurs: Shanghai Industrialists in Hong Kong* (Hong Kong: Oxford University Press, 1988).

9. Benjamin K. P. Leung and Teresa Y. C. Wong (eds.), *25 Years of Social and Economic Development in Hong Kong* (Hong Kong: University of Hong Kong Centre of Asian Studies, 1994).

10. Leung Chi-keung, J. W. Cushman, and Wang Gungwu (eds.), *Hong Kong: Dilemmas of Growth* (Canberra and Hong Kong: Australian National University and Centre of Asian Studies, 1980), and Ian Scott and John P. Burns, *The Hong Kong Civil Service and Its Future* (Hong Kong: Oxford University Press, 1988).

11. Lau Siu-kai and Kuan Hsin-chi, *The Ethos of the Hong Kong Chinese* (Hong Kong: The Chinese University Press, 1988).

12. Kernial Singh Sandhu and Paul Wheatley (eds.), *Management of Success: The Moulding of Modern Singapore* (Singapore: Institute of Southeast Asian Studies, 1989).

13. Lee Ting Hui, *The Open United Front: The Communist Struggle in Singapore, 1954–1966* (Singapore: South Seas Society, 1996).

14. Ernest C. T. Chew and Edwin Lee (eds.), *A History of Singapore* (Singapore: Oxford University Press, 1991).

15. Riaz Hassan (ed.), *Singapore: Society in Transition* (Kuala Lumpur: Oxford University Press, 1976).

16. Lee Ting Hui, *The Open United Front: Communist Struggle in Singapore, 1954–1966* (Singapore: South Seas Society, 1996), and Chua Beng-Huat, *Communitarian Ideology and Democracy in Singapore* (London: Routledge, 1995).

17. Lynn Pan, *Sons of the Yellow Emperor: A History of the Chinese Diaspora* (Boston: Little Brown, 1990), 225–274.

18. Victor G. Nee and Brett de Bary Nee, *Longtime California: A Documentary Study of an American Chinatown* (New York: Pantheon Books, 1972).

19. Tu Wei-ming (ed.), *The Living Tree: The Changing Meaning of Being Chinese Today* (Stanford, Calif.: Stanford University Press, 1994), and Wang Ling-chi and Wang Gungwu (eds.), *The Chinese Diaspora: Selected Essays* (Singapore: Times Academic Press, 1998).

20. Wang Gungwu and Wong Siu-lun (eds.), *Hong Kong in the Asia-Pacific Region: Rising to the New Challenges* (Hong Kong: Centre of Asian Studies, 1997).

21. Ronald Skeldon (ed.), *Reluctant Exiles? Migration from Hong Kong and the New Overseas Chinese* (Armonk, NY: M. E. Sharpe, 1994).

22. Tu, *The Living Tree*.

8

Cultural China

The Periphery as the Center

WEI-MING TU

China, one of the longest continuous civilizations in human history, "may be visualized as a majestic flowing stream."[1] Chinese culture, the generic term symbolizing the vicissitudes of the material and spiritual accomplishments of the Chinese people, has undergone major interpretive phases in recent decades and is now entering a new era of critical self-reflection. The meaning of being Chinese is intertwined with China as a geopolitical concept and Chinese culture as a lived reality.

Question

The question of Chineseness, as it first emerged in the "axial age" half a millennium prior to the birth of Confucius in 551 B.C.E., entails both geopolitical and cultural dimensions. While the territory of China has substantially expanded over time, the idea of a cultural core area first located in the Wei River Valley, a tributary of the Yellow River, and later encompassing parts of the Yangtze River, has remained potent and continuous in the Chinese consciousness. Educated Chinese know reflexively what China proper refers to; they may not be clear about the periphery but they know for sure that the center of China, whether Xi'an or Beijing, is in the north near the Yellow River. The archaeological finds of recent decades have significantly challenged the thesis that China grew from the Wei River Valley like a light source radiating from the center. Even in Neolithic periods, there were several centers spreading across present-day China. The Central Country came into being as a confederation of several equally developed cultural areas rather than growing out of an ever-expanding core.[2] Yet regardless of this persuasive scholarly explanation of the origins of Chinese civilization, the impression that geopolitical China evolved through a long process centering around a definable core remains deep rooted.

If the presumed core area was instrumental in forming a distinctive Chinese identity, Chinese culture symbolizing a living historical presence made the sense of being Chinese even more pronounced; it signified a unique form of life profoundly different from other styles of living often condemned as barbarian. The expression *hua* or *huaxia*, meaning Chinese, connotes culture and civilization. Those who lived in China proper were, inter alia, cultured and civilized, clearly differentiable from those barbarians in the periphery who had yet to learn the proper ways of dressing, eating, dwelling, and traveling. On the surface, the classical distinction between Chinese and barbarians was predicated on the divergence of two drastically different modes of life: the agrarian community of the central plain and the nomadic tribes of the steppes.[3] But the rise of Chinese cultural consciousness was occasioned by primordial ties defined in ethnic, territorial, linguistic, and ethical-religious terms. Although it is often noted that culture, rather than ethnicity, features prominently in defining Chineseness, the cultured and civilized Chinese, as the myth goes, claim a common ancestry. Indeed, the symbol of the "children of the Yellow Emperor"[4] is constantly reenacted in Chinese literature and evokes feelings of ethnic pride.

This idea of being Chinese, geopolitically and culturally defined, is further reinforced by a powerful historical consciousness informed by one of the most voluminous veritable documentary records in human history. Indeed, the chronological annals have flowed almost uninterruptedly since 841 B.C.E. The collective memory of the educated Chinese is such that when they talk about Tu Fu's (712–770) poetry, Sima Qian's (died c. 85 B.C.E,) *Historical Records*, or Confucius's *Analects*, they refer to a cumulative tradition preserved in Chinese characters, a script separable from and thus unaffected by phonological transmutations. An encounter with Tu Fu, Sima Qian, or Confucius through ideographic symbols evokes a sensation of reality as if their presence was forever inscribed in the script. Whether or not it is simply a false sense of continuity, the Chinese refer to the Han (206 B.C.E–220 C.E.) and Tang (618–907) dynasties as if their greatness still provides practicable standards for contemporary Chinese culture and politics.

The Middle Kingdom syndrome or Central Country complex[5] may have made it psychologically difficult for the Chinese leadership to abandon its sense of superiority as the center and join the family of nations as an equal partner, but we must also remember that China had never been thoroughly challenged by an alien equal—if not superior—civilization until the penetration of the West in the mid-nineteenth century. The "Buddhist conquest of China"[6] entailed the introduction, domestication, maturation, and development of Indian spirituality in China for more than six hundred years, culminating in the intense Sinification of Buddhist teachings in distinctively Chinese schools of Tiantai, Huayan, and Chan.[7] The military and political domination of the Central Country by the Jurchens, the Khitans, the Mongols, and the Manchus in the last millennium was compensated, in cultural terms, by the Sinicization of the Jin, Liao, Yuan, and Qing into legitimate Chinese dynasties. China survived these "conquests" as a geopolitical entity and Chinese culture flourished. Nevertheless, if we take seriously the image of "a majestic flowing stream," we must acknowledge that these great outside influences altered this stream at various points. "As the stream moves on, the new forces may move forward more or less intact, swerve off into small eddies and side pools, form new currents through interaction with older ones, or be overwhelmed by newer currents entering farther down the stream."[8] Thus, China, or Chinese culture, has never been a static structure, but rather a dynamic, constantly changing landscape.

Challenge

The rise of Japan and the so-called Four Mini-Dragons (South Korea, Taiwan, Hong Kong, and Singapore) as the most dynamic region of sustained economic development since World War II raises challenging questions about tradition in modernity, the modernizing process in its different cultural forms. Does it suggest the necessity, indeed, the desirability of a total iconoclastic attack on traditional Chinese culture and its attendant comprehensive Westernization as a precondition for China's modernization?[9] Culturally, do these societies symbolize successful examples of advanced technology being combined with age-long ritual practices, or are they simply the passing phases of traditional societies?[10] In short, how does the rise of East Asia challenge our deep-rooted conceptions of economic growth, political development, social transformation, and cultural change?

Since traditional features of the human condition—ethnicity, mother tongue, ancestral home, gender, class, and religious faith—all seem to be relevant in understanding the lifeworlds of societies, both modern and developing, the need to search for roots, despite the pervasiveness of global consciousness, is a powerful impulse throughout the world today. If there is an alternative path to capital formation, then democracy, technology, and even modernization may indeed assume different cultural forms. To Chinese intellectuals in East Asia, the awareness that active participation in the economic, political, social, and cultural life of a thoroughly modernized community is not necessarily in conflict with being authentically Chinese implies the possibility that modernization may enhance rather than weaken Chineseness. Still, the meaning of being Chinese is itself undergoing a major transformation.

Although the phenomenon of Chinese culture disintegrating at the center and later being revived from the periphery is a recurring theme in Chinese history, it is unprecedented for the geopolitical center to remain entrenched while the periphery presents such powerful and persistent economic and cultural challenges. Either the center will bifurcate, or, as is more likely, the periphery will come to set the economic and cultural agenda for the center, thereby undermining its political effectiveness.

Discourse

Cultural China can be examined in terms of three symbolic universes.[11] The first consists of mainland China, Taiwan, Hong Kong, and Singapore—that is, the societies populated predominantly by cultural and ethnic Chinese. The second consists of Chinese communities throughout the world, including a politically significant minority in Malaysia (35 percent) and a numerically negligible minority in the United States. These Chinese, estimated to number 36 million, are often referred to by the political authorities in Beijing and Taipei as *huaqiao* (overseas Chinese).[12] More recently, however, they have tended to define themselves as members of the Chinese "diaspora," meaning those who have settled in scattered communities of Chinese far from their ancestral homeland. While Han Chinese constitute an overwhelming majority in each of the four areas in the first symbolic universe, communities of the Chinese diaspora—with the exception of Malaysia already mentioned— rarely exceed 3 percent of their country's population.

The third symbolic universe consists of individual men and women, such as scholars, teachers, journalists, industrialists, traders, entrepreneurs, and writers, who try to understand China intellectually and bring their conceptions of China to their own linguistic communities. Foreign journalists continue to exert a strong influence on the discourse of cultural China. Sinologists in North America, Japan, Europe, and increasingly Australia have similarly exercised a great deal of power in determining the scholarly agenda for cultural China as a whole.

My tripartite division of cultural China is admittedly problematic. Hong Kong, Taiwan, and Singapore have much more in common with the Chinese diaspora than they do with mainland China. Hong Kong is, at least in spirit, part of the Chinese diaspora. Although the Republic of Singapore established full diplomatic ties with the People's Republic of China in 1990, its leadership has had closer contact with the Nationalist government in Taipei than with the Communists in Beijing. After all, Singapore, as a full-fledged nation-state, is English-speaking and a loyal member of ASEAN; the overall linguistic proficiency of Singaporean Chinese seems not as high as that of the Chinese in Malaysia. Singapore is basically apprehensive about its Chineseness, for fear that its perceived ethnic and cultural chauvinism might alienate its own minorities and strain relations with its neighboring states. Nevertheless, Taiwan, Hong Kong, and Singapore are grouped together with mainland China as the first symbolic universe because the life orientation in these societies is based on Chinese culture. If we define being Chinese in terms of full participation in the economic, political, and social life of a Chinese community or civilization, the first symbolic universe offers both the necessary and the sufficient condition.

Divergence in economic development, political system, and social organization notwithstanding, the four members of the first symbolic universe share a common ethnicity, language, history, and worldview. To be sure, ethnic awareness has been diluted by the admixture of a variety of races that constitute the generic Han people; linguistic cohesiveness is threatened by the presence of numerous mutually incomprehensible "dialects" (in the case of Singapore, the situation is further confounded by multilingualism); historical consciousness has been undermined by varying interpretations of "Confucian China and its modern fate"[13] and, with increasing rapidity, worldviews have been affected by the importation of radically different belief systems. Still, if we view cultural China as being a psychological as well as an economic and a political interchange, then the nature of the interactions between mainland China and Hong Kong, Taiwan, and Singapore is sufficient to group these distinct nations together as integral parts of the first symbolic universe.

This does not necessarily mean that perceived convergence will eventually lead to a reintegrated China as a civilization-state. It is more likely that, as the peripheral regions of mainland China become "contaminated" by Hong Kong, Taiwan, and Singapore, relative economic prosperity and cultural richness will bring about a measure of political independence. Of course, the destructive power of the center is such that the transformative potential of the periphery can be easily stifled. The unpredictability of the Beijing leadership and the vulnerability of the status quo in Hong Kong, Taiwan, and Singapore make the first symbolic universe fluid and a fruitful interaction among its members difficult. Despite the so-called Central Country syndrome, a Chinese civilization-state with a variety of autonomous regions (including Tibetan, Mongolian, Zhuang, and other minority areas) or even a loosely structured Chinese federation of different political entities, remains a distinct possibility.[14]

Nevertheless, we are well advised to heed the observation of Lucian Pye, who maintains that "China is not just another nation-state in the family of nations," but rather "a civilization pretending to be a state."[15] Actually, Pye writes, "the miracle of China has been its astonishing unity." In trying to find an analogy in Western terms, Pye says of China today, it is "as if the Europe of the Roman Empire and of Charlemagne had lasted until this day and were now trying to function as a single nation-state."[16] We may not accept Pye's assertion that "the overpowering obligation felt by Chinese rulers to preserve the unity of their civilization has meant that there could be no compromise in Chinese cultural attitudes about power and authority"; but his general point is well taken: "The fact that the Chinese state was founded on one of the world's great civilizations has given inordinate strength and durability to its political culture."[17] The beguiling phenomenon of China as a civilization-state requires further elucidation.

The idea of the modern state involving power relationships based on competing economic and social interests is anathema to the Chinese cultural elite as well as to the Chinese ruling minority. To them, the state—intent on realizing its historical mission to liberate China from threats of imperialist encroachment and the lethargy and stagnation of the feudal past—symbolizes the guardian of a moral order rather than the outcome of a political process. The state's legitimacy is derived from a holistic orthodoxy informed by Sinified Marxism-Leninism, rather than from operating principles refined by political praxis and codified in a legal system. The state's claims on its people are comprehensive and the people's dependence on the state is total; the state exemplifies the civilizational norms for the general public and the leadership assumes ideological and moral authority. The civilization-state exercises both political power and moral influence.

It should be acknowledged, however, that for all her power and influence, China as a civilization-state often plays a negligible part in the international discourse on global human concerns. It is undeniable that for decades intellectuals in North America and Western Europe have been involved in supposedly global and ecumenical discussions of psychology, politics, society, religion, and philosophy without any apparent need to take China into serious consideration. Despite the persuasiveness of the third symbolic universe in determining the agenda for international discourse on cultural China, even the most prominent Sinologists lament the relegation of their intellectual pursuits to the backwaters of the modern academy. Generations of college students from leading Western universities have graduated without any exposure to East Asia, not to mention China. Some of the most impressive grand theories about the human condition make no reference to China, past or present. The asymmetry between its centrifugal pull in cultural China and its marginal role in the "global village" as a whole makes the first symbolic universe a challenging issue for analysis and contemplation.[18]

Diaspora

The second symbolic universe, the Chinese diaspora, presents equally intriguing conceptual difficulties. Diaspora, which literally means the scattering of seeds, has most often been used to refer to Jews outside Palestine after the Babylonian exile or to Jews living in a Gentile world. Until the establishment of the modern state of Israel, the salience of faith in Jehovah and the attendant observance of law and ritual, rather than membership in a political entity, characterized the distinctive features of the Jewish religious community.[19] By contrast, the state, or more precisely China as a civilization-state, features prominently in the Chinese diaspora. Because the Chinese diaspora has never lost its homeland, there is no functional equivalent of the cathartic yearning for Jerusalem. Actually the ubiquitous presence of the Chinese state—its awe-inspiring physical size, its long history, and the numerical weight of its population—continues to loom large in the psychocultural constructs of diaspora Chinese. For many, the state, either Nationalist or Communist, controls the symbolic resources necessary for their cultural identity. Although dual citizenship is no longer possible, both Beijing and Taipei routinely expect the loyal support of their *huaqiao* (overseas Chinese). Few diaspora Chinese ever speculate about the possibility of China's disintegrating as a unified civilization-state. The advantage of being liberated from obsessive concern for China's well-being at the expense of their own livelihood is rarely entertained. The diaspora Chinese cherish the hope of returning to and being recognized by the homeland. While the original meaning of scattering seeds suggests taking root and producing offspring elsewhere, many diaspora Chinese possess a sojourner mentality and lack a sense of permanence in their adopted country. Some return "home" to get married or send their children back for a Chinese education; they remain in touch with relatives and friends who keep them informed of the economic and political climate at home.[20]

The Chinese settlers who are scattered around the world come, historically, from a few well-defined areas along the southeast coast of mainland China—notably Guangdong and Fujian. For specific groups of settlers, the province was too extensive and diffuse an entity to provide a point of emotional identification with their homeland. Until the recent waves of immigration to North America, which began after 1949, the overwhelming majority of Chinese Americans identified themselves not as Cantonese—too cosmopolitan a term to evoke any real sense of roots—but as natives of subprovincial districts such as Taishan, Zhongshan, or Panyu. Similar phenomena occurred in Europe and Southeast Asia. As a rule, mutual aid associations in Malaysia, Thailand, and Indonesia were organized according to county or village, rather than provincial, affiliations.[21] Secret societies that crossed local boundaries were either politically oriented or economically motivated. It is understandable, then, that the Chinese diaspora was for decades so fragmented that there was little communication between groups within a host nation, let alone any transnational cooperation.

Nevertheless, despite apparent parochialism, the overseas Chinese have managed to adapt themselves to virtually all types of communities throughout the world. The impression that the overall cultural orientation of Chinese settlers has been shaped predominantly by the magnetic power of the homeland is simplistic. The reasons why overseas Chinese rarely consider themselves thoroughly assimilated in their adopted countries are complex. In the United States, racial discrimination against the Chinese was, until recently, blatant; and the Chinatown mentality, as a response to the hostile environment, may be seen as a psychosocial defense and adaptation. The post-1949 immigrants from Taiwan and Hong Kong have developed entirely different patterns of assimilation. The arrival of "boat people" and refugees from the mainland has initiated yet another process whereby new-style Chinatowns have emerged in such places as the Deep South and the Midwest in the United States.

The situation in Southeast Asia is radically different. The case of the Philippine Chinese, perhaps the smallest population of any major Southeast Asian country, merits special attention. In the 1950s and 1960s when the Nationalist government in Taiwan exerted profound influence in the Philippines, "the Philippine government, on the whole, gave over to Taiwan the responsibility for defining the nature of the Chinese culture to be taught in the Philippine Chinese schools."[22] As part of the united front between the Nationalist government and the Marcos regime to fight the spread of communism, Chinese schools were allowed to fly the flag of the Republic of China, to display pictures of Sun Yat-sen and Chiang Kai-shek, and to make use of textbooks from Taiwan. The recognition of Beijing in 1975 facilitated the Filipinization of the Chinese schools and prompted the Marcos government to grant full citizenship to about one-sixth of the entire Chinese population in the Philippines.

Perhaps the most encouraging sign was the approach of the newly established intellectual organization Kaisa Para Sa Kaunlaran, which advocated "the understanding and retention of one's Chinese culture while fully identifying oneself with the Philippines and with Filipinos of non-Chinese backgrounds."[23] Conceived in the 1970s by young university graduates of Chinese ancestry, the Kaisa vision intends to create a narrow ridge between cultural chauvinism and total assimilation.

The precariousness of being Chinese in Southeast Asia is demonstrated by the institutionalized mechanisms of de-Sinicization in Malaysia and Indonesia. For political reasons, the Malaysian and Indonesian governments consider Chineseness a potential threat to national security, not to mention national integration. Among the most tragic events in the second half of the twentieth century were the atrocities committed against the native population in Indonesia in 1965, which were brought on by the perceived threat of a Communist takeover supported by China. An estimated 250,000 to 750,000 people (including thousands of Chinese) died in a matter of months, partly as the result of a coup d'état engineered by President Suharto. The holocaust inflicted upon both Indonesians and the Chinese minority received little attention in the first symbolic universe of cultural China. The Mainland was embroiled in its own holocaust, the Cultural Revolution; Taiwan condoned the heavy-handed attack on Communism; Hong Kong was too remote to be affected; and Singapore's proximity to Indonesia—both geographically and politically—made it too vulnerable to offer a protest. It was actually in the same period that growing anti-Chinese sentiment in Malaysia pushed Singapore to become an independent state. Intent on demonstrating its good faith as a member of ASEAN, Singapore declared that it would establish a full diplomatic relationship with the People's Republic of China only if Indonesia chose to do so as well.[24]

Recent events have greatly improved the atmosphere for the Chinese in Southeast Asia, although the "Chinese question" continues to be a sensitive subject. In Malaysia and Indonesia, being Chinese remains a stigma; things Chinese, especially symbols of Chinese high culture such as the written script, are viewed with suspicion. The economic success of the Chinese makes them hungry for cultural expression, and the host countries, while tolerating their prosperity, are adamant about imposing cultural prohibitions. Signs of a Kaisa-like solution to the conflict between political loyalty and cultural identity of Chinese in Malaysia and Indonesia are yet to be found.

Another example of the impact of the first symbolic universe on the second is the emigration of professionals from Hong Kong to North America and Australia. This seems to be part of a broader pattern: Chinese immigrants in these cities are also coming from mainland China, Taiwan, Singapore,

Malaysia, Indonesia, the Philippines, and Vietnam. This phenomenon, which historian Wang Gungwu aptly depicts as a remigration of Chinese, is unprecedented and requires closer examination.[25] These financially secure Malaysian, Indonesian, Filipino, and Vietnamese Chinese have ostensibly emigrated from their adopted homelands for several generations in order to escape from policies that discriminated against their Chineseness. In order to combat the pressure to assimilate imposed by the new nation-states in Southeast Asia and to preserve a measure of Chineseness for their descendants, they have opted to immigrate to modern Western-style nations with strong democratic traditions. The irony of not returning to their ancestral homeland but going far away from China with the explicit intention of preserving their cultural identity seems perplexing, but as Wang Gungwu perceptively remarks, the transformation from a sojourner mentality to deliberate emigration is a new phenomenon. The meaning of being Chinese, a question that has haunted Chinese intellectuals for generations, has taken on entirely new dimensions.

Prospects

China has witnessed much destructiveness and violence in her modern transformation. In retrospect, what the Chinese intelligentsia has collectively experienced in the twentieth century is what Mark Elvin pointedly characterizes as the "double disavowal" of both Confucianism and Marxism.[26] The same indignation that Lu Xun's generation felt about Confucian authoritarianism is now being expressed against Marxist totalitarianism. The matter, however, is complicated: the real challenge to mainland Chinese intellectuals is not the modern West per se, but the modern West mediated through industrial East Asia. Surely the Yellow River must flow into the blue sea, but as it enters the ocean, it first encounters the Pacific.

What mainland China eventually will become remains an overriding concern for all intellectuals in cultural China. She may try to become a mercantilist state with a vengeance; she may continue to be mired in inertia and inefficiency for years to come; or she may modernize according to a new holistic humanist vision. Saddled with a population burden approaching 1.2 billion, can this state succeed at any of these ambitions without finding a workable means to liberate the energies of the people? Although realistically those who are on the periphery (the second and third symbolic universes plus Taiwan, Hong Kong, and Singapore) are seemingly helpless to affect any fundamental transformation of China proper, the center no longer has the ability, insight, or legitimate authority to dictate the agenda for cultural China. On the contrary, the transformative potential of the periphery is so great that it seems inevitable that it will significantly shape the intellectual discourse on cultural China for years to come. It is perhaps premature to announce that "the center is nowhere, the periphery is everywhere,"[27] but undeniably, the fruitful interaction of a variety of economic, political, social, and cultural forces at work along the periphery will continue to shape the dynamics of cultural China.

The exodus of the most brilliant minds from the Mainland, the emigration of Chinese professionals from Hong Kong, and the remigration of middle-class Chinese from Southeast Asia to North America and Australia suggest that it is neither shameful nor regrettable to alienate oneself voluntarily from a political regime that has become culturally insensitive, publicly unaccountable, and oppressive to basic human rights. The meaning of being Chinese is basically not a political question; it is a human concern pregnant with ethical-religious implications.

Is it possible to live a meaningful life as a Chinese individual if the dignity of one's humanity is lost? Does citizenship in a Chinese polity guarantee one's Chineseness? As a precondition for maintaining one's Chineseness, is it necessary to become a fully participating citizen of one's adopted country? While the overseas Chinese (the second symbolic universe) may seem forever peripheral to the meaning of being Chinese, can they assume an effective role in creatively constructing a new vision of Chineseness that is more in tune with Chinese history and in sympathetic resonance with Chinese culture? Is it possible or even desirable for someone in the third symbolic universe who is not proficient in the Chinese language and who has no Chinese family ties of birth or marriage to acquire an understanding of Chinese culture such that he or she can greatly shape the intellectual discourse on cultural China and significantly contribute to the definition of being Chinese? An obvious "no" to the first and a resounding "yes" to each of the remaining questions, and an understanding of the implications of these answers, will give rich texture to the provocative inquiry into the meaning of being Chinese.

Notes

This chapter was modified and reprinted from Tu Wei-ming, "Cultural China: The Periphery as Center," *Daedalus* 120, no. 2 (Spring 1991): 1–32.

1. Herbert Passin, "The Occupation—Some Reflections," *Daedalus* 119, no. 3 (Summer 1990): 125.

2. Kwang-chih Chang, *The Archaeology of Ancient China*, 4th ed. (New Haven: Yale University Press, 1986).

3. Owen Lattimore, *Inner Asian Frontiers of China* (London: Oxford University Press, 1940).

4. Lynn Pan, *Sons of the Yellow Emperor: A History of the Chinese Diaspora* (Boston: Little, Brown, 1990).

5. For a reference to the "Central Country Complex," see Lucian Pye, "China: Erratic State, Frustrated Society," *Foreign Affairs* 69.4 (Fall 1990): 62.

6. Erich Zürcher, *The Buddhist Conquest of China* (Leiden, Netherlands: Brill, 1959).

7. Arthur Wright, *Buddhism in Chinese History* (Stanford: Stanford University Press, 1959).

8. Passin, "The Occupation—Some Reflections," 125.

9. Tu Wei-ming, "A Confucian Perspective on the Rise of Industrial East Asia," 1687th Stated Meeting Report, *Bulletin of the American Academy of Arts and Sciences* 42, no. 1 (October 1988): 32–50.

10. Tu Wei-ming, "The Rise of Industrial East Asia: The Role of Confucian Values," *Copenhagen Papers in East and Southeast Asian Studies* (April 1989), 81–97.

11. The term "cultural China" (*wenhua Zhongguo*) is relatively new. A similar concept, "overseas China" (*haiwai Zhonghua*), was used to designate Chinese communities outside mainland China. Since the term carries the political connotation of a Chinese-style commonwealth encompassing the mainland, Hong Kong, Taiwan, and Singapore, it has generated much controversy on both sides of the Taiwan Straits. I propose adopting the term "cultural China," applied loosely, and invite the participation of all those trying to understand and bring understanding to China and Chinese culture—thus the idea of community defined by participation in an intellectual discourse. See Tu Wei-ming, "'Wenhua Zhongguo' chutan" [Probing "cultural China"], *Jiushi niandai* (The nineties) 245 (June 1990): 60–61.

12. For scholarly treatments of the subject, see Wang Gungwu, *A Short History of the Nanyang Chinese* (Singapore: Eastern University Press, 1959); Edgar Wickberg, *The Chinese in Philippine Life, 1850–1898* (New Haven: Yale University Press, 1965); G. William Skinner, *Chinese Society in Thailand* (Ithaca: Cornell University Press, 1957); and James L. Watson, *Emigration and the Chinese Lineage: The Mans in Hong Kong and London* (Berkeley: University of California Press, 1975).

13. Joseph R. Levenson, *Confucian China and Its Modern Fate: A Trilogy* (Berkeley: University of California Press, 1968).

14. Yan Jiaqi, as a political scientist, has been a consistent and articulate advocate of a federated China. See *Toward a Democratic China: The Intellectual Biography of Yan Jiaqi*, trans. David S. K. Hong and Denis C. Mair (Honolulu: University of Hawaii Press, 1992), 159–160, 269–270.

15. Lucian Pye, "China: Erratic State, Frustrated Society," *Foreign Affairs* 69, no. 4 (Fall 1990): 58.

16. Ibid.

17. Ibid.

18. I thank sociologist Ambrose King of the Chinese University of Hong Kong for illuminating discussions on this issue.

19. Ernest W. Nicholson, *God and His People: Covenant and Theology in the Old Testament* (Oxford: Clarendon Press, 1980).

20. For a typical example of these patterns, see Clarence E. Glick, *Sojourners and Settlers: Chinese Migrants in Hawaii* (Honolulu: University of Hawaii Press, 1980), 172–181.

21. For the intriguing subject of networking among Chinese based on religious affiliation, see the pioneering work of Kristofer Schipper, "The Cult of Pao-sheng Ta-ti and Its Spreading to Taiwan—A Case Study of *Fen Hsiang*," in *Development and Decline of Fukien Province in the Seventeenth and Eighteenth Centuries*, ed. E. B. Vermeer (Leiden, Netherlands: Brill, 1990), 397–416.

22. Edgar Wickberg, "Some Comparative Perspectives on Contemporary Chinese Ethnicity in the Philippines," *Asian Culture* 14 (1990): 23–37.

23. Ibid.

24. True to her word, Singapore recognized the People's Republic of China only after Indonesia had done so, in 1990.

25. Remarks by Wang Gungwu at the conference of "The Meaning of Being Chinese," East-West Center, October 1990.

26. Mark Elvin, "The Double Disavowal: The Attitudes of Radical Thinkers to the Chinese Tradition," in *China and Europe in the Twentieth Century*, ed. Y. M. Shaw (Taipei: Institute of International Relations, 1986), 112–137.

27. Professor Ying-shih Yu of Princeton, perhaps in jest, proposed this as the theme to underscore the intellectual and political significance of the periphery in cultural China. This is reminiscent of Ernst Cassirer's famous statement, "Its center was everywhere; its periphery nowhere." See E. Cassirer, "Giovanni Pico della Mirandola," *Journal of the History of Ideas* 3 (1943): 337. I am indebted to Professor Yu for this information.

9

On the Margins of the Chinese Discourse

LEO OU-FAN LEE

The word *exile* in Chinese is often associated with negative or passive meanings—banishment as a form of punishment by government (*fangzhu, liufang*); seldom, if ever, does it connote the meaning of self-exile, or exile by voluntary choice as an act of protest by an individual. The closest equivalent in traditional China for voluntary self-exile is eremitism, or voluntary withdrawal from political service in order to maintain one's own integrity or for the more practical reason of survival in times of great upheaval such as the change of dynasties. Often, however, an elegant way of seeking eremitism from the political center of power was, in fact, a return to one's home region, to indulge in such cultural pursuits as art, literature, and scholarship. This stance, partly inspired by Daoism, formed a counterpoint to the Confucian ethos of sociopolitical engagement. But it did not, in my opinion, constitute exile in all its implications of alienation and dislocation. In modern Chinese the phrase *liuwang*, literally "wandering in escape," comes perhaps closer to the dictionary definition of exile, prolonged separation from one's country or home, as by force of circumstances. The phrase often refers to circumstances of war and famine, connoting almost the state of a refugee. In premodern China, in fact, given the Middle Kingdom syndrome, it was all but unimaginable, even as punishment, to be exiled out of the country; rather, the faraway lands to which a criminal (and sometimes a guilty official) was banished were always on the peripheries of the nation's power center—for instance, Xinjiang in the northwest or Hainan Island in the far south. In post-1949 China, the well-known region of banishment was Beidahuang (literally, "the great northern wilderness") in Manchuria, where leading Party intellectuals castigated as rightists, men and women like the writer Ding Ling, spent years doing hard labor under miserable physical conditions. With hindsight, one may even consider the movement to send youths "downward to the countryside" during the Cultural Revolution as a collective form of banishment or internal exile.

In modern Chinese history, education abroad is a largely twentieth-century phenomenon. Waves of Chinese intellectuals first went to Japan at the turn of the century. They were followed by students seeking education in Europe and the United States in the early 1920s. By the end of World War II, the Chinese student population in the United States was sizable, their ranks soon being swelled by massive numbers of college graduates from Taiwan coming to pursue graduate education. This has been a well-documented, familiar story. Equally familiar, but not adequately analyzed, is the concomitant phenomenon of voluntary exile resulting from the majority of Chinese students choosing not to return to their home country. For an older generation of students abroad, this was certainly related to the watershed moment of 1949, when the triumph of the Communist Revolution and the establishment of the People's Republic presented them with a compelling choice. A great number, fired by patriotism, chose to return to serve the New China; even larger numbers chose, for one reason or another, to stay in their adopted country, in most cases, the United States. For younger generations of students from Taiwan, going abroad does not carry the same momentous trauma of choice. Still, it may entail other psychological consequences.

In an article written in English and published in 1976, the famed novelist from Taiwan Pai Hsien-yung (himself a self-exile resident in America), characterizes such voluntary self-exiles as the "Wandering Chinese":

> Deprived of his cultural heritage, the Wandering Chinese has become a spiritual exile: Taiwan and the motherland are incommensurable. He has to move on. Like Ulysses, he sets out on a journey across the ocean, but it is an endless journey, dark and without hope. The Rootless Man, therefore, is destined to become a perpetual wanderer. . . . The Chinese Wanderer yearns for the "lost kingdom," for the cultural inheritance that has been denied him. . . . He is a sad man. He is sad because he has been driven out of Eden, dispossessed, disinherited, a spiritual orphan, burdened with a memory that carries the weight of 5,000 years.[1]

These depressing remarks are partially triggered by Pai's reading of a novel by another writer, Yu Lihua, who first applied the then-fashionable term "rootless generation" to Chinese students, intellectuals, and professionals who had chosen to stay abroad. Yu's popular work, *Youjian zonglu* (Again the palm trees), depicts such a person, a young professor who teaches elementary Chinese at an obscure American college. The novel is a heavily sentimental account of his journey back to Taiwan, his "hunger for cultural identification," his incessant nostalgia for the lost Mainland, and his final mental debacle, being unable to find spiritual anchorage in Taiwan. The journey exemplifies the familiar truism: You can't go home again.

Is the Wandering Chinese so spiritually dispossessed that he or she is utterly incapable of either rediscovering or reinventing his roots? I may perhaps offer my own experience as a case study. When I first came to the United States as a graduate student some thirty years ago, the term *exile* never occurred to me, nor did the term *émigré*. The phrase that obsessed me during my first twenty years in the United States was *identity crisis*, defined, not only as a psychological stage of youth in the human life cycle, but also as a matter of culture. Instead of feeling culturally deprived, I was more concerned about a self-perceived "threat" from the other side—was I becoming too Americanized, thereby losing my Chinese identity? My psychological confusion stemmed from a deep-seated ambivalence (perhaps even more acute than that of most of my contemporaries) toward the established forms of Chinese cultural practice at that time—a structure of conventional ethics and wisdom in the name of Confucianism with which I became profoundly disenchanted. This antitraditional frame of mind, curiously reminiscent of the familiar ideological stance of the May Fourth Movement (which eventually became the subject of my first scholarly pursuit), made the other May Fourth position, total Westernization, a distinctly viable alternative to forge a new identity as my American sojourn became lengthened into permanent residence.

However, as the years went by and I came to middle age, I outgrew this identity confusion. I realized that my sense of being Chinese, though it has undergone several subtle ideological transformations, is so deeply rooted that it practically rules out the possibility of total Westernization. This has not led me to return to Chinese cultural conservatism; I continue to find certain of the intellectual "temptations" from the West—particularly from Central and Eastern Europe—irresistible. Such a psychological state is by no means uncommon among exiled Chinese in the United States, but it has not been fully articulated as an issue *beyond* the parameters of what is known as Chinese-American ethnic or minority discourse. Simply put, I would call this stance Chinese cosmopolitanism—a loose epithet, but one that embraces both a fundamental intellectual commitment to Chinese culture and a multicultural receptivity, which effectively cuts across all conventional national boundaries. It is, in other words, a purposefully marginal discourse, intended to recontextualize the margins.

My marginality has a double edge vis-à-vis the centers of both China and America. On the peripheries of both countries, I feel compelled to engage actively in a dialogue with both cultures. Perhaps it was this perceived need for intellectual engagement that saved me from feeling totally "lost" between two continents, like the protagonist of *Again the Palm Trees*.

The one novel that most vividly dramatizes this double dialogue is Hual-ing Nieh's *Mulberry Green and Peach Red* (*Sangqing yu taohong*, translated into English as *Two Women of China*),[2] discussed by Pai Hsien-yung as providing an example of the Wandering Chinese syndrome. In this novel, written in high-modernist style, the two personas—divided selves—of the same pro-tagonist address her dual marginal fate. As Peach Red narrates her recent journey as an exile in America in a series of letters to the American immigra-tion officer, her former self, Mulberry Green, confronts a much larger histori-cal experience of modern China—her move from central China to Taiwan (and, as Peach Red, to America). This tortured double journey infuses the novel with tremendous psychological power. Its prevailing pathos comes from an author equally committed to, and troubled by, both cultures "from the margins." Through a purposeful schizophrenic split of the two contrasting personalities, the author has not only described a heightened case of identity confusion but has located a special angle from which to decipher—and in a way to deconstruct—the master narrative of modern Chinese history. In doing so, the novel gives new meaning to being a self-exiled Chinese on the peripheries.

In the double frame of the novel, it is precisely Peach Red's tormented and anxiety-ridden outcry about her exiled existence on the edge of American society that compels her alter ego, Mulberry Green, to encompass the entire historical span of her personal past. In other words, it is her newly acquired American side—and the need to explain why she is in America—that forces her Chinese side to be engaged in a search for meaning through her personal journey in Chinese history. That journey, in both geographical and symbolic terms, is also a journey of chaos and fragmentation in which the protagonist invariably finds herself escaping from an endangered center. The beginning of the novel, set in wartime China (1945), finds Mulberry Green as a young girl of sixteen who has just escaped from home only to join up with a boat full of refugees fleeing from the Japanese. The second part has her trapped in and then escaping from the besieged city of Peking in 1949, before the impending entrance of the Communists. In the third part of the novel, the setting shifts to Taipei, a peripheral city in the eyes of Mainland refugees, which became the new political center of the evacuated Kuomintang in Taiwan. Here, Mulberry

Green, her husband, and her daughter are locked in an attic that, according to one critic, "is highly symbolic of the island itself."[3] In addition to suffering from claustrophobia and temporal disjunction, they are being hunted by the police on charges of embezzlement of government money.

Only after Mulberry Green reaches the end of her journey to the periphery as she arrives in America is she able to recall her past experience in China. At the same time, she rejects this old "historical" self by assuming a new name and identity, Peach Red. The most harrowing part of the novel concerns the escapades of Peach Red as she is hunted down by the U.S. immigration officers. Her identity confusion takes the form of both schizophrenia and nymphomania as she sleeps her way from man to man across the continental United States. Her rejection of Mulberry Green, the Chinese side of herself, plunges her into a state of "moral and sexual anarchy," which, according to Pai Hsien-yung, may also be "representative of the macrocosmic disorder of an entire nation"—China.[4] Peach Red's fragmented psyche is a reflection of her own confusion as an exile and of the historical fragmentation of her past experiences in China. Pai considers the novel an allegorical tale because it evokes the fate of the prototypical Chinese exile who, as a Wandering Chinese, becomes "eternally terrified, eternally uncertain, eternally on the run," because "this physical uprooting means also the spiritual dislocation."[5]

Unlike Nieh's emotionally disturbed Peach Red, I now realize, after more than twenty years of identity confusion, that the journey of exile need not be utterly traumatic, dark, and without hope. On the contrary, it is only on this marginal ground that I feel psychologically secure and even culturally privileged. By virtue of my self-chosen marginality, I can never fully identify myself with any center. Thus, I do not feel any compelling need to search for my roots. I believe that the aimless anguish of Peach Red stems from the anxiety of loss and an inability to anchor her new identity on the margins of American society and culture. The feeling of self-torment, perhaps representing the negative side of a bicultural marginal person, can be turned into a positive character strength. Hualing Nieh's most recent work—a large-scale historical romance entitled *Qianshan wai shui changliu* (Beyond the myriad mountains flows the river) in which a young girl of an interracial marriage arrives in America in search of her American roots—presents a more affirmative tone that embraces the values of both cultures and replaces the nihilistic mood of *Two Women of China*. Total freedom from such a centrist orientation should be both the privilege and the prerogative of a truly "peripheral" writer, a literary exile who chooses to be "unbounded" by his or her homeland.

The fact of the matter is often to the contrary: exiled writers, within their own communities or ghettos in their adopted country, tend to reproduce narrow facsimiles of the same habits and ways of thinking that they brought from their homeland. According to Joseph Brodsky, the Soviet poet in exile, this signifies the exile writer's peculiar vanity to retain his past—a desperate wish not to be forgotten by the homeland. My attitude toward exile writers is perhaps more charitable because I can easily understand the reasons for this misplaced obsession, especially among Chinese writers whose "obsession with China" has been something of a moral burden.[6] It is an obsession that privileges China's problems as uniquely Chinese that lay absolute claim to the loyalty of Chinese in all parts of the world. This omniscient nationalism, easily capitalized upon by every Chinese government to legitimize itself at the center, has so dominated the literary imaginations of modern Chinese everywhere that it is virtually impossible to imagine a Joseph Brodsky who writes in both his native language and the language of his adopted country in order to create an art that transcends national boundaries. When one thinks of some notable examples produced by Chinese exiles in the United States in addition to Hualing Nieh and Yu Lihua—Pai Hsien-yung's own collection of fiction, *Niuyue ke* (New Yorkers), and the post-Cultural Revolution writings of Ch'en Jo-hsi, for instance—emotional attachment to the homeland seems like an "unbroken chain." In the last two or three years a new subgenre has crept into Mainland Chinese writing, following in the footsteps of exile writers from Taiwan: *liuxuesheng wenxue* (literature of Chinese students abroad) in which both author and subject are in America but the language remains Chinese and the work is published in Mainland Chinese journals. Again the stories take place, as in real life, in the Chinese communities; American culture and characters make only an occasional, peripheral appearance.[7] Needless to say, the Chinese characters' obsessions continue to be with China.

This excessive obsession with their homeland has deprived Chinese writers abroad of their rare privilege of being truly on the periphery. In my view, only by being on the true periphery of China—that is, overseas—can they hope to rise above it, because a true peripheral perspective affords them a distance sufficiently removed from the center of the obsessions so that they can subject the obsession itself to artistic treatment. This can be done by turning this perspective into a new form of fantasy or mythology, as in the case of the work of the Jewish-Polish writer Isaac Singer (who lived mostly in New York), or it can be turned into a kind of philosophical, metafictional discourse, as Thomas Mann did when he created his version of *Doktor Faustus* while an exile in southern California. The Indian-English writer Salman Rushdie subjects an entire religious tradition to an elaborate, postmodernist satire in his controversial novel *The Satanic Verses*. The boundaries are again not so much geographical as intellectual and psychological.

These (somewhat idle and diverse) meditations on the meaning of being an exile have been triggered, ironically, by my association with a number of Chinese intellectuals and writers who left China partly as a result of the Tiananmen incident. In reflecting critically upon the cultural activities and discourses that they had initiated or helped to promote in China—including the "search for roots" (*xungen*) movement—they were struck by a notable lack of peripheral thinking, because for several years they had been at the center of a cultural movement that exerted great impact on urban intellectual society. For all its implications of breaking up the Party's monolithic hold on creative culture, the movement has not entirely changed their "centrist" frame of mind—the elitist belief that they can ultimately influence the reformist leaders in the Party to their way of thinking.

No longer at the center of action (and in a sense the failure of the student demonstrations signaled the failure of hasty action) these writers are turning inward to matters of thought and psyche. They are beginning to reflect actively on the internal ravages caused by the Cultural Revolution—the impact of the Maoist revolution on their individual souls. They have invented a number of metaphors in order to describe a situation for which their old language seems inadequate. The hegemony of the "official talk" has created "a prison-house of a language" that has "subjugated the soul." After repeated political campaigns in which they were ordered to "surrender their hearts" (*jiaoxin*) to Chairman Mao and the Party, they have no heart left—they have almost no inner resources with which to fortify their sense of self and to justify their individual existences, much less their dignity as human beings. The first step toward a reconstruction of the self has led them to the writings of Václav Havel in order to reaffirm what Havel has called "human identity" and the individual will to "live in truth."

What the Czech intellectuals would call internal exile—the voluntary act of individuals to keep a private mental space that is immune from the power influence of the state—embraces a more activist ethos than the negative freedom of the right to privacy: it is a state of mind created willfully by an individual to resist pressures from the outside. To that extent it becomes a value like freedom. Coming from a tradition in which voluntary self-exile hardly existed (except as eremitic withdrawal), it is understandable that the concept of internal exile was initially baffling to my newly arrived colleagues from China. At the same time, they found it appealing because, I suspect, it fills a certain psychological gap by suggesting an alternative form of individual resistance to a far stronger central power than that which Havel confronted. Internal exile does not mean physical banishment to the peripheries of the country but rather to turn inward—the construction of a sanctuary of the soul that stands in a peripheral position vis-à-vis the omnipotent center.

Is it possible, then, to internalize the *xungen* movement by conducting a search for the roots of Chinese culture in the abode of an exile's soul?

In trying to answer this question, I am reminded of Josef Škvorecký, a self-exiled Czech writer now living in Canada who wrote about Bohemia: "I love her soul, which is in her culture. And that is in exile with me. That is my loyalty. . . . That has always been the loyalty of exiles. Only tyrants stress geographical patriotism."[8] Škvorecký also quotes these lines from the nineteenth-century Slovak poet Jan Kollar:

Do not give the holy name of homeland
To the country where we live.
The true homeland we carry in our hearts,
And that cannot be oppressed or stolen from us.[9]

These words carry a timely resonance not only to perennial self-exiles like myself but also to those Chinese intellectuals who left their homeland because of the Tiananmen massacre. For the first time, nation and state become separate entities in their minds: it is the Chinese nation, instead of the state, that remains the central object of their loyalty, their motherland. In this regard, their thinking corresponds closely with that of their fellow intellectuals inside China and offers an amazing parallel to the situation of Central and Eastern European nations before 1989. In the memorable words of Leszek Kolakowski (an eminent self-exile from Poland), "the split between the State, which people feel is not theirs, though it claims to be their owner, and the motherland, of which they are guardians, has reduced them to an ambitious status of half-exiles."[10]

It is this new self-awareness of being "half-exiles" that has led Chinese intellectuals from the People's Republic to reexamine their current situation in an international context of cultural exile and cultural migration. Here they are confronted for the first time with the familiar twentieth-century phenomenon of the "intellectual in exile," which, according to Kolakowski, can indeed "boast an impressive spiritual pedigree" in the Western traditions. In fact, Kolakowski considers exile to be "the normal and inescapable lot of mankind on earth" and finds the myth of exile not only in the Judeo-Christian religious tradition but in all religions: "The fundamental message embedded in religious worship is: our home is elsewhere."[11] Echoing essentially the same view, the Chinese scholar Liu Xiaofeng, in Switzerland, published a learned article entitled "Exile Discourse and Ideology" (*Liuwang huayu yu yishixingtai*) in which he juxtaposes the "homeless discourse" of exile and the "homed discourse" of authoritarian regimes and finds that somehow in this century the former has been invariably associated with "the knowledge-value discourse called socialism."[12] Liu singles out, in particular, the year 1922 when the new Soviet regime suddenly arrested and then exiled some 120 leading Russian scholars, writers, and scientists, thus marking the first massive intellectual migration (followed by the exodus of Jewish and other European intellectuals to America during the Nazi era and that of the Eastern Europeans in the 1950s and 1960s). The post-Tiananmen exodus of Chinese intellectuals seems to complete this twentieth-century picture.

It is widely known that the European intellectual migrations exerted a powerful cultural impact on the countries of their resettlement. At the same time, a reverse impact—that of the diasporas on the homeland—has also taken place, especially when mutual communication is possible (such as between Jewish communities abroad and in Israel). Even in the case of Eastern European countries before 1989, outside émigrés had always maintained contact with semiexiles inside through underground or unofficial channels to help create a powerful counterculture opposed to official ideology. Since 1989, many exiles have returned to assume key government positions or otherwise participate in the political transformation from the post-totalitarian systems to democracy. But the phenomenon of Chinese intellectual migration and its possible contribution to both the homeland and their adopted country is somewhat more complicated by the existence since 1949 of two rival regimes in two separate territories. Contending loyalties have tended to splinter overseas Chinese populations. As Mainland China and Taiwan resumed unofficial contact and Hong Kong emerged as an intermediary zone with its formal "return to the motherland" in 1997, a different configuration of relations—and a different perspective on the problem of center and periphery—has become possible.

In his classic essay titled "Center and Periphery," Edward Shils defined the center not as a spatial location but as a central zone of symbols, values, and beliefs that govern a society.[13]

> The existence of a central value system rests, in a fundamental way, on the need which human beings have for incorporating into something which transcends and transfigures their concrete individual existence. They have a need to be in contact with symbols of an order which is larger in its dimensions than their own bodies and more central in the ultimate structure of reality than is their routine everyday life.[14]

It would seem that this consensus model has the opposite implication when compared with Havel's ideas, and the symbols of a larger order could easily be construed as ideology, which Havel calls "a specious way of relating to the world. . . . As the repository of something 'supra-personal' and objective, it enables people to deceive their conscience and conceal their true position and their inglorious modus Vivendi, both from the world and from themselves."[15] However, Shils is careful to differentiate his concept from the specious and "supertranscendent" ideologies "which are explicit, articulated, and hostile to the existing order" such as Bolshevism, National Socialism, and Fascism.[16] Thus, it would seem that they are in basic agreement about the utopian excesses of ideology—in Havel's case, of an ideology in the service of a post-totalitarian system. Both men stress the need of human individuals to be "in personal communion" with one another once they have "reached a certain level of individuation."[17]

Still, in a fundamental way, the consensus model—which emphasizes the necessity of an established center and (despite tensions) its beneficial incorporation of either rebellious individuals or the mass population on the peripheries of a society through the process of modernization—remains suspicious. Havel has vividly described the frightening, anonymous power of the inhuman automatized systems found in both post-totalitarian and capitalist countries. In the case of post-Tiananmen China, the political scene clearly manifests the symptoms of an emergent post-totalitarian system in which control no longer comes from charisma (Maoism, for example) but from a central authority wielding anonymous power. What is to be done, even for those who, as Shils perceptively puts it, "have a very intense and active connection with the center, with the symbols of the central value system, but whose connection is passionately negative"?[18] The *xungen* writers have offered one alternative solution by reinventing new centers on the peripheries. But even this reinvention has already split open the Maoist model of a popular consensus: it has "relativized" the significance of one center and paved the way for cultural pluralism.

In fact, the statement by Han Shaogong, one of the leading *xungen* writers, already intimated such a pluralism. He has argued that the orthodox Han-Chinese culture is merely a dead "crust" resting on the "hot and turbulent" seedbed of a mixture of several unorthodox ethnic cultures, and it can only be revitalized if it is able to absorb the magma of these unorthodox cultures.[19] In Han's view the search for roots is not a search for lost purity but rather an attempt to uncover the vital pluralism of this cultural hybrid. To rephrase Han's point further, it is clear that in Chinese history orthodoxy is to be found in the center, whereas heterodoxy is to be found in the peripheries.

To render Han's argument in a different way, it celebrates the unorthodox cosmopolitanism that he has found in China's cultural past and contrasts it with the monolithic orthodoxy of present-day Chinese culture. The argument is not novel—the culture of the Tang dynasty comes readily to mind as a shining example of ancient cosmopolitanism. But its relevance to the contemporary world increases when the boundaries of the periphery extend to areas beyond the China coast. The prosperity of the Four Dragons may be used as an argument for the continuing influence of Confucianism. But I would rather see it as a continuation of a littoral vitality begun in the early nineteenth century, when new initiatives originated from coastal reformers (with a mixed cultural background such as the journalist-entrepreneur Wang Tao), which then became legitimized as policy by the hinterland center.[20] In the late twentieth century, this littoral zone has expanded to include two powerful new centers, Taiwan and Hong Kong, whose economic supremacy over the Mainland is also changing the cultural map of China. What Wei-ming Tu conceptualizes as the three Chinese cultural "universes"[21] makes increasing sense as the old national argument, based on territorial and ideological grounds, of a single China represented by a single government gradually loses its relevance. With increased influence from such central littoral regions, it is not unlikely that the more prosperous parts of China—the coastal cities on the lower Yangtze River and in the provinces of Fujian and Guangdong—will become part of the economic system dominated by Hong Kong and Taiwan. At the same time, what is known as the Pacific Rim has become increasingly internationalized as a large region of intermingling economies and cultures—both ancient and modern, Asian and Western. In this transnational and cosmopolitan framework, the old spatial matrix of center and periphery no longer has much validity. Even the notions of exile will have to be redefined. As we cast our gaze across the Pacific Ocean toward the future, perhaps Chinese of all regions and communities may take comfort in the vision that their boundaries will no longer close them off but instead crisscross each other to form interlocking networks in which there is no single center.

Notes

This chapter was modified and reprinted from Leo Ou-fan Lee, "On the Margins of the Chinese Discourse: Some Personal Thoughts on the Cultural Meaning of the Periphery," *Daedalus* 120, no. 2 (Spring 1991): 207–226.

1. Pai Hsien-yung, "The Wandering Chinese: The Theme of Exile in Taiwan Fiction," *Iowa Review* 7, no. 2/3 (Spring/Summer, 1976): 208–209.

2. Hualing Nieh, *Sangqing yu taohong* (Hong Kong: Youlian chubanshe, 1976). English edition, *Mulberry and Peach: Two Women of China*, trans. Jane Parish Yang (Boston: Beacon Press, 1981).

3. Pai, 211.

4. Ibid., 212.

5. Ibid.

6. C. T. Hsia, "Obsession with China: The Moral Burden of Modern Chinese Literature," in Hsia, *A History of Modern Chinese Fiction*, rev. ed. (New Haven: Yale University Press, 1971), 533–554.

7. An excellent example of this new genre is a short story by Zha Jianying, "Xiangei luo-sha he qiao de anhunqu" (Requiem for Rosa and Joe), *Renmin wenxue* (People's literature) 3 (1989). In this story the peripheral existence of an old American couple assumes central symbolic significance in the meaningless life of a young Chinese woman exiled in New York.

8. Josef Škvorecký, "Bohemia of the Soul," *Dædalus* 119, no. 1 (Winter 1990): 135.

9. Ibid., 132.

10. Leszek Kolakowski, "In Praise of Exile," in Kolakowski, *Modernity on Endless Trial* (Chicago: University of Chicago Press, 1990), 59.

11. Ibid., 57.

12. Liu Xiaofeng, "Liuwang huayu yu yishixingtai" (Exile discourse and ideology), *Ershiyi shiji* (Twenty-first century) 1 (October 1990): 115.

13. Edward Shils, *Center and Periphery: Essays in Macrosociology* (Chicago: University of Chicago Press, 1975), 3.

14. Ibid., 7.

15. Havel, 42.

16. Shils, 5.

17. Ibid., 7.

18. Ibid., 8–9.

19. Han Shaogong, *"Wenxue de 'gen'"* (The "roots" of literature), *Zuojia* (Writer) 4 (1985): 2–5. For some of my argument related to *xungen* fiction in this paper, I am also indebted to William Schafer, "Composing Roots: Dialogues of Center and Peripheries in Three Xungen Short Stories" (M.A. thesis, University of Chicago, 1990).

20. In Chinese studies, the notion of reform as a "littoral" initiative acting upon the "hin-terland" was first developed by Paul A. Cohen in *Between Tradition and Modernity: Wang T'ao and Reform in Late Ch'ing China* (Cambridge: Harvard University Press, 1973), chap. 1.

21. See chapter 8 by Wei-ming Tu, this volume.

10

The Structure of Dual Domination

Toward a Paradigm for the Study of the Chinese Diaspora in the United States

LING-CHI WANG

The primary purpose of this chapter is to critique the existing dominant paradigms for the study of the Chinese in the United States and to develop an alternative one. My other intention is to demonstrate both the importance and limit of transnational approaches in Chinese American studies within the framework of Asian American and ethnic studies.

The end of the Cold War in 1989 and the rise of a rapidly shrinking, but disorderly, world presented a unique opportunity to reexamine the history of the Chinese in the United States in a global context. The proliferation of demands for courses and programs in Asian American Studies among the top research universities and colleges, many of which have little to do with the kind of program originally conceived, likewise raises questions as to where Asian American Studies is heading and whether it is still considered a vital component of ethnic studies. To what extent is the Chinese experience in the United States similar to and different from the experiences of the Chinese in the other one hundred and thirty countries? How does the rapid transnational movement of labor and capital affect the structure and welfare of longtime Chinese communities throughout the United States? How has the reduction of hostility between China and Taiwan affected political alignments in Chinese America? In what ways have issues of Chinese American identity, lifestyle, and politics been affected by instant global communication and convenient access to popular culture from China, Taiwan, and Hong Kong? What are the relations between Asian American Studies and proliferating fields of studies, like multicultural education, cultural studies, and diaspora studies? What is the relevance of these questions to Chinese American and, ultimately, Asian American Studies?

Assimilationist and Loyalty Paradigms

Two major concepts have dominated and guided the study of the Chinese diaspora in the United States, and in most countries with a significant ethnic Chinese presence. In the United States, on the one hand, the concept of assimilation or Anglo-conformity has shaped public discourse on and dictated government policies toward the Chinese minority and guided both historians and social scientists in their studies of the Chinese in the United States.[1] The sole focus of the assimilationist paradigm is on the racial difference and conflict between the dominant Euro-Americans and the Chinese minority, how Chinese immigrants have become Americanized or failed to do so over time, and how society, through laws and policies, has treated Chinese immigrants.

In China, on the other hand, the dominant idea used by both scholars and government officials to study the Chinese diaspora in general and Chinese in the United States in particular is loyalty or how well the Chinese in the United States and in other countries have remained loyal or faithful, over time, to their loved ones at home (*xiaoshun*), to their native villages (loosely, *xiangyue*), to the Chinese culture (*baoliu* or *weihu*), or to the nation-state (*xiaozhong*) in China or Taiwan.[2] Two distinctive types of loyalty may be identified. Loyalty toward one's clan, village, and Chinese culture is intensely personal and cultural and decidedly apolitical. It is to be distinguished from the more formal and institutionalized loyalty one may or may not have toward the Chinese culture, nation, or a particular Chinese government or a political faction or party in the government. Retaining Chinese cultural identity, if not political and economic loyalty, of the Chinese overseas has been the primary preoccupation, if not the sole obsession, of both government policies and scholarly inquiries under the Nationalist government in Nanjing (1911–1949) and in Taiwan (1949–present), and, to a lesser degree, in China since 1956, even though both governments have very different policies toward the Chinese diaspora.

Aside from the fact that both notions of assimilation and loyalty are socially defined and historically conditioned (subject to periodical change and redefinition), there is virtually no common ground between the two paradigms. Each mirrors the view and interest of the respective state and dominant ideology. In general, books and articles using the loyalty paradigm are written in Chinese and published in China and Taiwan while books utilizing the assimilationist paradigm are written in English and published in the United States. At the theoretical and public policy levels, they stand on opposite poles, separated by linguistic, ideological, political, and cultural divides. Rarely do they cite, interact, or engage each other in intellectual dialogue or debate. Within Chinese America, a similar gap exists, complicated by difference in nativity, language, and class.

Beneath these two conflicting paradigms, as in the construction of any paradigm, are two entirely different visions of culture, society, and nation upon which the agenda for thought are set, dominant ideologies constructed, theories built, public policies formulated, and programs for action initiated. While there are many variations and even conflicting theories within each of the two paradigms over time, the difference in no way alters the basic premises, perspectives, and theoretical objectives of each.

This chapter, therefore, begins with a critique of the two dominant paradigms. Three separated, but interrelated levels of analysis for each paradigm can be identified: ideological, theoretical, and public policy. At the ideological level, the assimilationist paradigm is based on a widely accepted, though never fully articulated, vision in which the United States is seen as a nation peopled by successive waves of immigrants and guided by a set of principles articulated in the Declaration of Independence and the Constitution. This vision is reinforced by a widely held belief that the United States, by virtue of its superior constitution and democratic institutions, is capable of assimilating the immigrants equally and harmoniously into a great melting pot. This belief or dominant ideology is not just a national myth but also a national obsession. The myth is further linked to a promise of freedom, equality, and democracy for all. It is upon this dominant ideology that the U.S. government formulates its public policies and historians and social scientists interpret U.S. history and society.

Significant civil rights gains and social and economic progress for Chinese Americans did not begin until the Second Reconstruction in the 1960s. Even then, the racist vision and ideology of assimilation persisted. While Chinese Americans, unlike African Americans, were seen as having successfully achieved assimilation in selective social indicators, such as education, occupation, income, and residence, they were still treated as useful aliens, untrustworthy, therefore, to be kept powerless, subordinated, and at a distance. They became the indispensable technicians and technocrats in the emerging high-tech industries. The notion of assimilation, now reconceptualized for a new racial discourse in the post–civil rights era, came to be used as a political tool for pitting Chinese Americans and African Americans against each other. Chinese Americans were celebrated as a "model minority" while African Americans were equated to urban blight, crime, and welfare dependency. Yet, Chinese Americans remained excluded and powerless, and not infrequently the target of racist incidents. The persistence of exclusion can be seen readily in the economic and political conflicts between the dominant Euro-Americans and Chinese Americans in cities like San Francisco and New York and in middle-class suburbs like Monterey Park and Silicon Valley in California.[3] Overt racism may have subsided under the new legal and political climate, but covert racism manifests itself in new and refined discriminatory forms in college admissions, glass ceiling, immigrant bashing, zoning restrictions, English-only movement, backlash against affirmative action and bilingual education, and so forth.

Like the assimilation paradigm in the United States, the loyalty paradigm used in both Taiwan and China in the formulation of public policies and in the study of the Chinese in the United States and other countries is just as chauvinistic and ethnocentric. Historically, loyalty appeared in different forms and carried different meanings over time. It can be understood in cultural, economic, and political terms. Historically, both government and scholars played a crucial role in defining and redefining the terms of loyalty. Since 1949, the civil war in China divided the Chinese government into two camps, the Mainland and Taiwan, each claiming to represent the legitimate government of China and each having very different policies toward Chinese overseas, even as they adjust to changes in the global environment and their respective bilateral relations with different countries.

Loyalty, like assimilation, manifests itself in ideology, theory, and public policy in China and Taiwan. It also exists on two levels: formal and informal. Unlike Western society, the social and economic structure of traditional Chinese society is based on the family or clan and strong social ethics rather than on individual liberty and an elaborate legal system. Before the advent of modern Chinese nationalism at the turn of the century, loyalty for Chinese abroad, *xiao* (filial piety) and *shun* (obedience), meant simply obligations to one's family (*aijia*) and ancestral village (*aixiang*) or not forsaking or forgetting one's family and village. At the informal or personal level, it was one's obligation to remain faithful to one's family (*jia*), clan (*jiazu, zongzu, shizu* based on *xueyuan*, consanguinity), and village (*jiaxiang, xiang, xiangcun, xiangxia*) by being obedient to one's parents, sending regular remittances, remembering the living and the dead, and supporting charity and public works in the village. At the next level, still informal, loyalty also meant not forgetting one's cultural roots in China and the need to retain Chinese outlooks, values, and lifestyle. Racial and cultural superiority is assumed. At the collective or communal level cultural loyalty was maintained through community-based Chinese schools, temples, newspapers, public festivals and rituals, social institutions, like district associations (*huiguan*), and family or clan association (*gongsuo*). These reproduced institutions were deemed indispensable for mutual aid and cultural maintenance on alien or hostile soil, especially for those who stayed overseas for a long time and for those Chinese born abroad. Loyalty at the cultural level originally carried no political connotation before the rise of Chinese nationalism toward the end of the nineteenth century. This nonpolitical notion of loyalty exerted profound influence over the self-perception and development of Chinese communities in diverse settings and different countries.

However, with the advent of Chinese nationalism, traditional loyalty to the country (*guojia*) and emperor (*junzhu, tianzi, wangdi*) quickly acquired new meanings with strong political and legal connotations (*zhong, zhongzheng, zhong xin, xiaozhong, aiguo*). China's military and political defeats in the hands of Western powers and Japan militarism resulted in numerous unequal treaties, foreign domination, and national humiliation (*guochi*). Modern Chinese nationalism first emerged among the intelligentsia and Chinese overseas. To Chinese overseas, in particular, China's national sovereignty and honor had to be defended and, indeed, many attributed their mistreatment abroad to China's weakness.[4] To be loyal or patriotic for Chinese overseas was to support China's resistance, which can be both economic and political. Investing in China's modernization was a form of economic loyalty; sharing knowledge in science and technology is a contemporary counterpart. But the most controversial expression of loyalty was the support of various political movements, since late nineteenth century, aimed at strengthening, reforming, modernizing, or revolutionizing China.[5] Political reformers like Kang Youwei and Liang Qichao, and revolutionaries like Sun Yatsen at the turn of the century, and Chinese American critics of the Nationalist government in Taiwan like professor Wen-chen Chen and journalist Henry Liu (Jiang Nan) in the 1980s, were considered disloyal and seditious, therefore, subject to political harassment, intimidation, kidnapping, and assassination, if necessary.[6]

Anchored, therefore, in the new notion of loyalty were the government's attitudes and policies toward Chinese abroad. Since the turn of the century, elaborate laws and policies were enacted and government agencies established to instill cultural, economic, and political loyalty and to exercise its extraterritorial rule over the Chinese diaspora.[7] Since 1949, the Nationalist regime in Taiwan has been most aggressive in its intervention abroad and insistence on treating the Chinese diaspora as "external colonies," and its scholars dutifully wrote books from the same perspective. Its primary objective was to demonstrate the political loyalty of Chinese overseas to the Taiwan regime, which claimed to represent Mainland China. Since the late nineteenth century, the Chinese government's policies can be divided roughly into four periods: (1) strict prohibition of emigration, known as *haijin*, until 1868, to suppress Ming loyalists and political dissidents; (2) regulated emigration (1868–1911) and dual citizenship (*shuangchong guoji*) based on the principle of *jus sanguinis* (*xuetong zhuyi*); (3) progressive tightening of extraterritorial control under the Nationalist (Guomindang) government in Nanjing (1911–1949) and in Taipei (1949–1989); and (4) policies of decolonization, self-determination, and integration into host countries under the Beijing government, 1957–1989. These policies exerted a profound impact on Chinese America and Chinese overseas, yet scholars in Asian American Studies have largely ignored this transnational dimension.

Structure of Dual Domination

From the previous discussion of the two competing paradigms in the study of the Chinese diaspora in the United States, it is clear that both are simplistic, unidimensional, biased, and incomplete. Both erroneously assume Chinese America to be homogeneous and monolithic.

To construct an alternative paradigm for the Chinese diaspora in the United States, we begin with a vision of Chinese America that can be roughly represented by four methodological presuppositions. First, Chinese immigrants, like immigrants of all races and nationalities, came to the United States with cultural, social, and economic assets and with legitimate personal interests and aspirations. Second, we assume Chinese Americans to be an integral part of the vision of the United States as a nation peopled by Native Americans and immigrants, both voluntary and involuntary, in a great historic process in which they built not only their own communities but also the United States. Third, we further assume that Chinese Americans, like all Americans, are entitled to the same rights and privileges promised in the Declaration of Independence and in the U.S. Constitution. Lastly, China, by virtue of its size, history, culture, and by virtue of its rising influence on the global economy and politics, has been and will continue to have a profound influence over the identity formation of Chinese Americans and Chinese overseas in the shrinking world and in an age of instant global communication and transnational migration of capital and labor. All four presuppositions have been excluded from or only minimally considered by the two major paradigms discussed before.

The four methodological presuppositions necessitate the reconceptualization of assimilation and loyalty: the conditions for Chinese assimilation are reconceived as *racial exclusion* or *oppression* and the demand for loyalty to the homeland as *extraterritorial domination*. Both are seen as omnipresent and omnipotent powers or forces dominating all aspects of Chinese American life. Racial exclusion is driven by the ideology of white supremacy and notions of Chinese non-assimilability and alienage; extraterritorial domination is sustained by the loyalty imperative. Both are highly institutionalized and structurally integrated into the legal, political, economic, and cultural systems of their respective countries, sustained by public policies and dominant scholarship. *Under the new paradigm, racial exclusion or oppression and extraterritorial domination converge and interact in the Chinese American community, establishing a permanent structure of dual domination and creating its own internal dynamics and unique institutions.*

The structure is therefore not static; instead, it is dynamic, constantly undergoing change, driven by the respective domestic politics and bilateral relations between the United States and China. This is why not even periodical changes in respective governments and specific policies can substantively alter their hegemonic roles in the Chinese American community. To put it in another way, the structure of domination is supported by two pillars: one is domestic and racial and the other is extraterritorial and racial as well. Liberation from the structure of dual domination occurs only when there is fundamental change in the exclusionary vision and ideology in either or both countries and in the self-perception and assertion of self-determination by Chinese Americans. Its goal is the full realization of the vision outlined in the four presuppositions.

Within the structure of dual domination, the extraterritorial domination is grounded in the ideology of loyalty and is pervasive, extending into the political economic and cultural life of Chinese America. The extraterritorial domination of the Chinese government, however, did not go unchallenged. Resistance took many forms. The failure of the Chinese government to effectively repel Western and Japanese imperialism aroused nationalism overseas and made overseas communities, by virtue of their extraterritorial status, fertile grounds for instigating opposition movements and for generating new ideas for political reform and economic modernization in China. Passive resistance and supporting counter-hegemonic cultural activities and indigenous groups are other forms of resistance.

This brings us to the other pillar of the structure: the exclusion of the Chinese. Chinese Americans were systematically excluded from the basic rights and protection guaranteed by the U.S. Constitution. Grounded on the ideology of assimilation, their race and culture were the bases of their exclusion. The denial of citizenship to Chinese immigrants before World War II deprived the Chinese American community the most fundamental tool for redress in the United States. Chinese Americans were effectively relegated to a rigidly defined apartheid system under which they were economically subjugated, legally and socially segregated, culturally despised, and politically disenfranchised. It was a system established by democratic means and sustained by repeated judicial decisions. Chinese rights, privileges, and sanctuaries in the Euro-American society were permanently suspended. Under this system, a traditional Chinese society was reproduced and sojourner mentality reinforced.

We now turn to the relationship between racial oppression and extraterritorial domination in Chinese America. The relationship is linked *externally* by the changing bilateral relations between the United States and China and internally, as mentioned before, by their interaction with each other at the level of the Chinese American community. The structure of dual domination is, therefore, reinforced and constantly modulated by the bilateral international relations and by the collective resistance from the community. For example, the Nanjing Treaty of 1842 and Wanghsia Treaty of 1844 set the stage for the bankrupt Chinese peasants from the Zhujiang delta to migrate to California under labor contracts, the Burlingame Treaty of 1867 legalized Chinese emigration and extended treaty protection to Chinese in the United States, the migration and commercial treaty of 1880 led to the Chinese Exclusion Act of 1882, the mounting conflict over the mistreatment of the Chinese in the United States precipitated the 1905 boycott of U.S. imports, the U.S.-China alliance during World War II compelled Congress to repeal the Chinese exclusion laws, and the U.S.-China conflicts over Korea and Vietnam subjected Chinese Americans to a long period of political repression. It is not a static structure, confined geographically to traditional Chinatowns and historically to any period. Instead, by virtue of its structural links to the U.S.-China relations, the modus operandi of the two omnipresent, omnipotent powers are constantly interacting with each other and undergoing transformation, driven by domestic political changes and national interests in the United States and in China. For this reason, Chinese Americans can be seen as unwilling and unsuspecting participants, if not victims, of U.S.-China relations and dealings. It was their presence and resistance that exposed frequent political contradictions at home and abroad and caused these operating forces to act in domestic politics and in international relations. In this regard, Chinese Americans are both actors and victims of these great forces in history: they lay bare the practice of imperialism, racism, extraterritorialism, and political opportunism in Chinese politics and in

American democracy and the complicity played by intellectuals on both sides of the Pacific in their history writing.

To fully understand the structure of dual domination, the new paradigm requires the incorporation of the perspectives, feelings, and voices of Chinese Americans. This means the extensive use of individual, organizational, and collective voices and writings. Toward this end, Asian American studies has contributed significantly with books, video, and films. However, we cannot assume the community to be homogeneous and monolithic, a major flaw in the two dominant paradigms and in the privileging of the English-speaking world in Asian America studies to date. Particular attention must also be given to the segmentation of the community by nativity, gender, and class, glaringly missing in the works guided by the two dominant paradigms. The response to the structure of dual domination from each segment will be different. Less obvious are segmentation based on clan, religion, occupation, geographic and linguistic origin, and political party in China and Taiwan. Geographic origin is also important in light of the large influx of Chinese immigrants from countries in Africa, Southeast Asia, Europe, and Latin America in the last two decades. The diversity of voices and perspectives from opposing segments gives flesh and blood to the history and internal dynamic of Chinese America.[8]

Uncovering hidden knowledge of Chinese America is not an end itself in Asian American studies. If the structure of dual domination has robbed Chinese Americans of their identities and self-determination and prevented them from achieving equality and full citizenship in the United States, the sole appropriate response for Chinese Americans is to seek liberation from the structure of dual domination. It is here that we locate the genesis of Asian American studies and find the convergence of theory with practice and the integration of scholarship and advocacy. Separate resistance to racial oppression and extraterritorial domination is simply not sufficient in itself to achieve total liberation. The dynamic structural link between the two in the bilateral relations of the United States and China/Taiwan and in their interaction at the community level requires a comprehensive understanding of the structure of dual domination, a critical analysis of conditions faced by Asian Americans, and a coordinated program and strategy for self-determination and liberation. This is what defines the unique nature and mission of Asian American studies; it is also the soul of contemporary ethnic studies without which ethnic studies loses its uniqueness and becomes a subfield of either the social sciences or humanities. It is also an intellectual dilemma of all Asian Americanists.

By the early 1970s, some Chinese Americans, myself included, began to realize that their status, as citizens of the United States, was directly linked, not by choice, not only to the close relations between United States and Taiwan, then recognized as the sole legitimate government of China, but also to Taiwan's extraterritorial domination in Chinese America, which the nationalistic, progressive forces, the Old Left, in Chinatown fought vigorously against in the 1930s and 1940s. They acknowledged and took pride in their cultural heritage of China and recognized the important role China and U.S.-China relations played, both positive and negative, in the Chinese American experience, the last of the four methodological presuppositions. Accordingly, they added the demand for liberation from Taiwan's extraterritorial domination, even as they fought for their liberation from racial oppression and for full participation, as citizens of the United States, in the formulation and conduct of U.S. policies toward China and Taiwan. In short, they demanded self-determination and liberation from the structure of dual domination.

At the heart of the liberation movement was the rise of Chinese American consciousness and the development of a new Chinese American identity. This identity was derived neither from China nor from the United States; instead, it was rooted in the experience of Chinese America. Operating under the framework and promise of the U.S. Constitution, the new Chinese Americans demanded self-determination and guarantees of freedom, equality, and equal protection. They rejected the perception and treatment of themselves as non-assimilable foreigners or citizens of Taiwan (China) and refused to tolerate second-class American citizenship. Toward this end, they explicitly rejected the sojourner mentality (*luoye guigen*), the assimilationist mentality (*zhancao chugen*), and the accommodationist mentality (*luodi shenggen*). Instead, they posited their Chinese racial and cultural origin to be in China but insisted their identity and destiny to be exclusively rooted in and derived from the Chinese experience in the United States (*xungen wenzu*).[9] Uncovering the Chinese American past and reidentifying with the Chinese American community and its struggles for liberation were their first order of business. The Asian Community Center in San Francisco Chinatown, a student founded community action organization, and Chinese for Affirmative Action (CAA) of San Francisco, a community-based civil rights organization, are both the outgrowth of this development.

In the process, they also demanded Chinese American studies in universities on the one hand and promoted uniquely Chinese American creative expressions in arts, films, music, and literature on the other. It is this new movement that provides the perspective, inspiration, and space for Chinese American artists and writers like Frank Chin, Maxine Hong Kingston, David Henry Hwang, Maya Lin, Wayne Wang, Genny Lim, David Wong Louie, Gish Jen, Fae Myenne Ng, Fred Ho, Jon Jang, to name just a few.

Charting a New Destiny

The process of creating a new identity, redefining a new community, and charting a new destiny for the Chinese in the United States is long and arduous. It begins with an understanding of the structure of dual domination. Liberation from the structure of dual domination is therefore the goal for the emergence of a new Chinese America in the multiracial democracy of the United States envisioned by the Chinese Americans involved in the civil rights movement of the late 1960s and early 1970s. The changing relations between the United States and China/Taiwan have been shaping the process toward that liberation. As Taiwan becomes more democratic and its government less domineering in the Chinese American community, China moves toward greater openness and reform, and China-Taiwan tension reduces and the prospect of liberation improves. Resistance to change, however, is inevitable. The process has been made difficult with, if not undermined by, the consolidation of transnational capitalism and growing integration of the global economy. The steady influx of new Chinese immigrants and investment from China, Taiwan, Hong Kong, and countries in Southeast Asia and Latin America since the early 1970s has injected different interests and aspirations among the Chinese in the United States that are frequently at odds with the vision of liberation. Technological advances in telecommunication and transportation have likewise made not only the world smaller and more accessible but the presence of the cultures and lifestyles of China, Taiwan, and Hong Kong more visible and influential in the Chinese American community, transforming, in the process, the already segmented Chinese American community.

With some modifications, the dual domination paradigm, I believe, can be applied fruitfully toward uncovering and analyzing the rich, but still hidden, experiences of other Asian groups in the United States and other Chinese communities in different countries of the diaspora. Asian American studies began by focusing its political and intellectual attention and resources on the self-determination of Asians in the United States and their liberation from domestic racial oppression. It also correctly insisted on its intellectual autonomy from the field of East Asian studies. The proposed paradigm reaffirms the validity of the founding principles and approach of ethnic studies and supplements it with transnationality, but only to the extent they affect Asian American experiences, with two additional analytical dimensions: the diplomatic relations between the Asian American communities and their respective home countries. Both additions are transnational in nature and essential for enhancing our understanding for the Asian American communities in the past and in the future in the rapid trans-Pacific movements of information, capital, and people under global capitalism.

Notes

This chapter was modified and reprinted from Ling-chi Wang, "The Structure of Dual Domination: Toward a Paradigm for the Study of the Chinese Diaspora in the United States," *Amerasia Journal* 21, no. 1 (1995): 149–169.

1. The use of assimilation in the study on the Chinese in the United States may be divided into three periods: non-assimilation of the Chinese (1850–1924); assimilation of American-born Chinese (1924–1968); and Chinese American success in assimilation in comparison with other racial minorities (1968–present). Examples of the first period can be found easily in the polemic writings, legislative reports, judicial decisions, and scholarly publications. A representative work is Willard B. Farwell, *The Chinese at Home and Abroad* (San Francisco: A. L. Bancroft, 1885). Mary Coolidge, *Chinese Immigration* (New York: Henry Holt & Co., 1909) provides ample secondary documentation of this period. The second period is best represented by the Robert Park School's studies of the American-born Chinese and Japanese on the West Coast. Examples of this period range from R. D. McKenzie, *Oriental Exclusion* (New York: Institute of Pacific Relations, 1927), Elliot Mears, *Resident Orientals on the American Pacific Coast* (Chicago: University of Chicago Press, 1928), and William C. Smith, *Americans in Process: A Study of Our Citizens of Oriental Ancestry* (Ann, Arbor, Mich.: Edwards Bros., 1937) to Rose Hum Lee, *The Chinese in the U.S.A.* (Hong Kong: Hong Kong University Press, 1960), Shien-Woo Kung, *Chinese in American Life: Some Aspects of Their History, Status, Problems and Contributions* (Seattle: University of Washington Press, 1962), and Betty Lee Sung, *Mountain of Gold: The Story of the Chinese in America* (New York: Macmillan, 1967). The third period, characterized by the use of assimilation to contrast Chinese American success and African American failure, is best represented by numerous magazine reports in the 1960s and 1970s and studies, such as Ivan H. Light, *Ethnic Enterprise in America: Business and Welfare among Chinese, Japanese, and Blacks* (Berkeley: University of California Press, 1972).

2. The three-volume, 2,173-page history of the Chinese in the United States published in Taiwan by pro-Kuomintang historian Liu Bo-qi is representative of this approach: *Meiguo Huaqiao Shi*, Vols. 1 & 2; *Meiguo Huaqiao Yishi* (Taibei: Liming Wenhua Shiyue Gongsi, 1976, 1981, and 1984). Representative of the historical works on the history of the Chinese in the United States published in China in recent years is Li Chunhui and Yang Shengmao, *Meizhou Huaqiao Huaren Shi* (Beijing: Dongfeng Chubanshe, 1990) and Yang Guobiao et al., *Meiguo Huaoqiao Shi* [A history of the Chinese in the U.S.] (Guangzhou: Guangdong Gaodeng Jiaoyi Chubanshe, 1989). Earlier works include Liang Qichao, *Xindalu Youji Jielu* [Record of a 1903 trip to the New World] (Taibei: Zhongzheng Shuji, 1957), Feng Ziyou, *Huaqiao Geming Kaiguo Shi* [Overseas Chinese in the history of the Chinese Revolution] (Shanghai: Shangwu Yinshuguan, 1947), Wu Xianzi, *Zhongguo Minzhu Xianzhengdang Dangshi* [History of China's Democratic-Constitutional Party] (San Francisco: Shijie Ribao, 1952).

3. Victor and Brett Nee, *Longtime Calforn': A Documentary Study of an American Chinatown* (New York: Pantheon Books, 1972); Peter Kwong, *The New Chinatown* (New York: Hill & Wang, 1987); Timothy Fong, *The First Suburban Chinatown* (Philadelphia: Temple University Press, 1994).

4. This conclusion is best described in Renqiu Yu, *To Save China, To Save Ourselves: The Chinese Hand Laundry Alliance of New York* (Philadelphia: Temple University Press, 1992).

5. For a detailed analysis of Chinese American involvement in China's modernization, especially in political reforms, see L. Eve Armentrou-Ma, Revolutionaries, *Monarchists, and Chinatowns: Chinese Politics in the Americas and the 1911 Revolution* (Honolulu: University of Hawaii Press, 1990).

6. For example, in its effort to suppress dissident political activities in Chinese America, the Manchu government enlisted the Chinese Benevolent Association in San Francisco to send an intimidating letter in 1900 to exiled reformer Liang Qichao, suggesting its inability to guarantee his personal safety if he insisted on visiting the city. Liu Boqi, *Meiguo Huaqiao Shi,* Vol. 1, 449. For the death of Professor Wen-chen Chen of Carnegie-Mellon University, see U.S. House Subcommittee on Human Rights and International Organizations, and on Asian and Pacific Affairs, *Taiwan Agents in America and the Death of Prof. Wen-chen Chen,* July 30 and October 6, 1981. (Washington, D.C.: GPO, 1981). Similarly, ignoring repeated warnings not to publish his critical biography of Jiang Jingguo, president of the Nationalist government in Taiwan, Chinese American journalist Henry Liu was assassinated on October 15, 1984, in his own home in Daly City, a suburb of San Francisco, by agents sent by the Taiwan government. See Jiangnan Shijian Weiyuanhui, ed., *Jinian Jiangnan* (San Francisco, 1985) and David Kaplan, *Fire of the Dragon: Politics, Murder, and the Kuomintang* (New York: Atheneum, 1992). In both cases, the U.S. government chose to ignore the constitutional rights of the Chinese in the United States. L. Ling-chi Wang, "Justice Is Stonewalled: The Murder of Henry Liu: A Taiwanese Hit" in *Silenced: The Unresolved Murders of Immigrant Journalists in the U.S.,* 47–56, edited by the Committee to Protect Journalists (New York, 1994).

7. Most books on Overseas Chinese policies are written in Chinese, most of which are published in Taiwan. For English treatment of the subject, see Stephen Fitzgerald, *China and the Overseas Chinese: A Study of Peking's Changing Policy, 1949–1970* (Cambridge: Cambridge University Press, 1972) and Wang Gungwu, *China and the Chinese Overseas* (Singapore: Times Academic Press, 1991).

8. Peter Kwong's *New York Chinatown* (New York: Monthly Review Press, 1979) provides a good case study of this approach.

9. Tu Wei-ming, *The Living Tree: The Changing Meaning of Being Chinese Today* (Stanford, Calif.: Stanford University Press, 1994).

III

SITES AND ARTICULATIONS

The chapters in parts I and II of this volume lay out a spectrum and terrain for Sinophone studies thus far, addressing some of its major concerns and its potential interventions in dominant theoretical paradigms put forth by ethnic, area, postcolonial, literary, and cultural studies. Broadly scanning the "margins of China and Chineseness,"[1] the chapters in these first two parts compare and contrast different historical spaces of Chinese migration, expansion, and colonial incursion—contexts that have given rise to specific Sinophone conditions. Given the divergent historical trajectories of these variously formulated margins both within China and without, these chapters question the accuracy and appropriateness of China, Chinese, and Chineseness as labels, categories, and (assigned/chosen) descriptive modifiers of ethnicity, culture, nationality, and/or language. Both informing and informed by these more general debates, dialogues, and personal reflections, the chapters in part III offer examples of the type of close literary and grounded historical analysis that give shape to Sinophone studies as a discipline, as a "place-based practice,"[2] and as a method of critical inquiry.

Without claiming to be all encompassing, the chapters in part III nonetheless cover polyphonic voices that constitute the major chorus of the Sinophone. They are grouped together according to their specific sites of articulation—spanning North America, Taiwan, Oceania, Southeast Asia, Hong Kong, Tibet, Western Europe, Latin America, and the Caribbean. Here, "sites" are endowed with spatial-temporal significance, referring not only to these regions, nations, and territories, but also to the specific histories—colonial and postcolonial, national and transnational—that inform, shape, and construct the conditions for Sinophone cultural production—the medium for the specific "articulations"—discussed in the individual chapters. Some historical contextualization of the position of Sinitic languages and Sinophone cultural production within each site is a paramount feature of each chapter because it is intrinsically linked to the articulation, which engages in a dialogue with the political, cultural, and historical milieu of the specific site.

Since this volume is published in the United States and is largely the product of scholars working in the U.S. academy (although we have included the very generous, informative, and indispensible contributions of esteemed colleagues working at institutions in Taiwan, Hong Kong, Singapore, England, Spain, and New Zealand), let us first examine the Sinophone American context. The chapters by Sau-ling Wong, Te-hsing Shan, and Shuang Shen expose the exclusion of Sinophone American literature from the category of orthodox "American literature" and thus challenge the Anglophone-centric bias and basis of this discipline. Throughout the ongoing struggle since the Civil Rights era to establish, maintain, and fund ethnic studies programs in American academia, more and more non-Euro-American authors have gradually gained recognition from both (largely market-driven) U.S. publication outlets and academia, where they are, however, often relegated and confined to discussion in courses whose organizing principle is firstly ethnicity and secondly nationality (to say nothing of language). African American, Latino American, Native American, and Asian American literary voices have made steady (if occasionally tokenized) inroads into canonical anthologies of contemporary American literature. Yet one of the unspoken prerequisites for admittance into this oeuvre and for recognition as "American" is the composition of works in English. The monolingual hegemony of American literature, however, must be challenged. If ethnic, racial, and gender issues were integral to the counterhegemonic causes of twentieth-century U.S. politics, perhaps language is emerging as that of the twenty-first. By shifting works from the United States that are composed in the Sinitic script away from the category of overseas or diasporic "Chinese literature," Sinophone studies seizes the opportunity to assert the multilingualism of American literature and bring minor/minority languages, cultures, politics, and aesthetics to the fore of American literary studies.

Sinophone American literature is, of course, not the only site from which experiences of exclusion, marginality, and minoritization are articulated. Whereas "sites" indicate spaces of historical difference, particularity, and specificity, the "articulations" represent some of the common themes, dominant tropes, and strategic bonds of Sinophone cultural production across many of the sites where it is found. Together, the articulations help the reader see that the long historical trajectory of the construction of Sinophone identities, self-awareness, and senses of belonging are more than parabolic or allegorical. In several of the chapters on Sinophone literary production in the West, the experience of white racism, exclusion, and minoritization is a common theme. Monolingual educational structures and pressures for immigrant communities in the West to linguistically assimilate in order to be upwardly mobile have made the multigenerational continuity of Sinophone education, media, and literature difficult, yet the steady influx of Sinitic-language-speaking immigrants from China, Taiwan, Hong Kong, and Southeast Asia over the course of the last century has continued to replenish and revitalize these cultural and linguistic outlets. Many of the Sinophone authors in the West discussed herein are "China born," or belong to the "first generation," including those of an earlier era such as Lao She (see Prado-Fonts) and Lin Yutang (see Shen), or more recently, the Sinophone French author and Nobel laureate Gao Xingjian (see Bachner) and the Sinophone New Zealand poet Yang Lian (see Edmund). Whereas these more renowned (or privileged) Sinophone authors occupy a position in the West that allows them the freedom to self-identify as sojourners or students studying "abroad," or as ambassadors of Chinese culture or exiles who stand above nation and politics, the presence of Sinophone poetry anonymously etched on the walls of holding cells in San Francisco's Angel Island by sequestered immigrants (see Shan) narrates a far more entrenched genealogy of Sinophone literature in Western societies and challenges the stereotype of the uneducated, uncultured, non-literary immigrant figure of the earlier era.

In many sites, the Sinophone is shown as occupying not only an excluded or marginalized sphere, but also an ambiguous, in-between status that complicates conventional and simplistic configurations of colonizer-colonized/oppressor-oppressed relations. As Ignacio López-Calvo states, the presence of Sino-Latin American and Caribbean literature, largely Hispanophone but also Sinophone, in countries such as Cuba, Peru, Panama, Nicaragua, and Mexico, disrupts "the official black-and-white or indigenous-and-white discourse of the nation." From internalized and perpetuated racist stereotypes toward African Americans evinced in Sinophone Chinese American literature (see Wong) to the literary portrayal of ancestral Chinese settlers who become entangled agents in the British colonization of the indigenous Dayaks of Malaysian Borneo (see Bernards), the colonized and colonizing Sinophone demonstrates varying, situational access to the mechanisms of colonial, state, and financial power. This is particularly true of settler colonial spaces, where Sinophone settler communities sometimes form strategic anticolonial alliances with indigenous communities fighting for sovereignty, but at other times find themselves at odds with the indigenous struggle. This is the case with Sinophone New Zealand literature, which, as Jacob Edmund writes, "engages both Māori and Anglo-settler concerns with language, place, and identity, illuminating and entwining elements of their often opposed positions on these issues."

Where the legacies of settler colonial history intersect with conditions of postcolonial minoritization, Malaysia presents a unique case. Here, Chinese Malaysians are not only a very visible and indispensable minority with financial clout, but have established an entrenched (though oft-targeted) tradition of Sinophone education—primarily in Mandarin since the 1920s—which has helped give Sinophone Malaysian literature an autonomous, multigenerational longevity and vibrancy, despite its postcolonial exclusion from the category of "national literature." Since the Kuala Lumpur ethnic riots of May 1969 and the implementation of pro-Malay policies that marginalized the Sinophone from the public sphere, Sinophone Malaysian literature has gone transnational, particularly benefitting from its access to publication in Taiwan (see Tee).

Whereas Sinophone Malaysian literature is excluded from the "national" category by postcolonial Malaysia's ethnic hierarchy, in postcolonial Singapore (independent since the island's expulsion from the Malaysian Federation in 1965), Sinophone literature officially exists alongside national literary production in other languages, whether these languages carry indigenous (Malay), settler (Tamil), or colonizing (English) historical legacies and connotations. Yet as in Malaysia, Sinophone literature in Singapore has received an official ethnic/racial branding as "Chinese." Although here Chinese Singaporeans compose the ethnic majority, English is considered the common "interethnic" medium of communication through the discourse of "multiracialism" and "Chinese" (equated with Mandarin) is denied its internal multilingualism, both interethnic (incorporating other languages like Malay and English) and intraethnic (navigating across several commonly spoken Sinitic languages). Yet the Singaporean playwright Kuo Pao Kun reveals how the staging of a multilingual and creolized aesthetics—combining, for example, Hokkien and Tamil—presents a model of "Open Culture" that critically transgresses official state discourse (see Tan).

In their attention to language issues and politics, the chapters in part III demonstrate that multilingualism and creolization are crucial themes of Sinophone articulations across their many sites, composing the "discordant chorus" of Sinophone heteroglossia. Sinophone literature can be polyphonic, not simply intended to be read aloud in Mandarin, and the reader must also attend to the acoustics of indeed the Sino*phone* despite its visual trait. The work of the Hong Kong poet P. K. Leung, for example, is intended to be read in Cantonese: reading Leung in Cantonese amplifies the poetic resistance to the suppression of the local and the colloquial characterized by the hegemony of a vernacular literary standard based on spoken Mandarin (see Chow). One common theme of Sinophone literature is not only its resistance to an imposed Mandarin hegemony (whether in the name of ethnic or national unity/unification), but its exposure of the colonial context of that imposition. In her post-1997 rereading and reassessment of Sinophone Hong Kong literature, Mirana May Szeto foregrounds the literary articulation of resistance to the "seemingly inevitable 'vertical' relation to the cultures and traditions of the colonial and metropolitan centers, both Chinese and British." One of these sites of resistance is in the language of the literary works themselves—what Szeto calls the "Sinophone transgression"—that is exemplified, for example, in the Hong Kong author Wong Bik-wan's "stunning use of the crude Cantonese of peasant and working class Hong Kong women." The multivocality of the Sinophone gives rise to accented (re)citations, refuting the univocal claim of any national(ist) discourse, as well as calling out the disputable affiliation between language and identity.

Sinophone multilingualism and creolization may not necessarily demonstrate overt resistance to Mandarin hegemony in all their literary manifestations, but they certainly draw attention to the often highly self-conscious, politically volatile, identitarian decisions about language usage. Sinophone writers often *choose* the Sinitic script from a multilingual local milieu—a decision that is accompanied by an enormous burden with respect to one's community and is thus often not made easily or haphazardly—just as the decision for Taiwanese writers educated under Japanese imperial rule between 1895 and 1945 to write in Japanese and associate with transnational Japanese literary associations was a highly complicated one. As Chien-chung Chen points out, the belated and pejorative ascription of "fiction of imperialization" (*kōmin bungaku*) in 1943 to the work of Japanophone Taiwanese writers is indicative of this dilemma, because it suggests that Japanophone writers are complicit in their own colonization. By renaming the genre "fiction with themes of imperialization," Chen draws attention to the self-awareness of these Japanophone Taiwanese writers who also use Japanese as a medium to expose and narrate their condition of colonial subjugation.

The chapters on Taiwan account for the largest section in part III. The island's historical proximity to China, as well as its long history of serial colonization (Portuguese, Dutch, Japanese, and Chinese) and Han Chinese settler colonialism, have provided the context for a vast and diverse range of Sinophone articulations that individually demand critical attention. The four chapters included herein offer a survey of the varying and sometimes competing meanings of Taiwan as a place for different communities—Japanophone and Sinophone, settler and indigenous (Atayal, Bunun, Ami, Paiwan, etc.), so-called "Mainlander" (post-1949 settlers from China and their descendants), Taiwanese (Hoklo), and Hakka. For example, Pei-Yin Lin's chapter argues that for female writers whose families migrated to Taiwan from mainland China following the Kuomintang's (KMT) colonization of the island in 1945, Taiwan serves as a new frontier for exploring modern gender relations. Despite their nostalgia for the irrecoverable Chinese metropole of their past, these authors portray Taiwan "as a place with hopes and possibilities for renegotiating male-female relationships."

The chapters on Taiwan speak of the temporalities and relationalities of occupation and subjugation, settlement and migration, diaspora and indigeneity, and "guest" and "host" in shifting historical contexts. Chien-hsin Tsai's study of the Hakka writer Zhong Lihe offers an etymology and genealogy of "Hakka" as "a tailored example of a Sinophone articulation that bespeaks the politics of hospitality"—a term always defined through local relationships with non-Hakkas—first as ancestral guests in relation to Taiwan's aborigines, and later as hosts to Han Chinese settlers. In the case of aboriginal writers from Taiwan, the focus shifts away from ethnic Han perspectives to the other side of settler colonialism—indigenous communities that have been threatened, dislocated, displaced, and marginalized by the incursion of Han settlers. As the victims of numerous "civilizing missions" launched by different colonizing forces, aboriginal authors write in the Sinitic script to address, lament, contest, or satirize Han-centric portrayals of their communities as destitute, barbaric, primitive, or noble savages facing the disappearance of their livelihood (see Huang).

The articulations of Sinophone indigenous literature from Taiwan offer some parallels to those of Sinophone Tibetan literature. In both cases, sovereignty and self-determination are issues and themes of paramount importance. Also, the decision to write in the Sinitic script—the imposed language of the Han colonizers—is heavily fraught with and often implies a sense of *loss* of ethno-cultural identity as opposed to the reclamation of one. Sinophone Tibetan literature narrates the history of the westward continental expansion of the Chinese state (the Qing, the KMT, and finally the Chinese Communist Party [CCP]) from the perspective of the colonized Tibetan writers, several of whom are of mixed Han and Tibetan background. As Patricia Schiaffini writes, Sinophone authors exist "on the margins of Tibetanness," often "rejected as Tibetans by Tibetans" and proponents of "Tibetophone" literature (written in Tibetan), but also "treated as minority 'second class citizens' by the Chinese." Carlos Rojas, for example, describes the award-winning Sinophone Tibetan author Alai as "balanced on the knife-edge between an idealized national unity and the ethnic fault lines that perennially threaten to compromise that unity from within."

While part III, and indeed this entire volume, is heavily weighted toward the articulations of Sinophone literature emerging from the historical contexts of settler colonialism and overseas emigration, the case of Sinophone Tibetan literature in particular points to the glaring need to tend to and critically assess the cultural production of other non-Han communities, such as Uyghur and Mongolian, whose Sinophone articulations are tied to the legacies of the continental colonial expansion of the Qing empire.[3] Carles Prado-Fonts's chapter on the canonical modern Chinese author Lao She, for example, takes a step in this direction through a reexamination of the author's "double peripheral condition," both as a Sinophone writer in London, where Lao She reflected upon his Chinese national identity in the context of experiencing white racism, and as a Manchu writer in a modern China where the dominant strain of anticolonial Han Chinese nationalism was also formulated through expressions of anti-Manchu sentiment. Such analyses of the relationship between issues of language, ethnicity, and national identity, as well as conditions of coloniality and marginality, articulated from those sites "inherited" by successive Chinese regimes and now incorporated into the contemporary People's Republic of China's (PRC) (post)socialist model of multiculturalism offer a critical roadmap for future Sinophone studies.

Notes

1. Shu-mei Shih, *Visuality and Identity: Sinophone Articulations Across the Pacific* (Berkeley: University of California Press, 2007), 4.

2. Ibid., 185.

3. To call attention to Qing China's well-run colonial administrations is "to *open a space* for multiple forms of imperialisms and colonialisms, so that their historically particular and local manifestations can be discussed within the shared framework of postcolonial concerns" (Emma Jinhua Teng, *Taiwan's Imagined Geography: Chinese Colonial Travel Writing and Pictures, 1683–1895* [Cambridge: Harvard University Asia Center, 2004], 254).

11

Intra-Local and Inter-Local Sinophone

Rhizomatic Politics of Hong Kong Writers Saisai and Wong Bik-wan

MIRANA MAY SZETO

Vertical Articulation Under Erasure

Studies on Hong Kong culture "throughout the 1980s and 1990s—have often been assessed in terms of an overarching discourse, namely, the '1997 factor'"[1] and Hong Kong "in-between two colonizers,"[2] Britain and China. Such understandings of Hong Kong in vertical relation to the two dominant cultures have overwhelmingly "consolidated" into one "dominant viewpoint,"[3] overshadowing other variable readings, leaving the complicated dynamics of the intra-local and inter-local largely unexamined. A rereading after 1997 will likely reveal that many of the same works have in fact consistently questioned and elided these usual analytical frameworks and have gone beyond this vertical fixation to open up critical visions of an intra-locally and inter-locally related Hong Kong. It is not hard to find that a neglected horizontal Sinophone vision has been attentively portrayed all along.

Despite the generational and stylistic difference between Hong Kong writers Saisai (1938–)[4] and Wong Bik-wan (1961–),[5] they are both representative of Hong Kong's seasoned veterans of colonial global capitalism. Saisai, for example, can laugh at the drama of Hong Kong's spectacular growth[6] with the same ease that she deals with Hong Kong's status as "the doormat of a grand nation."[7] Feeling as entitled to Chinese cultural resources as she is familiar with European or Latin American influences, she concentrates on the quiet study of local Hong Kong's humble ordinariness and diversity, with details laid out like a Chinese scroll painting,[8] a Chinese medicine cabinet,[9] or a close reading of René Magritte's paintings.[10] She analyzes local street scenes and cultural phenomena not with the anxious claim of a local informant, but with the unimposing curiosity and "zero degree"[11] innocence of an alien observer. Like an archaeologist of the present in the future anterior tense, she records the fleeting presence of Hong Kong culture disappearing fast in her works like *Flying Carpet* and *My City*. Even the contemplation of Hong Kong's cultural marginality and hybridity is done with seasoned humor and intercultural references, such as in "Southern Barbarian"[12] and "The Fertile Town Chalk Circle."[13]

In the case of Wong Bik-wan, whether her works are read as national allegories, the usual women's writing, or in comparison to Lu Xun, Zhang Ailing, or Wang Anyi,[14] she has a set of tactics ready.[15] Literary studies tend to introduce writers in terms of their ambition vis-à-vis giants in the canon.[16] However, what is most interesting about the works of Wong and Saisai is rather their resistance against this seemingly inevitable "vertical" relation to the cultures and traditions of the colonial and metropolitan centers, both Chinese and British. Knowing that "vertical resistance" unwisely enhances the center by allowing it to remain the focus[17] and thereby, limits the vision and creative scope of the marginal, these creolized colonial subjects[18] cannibalize their multicultural heritage matter-of-factly.

A student recalls Professor Leo Ou-fan Lee giving a talk on the twin cities, Hong Kong and Shanghai, at the University of Hong Kong. After his lecture, a student naïvely asks, "why not Hong Kong and Tokyo?" For generations of Hong Kong people who have no living memory of the pre-1949 Shanghai, whose cultural link to China has been cut short by decades of Cold War under British colonialism, Hong Kong's cultural creativity is, indeed, much more intimately related to resources from Japan, Latin America, Eastern Europe, and New York rather than Shanghai.[19]

Moreover, in the age of *gaige kaifang* (Reform and Liberation), the difference that Chinese artists used to hold against the decadent capitalist world of Hong Kong has long been eroded. In an uncanny manner, the worst ghosts that Hong Kong stands for have become Shanghai's defining characteristics: kitsch, money, museumized colonial architecture, Shanghai *baobei*,[20] and nostalgia.[21] The vertical Hong Kong-Shanghai binary, China's "compulsion to claim precedence" and ownership are all undone,[22] as in Wong's collection of essays *Postcolonial Chronicles*:

> Hong Kong is not New York and London, will never be. New York and London are forced to acquire their diversity from their history. New York as a port of entry for immigrants, London as the ex-metropolitan center of the empire. If they had a choice, the Brits would want a white London. . . .

Shanghai can claim to be cosmopolitan because it looks European. It was a tiny little colony. . . . Why do we only dare to remember the Shanghai of Zhang Ailing, with the White Russian piano teacher, tap water and trams returning to their depot, but not the Shanghai of Rou Shi, Yan Fu and the 24 revolutionary martyrs?[23]

What begs contemplation is the historical amnesia in the suturing of colonial and Cold War history in some inter-Chinese studies. In the mainstream diasporic Chinese cultural imaginary of Shanghai, Hong Kong is merely a surrogate time and place, borrowed to suture the pre-1940s to post-1980s Shanghai. Hong Kong offers a familiar framework through which China can be reincorporated back to the capitalist worldview without having to deal with its Communist past. As Wong Bik-wan pointed out, people would rather look back to the trauma of invasion and semicolonialism in sensuous nostalgia than face up to the real Communist transformation of Shanghai into a paradigm proletariat city, which in fact created the material base for Shanghai's present transformation into the factory of the world, and the present exploitation of the *xiagang* and migrant workers. In this global capitalist suturing, the denizens of the colonized underclass, the racial others and migrant populations, all fall through the cracks. Thus, horizontally imagined Sinophone narratives that do not suture complex regional and local dynamics must take a different turn.

Rhizomatic Nomadology: Sinophone Subaltern Transnationalism

Refusing to massage the muscles of Westerncentrism and Sinocentrism through vertically imagined identity politics, Wong and Saisai's cultural and affective affinities are horizontal and rhizomatic.[24] The "Sinophone's favorite modes" tend to be "intertextual," "critical constellations" of the past and the present. They open toward a "nonlinear and discontinuous," "transnational and yet historically specific, imagined community."[25] They articulate "difference, contradiction, contingency" and "necessity" into "larger discursive" fields.[26]

Saisai's work is representative of this Sinophone, rhizomatic connectivity in Hong Kong literature. Her work connects with the enamored local audience because of her ability to open up intra-local, subaltern sensitivities to accommodate the greater issues of the day. As such, even her pre-1997 works covering the past 150 years of Hong Kong culture succeed to underlie the post 1997 sentiments in the city, where the preservation of vibrant old communities and traditional creative industries has converged into preservation movements burning all across the city, garnering broad-based, cross-class, and race alliances. The catalyst is the 2007 movement to preserve Queen's Pier from demolition. Significantly, this is not about colonial nostalgia for a British ceremonial pier. More important is the significance of the pier as a favorite grassroots public space, a sanctuary for Filipino migrant workers, a place of importance to silenced subaltern histories of local social movements, which gave birth to struggles for democracy, cultural rights, workers' rights, and anticolonial movements. This movement announces the quotidian effort to decolonize governmentality, to democratize city planning and policy, to preserve living subaltern heritage, and to insist on the quality of public space. The continuous reading and burning of Saisai's work *My City* in this preservation movement emblematize for the local citizenry the brutality of neoliberal privatization and destruction of their beloved city (see figure 11.1). The scenes in Saisai's 1996 *Flying Carpet* about local heritage preservation and its archaeology of transient local cityscapes and quotidian ways of life have been poignantly rediscovered during these struggles over local cultural entitlement. Thus, against the global and national denial of local historical agency and efforts of decolonization, Saisai's work emblematizes for Hong Kong people a vibrant local subjectivity in its production of vernacular chronicles and quotidian archaeologies.

What is most important is that Saisai's portrayals of everyday life are always already inclusive and intra-locally diverse. Her Hong Kong chronicle, *Flying Carpet*, is inspired by Turkish, Persian, German, British, and Chinese culture jam in Hong Kong. Unlike the neatly woven carpet (*tan*), hers is in fact a Turkish felt (*zhan*),[27] produced by the careful, arduous matting and meshing of forgotten legends, submerged histories, disappearing landscapes, and runaway fantasies. The symbolic flying mat is brought to Fertile Town by the Turkish merchant Fahriye (Hualiye). The overarching romance is intercultural, crystalized in the insomniac flights of his son Fahri Baba (Hualibaba) on his "Flying Carpet" together with the sleep-walking Cantonese beauty Fa Yim-ngan (Hua Yanyan).[28] The extended local Fa family and the neighborhood embrace the boy Fahri Baba into their social fabric without neatly weaving him in, all the while catering to his religious and cultural differences. Alike, they embrace the German entrepreneur Golz (Guluosi) and the fiercely independent wet nurse Mama Chang of pirate ancestry with the same large-hearted care as they cherish their own nerdy uncles Fa One and Fa Two, and their strangely disappearing Fa Three and his wife, Yip Chung-sang (Ye Chongsheng), who burnt the family homes down thrice by her sudden fires of despair.[29] With the same magnanimity they navigate the transformations of local businesses, industries, and banking and educational institutions, as well as the waves of urban renewals and the rise and fall of open markets, food stalls, herbal tea shops, artisan furniture shops, tenement

Figure 11.1 Anthony Leung Po-shan, "Public Act of Private Hearing: 'Book Burning' at the Queen's Pier," April 22 and 25, 2007. A burnt fragment of Xixi's novel *My City*, pp. 15–16. In this performance, each audience personally listens to the artist's recitation of two pages from the novel about the city of Hong Kong, which is then burnt, signifying the gradual destruction of the material heritage/basis in this city though which the cities stories can be embodied and told. (Photo courtesy of Poon Chi Hung.)

housing, and the like. In the chronicles of Fertile Town, everyone's travails are memorable, and the errand boy is just as legendary as anybody else.

Echoing Saisai's exuberant, intra-local diversity, Wong Bik-wan traverses the inter-local oral histories and oracular voices of the "wretched of the earth."[30] Her Cantonese working class women and peasants are imagined in affinity with the Romani "gypsies," the Communist rebels in Cuba, the nomadic Hakka women, and the migrating diasporic Chinese. Wong forces the Chinese language to accommodate cultural and ethnic differences. Hong Kong women's underclass Cantonese merges into the rhythm of the Flamenco, jams with the syntax of Spanish, and bursts into Hakka folk songs.

The connecting figure is the *Meixingzhe*,[31] the charming ascetic, who traverses the suffering of humanity.[32] This figure subverts the patriarchal interpretation of *meixing* in the *Lüshi chunqiu*, where it refers to the subdued and demure posture of the proper bride, constantly under the patriarchal gaze.[33] In *Meixingzhe*, Wong juxtaposes her personal Hakka heritage with the European Gypsy heritage. Wong becomes a travelling character, her Hakka mountain song heard within the intersubjective voice of the Romani Gypsy woman: "a Chinese woman, possibly a Mexican woman, I do not know. She comes from afar, why come from afar, your language I do not know. But she sings for us":

In the west the sun descends into hazy yellow
In my room so dimly lit, I cast a solitary shadow
Thinking of you makes the day an eternal glare
Yearning for you makes the night hardest to bear.[34]

The Hakka's exclusion by resident Chinese communities parallels the persecution of the Romani Gypsies by the Europeans. The Hakka and Romani, neither only nomad nor permanently settled, reminds us of a transnational Sinophone sensibility, a "mobile conception of homeness that is also more place-based." Together, they "decouple homeness and origin, and politicize routes and roots."[35] In the language of tarot cards, Wong writes about the sufferings of the Bohemian and Romani Gypsies in Auschwitz. Romani "grandma Red Hair Baba's . . . number in Auschwitz was M 1313. . . . M is also the thirteenth letter in the alphabet." Before she can read the thirteenth card in her set, the whole family was sent to Auschwitz.[36] But in the end, she did not die, although 1,300,000 Gypsies were killed in the concentration camps, even more than the Jews. She, the survivor, reduced to bare life, is like the subaltern Hakka persecuted during the *Taiping Tianguo* in China[37] or the victims among warring Balkan ethnicities. Their transnational "linguistic dissonance," their "heteroglossia"[38] are articulated through the "multiaccented"[39] Sinophone writings of Wong.

These stories show an inter-local resonance between Wong Bik-wan's subaltern women and what Giorgio Agamben conceives as the *Homo Sacer*, the Greek concept of bare life (*zoē*). The *homo sacer* is the one banned and scapegoated from society, both as the sacred and the damned. Thus, killing her does not constitute murder or sacrifice. She is the opposite of the martyr, whose "sacrifice" agrees with the values of the dominant. The Chinese rendering of bare life (*cangsheng*) as comparable to ants (*liuyi*) evokes a similar meaning. To those in power, they are but dispensable lives, not even considered human. Thus, to Wong, the ethical representation of bare lives must desanctify and de-aestheticize sacrifice.

Sinophone Subaltern Resistance: The CUNTonese of the *lienü*

Thus, when Hakka women do appear in the local dynastic chronicles rendered in Wong's *Meixingzhe*, they appear as a very particular kind of *lienü*. During the Chongzhen reign, one strategist suggested a way to invade a city by offsetting its power with the foulest of all matter—the cunt. Thus, more than a hundred women were rounded up, their heads and limbs chopped off, their cunts exposed, to counter the city's cannons. One such woman was a Hakka. Her leg severed, her cunt exposed, she was dying and unable to move when the city showered cannons over the field and all the men ran. Incredibly, she did not die. They gave her the infamous title Lazy Corpse Ma. From then on, Hakka people call prostitutes who languish lazily in bed Lazy Corpse Ma.[40] Thus, while the patriarchal community condemns its victim, she nonetheless survives, like a wart on the page of the scholar official's annals.

Rather than succumbing to the lure of collective and traditional concepts of victimhood, Wong offers a very different conception of these transgressive women by transforming the traditional Chinese understanding of a radical woman—a *lienü*. Traditionally, women enter history positively only when they go to extremes of martyrdom and self-sacrifice for upholding their community's Confucian virtues. In Wong, the traditional pious woman's (*lienü*) extreme sacrifice has become the extreme (*baolie*) tactics of transgressive women. The sense of extremity in the term *lie* in Wong's work is no longer directed toward excessive obedience to patriarchal, national, and communal imperatives, but has been taken as an extreme and violent form of transgression that confounds those very values.

It is against the threat of being cannibalized by colonial, national, and patriarchal identity that these women's paradoxical violence must be understood.

They are surviving as unprotected bare life, decomposing and scavenging the violence of the nation and the patriarchal home. Their politics cannot be understood in the existing political terms of their community, nor can this *"dirty feminism,"* which questions the dubiousness of law and morality, be incorporated easily by feminism itself. No matter how violent their experience, Wong's *lienü* neither give up nor give in. They refuse sympathy, resist "fate" ruthlessly, and devour suffering with a formidable, unrepentant savagery.

This subaltern Sinophone transgression is embedded in Wong's stunning use of the crude Cantonese of peasant and working class Hong Kong women in *Lienütu*, written with the pronoun *you*. The voice of "your" maternal grandma Sung Heung tells "you" the story of another maternal grandma Lam Hing (Lin Qing), the child bride. She carried her sickly child husband across the hills from the New Territories to Kowloon to see the doctor. After she carried him back, she had to immediately work in the fields, make compost, and fetch firewood. Exhausted and hungry, she went to the kitchen for some food, only to be driven out by her mother-in-law Li with a broom. She was so hungry she stole Granny Choi's potatoes, but got whacked in the head with a spade. When her menstrual blood came, her child husband was already dead. From then on, "the father-in-law of your maternal grandma pulled down her trousers, and pricked his hairy noxious dick right into her deep cunt . . . pushing, pulling, pushing, pulling, until, ah, he makes out." After raping her, he slapped her for not being a virgin. The one before was her uncle, who raped her in the cowshed. He "shuffled a handful of hay into her mouth, pushing, pulling, pushing, pulling." That was why her mother sold her as a child bride.[41]

But your grandma Lam Hing did not give up. She killed her father and mother-in-law, left Fei Ngo Shan, and married the handsome Ah Yuet Zai, who is half Cuban half Chinese. However, he already had a wife. Alas, the men were useless, the rich ones smoked opium, the poor ones gambled, but Lam Hing did not give in on her desires. She went after other men, like Ah Biu, the sailor. Your mom Lam Bao-bao (Lin Baobao) is the daughter with Ah Biu.[42] Moreover, the first wife Sung Heung and the concubine Lam Hing reconciled. When Lam Hing gave birth to your mom, it was Sung Heung who asked the wet nurse to bring her *danggui* soup. In turn, when your grandma Sung Heung broke her arm, your grandma Lam Hing came to see her and chatted about that doctor, already seventy, "teeth falling off, face like a rotten winter melon," still wanting to crawl on her breasts "like a blind-mute monkey on a papaya tree." The two old women giggled.[43]

In the end, after surviving all the atrocities, the old women came together at the mahjong table. "Your maternal grandma Sung Heung fell and broke her arm, but managed to drag herself over to her sister Sung Jing's place to play mahjong with their neighbors Granny Chan and Long Leg Six. The two sisters, one with a broken arm, one half paralyzed, each played with one hand. Granny Chan had cancer of the bladder and a urine bag on the side. Long Leg Six was diabetic, had her rotten leg amputated, and was still in her plaster casting. The four of them, with six hands, seven feet and one urine bag, played eight hours of glorious mahjong. Long Leg Six died the very next day."[44]

Thus, Wong Bik-wan makes "use of the polylingualism" of her own language to make us hear the gruesome but also triumphant oral histories of peasant women, from the Ming to contemporary Hong Kong. Her Hakka-infused crude peasant Cantonese forces itself into standard written Chinese (*shumianyu*), to make a "minor or intensive use" of it.[45] She opposes the "oppressed quality" of underclass Cantonese to the "oppressive quality" of *shumianyu*. This Sinophone intervention invents "linguistic Third World zones" in the major Chinese language through the "willed poverty" of the underclass Cantonese. In its very poverty, this minor language decomposes and scavenges the violence of patriarchal language. With the blunt CUNTonese deterritorialized out of the foul mouths of men, these women "proceed by dryness and sobriety" to "arrive at a materially intense expression"[46] of profound suffering, unrepentant savagery and triumphant survival.

Sinophone Rhizomatic Nomadology: The Subaltern Charming Ascetic

There are no/mad women in this attic.
Berteke Waaldijk

When Wong Bik-wan's women are stuck and stay put, they find alternative lines of flight through what Deleuze and Guattari calls nomadology. Nomads fare miserably under today's national regimes, but nonetheless, they insist on maintaining their patterns of inhabiting a landscape despite their being forced to move. Thus, nomado-logic in struggles is hard to maintain, like "the Bedouin galloping, knees on the saddle, sitting on the soles of" her/his "upturned feet . . . a feat of balance."[47] It is about letting go but not letting down: the stance of the *meixingzhe*. In this way, the working class women in Hong Kong take flight in Wong Bik-wan's *Lienütu*. Your mom Ngun Chi and your mom Tai Hei were lesbians stuck in factory jobs. They were called names: Double braids sisters, Tofu-po, Leftist girls. But they each took a different path, following their desires. Ngun Hei followed other leftists back to

China from 1959 to 1961[48] while Dai Hei joined the sister's hostel with other girls from the factory. When Ngun Chi was in China, there was a great famine and all the leftist guys chickened out. She therefore, returned to Hong Kong and married someone who understood her political passions.[49] Dai Hei's love was unrequited, but she does not give in. Every time when ordinary Hong Kong people took to the streets, the two would somehow find each other again. The April 1966 anti-Star Ferry price hike demonstration developed into riots in Nathan Road.[50] Ngun Chi, now a mom, wrote big banners and went to the demonstration. Dai Hei put on men's clothes and joined her, sleeping and demonstrating together (Chapter 23). Then twenty years passed. With their daughters they meet again at the 1989 march against the Tiananmen Massacre, hand in hand again.[51] Thus, their liberating subjectivities are still alive and kicking, despite being told to stay put in life. They can actually travel far around their kitchen sink.

Other women in Wong Bik-wan's oeuvre take more drastic transcontinental mental and physical drifts. They discover that "to forget is not knowing that you forgot."[52] The *meixingzhe* becomes a wandering journalist in search of a female rebel, Tania, a double spy and a guerrilla fighter in Latin America (see figure 11.2). Here, Wong learns to use Spanish punctuations and syntax, but in her own way, flipping the upside-down question mark from right facing to left facing, like the leftist politics of the woman she pursues (see figure 11.3).

As a spy, "Tania's" identity is forever slippery. *Meixingxhe*, the narrator, goes in search of her in just as slippery a manner, using a fake visa from the US to enter Cuba via Mexico. Her meandering trajectory is both multiphonic and graphically like the embodied physicality of the English novel, *Tristram Shandy* (see figure 11.4).[53]

What she discovers in Cuba however, is not the magic formula of freedom, but its greatest risk, a biting but empowering irony: to forget is to be free, to be homeless is to be at home with oneself. Thus, what she discovers is not the glory of revolution, but the striking similarity between ordinariness and life's horrors, between ordinariness and triumphant living, whether in Communist China and Cuba, or in capitalist Hong Kong. This is expressed in her very interesting translation between Chinese and Spanish:

> "He reads from his note book, in Chinese: Greatness–Victory–Eternity" and "teaches me the Spanish, ¡Hasta la victorie Siempre!"
> "I smiled and said, do you know, Everyday—Failure—Always?"[54]

The travelling ascetic grounds her transculturally inspired awakening in humility.

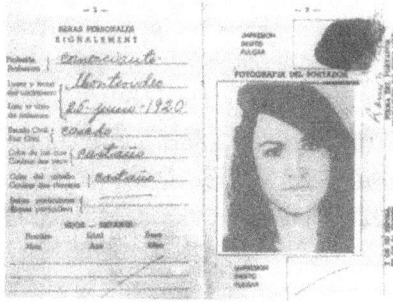

”那不是她。“

”﹖她在這裡做甚麼？“

”她一定有甚麼不可告人的目的。“

我慌忙闔上了護照。莎維拉是座漂亮的殖民地建築，米黃色，窗子高高的，窗外哈瓦那的藍天那麼藍，那麼遠，那麼高，微笑那麼大——不對，那是個人的微笑，蔗糖色的一個人，站在窗前看我，大大的微笑著。我站起來，啐貓一樣啐他，急起來，就說廣東話：喂，你做乜。那個蔗糖人還給我揮揮手，就不見了。窗上留他留下的一個印記，

Figure 11.2 Page 213 of the novel *Meixingzhe* with Tania's fake/true passport. In the text, we see the Spanish punctuations being flipped left to right and right to left deliberately.

Tania, in Buenos Aires, writes a poem:

Thus, thus ¿ must I depart? ¿ like withering flowers?

My name, will be forgotten

¿ Can we not leave behind something in this world?

Could there still be, flowers and song

Figure 11.3 This is my translation of a fragment of the poem supposedly written by Tania in April 1966, taken from the novel *Meixingzhe*, p. 209. I have kept the punctuation and syntax intact.

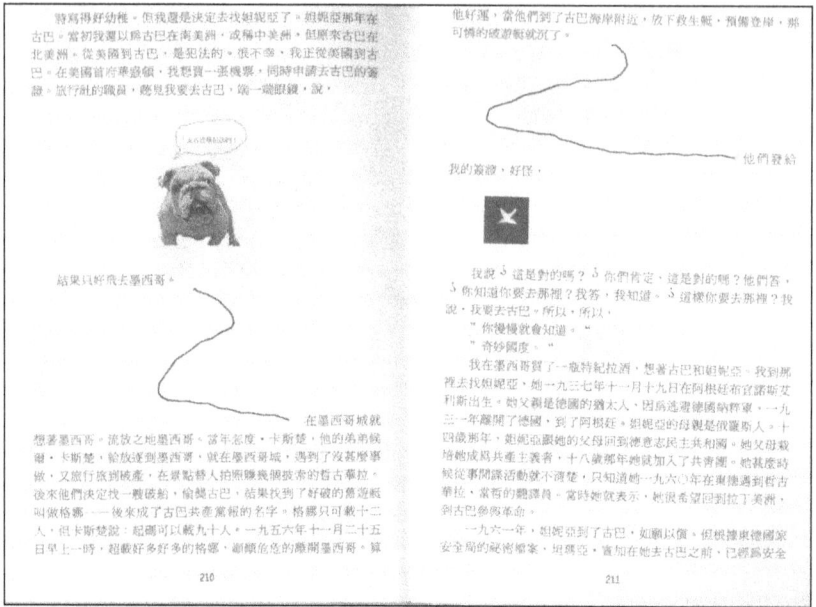

Figure 11.4 The Tristram Shandy-like representation of Tania's meandering trajectory (from the novel *Meixingzhe*, pp. 210–211).

Conclusion

Whether one is humbled by the inter-local pathos of Wong's dignified subaltern women, or uplifted by the endearing intra-local flights of Saisai's diverse communities, one is impressed by the polyphonic, complex dynamics of Sinophone politics in Hong Kong literature. These writers bring forth the best of Hong Kong literature's strength in humility, the quiet composure of a seasoned postcolonial Sinophone culture, extraordinary in its ability to accumulate local life's imperceptible traces despite the global prophesies of its disappearance.

Notes

1. Julian Stringer, "Boat People: Second Thoughts on Text and Context," in *Chinese Films in Focus: 25 New Takes*, ed. Chris Berry (London: British Film Institute, 2003), 15.

2. Rey Chow, "Between Colonizers: Hong Kong's Postcolonial Self-Writing in the 1990s," *Diaspora* 2, no. 2 (1992): 151–170.

3. See Stephen Teo, *Hong Kong Cinema: The Extra Dimensions* (London: British Film Institute, 1997); Patricia Brett Erens, "The Film Work of Ann Hui," in *The Cinema of Hong Kong: History, Arts, Identity*, ed. Poshek Fu and David Desser (Cambridge: Cambridge University Press, 2000), 176–194; Leung Ping-kwan, "Urban Cinema and the Cultural Identity of Hong Kong," in Fu and Desser, *The Cinema of Hong Kong: History, Arts, Identity*, 242.

4. I will use Cantonese romanization for the Hong Kong writers throughout. Saisai in Cantonese romanization and Xi Xi in Mandarin pinyin is the pseudonym of the popular Hong Kong novelist and poet Cheung Yin (Zhang Yan). She is Cantonese, was born in Shanghai and settled in Hong Kong with her family since she was twelve. She has published more than twenty volumes of fiction, ten volumes of essays, and two volumes of poetry, with translations in various languages. She is the winner of multiple literary awards both local and global, including the prestigious *Huazong shijie huawen wenxue* award of 2005.

5. Wong Bik-wan in Cantonese romanization (Huang Biyun in Putonghua) was born into a Hong Kong Hakka family, did her high school partially in Taiwan, and returned to Hong Kong for degrees in journalism, criminology, and law. She has published fifteen volumes of fiction and two volumes of essays and cultural critiques. A winner of multiple literary awards, both local and abroad, she is also an experienced war-zone reporter, a practicing lawyer, and dances the Flamenco in earnest.

6. See Saisai, "The Story of Fertile Town" (*Feitu zhen de gushi*) in *Huzi youlian* (Taipei: Hongfan shudian, 1986), 39–80. The soil infused with the by-products from nerdy uncle Fa One and Fa Two's experiments became so fertile and famous it was bought all over town and by tourists and companies throughout the world. However, the consumers soon got overridden by the monstrous growths emerging from the soil.

7. Saisai, *Fei zhan* [Flying carpet] (Hong Kong: Sue Yeh Publishing, 1996), 5.

8. The comparison of Saisai's work to the famous scroll *Along the River During Qingming Festival* by the North Song painter Zhang Zeduan is made by the literary critic He Furen in "One reading of *My City*" in *Wo cheng* [My city], by Saisai (Taipei: Yunshen, 1986), 219–230.

9. A comparison made by Saisai herself, in her novel *Meili daxia* [Beautiful building] (Taipei: Hongfan shudian, 1990), 175.

10. This is how Saisai's "Marvels of a Floating City" is written, a sarcastic, surrealist comment on the local through a conjunctive analysis of the paintings of Belgian artist René Magritte.

11. Hong Kong writer Dung Kai-cheung (Dong Qizhang) argues that Saisai's tone of naïveté is not an attempt to be childlike as is often supposed. Coming from an adult character with a high school degree and a technician's job, this wide-eyed curiosity about ordinary objects like the typewriter is written not with affected ignorance, but rather, is the result of a "zero degree" writing that aims at recording the present as if it is experienced for the first time. See Dung Kai-cheung, "Actual and Textual Experience of a City: Reading *Drunkard, My City* and *Paper Cuttings*," in *Hong Kong Literature as/and Cultural Studies*, ed. Cheung Mei-kwan and Chu Yiu-wai (Hong Kong: Oxford University Press, 2002), 394–407.

12. In the story "Southern Barbarian" is the name of the narrator's pet, a lama glama from Peru, neither camel nor goat, a gift from her aunt in Latin America. This is a good-natured displacement of the dominant vertical cultural imagination of China-Hong Kong by linking the story of a Hong Kong retiree to an old aunt married to a multicultural family spread all

over Latin America. Saisai, "Southern Barbarian" (*Nan man*), in *Muyu* [Mother fish] (Taipei: Hongfan shudian, 1990), 63–107.

13. She draws upon Persian, Chinese, and German literary antecedents of the "chalk circle" legend. Thematic localization happens through a traditionally silent character, the boy in Saisai's "The Fertile Town Chalk Circle," who speaks out against the silencing of his voice. As a child, his sophisticated analysis of the duel between two hostile camps of adults making claims on him parallels the neglect of Hong Kong people's opinions in the Sino-British negotiations over Hong Kong's political future. Saisai, "The Fertile Town Chalk Circle" (*Feitu zhen huilan ji*), in *Shoujuan* [Hand scrolls] (Taipei: Hongfan shudian, 1988), 77–120.

14. Other scholars have done magnificent studies in illustrating how Wong Bik-wan relates her own work to that of Lu Xun, Zhang Ailing, and Wang Anyi. See, David Der-wei Wang, "Hong Kong: Story of a City," in *The Making of the Modern, the Making of a Literature: New Perspectives on 19th and 20th Century Chinese Fiction* (Taipei: Maitian, 1998), 279–305; David Der-wei Wang, "Preface: Violent Gentleness: Huang Biyun's Fiction," in Huang Biyun, *Shiernüse* (Taipei: Maitian, 2000), 9–36. For a study of the relation between Wong Bik-wans's work and women's writing, see Liu Liang-ya, "Love and Desire in Hong Kong: Women and Hong Kong Subjectivity in Huang Biyun's Lienütu," in *Gender, Sexuality, and the Fin de Siècle: Studies in Erotic Fictions* (Taipei: Jiuge, 2001), 165–196.

15. Wong did not waste her major novel-length works on such "vertical models of resistance." With a kind of studied impatience, she quickly dealt with such issues in some of her earlier short stories. Like cannon to canons, she throws creative myths both East and West on their heads. Like meanness to meaning, she cannibalizes: Lu Xun's seminal "Diary of a Madman" and his rewriting of creation myths in *Old Stories Retold*; Guo Pu and Hao Yixing's *The Book of Mountains and Seas*; Liu Xiang's *Stories of Exemplarious Women*; the "Youyuan jingmeng" act of Tang Xianzu's *The Peony Pavilion*; the Bible's "Genesis" and "Book of Revelations," and Nietzsche.

16. Like how Huang Nian-xin has aptly written about Wong Bik-wan in Huang Nian-xin, "Reminiscence of a Life Foretold—Preliminary Study of the Anxiety of Tradition: Huang Biyun vs. Zhang Ailing," in Wong Bik-wan, *Shiernüse*, 259–274.

17. Françoise Lionnet and Shu-mei Shih (eds.), *Minor Transnationalism* (Durham and London: Duke University Press, 2005), 3–4.

18. The idea comes from the concept of "créolité" in Jean Bernabé, Patrick Chamoiseau, and Raphaël Confiant, *Éloge de la Créolité/In Praise of Creoleness* (Gallimard: 1993 / John Hopkins University Press: 1990, edition bilingue, 1997).

19. More Hong Kong people would have read Murakami Haruki, Gabriel Garcia Marquez, Milan Kundera, and Paul Auster rather than Wang Anyi.

20. Wei Hui, *Shanghai Baby* (New York: Washington Square Press, 2001).

21. For a broad outline of these characteristic cultural analyses of Shanghai, see Ban Wang, "Love at Last Sight: Nostalgia, Memory, and Commodity in Contemporary Chinese Literature," in *Illuminations from the Past: Trauma, Memory, and History in Modern China* (Stanford University Press, 2004), 212–234.

22. Shu-mei Shih, *Visuality and Identity: Sinophone Articulations Across the Pacific* (Berkeley: University of California Press, 2007), 37.

23. Wong Bik-wan, *Houzhimin zhi* [The postcolonial chronicles] (Hong Kong: Tiandi, 2004), 237–8. Similarly, Zhang Xudong examines the privileging of Zhang Ailing as the "origin" of a rewriting of modern Chinese literary history in Taiwan and diasporic Chinese literary history from the 1950s to the 1980s and beyond. He criticizes "the current Zhang craze" and craze for "Zhang's Shanghai" as a "coercive ideological discourse of free-market dogmatism and empathy with a bourgeois universal history." Zhang Xudong, "Shanghai Nostalgia: Postrevolutionary Allegories in Wang Anyi's Literary Production in the 1990s," *Positions: East Asia cultures critiques* 8, no. 2 (2000): 354.

24. Gilles Deleuze and Félix Guattari, *A Thousand Plateaus: Capitalism and Schizophrenia*, trans. Brian Massumi (London: Atlone Press, 1988); Gilles Deleuze and Félix Guattari, *Kafka: Towards a Minor Literature*, trans. Dana Polan (Minneapolis: University of Minnesota Press, 1986); Gilles Deleuze, "Nomad Thought," in *The New Nietzsche: Contemporary Styles of Interpretation*, ed. David B. Allison (Boston: MIT Press, 1985).

25. Shih, *Visuality and Identity: Sinophone Articulations across the Pacific*, 35–36.

26. Ibid., 35.

27. The metaphor of felt is important to the form of this novel. Felt is the oldest form of fabric known to humankind, some remains of which were found in Turkey, dating back at least to 6,500 b.c.e.

28. Wong Bik-wan, *Flying Carpet*, 204–205.

29. Ibid., 77–81, 110–111, 144, 150–155, 158, 169–170, 188–189, 202–205, 234–238.

30. Frantz Fanon, *The Wretched of the Earth* (New York: Grove Press, 2004).

31. *Meixing/zhe* or *mei/xingzhe*: the demure and alluring woman and/or the charming ascetic.

32. Wong Bik-wan, *Meixingzhe* (Taiwan: Datian, 2000); Wong Bik-wan, *Chenmo, anya, weixiao* [Reticence, muteness, humility] (Hong Kong: Tiandi / Taiwan: Datian, 2004). In *both novels,* the charming ascetic empathizes with those who suffer.

33. Lü Buwei, *The Annals of Lü Buwei*, trans. John Knoblock and Jeffrey Riegel (Stanford: Stanford University Press, 2000), 18/6.4 "Bu qu" (Not Complying): "When the bride first arrives at his home, she is compliant, shyly squints her eyes, and acts seductive" (463–464).

34. Wong, *Meixingzhe*, 161–163.

35. Shih, *Visuality and Identity: Sinophone Articulations across the Pacific*, 190.

36. Wong, *Meixingzhe*, 187–188.

37. Ibid., 172–174.

38. Shih, *Visuality and Identity: Sinophone Articulations across the Pacific*, 4.

39. Ibid., 38.

40. Wong, *Meixingzhe*, 185.

41. Wong Bik-wan, *Lienütu* (Taiwan: Datian, 1999), 29–32.

42. Ibid., 114.

43. Ibid., 108.

44. Ibid., 27.

45. Deleuze and Guattari, *Kafka: Towards a Minor Literature*, 27.

46. Ibid., 19.

47. Gilles Deleuze and Félix Guattari, *A Thousand Plateaus: Capitalism and Schizophrenia*, trans. Brian Massumi. London: Atlone Press, 1988, 381.

48. Wong, *Lienütu*, 138.
49. Ibid., 157.
50. Ibid., 164.
51. Ibid., 206–207.
52. Wong, *Meixingzhe*, 106–107.
53. Ibid., 208–210.
54. Ibid., 228–230.

12

Things, Common/Places, Passages of the Port City

On Hong Kong and Hong Kong Author Leung Ping-kwan

REY CHOW

The point of this chapter is to argue, through a discussion of Hong Kong and Hong Kong author Leung Ping-kwan/Liang Bingjun (pen name Ya See/Ye Si),[1] a way of reading coloniality and colonial literature that is alternative to the perspectives that are currently available. Hong Kong, a city in which I grew up, is a particular kind of passageway, which was created by an accident of history but which nonetheless persists from the nineteenth century to the present with a uniqueness and resilience that is otherwise unknown in world history.

Hong Kong's economic success has always been interpreted more or less as the compensation for a fundamental lack, as the sign of something gone wrong. Typically, this kind of interpretation goes as follows: Hong Kong thrives economically only because it is lacking in political autonomy and self-determination. For instance, Lau Siu-kai expresses it this way:

> The closing of the political path naturally leads to whole-hearted devotion of efforts to economic pursuits, opportunities for which are plentiful. The rise of apolitical materialism is a logical response of the Hong Kong Chinese to the unequal availability of political and economic opportunities in the unique setting which they find themselves.[2]

While Lau's comments are still largely descriptive, a sense of contempt for Hong Kong's "economism" and "materialism" is much clearer in the following passage by Ackbar Abbas, largely because of the author's wit:

One of the effects of a very efficient colonial administration is that it provides almost no outlet for political idealism (until perhaps quite recently); as a result, most of the energy is directed towards the economic sphere. Historical imagination, the citizens' belief that they might have a hand in shaping their own history—this gets replaced by speculation on the property or stock markets, or by an obsession with fashion and consumerism. If you cannot choose your political leaders, you can at least choose your own clothes. We find therefore not an atmosphere of doom and gloom, but the more paradoxical phenomenon of doom and boom: the more frustrated or blocked the aspirations to "democracy" are, the more the market booms.[3]

There is no description of economics that is not at the same time a moral judgment. For Lau and Abbas, it is because the people in Hong Kong are lacking in something essential—political power—that they have to turn their energies elsewhere, to economics. And yet this elsewhere, this other development, which is assumed in an a priori manner as compensatory in function, is then judged to be superficial, excessive, and pathological. As Abbas's clever rhyme of "gloom-doom-boom" suggests, the more Hong Kong excels in its materialistic accomplishments, the more this excellence must be taken to be a sign of its deficiency, degeneracy, abnormality, and hence basic inferiority. To expose the untenability of this type of argument, we can ask a simple question: if Hong Kong's materialism is "compensatory," then how should we understand the materialism of, say, the United States, where people do have political self-determination? Would such a materialism be more "natural"?

Reading as a feminist, I suggest that this kind of discriminatory judgment about Hong Kong's materialism, even though it does not seem at first sight to have anything to do with women, can be juxtaposed with Sigmund Freud's writings on femininity. Like "Hong Kong" for many an interested observer, female sexuality for Freud (especially in his later years) was an enigmatic libidinal economy to be interpreted. And yet this fascination, which establishes a discourse for femininity to be examined closely, ironically also dismisses femininity as pathological. In Freud's readings, as is well known, femininity is a sexuality that must make up for its lack of the penis in order to be. Because this lack is viewed by Freud (rather than by women) as so very basic (since the penis is, for Freud, indispensable), femininity becomes—except in the case of motherhood in which the production of a son equals a woman's possession of a penis at long last—a tragedy, an unpleasant fate to which women's libidinal precociousness and inflexibility, which stand in contrast to men's youthfulness and spontaneity, testify. Everything women do and excel in—Freud's example is specifically the technique of plaiting and weaving—becomes simply a concealment of their fundamental lack. The better women do, then, the more they prove their shame about not having "the real thing."[4]

The juxtaposition of Freud's reading of femininity and the prevalent reading of Hong Kong's materialism reveals much more than the traditional negative equation of femininity and the city. Rather, it shows how both kinds of readings, which emerge from very different cultural contexts, nonetheless share a common premise—namely, the identification (which takes place at the invisible/inarticulate part of discourse) with established, "proper" realms of power—an identification that must, in the course of asserting itself, denigrate the non-established and the "improper." In Freud's case, the patriarchal nature of such an identification is made clear (conveniently) by the explicit content of his discourse—sexuality. However, if it is the identification with power, rather than simply the discourse about sexuality, that is symptomatic of a certain kind of masculinism, then what the juxtaposition with Freud clarifies is that in the typical dismissal of Hong Kong's materialism as disease and compensation, a dismissal that does not apparently concern sexuality or women, the forces in play are, in fact, also masculinist and misogynistic.

The analogy between Hong Kong and feminine sexuality would seem even less fortuitous once we turn to the conceptions of Hong Kong by some of the most well-known Mainland Chinese writers. From the perspective of the Mainland Chinese, Hong Kong's "lack" has to do with its coloniality, a coloniality that, in the language of sexuality, is equated with Hong Kong's loss of her sexual integrity. Consider these lines from the writer Ai Wu at the point of his departure from Hong Kong: "When the ship had travelled a good distance, there seemed to be a low, plaintive call coming from the direction of the Colony. 'Will those who love me please forgive me? I'm being raped by the British imperialists!'"[5] And this poem, "Hong Kong," by the poet Wen Yiduo:

Like the yellow panther guarding the gates of the imperial palace
Oh, Mother! my post is a strategic one, yet my status so humble.
The ferocious Sea Lion presses upon my body,
Devouring my flesh and bones and warming itself on my blood.
Oh, Mother! I wail and cry, yet you hear me not.
Oh, Mother! quick! let me hide in your embrace!
Mother! I want to come back, Mother![6]

While the male writers from contemporary Hong Kong see Hong Kong's economic success as a compensation for the basic lack of the real thing, political power, the Mainland male writers focus on Hong Kong's status as a colony.

Once again, Hong Kong's condition is analogized to certain pejorative notions of femininity. Ai Wu sees Hong Kong as a woman who has been sexually violated; Wen Yiduo sees Hong Kong as a child in need of Mom. For them, Hong Kong's "lack" becomes the occasion for Chinese political idealism. This political idealism, moreover, takes a particular form—the form of rescue. Hong Kong is, in the eyes of these passionate literary men, the maiden who cannot defend herself against the dragon, the imperialist, and must therefore be delivered from her plight by the rescue operation of a St. George. Alternately, Hong Kong is in need of a mother: she is longing to be reunited with China; her "real" source of identification is Mainland China, and so forth.

The moral righteousness of these masculinist interpretations shows us how, as a modern city, Hong Kong cannot be considered apart from the two dominant historical issues of its "economism" and its "coloniality." Given that these are the facts of Hong Kong's origins (on which I will elaborate in a moment), the question I want to raise is: Is there a way of thinking and writing about Hong Kong without repeating the compensatory logic and salvational motives of these familiar interpretations? Without attributing to Hong Kong the derogatory sense of lack or the need of a savior, how might we go about describing its uniqueness and its difference—how might we go about thinking of it as a city? Instead of asking how Hong Kong falls short of other major cities, what does Hong Kong tell us about our assumptions about cities in general? What is it about Hong Kong as a city that offers us new insights into the conceptualizations of modern city culture?

If, for the time being, we stay with the analogies of "rape" and "need for a mother," we realize that the "rescuer" of Hong Kong, the "mother" that Wen Yiduo assumed to be China proper, is itself not innocent of the crime of rape. For Ai Wu and Wen Yiduo, who were writing in the pre–World War II period, anti-imperialism from a Chinese perspective was in many ways a justifiable cause because of European and Japanese territorial aggression against China. In the 1980s and 1990s, however, anti-imperialist claims from the People's Republic become in the main a way to mask Chinese imperialism, an imperialism that is well known and very visible in areas such as Tibet and, increasingly, Hong Kong. By pointing fingers at "Western" imperialists, China veils its own violence against its people and its colonized territories. As is the case of Chinese politics after the Tiananmen Massacre of 1989, the history of "Western imperialism" and "Western colonialism" is recalled strategically as a means to gain allegiance from the people and thus make them forget China's own far from innocuous complicities. By making "the West" and "Western imperialists" their overt enemy, the People's Republic thus allows itself to hold on to the status of a victim (whose people and land are being appropriated from her) while it openly acts as a militaristic empire.

This is the reason why a contemporary Hong Kong essayist, Ha Gong, attributes the act of raping Hong Kong to China as well as Britain, revealing thus the complicity and collaboration between colonizer and "rescuer" rather than their opposition. Referring to the talks conducted since 1984 between China and Britain over Hong Kong's fate after 1997, Ha Gong offers an image that sums up Hong Kong's predicament:

> The Sino-British talks closely resemble two men gang-raping Hong Kong, with the victim being denied the right to scream or protest. After the event, a member of a certain legislative body appeared on the scene and demanded a detailed enquiry into the background of the rape. But a number of staunch supporters of rapists' rights stood up and called for the legalization of rape, shouting at the victims that they were entirely without shame.[7]

Once it is clear that the motherland itself too is a "rapist" driven by its own unscrupulous self-interest, it becomes necessary to wrest Hong Kong from the sentimental metaphors of ethnic bonding and point to the exploitative realities involved in Hong Kong's "return" to China. My point is, of course, not a defense of British colonialism, but rather that we need to dispel as well the myth of a Chinese nationalism masquerading as savior and possessor of a community that has, in fact, very little in common with the People's Republic at this point. And this, I think, is the most unique feature of Hong Kong's postcoloniality: the end of British colonialism followed by a new colonialism, that of its "motherland." Hong Kong's colonization by the People's Republic in the name of a reunion and repatriation violates the telos of the conventional thinking about coloniality, in which coloniality is followed by emancipation. Hong Kong's return to China forces us to ask, what happens when colonialism is not a past but a future, when colonialism has not yet left all its tracks but is looming in the time we normally associate with hope, change, and freedom?

It is here—at the limits of land, space, political power, self-determination, and future emancipation, all of which Hong Kong supposedly "lacks"—that I would plot my reading of Leung. In this reading, identifying what Hong Kong does not have does not mean seeing what it has in terms of compensation, since to do so would be to follow the type of interpretative move that, however well intentioned, continues to valorize and privilege what is believed to be "lacking." Instead I would suggest that cultural workers such as Leung can be seen as actively producing and remaking the very origins of Hong Kong's coloniality in their "representations." These representations do not seek the impossible task of overturning those origins, nor do they assume the mode of a *ressentiment* that envies what Hong Kong never had in the first place. Rather, these representations accept these origins as Hong Kong's fateful difference—its own libidinal economy—and invent their own survival space therein. What results is neither a compensatory transcendence of these origins nor a negative aesthetics antithetically posed toward its society, but modes of writing that become themselves a special form of passageway, a material working through the most difficult of times.

The Port City, the Common/Place

Hong Kong, like most colonial cities,[8] has always been a port. The history of Hong Kong as a city is relatively short, dating back to the mid-nineteenth century when it was ceded by China to Britain as a result of the Opium War of 1839–1842. Before then, Hong Kong was a fishing village with a population of about 7,000. As a city, therefore, Hong Kong did not evolve into its modern form of a commercial center from a long history of internal culture accumulation; it does not possess the typical symbols of long civilizations—national treasures and precious monuments—that make up the appeal of ancient cities. Far away from London and Beijing, Hong Kong has always thrived on its local cultural practices, customs, and rituals. This is one reason why, for a long time, it was dismissed as a "cultural desert." Hong Kong's cityness—that is, its international or cosmopolitan status—is indistinguishable from the violence that established it as such, namely, British mercantile imperialism. As pointed out by some scholars, Britain's acquisition of Hong Kong was much less motivated by territorial gain than by the wish to have a point of entry into the "Far East." In acquiring Hong Kong,

> what was sought was a commercial and not a territorial empire, and the island was taken over reluctantly, primarily for the purpose of establishing the necessary organs of law and order and administration, free from Chinese intervention or control. . . . The Colony was not thought of in terms of territorial gain, but as the minimum space required for what were thought to be the necessary British institutions. Its function was to be the headquarters of British trade, administration and general influence in the Far East.[9]

With its coloniality, then, economics and commerce are Hong Kong's "origins"; there has never been any alternative social framework. When critics lament and disapprove of Hong Kong's mercenary degeneracy, they are ignoring and forgetting these origins. What they need to come to terms with,

I suggest, is not the extent of this degeneracy, but the ways Hong Kong has carved out its own space in the past century and a half within the environment permitted by this originary violence—not, in other words, how Hong Kong makes up for its lack, but what it has made of this lack, this original exploitation, which is its only condition of possibility.

Etymologically, the word *port* illuminates all the aspects of Hong Kong's "origins" that are suppressed in the eventual interpretations of the city. *Port* refers, of course, to Hong Kong's status as an entrepôt, an entrance point or portal to China and Asia. It also refers to Hong Kong's amazing economic development, to Hong Kong's status as a vast emporium with a plenitude of exports and imports. More significantly, though, it alludes to the transporting function that is part and parcel of Hong Kong's intended role as a carrier of valuables and values between cultures. In performing this function to its utmost capacity, Hong Kong has fully established itself as a land of opportunities. If Hong Kong remains in the avant-garde of world city culture, it is because it makes portability, including the portability of postmodern cultural identities, a fact of life.

Some might say that this port status of Hong Kong—as the convergence point between East and West—is a cliché, a commonplace that has been repeated over and over again. My point is exactly that we need to think more closely about the implications of the commonplace. Why is the commonplace always the sign of inferiority? Why is it always repressed— brought up in interpretations only to be quickly sidestepped, dismissed as insignificant?

The commonplace might be seen as occupying the same kind of status as the "center" in Jacques Derrida's early writings. Like the center, the commonplace is the place of value, the place where evaluation "takes place."[10] However, despite their similar function, the commonplace and the center have entirely different destinies. The center is always viewed as some metaphysical bestower of value. Even after the lesson of deconstruction, after it has been put "under erasure"—which means that we recognize its necessity without endorsing it as a virtue—the center continues to function as central. The commonplace, even though it is as indispensable as the center, occupies instead the place of the debased.

What does this mean in the culture of modern cities? If the center is the value that transcends its local, material body to become the "general equivalent," the commonplace is the value that, in spite of its general use, remains confined to the local and the material. Paris and London, capitals of imperialism, remain to this day "centers" of world civilization despite their bloody histories; Saigon, Vientiane, Calcutta, and Hong Kong, even though they have partaken of the same histories, are consigned to the margins. The European capitals persist as "origins" from which universal value rises and flows; the (post)colonial port cities, imagined as mere recipients of such value, live the lives of the forever "local" and negligible.

To underline Hong Kong's port status is thus to think about the significance of the commonplace the way deconstruction has taught us to think about the center—with a different emphasis. For deconstruction, the center is a necessity, but it cannot be endorsed as a virtue. The commonplace, we might say, may be the unvirtuous, but it is always necessary. In particular, we need to think about what may be called the commonplace of the commonplace—the "money" of Hong Kong. As I already mentioned, Hong Kong's economism and materialism have always been viewed pejoratively as a kind of disease, even in readings that recognize the central nature of Hong Kong's economic reality. My proposal is that it is only when we take the "diseased," excessive nature of Hong Kong's "economism" and "materialism" seriously, that we will be able to see the inextricable mutuality between center and commonplace, and to return to the commonplace the function it shares with the center, namely, that for all its dirty, smelly, unpleasant reality, it is the origin of value, the place that everyone, regardless of identification and social status, passes through.

As a manner of interpretation, this would mean reading even Hong Kong's creative and artistic cultures in terms of, rather than in opposition to, its material reality. Rather than locating the point of Hong Kong's "creative culture" away from its material bases, away from the commonplace of its "economism," how might we go about reading this culture as part and parcel of the port-ing of value? And, once we have done this, how might we use the commonplace to read the center? What might Hong Kong tell us about London and Beijing, rather than vice versa?

For the following discussion, I read the poetry of Leung, one of Hong Kong's leading writers (who also writes novels, short stories, critical essays, and filmscripts), not by opposing him to the material economic culture of Hong Kong, but by showing how he makes the "origins" of Hong Kong—origins that are economic and colonial—part of the process of his writing. Leung himself has described his poetry as "homeless." As he tells us in an essay, in order to write as a poet in Hong Kong, he must be "accommodating" and be willing to exchange his role with more marketable ones.[11] Even so, as a poet, Leung does not hold himself aloof from the material reality around him in a superior manner; rather, he is so thoroughly immersed in the materialisms and infatuations of his society that he does not write without at the same time showing us how that society works, without at the same time taking us through the passages that constitute "Hong Kong."

The Poems of Leung Ping-kwan[12]

The first feature about Leung's poems that needs to be mentioned is that they are meant to be read in Cantonese, the language used by most of the inhabitants of Hong Kong. While Cantonese can be written in the same Han characters of standard Chinese (Mandarin/Putonghua), which have been unified since the Qin dynasty (221–206 B.C.E.), the language has its own grammar, syntax, expressions, and set of tones. Writing "Chinese" for people whose mother tongue is Cantonese is therefore already learning to use a different language whose preeminence comes primarily from its long status as script. In Hong Kong especially, this has always meant negotiating between the "standard" that is Mandarin/Putonghua and the colloquial daily usages of Cantonese that one actually speaks and hears, suppressing the latter's "local" features, and translating such features into "readable" Chinese, which exists as a kind of common, viable currency. On the other side, meanwhile, has always been the "currency" of English, which is the "general equivalent" toward which all non-Western cultures are obliged to move in the postcolonial world. Like standard Chinese, English is not just a means of communication; rather it is a usurper of linguistic and cultural space, a usurper that itself has become the standard of evaluation. As Leung writes:

> I think various attitudes towards language are the products of specific ways of looking at and talking about the world. Not only would retired English professors from Oxford or Cambridge claim that this is the place that speaks the worst English, some Mainland or Taiwan writers who have advocated the purity of the Chinese language also say that Hong Kong writers are handicapped in the Chinese language because Mandarin (Putonghua) is not the native tongue here.[13]

Articulating a space between English and Chinese, between standard Chinese and Cantonese, Leung's poems constitute the kind of "minor literature written in a major language" that is spoken of by Deleuze and Guattari.[14]

A second feature of Leung's poems is that they are full of descriptions of the material world. This is a poetry of wandering, traveling, observing, and talking with people from different places and cultures. A list of some of Leung's titles suffices to show this: "The Bakery," "Sleeping on the Beach," "At the North Point Car Ferry," "At the Old Bull-Fighting Ring," "The Moon in La Jolla," "Ode to a Daoist in Del Mar," "The Visit to the Museum of Modern Art," "Tokyo Story," "Beijing Train Station," "Seagulls of Kunming," "Brechthaus, Berlin," and "Postcards from Prague." Even when he is still, the poet's eye is constantly on the move, bringing with it multiple perceptions that are constantly changing. And even in their rural images, Leung's poems attest to a material city culture with its variegated technologies of external as well as internal journeying, technologies that enable the poet not only to roam the world but also to approach, examine, and penetrate things from a variety of visual perspectives created by photography and film, from close-ups to long takes, from microscopic detailing to distant appreciation.

At the same time, precisely because of the technical multiplication of the optical as well as other kinds of sensorial "unconscious," a host of things are admitted into writing: fruits, flowers, trees, leaves, shoes, clogs, furniture, paintings, films, music, postcards, food, drinks, and so forth. As Leung describes it, one of the conventions he follows consciously is the classical Chinese *wing mut see/yongwu shi*, the type of poetry that eulogizes things.[15]

But what exactly do things do in Leung's poetry? As "the camera looks around, gorging on imagery," the "surplus images of the city" can, in many respects, be "discarded like garbage."[16] Unwanted things can form a ridiculous environment, which sometimes expresses itself as a senseless compulsion to acquire. In the poem "Lucky Draw," acquisition becomes a form of absurdity:

> She gets a canned husband,
> and a bunch of motorized relatives.
> She gets a new set of fingernails,
> eyebrows and nose.
> She gets the title of vice-chairman
> of all associations. She gets four crocodiles that can sing,
> a hippopotamus that sends flowers regularly,
> a rhinoceros that waits at the corner of the street,
> a big hairy tortoise that requires talk.
> She gets a hairnet.
> She gets two bloody hearts.
> She gets the kind of vacuum cleaner
> her neighbor Asou bought just last week.
> She gets identical dust to go with it.
> She gets twelve certified university entrance examination approvals.
> She gets as bonus small dishes offered by all the
> different brands of soy sauces.[17]

The awareness of the potential absurdity of thing-culture does not mean that Leung would therefore turn away from things. Instead, his poetry indicates alternative directions. If the convention of thing-poetry allows Leung to capture the world in the form of things, the multiple material presences in his poems also tell us about basic changes in the technology of representation.

The rich array of things makes us realize that the poet is not simply a poet but also a painter and a photographer. Poetry, in the sense that it allows juxtaposition of images much more effectively and literally than narrative—thereby preserving the physicality and crudity of such juxtaposition—becomes in the postmodern age a kind of verbal photography; poems are snapshots made with words. What comes across through thing-images is not the continuity of narrative prose but brokenness, the disjointed and hence stark presences of things as they impinge upon consciousness. Meanwhile, if the poet is now a painter and photographer, the "thing" in Leung's poetry is also multimediatized: it is no longer the thing in classical Chinese poetry but an intersemiotic object that is created between classical poetry, painting, and photography; between a classical poet's eye and a modern photographer's eye; between verbal and technologized visuality. The compact thing-images are now portable, miniscule worlds we can carry with us because time has been manipulated to become a synchronized object containing different worlds.

In the busy, kaleidoscopic variety of imagistic fragments, a predominant impression of the things in Leung's poetry is that they are utterly unremarkable—a hibiscus flower, a pair of clogs, a green salad, a morning cloud, the evening fog, lights, colors. These things are unremarkable not in the sense of "uninteresting" but rather in the sense of that which is beyond remark, beyond the smooth fluency of words. Instead, words have now become a means of bricolage—a bricolage of sensations as well as of practices—in which things are put together in small, detailed, varied angles that produce new relations. Each phrase introduces a slightly different perspective, asking us to see a familiar thing anew, with surprising results. It is as if hundreds of images are clicked and processed in front of us in order to demonstrate their lack of heroic aspirations, their sheer material but mercurial presence. Consider, for instance, the implications of the last stanza of this poem, "The Flame Tree":

How does something change colors?
Does green always mean the gentleness of tolerance? Red
the violence of revolution? No. Analogies
are mere restrictions. I am unwilling to classify.
As I look at you, I wish to know –
Are you what secretly emerges from tangles of green
to become a bright new red blossom, wide open toward
the white clouds?
Or are you stamens and pistils that laugh and shake at
the unending games of creeping branches and flirting leaves?
This way of thinking forms with my gaze, until the bus

turns the corner, and the scene disappears –
and you form yet another new relation with the world.[18]

The bricolage of sensations and practices means that Leung's poetry is, ultimately, a poetry of consumption—consumption not in the sense of passive mass indoctrination but in the sense of the use of objects by those who are not the producers, in spaces that were not intended for them. In this latter sense, consumption is the representational mode of those Michel de Certeau calls "the weak," who "must continually turn to their own ends forces alien to them."[19] In Leung's poetry, consumption consists in inventing uses of the world that clearly fall outside the design and purpose of the space that is the "British colony." Watching the mist and fog on an outlying island, listening to the voice of a man selling bamboo poles for drying clothes, walking through the empty corridors of a colonial building, studying the patterns of lotus leaves—such quotidian activities consume the world around them in useless, unglamorous modes, but they also bring with them surprising illuminations. Instead of establishing permanent, fenced-off spaces, a poetry of consumption in this context specializes in a tactic of seizing opportunities as they reveal themselves momentarily in time.[20]

If the things in Leung's poetry are ordinary, they also become in the process of consumption agents of a democratic space, a common ground, where even the most ordinary thing can be appreciated on its own terms and shown to give unexpected delight, where the plenitude of things is not about luxury, extravagance, or passive consumerism but about accommodation, about making room and letting be. Leung always writes in dialogue, be it a dialogue between subject and object, subject and subject, or object and object. His poems offer themselves as passages that people can enter without violence and trauma, and which establish themselves as a new kind of value making.

And yet such passages, because they intend genuine openness, are very fragile. For Leung, Hong Kong itself is such a fragile, vulnerable space, which is as easily appropriated as it is open:

> The space we have is a mixed, hybrid space, a crowded and dangerous space, carnival-like even in times of crisis, heavenly and not far from disasters. It is a field where many forces struggle together, a space we as well as everybody have to find ways to make better use of, but it will also be easily appropriated by other forces, political or economical. This space that is open to us could easily be lost to us.[21]

Leung's poems, which he writes in ways that do not "simply chime in" with Hong Kong's commodified culture, nonetheless participate in that culture in a deeply committed way. While Leung does not endorse Hong Kong's "materialism," neither does he simply repudiate it with contempt nor withdraw into an otherworldly metaphysics. The figure of the poet that is conjured by his work is not someone who fantasizes himself to be a virgin untainted by social reality; rather he involves himself in Hong Kong's materialism by making visible its abundant and overdetermined forms. The immanence and centrality of the material in his poems becomes both an expression of the commonplace—clichéd, ordinary, unremarkable things, things which are simply there—and a common place, the place where people meet, things converge, and mutualities and reciprocities are actively reinvented. As he puts it in the preface to one of his prose collections, *Books and the City*, the topic he is most concerned with is the relation between cultures.

The distinctive use of things in a poetry that does not think of itself as "representative" of Hong Kong thus tells us much more about Hong Kong than many other writers with conscious aspirations. The Hong Kong that comes across in Leung's writings is not one that is politically correct ("Down with the British imperialists! Down with mainland Chinese chauvinism!"); yet neither does it imagine itself as lacking or pleading for pity. Rather, it is a Hong Kong that reinvents its imposed fate as transporter in a new kind of production. What this Hong Kong transports is not only things; it is also the practice of things as opportunities whereby alternative values materialize in the process of allegorical juxtaposition and unconventional dialogue. In this way, postcolonial "city culture" is redefined not simply in the form of a new identity politics emanating from a specific "local" space, but also as the surprising encounters between things and human beings in common/places.

Coloniality: A Condition to Be Used

As I already indicated, the materialism of Leung's writings can be seen as a kind of tactic within the overdetermined historical situation of Hong Kong, where people are not "free" to "choose" their political system. For those who expect heroic proclamations of anticolonialism, it would be disconcerting to hear a poet from a colony describing his work primarily in terms of the pleasure of consumption: "I am more removed from poets who meditated on immortality, or those who believed their works were timeless artifacts. I would feel more comfortable with poets who wrote after dinner to tell their friends how tasty the yellow fish was."[22] What Leung's poetry makes us realize is the untenability of heroic narratives, especially as the latter continue to be mobilized with expedience by those who are in power, in the manner of refurnishing a home with grand old furniture even in the aftermath of a major catastrophe. Such heroic narratives are dismantled in the ironic poem "Refurnishing," which is one of a series of poems Leung wrote after the Tiananmen Massacre of 1989.[23] Once heroic narratives are dismantled, how do we deal with coloniality?

The founding of Hong Kong as a city converges with an epochal change in the world's value system, from the stability of landed culture to the speeds and currencies of trade. And yet, in the evaluation of culture, we seem to remain as fixated on stability as we are on the center. Leung's writings alert us to the necessity of reversing the conventional narrative of colonialism by de-fixating on such stability. The implications of this de-fixation on stable culture are vast. Chief of all, they necessitate a rigorous revaluation of the marginal. Rather than beginning with Europe as the origin, an origin that goes out to conquer and "civilize" other lands, we might say that it is "primitive" outposts like Hong Kong and Macau, which are far away from the "motherlands" of Britain and Portugal, that provide, through their economic, materialistic, transitory status, the "stability" of the notions of nation, people, land, and tradition that are such a crucial part of the discourse of empire building. To use the language of territorial possession, it is the utter deprivation of land in the colony—because land has been turned into a commodity—that enables the grandiose patriotic rhetoric of "England, my England" that we find in the reflections of English national culture in modernity, as well as in the ponderous musings about the Great Wall, the Yellow River, the Central Plains, and so forth that are the symbols of Chinese national culture. To use the language of legal identity, it is the denial of secure protection to the colonized, who are reduced to "transients" and "migrants," that enables the pride and respectability of those who possess the right documents of permanent citizenship. Finally, to use the language of sexual crime and discipline, it is the "rape" or "violation" of Hong Kong that makes possible the pious equation, in masculinist nationalistic discourse, between sexual chastity and national integrity, between virginity and cultural purity.

In terms of the formation of modern city culture, the violence of the trading port is thus originary rather than derivative in significance. But precisely because of this, port cities such as Hong Kong often become associated with that which is of lesser and less authentic value. In their vulgar, consumerist, debased form, such port cities stand, ultimately, as the "thing" that gives colonialist imperialism its consistency: colonialist imperialism cannot thrive except with the functioning of places like Hong Kong, and yet this "thing" that gives life to the system, that makes colonialist imperialism colonialist imperialism, is at the same time what is continually treated with contempt, as feminine disease, as native degeneracy—as what is "outside" the rooted civilizations of London, Paris, Beijing.

In Leung's writings, not only are the thing qualities and associations of Hong Kong given their due place, but coloniality itself is rethought as well. Coloniality is not only the historical violence committed by the powerful of the world against the powerless, it is also a basic economic condition—for many the only condition of value—in which to live, think, and make changes. When asked what Hong Kong's colonial past means to him, Leung answers:

> I think of it in relation to the inability to tell one's past, to express one's confusion about identity, and to articulate one's feeling about this place. I think of it in relation to the education, the imbalanced cultural policies, the silence and suppression, and the actual ignorance about one's own context. But it is not just that; it is also very much in the background of everything we do. Ironically, Hong Kong as a colony provides an alternative space for Chinese people and culture to exist, a hybrid for one to reflect upon the problems of a "pure" and "original" state.
>
> It is very much part of my background, it is there, hindering me as well as consoling me, making me uneasy, alerting me to my lack, urging me at an early age to doubt what could be easily taken for granted.[24]

Once again a certain conventional narrative of colonialism has to be reversed. Rather than beginning with Europe, whose colonizing acts leave the colonized in a pathetic state of deprivation and make the freedom from coloniality the ultimate telos, we might say that the condition of coloniality is also the means with which the colonized must fight the violence of colonialism. In other words, coloniality, a transindividual condition of history that carries with it all the tragedies of marginalization, can nonetheless become a form of opportunity, in which the daily experience of oppression is synchronized with a self-conscious search for freedom in alternative forms.

At this point, it would be relevant to return to one of the interesting facts of Hong Kong as a colony. Hong Kong's population is made up largely of immigrants. Unlike the classic colonial situation in which European powers force their way into lands that are already populated with indigenous peoples, most of the people who live in Hong Kong came voluntarily (many by risking their lives) in order to escape the harsher conditions in China. (The more appropriate comparisons here would be with Hispanic immigrants from Latin America in the United States, or with refugees from Eastern Europe and the former Soviet Union in Western Europe.) As Kwai-cheung Lo writes:

> The Chinese who came to Hong Kong after the colony was set up primarily aimed at gaining economic improvement or seeking refuge from political turmoil and persecution. They did not come to wage a nationalistic

battle against the colonial rule, especially when the only alternative to colonial rule was the domination of the authoritarian Communist regime. Thus the "China factor" ironically buttresses colonial rule by making it invulnerable to being toppled by the colonized. . . . It renders the colonial institution more benign and attractive to immigrants. It could be said that the colonial subjects are a self-select group who voluntarily subscribe to the colonial rule.[25]

By the mid-twentieth century, not only Chinese, but a host of other peoples, from India, Pakistan, Southeast Asia, as well as England, had also established permanent residency in Hong Kong in order to have—scandalous though it may sound—a better life under colonial rule than at home. Coloniality in Hong Kong is therefore not simply the condition of deprived enlightenment that critics of colonialism usually make it; rather it is something that the colonized actively use as a way of life—it is a form of violence, yes, but a form of violence that is lived as an alternative to greater violence elsewhere. In Hong Kong, the violence of coloniality is, we might say, a practicable way of escaping the violence that comes with living as "nationals" and "citizens" of independent countries.

This is why, much as Hong Kong culture is a marginalized culture, Leung's loyalty to the city is not an attempt to idealize the position of the marginal.[26] Rather, marginality is as much a personal discipline and a form of social instruction as it is the reality of living in Hong Kong. It is not marginalization alone, but the conscious effort to reflect on one's own culture by means of others, an effort that perhaps comes more "easily" with marginalization, which makes one develop a bi- or multicultural consciousness: "I don't think the special situation of Hong Kong makes its artists automatically bi-cultural or poly-cultural. . . . It is when one reflects upon one's culture by means of another that one eventually develops 'bi-cultural' awareness."[27] And, precisely because marginalization alone does not necessarily prevent one from chauvinism or violence, one needs to be very careful when approaching questions of coloniality and postcoloniality:

We should not look upon ourselves as victims, in self-pity, but should be conscious of victims turned tyrants, as in the way some Hong Kong people treat the Vietnamese boat people, Filipino maids, or new Mainland immigrants. But of course I am also skeptical towards people who shift the attention by pointing out these latter examples so as to level out all issues, to universalize colonialism and in the end successfully avoid the issue of British colonialism.[28]

Leung's work can be summarized by a line from his poem "Images of Hong Kong": "Always at the edge of things and between places."[29] In this line we find a special kind of agency, which is not that of a call for the end of coloniality, but the insistence on an openness, an insistence that comes paradoxically with the much more difficult task of living as the continually colonized. Leung warns that coloniality will always live in us if we are not careful: "one has to be conscious of not just the marker on the outside, the year 1997, for example, but rather the ways people think and reflect upon themselves; otherwise one would carry the colonial mentality into another phase of colonialism."[30]

I would like to conclude with stanzas from one of Leung's poems, "An Old Colonial Building." This title refers to the main building of the University of Hong Kong. It is here, in his professional environment, that he experiences first-hand the tensions and conflicts of coloniality as it impinges upon the practices of education. In spite of the frustrations he encounters daily, Leung persists in his work, refusing to give in to the powers that be:

So much dust swirls through sunlight and shadow,
through the scaffolding and the wooden planks raised-up around
the colonial edifice, as if
to dismantle it brick by brick. Perhaps
its basic shape will remain, perhaps
the bitterness deep in the soil will emerge.
The noble rotunda and the wide hollow corridors
are still facing a blocked wall. Perhaps when it's all knocked
open,
there will be stairs leading to more ordinary places . . .

Might the pieces of ruins put together compose
a new architecture? Ridiculous are the portraits of leaders,
laughable those with power. We meet in the corridor.
Looking by chance: the surface of the lotus pond is changing.
Thinking does not evade ripples, and does not bend with the wind.

I know that you don't believe in flags or fireworks.
I will give you fragmented words rather than "realistic" portrayals,
(showing that you are) not a center surrounded by magnificent
. . . buildings,
but simply a (circular) pond
of ripples, where moving signs come and go.[31]

Notes

This chapter was modified and reprinted from Rey Chow, "Things, Common/Places, Passages of the Port City: On Hong Kong and Hong Kong Author Leung Ping-kwan," *differences* 5, no. 3 (Fall 1993): 179–204.

1. In transcribing Chinese names, I will give first the Cantonese and then the Mandarin/Putonghua pronunciations. Even though such transcriptions are cumbersome, they serve as markers of resistance against Mainland Chinese imperialism in the present context.

2. Lau Siu-kai, *Society and Politics in Hong Kong* (Hong Kong: The Chinese University Press, 1982, 1984), 173.

3. Ackbar Abbas, "Introduction: The Last Emporium: Verse and Cultural Space," in *City at the End of Time*, by Leung Pink-kwan, trans. Gordon T. Osing (Hong Kong: Twilight Books Co. in association with the Department of Comparative Literature, University of Hong Kong, 1992), 5–7. Notably, instead of criticizing the "very efficient colonial administration" he mentions, Abbas goes on to mock Hong Kong people for their "false consciousness"—for being motivated by selfish economic interests even in their political demonstrations. With determination, his passage continues as follows: "By the same logic, the only form of political idealism that has a chance is that which can go together with economic self-interest, when 'freedom' for example could be made synonymous with the 'free market.' This, I believe, is how one can understand the unprecedented mass demonstrations over the Tiananmen Massacre by the hundreds of thousands of the middle-class who have never before marched in the streets. June 1989 in Hong Kong was a rare moment when economic self-interest could so easily misrecognise itself as political idealism. There was genuine emotion and outrage to be sure, which does not preclude the possibility that many of the marchers were moved by how much they were moved. In any event, the patriotic fervor in most cases was short-lived and without political outcome" (Abbas, 5). Such a display of derision and sarcasm is unfortunate in an essay that otherwise contains interesting insights into Hong Kong culture.

4. Sigmund Freud, "Femininity," in *New Introductory Lectures on Psychoanalysis*, trans. and ed. James Strachey (New York: Norton, 1964, 1965), 117.

5. Ai Wu, "One Night in Hong Kong," trans. Zhu Zhiyu, *Renditions* 29/30 (1988): 62.

6. Wen Yiduo, "Two Poems," trans. Zhu Zhiyu. *Renditions* 29/30 (1988): 65–66. Wen also has a poem called "Kowloon": "While big brother Hong Kong tells of his suffering / Mother, have you forgotten your little daughter Kowloon? / Since I married that Demon King who ruled the sea, / I've been tossed upon endless waves of tears / Mother, I count the days until our joyous reunion / Yet fear my hope is only a dream. / Mother! I want to come back, Mother!" ("Two Poems," 66).

7. Ha Gong, "The Legalization of Rape," trans. Don J. Cohn, *Renditions* 29/30 (1988), 326.

8. With the exception of Spanish America, colonial cities are almost always ports. See Robert Ross and Gerard T. Telkamp (eds.), *Colonial Cities: Essays on Urbanism in a Colonial Context* (Dordrecht: Nijhoff, 1985), 6.

9. G. B. Endacott, *Government and People in Hong Kong, 1841–1962* (Hong Kong: Hong Kong University Press, 1964), vii–viii; qtd. in Lau, *Society and Politics in Hong Kong*, 41.

10. For Derrida, see "Structure, Sign, and Play in the Discourse of the Human Sciences," in *The Structuralist Controversy: The Languages of Criticism and the Sciences of Man*, ed. Richard Macksey and Eugenio Donato (Baltimore: Johns Hopkins University Press, 1970), 247–272. Even though I am not reading "economic" texts here, my understanding of "value" and the mutual implications between "economics" and "writing" owes much to Gayatri Spivak, "Scattered Speculations on the Question of Value," in *Other Worlds: Essays in Cultural Politics* (New York: Methuen, 1987), 154–175; and "Speculations on Reading Marx: After Reading Derrida," in *Poststructuralism and the Question of History*, ed. Derek Attridge, Geoff Bennington, and Robert Young (New York: Cambridge University Press, 1987), 30–62.

11. Leung Ping-kwan, "The Homeless Poems and Photographs," *NuNaHeDuo* [Dislocation] 2, no. 2 ["Public vs. Images" Issue]: 1.

12. My readings are based on the poems collected in *Leung Ping-kwan gun/juan*, ed. Jap See/Ji Si (Hong Kong: Sanlian shudian, 1989). In some cases, I use the English translations provided by Osing in *City* (often with significant modifications); in other cases, where no translations exist in English, I provide my own. In each case I try as much as possible to stay close to the tone and syntax of Leung's originals, which means that my translations tend to be literal and may not always read smoothly in English.

13. Leung, *City at the End of Time*, 165.

14. Gilles and Felix Guattari, *Kafka: Toward a Minor Literature*, trans. Dana Polan (Minneapolis: University of Minnesota Press, 1986). Lo Kwai-cheung has used Deleuze and Guattari's notion of "minor literature" to discuss Hong Kong literature in *Crossing Boundaries: A Study of Hong Kong Modern Fiction from the Fifties to the Eighties*, M. Phil. Thesis (University of Hong Kong, 1990).

15. For a brief discussion of "thing-poetry" in both China and the West, see *Leung Ping-kwan gun*, 171–172. It should be mentioned that thing-poetry has been viewed with suspicion in Chinese communist literary criticism because of its "fetishizing" tendencies. Poets who indulge in this genre are often regarded as limited because they spend too much time on things rather than on the "important" events of nation, people, revolution, and so forth.

16. Leung, "Ap-liu Street," in *City*, 36–37.

17. Leung, *City*, 83.

18. Ibid., 101 (translation significantly modified).

19. Michel de Certeau, *The Practice of Everyday Life*, trans. Steven Rendall (Berkeley: University of California Press, 1984), xix.

20. See de Certeau, *The Practice of Everyday Life*; see also Mark Poster, "The Question of Agency: Michel de Certeau and the History of Consumerism," *diacritics* 22, no. 2 (1992): 94–107.

21. Leung, "The Homeless," 2.

22. Leung, *City*, 168.

23. Ibid., 75.

24. Ibid., 182.

25. Lo, *Crossing Boundaries*, 163. See also Lau, *Society and Politics*, 174–176. "As most of the immigrants came to Hong Kong in pursuit of economic opportunities, they largely constituted a self-selected group whose intention is not to question or attack the political system in Hong Kong, which existed prior to their decisions to emigrate. The memories of political disorder in

their homeland would make them receptive to a political system whose avowed purpose is to maintain political stability and which has demonstrated a capability of doing so" (Lau, 174).

26. Leung, *City*, 175.

27. Ibid., 161–162.

28. Ibid., 185.

29. Ibid., 35.

30. Ibid., 185.

31. Ibid., 31 (translation significantly modified).

13

Taiwan Fiction Under Japanese Colonial Rule, 1895–1945

CHIEN-CHUNG CHEN

Colonial Modernity and Literary Modernity

For a long time following World War II, studies of Taiwan literature from the Japanese colonial period paid more attention to issues such as "resistance" or "national consciousness." This was related to anti-Japanese sentiments, anticommunist ideology, and martial law. On the one hand, under the reign of the Kuomintang (KMT) government, stories with an emphasis on native resistance and Chineseness as well as related reviews and critiques had better access to the different media dominated and controlled by the KMT. On the other hand, since they were deeply influenced by nationalism and the aesthetics of realism, these critics could hardly offer an unbiased and nuanced analysis of Taiwan's colonial conditions.[1]

Nevertheless, as the KMT loosened its tight control on literary and cultural production, research and studies of Taiwan fiction from the colonial period have gradually shifted from a review of ideological trends and the formation of canons of modern vernacular literature to an exploration of the various forces behind such trends and canon formation. This is an exploration of what I call the experience of multiple modernities that contributed to the hybrid nature of Taiwan literature by way of divergent languages and cultures. In other words, current studies on Taiwan literature pay more attention to the "process" than to the "result" of literary production. This is indicative of the gradual institutionalization of the academic field of

Taiwan literature. The crucial questions are: How do we understand material and cultural modernities brought on by colonialism? How do we understand the literary historical significance of transformations in literary modernity? These questions require us to return to the actual sociohistorical context of colonial Taiwan to examine the material bases for the production of these different modernities.

Reviewing the duration and the expansion of Japanese imperialism in the colony of Taiwan, it is clear that Japan did not uniformly exploit local capital and resources but initiated a limited modernization of Taiwan by establishing a sugar industry, reforming existing educational systems, and improving overall hygiene and sanitation. However, it should be recalled that these efforts represent a form of "forced modernization" complicit in the scheme of Japan's colonization of Taiwan. Taiwan's modernization was the groundwork for Japan's desire to further advance its capitalist plans. The people of Taiwan, rather than enjoying the benefits of this transformation, were left to face its dire side effects.

The handicapped capitalization and modernization of Taiwan can be compared to "raising the goose for the golden eggs," which brings together the colonial and the modern: How the goose fares does not matter as long as it lays the golden eggs, thus the paradox of "colonial modernity" that benefited the colonizers more than the colonized. Colonialism introduced the predetermined and superior authority that brought modernity/modernization to the colony. As local intellectuals sought to modernize, they were faced with the confusing imbrications of "the colonial" and "the modern."

The "Orient" was coerced into modernization. Asian countries were compelled to understand the cause of their colonization while fighting against colonialism. "Traditional systems" were facilely blamed to have brought upon their own colonization. The dilemma is that to critique the legacies of the so-called backward tradition as inviting colonization is to admit the inferiority of one's own culture. Those who voiced their support of enlightenment thus played an ambiguous role as harsh critics of colonialism and indigenous culture.

We may proceed to ask: Should the colonized take the national (nativist) stance and fight the colonizers? Do they have a legitimate claim against colonialism? How one may ascertain one's ties to the native, or how one finds a new footing between the pulling forces of modernity and nativism, remain the two historical concerns inevitably confronted by writers in colonial Taiwan.

The quest for modernity is the driving force behind the anticolonial and antifeudalist thinking of Taiwanese intellectuals. However, when we analyze works by colonial Taiwanese intellectuals and writers, we discover different modes for the reception of modernity. These intellectuals and writers also clearly pondered questions of native culture in their reception of modernity. In a situation where the coloniality of Taiwan was inseparably linked to modernity, intellectual discourses risked debasing native culture as outdated and backward. It is therefore crucial to note the entanglement between colonial modernity and nativism.

Following traces of Taiwanese writers and their resistance against (or pursuit) of modernity, we may begin to reflect on the varied themes, aesthetic forms, and other related topics of Taiwan fiction from the colonial period and their significance. Taiwanese intellectuals and writers facing the dubious intersection of colonial modernity and nativism expressed their diverse concerns in fictional works. A close reading will help cast new light on the complex mentality of these writers, and thereby offer a fresh and more nuanced perspective on the connection between literature and history.

Enlightenment, Leftist, Urban, and *Kōminka*: The "Multiple Modernities" of New Taiwan Literature

Enlightenment Fiction: An Anti-Traditional and Liberated Modernity

Fiction that incorporated enlightenment thought introduced new techniques of representation and liberal thinking to Taiwan literature in the 1920s. If Taiwanese intellectuals with a modern Japanese education inherited the Westernized and Japanized Enlightenment ideals—such as freedom, equality, reason, science, and democracy—during the Meiji (1868–1912) and Taisho (1913–1926) periods, they were also enlightenment figures who sought liberation from tradition. They played crucial roles in what Wallerstein calls the "modernity of liberation."[2]

Enlightenment figures in Taiwan who learned about ideals of enlightenment and liberation faced a complex situation. With their knowledge about modernity in the West, of which Japanese colonialism is an extension, they turned against and criticized native tradition. Meanwhile, they also had to fight imperialist invasion. To spread ideas of enlightenment, they relied on modern fiction, a literary genre from the West. This seemed an inevitable choice for non-Western writers. Focusing on the dynamics between "colony" and "literature," we may examine modern Taiwan writers since Lai He (1894–1943) and how their modern fiction reflects both colonial reality and personal struggle.

The mode of realism is a commonality shared by many minor/minority writers. The form of realism helps to effectively record and criticize the oppression of colonialism and imperialism. For anticolonial writers who felt the acute and immediate pressure of the colony to assimilate, realism with its focus on details of verisimilitude helped better preserve in writing the native way of life. This is one of the many important reasons why the colonized preferred realism and its form.

The appearance of writers such as Lai He, Yang Yunping (1906–2000), and Zhang Wojun (1902–1955) marked an important turning point. It demonstrated that Taiwan writers had become familiar with the styles and fictional techniques of modern fiction in the West. It was in this context that enlightenment fiction began to undertake the task of promoting a modernity of human liberation.

But how do we define the "human"? It is perhaps the primary concern of all adherents to the universal values of the Enlightenment. Those who believed in the Enlightenment's pursuit of freedom and equality witnessed "inhuman" practices in their own country. The goal of a new literary and cultural movement in Taiwan was thus not so different from those in other Asian countries during the process of modernization. In the fighting against colonialism and imperialism, the projects of demonstrating "disenchantment" with cultural backwardness and the pursuit of human rights, democracy, and science are indebted to the ideas of the Enlightenment.

A project of expressing disenchantment can be found in Lai He's "Her Tragic Death" (*Kelian ta sile*, 1931), in which the wealthy Ah Li—who already has three wives—purchases a fourth, the poor teenage girl Ah Jin, in order to satisfy his sexual impulses. Or, in "A Measuring Stick" (*Yi gan chengzai*, 1926), the character Qin Desen cries out as a Japanese policeman mistreats him: "I am no longer a human being. I am treated like an animal. Who would want that? What kind of world is this? Death would be more tolerable than life."[3] These are examples of expressions of Enlightenment ideals that call our attention to the dignity and values of humanity.

As an enlightenment intellectual, Lai He was the most representative of all writers from Taiwan. Also, as a nationalist, he was convinced that one must remain self-critical and not give up the fight against colonialism. His attitude toward the masses is critical and his cultural critique of the national character is persistent.

The understanding of "folk culture" among Taiwanese intellectuals reveals their struggle between modernity and coloniality.[4] They grappled with questions such as how one elevates one's culture while pursuing modernity and fighting against colonialism, or how one critiques one's own cultural backwardness without the limiting pitfall of Western (or Japanese) progressivism. What I call the literature of enlightenment—which addresses issues of nation, class, and gender so as to provide new ways of thinking about tradition and to establish the trend of individualism and liberalism in the modern fiction of Taiwan—is an important genre worthy of our attention.

Proletarian Fiction: Nativist and Critical Modernity

The New Taiwan Literature Movement of the 1920s and 1930s tried to change people's worldviews to assist in political and social modernization. Eventually it sought to rid Taiwan of Japanese control. Socialist ideals were introduced in response to practical demands from people in Taiwan. Different voices began to emerge in terms of defining "culture and arts for the people" and "literature for the people."

The development of proletarian literature, also known as "left-wing literature" (*zuoyi wenxue*), in Taiwan was by and large suppressed by the Japanese colonial government. Nonetheless, socialist ideas and nativist concerns in proletarian fiction still cast light on the multifaceted aspects of literary modernity in Taiwan.

Taiwan literature started to demonstrate more explicit leftist tendencies in the 1930s. Leftist journals were established one after another, and small communities of Taiwanese leftist writers were formed. The so-called "Cultural Enlightenment Movement" initiated by the Taiwan Cultural Association (*Taiwan bunka kyōkai* or *Taiwan wenhua xiehui*) in 1927 transformed into a proletarian literary movement. "Art and literature for the masses" became the leading principle in the literary field. *Wurenbao* was the first magazine to promote arts for the masses in the 1930s. In addition to *Wurenbao*, *Taiwan zhanxian* (Taiwan battlefront), in its inaugural issue, vows "to look after the poor and hard-working people by offering proletarian literature and art, and to liberate them from capitalist oppression."[5] The class-conscious statement and its tone against capitalism are overt.

Yang Kui (1905–1985) was the most productive writer under the banner of proletarian literature. Yang's proletarian story "Newspaper Boy" (*Shimbun Haitatsufu*) won a literary award in *Bungaku hyōron* (Literary review) in Tokyo, as Yang became the first Taiwanese writer to win a Japanese literary award. In the story, Yang strongly criticizes Japanese colonialism in Taiwan. He also proposes an internationalist ideal that attempts to bring together proletarians from all over the world, placing the colonial modernity of Taiwan in a larger, transnational and anticapitalist context.

Yang Shouyu (1905–1959) was another proletarian writer. Once an active anarchist, he wrote stories such as "A Group of Unemployed Persons" (*Yiqun shiye de ren*, 1931) and "Break up" (*Juelie*, 1932) that demonstrate his strong awareness of class struggle. With his characters—especially farmers, workers, and women—Yang vividly exposes social inequality. Struggling to make ends meet, these characters help define the margins and limits of a Taiwanese society troubled by Japanese colonialism and capitalism.

After Yang Kui, Lu Heruo (1903–1947) is another writer who has made a name for himself in Japan with his short story "The Ox Carriage" (*Gyūsha*, 1935). The story was also published by *Bungaku hyōron*. In the story, Lu, through the trope of the ox carriage, which is soon to be replaced by automobiles, criticizes the unforgiving force of Japanese colonialism and the adverse side effects of modernization that farmers must face.

In the meantime, like proletarian fiction's criticism of capitalism, nativism also refuted the "pseudo-progressive" side of coloniality and affirmed native culture and its legacy. The collection of folklore and the Taiwanese Language Movement (*Taiwan huawen yundong*) both of which occurred in the 1930s, were the result of nativist concerns about preserving and promoting the culture of the masses, echoing the basic tenets of socialism and nativism.

In August 1930, Huang Shihui ignited the heated quarrel now known as the "debate on nativist literature" with "How Couldn't We Promote Nativist Literature?" (*Zenyang bu tichang xiangtu wenxue*) and "Revisiting Nativist Literature" (*Zaitan xiangtu wenxue*). In July 1931, Guo Qiusheng started the "debate on Taiwanese language" with his "Constructing the 'Taiwanese Language,'" which was aimed at a proletarian readership. While Huang Shihui argued that art and literature must reverberate with the masses in a language that these hardworking people understand, Guo Qiusheng tried to transliterate the Taiwanese language (the Hoklo) using the Sinitic script, which he believed would help educate the illiterate.

Scholars have provided thoughtful studies on the debates,[6] widely acknowledging the influence of socialist ideas on such debates. In short, in terms of the critique of modernity, proletarian fiction and nativist fiction play an irreplaceable role in strengthening the connection between an emergent class consciousness and a traditional local culture. The two different forms of fiction, unlike the fiction of enlightenment that adheres to Western modes of modernity, maintain a vigilant critical distance from it.

Urban Fiction, Literary New Sensationism, and Ambiguous Modernity

The positioning of modernist literature from the colonial period requires further extrication because extant scholarship on colonial period literature tends to place emphasis on enlightenment and leftist writings. In Japan and the West, when urban modernity is placed at the center of literary representation, a new type of sensationism in tandem with urban life and literary aesthetics is thus created. Such literary new sensationism played a key role in the trend of modernist literature. But because modernism and imperialism arrived almost simultaneously in Taiwan, modernist writers had to deal with the crises of the deprivation and displacement of their cultural subjectivity while relying on new language and technique from the empire for their creation. As a result, in the annals of anticolonial literary historiography, these writers have not received fair and serious assessment for an extended period of time.

In his study *A History of Taiwan's New Literature* (*Taiwan xin wenxue shi*), Chen Fangming explains how urban fiction arose alongside proletarian and leftist writings.[7] Through Japan, Taiwan writers came to learn about modernism, a form with which they effectively explored human interiority. In the urban setting, the depiction of internal struggles is closely related to questions of coloniality and modernity, including the difficulties overseas Taiwanese students faced in an international city like Tokyo. Examples are found in Wu Yongfu's "Head and Body" (*Shou yu ti*) and "Camellia" (*Shanchahua*, 1935), Wu Tianshang's "Buds" (*Lei*, 1933) and "The Dragon" (*Long*), Weng Nao's "Remaining Snow" (*Canxue*, 1935) and "A Love Story Before Dawn" (*Tianliang qian de lian'ai gushi*, 1937); and Zhang Wenhuan's "A Prematurely Withered Bud" (*Caodiao de beilei*, 1933). These writers express their unhappiness with displays of romantic and bourgeois decadence. As a result, there emerged a group of romantic rebels and intellectual exiles.

Weng Nao's "Love Story Before Dawn" details Weng's personal experiences in Tokyo. Filled with sensuous imagery, the story features the protagonist's rambunctious internal monologue, which stands in vivid contrast to the city and a sense of fatigue with urban culture. The city and all its pressures consume the life of the protagonist. As he approaches his 31st birthday, the protagonist exclaims: "Oh! My youth has withered away. The day is coming to an end . . . For me, life is not life anymore without youth."[8]

In his new sensationist story "Head and Body," Wu Yongfu depicts the vacillation of an overseas Taiwanese student in Japan between colonial Taiwan and cosmopolitan Japan. The story is notable for its modernist technique of soliloquy that expands the depth and breadth in the depiction of the protagonist. In comparison to writers such as Lai He who focus on the "local" and the "native," Wu Yongfu writes about confusing challenges one faces in the metropole of the Japanese colonizers.

Spearheaded by Weng Nao and Wu Yongfu, sometimes this group of modernists who had studied in Japan before seem fully mesmerized by urban culture; at other times, they explain soberly how a big city such as Tokyo symbolizes their life's predicaments. Their stories about living in a big city are not concerned with enlightenment and anticolonialism; rather, they display a penchant for literature, art, and even romance. More individualistic and seemingly lacking nationalist sentiments, these stories accentuate the relationship between Taiwan modernism and Japanese urban modernity.

Fiction with Themes of Kōminka or Imperialization: Nationalism and Colonial Modernity

After the second Sino-Japanese War broke out in 1937, the colonial government in Taiwan started its policy of imperialization. The primary activities included the promotion of *kokugo*, the Japanese language, the adoption of Japanese surnames, a volunteer military, and the adoption of Japanese religious and social practices. The goal of the movement was to transform Taiwanese people into "children of the emperor." In particular, the volunteer military was an important topic in wartime fiction.

During wartime, both Japanese and Taiwanese writers were instructed to produce works that adhere to national policy. Many of the stories are inevitably propaganda. Zhou Jinpo's "Volunteer Soldiers" (*Shiganhei*, 1941) was a tailored example. Nonetheless, the official label of "fiction of imperialization" (*kōmin bungaku*) was not used until 1943, when Chen Huoquan's short story "The Road" (*Michi*) was published. Hamada Hayao, a writer in his own right, publicly praised Chen's story as a model for new literature in Taiwan in an article entitled "On 'The Road'": "This is unprecedented in Taiwan literature. This is Taiwan's own literature of imperialization through which we can envision a new literary landscape. In this sense, I am truly fascinated by this piece."[9]

The "literature of imperialization" (*kōmin bungaku*) was a label promoted especially by the Japanese state and its scholars and writers at the time. The label was meant to co-opt Taiwan writers. Postwar Taiwan scholars tend to critique "literature of imperialization" from a nationalist stance. They tend to despise and reject writings by those who collaborated with the Japanese colonizers during the period of imperialization.

I believe that the label "literature of imperialization" renders all Taiwan writers collaborators, and that we should stop using this label for self-referencing. Understanding how the "literature of imperialization" came into being historically, we should face the fact that Taiwan writers were also "the oppressed." Without the movement of imperialization, and without nearly five decades of colonial education, it would not have been possible for Taiwan writers to produce the so-called "literature of imperialization" under the condition of humiliation and distortion.[10] I propose to replace the term "literature of imperialization" with "literature with themes of imperialization" so as to better reconsider the nuanced positions taken by Taiwan writers who at first glance seemed to have aligned themselves with the Japanese colonizers.

Zhou Jinpo and his "Volunteer Soldiers" (*Shiganhei*), written in Japanese, often appears on the list of "literature of imperialization." This story discusses how a Taiwanese youth may become a "real" Japanese. Having formerly studied in Japan, the character Zhang Minggui takes a theoretical and rational approach to identity issues, which does not help him feel more Japanese. On the other hand, the less-educated Gao Jinliu is able to overcome barriers of "blood" and "race" to embody the Japanese spirit through the "handclapping" ritual. Gao even composes a letter in blood and throws himself into the war as a Japanese soldier. The sense of irony about the impossibility of truly becoming Japanese was probably shared by a great number of Taiwanese youths at that time.

Works by Japanese writers in Taiwan of the same period also require further research. Understandably, Japanese writers, as colonizers, have a different approach in terms of their depiction of Taiwan. For example, the opening chapter of Hamada Hayao's (1909–1973) *The Immigrants' Village* (1942), depicts how a Japanese doctor with no formal medical training is rejected by native Taiwanese doctors in central Taiwan. He decides to move to Lutian Village (an immigrants' village established in 1915) in Taidong county, where he works as a doctor for a sugar company run by the imperial government. His experience in the village recounts the treacherous life these immigrants have to face. *The Immigrants' Village* aims to reveal the conflicts between different classes in the colonial system, thereby exposing the hierarchy of colonial modernity.

Similarly, another Japanese writer, Nishikawa Mitsuru (1908–1999), was not considered a "formal" part of Japanese national literature. He belongs to the so-called *gaichi bungaku* (literature written by expatriates), or the "foreign literature of the Showa period" (*Ikyō no Shōwa bungaku*).[11] Perhaps the reason why Nishikawa is not included in the Japanese national literary canon has to do not simply with matters of literary achievement but also with the difficulty of defining expatriate writers in the colony. In this regard, Nishikawa's writings on the history of Taiwan are especially noteworthy. From 1940 to 1942, Nishikawa's writings were all centered on Taiwan history and geography. Nishikawa's writings during the Pacific War may be divided into two genres: the fictionalization of Taiwanese history and the romanticization of Taiwanese folk customs.

Here I shall use one story from the collection *Sekikanki* (1940) as an example to explain how Nishikawa fictionalizes history for various purposes. "Sekikanki" recounts the family history of Koxinga (Zheng Chenggong) and Chen Yonghua. With this fictional account of the lives of three generations of one family, the story contends that Chinese official history is not reliable. Nishikawa uses other sources such as Jiang Risheng's *Unofficial Record of Taiwan* (*Taiwan waiji*) to try to recover history. The ambition of Koxinga's grandson, who is part-Japanese, to expand the Ming empire to the south eventually falls short, and he is in the end murdered. The following monologue is significant:

> Ah! My grandfather [Koxinga] had conquered the Red Fort, and as his descendant I want to start from the spot that he had taken. What's the big deal in governing such a small island (Taiwan)? The restoration of the Ming Dynasty is my most important calling! I want to establish the Ming again in the south. Right! I have to leave here for the spacious southern seas. I still remember the story grandmother told me when I was young about the brave adventures of my grandfather. His mother was Japanese, and was very proud of his Japanese lineage. Let's sail to the south![12]

In addition to its historical vignettes, the true force of the story comes from its political agenda. Situated in the historical context of the time, the story's call to turn Taiwan into a military base for southern expedition echoes the colonial policy during the Pacific War. In other words, the story is as much a historical fiction about the Zheng family as a call to arms in disguise. Nishikawa uses Taiwan to display the fantasy of Japanese racialism (Koxinga is part Japanese) and colonialism (the vision for the southern expedition and expansion).[13]

Both literature with themes of imperialization and writings by Japanese expatriate writers reveal a pivotal point in Taiwan literature during the war period—the adherence of literature to colonial policies and Japanese imperialism. This is a crucial point that concerns all writers in Taiwan at the time. Becoming Japanese means the affirmation of colonialism and modernity. However, it is certain that there existed vastly different psychological mechanisms for writers who occupied positions as colonizers and those who were colonized.

Popular Charm: Modernity in Popular Narratives

If we observe the development of modern fiction in Taiwan only from the perspective of the New Literature Movement in the 1920s, a special portion of writings produced during the transition from traditional fiction written in the classical Sinitic script to modern vernacular fiction is neglected. In other words, the emergence of modern fiction in Taiwan was by no means sudden.

According to Huang Mei-e's recent study, as early as the early twentieth century in *New Taiwan Sinophone Daily* (*Hanwen Taiwan ririxinbao*) there were already discourses and literary compositions that were influenced by modern Western thought. Huang argues that Li Yitao (1897–1921) and his "reportage fiction" shows the influence of enlightenment beliefs and popular art. Li's stories during the years between 1905 and 1911 already challenged the structures of composition and reading in traditional literary communities.[14]

Moreover, Lu Chun-yu's study of "detective fiction" points out how such narratives have, since the beginning of Japanese colonialism in Taiwan, introduced readers to a number of novel themes of modernity: "Through detective fiction, whose rise bespeaks certain characteristics in an industrialized and modernized society, writers display their understanding of and their reaction to modernity."[15] The common themes of these popular narratives include the adoration of rationalism and science, the imagination of justice and social order in modern legal systems, sensitive issues related to repressed sexuality, violence and death, and the aspiration for modern civilization. These popular narratives can be considered products of a transitional period.

The appearance of the column for the serialization of fiction in *Sanliujiu xiaobao* (a tabloid published on the third, sixth, and ninth days of each month) in September 1930 marked the beginning of popular narratives in Taiwan. Every issue of the tabloid, established by poets from two poetry societies—Taiwan Southern (*Taiwan nanshe*) and Call of the Oriole (*Chunying yinshe*)—contains four pages and eight folios in total. They are titillating anecdotes provided by various authors and poets.

Besides the anecdotes, *Sanliujiu xiaobao* is also known for its serialized novels. In terms of theme and style, the stories serialized are reminiscent of popular novels from the Mandarin Ducks and Butterflies school in China. Before the popular narratives written in Japanese began to appear in 1932 in *New Taiwan Citizen* (*Taiwan xinminbao*), these serialized stories were representative of popular fiction.

In April 1932, *New Taiwan Citizen* posted a public announcement inviting writers to submit their works.[16] Thereafter, popular narratives written in Japanese began to appear. From the perspective of reader reception, the writing of the literary history of Taiwan cannot be complete without taking into account the heretofore ignored popular narratives and their audience. In a sense, popular narratives provide important insight into conflicts between the intellectual elite and the masses. Precisely because the power of writing was controlled by intellectuals who enjoyed literature with serious agendas, popular narratives continue to struggle to be accepted and written into Taiwan's literary history, which is largely dictated by nationalism and the love of highbrow literature.

Gendered Experience of Modernity: Women Writers

The strict boundaries separating the intellectuals and the masses—"serious" literature and popular narratives—have prevented the emergence of a more comprehensive assessment of Taiwan literature. Similarly, the lack of consideration over gender issues tends to ignore women writers, and their achievements also warrant more critical appraisal. Examining works by women writers will cast new light on the differences between male and female writers and on how such differences contribute to the shaping of a literary landscape.

In colonial Taiwan, women faced not only patriarchal oppression but also colonial and capitalist oppression, which relegated them further to the margins in a triple structure of oppression.[17] In a society that was both patriarchal and imperialist, women were expected to play a "supporting" role. The rise of women's consciousness did not help alter their position in the social hierarchy structurally. The supporting role was all the more rationalized and emphasized when the colonial government began the movement of imperialization. The goal was to rally women to safeguard their homes so that their husbands and sons could fight the "holy war" without lingering concerns for their households. In such a historical context, it is understandable that the constitution of national literature would "naturally" exclude women's writings because such texts do not usually adhere to the grand narrative of the nation-state, which is dominated by realism and anti-imperialist and anti-feudalist concerns.

In the fictional works containing themes of anti-imperialism and anti-feudalism written by male writers, the reader rarely finds a story with a strong focus on women and female subjectivity. During the colonial period, women writers were inclined to write and publish prose essays. Fictional works by women writers were scarce, and if we were to take into account that some male writers actually adopted a feminine pen name, the number understandably becomes smaller. In my discussion, I exclude controversial texts and focus only on those that are indisputably penned by female writers. With the following stories, I wish to highlight the limits of literary criticism that were dominated by masculinist discourses of the nation-state.

Huang Baotao's "Life" (*Rensheng*, 1935) describes a village where almost all villagers participate in self-preserving projects in the face of economic depression. Though poor and exhausted, the villagers find a way to humor themselves: "This is called trash life! . . . We were born like trash anyway."[18] Against the backdrop of economic depression, the author focuses on female protagonists to express her compassion for laborers. A worker named Jinying is constantly harassed for her youthfulness and beauty. In addition, pregnant workers are required to perform men's work and as a result one of them dies a horrendous death. Huang pays particular attention to female workers and their position in social hierarchy, thus revealing the intersection of class and gender perspectives as her unique point of departure.

Ye Tao's "The Beloved" (*Ai de jiejing*, 1936) is semiautobiographical. The heroine, Suying, is an elementary school teacher who falls in love with Ruichang, a social activist. Suying is forced to leave her job because of her indirect involvement in politics. The couple's beloved baby loses his eyesight because the parents fail to provide enough vital nutrients for him. The story implies that women under patriarchy and capitalism were denied the conditions for fostering happy marriages and healthy children. With her simple narrative voice, Ye stresses both class and gender consciousness. She calls attention to the ways in which women are left alone to suffer without support from their male counterparts in the face of modern challenges.

In romantic fiction, women writers take a different approach to female psychology and to the delicate changes of mood and desire that are absent in grand anticolonial and anti-feudal narratives. Yang Qianhe's "Season of Blossoms" (*Huakai shijie*, 1942) links marriage to a quest for the purpose of life. Even though the bride's desire for self-discovery is prominent, eventually she enters into an arranged marriage, symbolizing her succumbing to patriarchy. Despite certain shortcomings, these stories represent a burgeoning endeavor to explore female subjectivity.

As discussed previously, since the late 1990s, studies of Taiwan fiction from the colonial period tend to focus on the "process" rather than the "result" of literary production. This is indicative of "a modernist turn" in Taiwan literary studies. The issues of modernity, modernism, enlightenment, nativism, and colonialism discussed in this chapter require further study from both aesthetic and intellectual perspectives. They could be further analyzed in terms of the authors' biographies and the evolution of literary thoughts and practices in both Taiwan and elsewhere in the world. Besides issues that pertain to grand narratives of the nation, there are minor narratives in popular fiction and writings by female writers that have yet to be adequately studied. This chapter is but an initial inquiry into these larger and more complex issues that continue to shape the literary landscape of Taiwan fiction.

– Translated by Kuei-chih Evelyn Wu

Notes

This chapter was modified and reprinted with permission from Chien-chung Chen (Chen Jianzhong), "*Chayi de wenxue xiandaixing jingyan: Riben zhimin tongzhi shiqi de Taiwan xiaoshuo* (1895–1945)" [Divergent experiences of literary modernity: Taiwan fiction during the period of Japanese colonial rule, 1895–1945] (previously unpublished essay).

1. Chiu Kuei-fen, *Hou zhimin ji qi wai* [Postcoloniality, etc.] (Taipei: Maitian chuban, 2003), 83–89.

2. Immanuel Wallerstein, *After Liberalism* (New York: The New Press, 1995), 144.

3. Lin Ruiming, ed. *Lai He quanji, xiaoshuo juan* [The complete work of Lai He: Fiction] (Taipei: Qianwei chubanshe, 2006), 55.

4. See Xu Junya, *Jianshu you jianlin: wenxue kan Taiwan* [Seeing the trees, Seeing the forest: A literary look at Taiwan] (Taipei: Pohaitang, 2005) and Yin Haofei, *Rizhi shiqi Taiwan xiaoshuo zhi Hanren zhi xisu yanjiu* [A study of Han customs in the Taiwan novels under Japanese rule] (Taipei University M.A. Thesis, 2004).

5. Wang Shihlang, *Taiwan shehui yundong shi: wenhua yundong* [A history of Taiwan's social movements: Cultural movements] (Taipei: Douxiang chubanshe, 1995), 508–509.

6. See Matsunaga Masayoshi, "*Kuanyu xiangtu wenxue lunjing* (1930–32)" [On the nativist literary debates, 1930–32], in *Taiwan xueshu yanjiuhui zhi* [Proceedings of the Taiwan Academic Conference, Volume Four] (1989), and Liao Qisheng, *Sanling niandai Taiwan xiangtu huawen yundong* [The 1930s Taiwanese Language Movement] (Chengkung University M.A. Thesis, 1990).

7. Chen Fangming, "*Xieshi wenxue yu pipan jingshen de taitou*" [Realist fiction and the advancements of the critical spirit], *Lianhe wenxue* [United literature] 16, no. 5 (March 2000).

8. Chen Zaoxiang and Xu Junya (eds.), *Weng Nao zuopin xuan* [Selected works of Weng Nao] (Zhanghua: Zhanghua xianli wenhua zhongxin, 1997), 181.

9. Hamada Hayao. "On 'The Road,'" *Wenyi Taiwan* [Taiwan literature and art], 6, no. 3, 1943, 142.

10. For more discussion on this topic, see Chen Chien-chung, "*Faxian Taiwan: Riju dao zhanhou chuqi Taiwan wenxue shi jiangou de lishi yujing*" [Discovering Taiwan: The historical context for the early period of Taiwan literature from the Japanese colonial era to the postwar years], *Taiwan wenxue pinglun* [Taiwan literary criticism] 1, no. 1 (July 2001).

11. Kawamura Minato. *Ikyô no showa bungaku* [Showa literature on a foreign land or foreign literature of the Showa period] (Tokyo: Iwanami, 1990).

12. Nishikawa Mitsuru, *Xichuan Man xiaoshuo ji 2* [The collected fiction of Nishikawa Mitsuru, Vol. 2], trans. Chen Qianwu (Kaohsiung: Chunhui chubanshe, 1997), 33.

13. Faye Yuan Kleeman, "*Bendi wenhua yu zhimin xiangxiang: guiguai, jingguan yu lishi chenshu*" [Local culture and the colonial imagination: Monsters, landscape, and historical narrative], in *Houzhimin de Dongya zaidihua sikao: Taiwan wenxue changyu* [The localization of thought in postcolonial East Asia: The Taiwan literary arena], ed. Liu Shu-ching and Chiu Kuei-fen (Tainan: Guojia Taiwan wenxueguan, 2006), 186.

14. Huang Mei-e, "*Cong shige dao xiaoshuo: Rizhi chuqi Taiwan wenxue zhishi xin zhixu de shengcheng*" [From poetry to fiction: The birth of a new order of Taiwan literary knowledge in the early period of Japanese rule], in *Kua lingyu de Taiwan wenxue yanjiu xueshu yantaohui lunwen ji* [Collected essays from the Academic Conference on Interdisciplinary Taiwan Literary Scholarship] (Tainan: Guojia wenxueguan, 2006), 73.

15. Lu Chun-yu, *Rizhi shiqi Taiwan zhentan xushi de fasheng yu xingcheng: Yi ge tongsu xin wenlei de kaocha* [The appearance and formation of Taiwan detective narratives during the Japanese occupation] (Chengchih University M.A. Thesis, 2004), 151.

16. *Huang Deshi, Rizhi shiqi Taiwan xin wenxue yundong gaiguan* [Survey of the Taiwan New Literature Movement under Japanese rule], in *Wenxian ziliao xuanji* [Selected works on historical literary documents], ed. Li Nanheng (Taipei: Mingtai chubanshe, 1979), 300.

17. Yang Tsui, "*Rizhi shiqi Taiwan funu jiefang yundong*" [Taiwanese Women's Liberation Movement during the Colonial Period]. (Taipei: Shibao wenhua, 1993), 54.

18. Huang Baotao, "*Rensheng*" [Life], in *Taiwan wenxue ji 1: Riwen zuopin xuanji* [Taiwan Literature, Vol. 1: Selection of Japanophone Works], ed. and trans. Ye Shitao (Kaohsiung: Chunhui chubanshe, 1996), 187.

14

Sinophone Indigenous Literature of Taiwan

History and Tradition

HSINYA HUANG

From ignored to recognized, Sinophone indigenous literature of Taiwan emerged in the 1980s and deserves much attention and praise, yet also invites some perplexing and even troubling questions. What exactly is Sinophone indigenous literature of Taiwan? What are the characteristics that distinguish Sinophone indigenous literature of Taiwan? In what way does the Sinitic script provide the cultural translation that coded the indigenous past and present? How can Mandarin (and the vernacular Sinitic script), the colonist's language, be created and reinvented to name the indigenous self and to mediate between the colonial conquest and indigenous history? Before the arrival of Han Chinese, the Dutch, the Spanish, and the Japanese, there had already been thousands of narratives, ceremonies, songs, myths, chants, and speeches performed and passed down orally from generation to generation. All this constitutes rich cultural and oral traditions in indigenous Taiwan, yet these categories were hardly visible to literary critics and scholars. Anthropologists along with folklorists and historians appropriated the tribal materials to substantiate what Bruno Latour calls "the modern constitution"—"the modern constitution" evolved through the history of dichotomizing thought to establish the division of Nature from Culture as the two purified building blocks of the world.[1] The native/indigene, who confounded Nature and Culture, became a vanished/vanishing premodern phantom. To redeem their oral traditions—the words of their ancestors—from oblivion, is one of the important missions of modern tribal writers. The relationship between the "oral" and the "literary" is then of particular significance. How to characterize indigenous orality in a Sinophone literary text? This article traces the history and tradition of Sinophone indigenous literature of Taiwan and, in so doing, ventures possible responses to the aforementioned questions in the meanwhile bringing together a narrative, which attests to Taiwanese indigenous identity in transit, placing Taiwanese indigenous lived experience, memory, and identity under scrutiny.

Though indigenous groups of Taiwan hold varieties of creation stories, archaeologists suggest that the history of Taiwanese aboriginal ancestry dates back to the late Paleolithic Age, some thirty thousand years ago, while earlier historical records written in the Sinitic script on aboriginal people in Taiwan were found in such marginal texts as *Records of Waters and Lands* (*Lianhai shuitu zhi*) of the Three Kingdoms Era of China. In most of the recorded history, indigenous people of Taiwan are defined, contained, and appropriated by numerous "civilizing" projects, launched by their colonists to serve the colonial agenda. The plain indigenes of Taiwan intermarried with Han immigrants, were assimilated to the mainstream Han culture, and even adopted a Han identity whereas their traditional language and social structure became extinct by the late nineteenth century. A hundred years later, the remaining highland indigenous tribes fell scarce in numbers; to date, there are only fourteen recognized tribes, namely, Amis, Paiwan, Atayal, Bunun, Rukai, Puyuma, Tsou, Saysiyat, Yami (Tao), Thao, Kavalan, Truku, Sakizaya, and Seediq, while many more have either been assimilated or unrecognized. In recent years with an evolving politicized discourse on Taiwanese national identity, however, Taiwanese indigenes and their cultures and traditions exert a significant impact on the dynamics and efforts to establish a distinct Taiwanese identity. Taiwanese indigenes are Austronesian peoples. With their genetic, linguistic, and cultural ties to other Austronesian ethnic groups, such as peoples of the Philippines, Malaysia, Indonesia, and Oceania, they represent the missing link of an ethnic identity unconnected to the Asian continent. In other words, their cultures and traditions become one thread in the political discourse of distinct Taiwan-ness, as separated from mainland (continental) China. The unassimilated excess of indigeneity was interpolated to strengthen Taiwanese nativism by the Taiwanese state. The late Taiwanese author and critic Shih-tao Yeh was straightforward in pointing out that "the future of Taiwanese literature will be shouldered by indigenous authors."[2]

The indigenes on the margins were hailed as instrumental in defining and exemplifying a new cultural paradigm. To a certain extent, the indigenous were appropriated and incorporated by Han-Taiwanese writers in their hope to establish a distinct body of national literature and in constructing a narrative of Taiwanese national identity as native. In his novel *Remains of Life*

(*Yu sheng*), Wu He, for instance, used as his historical backbone the Wushe incident of 1930, in which Seediq people in Central Taiwan violently protested against Japanese colonial rule. The interpretation of the incident has long been the exclusive preserve of the Han people and the Japanese, whose power gives them a form of cultural hegemony. Han Taiwanese appropriate indigenous culture and history to enrich their imaginary trajectory and the indigenous uprising serves as a righteous case of Taiwanese resistance against colonial oppression. In 1987 and 1989, respectively, Wu Chin-fa published two collections, *Mountains of Sadness: Selected Works of Taiwanese Aboriginal Novels* (*Beiqing de shanlin—Taiwan shandi xiaoshuo xuan*) and *Wish to Marry an Aboriginal Man: Selected Works of Taiwan Aboriginal Essay* (*Yuan jia shandilang—Taiwan shandi sanwen xuan*), juxtaposing works by Han Taiwanese writers with those by indigenous authors. He proposed *shandi wenxue* (mountainscape literature) as a genre that incorporates any writings about the mountainscapes of Taiwan by either indigenous or nonindigenous authors. The indigenes were used to being pejoratively called *shandi ren* (mountain people), and in this marginalizing ideology, apparently, the indigenes and their cultures and histories were part of the "mountainscapes" (*shandi*). The Han Chinese used to call indigenous people *shandi ren*, considering them to be part of the wilderness and uncultivated space. Just as Europeans once broadly used the word *heathens* to refer to Native Americans, *shandi ren* has a derogatory connotation related to perceived lack of civilization in indigenous peoples.

In retrospect, the earliest work published in the Sinitic script by an indigenous author was a collection of short stories by Kowan Talall (Paiwan) entitled *Traces of Dream in Foreign Lands* (*Yu wai meng hen*; Taiwan Commercial Press, 1971). Kowan reworks Paiwan traditional myths, weaving together rich materials and the complexity of past legends. Linking past and present, he maps out the migratory trajectory of the Paiwan ancestors, which is intertwined with the lived experiences of the tribe. Through the reworking of tribal myths and the interplay of orality and writing, Kowan recaptures multiple layers of reality, which impinge on the here and now. Cultures merge in the storytelling. He is one of the very few visible indigenous authors before the indigenous writings in Chinese bloomed in Taiwan in the 1980s.

Drastic changes took place in the 1980s with an outgrowth of political, social, and cultural metamorphosis in the Taiwanese context, in particular, after the lifting of martial law in 1987. A generation of Taiwanese indigenes was coming of age, who were the first of their tribes to receive a substantial Sinophone education. Inspired by the rise of the indigenous movement, indigenous authors used the Sinitic script to address a wide range of issues including the autonomy of indigenous people, and protest against assimilation, subordination of the indigenous culture, loss of cultural memory, communal identity, and authorial responsibility. One representative publication during this early era was *High Mountain Youth* (*Gaoshan qing*) magazine (1983–), which initiated writing projects to document, from indigenous perspectives, the history of colonial invasion and tribal resistance. Morning Star Publishing (*Chenxing*) was founded in 1980 and has published numerous indigenous works as their specialized series since 1987, which were among the well-recognized Sinophone writings of indigenous Taiwan. The launchings of *Hunters' Culture* (*Lieren wenhua*) and *Mountain-Sea Culture* (*Shanhai wenhua*) in 1990 and in 1993 were yet other milestones for the Sinophone indigenous literature of Taiwan. They sponsor and support numerous indigenous authors, while later Unitas Publisher (*Lianhe wenxue*) and Yelu Diverse Knowledge Management International Cultural Publishing, Ink Publishing, and other similar publishing companies followed suit. Fragrant Rice (*Daoxiang*) Publishing and Taiwanese Indigenous (*Taiwanyuan*) Publishing offered sponsorship for the publication of indigenous Sinophone writings. All these endeavors increased the interest in and chances to be published for new indigenous voices of Taiwan. Meanwhile, Taiwanese indigenous literature was established as a distinct discipline of research and study in the late 1990s. National Dong Hwa University in Hualian founded the College of Indigenous Studies and set up the Department of Indigenous Languages and Communication in 2001.

During the time of change, a group of native writers emerged. Essayists, poets, and novelists, in only two decades, significantly expanded the indigenous literary canon, which is powerful with its direct expression of demands for indigenous autonomy, political participation, land rights and other civil rights, and for the recovery of tribal memories, ceremonies, and names. The term "mountainscape literature" was replaced by "indigenous literature" (*yuanzhumin wenxue*). As defined by Wu Chin-fa, "mountainscape literature" includes writings by non-indigenes whereas "indigenous literature" is writings by indigenous authors: "Facing the increasing currents of social change, the indigenous faithful literary recorders held their pens with confidence to resist the oppression imposed upon the indigenous people; here indeed emerged the first group of excellent indigenous writers."[3] From "mountainscape" (*shandi*) to "indigenous" (*yuanzhumin*) is a shift of focus from topology and space to ethnicity and history. The ills of colonialism cannot be romanticized into the appreciation of beauty and tranquility of "mountainscapes"; neither can the native people of Taiwan be subjected to topology.

The indigenous authors write in the "colonist's language" to tell their own stories, remember their ancestors and rituals, and in so doing, retrieve a voice and self-hood long buried. Tribally identified, the authors directly experience a sense of being indigenous in their everyday lives. In order to make their cultural traditions accessible to a larger audience, they face the demand to write and record their collective and individual stories and experiences in the Sinitic script. Some of them incorporate native language, inscribing their tribal orality in the written texts. Others subvert the Taiwanese literary canon from within by retrieving the memories and voices long suppressed and by uncovering the indigenous lost tradition to amend the lack in history and culture. In "reinventing" the Sinitic script and turning the indigenous into a writing subject, there is hope that they will turn the process of colonization around. Their literature represents a form of cultural survival, which is read and viewed as a process of resistance, opposition, and decolonization.

And yet, the indigenous literature of Taiwan should be traced back to the oral tradition from the remote past in the forms of myths, songs, and legends, and the efforts to record such materials have been made since the Japanese Occupation period (1895–1945). Japanese anthropologists and linguists have consistently produced works on the indigenous people of Taiwan. The colonial intention involved in their knowledge production is obvious, for, one way to incorporate and contain Taiwan is through appropriating its local/native cultures and traditions. The act of writing serves as a tool of colonialism and a way to legitimate the political power, as Michel de Certeau indicates in his famous work *The Writing of History* (1988). *Report on Barbarian's Customs: The Taiwan Governors Office Provisional Investigation Committee on Taiwan Traditional Manners and Customs, 1915–1920*, edited by Yoshimichi Kojima, and *A Century of Japanese Anthropological Studies on Taiwan Aborigines. The Taiwan Governors Office Provisional Investigation Committee on Taiwan Traditional Manners and Customs, 1913–1921*, edited by Yukichi Sayama, are two distinct examples. In both instances, the Japanese anthropologists referred to indigenous peoples of Taiwan as "barbarians" and subjected them to the colonial power and written text while their "pens" are tools of "civilizing" and "converting" the barbaric native inhabitants.[4] In 1935, Japanese linguists Ogawa Hisayoshi and Asai Erin published a collection of nearly three hundred stories and legends, which remains an important source of reference in Taiwanese indigenous scholarship.[5] The indigenous culture was then the object of research by the outsiders/foreigners, be they missionaries, anthropologists, or linguists. In a nutshell, the materials gathered and assembled by non-indigenes contain roughly the following categories: historic accounts of wars and appeasement of aboriginal tribes by Han people; records based on travelogues by Han Chinese and Westerners, and accumulated archives about aboriginal societies and customs over fifty years of Japanese Occupation; and references gathered and produced by Japanese anthropologists and linguists of aboriginal dialects and phonetic symbols, alongside records of oral traditions containing rich mythical legends. As a matter of fact, the first written language learned and used by indigenous people was Japanese. During the Japanese Occupation period, indigenous people who received Japanese education wrote messages of appreciation to the Japanese colonizers for bringing them into civilization, which were published in a Japanese official journal in colonial Taiwan, entitled *Governing the Taiwanese Aborigines* (*Rihan no tomo*) from 1932 onwards to the end of World War II.

In the last two decades, while indigenous writers became highly aware of the power of their oral tradition and its effects on their identity and self-esteem, they have undertaken the mission to record their family stories before they vanish. Sun Ta-chuan and Syaman Rapongan, among many others, have lamented that the indigenous groups face a cultural crisis of losing their tribal roots: as the elderly pass away gradually, the stories, which sustain their ethnic survival, will vanish with them. Indigenous writers of the older generation, such as Lifok Oteng, Tiway Sayion, and Wu Ming-Yih from Amis, Masaw Mowna from Atayal, Siyapenjipeaya from Tao, and Dangalo Kingzi from Puyuma, rely heavily on oral tradition rather than regard themselves as creative writers. Works like Walis Loqang's *Atayal Footprints* (*Taiya jiaozong*) published in 1991, Syaman Rapongan's *Mythology of Eight-Generation Bay* (*Badaiwan de shenhua*) in 1992, Siyapenjipeaya's *The Yami Who Fished Rain Shoes* (*Diao Dao yuxie de Yameiren*) in 1992, and Yubas Naogih's *Stories of Atayal* in 2003 attempt to compose modern texts out of traditional stories mingling Chinese with the indigenous language, which Sun Ta-chuan called the "literature of the indigenous language" (*zuyu wenxue*).

Before colonial invasion, the indigenes did not use "writing" but poetic chanting to pass on their stories. Despite risking the loss of beauty, rich vocabulary, and expressiveness of their oral cultures, writing and the use of a single language as the means for a dialogue between the tribes as well as between the indigenous and other ethnic groups in Taiwan became a necessary evil. The emergence of indigenous Sinophone writing in the 1980s signifies the native articulation from liminality and their trajectories into modernity as well as the identity-seeking desire of the various indigenous groups. The indigenes are able to articulate their stories, from their subject positions. To think of "indigeneity" as "articulated" is, as James Clifford insightfully comments, to "recognize the diversity of cultures and histories that currently make claims under this banner."[6] This indigenous diversity in turn feeds back into local native traditions to define what "Taiwan-ness" is. Syaman Rapongan's ocean, Topas Tamapima's mountains, Walis Norgan's island, and a plethora of mythology and imagination of the universe encompassed in the contemporary indigenous literature in Taiwan represent a completely different subjectivity from that of the realist and heavily political Han Taiwanese local writings. The indigenous literature makes a breakthrough not only by offering an entirely different worldview but by restructuring relations between human and nonhuman and among humans.

In his autobiographical narrative "Surviving History—the Past, Present, and Future of the Indigenes," Sun Ta-chuan mentions that he was born in the early 1950s, a time when the Nationalist government promulgated "The Outline Plan for Improving Administrative Construction in Mountainous Areas," which officially proposed the working objective of "cultivating the mountains into flat land." He laments, "My childhood passed in the shadow of this national objective. In a way, my childhood was spent in the vanishing history and memory of tribal traditions." He witnesses his tribal elders shedding tears at the annual ceremony: "There was no familiar singing and dancing, no solemn ceremony, no speaking in the language of ancestors anymore. . . . At that moment, I realized why the elders wept at the ceremony."[7]

Indeed, the articulation of the indigenous groups as displaced and dispossessed cultures permeates contemporary Sinophone indigenous writings of Taiwan. It is the separation anxiety from home that propels one of the best-known contemporary Tao authors, Syaman Rapongan, to write. Syaman left Orchid Island for school when he was a teenager. He worked in the city throughout the next decade and participated in the indigenous demonstrations of the 1980s, of which the most significant was the Tao people's protest against the storage of nuclear waste on Orchid Island. At the end of the 1980s, Syaman decided to return to his homeland and resolved to be a "real Tao man":

> As I recall, for the last several years, I learned to dive and spearfish alone, trying to be a real Tao man to have the skills to support my family and to foster my self-confidence from the life experience of struggling with the ocean with the primitive physical strength of my ancestors. I tried to show my filial piety by providing fresh fish to my parents, to raise my children with sweet fish soup, just like my parents did when they raised me.[8]
>
> My great-great-grandfather and all my forebears lived in this small island. The moment they were born, they fell in the love with the sea, entertaining themselves by watching, worshiping, and adoring the sea. The sea-loving genes are already contained in my body, passed down from generation to generation. I love the sea fervently, almost to the degree of mania.[9]

Syaman's depiction of an intimacy and immediacy of that long-ago moment when his beloved ancestors were very much present links the tribal body with the individual, whereas the individual was empowered and became an agent of change at the time he returned to the tribe. Syaman formulates the indigenous body in its capacity to represent the hidden past and repressed memory, invoking the body as the site of vibrant connection and tribal knowledge. This ancestral immediacy and intimacy as the memory in the body permeates Syaman's narratives. It is further sustained and strengthened by his cultivation of the proprieties and techniques of his body. The acquisition of his bodily proprieties and techniques in order to interact with nature in a proper and traditional fashion bespeaks not only his desire to "savor" the waves but his urge to "save" the ocean, to set it straight.

Syaman's concerns pivot on environmentality, one of the most popular themes in the Taiwanese indigenous literature written in Chinese. As Syaman and his father select a tree, cut it down and make it into a boat, the process is deemed not only as a sacred ritual but as an ecological lesson. Syaman's father names the trees, delineating a rich tribal vocabulary as well as knowledge of the woods:

> Father (which is what "Syaman" means) of my grandchildren, this tree is apnorwa, and that one is isis. That tree is pangohen. . . . They are all excellent timber for building boats. This apnorwa has been waiting for you for more than a decade; it's the best timber for the middle pieced together on the two sides of the hull. This kind of timber rots the most slowly. This tree is a syayi, and it's the one we will cut down today for the keel.[10]

With prayers and poetry, furthermore, Syaman reveals an older Tao's attitude toward life, livelihood, and nature. His father mutters his prayers as the son listens and learns:

> Oh, mountain god of the forest, I am a grandfather; you know my voice and the smell of my body. The father of my grandchildren also comes to pray to you with me. Don't let the knife and axe in our hands became dull, so that you can show off your heroism by breaking the surging waves on the sea.[11]

Syaman's poetic sentiment revolves around humility and respect. Depicting his father, like his other tribal elders, engaging in an intimate conversation with mountain gods and tree spirits, Syaman expresses an awe of nature as he forges an itinerary for a bonding experience with nature. The generational continuity is made possible by the practice of responsibility and respect: "I tried to show my filial piety by providing fresh fish to my parents, to raise my children with sweet fish soup, just like my parents did when they raised me."[12] The acquisition of bodily skills for diving and spearfishing awakens his repressed genetic memory. It is central to the transmission of Tao tradition, which is based on intimate association with the sea, and it provides a platform of interaction between the old and the young, performing the dynamics of their rich culture together.

The homing-in motif is crucial to Sinophone indigenous writings of Taiwan, for instance, in the life narratives as different as Syaman Rapongan's *Cold Sea, Deep Passion, Black Wings,* and *Memory of Waves* and Walis Norgan's *Eternal Tribe, The Call of Wilderness,* and *Flying Squirrel with Sunglasses.* But the complexity of the homing-in motif is increasing as the concept of home evolves with time. What happens to those indigenes who, estranged from their original home base, try to make the urban setting a home away from home? What about the many indigenes whose sense of place is not firmly grounded? In fact, it is difficult to establish a sense of place given the loss of tribal lands and the limits of indigenous sovereignty in their traditional territories. Awareness of this continuing absence takes the form of a painful consciousness of places lost and constitutes a geographical inquiry into colonial and tribal history.

These writings are characterized by strong literary heteroglossia: history, language, and culture, social injustice, conflict and mediation between modernity and tradition, and the dilemmas facing urban indigenous people and numerous narratives of trauma in poetry, prose, personal and collective stories, and so forth. Indigenous authors work through the traumatic aftermath through language, turning testimony into history. The insistent return of the historical trauma, evidences of the scars and still-open wounds as a collective experience, and the memory shared and spread among the members of an oppressed group can be transformed into an iconic identity and the instrument of communal identification. Indeed, writings of traumatic processes work for the oppressed group to reclaim a history and transform it into a more or less enabling basis of life in the present. Monanen Malialiaves's poetry in *Beautiful Ears of Rice* (*Meili de daosui*) makes a drastic appeal by using prostitution as a metaphor for the demoralized and dehumanized condition of the indigenes deprived of their autonomy. By contrast, Lavulas Geren tones down to a moderate style and yet composes an equally strong resistance discourse. Taiban Sasala's *Looking for the Lost Arrow: Vision and Action of Tribalism,* Lyiking Yuma's *Heritage: Walking out of Accusation,* Topas Tamapima's *The Last Hunter* and *Notes of a Doctor in Orchid Island,* and Walis Norgan's poetry and narratives, among others, explore the impact of colonialism and capitalism on tribal life, the clash between national and tribal sovereignty, the indigenous people's everyday struggle, the devastation of colonialism and tribal resistance.

Indigenous women who write in the Sinitic script are relatively few though there are numerous grandmother storytellers who transmit and preserve tribal oral heritage: Liglav Awu's VuVu is a distinct example. Liglav A-wu, half-Paiwan, works on the intersection of gender, ethnicity, and class as oppressive matrix and discloses the confrontation and conflict of a mixed-blood woman. Her prose collection *Who Will Wear the Beautiful Clothes I Weaved* is among the most widely read indigenous pieces in Taiwan, in which she records her mother's life and her unhappy childhood memory and gives voice to marginalized indigenous women. Specifically, Liglav Awu problematizes the universal statements of "women" and challenges mainstream feminism for not seeing the predicament of the indigenous woman in her own right but forever appropriates her for its own ends. She is one of the four women writers selected by Sun Ta-chuan to be included in his 2003 *Anthology of Sinophone Indigenous Literature in Taiwan*, the other three being Paiz Mukunana, Dong Shuming, and Rimui Aki. Though small in number, they register a powerful cross-cultural feminist/female vision, which originates within their personal experience.

At the turn of the twenty-first century, Sinophone indigenous literature of Taiwan not only carries on the traditional forms and contents, such as the allusions to taboos, ceremonies, and storytelling traditions but also moves with the times. Now and then indigenous writers adopt a global and trans-cultural vision. Their works focus on diverse subjects including ecology, modernity, globalism, and planetary awareness. They transcend antagonistic colonizer-colonized consciousness to articulate their histories through epic narratives. By extending their respective tribal orality into their work, they mediate between the traditional and modern. Their texts are communicative because the stories provide the missing link between the ancestral past and the global-local present. They are furthermore transformative, converting cultural nothingness into insight. Some are realistic while others are fantastic, using the techniques of magical realism to structure their narrative paradigm. Their texts are above all healing since in them myth and history converge to make the "hurt" become the "hope": Masao Aki's (Atayal) *Atayal's Chi-chia Bay Creek: Atayal Tribe's Chronology and Memory* published in 1999, Bukun Ismahasan Islituan's (Bunun) *Brown Mountain and Moon Shadow: Bunun Poetry and Proverbs* in 1999, Ahronglong Sakinu's (Paiwan) *Wild Boar, Flying Squirrel, Sakinu* in 2000 and *Wind Walker: My Hunter Father* in 2005, Rimui Aki's (Atayal) *The Sound of a Flute in the Mountains* in 2001, Paiz Mukunana's (Tsou) *Don't be Angry, Dear A'ki* in 2003, Dadelavn Ibau's (Paiwan) *Goodbye, Eagles* in 2004, Rahic Talif's (Amis) *Muddiness* in 2006, Auvini Kadresengan's (Rukai) *Mysterious Disappearance: Rukai in Poetry and Essay* in 2006, Li Yong-song's (Atayal) *Goodbye Snow Country* in 2006, Badai's (Puyuma)

Deekwan the Witch: Tabalaw Tribe in Taisho Years in 2007, Nequo Sokluman's (Bunun) *Tonku Saveg* in 2008, and It Ta-os's (Saishiat) *Legends and Stories of Baka Mountains* in 2008.

Indigenous people of Taiwan do not have an exact word for literature. The Bunun call the mythological narratives and other stories *halihabasan*, literally meaning "(strange) things that happened in the ancient past"; Atayal and Paiwan counterparts are respectively *ywaw raran* and *milimilingan*. The Puyuma refer to myths, tales, and legends as *tinu pa'ti Ta tomuamuan*, that is, "ancestors' words," or *tinu pa'ti Ta ma'I Tangan*, that is, "the words of the elderly," while stories about the ancient heroic deeds set as model are *mutu ngayingayan* or *mutu ngayingai*.[13] To them, the way of life is the practice of "literature" or orature. Indigenous people fully demonstrate their ability to tell stories that mingle lived experience and living imagination in poetry, prose, and fiction and create a productively unique style: Monanen Malialiaves and Walis Norgan in poetry; Sun Ta-chuan, Syaman Rapongan, Topas Tamapima, Walis Norgan, Liglav Awu, and Ahronglong Sakinu in prose; Husluma Vava, Topas Tamapima, Yubas Naogih, and Nequo Sokluman in fiction.

The first and foremost problem facing indigenous writers is the writing system. When indigenous authors write, they have to cross the lines of difference between the indigenous and the mainstream culture, language, and ideology. The key term is translation or mediation, both cultural and linguistic, which suggests a bridging and connecting of two different cultural entities—from the traditional, oral, and communal to the modern, written, authorial/authoritative. The literature we encounter is always already at some distance from the communal and oral tribal culture and yet this does not give it a lesser claim to be called indigenous literature. The Sinophone indigenous writers are intercultural translators/mediators, who work to explore and challenge the clear-cut boundaries. Writing and identity are not conceived as a boundary to be maintained but rather as a nexus of relations and transactions, translation and mediation, actively engaging a subject. Although there has always been the call that emphasizes the importance of writing in the tribal languages, the indigenized Sinophone writings open up possibilities for tribal voices and richly hybridized dialogues between the indigenous and the mainstream groups. This hybridization is subversive. Situated between two worlds, the indigenous writers violate Chinese writing and cultural boundaries and effect a(n) (un)conscious subversion and remaking of the language, culture and history, filled with an extensive indigenous vocabulary, tribal expressions, and voices.

Despite the boom the indigenous literature has entered, Sun Ta-chuan seems to be pessimistic about the future of the indigenous culture, as he writes in his *Drinking Once in a Long Time*:

Like the twilight that possesses both the daybreak and nightfall, we cannot pronounce that the indigenous culture is dead/vanishing; neither can we encourage the illusion that it is on its peak. On the contrary, we should bravely accept the death or dark night of the indigenous culture and prepare the lamp to light through the long dark night positively.[14]

The indigenous language and culture are disappearing rapidly as assimilation continues apace. Yet, Sun's remarks involve not only the anxiety of facing cultural genocide and crisis of identification but strong criticism and self-reflection, open and introverted, and the commitment to act. The Sinophone indigenous writers not only compose writings in Chinese but also portray, at their best, the past, present, and future of indigenous communal experience, psyche, and their shared dreams. How to create unique artistic forms? How to maintain and revive the tribal cultures and oral traditions in writing? The Sinophone indigenous writers are appropriating an externally imposed/"other" language and thus entering into dialogue with the language itself and the history, ideology, and culture it signifies. In so doing, they are bridge builders and border crossers and confound the outside and the inside. The enfolding of the outside and inside and the blurring of boundaries require that we view indigenous literature as a continuum in history and culture.

Notes

1. Bruno Latour, *We Have Never Been Modern* (Cambridge: Harvard University Press, 1993), 13.

2. Yeh Shih-tao, "*Wode Taiwan wenxue liushinian*" [My Taiwanese literature for sixty years], *Wenxue Taiwan* [Literary Taiwan] 44 (2002): 48.

3. Wu Chin-fa, "*Lun Taiwan yuanzhumin xiandai wenxue*" [On Taiwan indigenous modern literature], *Gaoxiong wenxian* [Literature of Kaohsiung County] 12 (July 1992): 175.

4. For an overview of oral traditions of indigenous tribes of Taiwan, see Basuya, *Taiwan yuanzhumingzu shigang* (The history of Taiwan indigenous literature), 1–38, 1154–1174. For references to Japanese anthropological work on indigenous peoples of Taiwan, see Basuyu, *Taiwan yuanzhumingzu shigang* (The history of Taiwan indigenous literature), 1155–1157, 1182–1185.

5. Ogawa Naoyoshi and Asai Erin (eds), *Gengo ni yoru Taiwan takasago-zoku densetsu-shu* [The myths and traditions of the Formosan native tribes] (Taihoku [Taipei]: Institute of Linguistics, Taihoku Imperial University, 1935).

6. James Clifford, "Indigenous Articulations," in *Cultural Rupture and Indigeneity: The Challenge of (Re)visioning "Place" in the Pacific*, ed. David Welchman Gegeo (Honolulu: U of Hawai'i Press, 2001), 472.

7. Sun Ta-chuan, *Jiujiu jiu yi ci* [Drinking once in a long time] (Taipei: Living Psychology, 1991), 112–114.

8. Syaman Rapongan, *Leng hai qing shen* [Cold sea, deep passion] (Taipei: Unitas, 1997), 213.

9. Syaman Rapongan, *Heise de chibang* [Black wings] (Taichung: Morning Star, 1999), 80.

10. Syaman Rapongan, *Leng hai qing shen* [Cold sea, deep passion], 56–57.

11. Ibid., 57–58.

12. Ibid., 57.

13. Basuya Boyijernu, *Yuanzhumin de shenhua yu wenxue* [Indigenous mythologies and literature] (Taipei: Taiwan Aborigine, 1999), 1103–1104.

14. Sun Ta-chuan, *Jiujiu jiu yi ci* [Drinking once in a long time] (Taipei: Living Psychology, 1991), 118.

Writing Beyond Boudoirs

Sinophone Literature by Female Writers in Contemporary Taiwan

PEI-YIN LIN

In the age of globalization, scholars have shown burgeoning interests in Chinese-language literatures produced in different diasporic communities. Just as the notion of "Chineseness" has been constantly renegotiated, several attempts were made to remap the new configuration of Chinese-language literature.[1] Regarding the concept of the "Sinophone," Shu-mei Shih's definition excludes Chinese literature from China in general but includes those by Tibetan and other minority writers, whereas David Wang uses the paradoxical term "to include without" (*baokuo zaiwai*) to describe Sinophone writers' strategic appropriation of the Chinese sign in order to articulate their local sensibilities.[2] In short, Chinese literature from China in Wang's view is part of the Sinophone literature, but should not be considered more authentic than the Chinese-language writing produced by diasporic writers. Outside the U.S. academic circle, Chen Kuan-hsing and Chien Yung-hsiang advocated the network of *huawen guoji* (Chinese-language International) to urge different Sinophone communities to serve as each other's reference points, and Chiu Kuei-fen insists on the use of "literatures in Chinese."[3] Among the numerous Sinophone communities, Taiwan plays a significant role both as a producer and as a publisher. Sinophone literature from Taiwan, particularly the modernist and nativist fiction by male authors, has received considerable scholarly attention. To fill the lacuna, this chapter focuses on women writers' works. Rather than aiming for a comprehensive survey, it examines some important characteristics of this literature and explores how women writers have creatively responded to Taiwan's social reality. It argues that the vitality of Sinophone works by Taiwan's women writers lies in its flexibility, which allows their works to be socially engaging yet simultaneously personal.

Breaching the Limits of the Anti-Communist Framework

After its retreat to Taiwan in 1949, the Nationalist (Kuomintang) government exerted control over Taiwan's literary production through various means. The popularization of Mandarin as the only "national language" (*guoyu*)[4] and the establishment of official literary associations were two influential strategies. The advocacy of Mandarin began in 1946 as an integral part of the Kuomintang's cultural reconstruction projects in Taiwan.[5] Due to the linguistic switch from Japanese to Mandarin, most female writers proficient in Mandarin and therefore active during the early postwar Taiwan were émigré writers arriving in Taiwan in the late 1940s and early 1950s.[6] Besides promoting Mandarin, the Nationalist government established the Chinese Literary Awards Committee (*zhonghua wenyi jiangjin weiyuanhui*) to promote anti-Communist works in the early 1950s. In 1955, Chiang Kai-shek explicitly advocated "combat literature" (*zhandou wenyi*) to further reinforce the anti-Communist ideology. It is in this year that the Taiwan Province Women Writers' Association (*Taiwansheng funü xiezuo xiehui*) was established, which quickly attracted a large number of women writers.

Due to the exilic experience of these émigré writers, women's literature in this period is largely tinted with nostalgia for China and often categorized as literature of "anti-Communist nostalgia" (*fangong huaixiang*). Nevertheless, their works display rising gender awareness.[7] Pan Renmu's *My Cousin Lianyi* (*Lianyi biaomei*, 1952) and *Malan's Autobiography* (*Malan zizhuan*, 1952), though hailed as anti-Communist works, can be read as early examples of female bildungsroman. The former tells of a beautiful and spoiled heroine Lianyi's tragic life, whereas the latter narrates how Malan gradually turns into a mature woman after experiencing different adversities in life. Similarly, Lin Haiyin's *Memories of Peking* (Chengnan jiushi, 1960) touches upon the miseries of Chinese women trapped in a feudal society: Xiuzhen's pursuit of freedom of love ends tragically, and nanny Song's diligence is met with continuous setbacks. A possible way out is represented by Aunt Lan, yet whether she will find happiness with her lover remains unknown. Centering on female protagonists,[8] these works are more than simply anti-Communist nostalgic narratives. Instead, they provide gender-sensitive visions relatively uncommon at the time. They also point to the self-dissolving feature of nostalgic writing, as the more one strives to record one's hometown, the more one comes to realize that it is only sustainable through fictive, literary imagination.

If China represents a longing for one's past glory and bygone innocence, then Taiwan is frequently portrayed as a place with hopes and possibilities for renegotiating male-female relationships. Tong Zhen's "The Woman in the Wilderness" (*Chuanguo huangye de nüren*, 1960)[9] offers a salient example. Told in flashback, the divorced female protagonist in southern Taiwan gradually recognizes that the two families she has in China (her natal family and her ex-husband's family) are shackles for her, and the way forward is to be self-reliant. Other popular themes treated by female writers in the early postwar period include the misfortune of adopted daughters (*yangnü*) in Taiwan, and intermarriages (usually between Mainlander males and Taiwanese females). An ambitious work covering both topics is Zhang Shuhan's *Blossoms in Yunqiao* (*Yunqiao feixu*, 1969). The novel depicts how women are exploited as adopted daughters and prostitutes including serving as comfort women in wartime. Despite her longing for China and haplessness in Taiwan, the protagonist marries a Taiwanese man and later becomes a successful businesswoman in Yunqiao of southern Taiwan. The Mainlander/Taiwanese intermarriage is endowed with an amusing linguistic twist in Lin Haiyin's "The Story of Blood" (*Xie de gushi*, 1957), accounting how the Mainlander Mr. Peng's marriage with his Taiwanese wife Xiuluan finally wins his father-in-law's approval after he voluntarily donates his blood to help his father-in-law. The plot is plain, but the lingustic features of the text make this story unique.[10] For instance, to thank his son-in-law, Xiuluan's father utterance "You are truly kind" is rendered in Taiwanese sound: "你金家伙," which in literal Mandarin means "You gold guy." Lin's rendering "What's the matter?" as "新媽逮雞?" (new mother catches the chicken), and "wait a moment" as "burning eggs" (燒蛋) are other examples. This device is a humorous way to register the protagonist's linguistic difference, which subverts standard Mandarin expressions imposed by the exiled Mainlander government.

Thematic/Formal Innovations and Popular Romances

Per Nationalist government's ideological guidelines, works by women writers were usually considered "trivial" or "conservative." Ye Shitao states female writers' works offer "little social perspectives" and their popularity is because they "cater to the general readers' escapism."[11] Yvonne Chang argues that those female writers were too concerned about the stability of the Nationalist regime to examine patriarchal domination on a social level, whereas Chi Pang-yuan concludes that female writers in early postwar Taiwan were "full of talents yet no boudoir complaints."[12] However, scrutiny reveals that works by female writers do not strictly adhere to the principle of healthy and combat literature; quite the opposite, their works are often socially engaging and even potentially subversive. One of the most controversial cases is Guo Lianghui's *The Lock of the Heart* (*Xinsuo*, 1962), a novel about a young woman who follows her sexual pleasure and engages in an incestuous relationship. Guo's description of female desire and the subject of incest stirred up heated debates soon after the work was serialized in *Credit News* (*Zhengxin xinwen*) from January to June in 1962. Xie Bingying criticized the depiction of incest as "seeds of evil" and Su Xuelin accused Guo of trying to cater to readers. Guo's membership with the Taiwan Province Women Writers' Association was soon cancelled, and the Association asked the government to ban the work in November 1962.[13] In January 1963, the Ministry of Interior (*Neizheng bu*) banned it for "moral offenses" (*fanghai fenghua*),[14] and Guo was expelled from the Chinese Literary Association (*Zhongguo wenyi xiehui*) afterward.[15] This example highlights writers' practice of self-censorship, the impact of social conservatism, and the governmental control in literature. Moreover, it exposes the gap between writers' expected role as the arbiter of social morality and their thematic avant-gardism. Fortunately, this did not completely impede women writers from exploring controversial or taboo topics.[16]

Among those who consistently challenged the subservient role imposed on women, those young female writers surrounding the avant-garde journals of *Modern Literature* (*Xiandai wenxue*) and *Literature Quarterly* (*Wenxue jikan*) were prominent. Similar to their male counterparts, those young female writers are mainly well-educated intellectuals keen to breach the old thematic and formal conventions. Ouyang Zi's "Vase" (*Huaping*, 1961) depicts women not to be just beautiful objects to be appreciated by men, but independent individuals with their own thoughts. In the story, Shi Chuanzhi treats his wife Feng Lin like the delicate vase in their house. He yearns to own the vase completely, resembling his wish to dominate Feng Lin's life. When he fails to control her, he attempts to smash the vase. The vase remains unbroken, signifying the triumph of women's autonomy. "Devilish Woman" (*Monü*, 1967), as the title suggests, exposes the bleakness of the female psyche, which goes against the traditional demands on women as virtuous wives and good mothers (*xianqi liangmu*). The story tells how Qianru endeavors to sabotage her mother's second marriage, but without much success. What's more, the mother admits that she has never loved her late husband (Qianru's father) or Qianru, and has all the while been dreaming to be together with her lover.

As the 1960s was a decade in which cultural Westernization was prevalent and studying abroad relatively common,[17] significant formal and thematic changes to literary writing occurred in conjunction with cultural transformation. On the one hand, Ouyang Zi, for example, employed symbolism in "Vase" and the stream of consciousness technique in "Devilish Woman." Likewise, Shi Shuqing's "Gecko" (*Bihu*, 1962) is a highly symbolic and grotesque piece narrated in the form of the revengeful female protagonist's monologue. These women writers were fully participating in the modernist movement. On the other hand, following several writers' moving abroad (mainly to the United States) for further studies, "overseas student literature" (*liuxuesheng wenxue*) emerged.[18] It later developed into a distinct literary genre, and the term "rootless generation" (*wugen de yidai*) is occasionally used to characterize Taiwan literature of the decade. Yu Lihua's *Again, the Palm Trees* (*Youjian zonglü youjian zonglü*, 1965) vividly illustrates the rootless psyche of overseas students. For the generation of the male protagonist such as Tianlei, China has become too distant to return, the American dream is not as glorious as it seems, and Taiwan is merely an expedient sojourn. Torn between staying in Taiwan and returning to America, neither of which is home, Tianlei is unable to find a place where he can be fully content. Eventually he realizes that he can never rekindle his youthful ambition and becomes overwhelmed with loneliness.

Although overseas student literature and the aforementioned modernist works both reflect the zeitgeist of Taiwan during the 1960s, their orientation remains rather elitist. Concurrent to these thematically and formally experimental works, Qiong Yao's romances became popular and incited vigorous discussion among critics. Regarding her quasi-autobiographic novel, *Outside the Window* (*Chuangwai*, 1963), some scrutinized its conservative ideology while others considered the piece to be excessively contrived and sentimental.[19] Among her more than forty published books, Qiong Yao shifted effortlessly from slushy love stories in the earlier period, to happy-ending novels set in contemporary Taiwan, and then to stories set in premodern Chinese courts. Despite different settings and narrative styles, most of her romance novels contain dramatic plot twists, highly literary language, and clear characterization. Those elements prove to be well loved by readers, especially those seeking entertainment. As a commercially successful writer, Qiong Yao and her fame invite us to rethink the division between highbrow and popular fiction, on which criticism about her works in the 1970s was focused. Although in the 1980s scholars began to examine her case as a social phenomenon, the literary dimension of Qiong Yao's fiction is yet to be fully evaluated.

Multifarious Literary Activism

The 1970s witnessed the emergence of Taiwanese nativist consciousness, as a response both to the increasingly individualistic writing of the modernists, and to the Nationalist government's Western-style modernization policies that left manual workers heavily exploited. Though some modernist writers published their more mature works in the decade, the mainstream literature of this period consisted of works describing Taiwan's social reality. Representing the underprivileged groups such as factory workers, fishermen, and urban proletariats became common in this literature. The growing dissatisfaction with the modernist camp later triggered the nativist literary debate in 1977 and 1978, during which Ye Shitao's Taiwan-centered viewpoint, Chen Yingzhen's leftist and China-leaning nationalist stance, and Wang Tuo's reformist and realist tendency represent the three major views. Although the virulent debate cooled down after Wang Sheng advocated a "pure" nativist literature, the ideological difference between Ye Shitao and Chen Yingzhen was deep and remained not fully articulated during the debate. In contrast to the polemical nature of the debate among male writers, works by female writers appear less ideologically oriented. Hsiao Li-hung's (Xiao Lihong) family saga *A Thousand Moons on a Thousand Rivers* (*Qianjiang youshui qianjiang yue*, 1980)[20] is such a case in which Taiwanese nativism and yearning for China can somehow harmoniously coexist.

Generally speaking, works by women writers in the 1970s can roughly be divided into three types—reformist, China-longing, and popular (essay) writing—and all of them can be considered literary activism. For the first type, an example in point is the socially active writer Zeng Xinyi. With her concerns for female manual workers, Zeng's works attended to the gap left by her contemporary male writers.[21] "Caifeng's Wish" (*Caifeng de xinyuan*, 1977) depicts how a department store deceives Caifeng by asking her to work as a prostitute, and how saleswomen were routinely not compensated for overtime work. In the story, Caifeng's "client" is a Japanese man, through whom Caifeng recalls all the atrocities committed by Japan. The text thus registers concerns for female laborers and critiques foreign, neocolonial dominance in Taiwan.

Simultaneous to the nativists' call for writing about Taiwan's reality, however, some young writers formed a literary group in 1977, the Double-Three Club (*sansan jikan*), to express their penchant for an idealized, ancient Chinese culture and to promote love in order to redress the increasingly tense ideological conflicts. Consisting of young Chu T'ien-wen (Zhu Tianwen) and Chu T'ien-hsin (Zhu Tianxin), the Club epitomizes the second type.[22] Under the influence of Mainlander exile Hu Lancheng, the members aspired to have the ambition of traditional Chinese literati (*shi*) with youthful patriotism. Their works are largely romantic, idealistic, and China-leaning, which to some extent can be seen as a means to counter the separatism associated with some of the nativist writings.[23] The third type is found in San Mao's essay collections such as *Sahara Stories* (*Sahala de gushi*, 1976) and *Crying Camels* (*Kuqi de luotuo*, 1977) that recall her life in Africa. They describe guerrilla warfare in the Sahara, numerous exotic adventures, and cross-cultural encounters. Most of the pieces are narrated in the first person and told with humor and wit. San Mao's bohemian image, built on her extensive travels and interracial marriage, to some extent displayed a fulfillment of romantic love, and a kind of freedom-loving and self-searching activism. Its continuous appeal, particularly to young people, is hardly surprising.[24]

Pluralism, Identity Politics, and Post-National Writing Since the 1980s

After Annette Lü's calling for New Feminism in 1972 and with the establishment of Awakening Foundation Press (*Funü xinzhi zazhishe*) in 1982, the 1980s witnessed the continued development of female consciousness. Although works by young women writers active during this period have been labelled as "boudoir literature" (*guixiu wenxue*), many of their works actually reveal feminist ideas. For instance, in *The Butcher's Wife* (*Shafu*, 1983), Li Ang subverts the demeaning attitude toward women by telling readers that not all women guilty of killing their husbands must be promiscuous, and Ping Lu in a sci-fi story creates a female robot to rewrite the male-centric myth of creation. In the works of Liao Huiying, Xiao Sa, and Yuan Qiongqiong, the female protagonists[25] are also usually self-sufficient whether with or without a marriage, illustrating that women now enjoy more choices and sexual mores have become more liberated than before as a result of economic prosperity.

With the waning of the Kuomintang power and the lifting of martial law in 1987, political ecology in Taiwan underwent profound changes. Accordingly, literary works stressing one's cultural identity and ethnic memories surged,[26] including those tackling the long-repressed February 28 Incident of 1947, when the exiled Mainlander government massacred thousands of protesting Taiwanese.[27] Chu T'ien-hsin's works, particularly, "In Remembrance of My Buddies from the Military Compound" (*Xiang wo juancun de xiongdimen*, 1992) and *Ancient Capital* (*Gudu*, 1997), typify this wave of identity narration.[28] Similar efforts are also found in the works by Li Ang and aboriginal female writers such as Liglav A-Wu and Rimui Aki.[29] Weaving two important events (the cessation of Taiwan to Japan in 1895 and the February 28 Incident of 1947) into the plotline, Li Ang in her *Labyrinthine Garden* (*Miyuan*, 1991) provides a political allegory of Taiwan through a saga that depicts the female protagonist Zhu Yinghong's family. After her father's death, Zhu Yinghong is expected to restore the family garden filled only with native plants and fauna of Taiwan. With the financial help from her entrepreneur lover Lin Xigeng, Zhu establishes a trust and donates the garden to the trust. If we take the garden as an emblem of Taiwan, then Taiwan's nation-building requires the combination of old cultural capital (symbolized by Zhu's father's cultural sophistication) and the new economic capital (represented by Lin's aggressive capitalist endeavors). It also suggests that reconstructing Taiwan has chiefly been a male-centered project. Toward the end of the novel, Lin becomes impotent, and Zhu hopes to have a last glance at the garden. She is afraid that "everything in it might disappear, as if nothing has ever happened or existed."[30] Lin's impotence implies a demotion of male power, while the garden's fate suggests that (male) nation-building (garden-restoration) might simply be nothing but myth.

The Seven-Generation Affectionate Bonds Between Taiwan and China (*Qishi yinyuan zhi Taiwan-Zhongguo qingren*, 2009), Li's latest work, is written in a similar self-reflexive fashion. Through a romance between a Taiwanese female writer, He Fang, and a Chinese government official, Zhou Xiaodong, this novel reflects the complex China/Taiwan relations on mythical, socio-economical, and politicohistorical levels. Through He Fang's ambivalence toward Chinese men (she finds them attractive but dangerously aggressive), Li Ang explores how China and Taiwan are "so much the same yet totally different"[31] and contemplates Taiwan's position in an era of globalization. It appears that neither leaning toward China nor remaining insular, two positions often reduced to the Nationalist Party's versus the Democratic Progressive Party's attitude toward China, presents a productive solution. Without lining up with any particular ideology[32] and deliberately employing the overgrown genre of a love story in which the male protagonist dies, Li Ang demonstrates that the female's (and female writer's) "soft" strategy may be, in the end, much more enduring.

In addition to the trend of narrating identity and the nation, stylistic experiments in the works of female writers are worth noticing. Su Weizhen's dual narrative, Ping Lu's alteration from sci-fi fantasy to historical narrative, Chu T'ien-hsin's playful narrative voice, and Qiu Miaojin's self-writing are all impressive new developments. Many of their practices can be seen as deliberately counter-hegemonic, although the hegemonies targeted are not all the same. In *Silent Island* (*Chenmo zhi dao*, 1994), Su Weizhen unfolds the plot in a form of dual narrative. Each centers on one female protagonist, but interestingly, both female protagonists are called Chenmian. One travels between different places and later becomes a single mother, while the other is a married woman residing in Taiwan and opts for an abortion. Wanderings, continuous pursuit of sexual adventures, and a sense of alienation are the similarities shared by the two otherwise unrelated characters. The narrative continuously shifts between the two Chenmian, which is likely an effort to decentralize a single dominant voice. Ping Lu's "Taiwan Miracle" (*Taiwan qiji*, 1989) takes the form of sci-fi fiction to mock the social disorder of Taiwan. But after the mid 1990s, she gradually turns to gendered historiography. *Love and Revolution* (*Xingdao tianya*, 1995) rescues Song Qingling (wife of Dr. Sun Yat-sen) from the nationalist discourse, stressing her experience as an individual and a woman. After the millennium, Ping Lu changes gears again. Based on the death of the legendary singer Teresa Teng, *When Will You Return* (*Heri jun zailai*, 2003) mingles historical, medical knowledge and popular memories in a form close to detective or espionage fiction involving the Nationalist Party's secret agents. In her latest novel *East and Beyond* (*Dongfang zhi dong*, 2011), though focusing on the male-female relationship, Ping Lu weaves a complex picture of the China-Taiwan interactions during the premodern and modern periods and this resonates ambitiously with Li Ang's attempt mentioned earlier.[33]

Among women writers in contemporary Taiwan, Chu T'ien-wen is an acclaimed stylist.[34] Her short story "Fin-de-siècle Splendor" (*Shijimo de huali*, 1990) is a collage composed of exotic fabrics, scents, and colors. The twenty-five-year-old protagonist Mia lives in a fluid and culturally amalgamated world, identifying the network of the global as her "homeland." Mia for sure can be called a fetishist of material objects. However, as she is able to explore and trace the implied meanings of objects, her fetishism indicates that she is an accomplice, instead of a victim, in the ultra global and hybrid world. The story ends with Mia's claim that she can not only survive, but also rebuild the collapsed world of men with her memories of scents and colors. We can consider this story a playful post-national account of Taipei with a distinctive feminist hue.

The celebration of hybridity and alterity is taken further in works concerning homosexual desires such as Chu T'ien-wen's *Notes of a Desolate Man* (*Huangren shouji*, 1994), which depicts the relationship between two gay men—the middle-aged timid Xiaoshao (the narrator of this novel) and his gay activist friend Ayao. Throughout the novel, Xiaoshao oscillates between taking the position of heterosexual morality (revealed through references to Levi Strauss's structuralism) and that of gay hedonism (with references to Foucault). The protagonist, however, harbors an androgynous identity (he views himself as a feminine soul in a masculine body), which undercuts the novel's resistance against the paternal and heterosexual culture. Although critics have pointed out various problems with this novel,[35] Zhu's fragmentary narrative and elaborately wrought language seem effective in representing the fluidity of sexuality. This novel can perhaps be read as an attempt to reflect on the power embedded within gender discourses in general. In addition to a gender-centered interpretation, this novel also demonstrates how writing can be a radical act enabling the potentiality of an autonomous space of literary creation beyond all hegemonic discourses.[36]

While Zhu elevates writing to such intellectual height, Qiu Miaojin takes it to the private realm where there is little demarcation between textual life and real life, such as in her *Testament of Montmartre* (*Mengmate yishu*, 1996). Qiu established her fame as a lesbian writer after the publication of her controversial novel, *The Crocodile's Journal* (*Eyu shouji*) in 1994. The novel was received warmly among Qiu's many young lesbian readers, but scholars' views on this work diverged. Some were concerned that Qiu's accentuation of T (close to the English term butch) narrators risks reproducing oppressive, masculinist gender relations, while others credited Qiu for presenting Taiwan's local version of lesbian culture.[37] In my view, what makes Qiu stand out from other authors of queer fiction is the honest self-exploration and autobiographic tendency in her works. Written in retrospection and introspection, *Testament of Montmartre* is such a case in which the narrator tells about her nearly fascist love for her lover Xu, a love tinted with sadomasochistic passion and violence. Love for the narrator is closely intertwined with her pursuit of the beauty of life and art, hence writing love letters to Xu is roughly analogous to drawing up her will. Toward the end, it becomes almost a logical choice for the narrator (and perhaps for Qiu also) to declare "eternal love" through death. On the surface, the letters are written for Xu, but the narrator's aesthetic style is so dominant that the letters become more a monologue or diary of the narrator. It is this self-writing, or even life-writing, which differentiates Chiu from her contemporaries in queer writing. Paradoxically, it is the public domain—a collectively shared lesbianism Qiu's works potentially projects—rather than the private domain of self-realization that has caught the attention of critics and Taiwan's local lesbian communities.[38]

Conclusion

Sinophone literature by women writers in Taiwan over the past six decades has displayed a great diversity and vitality. The issues with which female writers are concerned can be small ones, such as personal love, or big ones, such as social inequality and identity construction. The diversity of their writing is so vast that it is impossible to pin down one thematic focus that can be considered unique to Taiwan fiction written by women writers. Some are well engaged with topics of the day, while others strive to write for their own sake regardless of political correctness. Stylistically, women's literature from Taiwan also proves to be highly adaptable. The writers discussed in this chapter demonstrate that they can be equally at home with popular romances, travelogues, and aesthetically experimental modernist writing in form, or with nativist rhetoric and postmodern playfulness in tone. Their works collectively offer profound insights into Taiwan society, continuously challenging different structures that may be detrimental to their creativity, be it the anti-Communist ideology, conservative mentality, gender bias, or readers' tastes. With their gender-sensitive perspectives, they have produced works that are on a par with male writers' accomplishments in quality and quantity, and some have deservedly received international accolades.[39]

There are two phenomena related to Taiwan's Sinophone writing that are worth mentioning separately at the close of this chapter. One is that even though writers are obsessed with Taiwan, they also simultaneously endeavor to go beyond the narrow framework of narrating the nation. Looking back at the path of women's literature in Taiwan, we can see that writers in different periods have consistently tried to challenge and negotiate the boundaries regulated either by the nation or by men. Many of their works reflect the oppression suffered by women, critiquing male-centered social order in no uncertain terms. The gendered nostalgic writing of the 1950s and Guo Lianghui's and modernist writers' works in the 1960s illustrate this well. In the 1970s, women's writing was most fruitful either in the vein of nativist writing, or the often castigated popular romance genre, represented by the work of Qiong Yao. By the 1980s, especially after 1987, women's literature became bifurcated into the postmodern practice of playfulness and postcolonial obsession with identity. So far, however, attention has been largely focused on highbrow literature. Popular female authors in this regard are often "doubly marginalized." On the list of "30 Classics of Taiwan Literature," only five female writers were included.[40] Other instances, such as *Asia Weekly*'s ranking of "Top 100 Works of Twentieth-century Chinese Fiction" and Columbia University Press's "Modern Chinese Literature from Taiwan" series further confirm this predilection for high-brow literature that tends to marginalize women writers.

This question of style presents an urgent issue concerning Taiwan literature in the global context. Chu T'ien-hsin once observed from her personal experience that a likely crisis for Taiwan writers is due to globalization and urbanization: "There are no stories in cities" (*chengshi wu gushi*).[41] In other words, Taiwan writers writing about globalized cities of Taiwan tend not to show anything that is locally unique to Taiwan. This may well be a relief for those optimists as it means Taiwan writers are less likely to be accused of self-orientalization to cater to the Western readership. Still, how to enhance visibility locally and gain recognition globally remain two paramount challenges for Taiwan writers. Female writers are no exception. Their work has undoubtedly surpassed the narrow boudoir vision of traditional feminine writing. But, in addition to writing good works, the future of their writing is likely to be shaped by a global Sinophone readership beyond Taiwan and a global non-Sinophone readership through translations.

Notes

1. Earlier relevant terminologies include "the commonwealth of modern Chinese literature" used by Helmut Martin in 1966, "overseas Chinese literature" (*haiwai huawen wenxue*) used by Chinese scholars since the 1980s, and "world literatures in Chinese" (*shijie huawen wenxue*) proposed in early 1990s. In 2003, the 'Studies on World Chinese Literature" Web site was established.

2. See Shih's "Global Literature and the Technologies of Recognition," *PMLA* 119, no. 1 (2004): 29 fn. 5, and her *Visuality and Identity: Sinophone Articulations Across the Pacific* (Berkeley: University of California Press), 30. As for Wang's idea, see his "*Wenxue xinglü yu shijie xiangxiang,*" [Literary trajectories and world imagination], *United Daily News* (July 8 & 9, 2006).

3. See Chen's and Chien's "*Xin ziyou zhuyi quanqiuhua zhixia de xueshu shengchan,*" [Academic production under neoliberal globalization] in *Quanqiuhua yu zhishi shengchan: Fanxi Taiwan xueshu pingjian* [Globalization and knowledge production: Reflections on Taiwan's academic evaluations] (Taipei: Tangshan, 2005), 3–30. Chiu's notion can be found in her "Empire of the Chinese Sign: The Question of Chinese Diasporic Imagination in Transnational Literary Production," *Journal of Asian Studies* 67, no. 2 (May 2008), 594 fn. 1.

4. According to Wei Jiangong, a linguistics scholar from China and one of the earlier postwar Mandarin promoters, anything that Chinese people speak can be considered "*guoyu*" as long as it does not use abcd or ㄅ ㄧ ㄨ ㄧ ㄝ. Unfortunately, Wei's definition does not correspond well with the Kuomintang's language policy in which the use of local languages such as Taiwanese in public settings is restricted and exclusive use of Mandarin enforced.

5. The domination of Mandarin Chinese in public sectors such as schools and on television lasted until the 1980s. With the democratization progress, more and more Taiwanese language programs appeared. Although nowadays children can learn their "mother tongues" (Taiwanese, Hakka, or aboriginal languages) at schools, the legitimacy of Sinophone Taiwan literature remains questionable for certain radical promoters of Taiwanese language, who also demand an apology from the Ministry of Education for their changing Taiwanese language (*taiyu*) to Southern Min language (*minnan yu*). A recent confrontation took place in a public lecture held in Tainan during which Jiang Weiwen accused Huang Chunming's not writing in Taiwanese language as "shameful."

6. It is, however, notable that there were few female writers during Taiwan's Japanese period. Yang Qianhe, Huang Fengzi, and Huang Baotao are some of the more well-known names.

7. As early as in 1950, Meng Yao discusses women's dilemma between individual fulfillment and family duties as mothers and wives in her essay "The Weaker, Are Your Names Women?"

8. In addition to Lin Haiyin's aforementioned *Memories of Peking*, examples can be found in Yu Lihua's *Recollections of Qing River* (*Menghui qinghe*), which is set in Zhejiang; Nie Hualing's *Shiqu de jinlingzi*, which is set in the suburb of Chongqing; Zhang Shuhan's *Unforgettable Reminiscences* (*Yi nanwang*); and Qi Jun's essays.

9. Tong Zhen, "Chuanguo huangye de nüren," in *Heiyan* [Black smoke]. Taipei: Minghua, 1960, 158–176.

10. Similar phenomenon of linguistic hybridity can be found in the works of other writers either from the colonial period (such as Lai He) or later period (such as Wang Chen-ho).

11. *Taiwan wenxue shigang* (Kaohsiung: Wenxuejie, 1998), 96.

12. See Chang's "Three Generations of Taiwan's Contemporary Women Writers: A Critical Introduction," in *Bamboo Shoots After the Rain* (New York: Feminist Press at the CUNY, 1990): XV–XXV, and Chi's "Guiyuan zhiwai" (Beyond the Resentment in Boudoirs), *Qiannian zhi lei* [Tears of a thousand years] (Taipei: Erya, 1990), 109–147.

13. See *United Daily News*, 2nd ed. (November 4, 1962).

14. Publications were strictly managed by the Taiwan Garrison Command and regulated by the Publication Control Act during the martial law era.

15. A detailed examination can be found in Edel Lancashire's "The Lock of the Heart Controversy in Taiwan, 1962–63: A Question of Artistic Freedom and a Writer's Social Responsibility," *The China Quarterly* 103 (September 1985), 462–488.

16. Though Guo claimed "self-censorship" after *The Lock of the Heart* controversy, her works remain comparatively radical thematically. A good case in point is Guo's novel entitled *Liangzhong yiwai de* [Beyond the two types, 1978], which tackles women's same-sex desire.

17. According to the statistics of the Ministry of Education, the number of females who went abroad between 1962 and 1971 is 24,241, amounting to about one-third of the total student number. This "wave" of studying abroad (especially in the United States) was partly because the restrictions of studying abroad were loosened in 1962, and partly because of the attraction of Western world, which is often associated with openness and advancement.

18. Bai Xianyong [Kenneth Pai], Zhang Xiguo, Yu Lihua, and Nie Hualing are some of the representative writers of overseas students literature.

19. For the discussion of the conservatism in this story, see Li Ao's "*Meiyou chuang, nayou 'Chuangwai'?*" [Without a window, where is 'Outside the Window'?], *Wenxing* 93 (1965): 4–15. For a negative reception of Qiong Yao's style, see Hen Tu's "*Ping banben xiaoshuo 'chuangwai': Jianlun zuopin de 'shendu' yu 'guangdu'*" [On half 'Outside the Window': And also on the 'depth' and 'breadth' of the work], *Zuojia* 1, no. 2 (1964): 54–55. For a comprehensive sociological analysis on Qiong Yao's works and popularity, see Lin Fangmei's *Jiedu qiongyao aiqing wangguo* [Reading Qiong Yao's kingdom of love] (Taipei: Taiwan Shangyu yinshuguan), 2006.

20. It was serialized in *United Daily News* in 1980 and was also the winner of the 1980 *United Daily News* Literature Competition. After its publication in 1981, it became an instant bestseller and remained popular for a long period. Hailed as one of the bestselling books by native Taiwanese writers, this novel's 25th-year special edition was published in 2006 by Renmin Wenxue in Beijing.

21. Zeng was inspired by the nativist literary debate, and was involved in social movements calling for Taiwan's democracy and aborigines' rights. As for the genre poetry, several of Chen Xiuxi's works show strong Taiwanese consciousness.

22. For instance, in Chu T'ien-hsin's *Danjiang ji* [Record from Tamkang], China is referred to as "an eternal lover." Shenzhou Poetry Society, calling for returning to tradition and individuals' social devotion, is another example exhibiting longing for China.

23. Yvonne Chang further points out that the Double Three's evoking ancient China is useful for them to reiterate that Taiwan's aborigines also inherit the same cultural tradition. See Zhang's "Zhu Tianwen and the New Orientations of Taiwan Culture and Literature," *Chungwai Literary Monthly* 22, no. 10 (March 1994): 81.

24. For more about San Mao, see Miriam Lang's "San Mao Goes Shopping: Travel and Consumption in a Post-Colonial World," *East Asian History* 10 (December 1995): 127–164 and "San Mao and Qiong Yao: A 'Popular' Pair," *Modern Chinese Literature and Culture* 15, no. 2 (Fall 2003): 76–120.

25. Such as Ahui in Liao Huiying's *Youma caizi* [Rape seeds], Fan Anping in Xiao Sa's *Weiliang de ai* [Weiliang's love], and Jingmin in Yuan Qiongqiong's "Ziji de tiankong" [A space of one's own].

26. Examples include Yuan Qiongqiong's *Jinsheng yuan* [This love, this life, 1988], Chu T'ien-hsin's "Xindang shijiu ri" [19 days of the new party, 1989], and Su Weizhen's *Likai tongfang* [Leaving Tongfang, 1990].

27. Works tackling the February 28 Incident by female writers include Chen Ye's *Nihe* [Muddy river], Xiao Lihong's *Baishuihu chunmeng* [Spring dreams over white water lake], and Li Ang's short story "Caizhuang xieji" [Bloody sacrifice with color makeup].

28. In the 1990s, Chu T'ien-hsin can easily convert herself to her maternal side (for her mother was born in Taiwan) to be "ideologically correct." However, she chose to narrate the anxiety of "not being included" encountered by the second-generation mainland immigrants. In the nativist critics' eyes, Chu T'ien-hsin's works become evidence of her "self-alienation." Her works, however, are not necessarily an inscription of the second-generation mainlanders' memory per se, as they also address the general sense of displacement encountered during the process of modernization.

29. Liglav's father is a mainlander, and her mother belongs to the Paiwan tribe. She grew up in the Nationalist government officials' dependents compound and identified herself as the second generation of mainlanders until she returned to the Paiwan tribe with her mother after her father's death. *Hometown of Taiwanese Cherries* (2010) by Rimui Aki (Atayal tribe) marked the first full-length novel by one of Taiwan's aboriginal female writers. Many aboriginal writers choose to compose in Chinese in order to reach a wider readership. Some, however, do try to write in the aboriginal languages. For more about the aboriginal writing in Taiwan, see the chapter in this volume by Hsinya Huang.

30. Li Ang, *Miyuan* [Labyrinthine garden] (Taipei: Yueyi chuban, 1991), 312.

31. *Qishi yinyuan zhi Taiwan-Zhongguo qingren* [The seven-generation affectionate bonds between Taiwan and China] (Taipei: Lianjing, 2009), 45, 92, and 139.

32. When showing the draft of the story to her friends in different political camps, Li said that it pleased no one. Her Taiwan-centered friends were unhappy with the plot (a Taiwanese woman falls for a Chinese man) and Li's positive portrayal of Zhou Xiaodong in the work, and

her China-inclined friends felt that Li's depiction of China ought to be more positive. Some were even concerned that China will be unhappy with it, presumably because of the section on Tibet in this novel. See Su Huizhao's "Li Ang Attempts to Write Romance with New Techniques" (*Li Ang changshi yong xinde jifa shuxie aiqing*) (January 19, 2009), http://books.yam.com/publish/publish_detail_2.asp?pub_date=2009/01/19&kind=1&ID=817

33. Another extremely ambitious project of historical construction is Shi Shuqing's *Taiwan sanbuqu* [Taiwan trilogy]. The first one accounts Shi's hometown Lugang's rise and fall during the Qing dynasty. The other two are set under the Japanese rule, with one focusing on Japanese women and the other on a Taiwanese gentry family.

34. Ah Cheng describes Chu T'ien-wen's style as "sumptuous" (*shehua*) and David Wang refers to Zhu as a writer possessing the ability of "alchemy of words" (*wenzi lianjinshu*).

35. Liou Liang-ya questions whether it is possible to resist if one's (Xiaoshao's) subjectivity is yet to be constructed. See "Oscillating Between Modernism and Postmodernism: Issues on Nation, Generation, Gender, and Sexuality in Chu T'ien-wen's Recent Works," in *Yuwang gengyishi: Qingse xiaoshuo de zhengzhi yu meixue* (Taipei: Yuanzun, 1998), 23–25. Liou's point echoes with Padmini Mongia's notion that the hybrid subject may be in danger of "aspecificity and ahistoricity." See "Introduction", *Contemporary Postcolonial Theory: A Reader*. London: Arnold, 1996, 1–18. Yvonne Chang considers Xiaoshao's worldview conservative. See Yvonne Sung-sheng Chang, *Literary Culture in Taiwan: Martial Law to Market Law*. New York: Columbia University Press, 2004, 177.

36. On July 24, 2008, at the Hong Kong Book Fair, Zhu claimed that her work *Wuyan* [Abracadabra, 2007] is written from a position as "left" as possible to interlocute with the "right"—either socialization or mainstream system, corroborating the latent radicalism in her works.

37. See Fran Martin, "The Legacy of the Crocodile: Critical Debates Over Taiwan's Lesbian Fiction," *IIAS Newsletter* 29 (November, 2002).

38. Deborah Tze-lan Sang argues that Qiu's representation of lesbians as the embarrassing crocodile in *The Crocodile's Journal* is to point out and hopefully to resist against the general stigmatization of lesbianism. For Sang, Qiu's suicide is an act of self-publicization. See Sang's *The Emerging Lesbian: Female Same-Sex Desire in Modern China* (Chicago: University of Chicago Press, 2003), 262. Taiwan's lesbian communities considered Qiu an idol after her suicide, appropriating her death to a fight for social recognition.

39. On August 22, 1999, the *New York Times* published a positive review introducing the English translation of Chu T'ien-wen's *Note of a Desolate Man*. In 2004, Li Ang was awarded the Chevalier de l'Ordre des Arts et des Lettres by the French Minister of Culture and Communication in recognition of her contribution to world literature.

40. The survey was commissioned by the Council for Cultural Affairs. The five female writers selected are Qi Jun and Jian Zhen for the prose category, Zhang Xiaofeng for the drama category, and Eileen Chang (Zhang Ailing) and Li Ang for the fiction category.

41. Zhu discussed this in a forum held in 2003 during which she presented a short report entitled "Yichang yu xiandaihua de zaoyuzhan – Wode Taibei chengshi shuxie" [An encouter with modernization – My urban narrative about Taipei]. It is inspired by Ye Shitao's thought-provoking statement made in 2002 in Tokyo in which Ye claimed the future of Taiwan literature lies in aboriginal writing.

Of Guest and Host

Zhong Lihe, Hakka, and Sinophone Hospitality

CHIEN-HSIN TSAI

Granny hummed a strange tune from time to time. This tune was soft, passionate, curious, and different from all others people would sing. She strode the mountain path effortlessly while humming. Her face had a mesmerizing radiance and her eyes rolled with liveliness. Her entire body exuded a youthful vitality. I thought she was much younger than her usual self.

The pitch of her humming got higher and higher, but not loud. Her voice was filled with wholehearted happiness and excitement as if a long latent being suddenly woke up with a joyful emotion. At times, she would stop abruptly and look at me as if wanting to know what I thought. She would always smile, and would continue her singing.[1]

In the preceding passage from an autobiographical short story, "A Gali Woman," the young Zhong Lihe (1915–1960) thinks his singing grandmother is charming. Nevertheless, the young boy eventually breaks down in tears and begs his grandmother to stop. The young boy is much perplexed, troubled, and saddened by the sight and her humming. He is unfamiliar with the tune and this joyful stranger who resembles his grandmother. For him, his grandmother's nameless tune is a world created only for her from which he is coldly left out. Surprised by the teary pleading, or perhaps more so by her carelessness in letting her repressed emotion show, the young boy's grandmother immediately stops singing and remains silent the rest of their way home.

This is an intriguing episode that showcases well Zhong Lihe's auditory sensibility and sensitivity at a young age. More importantly, this is an episode when (sonic) identification comes into contestation with nostalgia for both the grandmother and the young boy, who had grown up. As a young boy, Zhong Lihe could already tell something was different about the humming on the mountain path even though he could not quite fathom or pinpoint the strangeness. It was not until he became an adult that he realized his grandmother was indeed different. She was a *gali*, a tattooed non-Han aborigine. She was not the mother of his father but the stepmother. Zhong Lihe's biological grandmother had passed away without leaving any impression on him and his siblings. Since then, they just referred to this second wife as grandmother.

His grandmother's joy was immense as she walked on the mountain path. She felt back at home. Her humming was both a sign of relaxation and an enactment of nostalgia. When she married into the Zhong family, she left her past. She also concealed much of her expressiveness. Marrying someone outside of her tribe meant that she became a guest awaiting reception, acceptance, understanding, and hospitality from the new family. However, our reading of this particular story should not just end here. The story has yet another layer concerning the complex relationship between the host and guest, one that concerns what I will call "Sinophone hospitality."

Zhong Lihe's Hakka ancestors came from China as guests to the island of Taiwan. They settled down and made this foreign place of Taiwan their home. This is to say that Hakkas were ultimately the guests in relation to the aborigines and later, the so-called Taiwanese. Just as the young Zhong Lihe thought his grandmother had turned into a stranger when she sang, he was in fact the real stranger, or even intruder, in the eye of the aborigines. As a young boy, Zhong did not know that the moment he begged his grandmother to stop was the moment he reversed the host-guest relationship and changed from guest to host, the one who laid down the rules and extended hospitality to the guest. Zhong Lihe had good reason to invest much sentiment in makeshift definitions of the host and guest. Born to a wealthy Hakka family in southern Taiwan, Zhong led a life full of erratic adventures emblematic of numerous unexpected migrations of Hakka. The symbiosis of host and guest manifested in the ethnic community of Hakka is ultimately about the ethics of hospitality.

Zhong Lihe was one of the few second-generation writers born in colonial Taiwan who wrote very well in Mandarin. In addition, his ethnic background and his travels to China added much unique breadth and depth to his stories. As an heir of a plantation owner, Zhong Lihe married Zhong Taimei (1911–2008), who worked in the plantation for the family; their marriage created much commotion in the village because the two shared the same surname (same-surname marriage was taboo) and Zhong Taimei was a few years older than Zhong Lihe and poorer. The villagers and their families refused to give the two lovers their blessings because of these three factors.

In 1938, Zhong Lihe left Zhong Taimei temporarily to go to Manchuria, then a puppet state of Japan, hoping to make a living so that he could return to take his lover with him. In 1940, Zhong did return for his lover as promised. Together as a couple struggling to start a new life of and on their own, the two traveled from place to place. They lived in Mukden and Beijing but returned to Taiwan in 1946 after the end of the second Sino-Japanese War. Before they had left, the couple had planned never to return because they did not think Taiwan would be returned to China or that their family would embrace them again. Their departure, however, marked only the beginning of their hardship. The life journey and stories of Zhong would not have been so intriguing had they been ones about daily life in a peaceful countryside.

In the Name of Hakka

Zhong Lihe's life journey is an intriguing microhistory of Hakka migrations.[2] There are no other writers in modern Taiwan literary history whose writings engage the various dimensions of being Hakka with so much affective force and even political implications. His life journey is inextricably linked to the making of what I call "Sinophone hospitality," one that involves the migration experience of Sinophone writers, their writings about the Chinese homeland, and their guest status in China. Zhong's life stories enrich our current understanding of the entangled relationship between host and guest, China and Sinophone communities. In the following, I will discuss the meaning of Hakka and how Hakka people's belief of homeland (*yuanxiang*) can be studied anew in relation to hospitality, a concern of host-guest relation that runs through Zhong Lihe's Hakka stories.

First, what is Hakka, and why is Hakka important? A shorthand answer: the name and naming of Hakka is a tailored example of a Sinophone articulation that bespeaks issues of hospitality. Estimated to number in the tens of millions today in different parts of the world, Hakka represents an ethnic and cultural group whose ancestors are widely believed to have originated in the Central Plains of China, the middle and lower reaches of the Yellow River basin.[3] Scholars have yet to reach consensus with regard to the origins of Hakka people. In his study of the formation of Hakka ethos, Sow-Theng Leong even suggests that, although the traits of Hakka as a cultural group are objectively verifiable, the origin and the culture of Hakka tend to be mythmaking.[4] Nonetheless, mobility, military prowess, strong women with unbound feet, and language are certain traditional strengths people associate with Hakka.[5] Like many other ethnicities, Hakka is also a product of interethnic interactions. It was through Hakka people's encounters and interactions with others who had distinctly different cultures that the so-called Hakka as an ethnic group started to emerge in the seventeenth century. By the mid-nineteenth century, Hakka became prevalent as an ethnic label. Needless to say, the term Hakka itself carries a broad range of references, stressing not a kind of sociocultural and ethnic homogeneity but the continuous tension and interdependence between natives and nonnatives, hosts and guests.[6]

Throughout the course of Chinese history, each migration pushed Hakka people further away from the Central Plains. With each migration, Hakka people inevitably face the destruction and reconstruction of a homeland in a foreign land. Their relationship with non-Hakkas, those who settled before their arrival, was always intense and confrontational. Negatively, it was through a series of conflicts that Hakka people became famous for their military prowess. Positively, the conflicts can be viewed as a dialogical or reflexive process through which ethnic identity is created and maintained and adherence to an ethnic group reinforced. As Hakka people moved further away from the Central Plains, the more their memories of the Central Plains blurred. Eventually homeland becomes one secured only in *terra incognito*. A homeland secured in *terra incognito* is a homeland that is suspended and imagined. In other words, what Hakka people harbor since their first migration is no different from a kind of imaginary nostalgia.[7]

Even the name Hakka bespeaks an imaginary or even uncanny quality. Hakka demonstrates sonically a linguistic extension of cultural differences. By that I mean Hakka is a Sinophone articulation (the Cantonese pronunciation) of the Mandarin *Kejia*, with *hak* 客 meaning "guest" and *ka* 家 meaning "home," "family," and so forth. One reason Hakka is an uncanny compound is that both *hak* and *ka* have numerous synonyms. Together, *hak* and *ka* further suggest a number of heterogeneous yet interrelated features that govern the production of textual meaning. In addition to guest—the most common English equivalent adopted by scholars of Hakka—*hak* also refers to foreigner, visitor, stranger, sojourner, customer, and even prisoner. Even though some meanings apparently carry more negative nuances than others, *hak* references a person. *Ka*, on the other hand, is a nonperson word. It connotes home, family, house, settlement, shelter, a private sphere of closure or confinement, especially from a feminist standpoint. Hakka thus is also a conflation of personhood and hominess. This conflation is a perilous, uncanny one because, given the inclination of guest and host to make themselves feel "at home"—a gesture of hospitality—the representations of such people and spaces become ever elastic. What is at stake here is a longing for the inaccessible homeland—inaccessible because the homeland in reality always betrays the homeland in memory. I go one step beyond, however, and suggest that Hakka people strive on this feeling of the uncanny. Their search for the only location in which they as guest can feel at home is deemed futile. Being at home negates the guest status of Hakka. The term *Hakka*, therefore, posits itself as a semiotic (and, of course, ontological) configuration of identity and refers one to the politics and ethics of hospitality that keeps guest and host on a motion equilibrium.

A Stranger in His Homeland

Zhong Lihe and wife embarked on their journey to China in search of a place where they could claim a home. Coming from colonial Taiwan, the two had to first go to Japanese-occupied Manchuria and then wait for an opportunity to go to China proper. They first stopped in Mukden, the capital of Manchuria, controlled by the puppet regime of Japan. Mukden was a railway artery that connected Japan, Korea, and the rest of China. For many—Taiwanese, Chinese, Japanese, and Koreans alike—it was a spacious "new world," an embodiment of hospitality where adventurous immigrants pursued their dreams. However, Zhong Lihe soon found himself disillusioned.

Zhong Lihe details his life in Mukden in a few stories. In "Fungus of the Earth" (*Diqiu zhi mei*), Mukden is presented as the most developed city in northeastern China crowded with modern buildings, nice restaurants, and shops—indeed a double of the cosmopolitan Shanghai. If not given the title or the name of the author and judging solely on its content and style, a reader might suspect this is a story by one of the New Sensationist writers such as Liu Na'ou (1905–1940), Mu Shiying (1912–1940), or Shi Zhecun (1905–2003). Yet the fundamental difference between Zhong and the New Sensationist writers is that, although the latter embrace the thrills of the city, the former finds the urban development distasteful. As Zhong insinuates in the gloomy title, he considers the modern advancements in Mukden none other than mind-consuming fungus. Not a sensationist after all, he is even more critically direct in "The Door" (*Men*), which characterizes this "new world" as a "city of cruel animals," always "unclean," "topsy-turvy," and "desolate."

In *Taidong Hotel* (*Taidong lüguan*), Zhong gets to the core of what frustrates him in Mukden. What he feels is hostility disguised in hospitality that turns him into a stranger in his ancestral homeland. A portrayal of the vicissitudes of a number of hotel guests in Mukden during the second Sino-Japanese War, *Taidong Hotel* is rife with details and characters of a standard realist novel. It is not Zhong's best work (and it is incomplete), yet it merits attention because of the emblematic site of the human network in the story—a hotel, especially one in the city of Mukden. Etymologically, perhaps it is not coincidental that the following words all have the same, or related, root: *hospice, hospital, hotel, hostel, host,* and *hospitality.* These words share a commonality: either the reception of a guest or the place for such reception. In modern usage, the host stands on the opposite side of the guest; the former displays hospitality whereas the latter demands hospitality. However, in *Taidong Hotel,* where the host greets the guest, one finds ample evidence of Zhong Lihe's retrospection on being a guest in one's homeland, a stranger to oneself.

The most unexpected episode in the story occurs when the host, the hotel manager, quizzes a guest from colonial Taiwan, Mr. Chen, on two Sinitic scripts. The hotel manager writes down the compound word *wanku,* which means a rich good-for-nothing, and asks the protagonist to explain its meaning. The inquiry amounts to a humiliating dilemma: if the guest admits his ignorance, he is immediately labeled as Japanese from colonial Taiwan even though he has ancestral ties to China; if the guest exercises his knowledge, he would be embarrassing the host who is convinced that the guest does not know the two scripts. After some internal struggles, the guest decides to fake incomprehension to prevent shaming the host.

The hotel manager ascertains from the guest's accented Mandarin that he is not local. With the quiz, the hotel manager draws attention to his own status as not only the host of the hotel and a local resident, but, more important, the authentic owner of Chinese culture, who thinks his guest from colonial Taiwan is not "Chinese" enough. Although both the host and the guest pretend that they are unfamiliar with the two Sinitic scripts, their intentions are drastically different. The hotel manager aims at self-aggrandizement whereas the guest focuses on being amicable at the expense of self-humiliation. In this episode, curiously, the guest then becomes the host who extends hospitality to the hotel owner. Here, a paradox intrinsic to Hakka and hospitality is exposed: to be welcomed as a guest, a guest can never take for granted the host's imperative of "make yourself at home," which ineluctably destabilizes and inverses the guest-host relationship.[8]

Zhong compels the reader to consider the following questions: Can one still be awaited and received as a guest if there is no strangeness to claim? More curiously, must one negate one's very own Chineseness, namely, one's very native knowledge of China/Chinese, so as to be welcomed as Chinese? If one is to return home as a guest—as a stranger to one's home—then what is the condition of the (im)possibility of homecoming? Or most simply, what is home and what is homecoming? With the hostile quiz in disguise, the guest protagonist comes to a realization that he must sever any ties he has to the ancestral homeland in order to be welcomed back. *Taidong Hotel* thus gives us a good opportunity to reconsider Ien Ang's essay in the first section of this volume. "Can one say no to Chineseness?" (and how and why) remains a question that not only Zhong Lihe but perhaps all Sinophone writers face.

Upset with life in Mukden, Zhong Lihe and his wife moved to Beijing. They thought life in Beijing, the old capital of China with a long history, would be much more enjoyable. Zhong was convinced that he would feel much more "at home" in Beijing than in Mukden. Nevertheless, the couple would soon find themselves disillusioned again. Living in Beijing as guests from colonial Taiwan turns out equally, if not more, frustrating.

In Beijing in 1945, Zhong Lihe published *Oleanders* (*Jiazhutao*), a collection of four stories. These stories represent the first by any writer from Taiwan to detail everyday life in Beijing. In one of the stories, "Oleanders," Zhong's protagonist from Taiwan, Zeng Simian, observes life in Beijing with such an authoritative voice that the reader may mistake him as a Beijing native. Yet it is not difficult to hear undertones of melancholia and disappointment in his voice. In the eye of the protagonist, Zeng Simian, Beijing is squalid and noisy, and her people conniving and untrustworthy. Try as he might, the protagonist falters at adaptation, and continues to think of his hometown in southern Taiwan. His failure to adapt to Beijing, indeed, mirrors a strong nostalgia for Taiwan. Nostalgia aside, his negative portrayal of Beijing raises yet another set of questions pertaining to Sinophone hospitality: Must one do in China as the Chinese do? Must the guest act as the host so as to deserve hospitality? By not acting as the Beijing native, does the guest not invite hostility upon himself? In "Oleanders," Zhong explores a different dimension of the host-guest relation. If the guest in *Taidong Hotel* is self-deprecating, the guest in "Oleanders" is much more aggressive as he demands hospitality from local Beijingers.

Curiously, the guest's refusal to assimilate makes the host's extension of hospitality possible, for if the guest is assimilated, hospitality is no longer necessary. In other words, a Beijing host can only demonstrate his hospitality if, and only if, his guest remains a demanding guest. Like *Taidong Hotel*, "Oleanders" compels the reader to think more critically about the condition of the possibility of hospitality. On a larger allegorical scale, Zhong Lihe's stories of Beijing represent the negotiation between not only hospitality and hostility but also the Sinophone and the Beijing centered.

Life in Beijing grew more disconcerting as the Japanese surrendered in 1945. Before, Zhong Lihe was considered Japanese, and now he was Taiwanese—still not Chinese. In fact, the Beijing natives started to refer to people from colonial Taiwan as "sweet potato" with Japan's defeat. The nicknaming was indicative of a problematic redirection of anti-Japanese sentiments to people from Taiwan. The distinction between colonial victimizer and the victimized was willfully overlooked to help restoration of order in Beijing. Trapped in an ongoing political swirl and identity shuffle, it is no wonder that Zhong puzzles over the meaning of being a guest in China whose ancestors came from China. Accordingly, the meaning of homeland also varies throughout Zhong Lihe's writings. When in China, Taiwan is home, and vice versa. With this in mind, more fruitful questions the reader may ask are: *Can* one have only one homeland? As opposed to *which* one is the true homeland? Is the notion of homeland and foreign land so fixed upon consanguinity that the opposites must remain mutually exclusive? Is homeland per se not an ideal, a manifestation of imaginary nostalgia, to which one returns not through physical visitation but textual rendition, and to which one returns never as a native but as a guest, a foreigner?

A Second Homecoming

In 1946, life in Beijing became too chaotic for Zhong Lihe and his wife. They decided to stop pursuing their Chinese dream and return to Taiwan. Much to their dismay, life was not any better; in fact, it was worse after the two returned to Taiwan. Not too long after his return, Zhong was struck down by tuberculosis and related complications. In times of sickness and poverty, Zhong Lihe continued to write, for writing had become a way of self-consolation, a way of living, and a way of ascertaining his own life. Blessed or cursed, Zhong remained productive on his sickbed, leaving the economic burden on his wife. Just when Zhong was steadily receiving praises for his stories, his literary career came to a sudden halt. On August 4, 1960, while working on the revision of his novella *Rain* (*Yu*), Zhong Lihe coughed up blood and soon passed away.

Many of Zhong's most memorable works—*Lishan Plantation* (*Lishan nongchang*), his tetralogy of "Hometown" (*Guxiang*), and certainly "Old Country Folk" (*Yuanxiang ren*), to name but a few—were all written during the last ten years of his life. These stories about his hometown in southern Taiwan anticipate the rising of "native-soil" literature in Taiwan during the 1970s and 1980s. *Lishan Plantation*, particularly, is a Hakka family saga that lends itself to a reading of the Japanese "I-novel" as it carefully retells Zhong Lihe's forbidden romance on the one hand, and the rise and fall of his family during the colonial period on the other. Indeed, all stories by Zhong Lihe carry an aura of autobiography that is difficult to miss. Among all, "Old Country Folk" represents Zhong Lihe at his best. Hakka people refer to their ancestral homeland as the "old country" (*yuanxiang*). "Old Country Folk" is an autobiographical short story that has attracted many contradicting interpretations. Notwithstanding critics' disagreement, Zhong's familiar musings on Hakka, hospitality, and homeland are difficult to miss.

"Old Country Folk" begins with what Zhong calls a valuable lesson on "racial anthropology" (*renzhongxue*). The lesson introduces three types of people: the Japanese, Fukienese, and Mainlanders, also known as the old country folks. The Japanese are stoic, and the Fukienese good at doing business. The two, nonetheless, pale in front of an old country folk who loves dog meat and whose brutal dog killing scars the young protagonist. As the young child turns to his grandmother for consolation after witnessing the death of a dog, he is faced with another unsettling revelation: Hakka people, too, are old country folks from the other side of the Taiwan Strait. Stunned, the boy immediately asks more questions that are naïve but movingly poignant: If we are also heirs of old country folks, why don't we eat dogs like that old country folk does? Are we, or are we not old country folks? Unable to provide a satisfying answer, the grandmother can only try to comfort her grandson.

Both the dog killing and the comforting words of the grandmother serve as a lesson of awakening and loss, indeed a premature coming of age. For the first time, the young boy learns about his guest status in this place he calls home. He is shocked to find out that the real home is far and away. Written in 1959, thirteen years after Zhong's return from China, the story is perhaps not so much a reminiscence of childhood trauma as a confession of his homeland complex. From a young age, he has been wanting to go to China, to confirm or dismiss such animal cruelty, to fulfill the Hakka dream of homecoming, and, in a sense, follow his older brother's footsteps. After the episode of dog killing, Zhong explains how his perception of the old country is also influenced by his older brother, who later joins the Communist Party and moves to China. This is the same brother who stands next to the young Zhong Lihe at the site of dog killing. Zhong has come to depend on him since a very young age.

With his brother, his example, and their shared experience in mind, Zhong ends the story with his most famous statement: "Old country blood must flow back to Old country before it can stop seething."[9] The reader may proceed to ask: What does it mean for the blood to stop seething? What is the significance of blood? If blood symbolizes passion and dream, does the statement refer to Zhong's disillusionment in Mukden and Beijing? Or if blood connotes vitality, does the statement then mean that a Hakka can finally rest in peace once he returns to China? Zhong refrains from giving his audience a definitive answer, which gives rise to a plethora of interpretations.

Here, I analyze how the concluding statement implies a convergence of future time and historical time that has escaped critical attention thus far.

This temporal convergence is crucial to our understanding of Sinophone hospitality and Hakka. First, the temporal convergence implies that there will be a future event that will have taken place: Old country blood will have flown back to old country and will have stopped seething. Second, because the story is written after his return from China, Zhong has perfect hindsight. As mentioned, he has visited the old country, he has become disillusioned, and he has become a guest in his ancestral homeland. Despite the fact that in the story the future event has yet to happen, in reality it has already come to pass. With perfect hindsight, the future time is also the historical time. If the future time is written into history as historical time, history may then repeat itself in the future. With this convergence of different times/temporalities, "Old Country Folk" is to tell the reader: what Zhong as a Hakka writer has experienced in the past—the volatile host-guest relation, the issues pertaining to hospitality and the multiplying meaning of homeland—may be experienced by many others in different Sinophone communities in the future. In this sense, he was truly a writer with an unmistakable vision.

In relation to his Hakka background, Zhong's dilemmas are his repeated shuffles between the China-centered and the Sinophone, between being a host and a guest, as well as the uncanniness of feeling out of place at home and feeling at home outside of homeland. Writing during the apogee of Japanese imperialism and immediately thereafter, Zhong Lihe was able to capture the challenges and the opportunities faced by many Sinophone writers and to articulate the need to remap an extensive sense of responsibility towards others. His stories bring to relief a China-centered arbitrariness of host-guest relation in border-crossing contexts that Sinophone studies sets out to critique. Even at the turn of the twenty-first century, Zhong's writings from more than four decades ago still (perhaps more so now than before) warrant our attention.

Notes

1. Zhong Lihe, *Zhong Lihe quan ji*, Vol. 1 (Taibei: Yuanxing chubanshe, 1976), 87.

2. According to Luo Xianglin, a pioneer in Hakka studies, there were five major periods of Hakka migrations. See Luo Xianglin, *Kejia yuan liu kao* (Beijing: Zhongguo huaqiao chuban, 1989). Aligned with Luo's research is Myron Cohen's detailed study, which focuses on the use of language in the five major periods of migrations in his "The Hakka, or 'Guest People': Dialect as a Sociocultural Variable in Southeastern China," in the American Society for Ethnohistory, *Ethnohistory* (Durham, NC: Duke University Press, 1954), 237–292. For various enlightening discussions of the Hakka migrations to different parts of the world and their significance, please see Nicole Constable, *Guest People: Hakka Identity in China and Abroad* (Seattle: University of Washington Press, 1996).

3. There are also scholars, such as Fang Xuejia, who argue that the original Hakkas were neither immigrants from the Central Plains nor entirely barbarians in the south. They were, according to Fang, a mixed community of remnant subjects of the ancient Yue tribe (Guyu-ezu) and some immigrants from central and northern China after the Qin dynasty unified China. See Fang Xuejia, *Kejia yuan liu tan ao* (Guangzhou: Guangdong gao deng jiao yu chu ban she, 1994).

4. Sow-Theng Leong, Tim Wright, and G. William Skinner, *Migration and Ethnicity in Chinese History: Hakkas, Pengmin, and Their Neighbors* (Stanford, Calif.: Stanford University Press, 1997).

5. Mary Erbaugh, "The Secret History of the Hakkas: The Chinese Revolution as a Hakka Enterprise," in *The China Quarterly* 132 (1996): 937–968.

6. As Nicole Constable indicates, the Hakkas and their descendants who emigrated for economic and political reasons "speak different languages, eat different foods, and belong to different economic classes and political parties, yet they may retain the name Hakka and identify themselves as such. Constable, *Guest People: Hakka Identity in China and Abroad*, 5.

7. See David Der-wei Wang's discussion of imaginary nostalgia in Chapter 7 of *Fictional Realism in Twentieth-Century China: Mao Dun, Lao She, Shen Congwen* (New York: Columbia University Press, 1992), 247–289.

8. For a more in-depth, critical discussion of (unconditional/absolute) hospitality, please refer to the following: Jacques Derrida and Anne Dufourmantelle, *Of Hospitality*, Trans. Rachel Bowlby (Stanford, Calif.: Stanford University Press, 2000).

9. *Zhong Lihe quan ji*, Vol. 2, 6.

On the Margins of Tibetanness

Three Decades of Modern Sinophone Tibetan Literature

PATRICIA SCHIAFFINI

Disciplinary practice has [...] decried "bastard traditions," thus continually upholding the fallacy that cultural purity rather than hybridity are the norm.
—Regina Bendix, *In Search of Authenticity*[1]

Sinophone Tibetan literature is rooted in the contradictions of modern colonial Tibet. Half a century of Chinese political and cultural domination of Tibet have rendered many Tibetan intellectuals unable to use their native language to write. Educated in a Chinese-language medium, Sinophone Tibetan writers are solely able to express themselves in the language of the colonizers. In spite of this, they have not become mouthpieces of the Chinese government, as their literature is not a copy of that of their Chinese counterparts. Sinophone Tibetan writers have articulated an array of original voices to vindicate their Tibetan identities, to master innovative writing styles, and even to challenge the Chinese colonial presence in Tibet. Their many literary accomplishments, however, have not come at an easy price. As in the case of many other culturally hybrid writers around the world, most of them are the product of colonial situations, the hybridity of Sinophone Tibetan writers has been criticized and contested. The same way as scholars have debated ad nauseam whether Anglophone literature in India should be considered Indian literature, similar language debates have both shamed and marginalized Sinophone Tibetan writers.[2] This chapter examines the evolution of modern Sinophone Tibetan literature through thirty years of political changes in Tibet, the reasons behind the use of the Chinese language by

Tibetan writers, its effect on how they are perceived by other Tibetans, and some of their stylistic and political choices.

The Emergence of Modern Literature in Tibet

The lack of a secular Tibetan literary tradition, and the fact that many Tibetan scholars fled to India after 1959, delayed the emergence of modern literature in Tibet. Although its origins are usually traced to the post-1959 period, and even more so to the post-Cultural Revolution liberalization in China, the fact is that some early Tibetan writers who wrote in Tibetan (hereafter noted as "Tibetophone" writers, to distinguish them from Sinophone writers) had already engaged in innovative literary creation during the pre-Communist period. Gendün Chömpel (1903–), an Amdo-born[3] Tibetan scholar and monk, is considered to be the father of modern literature for his progressive ideas, his use of vernacular language, and his knowledge of foreign literature, history and science.[4] In what pertains to Sinophone Tibetan literature, the main figure of the earliest generation of writers is the poet Yidam Tsering (Yidan Cairang in Mandarin, 1933–). Born to a humble family in Tsongkha, a Tibetan area that became part of Qinghai province in 1928, Yidam Tsering was educated in a Chinese school and never learned to write in Tibetan. He began writing at a time when literature in China still followed Mao Zedong's mandate "to serve the masses." Although his early career was marked by idealized poems about the Chinese Communist Party, he soon found his own literary voice in poetry that celebrated the Tibetan nationality. Full of references to folk stories and traditions, his accessible and heartfelt poetry appealed to the national pride of Tibetans, at the same time that it made Tibetan culture accessible to a Chinese audience.[5]

After the Dalai Lama fled to India in 1959, the Chinese government sent "cultural workers" to Tibet to write for propaganda and educational purposes. Although most of them were Chinese of Han ethnicity, some Tibetans from Amdo and Kham were also recruited, educated, and sent to Tibet by the People's Liberation Army (PLA).[6] These army writers monopolized modern Sinophone literature in Tibet during the 1960s and early 1970s with romanticized descriptions of the "land of snows" and eulogies to the Chinese occupation.[7]

While these earlier romantic poems in Chinese helped pave the way for the development of other forms of modern literature in Tibet, true literary innovation and experimentation did not start until the late 1970s and early 1980s. China was opening up after decades of intellectual intolerance and political repression. This is the time when a second wave of Han cultural workers volunteered to go to Tibet driven by their romanticism and spirit of adventure. Many of them would soon become writers and editors of the recently created Sinophone journal *Literature from Tibet* (Ch. *Xizang wenxue*). This generation of Chinese intellectuals included the writers Ma Lihua and Ma Yuan, and the painter Han Shuli, who exerted a tremendous influence in Lhasa's literary and artistic worlds, becoming famous also in China for their long-lasting association with Tibet. Soon, Tibetan graduates from Tibetan populated areas outside the Tibet Autonomous Region (TAR) also converged in Lhasa, clustering around the Tibetophone journal *Literature and Arts from Tibet* (Tib. *Bod kyi rtsom rig sgyu rtsal*) to promote the emergence of modern literature in the Tibetan language.[8] The historic visit of Chinese leader Hu Yaobang to Lhasa in March 1980, together with his recommendations to promote Tibetan culture, gave official sanction to the vibrant cultural renaissance the Tibetan capital was experiencing after the devastating decade of the Cultural Revolution.[9]

Lhasa and the 1980s Sinophone Literary "Boom" in Tibet

The two main literary journals published by the Association of Chinese Writers in Tibet, the Sinophone *Literature from Tibet* and the Tibetophone *Literature and Arts from Tibet*, grouped Tibetan writers by their choice of language. While only Tibetan writers published in the Tibetophone journal, its Sinophone counterpart published works by both Sinophone Tibetan writers and Han authors residing in Lhasa. Although both literary worlds were under the umbrella of the same institution, the Tibetan branch of the Association of Writers and Artists of China, they followed different paths and had little communication with each other.[10]

During the 1980s, the Sinophone literary scene seemed to be more energized than the Tibetophone one due to the convergence in Lhasa of charismatic figures such as the Han writer Ma Yuan and the Tibetan writer Tashi Dawa (Zhaxi Dawa). Writers and artists would meet in Lhasa's famous tea houses or in their own homes to discuss literature and art, to show each other their recent works, and to pass around books they had recently read, many of which were foreign novels and studies about literary or artistic theory recently translated into Chinese.

The most prolific and acclaimed Sinophone Tibetan writers of the time are Tashi Dawa (Zhaxi Dawa in Mandarin, 1959– , and also known by his Chinese name, Zhang Niansheng) and Sebo (Tib. Gsal po, 1956– , and also known by his Chinese name, Xu Mingliang), two youngsters educated in China and born to ethnically hybrid Han-Tibetan families.[11] Virtually ignorant of Tibetan language and traditions when they first arrived in Tibet, they were soon encouraged by Han editors and writers to undergo a process of "Tibetanization" (i.e., writing about Tibet and under a Tibetan name). The publication of literary works by minority writers was officially envisioned as one of the most visible signs that the new Chinese government was committed to the recovery of minority cultures, which had been heavily damaged during the Cultural Revolution. During the 1980s, the educated Han elite experienced a "minority fever"—an intellectual and aesthetic need to look for the authenticity, primitivism, and purity they felt had been lost in Chinese culture. Ethnically hybrid Tibetans like Tashi Dawa and Sebo were soon embraced as "the true voice of Tibet"—the only ones able to decode the "mysterious" Tibetan world for a Chinese audience.

The literary universe of Tashi Dawa and Sebo changed substantially in the course of a decade. Their earlier stories were characterized by descriptions of Tibetans as honest and innocent. In the romanticized Tibet portrayed in short stories such as Tashi Dawa's "Buddhist Pilgrimage" (*Chaofo*, 1980) or Sebo's "Going Back" (*Guisu*, 1983) Tibetans and Han are portrayed as caring about each other and living in harmony.[12] However, this idealization of Tibet, shared by most Chinese intellectuals during the early 1980s, turned progressively into a darker and chaotic reality wrapped in surreal images, complicated metaphors, and magical-realistic turns. As I have shown elsewhere, this change was due to a combination of different factors: a deeper understanding of the hopelessness of Tibet's colonial situation—including Han cultural chauvinism and political repression, as well as Tibetan collaborationism or violent dissent; disillusionment with the failure of their own process of Tibetanization, having been rejected as Tibetans by Tibetans, yet treated as minority "second class citizens" by the Chinese; and reaching a personal and literary maturity that no longer allowed them to portray Tibet in socialist-realistic terms.

In this period, Tashi Dawa moved his attention from modern Lhasa, the setting of most of his early stories, to the Tibetan countryside, the stronghold of Tibetan traditions. While his early stories portrayed traditional Tibetans adapting to a Chinese "modernity," his later works show a traditional Tibetan countryside detached from the modern world and impermeable to change. Tashi Dawa hinted to this impossibility of change in Tibet through topics such as cyclical time and cyclical revenge.[13] He often referred to common misunderstandings between Tibetans and Hans based not only on different languages but also on irreconcilable belief systems.[14] His choice of magical realism, initially playfully mixed with surrealism, soon became his quintessential way of expression. A magical realistic veil allowed him to deal with political issues sensitive for the Chinese, or religious taboos for the Tibetans.[15]

It also allowed him to transcend the identity limbo of not belonging to Tibet or to China. By the beginning of the 1990s, having become already a skilled magical realistic author—translated into many foreign languages, and often hailed in China and the West as the "Tibetan Gabriel García Márquez"[16]—he could finally feel he belonged somewhere—not necessarily to China or Tibet, but surely to the world.[17]

In Sebo's mature stories, Tibetans were not happy about the Chinese presence, as exemplified by the complaints of one of Sebo's Tibetan characters about the way the Chinese showcased Tibet so as to please Western tourists.[18] Han characters rarely appear in Sebo's later stories and when they do, it is just as part of Lhasa's chaotic urban scene. The clumsy Han girl who asks a dozen times the prices of different wool sweaters until she realizes that all of them cost the same, or the Chinese Muslim peddler running after a goat who has just eaten part of his mat, are just quick comic sketches in stories that are not meant to deal with Chinese people. Tibetans, previously portrayed by Sebo as models of loyalty and friendship, behave now despotically and egotistically, like the stranded travelers of his short story "Board the Boat Here."[19] Images of Tibetan teenagers dreaming about dates and provocative clothes, rumors of sinful relationships by incarnate lamas, and Tibetan nomad couples making out in public fill Sebo's more recent literary canvas, previously populated only by Tibetan models of morality and family values.[20]

Lhasa's Literary "Goddesses" of the 1990s

In the 1990s, after a little over a decade of success, Sinophone Tibetan literature in Lhasa began to decline. The materialistic spirit of 1990s China (summarized in Deng Xiaoping's famous statement "to become rich is glorious" [zhifu guanrong]) diverted official resources and talents from culture-related endeavors to more profitable activities. To make things worse, several Tibetan popular unrests in Lhasa in the late 1980s brought about a severe tightening of the Chinese control and censorship inside the TAR. The political repression following those Tibetan pro-independence demonstrations interrupted all Chinese efforts to promote Tibetan culture. Discouraged, many writers left Tibet or discontinued fiction writing in the early 1990s; Tashi Dawa remained in his editorial post, alternating it with a new career in film production and script writing;[21] Sebo left Lhasa to work as an editor in Chengdu.

The absence of the prevalent male Sinophone Tibetan voices of the 1980s left space for the emergence of a small group of talented female Tibetan writers in Lhasa. Educated in Chinese schools and unable to write in Tibetan, these young writers made themselves known by novels, short stories, and poems written in a realistic style with an abundance of female Tibetan characters, symbols of Tibetan culture, and praises to Tibet's past. Dominated by the works of these female writers, this literary decade was saluted by long-time Lhasa resident and writer Ma Lihua as "the age of the Goddesses."[22] Although less innovative than the works of their previous generation, Weise (Tib. Özer, 1966–), Yang Zhen (Tib. Yangdrön, 1963–), and Ge Yang (1976–) managed to produce solid literary works amidst Lhasa's repressive intellectual environment in the 1990s. Initially nurtured in Lhasa by famous writers and editors such as Tashi Dawa, Sebo, and Ma Lihua, these female writers were also trained in prestigious academic institutions in Beijing, where they were exposed to the new realistic currents prevalent in China in the 1990s.[23] The Lhasa "goddesses" harvested most of the minority writers' prizes of the decade, one of the most celebrated novels being Yang Zhen's *A God without Gender* (*Wu xingbie de shen*, 1994).[24]

Weise, Yang Zhen and Ge Yang also shared an interest in Tibetan traditional culture and Buddhist religion. Their choice of themes (traditional Tibetan lives, monastic lives, the lives of women) and their literary choice (realism) denote a stronger nationalism than that of the previous generation. Their favorable portrayal of the old Tibet and Buddhist religion directly oppose official Chinese dictates. In 1995, the secretary of the Communist Party in Tibet, Chen Kuiyuan, addressed writers and editors in Lhasa, warning them not to portray "backward habits" such as "pilgrims worshipping on bended knees" or "the mystery and splendor of religion."[25] Far from discouraging them from writing about these issues, the Chinese attempts to control Tibetan intellectuals did nothing but strengthen their sense of national pride and responsibility. The exalted view of Tibet's free past, expressed below in Weise's poetry, became for them a hopeful image for Tibet's future:

> The past, ah, how beautiful the past was,
> How beautiful, how beautiful,
> A beauty which cannot be expressed
> A beauty which cannot be imagined
> My past,
> Our past,
> How beautiful, how beautiful, how beautiful.[26]

For this generation of Sinophone Tibetan writers who, unlike Tashi Dawa and Sebo, had deeper roots in Tibetan culture and ways of life, writing about Tibet in a magical realistic or otherwise experimental flair was felt as disrespectful.[27] As demonstrated in the following discussion, their ethnic pride and responsibility was also spurred by their regrets at not being able to write in the Tibetan language. The climax of intellectual repression they experienced in Lhasa during the 1990s reminded them constantly of the fragile situation of Tibetans inside the Chinese "motherland," and their own contradictions at using the language of the oppressor to praise the oppressed.

The Center Transfers to the Periphery

Fortunately for Tibetan literature, while Lhasa was experiencing its climax of intellectual repression, Tibetan writers residing in Tibetan areas of Qinghai, Gansu, and Sichuan provinces (called Amdo and Kham in Tibetan) suffered less official control and censorship. Many literary journals continued to be founded all through the 1990s in these areas. As Lauran Hartley has explained, one other reason for the shift of the Tibetan cultural center from Lhasa to the "peripheries" of Tibet was the consolidation of a Tibetan intelligentsia around centers of higher education such as the Northwest Nationalities Institute in Lanzhou (Gansu), and the Qinghai Nationalities Institute in Xining (Qinghai). This ensured the flourishing of literary creation and intellectual debates regarding Tibetan culture, both in Tibetan and Chinese.[28]

This environment of relative tolerance outside the TAR produced several impressive Sinophone Tibetan writers, among them the Amdoan writer Medrön (Meizhuo, 1966–) and Sichuan-born novelist Alai (Tib. A legs). While Medrön's use of realism (although mixed with legendary elements) and her thematic inspiration in Tibet's past situate her close to the group of Lhasa female writers previously discussed, Alai's conscious distortion of reality places him at the core of Tibet's magical realism.

Medrön began her writing career in the late 1980s, but she became known nationally in 1998 when she published her novel *The Clan of the Sun* (*Taiyang buluo*), which won the national award for minority writers.[29] A story about love and competing clans situated in China's republican period, the novel contains some common elements with Medrön's earlier poetry: a preference for historical themes, and an emphasis for an accurate representation of Tibetan culture.

Since another chapter in this volume by Carlos Rojas is devoted to Alai, I will merely mention here some biographical notes that tie him to this group of ethnically and culturally hybrid Sinophone Tibetan writers. Born in 1959 in Sichuan province to a peasant family, he has been defined by literary critiques as "'hybrid' twice over," being the offspring of Tibetan and Hui parents.[30] His literary career began as a poet and editor of the journal *Science Fiction World* (*Kehuan shijie*). Although he is an accomplished poet, he became well known, not only in China but also in the West, for his novel

Chen'ai luoding (translated into English as *Red Poppies*) which was awarded the Mao Dun Prize, China's most prestigious literary award, in 2000.[31] A story about Tibetan chieftains in an area in Sichuan where historically Chinese and Tibetans have coexisted, his multilayered magical realistic novel has rendered a wide variety of readings: from an attempt to destabilizing pure Tibetanness and vindicating Alai's own hybridity,[32] to an open critique to the Chinese, who in the end are seen as culprits for the corruption and demise of the Tibetan chieftains Alai describes.[33]

Perceptions of Sinophone Tibetan Writers

For educated Han readers, with no access to the works of Tibetophone writers, Sinophone Tibetan writers are the most "authentic" resource to approach Tibet.[34] The opinions of Chinese literary critic Zhang Jun exemplify the tendency in China to give absolute ethnic agency to the works of Sinophone Tibetan writers. He maintains that writers like Tashi Dawa "opened a door to Tibet for many people [in China]."[35] He goes on to credit the works of Sinophone Tibetan writers while clarifying some common misconceptions about Tibet among the Chinese: "For example, I used to think that Tibet was a backward place, but after reading these stories I understood that this was not the case. I learned that Tibetan society had traditionally emphasized the development of spirituality over the pursuit of material concerns."[36]

It is interesting to point out that while Chinese consider ethnically Sino-Tibetan writers to be "authentic" Tibetans, their half "Han side" is always neglected by their fellow Chinese citizens. Contrary to common Chinese knowledge, writers like Tashi Dawa, Sebo, or Alai have received most of their educational and intellectual influences from China, due to the fact that they were raised and educated in a Chinese environment and their primary language is Chinese. However, it is their nominal Tibetan identity that carries more tokenized cultural capital. Thus, they are always introduced as "Tibetan" or "minority writers," and they are expected to write solely about Tibet.

However, most ethnically hybrid Tibetan writers are only considered to be Tibetans by the Chinese. As Yangdon Dhondup reminds us, they are often described by Tibetophone Tibetans as "neither Chinese nor Tibetan" (Tib. *Rgya ma Bod*), a term previously used to describe the geographical border areas in between China and Tibet, such as the area where Alai was born, and the one he describes in *Red Poppies*.[37] It does not matter how hard they try to "become Tibetans" by writing under Tibetan names or learning about Tibetan culture. Their hybridity, their marked Han cultural sensibility, their use of Chinese, and their choice of "foreign" surrealistic and magical-realistic literary styles always make them the object of critique in Tibetophone cultural circles. The two most notorious exceptions are Sinophone Tibetan poets Yidam Tsering and Weise, who have gained the admiration and respect of Tibetans due to the marked nationalistic overtones of their poetry, and, in the case of Weise, her open political dissent.

Some Tibetans in exile do not bestow much respect on Sinophone Tibetan writers. Take, for instance, the opinions of exiled Tibetan intellectual Jamyang Norbu about Tashi Dawa, whom he accuses of perpetuating "age-old Chinese racist calumnies about Tibet: about people barely more civilized than beasts, clinging superstitiously to a dark and savage religion."[38] Luckily for Alai, although his *Red Poppies* was a "great hit" in China, it has gained much better reviews by Tibetans in exile than the works of his predecessor.[39]

When Sinophone Tibetan writers are discussed among Tibetophone Tibetans, the main considerations are whether the writer speaks and writes in Tibetan, whether his/her literature reflects on Tibetan culture and ways of life, and whether he or she has a marked sense of national responsibility. However, not all these characteristics need to be met for a work or an author to be considered Tibetan. Above all, among Tibetans, it is the use of language that determines the perception of one's identity. For example, as we have seen, in Tibetophone circles, although Tashi Dawa's works always dealt with Tibet, he was never considered to be a Tibetan due mostly to the fact that he did not write or speak in Tibetan. On the contrary, the works by the talented Tibetophone writer Dorjé Tsering Chenaktsang do not always deal with Tibet and do not necessarily possess a strong Tibetan flavor, but his use of Tibetan (as well as his many literary accomplishments) elevates him to be regarded as one of the best Tibetan writers alive.

The passionate debate in Tibet about what constitutes Tibetan literature has highlighted the Tibetan-language incompetence among Sinophone Tibetan writers, thus casting a shadow on their Tibetan ethnic identities. Similar acrid debates in other parts of the postcolonial world, wonderfully described by African authors such as Ngũgĩ wa Thiong'o or Chinua Achebe, remind us that these "feudal" literary wars on the battle fields of language, literature, and national identity are yet one more consequence of colonialism.[40]

Sinophone Tibetan writers are acutely aware of the fact that many Tibetans criticize them for writing in Chinese. Over the course of months of research conducted in 1999 in China among Sinophone Tibetan writers, all authors I interviewed voluntarily brought up the issue of their lack of knowledge of written Tibetan. Weise continued this conversation with me in an e-mail exchange after I returned to the United States, in which she affirmed: "Those of us who do not use our native language to write feel a sense of embarrassment in the bottom of our hearts."[41]

From the Margins to the Center: The Change in the Perception
of Weise's Identity

Although born in Lhasa, Weise moved to Sichuan when she was a child and
grew up in a Chinese speaking environment. Of mixed ethnicity herself (she
is a quarter Han), she was still the object of the same discrimination other
Tibetans endured in China; this made her painfully aware of ethnic differences. Although naively proud of being a Tibetan, she was unable to speak
and write in that language, and lacked fundamental knowledge about Tibetan
culture and ways of life. She studied Chinese at the Southwest Institute for
Nationalities in Chengdu, where she graduated in 1988. In 1990, she moved
back to Lhasa where she became editor of the Sinophone magazine *Literature
from Tibet*. Weise's process of "Tibetanization" began with her resolution to
learn the Tibetan language. At the same time, she traveled extensively around
Tibet and began her study of Tibetan culture and religion, which would eventually lead her to become a fervent Buddhist.[42] When I met her in Lhasa in
the fall of 1999, she had already gained the respect of the Tibetophone writers' community for her efforts to learn the Tibetan language.

Some short stories and poems from the 1990s already show her concern
with Chinese abuses in Tibet, as well as her respect for the figure of the Dalai
Lama. Preoccupied for her outspoken nature, both Tibetan and Chinese
friends in Lhasa warned her by the late 1990s of the possible consequences
of her open views on the Chinese presence in Tibet. In 2003, she published
Notes on Tibet (Ch. *Xizang biji*), a compilation of her research and reflections on Chinese migration to Tibet, religious repression, and other very
sensitive topics.[43] A year later the book was banned in China. She was sent
to reeducation, removed from her job, deprived of her health and retirement
benefits, and forbidden to leave China. Weise left Lhasa, moved to Beijing,
and became Tibet's most outspoken dissident. Her popular blog, followed
by Tibetans, Hans and Westerners alike, was blocked in China in 2006. Since
then she has published several books in Taiwan and Hong Kong, and continues communicating with her followers through her Sinophone blog on a
foreign server.[44]

The impact of her poetry has always relied on her lyrical imagery and her
mastery of the Sinitic script, which makes her one of the most compelling
poets in China. The impact of her lucid political writing relies on her clever
use of the media and again, her mastery of the Chinese language. By choice
and by force, Weise has transformed what made her feel most embarrassed—
and what separated her from other Tibetans—into a source of pride that
both unites her fellow countrymen and helps the Tibetan cause. Weise's use
of the Sinitic script to oppose the Chinese occupation of Tibet is, borrowing

Audre Lorde's words, an attempt to "use the master's tools to dismantle the master's house." It is debatable whether or not this attempt will be successful. What is clear is that, having taken the courageous step of becoming a dissident, Weise has finally purged her "sin" of being a Tibetan who is only able to write in Chinese.

Conclusion

Tibetan writers, no matter the language they choose, write in the certainty that their work will always be subject to criticism, either by the Chinese authorities or by the Tibetan community inside and outside Tibet. The sociopolitical environment of Tibet deeply influences the choices of Tibetan writers. The education they have received determines whether they would use the Sinitic script or Tibetan to write. This, in its turn, influences the way in which their identity will be perceived by Chinese, Tibetan, and even Western observers. Their choice of language will have also a huge impact on their literary and personal careers. The market for Sinophone writers is usually larger, and their chances to get translated into foreign languages, and therefore known abroad, are also higher than those of their Tibetophone counterparts.[45] However, this comes at the expense of carrying a heavy burden of "identity doubt" on their shoulders: Sinophone Tibetan writers will never be considered Chinese by the Chinese, or Tibetan by the Tibetans.

Even though the road has been arduous, Sinophone Tibetan writers have garnered many accomplishments. Just as Tashi Dawa and Sebo were well read by Chinese educated readers during the 1980s, Alai has captivated Chinese audiences from the late 1990s on, having an international projection far beyond that of his previous generation. The Tibetan magical realism initiated by Tashi Dawa in the 1980s has permeated the works of both Sinophone and Tibetophone writers such as Alai and Dorjé Tsering Chenaktsang.[46] Moreover, it is now present also in Tibet's emerging film scene through the work of the rising star of Tibetan film, Pema Tseden. After publishing a Chinese-language anthology with magical realistic short stories in 2010,[47] the bilingual writer and filmmaker Pema Tseden will soon release his magical realistic movie "An Everlasting Day," an allegoric reference to Tibet's modern history through the story of a Tibetan herdsman.

The accomplishments of Sinophone Tibetan writers go beyond the literary field. Weise's tenacity and courage in opposing the Chinese occupation of Tibet has shown Tibetans inside and outside China that language does not determine who you are. Contradictory as it sounds, in recent years it has been Weise's Sinophone writing that has given hope to Tibetans around the globe, uniting Sinophone and Tibetophone Tibetans, Tibetans in China, and Tibetans in exile, in the pursuit of a common dream.

Notes

1. Regina Bendix, *In Search of Authenticity: The Formation of Folklore Studies* (Madison: University of Wisconsin Press, 1997), 9.

2. See, for example, the case of Anglophone Indian writers discussed by Salman Rushdie in his introductory study to *Mirror Work: Fifty Years of Indian Writing: 1947–1997*, ed. Salman Rushdie and Elizabeth West (New York: Henry Holt, 1997), vii–xx.

3. The Tibetan Autonomous Region (TAR), also commonly referred to in Chinese as Xizang and in English as Tibet, was established by the Chinese government in 1965. Only half of the 5.4 million Tibetans who live in China call the TAR home. The rest of the Tibetans mostly live in what are now areas belonging to the Chinese provinces of Sichuan, Qinghai, Gansu, and Yunnan. These areas are called Amdo and Kham in Tibetan.

4. For more on Gendün Chömpel and other Tibetan literary innovators in the pre-Communist era, see Lauran R. Hartley, "Heterodox Views and the New Orthodox Poems: Tibetan Writers in the Early and Mid-Twentieth Century," in *Modern Tibetan Literature and Social Change*, ed. Lauran R. Hartley and Patricia Schiaffini (Durham: Duke University Press, 2008), 3–31.

5. For more on Yidam Tsering, see Yangdon Dhondup, "The Road of the Snow Lion: Tibetan Poetry in Chinese," in *Modern Tibetan Literature and Social Change*, 32–60.

6. China has fifty-six recognized ethnic minorities, Tibetans being one of them. The Han, included in the list of these fifty-six ethnic minorities, comprises in fact more than 90 percent of the Chinese population, according to official statistics. In this chapter, the term *Han* will be used as a synonym of Chinese people.

7. Even though the writings of this generation of PLA writers are not relevant or influential from a literary point of view, they are frequently reprinted by the official Chinese media in Tibet. Some of the most representative works by army writers can be found in *Xizang wenxue* 45 (1984), *Xizang wenxue* 105 (1989), *Xizang wenxue* 116 (1991), and *Xizang wenxue* 129 (1993).

8. This is the case of Amdoan Tibetophone writer Dorjé Tsering Chenaktsang, also known as Jangbu. Upon his arrival in Lhasa, he inspired many young Tibetan writers to write in their own language. In an interview with the author, he related how he decided to move to Lhasa: "When we read the first issues of *Literature from Tibet* we were extremely excited. It did not matter that it was written in Chinese; what mattered was that Tibetan writers at last had a forum. Later on, they began publishing [the Tibetan language journal] *Literature and Arts from Tibet*. It was really unbelievable, we were thrilled. [. . .] At the time, Lhasa was the center of [Tibetan] literary development, and it exerted a powerful attraction over us back in Amdo. Many people wanted to come to Lhasa and be part of the literary movement. That is how I came here." (Personal interview with Dorjé Tsering Chenaktsang , Lhasa, October 10, 1999.)

9. On May 29, 1980, Hu Yaobang gave an emotional speech in Lhasa where he acknowledged the wrongdoings of the Chinese government in Tibet. He then summarized the main

points of his vision for Tibet: to promote economic recovery; to develop science, culture, and education; to establish the University of Tibet; and to exercise national autonomy in the region. This translated into new regulations on religious and cultural freedom, the reconstruction of temples, shrines, and monasteries destroyed during the Cultural Revolution, and the reprinting of the Tibetan classics. The local government obtained a high degree of autonomy in dealing with religious, cultural, and educational issues. The living standard of the Tibetan people improved considerably as well, due to the liberalization of the economy and to the number of projects on infrastructure and development carried out by the Chinese authorities. But, as we will see, the golden years of freedom and creativity in Lhasa came to an end by the 1990s, when the Chinese government reverted to its repressive policies.

10. For more on language diglossia in Tibet, as well as the debate on what constitutes Tibetan literature, see Lara Maconi, "One Nation, Two Discourses: Tibetan New Era Literature and the Language Debate" in *Modern Tibetan Literature and Social Change*, 173–201, and Patricia Schiaffini, "The Language Divide: Identity and Literary Choices in Modern Tibet," *Journal of International Affairs* 57, no. 2 (2004): 81–98.

11. For more on Tashi Dawa and Sebo see Patricia Schiaffini, "Changing Identities: The Creation of 'Tibetan' Literary Voices in the PRC" in *Contemporary Tibetan Literary Studies: Proceedings of the Tenth Seminar of the International Association for Tibetan Studies, Oxford 2003*, ed. Steven Venturino (Leiden, Netherlands: E. J. Brill, 2007), 111–131. See also Patricia Schiaffini-Vedani, "The Condor Flies Over Tibet: Zhaxi Dawa and the Significance of Tibetan Magical Realism" in *Modern Tibetan Literature and Social Change*, 202–224.

12. Zhaxi Dawa, "Chao fo" [Buddhist pilgrimage], *Xizang wenyi* 17, no .4 (1980): 3–9. Sebo, "Guisu" [Going back], *Xizang wenyi* 34 (1983): 79–85.

13. See Zhaxi Dawa, "Xizang: Yinmi suiyue" in the anthology under the same title *Xizang: Yinmi suiyue* [Tibet: The mysterious years] (Wuhan: Changjiang wenyi chubanshe, 1993), 1–46. See also Zhaxi Dawa, "Meiyou xingguang de ye" [A night without stars], in his anthology *Xizang, ji zai pisheng jieshang de hun* [Tibet: A soul knotted on a leather rope] (Tianjin: Baihua wenyi chubanshe, 1986). This story was partially translated into English in the journal *China's Tibet* 3 (1995): 32–35.

14. Zhaxi Dawa, "Xizang: Yinmi suiyue," 38–39.

15. For Tashi Dawa's hinting at the taboo issue of homosexuality in monasteries, see Zhaxi Dawa, "Weigan dingshang de zhuiluo zhe" [Those fallen from the mast], *Xizang wenxue* 131 (1994): 4–25.

16. For better or for worse, Tashi Dawa has been compared to Gabriel García Márquez in virtually all Western, Chinese, and Tibetan studies. For some English-language studies, see Geremie Barmé and John Minford, *Seeds of Fire* (New York: Hill and Wang, 1988), 450; Cai Rong, "The Subject in Crisis in Contemporary Chinese Literature," (Diss. Washington University, 1995), 207–232; Lü Tonglin, *Misogyny, Cultural Nihilism and Oppositional Politics* (Palo Alto: Stanford University Press, 1995), 104–128.

17. Interview with the author (Beijing, February 3, 1994).

18. Sebo, "Zai zheli shang chuan" [Board the boat here], *Xizang wenxue* 83, no. 9 (1987), 17. For an English translation see Herbert Bat, trans. "Get the Boat Here" in *Song of the Snow Lion: New Writing from Tibet*, ed. Frank Steward, Herbert J. Batt, and Tsering Shakya, Spec. issue of *Manoa*, 12, no. 2 (2000): 42–48 (Honolulu: University of Hawai'i Press).

19. Sebo, "Board the Boat Here," 14–19.

20. Sebo, "The Circular Day," trans. Herbert Batt, *Tales of Tibet: Sky Burials, Prayer Wheels and Wind Horses* (New York: Rowman and Littlefield, 2001), 206, 213–14.

21. For more on Tashi Dawa's interest in script writing and film producing see Patricia Schiaffini, "An Interview with Tashi Dawa," Latse Tibetan Library Newsletter, 4 (Fall 2007).

22. Ma Lihua, *Xueyu wenhua yu Xizang wenxue* [Snowland culture and the literature from Tibet] (Changsha: Hunan jiaoyu chubanshe, 1998), 144.

23. Geyang and Weise studied at the Lu Xun Institute in Beijing. Yang Zhen studied at Beijing University.

24. Yang Zhen, *Wu xingbie de shen* (Beijing: Zhongguo qingnian chubanshe, 1994).

25. Chen Kuiyuan, "Speech at the Meeting for Summarizing and Commenting on the Creation of the Thematic Concert 'Praising the Return [of Hong Kong to the People's Republic of China]' " [*Zai zhuanti yinyuehui 'Huigui song' chuangzuo zongjie biaozhang dahui de jianghua*], *Xizang ribao* [Tibet Daily] July 16, 1997.

26. From the poem "Another embodiment" (*Ling yige huasheng*), qtd. in Yangdon Dhondup, "The Roar of the Snow Lion: Tibetan Poetry in Chinese," *Modern Tibetan Literature and Social Change*, 32.

27. This information has been extracted from a series of interviews I conducted with these writers in the fall of 1999 in Lhasa (for Weise and Geyang) and in Beijing (in the case of Yang Zhen).

28. For more on recent public debates regarding Tibetan culture that were held in Amdo, see Lauran Hartley, "Inventing Modernity" in "Amdo: Views on the Role of Traditional Tibetan Culture in a Developing Society," in *Amdo Tibetans in Transition, Proceedings of the Ninth Seminar of the International Association for Tibetan Studies*, ed. Toni Huber (Leiden, Netherlands: Brill, 2002).

29. Meizhuo, *Taiyang buluo* [The clan of the Sun], Beijing: Zhongguo wenlian chuban gongsi, 1998.

30. See Gang Yue, http://mclc.osu.edu/rc/pubs/reviews/yue.htm. The Muslim Hui minority is another of the fifty-six recognized minorities in China.

31. Alai, *Red Poppies*, trans. Howard Goldblatt and Sylvia Lin (Boston: Houghton Mifflin, 2000).

32. See Howard Choy "In Quest(ion) of an 'I': Identity and Idiocy in Alai's *Red Poppies*," in *Modern Tibetan Literature and Social Change* (Durham: Duke University Press, 2008), 225–235.

33. See exiled Tibetan writer Tenzing Sonam's review of *Red Poppies* in http://www.whitecranefilms.com/other/red_poppies-review.html.

34. Tibetophone literature is rarely introduced to Chinese audiences. Chinese readers are usually not aware of the wealth of modern literary works produced in the Tibetan language. The occasional Sinophone translations of Tibetophone works are read mostly by Sinophone Tibetan writers and not by Chinese readers.

35. Personal interview with Zhang Jun (Chengdu, November 3, 1999).

36. Ibid.

37. Yangdon Dhondup, "Roar of the Snow Lion: Tibetan Poetry in Chinese" in *Modern Tibetan Literature and Social Change*, 49.

38. Jamyang Norbu, "Cultural and Literary Conjectures on Directions in China," Jeanne Marie Gilbert and James D. Seymour, ed., *The Potomac Conference Proceedings. Sino-Tibetan Relations: Prospects for the Future* (New York: Columbia University Press, 1992), 110.

39. See Topden Tsering, http://www.phayul.com/news/article.aspx?id=6965&t=1.

40. For the language debate in African literature, see Ngũgĩ wa Thiong'o, *Decolonising the Mind: The Politics of Language in African Literature* (London: James Currey, 1986), 6; and Chinua Achebe, *Morning Yet on Creation Day* (New York: Anchor Books, 1976), 74–75.

41. E-mail from Weise (March 31, 2001, 00:51:26). Original in Chinese.

42. Information gathered in a series of interviews conducted with Weise in Lhasa, Fall 1999.

43. Weise, *Xizang biji* [Notes on Tibet] (Guangzhou, Huacheng chubanshe), 2003.

44. http://woeser.middle-way.net

45. There has been a steady flow of English translations of works by Sinophone Tibetan writers, previously mostly Tashi Dawa, and more recently Alai's *Red Poppies* and Weise's *Tibet's True Heart*, trans. A. E. Clark (Ardsley: Ragged Banner, 2008). *Red Poppies*, for example, was translated into English in 2002, in a paperback edition that has sold well and has received much attention in the wide community of Western scholars of China. On the contrary, the first English translation of an anthology by a Tibetophone writer, Dorjé Tsering Chenaktsang's *Nine-Eyed Agate* (published under his pseudonym, Jangbu), has taken many more years to attain visibility in the United States. Although it is a highly accomplished work of translation, and a masterpiece of Tibetan writing, its high price (only published in hardback) and the much reduced market for Tibetan scholarly works in the West, will not grant this translation the attention it deserves (Jangbu, *Nine-Eyed Agate,* trans. Heather Stoddard [Lanham, Md.: Rowman and Littlefield, 2010]).

46. For more on Alai, see the essay in this volume by Carlos Rojas. See also Howard Choy's "In Quest(ion) of and 'I': Identity and Idiocy in Alai's *Red Poppies*" in *Modern Tibetan Literature and Social Change*, 225–235. The use of magical realism in Tibetophone literature is explained in Franz Xaver Erhard's "Magical Realism and Tibetan Literature" in *Contemporary Tibetan Literary Studies*, ed. Steven Venturino, 133–146.

47. Wanma Caidan, *Liulang geshou de meng* [The bard's dream] (Xizang renmin chubanshe, 2010).

18

Danger in the Voice

Alai and the Sinophone

CARLOS ROJAS

Danger in the voice. Sometimes in conversation the sound of our own voice confuses us and misleads us to assertions that do not at all reflect our opinion.

Friedrich Nietzsche, *Human, All Too Human*

"Let's have ourselves a national unification."

Every weekend that all three of the protagonists of Alai's story "The Hunt" (*Shoulie*)[1] happen to be in town, they call each other up to propose a "national unification" (*minzu tuanjie*). One of the People's Republic of China's (PRC) standard nationalistic mottos, this phrase literally means "ethnic unity" and is reappropriated here to function as a call for a weekend hunting expedition. The story's protagonists treat this call for a reunion as a sort of private joke, alluding ironically to the fact that they themselves are comprised of an ethnically Tibetan military scout named Yinba, a Han Chinese driver named Qin Keming, together with the story's partially Sinified Tibetan narrator, who is described as being "the product of an intimate unification (*tuanjie*) of two ethnicities (*minzu*)" (128).

Beyond its specific function in this story, this *national unification* phrase could also be seen as a sort of coded reference to Alai himself—who, like his narrator, is literally the product of an "intimate unification of two ethnicities." As an ethnically Tibetan author who writes exclusively in Chinese, Alai is balanced on the knife-edge between an idealized national unity and the ethnic fault lines that perennially threaten to compromise that unity from within. Some of the implications of Alai's complicated relationship to

Chinese nationalism are illustrated, for instance, in the reception of his first novel, *Red Poppies* (*Chen'ai luoding* 塵埃落定, or literally, "The dust settles," 1998), which in 2000 was awarded two of China's most prestigious literary prizes: the Mao Dun Prize for novels by Chinese nationals, and the *Junma* Prize given to works by Chinese ethnic minorities. The Mao Dun Prize celebrates literature representing the quintessence of modern Chinese culture, while the *Junma* Prize recognizes the ethnic and cultural diversity that implicitly provides a foil for a discourse of normative "Chineseness"; together they reflect the mutually opposed political logics underlying the nation's status as a product—but also a strategic elision—of the ethnic diversity of which it is comprised.

The real "joke" in Alai's use of the *national unification* phrase, however, is not so much that his hunters are borrowing an official motto to propose a private excursion, but rather that this assertion of ethnic unity is *itself* internally fractured. Whether applied to the weekend hunting expedition, to the author, or to the Chinese nation as a whole, this formulaic appeal to the possibility of transcending internal differences paradoxically underscores the continued relevance of those same distinctions. Even as this political motto draws attention to its own indeterminacy, it also signals more generally the possibility that language may diverge from, and even undermine, the meaning it has been assigned. The story's *national unification* phrase, in short, illustrates the inherent danger that a speaker may lose control of his or her own language, but also the problem that language may at the same time reveal certain unintended truths about itself.

I will take "The Hunt"'s ironic call for a "national unification" as my entry point into the intersecting concerns of nationalism and language at the heart of Alai's literary project, and will consider how his work critiques not only the possibility of national unity but also the reliability of the very language used to affirm it. These issues, furthermore, have a direct bearing on our understanding of Alai's general literary oeuvre. His interrogation of the possibility of national unity brings into question the feasibility of classifying his work in conventionally national terms, just as his interrogation of the possibility of linguistic coherence complicates the possibility of classifying his works based on the language in which they are written. I propose we may instead use a notion of authorial "voice" to develop a new literary taxonomy that would take as its starting point the disunity and indeterminacy that undermine traditional notions of nation and language.

On the surface, "The Hunt" appears to be a straightforward account of three friends on an ill-fated hunting expedition. Between the lines, however, the work presents a complex exploration of the limits of language and national identity. We find a hint of the text's double voicing in a curious anecdote about how the driver Qin Keming once discovered that he could switch the frequency of his car's radio to surreptitiously listen in on other people's private telephone conversations. The seemingly random series of conversations he overhears succinctly introduce several of what will prove to be the central concerns of the story as a whole, including issues of authority (a conversation about his boss), mortality (a conversation about the death of an acquaintance), and desire (a bout of phone sex).

At the same time, Qin's very act of eavesdropping presents a useful model for our own reading (and figurative decoding) of the work itself. This theme of linguistic decoding is explicitly introduced in the narrator's specification that the hunters' call of a "national unification" functions as a sort of "secret code" (*yinyu*) (128). The narrator notes that hunters have used this sort of coded language from time immemorial, and describes how he and his companions are particularly attracted to the sense of "mystery and allure" that results from the cloud of regulation under which hunting is currently enveloped. As national wildlife protection regulations have placed under legal protection "virtually all of the birds and animals [the hunters] crave most" (128), hunting itself has increasingly become wedged between the proscriptive authority of the state and the private desires (cravings) of the hunters themselves.

The narrator notes that these protected game include goat-like serows, black bears, ring-necked and white-eared pheasants, and red deer, together with the eastern roe deer that is the primary focus of the story. The roe deer makes its initial appearance when Qin Keming notices some deer droppings outside their tent and wonders aloud whether they were left by a male or female. The narrator teases him, saying, "Even if it were a female, it still wouldn't give you that sort of phone call," but immediately regrets his remark upon seeing Qin's face drop in embarrassment. The next morning they are awakened by the plaintive bleating of a doe standing just outside their camp "with milk dripping from its swollen teats, looking as though it had been a long time since it last nursed." It turns out that the doe is searching for a fawn that had hidden inside the hunters' tent overnight without their notice, and Qin Keming and the narrator accidentally break the fawn's leg attempting to remove it from the tent. As the hunters fashion a splint for the injured fawn and try to feed it mushrooms, the doe continues to hover anxiously nearby, desperate to nurse her offspring. The doe's incessant bleating eventually annoys Qin Keming to the point that he takes his double-barreled shotgun and shoots the ground at the doe's feet, knocking her head over heels down the hill. Qin then turns to the narrator and calmly notes, "I didn't kill it" (135).

Despite being the ostensible subject of the story, the roe deer is presented here not so much as an object of the hunt but rather as an overdetermined node within a conflicted knot of attitudes toward maternity and femininity. From Qin's embarrassed reaction to the joke about his interest in the doe, to his subsequent attempt to "mother" her injured fawn, to his violent attack on the lactating doe herself, Qin's attitude toward the mother deer oscillates wildly between desire, aggression, and vicarious identification (e.g., his insisting on feeding the fawn even as its mother is standing nearby). The doe functions not merely as a maternal figure in her own right, but more generally as a figurative screen against which the work's own ambivalences about maternity and identity are played out.

Paralleling the story's fascination with maternity, there is an underlying concern with mortality. The first night of the expedition, for instance, Qin Keming dreamed of white mushrooms that he felt were a premonition of death, and it is precisely as he is feeding these same mushrooms to the injured fawn the next morning that he—in a bizarre act of aggression that comes back to haunt him—attacks and almost kills the fawn's mother. It turns out that just as Qin is shooting at the fawn's mother, Yinba is simultaneously hunting a wolf that had just killed a roe buck he speculates may have been the fawn's father. When Qin Keming goes to retrieve the wolf's pelt for his arthritic wife, the wounded animal unexpectedly lashes at him with its hind claw and rips open a deep gash in his belly, thereby providing a sort of karmic retribution for Qin's own unprovoked attack on the doe earlier that same morning.

Yinba and the narrator bandage Qin up as best they can, and construct a makeshift stretcher to carry him back down the mountain. As they are about to leave, Yinba suddenly curses at the fawn, "*X your mother, go back home,*" and then turns to his companions and repeats, "*X your mother, let's go.*" This curse marks the conclusion of both the expedition proper as well as the story as a whole, and furthermore it neatly bookends the call for a "national unification" at the beginning of the work. Whereas the *national unification* phrase used an ironic appeal to nationalism in order to introduce a critical perspective on language, this final *X your mother* curse instead uses a focus on language to reevaluate the significance of one's own "mother tongue."

Yinba's ejaculation is a familiar variant on the nearly universal "your mother" formula,[2] and in transcribing it Alai follows the common convention of using the letter X in place of the initial verb, *cao*—which in this context could be translated literally (and euphemistically) as "to do."[3] Although strategically omitted from Alai's transcription, this same *cao* character makes an uncanny return in the narrator's description of the pleasure Yinba derives from "manipulating" (*caozuo*) the foreign language of the curse itself:

We never made any attempt to restrain Yinba's curses. This was the first phrase he had learned when he started studying Chinese as a teenager. He still speaks Chinese with a heavy accent, and this curse—which he pronounces distinctly and melodiously—is the only Chinese phrase he is able to utter fluently. You simply can't imagine depriving him of the rush he derives from smoothly manipulating (*caozuo*) a foreign language (139–140).

At a linguistic level, the curse folds back upon itself, with Yinba's vulgar reference to taking pleasure from "using" (*cao*) someone else's mother suggestively mirroring his own pleasurable "use" (*caozuo*) of a curse that is very explicitly *not* in his "mother tongue." The *X* in the curse literally marks a space of linguistic erasure, underscoring the necessary divergence of oral speech from the written language used to transcribe it. At the same time, this *X* points to Yinba's conflicted position at the intersection of two language systems and their respective ethnic associations, the sensuous "rush" (*kuaigan*) he derives from using a language that is not his own standing in contrast to the "heavy accent" that reveals his continued loyalty to his native tongue, together with the ethnic identity with which it is associated.

The linguistic and ethnic chiasmus graphically represented by the *X* in Yinba's curse could also be compared to the interstitial region of northwestern Sichuan where Alai himself was born and has lived most of his life, and where all of his fiction is set. Comparable to Faulkner's Yoknapatawpha county or Mo Yan's northeast Gaomi county, Alai's Maerkang county is located in Sichuan's Ngawa Tibetan and Qiang Autonomous Prefecture and belongs more broadly to what is known as Cultural Tibet (and which includes not only Tibet proper but also regions with high concentrations of Tibetans in adjacent Sichuan and Qinghai provinces). In a lecture Alai delivered in the United States in 2001, he explained that his hometown was located in a region that extended

> from the rich Chengdu plains north and west to the Tibet-Qinghai Plateau, [where] there lies a transition zone comprised of a series of mountains and valleys. This zone is called *Jiarong* in Tibetan, and a linguistic study reveals that this classical Tibetan word literally means an agricultural area adjacent to a mountain pass leading to an ethnically Han region (156).[4]

Alai's etymological reading of *Jiarong* as signifying a sort of ethnogeographic "transition zone" is fitting, given his own emphasis on his hometown region's significance as a meeting point between China and Tibet and their respective languages and cultures. He adds that that it was as a result of having grown up in this border region that he therefore found himself "destined to roam between two languages" (157), educated in Chinese but accustomed to using his native "mother tongue" for casual conversations.

Elided from Alai's discussion of the linguistic significance of his hometown region is a language linguists call *Jiarong*, after the region where it is traditionally spoken. Jiarong shares many cognates with Tibetan, though it is formally classified as a distinct language with several dialects of its own (including one named after Alai's own Maerkang county).[5] Despite being the mother tongue of many of the residents of the region—and quite possibly of Alai himself[6]—Jiarong nevertheless occupies a curiously indeterminate position in Alai's writings. Alai never refers to this language directly, and instead it can only be glimpsed in his references to characters speaking an unspecified "hometown speech" that is neither "standard Tibetan [nor] Mandarin Chinese." Jiarong, in other words, appears in Alai's fiction as a local speech that, like the author himself, is "fated to roam between two languages."[7]

Alai notes that it was precisely his position at the interstices of disparate languages and their corresponding cultures that led him to develop an interest in other "nonmainstream" (*fei zhuliu*) authors such as Jewish American writers including Isaac Bashevis Singer and Philip Roth and African American authors such as Toni Morrison and Ralph Ellison, all of whom, he concludes, use English to "express themselves in a distinctive yet authentic manner" (159). What Alai here calls nonmainstream authorial production— and which Deleuze and Guattari similarly call minor literature—refers to a minority author's ability to internally colonize the dominant literary language within which he or she is working. It is precisely this potential disjoint between an author's subject position and the language in which he or she writes that has motivated a move from a traditional nation-based system of literary classification to one that also includes hybrid postcolonial categories such as Francophone, Anglophone, Hispanophone, and Lusophone literatures. This "linguaphone" model, however, is rhetorically at odds with itself, in that although in principle it might be understood as referring to *all* literature written in a certain language, in practice it has been used more narrowly to designate only literature originating from *outside* the "home" nation itself. As a result, the linguaphone has not supplanted the earlier national literature model, so much as it has merely supplemented it, implicitly reaffirming the normative nationalism that the category was ostensibly attempting to challenge in the first place.[8] Even if approached in strictly linguistic terms, the linguaphone is grounded on an internal tension, in that etymologically it refers to *spoken* language (the suffix *phone* is Greek for "voice" or "sound"), though in practice is it used primarily to refer to written—rather than oral—texts. This distinction is particularly significant in the Chinese cases, in that it is precisely the comparatively loose link between Chinese characters and their pronunciations that has permitted the Chinese writing system to anchor a vast population speaking an array of mutually unintelligible "dialects."

The concept of the Sinophone, consequently, is deeply at odds with itself, to the point that one might perhaps be tempted to discard the entire category altogether. Instead, we may follow the story's example of a strategic appropriation of a politically orthodox phrase ("national unification"), and capitalize on conceptual indeterminacies inherent in the notion of the Sinophone in order to develop a literary taxonomy grounded not on strictly national or linguistic considerations but rather on what we might instead call an authorial "voice." Rather than simply substituting one taxonomical criterion ("nation" or "language") for another ("voice"), this notion of a national voice could make possible a systematic rethinking of the very logic of literary taxonomy itself. Many existing models of literary classification assume it is possible to make reasonably clear-cut determinations of an author's national affiliation or a work's language, despite the fact that neither of the two is a unitary and homogenous category to begin with. An author's "voice," by contrast, is not determined by any single necessary and sufficient condition, but rather is informed by a loose set of what Wittgenstein calls family resemblances.[9] Alai's literary voice, for instance, is shaped not only by his nationality and the language in which he writes, but also by the cultural region and the vernacular with which he identifies, the subject matter about which he chooses to write, the authors by whom he is influenced, his relationship to the political regime under which he is writing, and so forth. To classify Alai as a Sinophone author, therefore, may reflect any and all of these factors, some of which ally him in suggestive ways with other writers who are conventionally categorized as Chinese or Sinophone, while others distance him from many such writers and instead point to other networks of affiliation.

In his 2001 discussion of the ability of "nonmainstream" authors to "express themselves in a distinctive yet authentic manner," discussed previously, Alai cites a Buddhist expression to describe the possibility that one's writing might succeed in "reach[ing] the sky" and becoming a "great voice" (*da shengyin*). For Alai, this notion of a great voice speaks to the possibility that a writer might succeed both in transcending his or her origins and being "heard by a larger audience," while at the same time reaffirming the distinctiveness of his or her positionality and ensuring that "their boiling blood and true emotions [will] become embedded within their words and between the lines of their writing" (160).

The use of a multifaceted notion of authorial "voice" (rather than simply language, ethnicity, or nationality) to approach Alai's status as a "Sinophone" author similarly underscores his distinctiveness while at the same time inviting productive comparisons with a wide variety of other authors working throughout China, the global Chinese diaspora, and beyond. This approach attempts to find the meaning embedded within the work's words and between the lines of the text, inviting a reading process that approaches the text as a sort of "secret code" potentially at odds with itself—a reading process, in other words, that approaches literature as being a peculiar product of what Alai's hunters might call a "national unification."

Notes

1. Alai, "Shoulie" [The hunt], in *Gela zhangda* [Gela grows up] (Shanghai: Dongfang chu-banshe, 2007), 127–140. Subsequent page numbers will be noted parenthetically in the text.

2. This same curse recently became the focus of a similar debate over language and pro-hibition when a reference to "straw-mud horse"—or *cao ni ma* in Chinese—began circulating virally over the Chinese Internet. The joke is that the Chinese name of this imaginary animal is a near homophone for the "X your mother" curse—*cao ni ma*—and its usage symbolizes the possibility of circumventing more general restrictions on public discourse over the Chinese Internet.

3. The elided character is also sometimes read as *gan*, which in this context could also be translated euphemistically as "to do."

4. Alai, "Zai Meiguo bijiao wenxue xuehui nianhui shang de yanjiang" [A lecture delivered to the American Comparative Literature Association's annual conference], in Alai, *Aba Alai* [Ngawa Alai] (Beijing: Zhongguo gongren chubanshe, 2004), 156–160.

5. See Raymond G. Gordon, Jr. (ed.), *Ethnologue* (Online version: http://www.ethnologue.com/show_language.asp?code=jya)

6. Robert Barnett, personal communication, June 2007.

7. For a more comprehensive discussion of this story and of the linguistic issues it raises, please see Carlos Rojas, "Alai and the Linguistic Politics of Internal Diaspora," in *Global Chinese Literature: Critical Essays*, ed. Jing Tsu and David Der-wei Wang (Leiden, Netherlands: Brill Press, 2010), 115–132.

8. A partial exception to this rule can be found with Anglophone literature, which is fre-quently used to refer to all English-language literature from the former British Empire, with the exception of literature from Great Britain and, oddly, the United States.

9. See Ludwig Wittgenstein, *Philosophical Investigations* (New York: Blackwell Publishing, 2001).

19

Sinophone Malaysian Literature

An Overview

KIM TONG TEE

The term "Sinophone Malaysian literature" denotes Malaysian writings in Chinese, suggesting, on the one hand, the existence of Malaysian literatures written in languages other than Chinese, namely Malay, English, and Tamil. On the other hand, it is also possible to talk about "Malaysian Sinophone literature," which implies the existence of global writings in Chinese produced in other places outside China—for example, Singaporean Sinophone literature, Indonesian Sinophone literature, and so forth. Both Sinophone Malaysian literature and Malaysian Sinophone literature refer to the same object or body of literature, which is generally categorized as *Ma Hua wenxue*, but the discursive contexts differ.

In the early twentieth century, following the May Fourth "New Literature" Movement (*Xin wenxue yundong*) of China, a vernacular Sinophone literature emerged in colonial Malaya, marking the beginning of a modern literary tradition in the Nanyang, or the South Seas, as Southeast Asia as a region was known to the Chinese at that time. This literature was produced by Chinese sojourners and settlers, who had formed various diasporic communities outside China since the mid-nineteenth century or earlier. These diasporic Chinese communities in Malaya, particularly in the Straits Settlements of Singapore, Melaka (Malacca), and Penang, were able to maintain some cultural activities and establish their literary fields, though minor and marginalized. After World War II, most colonial Southeast Asian countries achieved their independence. Malaya gained her independence in 1957, and Singapore became self-governing in 1959. Sinophone literary texts produced in both Malaya and Singapore before the early 1970s are categorized as *Mahua wenxue.*

The Sinophone literature produced in Malaya is generally referred to as either "overseas Chinese-language literature" (*haiwai Huawen wenxue*) or "world Chinese-language literature" (*shijie Huawen wenxue*) by critics and scholars in Taiwan and China. As an imprecise label with geopolitical connotations, overseas Chinese-language literature indicates the dominant position, marginalizing ideology, and co-optative motivation of Chinese literature as both national and ethnic literature. Likewise, world Chinese-language literature minoritizes the Sinophone literary articulations around the world as writing in "world Chinese." Terms such as "Sojourning Chinese literature" (*Huaqiao wenxue* or *qiaomin wenxue*) were used particularly in the older days by literary historians and critics from both sides of the Taiwan Straits, who claimed that such literary works were produced by Chinese who resided overseas.

On October 6, 1919, the *Sin Kok Min Jit Pao* (*Xin guomin ribao*) published an editorial by Zhang Shunai, explaining the newspaper's cause for adopting the vernacular *baihua* as the medium of expression in its *Sin Kok Min Magazine* (*Xin guomin zazhi*) supplement.[1] Zhang explained that the literary works he published in the supplement were meant to cultivate learning and morality in readers and to promote social progress. To these ends, the newspaper would welcome articles in the vernacular because "the classical language is difficult to comprehend; simple words, however, are easy to understand."[2] Moreover, Zhang added, as China was in a critical state, the newspaper was obliged to preach patriotism toward China, and in order to arouse the public its language should be in the form of simple vernacular Chinese. The newspaper's promotion of Chinese patriotism toward China is understandable because its readers were Chinese sojourners and settlers in Malaya.

While the presence of the immigrant Chinese community in Malaya was the result of British efforts, the arrival of a Chinese intelligentsia (notably journalists and writers) in the region, especially during the 1920s, was due to political controversy in China. When the Nationalist-Communist coalition finally fell apart in 1927, many leftist intellectuals fled to the Nanyang to avoid imprisonment and political suppression. The influence of the transformation of ideology in Chinese literature on the embryonic Sinophone literature in Malaya and the Straits Settlements in the 1920s was obvious, for the Emergent Literature (*Xinxing wenxue*) movement launched in 1925 by Guo Moruo and Jiang Guangci was soon engaged by the local literati. In 1927, some Sinophone Malayan men-in-the-culture launched a "Nanyang Emergent Literature" movement to echo the Chinese proletarian or revolutionary literary movement. It is evident that the use of the term "Nanyang Emergent Literature" was to de-radicalize the socialist implication of terms like "revolutionary literature" and "proletarian literature." The movement was also a reorientation of the local literary institution regarding the function of literature, for since then, literary ideology manifesting the sociocultural code became dominant in Sinophone Malay(si)an literature. The movement was culminated in the editorial work of Xu Jie, a short story writer who came from China in 1928.

Xu Jie became the chief editor of *Yik Khuan Pao* (*Yiqun bao*) after he arrived in Kuala Lumpur. Soon *Barren Island* (*Kudao*), the literary supplement Xu edited, became an arena for budding Sinophone Malayan writers to express their literary interest and talents. Kuala Lumpur, now after Singapore and Penang, became an important literary center in the late 1920s. Promoting proletarian or revolutionary literature in the *Barren Island* supplement, Xu moreover encouraged local writers to express their true feelings on local subject matter. This suggests that a joint effort between Emergent Literature and literature of "local color" in establishing a new literature in the Nanyang. Xu's intention, however, was to make use of the Nanyang local color to reinforce the revolutionary Emergent Literature movement, which virtually ended after he left Malaya in 1929.

In the colonial Malayan period, the earliest attempt to advocate the concept of "Nanyang local color literature" (*Nanyang secai wenxue*), however, was made by Zhang Jinyan, a Singapore-born tailor and short-story writer, and his colleagues of the *Desert Island* (*Huangdao*) supplement in the *Sin Kok Min Jit Pao*. This early endeavor of the *Desert Island* supplement to promote a literature of local color in theory and practice was based on Zhang's idea of "inscribing Nanyang local color in literary texts to create something of interest."[3] The *Desert Island* supplement, which ceased to exist after September 1929, marked an initial stage of the Sinophone Malayan literary agenda of nationalizing an immigrated literature by abandoning the ready-made matrix of Chinese literature imported from China and fitting it into local sociocultural codes.

Other efforts during the late 1920s to localize Sinophone literature and help encourage the emergence of a nationalized Nanyang literature in the *Mahua* literary institution was from Zhang's counterparts in other newspapers such as Zeng Shengti, who founded the *Literary Weekly* (*Wenyi zhoukan*) of the *Nanyang Siang Pau* (*Nanyang shangbao*), and Chen Lianqing, a China-born writer, who edited the *Coconut Groves* (*Yelin*) literary supplement of *The Straits Gazette* (*Lat Pau*). While Zeng urged his fellow writers "to work together under tall coconut and rubber trees to construct the tower of Nanyang literature with blood and sweat,"[4] Chen proposed the creation of a Nanyang culture in the immigrant Chinese community. To promote a literary Nanyang consciousness, Chen encouraged writers to explore life in the equatorial region with its "verdant coconut trees, lush rubber estates, dense banana groves, and upright old-growth trees," all of which were by no means less beautiful than any seen in China.[5]

The idea of "Nanyang literature" was later translated into "local Malayan literature," a term eventually leading to the concept of *Ma Hua wenxue/Ma Hua wenyi* as an abbreviation for *Malaiya Huaqiao wenyi* (Overseas Chinese literature in Malaya). Such a Malayan turn in immigrant Chinese literature was the consequence of two heated debates that occurred in 1934 and 1936, respectively. In 1934, Qiu Shizhen, author of *Baba and Nyonya* (*Baba yu niangre*), published an article entitled "On Local Writers" (*Difang zuojia tan*) in the *Lion's Roar* (*Shi sheng*) supplement of the *Nanyang Siang Pau*, urging local writers to identify themselves as Malayan writers since Malayan literature is produced by writers who are born or who reside in Malaya. Two years later, Zeng Aidi published "A Sketch of the Malayan Literary Scene" (*Malaiya wenyi jie manhua*) in the *Publishing World* (*Chubanjie*) supplement of *Sin Chew Jit Poh* (*Xingzhou ribao*), in which he bitterly attacked those local short satirical essay (*zawen*) writers who simply imitated or copied whatever was advocated by their counterparts in China. He further argued for the importance of local uniqueness in literary creation by pointing out that Malayan literature should endeavor in exploring local subject matters and should not simply and mechanically carry over (*banshi*) theories from China.[6] Zeng's emphasis on literary localness was discussed enthusiastically by other local writers such as Yi Jiao and Yang Ru, who used the abbreviated term *Mahua* for the first time in the history of Sinophone Malay(si)an literature.

However, it was during these post-Emergent Literature years that immigrant and local-born Chinese writers alike expressed their strong Chinese cultural identity and Chinese nationalism. The main cause was of course the Japanese invasion of China in 1937. This interference through the introduction of the dominant patriotic "Resistance Literature" (*kangzhan wenxue*), on the one hand, put Sinophone Malayan literature back into the grand narrative of Chinese literature. On the other hand, the occupation of Malaya by the Japanese in the Pacific War had led to the formation of a new consciousness for the Chinese in Malaya and Singapore. They now realized that their fate was closely tied with Malaya as a whole. After the war, various factions of the crown colony organized themselves and thought about ways to gain self-government and independence from the British. When China turned Communist in 1949, the Chinese in Malaya and Singapore had to make a choice regarding their own future. Malaya was now the object of identification and loyalty for all the people.

In the 1950s, Malaya and Singapore witnessed an era of political nationalism. After the Japanese occupation of 1942–1945, like many Third World countries that fought for their liberation from colonial rule in the postwar years, Malaya sought independence from British colonization. For the Chinese in Malaya, there were questions of identity, loyalty, citizenship, constitutional status, language, education, and culture to be solved. In spite of this, most Chinese in Malaya chose to stay and become citizens of the newly independent country.

Meanwhile, Chinese writers in Malaya and Singapore who produced literary texts with a China background became the target of attack for some Chinese Malayan writers who embraced a local consciousness. In the eyes of these writers, those who still wrote about things China in the postwar years were regarded as "sojourning writers" (*qiaomin zuojia*) and their works "sojourners' literature" (*qiaomin wenyi*). In contrast, the local writers advocated the idea of "the distinctive features of Sinophone Malayan literature" (*Ma Hua wenyi dutexing*) in 1947, when a group of writers in Singapore gathered in a literary forum to express their views and opinions. In response to the suggestions raised in the forum, in which the local writers were urged to learn from writers with China background and the latter were encouraged to pay attention to local social reality, the local Sinophone Malayan writers started a series of debates in various newspaper supplements, and soon the central issue of their argument became one about form and content, literary universals and particulars, as well as ideology and stance. An important intention of the local writers in this debate was to distinguish Sinophone Malayan writings from Chinese literature.

This nationalized advocacy was what gave the debate an ideology different from the prewar localized endeavors contributed by Zhang Jinyan, Zeng Shengti, Huang Seng, Chen Lianqing, or those involved in the Malayan turn or debate. It was the first time the Sinophone Malayan men-in-the-culture raised the question of identity and mounted a strong pro-Malayan position. Ling Zuo, for example, raised a strong voice in his view of upholding a local stance: local Sinophone writers should identify themselves as Malayan.[7] Ling's view was obviously supported by many local writers, for the debate soon turned into one with an attack on "sojourners' literature." The attack was started in 1948 by Zhou Rong (aka Jin Zhimang) in his "On Sinophone Malayan Literature" (*Tan Mahua wenyi*), an article emphasizing the distinctiveness of literature, and "Another View on Sojourners' Literature" (*Ye lun qiaomin wenyi*), a long rebuttal of the counterattack from those holding the opposite opinion. Zhou suggested that local literature must express a sense of being "here and now," otherwise it would be sojourners' literature. In his view, Sinophone Malayan writers had to distinguish themselves by expressing a sense of "place" and a sense of "contemporaneity."[8]

Though not written in Malay, in the early Federation period, Sinophone Malayan literature already self-consciously functioned as part of the operating force in promoting a Malayan nationalism. In other words, Malayan literature before and after the periods of independence should be understood in its sociocultural context and viewed respectively from the nationalized projects of Sinophone, Anglophone, Malay, and Tamil literatures. Such a redefinition would restructure and represent a Malay(si)an literature as a polysystem, emphasizing the intrasystemic relations of the different literatures.[9] Furthermore, the nationalized project of Sinophone Malayan literature also helps clarify the question of double cultural identities in migrancy and its historical relationship with a Nanyang consciousness.

During the early postcolonial period, the Sinophone Malayan literary scene presented a diversity of literary ideologies and expressive forms, though later on they were vulgarly and dichotomously categorized as the realist and modernist schools. The widely used catchphrase "*Mahua* Modernist school" was actually an abusage invented by some conservative critics who upheld the social-realist literary codes to attack the new generation who began to turn away from the polemical nationalization of literature. Followers of the leftist social-realistic literary ideology became a dominant force in the 1960s and 1970s. For at least two decades, works published in the literary supplements of *Nanyang Siang Pau* and *Sin Chew Jit Poh* were mostly of the social-realist style. However, there were writers like Miao Xiu, Wei Yun, Yu Mowo, and Fang Beifang who clearly practiced realist writing techniques but did not embrace leftist ideology. Similarly, *Chao Foon* (*Jiaofeng*), the literary magazine founded in 1955 as a fortnightly and which practiced a "Malayanized" editorial policy, published, in its founding years, mostly realist works. Its editor, Fang Tian, was interested in representing Malayan life realistically. To find inspiration in writing his short stories, he often visited tin mines, rubber estates, and shipyards where he observed laborers and coolies and took notes of their conversations.

In the 1960s, the two main forces in the local Sinophone modernist literary movement were *Chao Foon* and the *Student Weekly* (*Xuesheng zhoubao*) in Malaysia, as well as the *Literature* (Wenyi) and *Youth's Park* (Qingnian yuandi) supplements of the *Nanyang Siang Pau,* edited in Singapore by Liang Meng Kwang from 1967 to 1970. The modernist movement culminated in the emergence of the "Generation of 1968" (Tan Swie Hian and other modernist poets) in Singapore and the establishment of the May Publishers in 1968, the publication of the new series of *Chao Foon* in 1969, and the founding of the *Literary Miscellany* (*Wencong*) supplement of the *Nanyang Siang Pau,* coedited by Liang Meng Kwang and Tan Swie Hian, in 1971.

Though in the early 1960s Pak Yiu (Bai Yao), poet and editor of *Chao Foon* and the *Student Weekly,* had begun to write poems expressing a sense of modernity and essays introducing the concepts of Modernist poetry, and under the influence of Pak Yiu's colleague Huang Yai the novelist, many literary societies were set up and little magazines appeared throughout the peninsula, forming a pro-modernist literary constellation, it was not until 1969 when Tan Swie Hian joined the editorial board of *Chao Foon* that Sinophone literary modernism became a local movement. Chao Foon's modernist project marked a renovation and the joining together of the most outstanding Sinophone writers and editors from Singapore and Malaysia—the two once-merged regions having become two separate political entities in 1965.

In Singapore, the modernist movement was launched by Liang Meng Kwang in the second half of the 1960s. From 1967 to 1970, after Liang succeeded Yang Shoumo (aka Xing Ying) as the literary page editor of *Nanyang Siang Pau,* the *Literature* and *Youth's Park* supplements became important fields for budding writers from both sides of the Malaysia-Singapore Causeway to cultivate their literary talents. During the three years that Liang was the editor, the most remarkably talented writer was Tan Swie Hian, who later helped Liang edit *Literary Miscellany.* In the *Nanyang* supplements, Tan's talent was fully expressed through his poems, short stories, translations, and prose. In those years, members of the "Generation of 1968" devoted themselves to the art of modernist poetry, though they signed no manifestos. Joining in a poetical revolt against the social-realist predecessors, Tan and his comrades shared a common pursuit in poetry and art at large—a pursuit detached from social and political engagements inspired by the Chinese Cultural Revolution. For them, modernism was precisely an aesthetic taste and belief in literature. It served as an alternative model, rather than a doctrine, for their generation to seek an autonomous aesthetics of their own.

Compared with Liang's literary supplements, *Chao Foon* had more than a whole decade to promote Sinophone literary modernism in Malaysia. Yet, its modernist project was generally an incomplete one. For some reasons the magazine never openly declared its modernist stance. It defended at most innovative techniques in literary creation. But such a lack of radical and systematic culture planning in its editorial policy led the magazine to its failure of meeting the challenge of cultural, social, and ideological changes in the 1970s. Many writers from Malaysia and Singapore who contributed to the magazine looked upon themselves as disciples of literary modernism, but owing to the lack of a Modernist tradition and the limitation of individual talents, they failed to create a new Modernist wave after Tan turned wholeheartedly to painting as well as religious meditation and thus became less enthusiastic about literature. Similarly, in Singapore the Modernist movement slowed down its pace and eventually died away after the three supplements edited by Liang ceased publication. So after the mid-1970s, while some poets of the "Generation of 1968" re-embraced the realist or nationalized code, others practically abandoned their literary careers. But, significantly, some former contributors of *Chao Foon*, including writers of fiction such as Wan Kok Seng (Wen Xiangying), Tan Kee Keat (aka Xiao Hei), Ng Neoh Leng (aka Song Tzyy Herng [Song Ziheng]), and Tan Cheng Sin (Chen Zhengxin), as well as poets such as Moy Sook Chin, Tan Boon Hong (aka Sha Qin), Wee Juan Hiong (Huang Yuanxiong), and Woon Swee Tin (aka Wen Renping) still remain major figures in the Sinophone Malaysian literary scene today.

In the post-1969 years, Malaysia's pro-native cultural and pro-Malay economic policies, commonly known as *Bumiputraism*, have aroused feelings of estrangement in the non-*Bumiputra* communities. The two policies, part of the agenda of the government's social restructuring project to strengthen the ruling party's power and improve the financial status of ethnic Malays, were implemented as an affirmative action in the early 1970s. Sinophone Malaysian writers who continued to write in the contemporary era were caught in a difficult situation. Since literature of political engagement was quite impossible, and questions of political, ethnic, religious, and education were "critical or sensitive issues" that the government deemed off limits for discussion in the public sphere, some Sinophone Malaysian writers turned inward by appropriating the modernist techniques of contemporary writers in Europe and Taiwan to explore the fragmented self—fragmented because of discrepancies between their national, ethnic, and cultural identities. Followers of socialist realism, on the other hand, failed to reflect social reality and depict the contemporary political situation. As the literature of resistance could not find an outlet under the tense atmosphere and the government's anti-Communist policies, many Sinophone Malaysian writers of both the modernist and realist camps in this period produced either modernist works indulging in personal emotions and feelings or realist texts that were only skin deep in representing society. Some important writers who were active in the roaring 1980s were Xiao Hei (Tan Kee Keat), Hong Quan, Liang Fang, and Ding Yun.

Another consequence of the adoption of this autochthonous, monocultural ideology of Malay supremacy was the voluntary exile of many non-*Bumi* intellectuals to other countries. However, the existence of Sinophone Malaysian writers in Taiwan has even earlier origins. As early as the late 1950s, young ethnic Chinese Malaysians went abroad to Taiwan to further their higher education. Some of these students were already budding writers in Malaysia, but there were also those who began to write poetry or stories only after their arrival in Taiwan. In the 1960s and 1970s, they not only contributed to local literary magazines but also established their own literary society and launched their own literary magazines in Taiwan. In fact, before the 1980s, many Chinese Malaysian students who went to Taiwan were regarded as overseas compatriot students (*qiaosheng*), suggesting that they were Chinese born outside China and were sojourners in foreign countries. On the other hand, before the 1990s, the educational passage of these Chinese Malaysian students was also regarded as their "return to the motherland" (*huigui zuguo*) by the Nationalist (KMT) government in Taiwan. In the literary field, however, there was a debate on the position and identity of these "overseas Chinese" writers who reside in Taiwan (outside their nation of birthplace and citizenship), where they still write about the tropical rainforests and rubber estates of their Malaysian homeland.

The debate on the issues of "cultural return" and "self-exile" among these "overseas Chinese" writers is in fact a controversy over cultural identity. The question, of course, is what is their cultural identity? In the 1960s and 1970s, Sinophone Malaysian poets in Taiwan, in fact, joined forces with modernist poets there to actualize their "Chinese imagination," claiming their stay in the island was a cultural return. For writers like Wen Rui'an, Li Yung-p'ing (Li Yongping), Lim Chin Chown (Lin Xingqian), and, to a certain extent, Chang Kuei-hsing (Zhang Guixing),[10] their respective "return" no doubt indicates an embrace of the dominant Chinese literary and cultural ideology in Taiwan. Li, for example, attempts to construct a linguistic utopia of "pure Chinese" in his novels, particularly *The Jiling Chronicles* (*Jiling chunqiu*) and *Haidong Blues* (*Haidong qing*).[11]

From the late 1980s onward, a number of Sinophone Malaysian writers of the younger generation, such as Ng Kim Chew (Huang Jinshu), Chan Tah Wei (Chen Dawei), and Choong Yee Voon (Zhong Yiwen), have emerged on the Taiwanese literary scene. Travelling to Taiwan to further their studies in higher education, they have established themselves by winning prominent literary prizes and hence forming a small community of Sinophone Malaysian literature there. For these writers, their journey to Taiwan is an educational passage and, subsequently, a professional choice. They teach at various universities in Taiwan, but occasionally return to Malaysia. Moreover, they mostly write about things past and bygone days in Malaysia.

However, while Taiwan serves as a flexible and resourceful literary environment for the transnational/diasporic/expatriate producers of literatures in Chinese, the position of Sinophone Malaysian literature in Taiwan remains somewhat ambiguous. On the one hand, Taiwanese literary critics complain that writers of Sinophone Malaysian literature in Taiwan tend to write more about the world that they have left behind than their present place of inhabitance. On the other hand, they are accused, by some Sinophone Malaysian critics, of misrepresenting their tropical homeland. Such a double disposition of these writers actually provokes reflections on the mobility and transnationality of contemporary Sinophone Malaysian literature, Taiwanese literature, and Sinophone literatures at large. In other words, these writers illustrate the diasporic phenomenon of the Sinophone by leaving their country and writing outside the nation.

For those Sinophone Malaysian writers who stay in their country and are still writing in their mother tongue today, the literary field basically remains the same as in the previous century. In fact, from the 1980s onward, a blend of the realist and modernist modes of expression has replaced the heated debates and tension between the two camps. Western writers like Italo Calvino, Jorge Luis Borges, Milan Kundera, and Gabriel Garcia Marquez, and new trends such as magical realism and postmodernism, have received much attention from writers of younger generation. They have also sought inspiration from outstanding writers of various Sinophone regions, such as Su Tong, Mo Yan, Wang Anyi, Saisai (Xi Xi), Chang Ta-chun (Zhang Dachun), Hsia Yu (Xia Yu), or Lo Yi-chin (Luo Yijun). A new generation of promising Sinophone Malaysian poets and novelists has appeared on the scene. Some notables among them are authors of fiction such as Lim Pow Leng (aka Li Zishu), Lee Tian Poh (Li Tianbao), Tan Chee Hon (Chen Zhihong), Seen Mun Kong (Xian Wenguang), and King Ban Hui (Gong Wanhui), or poets such as Looi Yook Tho (Lu Yutao), Mu Yan, Fang Sini, Law Yee Wan (Liu Yiwan), and Chen Lin Loong (Zeng Linglong). If these young writers continue to cultivate their talent and craft to represent their Malaysian experiences and backgrounds, they will help produce a remarkable repertoire of Sinophone Malaysian literature.

Notes

1. Zhang Shunai, "Xin guomin zazhi liyan" [Preface to the *Sin Kok Min Magazine*], in *Mahua xin wenxue daxi* [Compendium of modern Sinophone Malayan literature], Vol.10, ed. Fang Xiu (Singapore: Shijie shuju, 1972), 3–4.

2. Zhang, "Xin guomin zazhi liyan" [Preface to the *Sin Kok Min Magazine*], 3.

3. Zhang Jinyan, "Manlang Nanyang yinian de huangdao" [Desert island: A year in the Nanyang], in *Mahua xin wenxue daxi* [Compendium of modern Sinophone Malayan literature], Vol. 10, 100.

4. Zeng Shengti, "Wenyi zhoukan de zhiyuan" [Prospects of the *Literary Weekly*], in *Mahua xin wenxue daxi* [Compendium of modern Sinophone Malayan literature], Vol. 10, 112.

5. Chen Lianqing, "Wenyi yu difang secai" [Literature and local color], in *Mahua xin wenxue daxi* [Compendium of modern Sinophone Malayan literature], Vol. 1, 144.

6. Zeng Aidi, "Malaiya wenyi jie manhua" [A sketch of the Malayan literary scene], in *Mahua xin wenxue daxi* [Compendium of modern Sinophone Malayan literature], Vol. 1, 280.

7. Ling Zuo, "Mahua wenyi de dutexing ji qita" [The uniqueness of Sinophone Malayan literature and other issues], in *Xinma huawen wenxue daxi: lilun* [Compendium of Sinophone literature in Singapore and Malaysia: Criticism and theory], ed. Miao Xiu (Singapore: Jiaoyu chubanshe, 1974), 201.

8. Zhou Rong, "Tan Mahua wenyi" [On Sinophone Malayan literature], *Zhanyou bao* 26 (December 1947): 4.

9. For a polysystemic study of Sinophone Malaysian literature, see my dissertation entitled *Literary Interference and the Emergence of a Literary Polysystem*, Diss. National Taiwan University, 1997.

10. Lin Chin Chown later moved to Hong Kong and established himself as a writer and scholar there.

11. Kim Chew Ng discusses this linguistic endeavor in his essay included in this volume.

20

Transcending Multiracialism

Kuo Pao Kun's Multilingual Play Mama Looking for Her Cat and the Concept of Open Culture

E. K. TAN

In 2002, Singapore lost its most influential playwright, Kuo Pao Kun. Kuo left behind a legacy of works that both documented and shaped Singapore's postindependence history. As a key representative of Singapore's multilingual theater, Kuo's works examine and comment on the island city's multiracial policies. This essay documents the history of Singapore's policy of bilingualism, using Kuo's multilingual play *Mama Looking for Her Cat* as an illustration of the effects of this policy. It then presents Kuo's notion of "open culture" as a generative concept that embodies the potential to transcend the limits of multiracialism and multiculturalism as currently practiced in Singapore. Open culture, as represented in Kuo's multilingual theater, promotes exchange, diversity, inventiveness, and transformation in the production of a cultural identity unique to the Singaporean experience. In contradistinction to government policies of multiracialism, Kuo's open culture celebrates the intermingling of cultures (past, present, local, and global) beyond the constraints of racial and linguistic origins.

In the Name of Multiracialism: Language Policies in Singapore

One hundred and forty years of British colonial rule transformed Singapore into a venue where cultures and civilizations convene, contact, and comingle. The decolonization process, which began with Singapore's independence in

1965, provided the burgeoning nation with the challenge to create channels of mediation not only among its many diverse ethnic cultures (including a conglomeration of local Malay, immigrant Chinese, and Indian Singaporeans) but also with the remnants of British colonial culture. The nation and its people inherited the richness of this diversity and have reinvented a unique cultural heritage while maintaining harmony among Singapore's various ethnic cultures. The nation's postcolonial agenda at the time of independence was to establish racial unity by constructing a multiracial and multicultural environment in order to facilitate the development and modernization of the new city-state.

Since no unified Singaporean identity existed in the historical sense, the People's Action Party (PAP), led by Prime Minister Lee Kuan Yew, urgently sought to formulate the terms for a common identity capable of at least potentially uniting all members of Singapore's multiethnic population for the sake of promoting the nationhood of the city-state. Without kinship or any specific ethnic culture as a unifying factor, the role of the government was crucial: the government was responsible for supplying its people with common markers of identification, such as citizenship, benefits, welfare, and economic opportunities. However well thought out this plan may have been, the lack of a common language hindered the project of unifying Singapore's diverse population. The most convenient and pragmatic approach to creating a common identity then, became adopting the colonial language, English, as the lingua franca. Adopting a neutral[1] common language meant that the people could communicate with relatively little conflict. It also enabled the construction of a new political and cultural identity in which every citizen, regardless of ethnicity, could play a constituent role.

This agenda to unite Singaporeans through the construction of a new identity resulted in the implementation of a new bilingual language policy aimed to promote the use of English as a common language, while encouraging citizens to learn their own mother tongues too. This policy recognized English, Mandarin, Tamil, and Malay as the four official languages of Singapore, yet, as linguist Braj Kachru points out, the bilingual policy—a strategy within the government's discourse of multiracialism—is after all, an "English-knowing bilingualism"[2] that privileges English over Singapore's other ethnically ascribed languages.

Of course, following the implementation of the bilingual policy, education became a focus of reform. Although most pre-tertiary institutions complied with the policy of bilingualism, not all adopted English as the language of instruction—independent Sinophone schools were especially resistant to the new rule. By contrast, the change in tertiary institutions was rather uniform: English was given a marked priority over other languages, contradicting the very nature of bilingualism as public policy. Such lopsided treatment of languages in a multiracial society contributed very little, if anything at all, to maintaining racial peace or facilitating the people's understanding of each other's cultures. Simply put, the hidden agenda behind the policy was the government's push toward "rapid industrialization, modern education, bureaucratic efficiency, urban resettlement, and social mobility."[3]

It was not until 1979 that the government officially declared English as the national "first language" to further the project of transforming Singapore into a global village, and in so doing to promote international trade and facilitate increased development in science and technology.[4] This privileging of the English language formally consigned ethnically ascribed languages of the Malay, Chinese, and Indian populations to roles as "mother tongues." For the Chinese Singaporean community, the official appointment of standard Mandarin as their mother tongue not only demoted Mandarin to the status of a second language but also discouraged the use of other Sinitic languages (the so-called "dialects") specific to various Chinese Singaporean communities. This denied Chinese Singaporeans an important link to their ancestral cultures, represented by the ties between language and home village (*xiang*).[5] The paradox of such official policy for nation building lies in the contradiction between maintaining racial harmony and regulating ethnic cultures and expressions. This also marked the very first time in Singapore's history that race was directly linked to language by way of a government policy.[6]

Realizing the potential problems with declaring Mandarin the mother tongue for the Chinese Singaporean community, the government launched its "Speak Mandarin" Campaign in the same year English was declared the nation's first language. The campaign successfully promoted Mandarin as the common language among Chinese Singaporeans (aside from English). It also set the path for Singapore's venturing into the mainland Chinese market.[7]

Though not unproblematic, the government's commitment to promoting the nation-state as multiracial and multicultural has played a crucial role in establishing the state of harmony among the people for at least five decades. The policies of multiracialism and bilingualism have established a consciousness of diversity in race, culture, and religion among the people and have created equal economic opportunities for Singapore's citizens, regardless of ethnic background. The emphasis placed on racial peace in the government's advocacy of multiracialism and multiculturalism through language policy has unfortunately restricted the development of cross-cultural exchange between racial groups, impeding the necessary production of a common local culture and identity. On the one hand, the state challenges old systems and traditions; on the other hand, it regulates these systems and traditions within the boundaries of individual ethnic communities, a move that has ended up compartmentalizing these communities. Such compartmentalization, as sociologist Kwok Kian Woon has argued, results in the managing of different ethnic communities "within a polity as racially distinct and culturally separate."[8]

While acknowledging the government's effort in maintaining racial harmony with the policies of bilingualism and multiracialism, Kuo Pao Kun, the doyen of Singaporean theater, warned of Singapore's "extraordinary act of voluntary uprooting, preferring to its own language (a major world language) one which its former colonizer forced upon it"[9] and called for strategies to construct a culture Singaporeans could claim as their own. Instead of promoting a multiethnic culture based on diversity and respect, the focus on the colonial English ended up restricting the interactions between various ethnic communities in Singapore. As Kuo points out, though "[t]aboos are there for each other to behold and respect," citizens had grown ignorant, and were indifferent and oblivious to the complexity and richness of each other's cultures.[10]

This ignorance and insensitivity to the complexity and richness of the nation's multicultural makeup prompted Kuo to write "Uprooted and Searching," an essay that addresses the status of Singaporeans as cultural orphans. For Kuo, the sentiment of a cultural orphan is not an individual affect, but rather, a collective mentality and awareness constituted by the colonial and immigrant history of Singapore. Without a culture they can claim as their own, the nation and its citizens as a whole experience a sense of loss and alienation. In other words, when encountering the question of identity, Singaporeans recognize their own displacement from their cultural heritages, making them cultural orphans.[11] This awareness is heightened when Singaporeans embark on journeys to visit their ancestral homelands such as China and India. Simply identifying with general cultural traits and romanticizing a sense of belonging with their remote ancestral homelands only serves to reinforce the status of Singaporeans as cultural orphans in need of a culture they can call their own.

Although the material reality of Singaporean culture is a multicultural one, they remain, according to Kuo, in a state of psychological wandering and searching. What Singaporeans regard as their culture is merely a conglomeration of culture remnants culled from ancestral rituals and beliefs that have survived the immigrant histories of their forebears. These second-hand cultural traditions and practices cannot fully circumscribe the Singaporean experience and identity. The government's multiracial agenda has effectively prevented Singaporeans from searching across official racial boundaries to absorb the essence of other cultures and to imagine and invent a culture of their own.

A strong believer in the transformative power of art and culture, Kuo Pao Kun proclaims that it is important for Singaporeans to move beyond multiracialism, a national ideology stratified by language policies, to build a common culture shared by the state's various ethnic communities on the basis of racial peace, thus offering a "qualitatively larger sharable space in culture."[12] One such space in Kuo's context lies in Singaporean theater. Kuo believes that knowledge acquisition and production through art will help Singapore, as a nation and a people, transcend the compartmentalization of multiracialism.

Contesting Multiracialism: Kuo Pao Kun's *Mama Looking for Her Cat*

Written and first performed in 1988, Kuo Pao Kun's multilingual play *Mama Looking for Her Cat* is a reflection on Singapore's multiracial and multilingual policies. While showcasing the result and impact of these polices on society, the play also illuminates the problems underlying them. As Singapore's first multilingual play, *Mama* was both groundbreaking and controversial. The linguistic experiment Kuo employed with the staging of this project was not one of comprehension and intelligibility; rather, the potpourri of languages—including Singapore's four official languages, English, Mandarin, Malay, and Tamil—as well as other Sinitic languages such as Hokkien, Teochiu, and Cantonese—in the play suggests a diversity that cannot be taken for granted as a mere result of the interaction between languages. The lack of communication among the characters and their inability to understand one another is both a problem and a product of linguistic and cultural diversity. The problem of language lies in the reality that there is no one common language that can wholly define a multicultural nation and people. The implementation of English first as an official language at the dawn of Singapore's independence, and then the declaration of it as the "first language" in 1979, leads to miscommunications between the characters in the play. Not only are characters unable to communicate well due to varying linguistic abilities, the instrumental purpose of the English language also fails to account for the affective meanings of individual speech—in the case of the play, Mama's words. No translation was provided for the audience during performances of the play, imparting upon viewers a strong sense of alienation and frustration. Ironically, it is this very alienation that provides the grounds of solidarity for the audience to acknowledge and reevaluate the reality of their cultural identity, one that is marked by diversity and difference.

Mama Looking for Her Cat tells the story of a Hokkien-speaking mother's alienation in a rapidly modernizing Singapore. As the communication between Mama and her children becomes increasingly sporadic, due to their adoption of the "official languages" (Mandarin and English) over Hokkien, she turns to her cat for companionship. The dilemma of miscommunication at the heart of the play is multilayered: it connotes the neglect for the elders in a modern society and the loss of particular cultures with the suppression of "unofficial" languages, among other things.

The powerful opening scene of the play summarizes the impact of Singapore's language policies on its citizens, especially on Mama. The scene begins with the characters playing the role of the children singing "The ABC Song" as they proceed onto the stage. They gradually form a circle, trapping Mama within. She tries to break out of the circle but is unable to do so. Subsequent scenes show Mama teaching her children a Hokkien lullaby and telling them the popular parable of the hare and the tortoise.[13]

The government's decision to adopt English as the common language for Singaporeans leads to the restriction of Mama's freedom in her own home and creates a (language) barrier between her and her children, as represented by "The ABC Song." The lullaby and parable are memories Mama preserves for herself after her children have grown up and abandoned Hokkien for English and Mandarin. Immediately after Mama goes missing, her children's dialogue switches from Hokkien to a mix of English and Mandarin. The shift in language dramatizes Mama's displacement as a loss of her personal experience, memories, and cultural identity.

Mama's bleak plight does not monopolize the overall tone of the play. Halfway into the play, as the children's search for Mama proceeds, Kuo orchestrates a poignant scene of affective interaction between two individuals that transcends language, race, culture, and gender. While looking for her cat, Mama encounters an old Indian Singaporean man praying motionless in a prostrate position. Wondering if he is alive, Mama touches him, causing him to jump and retreat to a corner. When he finally returns, Mama and the Indian man try to communicate in their respective languages, Hokkien and Tamil, to no avail. But soon, "aided by the most expressive mime gestures, through a painfully but joyfully grueling process, [they] manage to communicate." They realize that they have both lost their cats. Her cat is big and she cries, "meow meow," mimicking its call; his is small and he cries, "miu miu." Lamenting the fact that their children have chased their cats away, they begin comforting each other. At the same instant, the old man's cat appears. Upon several attempts by the old man to coax his cat over to him, the cat finally sidles over to greet Mama. "Both he and Mama are elated that the kitten has recognized a new friend."[14] This touching moment of empathy between two individuals who do not share a common language or ethnicity exemplifies how human beings can connect through experience and a common understanding of humanity. The scene closes with a reinforcement of the affective connection between the two as, "[v]ery reluctantly," the old man says goodbye to Mama as he tends to his cat.

In this scene, verbal language fails as a tool for communication. Unlike the children who know English, Mandarin, and Hokkien, and yet still fail to understand Mama and her needs, the old Indian Singaporean man, without the mediation of verbal language, empathizes with the pain Mama feels after losing her cat. Mama and the old man do not need a state-implemented common language to understand each other. In other words, Kuo's *Mama Looking for Her Cat* does not stop at criticizing the utility of Singapore's language policies and strategies of multiracialism and multiculturalism; instead, it aims at ushering the nation and its citizens forward, beyond the constraints of policies, to imagine a common culture that transcends the compartmentalization of the country's diverse communities while still appreciating their differences.

Transcending Multiracialism: Open Culture

Ten years after the production of *Mama Looking for Her Cat*, Kuo conceptualized his pursuit of a common culture that embraces diversity, difference, and openness—an agenda hinted at in his works as early as in *Mama Looking for Her Cat*—in his essay "Contemplating an Open Culture: Transcending Multiracialism." This essay introduces an innovative approach to cultural production. Rather than regarding Singaporeans as "cultural orphans" capable only of replicating their ancestral cultures, Kuo argues that Singaporeans are capable of forging a cultural identity that embraces racial and cultural difference within and beyond the scope of the nation and traditions. This new "open culture," built upon the structures of multiculturalism and multiracialism, develops out of a generative practice beyond the constraints of state governance. It is a practical concept that does not privilege racial or ethnic origins; it is a virtual (cultural) space that advocates the intermingling of cultures as a point of departure for new possibilities and meaning in the production of identity. Kuo uses theater to exemplify the potential of open culture and describes the collaborative nature of his plays as offering a shared space for ethnic communities (Chinese, Indian, Malay, Eurasian) to grow and interact with their peers of diverse backgrounds just as different types of trees coexist in the forest. Though distinct and separated from each other, their roots absorb the same nutrients and are entwined; cross-pollination takes place as their branches and leaves touch. These interactions and exchanges of cultures rely on an openness toward rebuilding and transformation. Kuo's work reflects his strong belief in the creative capacity of both the individual and the nation to embrace diversity and explore "different dimensions, different ways of seeing." For Kuo, "openness can only be expressed in diversity," and this openness can offer a qualitative transformation to consciousness and being from the intermingling of various traditional cultures to a broader understanding of humanity.[15]

In "Contemplating an Open Culture: Transcending Multiracialism," Kuo Pao Kun asks, "[S]hould Singapore not reach out to the global culture rather than confine itself to the current four-culture-framework of Multiculturalism founded on Multiracialism?"[16] As pointed out earlier, though multiracialism implemented by the government through language policies to promote racial harmony has achieved significant success, it has also proven to be little more than a set of rules instituted to prevent conflicts between different racial groups by compartmentalizing Singapore's diverse population. This results in hindering interracial interaction and the cultural maturation of Singaporeans by numbing their sensitivity and sensibility toward other cultures.[17] In such a context, cultural exchange is limited and does not lead to significant transformation. Kuo suggests open culture as an alternative foundation of a common local identity and culture. Kuo's open culture is based on a set of fundamental ideas:

1. Every individual should be deeply rooted in at least one culture.
2. Every individual should be given the choice to begin one's "opening up" by first deepening the organic culture one is living by—that is, one's parent culture.
3. The cultural development of the individual should be de-linked from the racial and linguistic origin of the individual.
4. Every student should be exposed, generally, to an overview of the cultures of the world and, specifically, to at least two culture(s) in depth.
5. The state should recognize culture as a primary, core area of study, and, because of the serious handicap caused by past disregard, Singapore should give culture urgent priority in terms of education, acquisition, and accumulation both in breadth of diversity and depth of reach.[18]

The first three fundamentals focus on the individual while the last two look to the state to support the fostering of an open culture that benefits the individual, the people, and the nation as a whole. The main responsibility falls on the individual, while the state functions as the engineer that supplies the necessary infrastructure. Instead of lamenting the loss of one's roots and ancestral culture, open culture facilitates a re-rooting and rerouting of one's cultural parentage that intermingles lived experience, history, and memory filtered through the active participation of an individual to open up new possibility and meaning. Open culture does not insist on which culture is embraced; its only concern is that "one is *deeply rooted in any culture.*"[19]

Conclusion

The building of a multiracial and multicultural state requires both the effort of the ruling party and the individual. On the part of the government, policies are necessary to maintain the stability of the society as it matures into an independent and self-sufficient nation. Upon independence, Singapore required the restructuring of the economic, political, and social domains to work its way out of the inequities and injustices of the colonial past. To transform the society and usher its citizens into a new, more egalitarian society—one that celebrates multiracialism—the government regarded racial peace as the single most urgent issue on its social agenda. Hence, language policies such as the bilingual policy were launched to connect Singaporeans by way of a common language, English. Such an approach that focused on linguistic policies soon proved to be restrictive rather than generative in the building of a common culture. Realizing the lack of a cultural identity among Singaporeans, the Singaporean playwright Kuo Pao Kun channeled his energy into cultural work in the realm of theater. In 1988, Kuo began working on multilingual theater as a way to expose and contest the limits of multiracial policies in forging a common national culture. Years of experimentation facilitated Kuo's conceptualization of a practical strategy to enable Singaporeans to imagine a culture they can call their own—an open culture. Kuo himself is an example of the product of such practice. Grounding himself in his choice of a primary culture, his Chinese heritage, Kuo embraces characteristics of worldly cultures from Russia to Europe to India to Indonesia, and so forth, to promote art as the advocate of truth and humanity, and as the producer of culture. For Kuo, the difference between open culture and the state policy of multiracialism is the disengagement with racial and linguistic origins as primary factors in the reconstruction of one's cultural identity. Open culture, by transcending the policy of multiracialism, frees individuals from the constraints of their ethnic identities and in the process encourages them to absorb and mingle with cultures of the world in search of new forms of being and identity.

Notes

1. English was chosen as the common language because it was not tied to any racial identity in Singapore. Hence, it could function as a neutral working language for administrative purposes and facilitate communication among various ethnic groups. See Eddie C.Y. Kuo and Bjorn Jernudd, "Balancing Macro- and Micro-Sociolinguistic Perspectives in Language Management: The Case of Singapore," in *English and Language Planning: A Southeast Asian Contribution*, ed. Thiru Kandiah and John Kwan-Terry (Singapore: Times Academic Press, 1994), 70–91.

2. Braj B. Kachru, "Models for Non-Native Englishes," in *The Other Tongue: English Across Cultures* (Illinois: University of Illinois Press, 1992), 48–74.

3. Stanley S. Bedlington, "Singapore: The Contemporary Setting," in *Malaysia and Singapore* (Ithaca: Cornell University Press, 1978), 214–215.

4. Kuo Pao Kun, "Uprooted and Searching," in *Drama, Culture and Empowerment: The IDEA Dialogues* (Australia: IDEA Publications, 1996), 168.

5. For information on how the early Chinese Southeast Asians from Fukien (Fujian) and Kwangtung (Guangdong) regarded their village (*xiang/hsiang*), rather than the nation (China or *Zhongguo*), as their homeland, see Lynn Pan, *Sons of the Yellow Emperor: The Story of Overseas Chinese* (Boston: Little, Brown and Company, 1990), 3–22.

6. Kuo Pao Kun, "Contemplating an Open Culture: Transcending Multiracialism," in *Singapore: Re-Engineering Success* (Singapore: Oxford University Press, 1998), 53.

7. S. Gopinathan, "Language Policy Changes 1979–1992: Politics and Pedagogy," in *Language, Society and Education in Singapore: Issues and Trends*, ed. Saravanan Gopinathan, Anne Pakir, Ho Wah Kam, and Vanithamani Saravanan (Singapore: Times Academic Press, 1998), 70.

8. Kwok Kian Woon, "Cultivating Citizenship and National Identity," in *Singapore: Re-Engineering Success*, 116.

9. Kuo Pao Kun, "Uprooted and Searching," 168.

10. Kuo Pao Kun, "Contemplating an Open Culture: Transcending Multiracialism," 52–53.

11. Kuo Pao Kun, "Considerations of a Cultural Orphan: Choices and Challenges of the Singapore Theatre," in *Guo Baokun Quanji: Volume Seven*, ed. Beng Luan Tan and Sy Ren Quah (Singapore: Global Publishing, 2008), 212–214.

12. Ibid.

13. Kuo Pao Kun, "Mama Looking for Her Cat," in *Images at the Margins* (Singapore: Times Books International, 2007), 120–125.

14. Ibid., 129–130.

15. Alvin Tan and Sanjay Krishnan, "Between Two Worlds: A Conversation with Kuo Pao Kun," in *Nine Lives: Ten Years of Singapore Theatre 1987–1997* (Singapore: The Necessary Stage, 1997), 141.

16. Kuo, "Contemplating an Open Culture: Transcending Multiracialism," 59.

17. Ibid., 52–53.

18. Ibid., 60.

19. Ibid., 57.

21

Plantation and Rainforest

Chang Kuei-hsing and a South Seas Discourse
of Coloniality and Nature

BRIAN BERNARDS

Theories of postcolonialism have by and large ignored potential discursive formations emerging out of the former colonies of East and Southeast Asia and the unique perspectives these regions bring to a comparative postcolonial framework.[1] The histories of these spaces not only offer stories of encounters with multiple forms of imperialism but also various forms of settler colonialism. In particular, the historical interaction between China and Southeast Asia, quite often mediated by a series of different foreign colonial powers and forms, adds complexity to and reveals layers of colonial crossings in the interactions between colonizer and colonized, perpetrator and victim. Furthermore, communities of descendants of immigrants from predominantly southeastern China to Southeast Asia have "localized" in various ways depending on discourses of race and ethnicity in the different colonies and nation-states that supplanted them. Minority Sinophone Malaysian communities, for example, have historically been cast as "outsiders" or "nonnative" and denied participation in the political project of narrating the nation.[2]

This chapter examines the fiction of the Sinophone Malaysian author Chang Kuei-hsing (Zhang Guixing, 1956–). In his unveiling of the heavily layered matrix of the island of Borneo's colonial history, Chang contributes richly to the formation of a "South Seas" postcolonial discourse.[3] Chang, who now lives in Taiwan, is frequently compared to the likes of literary giants such as Gabriel García Márquez, William Faulkner, and Joseph Conrad, and his work has received many awards and much critical acclaim in Sinophone literary circles. Chang is best known for his "Rainforest Trilogy" (*Yulin sanbuqu*) three novels about his former homeland of Malaysian Borneo, composed of *Siren Song* (*Sailian zhi ge*, 1992), *Herds of Elephants* (*Qun xiang*, 1998), and *Monkey Cup* (*Hou bei*, 2000).

Here, I draw a historical and theoretical analogy between the discourses of two tropical, postcolonial "southern seas"—the Sinophone South Seas as evinced in the work of Chang Kuei-hsing, and the Francophone Caribbean as theorized by Édouard Glissant in his *Caribbean Discourse* (*Le discours antillais*, 1981). I argue that Chang Kuei-hsing's South Seas is a site of a multilingualism that is articulated not through the same historical conditions of hybridity or creolization as in the Caribbean but rather through the evocation of competing colonial and counter-colonial spaces and the contrasting languages and types of knowledge these spaces produce. The first space is the plantation, expressing a coloniality whereby language and ethnicity are hierarchically layered according to colonizing methods of knowledge production and control. In this hierarchical context, languages, ethnicities, and cultures do not blend harmoniously but clash dissonantly. The second space is the rainforest—as opposed to the plantation, it is the source of a language that is molded by nature rather than the other way around. This language reverses the hierarchies of plantation coloniality and can thus be read as a kind of counter-colonial poetics.

Plantation Thinking: A Language of Coloniality

As a colonial power mechanism and capitalist form of economic dominance, the plantation system best captures Western imperialism's "desire for expansion and accumulation."[4] It is an imported system that attempts to extract resources and labor, to displace other landscapes and forms of subsistence, to enclose its territory and internal environment from the outside, and to vertically layer its labor according to an ethnicized and racialized hierarchy. In offering a theoretical vision for a nonhierarchical, non-totalizing alternative to "plantation thinking," Édouard Glissant, in *Poetics of Relation* (*Poétique de la relation*, 1990), recognizes the necessity of first confronting that system by which colonized minds and subjectivities were historically produced. Theorizing from his native Martinique, a Caribbean island still under French colonial rule and thus still grappling with the immediate and necessary process of decolonization, Glissant argues that the plantation is "an organization formed in a social pyramid, confined within an enclosure, functioning apparently as an autarky but actually dependent, and with a technical mode of production that cannot evolve because it is based on a slave structure."[5]

The plantation system mandates dependency on the metropole's demands within a global international market, thus obscuring, displacing, and even obliterating other possible methods of local survival. The plantation survives through expansion—the continual layering of its internal hierarchy through the importation of indentured labor to feed the bottom rungs of that hierarchy as well as the mercenaries to enforce it.

The desire to expand and accumulate that defines the direct colonial rule characteristic of the role of the West in the Caribbean, Southeast Asia, and other postcolonial spaces of the world is different from the type of desire for land and survival that defined the settler colonialism of Chinese immigrants and their descendants, known as the "Hua people" (Huaren), to the South Seas.[6] These two types of colonial desire, to which Hua people in Southeast Asia were both subjected to and proponents of, and which layered their specific yet diverse experiences there, become entangled and woven into the plantation system and its hierarchical formation. Chang Kuei-hsing evokes this condition in Monkey Cup, as the protagonist Zhi embarks on a journey home to the state of Sarawak in Malaysian Borneo from Taiwan that is also a journey into the "heart of darkness" of the memories and legacies of the colonial past.[7]

Zhi, who works as a high school English teacher in Taipei, is forced to leave when he sleeps with a young prostitute who, unbeknownst to him, turns out to be his student. Zhi returns to his home in Sarawak only to find that his younger sister, who is likely an adopted Dayak, the aboriginal people of Borneo,[8] has run off into the rainforest with her deformed newborn (apparently fathered by Zhi's grandfather). Zhi, with the help of a Dayak girl named Yanini, hires a guide to take him into the rainforest in search of his sister. The journey is interspersed with stories of Zhi's family history, dating back to his great-grandfather. In the "age of colonial pioneering," Great-grandfather's desire for land and survival (settler colonialism) gets caught up in the desire for expansion and accumulation (direct colonial rule) that defines his ascension to the role of plantation headman. He comes to stand in as the face of British colonial power to both the laborers enclosed within the plantation hierarchy and the displaced aboriginal peoples, the Dayaks, beyond the plantation's ever-expanding periphery: "The plantation headman had already been dead for more than a month. None of the British were willing to end up as the next sacrifice by the aborigines. Since eighty percent of the workers were Hua, the governor-general had long hoped to find a Chinese man who could be their representative plantation owner."[9]

The British search for a local "face" to represent their authority in Sarawak is similar to what Glissant, in the case of the Caribbean, calls the colonizer's "urgent need to form an elite" among the colonized that could represent as well as protect the plantation system.[10] Like the plantation, which demonstrates the attempt to convert the nature of other topographies into a transparent, functional product, the colonized local elite are the "functional product" through which local cultures can be rendered transparent or knowable to the colonizer. Transparency, according to Glissant, assumes the reducibility of the unknowable to the knowable through a process of translation into the "vehicular" language of the colonizer, which assumes universal expressiveness.[11] The "mastery" of knowledge of the other by rendering his or her language transparent is, as in most colonial situations, the attempt to master the person of the colonized.

In *Monkey Cup*, Great-grandfather, integrated into the colonial hierarchy, explains the strategic function of learning the aboriginal Dayak language to his son, saying, "If you don't speak the barbarian language well, how can you rule this barbarian land? How can I feel assured in letting you inherit my legacy?"[12] This advice comes from Great-grandfather's having "spent ten years luring and bribing the natives, intimidating and threatening them, sowing dissension among them, and forming strategic alliances with them" in his attempts to "pacify, control, and exterminate" them.[13]

Great-grandfather is shown to be deluded by power and the thirst for land accumulation, thus becoming not only complicit in, but actively advancing, the colonial cause and the violence of the plantation system. *Monkey Cup* brings to light multiple forms of plantation violence. First, there is the introduction of exclusive land-as-property ownership in a traditionally maritime society where an abundance of land provided for everyone and many people moved across the archipelago according to seasonal monsoon winds. Small-scale plots of crop cultivation by both immigrant settlers and various indigenous peoples that had existed for centuries had a different relationship to the surrounding land and people than the plantation. Thus, in the earlier period of Chinese, Arabic, Portuguese, and Spanish colonialism in Southeast Asia, trading ports such as Malacca (Melaka) were sought after to profit from the flow of production, not from the direct control of its means. What Glissant calls the period of the plantation system in Martinique's history (1800–1930) similarly registers this shift and its effects. He writes that the plantation system created a situation of balkanization, indicating both internal stratification on the plantation and external isolation from other islands in the Caribbean.[14] The following scene from *Monkey Cup* highlights the introduction of this type of plantation violence, as Great-grandfather resorts to the "land permit" issued by the British to dispossess the native Dayaks of a now "exclusively-possessed" territory:

When Great-grandfather brought the colonial government's permit and settlement agreement, allowing him to cultivate the virgin soil, and ordered the workers to begin opening up the plantation area, the Dayaks, with bare upper bodies, wearing only loincloths, and brandishing bush knives, bows and arrows at their sides, rowed their longboats to pay a visit to the colonial government officials in their air-conditioned office down-river. Most of the British officials wore long silvergrey moustaches resembling the fangs of wild boars, their cheeks red and tender like a baby's buttocks, their eyes an emerald blue like the tree frog that camouflages itself the color of a plantain leaf, their skin too delicate and transparent. They spoke as if squeezing milk from cows—their Adam's apples were soft like boiled sea-turtle's eggs: "Although you say that you have lived there for generations, you have just let that excellent expanse of arable soil go to waste." After a long moment of rumination the Dayak representative said softly, "We also do some cultivating of that land—it's just that we don't depend entirely on cultivation. We just turn the soil over once every so often. The Chinese know that." The colonial official nodded, "That's why we want to make better use of it."[15]

For the Dayaks the piece of paper may only symbolize the arbitrary claim to power by the British on their own terms (as the Dayaks continue to take crops from the plantation fields), but it gives Great-grandfather direct access to other mechanisms of plantation violence within the colonial hierarchy.

By way of purchasing guns and gunpowder from the colonial government and organizing a mercenary patrol team, Great-grandfather captured and injured dozens of Dayaks. Then, he had them sent to the colonial government for sentencing. After the Dayaks ate prison food for several months they would continue to disturb and destroy the plantation fields and the workers' quarters on them. After Great-grandfather led the patrol team in shooting and killing two Dayaks and had his dog bite and kill an old man, the plantation fields and workers' quarters went undisturbed for two months.[16]

The Dayaks, taking food from the same parcels of land that had sustained them for years, are now, in the language and logic of colonial law, construed as "thieves."

The narrative of *Monkey Cup* involves continual leaps back and forth in space (between Sarawak and Taiwan) as well as in time. As it follows Zhi deeper into the heart of the Borneo rainforest in search of his sister Limei, it also follows Great-grandfather as he gets mired deeper in the mechanisms of colonial rule. Plantation violence escalates into a full-scale war, referred to as the "Coffee Plantation War," between Great-grandfather's hired mercenaries and the displaced Dayaks:

> The first time they waged war, although the mercenary patrol was few in numbers, they had absolute superiority in weaponry. In less than a half hour they had driven their enemies out of the coffee plantation, where-upon the two sides, separated by over a hundred meters, exchanged shouts. A round of bullets and arrows were feebly shot out in an arc. The Dayaks lost 70 or 80 warriors, but they weren't willing to leave in defeat, and they prepared to call in reinforcements for a counterattack. The mercenary patrol and the coolies lost over 30 of their men. Two hundred coolies formed a support unit and joined in the action, and just like that they far outnumbered the Dayaks.[17]

The violence of the Sarawak plantation in *Monkey Cup* rejects the idyllic romanticism of white European novelists, who, as Chang Kuei-hsing writes in the novel *My South Seas Sleeping Beauty* (*Wo sinian de changmian zhong de Nanguo gongzhu*, 2001), "followed the gunboats to the South Seas, where they drank wine in splendid estates and hotels, attended by legions of servants, and occasionally took up their pens to portray a bit of the sentimental flavor of these foreign lands."[18] This is the contradiction between written literature (by those complicit in colonization) and the lived reality within not only the plantation but the entire "plantation matrix." For Glissant, this matrix includes the urban shantytowns, brothels, slums, and all of the "violently dehumanized" spaces and destitute means of existence that appeared alongside plantations and after their disintegration in the Caribbean.[19]

In *Caribbean Discourse*, Glissant charts a history of literary production in Martinique alongside a history of economic production—it is during the era of the plantation system that a Creole oral literature emerges, speaking tales much different from the exotic written literature of the elite, and the plantation thus becomes the site of the opposed forces of the two forms of literature.[20] In *Monkey Cup*, however, the plantation matrix does not produce a creolized orality, but rather an aural discord. The language of coloniality is here one that produces visual, aural, and olfactory dissonances, a cacophony of surface images, sounds, and smells that do not harmonize, hybridize, or creolize, but rather clash in their distinction: "Malay, Indonesian, Indian, and

Dayak languages made of rice wine, spice, and pickled chili-pepper. Mandarin, Cantonese, Hokkien, full of the pungent aromas of tree bark, grassy roots, and mud. English and Dutch, a mixture of the flavors of cigar, alcohol, and lead."[21]

As Glissant argues in *Caribbean Discourse* and as is evident in *Monkey Cup*, the heavily layered and hierarchical encounters that form the plantation system are not ideal forms of "multicultural" encounter and subject formation. In Glissant's *Poetics of Relation*, the history of plantation creolization is a starting point from which another, more ideal form of encounter and creolization that is nonhierarchical and non-enclosing (which Glissant calls "Relation") can be envisioned and opposed to plantation thinking.[22] In *Monkey Cup*, the plantation is not a site of an oral *créolité* but a site of sensual discord, and it is the sensual stirring of the rainforest that provides a counter discourse—a language molded by nature—to the plantation hierarchy.

Rainforest Imaginary: A Language Molded by Nature

In *Caribbean Discourse*, Glissant ponders the symbolic force of the forest in the fiction of Gabriel García Márquez and William Faulkner:

> The forest is defiant and compliant, it is primitive warmth. Conquering it is the *objective*, to be conquered by it is the true subject. This is not the Eternal Garden, it is energy fixed in time and space, but which conceals its site and its chronology. The forest is the last vestige of myth in its present literary manifestation. In its impenetrable nature history feeds our desire. The forest of the maroon was thus the first obstacle the slave opposed to the *transparency* of the planter. There is no clear path, no *way forward*, in this density. You turn in obscure circles until you find the primordial tree.[23]

The subjectivity produced by the forest, as envisioned by Glissant, challenges on multiple levels the logic of colonizing knowledge and the transparency assumed by "plantation thinking." First, this subjectivity reverses the subject/object relations of colonizing knowledge: instead of making the forest the objective space that the subject, who is given agency, sets out to conquer, the "true subject" allows the forest agency through its own subjectivity. Second, the forest, as both defiant and compliant, can be considered anticolonial at the same time it assumes the position of the colonized. Finally, representing "the last vestige of myth" that presents no clear path but only a dense obscurity that leads one in circles, the forest challenges the linearity or arrow-like trajectory of history. In *Poetics of Relation*, such challenges to transparency are what Glissant calls "opacity," a reserving of the right on the part of the colonized subject not to be transparent, fully understood, and explained by the knowledge mechanisms of the colonizer.[24] The forest subjectivity is opaque, challenging the transparency of the hierarchies in the plantation's pyramid-like formation.

In *Monkey Cup*, the Borneo rainforest reverses the linguistic hierarchy of the plantation, where English is at the apex and Sinitic languages are second in command. Dayak becomes the "royal language," while Mandarin and English become linguistic descendants who "fell from grace."[25] Whether owned by its inhabitants or owner of its inhabitants, the rainforest is always for Chang Kuei-hsing a site of the contestation between the subjects it produces and those who seek to conquer and objectify it. Dayaks protesting massive timber harvesting by multinational Japanese corporations, for example, burn the Japanese base camp, and then are hunted after by Malay state police.[26] In the face of the obliteration of the rainforest, Chang seeks, through language, to evoke a different relationship with nature. This language is something like the discourse that Glissant reads as emerging in Marquez's *One Hundred Years of Solitude*:

> The relationship with the land, one that is even more threatened because the community is alienated from the land, becomes so fundamental in this discourse that landscape in the work stops being merely decorative or supportive and emerges as a full character. Describing the landscape is not enough. The individual, the community, the land are inextricable in the process of creating history.[27]

Glissant recognizes that the "civilizing" project of colonization teaches colonized peoples that they have no culture, no history, and that these things are imported from the metropole where they allegedly originate. This process serves the colonizer's needs in that it alienates colonized peoples from the local landscape, distracting and blinding them to the colonizer's exploitation of the land for profit. Thus, in the project of decolonization, a discourse of nature that not only recognizes but gives critical agency to the local landscape is not a reaffirmation of the colonizing logic of an age-old nature/culture binary, in which the colonizer possesses "civilized culture" while the colonized has only "primitive nature," but is rather a necessity in the ongoing struggle for the colonized to claim culture for themselves.

When the counter-colonial potential of this discourse is considered, the language molded and inhabited by nature that emerges in Chang Kuei-hsing's fiction can be understood as doing something more than mere exoticizing. The opacity of the rainforest manifests itself in the language and word choice of the narrative. Language's transformation by nature brings it to life on the page as a living, breathing, and continually metamorphosing organism. Consider the ways that language comes to life in the description of the jungle vegetation in the following scene, in which Zhi's grandfather runs away from the tyranny of his father with Little Spot, the daughter of a coolie executed by Great-grandfather. After her father's execution, the orphaned Little Spot was groomed by Great-grandfather on the plantation for sale into prostitution, but Grandfather falls in love with her and makes plans for their getaway:

Grandfather planned to flee to the town of Lutong, and from Lutong take a ferry along the coastline of the sea to the First Division or the Third Division of Sarawak, forever leaving behind Great-grandfather's plantation. [. . .] After a half hour, the plantation speedboat, at double the speed of their longboat, appeared behind them. Its searchlight lit up all of the Baram River like the light of day. Grandfather immediately steered ashore. Pulling Little Spot, he leapt up onto the bank and led her away in a hurry, taking only his bush knife and flashlight. They hid, relying on the moonlight, and only after a half hour passed did he turn on the flashlight. They kept walking until the battery ran out. At this time they could sense they were already covered underneath the shade of lush, giant trees, and they couldn't even see their five fingers in front of them. [. . .] Then, just over ten meters ahead of them, a vast expanse of the rainforest floor suddenly lit up brightly, like the hazy lights of the opium den on the plantation illuminating when night falls, or the flashiness reflected off a luminous mineral. Dazzling and dizzying, it seemed they had entered the realm of the immortals. Grandfather led Little Spot into the light, and they saw that out of the tree trunks, the ground, the rocks, the withered branches, and the fallen leaves, millions of strange fungi grew in the most bizarre shapes, like soup ladles, like small umbrellas and hats, like soles of hooves and ram horns, like full breasts rich with milk and flashy buttocks. It seemed as if beams of neon light dispersed everywhere, stretching out across a hundred meters, and lighting up a twisting and winding path in the deep, dark rainforest. Grandfather and Little Spot followed this path, and after walking for another fifteen minutes they stopped to sleep on the protruding roots of a giant tree. A slight breeze blew all through the night, and the meaty fungi, under their umbrella cover, kept shooting out dense spores of foamy mist. The next morning Grandfather finally discovered the droplets of blood dripping from Little Spot's groin, and there were bruises on her hands and feet that appeared to have been left by a whip. [. . .] Grandfather decided to follow the rim of the Baram River heading in the direction of Lutong, but after walking all morning they still hadn't emerged from the humid and stuffy embrace of the jungle. They ate wild fruit and drank the rainwater out of the nepenthes pitcher plant. At noon they suddenly stepped into a neatly-arranged plantation field, and it was then that Grandfather realized that all along they had just been going around in circles in Great-grandfather's vast plantation fields.[28]

The language in this scene is rich with imaginative detail, particularly in its description of the "meaty fungi" that change shape, pulsate, and exhale mist. The numerous metaphors and similes, comparing these fungi to all sorts of objects as well as human and animal parts, do not allow the reader to hold onto any one image of them. Thus, the language does not exhaust the transformative potential of these fungi, and they remain opaque beings. Also, this scene contrasts the "twisting and winding" paths of the "deep, dark rainforest" with the "neatly-arranged" rows of Great-grandfather's plantation fields, positing the density and impenetrable nature of the rainforest (to return to Glissant) against the transparency of the colonizer. Yet to the characters' as well as the reader's surprise, the forestscapes described turn out to be uncultivated areas on Great-grandfather's plantation property. This mystifying twist is open to different interpretations: more cynically, it signals the ongoing colonization of the rainforest and its process of transformation into objective property; more optimistically, it represents the resistance of the rainforest to colonizing mechanisms of control and manageability. While a colonizer's map may clearly delineate the geographical borders between the plantation and the rainforest, those who see and experience the local landscape in its full dimensionality recognize that such borders are not easily determinable. As a mechanism of the colonizer's transparency, cartography graphs knowledge onto paper in an attempt to objectify and make static a nature that is not. Through his rainforest imagery and a living language conquered by dynamic, changing nature, Chang Kuei-hsing exposes the limits of the cartographic mechanism in *Monkey Cup*. Zhi, from his desk at his teacher's office in Taiwan, watches a map of Borneo come to life:

On the top of Zhi's glass desktop there remained a generous amount of his sweat stains. They made the map of Borneo underneath the glass desktop wet and slick, resembling a hibernating tree frog. The tree frog's head faced northeast, its left leg and half of its midsection formed Sarawak, its head and neck Sabah and Brunei, and the rest of its body was Kalimantan. Distributed across the frog's back were strings of warts and stripes: they looked like the mountain ranges concentrated in the island's center and the scattered small lakes and swamps that covered the entire island. The whisker-like green veins on the frog's skin resembled rivers.[29]

Animated as a tree frog, the map of Borneo rejects the sense of stasis that the map as object signifies, turning a motionless, two-dimensional reduction into a three-dimensional organism in motion.

As the examples from *Monkey Cup* suggest, the language conquered by nature is a move away from reduction and deduction and toward multiplicity and opacity. Words and tropes of nature are chosen that are not meant to deduce meaning but to multiply it. This is evident in the very titles of some of Chang's works, such as *Qun xiang* (Herds of elephants), where *xiang* can also be understood as "ideogram" or the verb "to resemble," and *Hou bei* (Monkey Cup), a nickname for the pitcher of the tropical nepenthes plant that captures rainwater occasionally drunk by monkeys or humans lost in the forest. Language enchants (drawing the reader closer) but simultaneously defamiliarizes (keeping the reader at a distance). For example, the noun "leech" (*zhi*) takes the position normally occupied by an adverb to describe the way Zhi's sister Limei lays down like a leech ("leech-lays") on the bed or crawls like a lizard on the forest floor.[30] Four-character, or quadrisyllabic, idiomatic expressions, commonly used in Chinese to express insider cultural knowledge, allusion, and references, here, in a Sinophone articulation, become inhabited by the South Seas and create a defamiliarizing effect that creates an explosion of meaning. In *Herds of Elephants*, it is the "wild scripts and untamable words" (*huang wen ye zi*) that the protagonist finds inhabited by cockroach corpses and skeletal leaf veins in the pages of his uncle's elephant hunting diary.[31] In *Monkey Cup*, it is the grandiose "dolphin words and whale dreams" (*tun yu jing meng*) that the Dayak tattoo artist and shaman-like figure, Abanban, speaks and dreams from the corner of the longhouse.[32] While these expressions are not a form of creolized language, they inject the written script of the narrative with a Sinophone multiplicity positing a Borneo rainforest/South Seas imaginary as the central perspective. This is Chang Kuei-hsing's counter-colonial poetics—a language molded by nature.

Conclusion

In Chang Kuei-hsing's preface to *Monkey Cup*, entitled "Return to the Rainforest," the author describes this "return" and what inspired it: "My mother, the rainforest, mother earth, and the lungs of the world—please let me twitch. Let my filthy genes seep below your roots, and through your nurturing soil, let them be reincarnated and have a chance to live again."[33] This "return," upon which Chang's earthy idols are reincarnated in his literature, can be considered what Stuart Hall calls the "displaced 'homeward' journey," which for Hall refers to the "return to the Africa" that is a "necessary part of the Caribbean imaginary" but not in fact a literal return.[34] In the preface, Chang acknowledges that he cannot physically enter the Borneo rainforest so crucial to his imaginary and historical memory: "I paced back and forth on the margins of the rainforest, and for a while could not find an entrance. It was as if man had already slashed much of the rainforest, turning it into a cold, closed off world."[35] The only entrance Chang can find to the rainforest of his South Seas imagination is through the gateway of literature. This type of literary "return" has imaginative and figurative value with respect to its local context of articulation.[36] As the Sinophone, according to Shu-mei Shih, is a place-based practice,[37] the condition of a perpetual "imaginative return" in Sinophone Malaysian literature from Taiwan can be read as a Taiwan-based practice.

Sinophone Malaysian literature in Taiwan, such as that by Chang Kuei-hsing, evokes both "doubly colonial" and "doubly diasporic" conditions, and in this manner offers a unique perspective to comparative postcolonial studies. By "doubly colonial" I mean both the settler colonialism as well as direct colonial rule that define the Sinophone historical experience in Malaysia,[38] and which, as we see in Chang Kuei-hsing's writing, can become entangled in the hierarchical mechanisms of colonial administration. By "doubly diasporic" I refer to those transnational Sinophone Malaysian authors such as Chang Kuei-hsing who were first part of a Sinophone community in Malaysia that was historically and politically construed as "nonnative," denied participation in the local, and thus, "diasporic Chinese." Written out of their own nation's literary canon, they became part of a Malaysian minority of writers in Taiwan who when they first arrived were recognized as "overseas students" in Taiwanese universities. Over the years, their access to Taiwanese citizenship has fluctuated.[39] The "doubly diasporic" condition of these writers evokes multiple imaginative "returns." First, there is the "return" to a linguistic and cultural "motherland" that prompted the movement from Malaysia to Taiwan, a trajectory that is not actually a "return" but rather a movement from an environment in which the Sinophone is minoritized to one where it is the majority. Second, there is the "return" to Malaysia in their literature. These "returns," perhaps better described as trajectories and searches, are a local but transnational condition arising at key moments in the histories of Malaysia, Taiwan, and China on the world stage. Chang's planting of his literary "genes" deep beneath the Borneo rainforest coupled with his continual tracing of trajectories and movements across the South Seas evoke an identity balancing "roots" with "routes."[40] In Chang Kuei-hsing's fiction, the "doubly colonial" condition is centered at the margins of plantation and rainforest, and the "doubly diasporic" condition locates the imaginative "return to the rainforest" of Sinophone Malaysian literature as a Taiwan-based literary practice.

These two conditions are crucial to not only gauging the position from where Chang Kuei-hsing's South Seas discourse is written, but also the language of coloniality and nature that this discourse produces.

Notes

1. One of the primary reasons for this absence is that the majority of postcolonial texts from East and Southeast Asia are not written in the languages of the former Western empires that dominate the attention of postcolonial scholars in the West. For more, see Chua Beng Huat, "Southeast Asia in Postcolonial Studies: An Introduction," *Postcolonial Studies* 11, no. 3 (September 2008): 231–240. Interested readers may also refer to the other essays included in this special issue on "Southeast Asia's absence in postcolonial studies."

2. For more on the term *Sinophone*, please refer to Shu-mei Shih's introduction to this volume, as well as her book *Visuality and Identity: Sinophone Articulations Across the Pacific* (Berkeley: University of California Press, 2007).

3. *Nanyang*, or the "South Seas," is the traditional Chinese term for Southeast Asia.

4. Walter Mignolo, "The Geopolitics of Knowledge and the Colonial Difference," *The South Atlantic Quarterly* 101, no. 1 (2002): 76.

5. Édouard Glissant, *Poetics of Relation*, trans. Betsy Wing (Ann Arbor: University of Michigan Press, 1997), 64.

6. For a definition of the "Hua people" (*Huaren*) and a theorization of its distinction from the term "Chinese" (*Zhongguoren*), see Kim Chew Ng's chapter in Part I of this volume.

7. For analogies between the narratives of Chang Kuei-hsing and Joseph Conrad, see Ng Kim Chew (Huang Jinshu), *Huangyan huo zhenli de jiyi: Dangdai Zhongwen xiaoshuo lunji* [The craft of falsehood or the craft of truth: Contemporary Chinese fiction criticism] (Taipei: Maitian chuban, 2003), 266–267.

8. *Dayak* is a loose term applied to all of the indigenous ethnic groups of Borneo, an island whose territory is divided among the nations of Malaysia, Indonesia, and Brunei.

9. Chang Kuei-hsing, *Hou bei* [Monkey cup] (Taipei: Lianhe wenxue, 2000), 179. As this passage demonstrates, Chang Kuei-hsing uses the term *Chinese* to refer to the British perspective of the Hua, which not only reveals the narrowness of English terminology but also the British policy in colonial Malaya of identifying the *Chinese* as nonnative. Since this perspective was also adopted by the Malays and Dayaks, Chang also uses *Chinese* when they refer to the Hua.

10. Édouard Glissant, *Caribbean Discourse*, trans. J. Michael Dash (Charlottesville, Va.: Caraf Books, 1989), 175.

11. Glissant, *Poetics of Relation*, 117.

12. Chang Kuei-hsing, *Hou bei* [Monkey cup], 217.

13. Ibid., 181.

14. Glissant, *Caribbean Discourse*, 90.

15. Chang Kuei-hsing, *Hou bei* [Monkey cup], 162.

16. Ibid., 163.

17. Ibid., 262–263.

18. Zhang Guixing, *My South Seas Sleeping Beauty*, trans. Valerie Jaffee (New York: Columbia University Press, 2007), 56.

19. Glissant, *Poetics of Relation*, 72–73.

20. Glissant, *Caribbean Discourse*, 95.

21. Chang Kuei-hsing, *Hou bei* [Monkey cup], 179.

22. Glissant, *Poetics of Relation*, 11.

23. Glissant, *Caribbean Discourse*, 82–83.

24. Glissant, *Poetics of Relation*, 111–120.

25. Chang Kuei-hsing, *Hou bei* [Monkey cup], 144.

26. Ibid., 122.

27. Glissant, *Caribbean Discourse*, 105.

28. Chang Kuei-hsing, *Hou bei* [Monkey cup], 220–221.

29. Ibid., 24.

30. Ibid., 83.

31. Chang Kuei-hsing, *Qun xiang* [Herds of elephants] (Taipei: Maitian chuban, 2006), 219–220.

32. Chang Kuei-hsing, *Hou bei* [Monkey cup], 108.

33. Ibid., 12.

34. Stuart Hall, "Cultural Identity and Diaspora," in *Identity: Community, Culture, Difference*, ed. Jonathan Rutherford (London: Lawrence and Wilshart, 1990), 232.

35. Chang Kuei-hsing, *Hou bei* [Monkey cup], 12.

36. Hall, "Cultural Identity and Diaspora," 232.

37. Shih, *Visuality and Identity*, 185.

38. For more on Malaysia's "doubly colonial" condition, see Wong Yoon Wah, *Post-Colonial Chinese Literatures in Singapore and Malaysia* (Singapore: Department of Chinese Studies, National University of Singapore/River Edge, NJ: Global Publishing), 1–5.

39. For more on the "doubly diasporic" condition of Sinophone Malaysian literature in Taiwan, see Tee Kim Tong (Zhang Jinzhong), *Nanyang lunshu: Ma Hua wenxue yu wenhua shuxing* [South Seas discourse: Sinophone Malaysian literature and cultural identity] (Taipei: Maitian chuban, 2003), 135–150.

40. Shih, *Visuality and Identity*, 190.

22

Inverted Islands

Sinophone New Zealand Literature

JACOB EDMOND

岛 从来在倒映心里一个岛 的形像
an island always mirrors an inverted image of an island in the mind
Yang Lian, 杨炼, 视觉, 或岛之五 ("Sense of Sight, or Island No. 5")

The Chinese are the non-European, nonindigenous ethnic and linguistic group with the longest history in New Zealand. Their literature therefore plays a unique role in complicating the dominant bicultural and bilingual narrative of New Zealand literary history. Sinophone New Zealand literature engages both Māori and Anglo-settler concerns with language, place, and identity, illuminating and entwining elements of their often opposed positions on these issues. Sinophone New Zealand writers share with their colonial and postcolonial Anglophone counterparts an ongoing anxiety about the relationship of their language and culture to the land they have settled and a closely connected need to define themselves in relation to a much larger literary culture abroad that is itself dispersed among multiple centers, be they London and New York, or Beijing, Hong Kong, and Taipei. At the same time, as a cultural and linguistic minority in New Zealand, speakers of Sinitic languages have shared with Māori speakers a need to use literature to preserve and assert their cultural identity in the face of an at times repressively dominant Anglo-European settler culture.

The first Sinophone New Zealand literature dates from the beginning of Chinese immigration to New Zealand in the second half of the nineteenth century, a period when questions of land, language, and identity led to war between the indigenous Māori and the British settlers. Significant numbers of Chinese began to arrive in the 1860s, two decades after the signing of the Treaty of Waitangi between Māori tribes and the British crown in 1840, and during a period of major hostilities in the North Island over the extension of British settler power and British breaches of treaty provisions. These early Chinese arrivals were mainly miners, overwhelmingly from the area in and around Guangzhou in the Pearl Delta region of Guangdong province. They were invited by the Otago Chamber of Commerce as a way to extend the term of the gold rush that had begun in 1861. Their population peaked at about 5,000 in 1881 before declining due to the introduction of a discriminatory Poll Tax designed to limit Chinese immigration.[1]

Literary culture was an important part of Chinese New Zealanders' lives from the very beginning of their settlement. The miners not only treasured every scrap of literary text in their possession but also participated in literary competitions, which probably took place annually. A missionary records that the results of the "rhyming couplets" competition generated excitement in 1884 at the prospecting site of Round Hill. Around "40 competitors entered from New Zealand and Australia, subscribing 750 couplets at 1s 6d each. These were sent to three literary men in China who made awards independently of one another."[2] As this account of nineteenth-century literary production illustrates, Sinophone literature in New Zealand functioned at this time as a marker of Chinese identity, a connection to the Chinese homeland and its arbiters of cultural value.

The transnational context of these founding works of Sinophone New Zealand literature reflects the "doubleness" of Chinese New Zealanders' diasporic experience, a part of their inhabiting of "more than one 'home'": most of the miners maintained close ties with their family homes in China, where many had wives and children.[3] Yet while the literary competitions inaugurate the history of Sinophone New Zealand literature through a relationship to the Chinese homeland, they also point to the more complicated web of relations that constituted nineteenth-century New Zealand culture in Chinese as in English.[4] They show an integration of New Zealand and Australian literary culture via papers such as the *Chinese Australian Herald* (*Guangyi hua bao*), which played a key role in establishing a Chinese Australian community, and which organized a Sinophone poetry competition in 1895 in which Chinese New Zealanders also participated.[5] Such linkages between Sinophone New Zealand and Australian literatures belie accounts of these communities that stress only a two-way relation between home and destination, anticipating the further complication of the Sinophone literary field in the twentieth century through the emergence of multiple competing centers of Chinese literary culture, such as Taipei and Hong Kong, and through the ongoing importance of linkages between Sinophone New Zealand and Australian literatures.

The doubleness of Sinophone New Zealand literature's engagements with the Chinese homeland and with their own community is reflected in the broader context of Chinese New Zealanders' search for recognition in domestic New Zealand politics and their engagement in the turbulent political situation of China in the first half of the twentieth century. The few New Zealand periodicals published in the Sinitic script at this time served both roles: they were engaged with the fate of China but also helped to construct a community of Chinese New Zealanders. Literature contributed to these two contrary responses to the issues of land, identity, and language. For example, a poetry recital was part of the event launching the short-lived KMT newspaper the *Man Sing Times* (*Minsheng bao*, 1921–1922).[6] The recital linked Chinese New Zealanders to the new Chinese republic while also building a local community identity.

The same double pull between the desire to assert a connection to China and the need to consolidate a community in New Zealand lay behind the small amount of literature included in *The New Zealand Chinese Growers Monthly*, or *Qiao nong yuekan*, which became the main national Sinitic language periodical after World War II. In supporting the local war effort, the Dominion Federation of New Zealand Chinese Commercial Growers had itself engaged in this dual role—it advocated both for China in its war with Japan by supporting the war effort in the Pacific, and for the local Chinese New Zealand community by lobbying the New Zealand government to reduce restrictions on immigration. The Federation's efforts led to the removal of the hated Poll Tax following World War II. Begun in 1949, on the back of this success, its journal negotiated the new political situation in China and helped consolidate the Chinese New Zealand community. From 1952, its monthly journal was the first Sinophone publication in New Zealand to be printed, rather than handwritten and mimeographed. The periodical thus represented a significant advance in the development of Sinophone print culture in New Zealand, while the purchase of the printing press for four thousand pounds symbolized the strengthening of the Chinese community's economic, social, and cultural position within New Zealand society.[7]

The journal also marked a further step in the establishment of Sinophone New Zealand literary culture. Though devoted to the general business, social, and cultural interests of the community, *Qiao nong yuekan* did publish a small amount of literary work that reflected the negotiation between local and Chinese affiliations, and between the Cantonese spoken by most Chinese New Zealanders and the Mandarin that dominated officially sanctioned literary culture in both Mainland China and Taiwan. The literature in *Qiao nong yuekan* was still largely limited to either Chinese writers who had established themselves within centers of Chinese literary culture, including Shao Ting and Huang Shaohong in its first issue published on July 1, 1949, and Li Xiangen, whose Cantonese poetry appeared in the August 1, 1951, issue. The journal also included some local amateur literary production. This tended to be highly conventional, as in the two poems in traditional seven-syllable form by Wu Yousheng published in the January 31, 1961, issue.[8] By the time *Qiao nong yuekan* ceased publication in 1972, knowledge of the Sinitic languages was diminishing among the New Zealand population.[9] The established local Chinese community was becoming increasingly educated but predominantly Anglophone, a result of assimilatory pressures from the dominant culture (which equally affected the speaking and writing of Māori at this time) and also of the relative isolation of this community as contact with and travel to Mainland China became more difficult. Thus, just as conditions grew more favorable for a Sinophone literary culture in New Zealand, that culture became more likely to find its voice in English rather than in the Sinitic script.

While a small number of Chinese were able to immigrate to New Zealand in the 1970s and 1980s, mainly from Hong Kong, Singapore, and Malaysia, the major changes in Chinese New Zealand culture and correspondingly in Sinophone New Zealand literature took place from the late 1980s onward. At this time, people from China were increasingly able to travel and live abroad, a tendency promoted by political events at home and educational and economic opportunities overseas.[10] This tendency coincided with a loosening of New Zealand's restrictions on immigration from China and other non-Anglo-Saxon countries. As a result, the Chinese population of New Zealand increased almost eight-fold over a twenty year period from 19,000 in the 1986 census to 145,000 in the 2006 census. Where in 1986 a large proportion of Chinese New Zealanders were Anglophone and had a long history—and a strong sense of location—in New Zealand, the more recent arrivals spoke various Sinitic languages and came from diverse parts of the Sinophone world, including Hong Kong, Taiwan, and Mainland China. Like their nineteenth-century predecessors, they also maintained strong connections with the communities and cultures from which they had emigrated. This new wave of migrants helped establish a diverse new internationally connected Sinophone media, publishing, and literary culture and thus the conditions for a new Sinophone New Zealand literature.

After June 4, 1989, a number of prominent Mainland Chinese writers settled at least temporarily overseas, and their influence was particularly felt in New Zealand where they contributed to the new wave of Sinophone New Zealand literature. They also further developed the uncertain relation of language to place and identity as a theme in that literature. The poets Gu Cheng and Yang Lian, who had been associated with the controversial modernist *menglong* poetry in the early 1980s, came to New Zealand in 1988 and 1989, respectively, to teach at the University of Auckland. Yang was also accompanied by his wife, the novelist and essayist Yo Yo (penname of Liu Youhong). These writers were in New Zealand at the time of the June Fourth massacre and afterwards chose to remain there rather than return to China. Yo Yo, Gu, and Yang were all based in New Zealand until the early 1990s, and during this time Gu and Yang in particular produced a substantial body of work that engages with their New Zealand experience. Yo Yo and Yang left the country permanently in 1992, eventually settling in London. The following year, Gu killed his wife Xie Ye and himself on Waiheke, an island in the Hauraki Gulf near Auckland. New Zealand thus suddenly appeared prominently on the international map of Sinophone literature for both literary and horrific extra-literary reasons.

In response to the June Fourth crackdown, Yang and Gu organized a number of literary actions that gave Sinophone literature a more prominent place than ever before in New Zealand culture. Soon after June Fourth, they held a memorial reading, at which a statement written by Yang and Gu was read and distributed. On September 17, 1989, Yang, Gu, and prominent Anglophone New Zealand writers such as Russell Haley, Albert Wendt, Kevin Ireland, and Murray Edmond participated in a memorial festival, "China: The Survivors." The festival included a theatrical event conceived by Yang and others, a concert of readings and musical and theatrical performances, and the laying of a commemorative stone. Yang wrote the dedication for the stone: *nimen yi wu yan, er shitou you le husheng* ("you do not speak, but the stone has a cry").[11] This epitaph not only commemorated those who died on June Fourth and so "do not speak" but also left a small but permanent marker of the presence of these major Chinese writers. Indeed Yang's implicit aural and visual wordplay on *shetou* and *shitou*, "tongue" and "stone," suggests an unstable connection between speech and location.[12] It thus inaugurates the radical disruption of relations between language and place that he would explore in his New Zealand work.

Both Yang and Gu used their experience of linguistic, cultural, and geographical displacement from their native Beijing to construct New Zealand as a particular topos in their work, though in quite different ways. Extending the construction of Sinophone New Zealand identity in relation to the Chinese homeland, Gu's New Zealand served as a utopian alternative to—or inversion of—an oppressive Chinese modernity. In 1988, just months after arriving in New Zealand, Gu Cheng and his wife Xie Ye moved to Waiheke Island. There, he began to construct a literary image of the island as a place of utopian escape from China, reality, and urban life, symbolized for him by the "city," a word contained even within his own name, as underscored in his major late cycle of poems "City" (*Cheng*) begun on Waiheke Island.[13] While the opposition of country to city predates Gu Cheng's association with New Zealand and is widespread in modern and especially post-Mao Chinese literature, Gu came to associate the country with Waiheke. This is evident in his final poem, addressed to his son Mu'er, or Samuel, in which Gu writes of returning "home" to Waiheke, where "the sea . . . cuddles your little island."[14] In setting his rural idyll in New Zealand, Gu not only appealed to the romanticized image of the South Seas promoted by artists such as Gaugin (Gu visited Tahiti just before his death), but continued a tradition within Anglophone New Zealand literature and culture of imagining the country as a utopia.[15]

Gu's murder suicide created a media storm. His posthumously published *Ying'er* (partly coauthored with Xie Ye) attracted the highest advance ever paid for a book in Mainland China at that time.[16] Thus Gu's strange and disturbing autobiographical story of a love triangle set on Waiheke Island became arguably the best-known work of Sinophone New Zealand literature. If seeing Gu's work as Sinophone New Zealand literature seems far fetched, one might consider how important place was to Gu's literary and personal fantasies of his final years and his notion of a "kingdom of girls" (*nü'er guo*). Connecting this fantasy to *Dream of the Red Chamber* (*Hong lou meng*), Gu wrote: "It was long after, when I started dwelling in the 'red chamber of the South Sea' that I came to realize that girlhood is the purest land in paradise."[17] Gu Cheng constructed a mythic New Zealand that was by definition detached from everyday reality. And his imagined Waiheke and New Zealand have also been central to the posthumous writing about him within China. Gu Cheng, Tang Xiaodu claims, "seems to have carried Waiheke Island with him and slowly turned himself into such an island."[18] Gu Cheng was resolutely opposed to learning English in case it ruined his Chinese but equally resolutely called New Zealand—and Waiheke in particular—his "home."[19] That such a writer, in many ways entirely resistant to any engagement with New Zealand culture and society, should have a strong claim to a central place within Sinophone New Zealand literature points to the complexities of defining the concept of Sinophone New Zealand literature in the first place.[20] These inversions also illustrate how that concept can serve to question too easily assumed relations between place, language, and identity.

Yang offers a less utopian, more complex view of New Zealand and Chinese identity, location, and language. Rather than depicting a return to a simple life on an isolated Pacific island, Yang picked a bridge near his home that spanned a motorway and was popular with suicide leapers as one of his key New Zealand poems when he first published four of these poems in Mainland China in 1991.[21] Yang's New Zealand, specifically the city of Auckland (by far the largest city in New Zealand and the main destination for Chinese immigrants), is threatening. Death lurks everywhere—in bridges from which people throw themselves, in the city's many extinct (or in Chinese literally "dead") volcanoes, in the forgotten graveyard beneath the suicide bridge that is also the focus of his highly poetic prose piece "Eclipse" (*Rishi*).[22] Likewise, while Waiheke becomes "home" in Gu Cheng's writing, Auckland never is for Yang Lian. Rather than remaining secure in both his Chinese identity and his new non-Chinese home, Yang's writing continuously insists on the impossibility of his reconciliation to any one place and language: home ceases to exist, and the poet writes neither in Chinese nor English but in "Yanglish" (*yangwen*).[23] Underscoring his uncertain location, his prose piece "City of One Person" (*Yi ge ren de chengshi*) superimposes Beijing on Auckland. Likewise, his poem "Winter Garden" (*Dongri huayuan*) refers to "snow" (*xue*), which is unknown in subtropical Auckland and least of all in the city's Domain hothouse to which the title refers.[24] Auckland comes to embody his condition of perpetual exile, thereby ironically founding a Sinophone literature intimately located in a New Zealand landscape on a condition of dislocation, reanimating a long tradition in Anglophone New Zealand literature and culture from its poetry of "unsettling settlement" to its "cinema of unease."[25] On the one hand, Yang's Auckland locations serve only, as in Gu, to underscore that this is a fantastic world, a "City in a Daydream" (the title of his most extensive cycle of New Zealand poems).[26] On the other, they lead his writing into a concrete engagement with place and have contributed to his acceptance as a New Zealand writer.

Although he has been based in London since the mid-1990s and frequently returns to China, Yang is a New Zealand citizen, maintains a presence within New Zealand literature, and continues to write work that addresses his New Zealand associations. His poem "Brian Holton Traveling in New Zealand" was written after Yang returned to Auckland in October 2001 for the official celebrations of the establishment of the New Zealand Electronic Poetry Centre and the launch of his author page on the Centre's website, a major online resource for New Zealand poetry based at the University of Auckland. Yang returned to New Zealand for a longer stay in July 2003, when he and his translator and friend Brian Holton participated in the international Poetics of Exile conference held at the University of Auckland. On this trip, Yang was presented with a tapa notebook in which he wrote the poem "Sense of Sight, or, Island No. 5," which is dedicated to Anglophone New Zealand poet Michele Leggott and which is clearly located in the Auckland landscape.[27] The tapa notebook and Yang Lian's papers from his time in New Zealand and Australia are now housed in the University of Auckland library's special collections, further establishing his position within New Zealand literature.

These renewed connections with New Zealand culminated in *Unreal City*, a collection of his New Zealand work in English translation published in 2006 by Auckland University Press. The editors' introduction to *Unreal City* seeks to establish Yang's place within New Zealand literature in a way that has provoked criticism from scholars of Chinese literature. Reflecting the persistent false dichotomy that the concept of Sinophone literatures seeks to overcome, these scholars insist that Yang's Auckland is a mere backdrop to his Chinese—not New Zealand—poetics.[28] By contrast, Anglophone New Zealand critics have welcomed Yang's association with New Zealand, perhaps as a result of the lessons learned from earlier debates over the relationship between Māori and Anglophone literature. They have even extended the comparisons put forward in *Unreal City* to other New Zealand writers, such as the modernist Robin Hyde: "Hyde begins two of her China poems with the question 'What is it makes the stranger?' . . . and variations on this question haunt Yang's fascinating, fractured Auckland poems."[29] Yang's ongoing presence in New Zealand literature has also been supported by Chinese Anglophone writer Tze Ming Mok, who published a poem by Yang Lian in Chinese along with her own creative and deliberate "mistranslation" into English in New Zealand's premier arts and culture journal, *Landfall*.[30] Mok, who was born in New Zealand to Chinese-speaking parents who arrived in the 1970s, writes predominantly in English, though words and phrases from various Sinitic languages play a prominent role in her writing, as they do to some extent with other Anglophone New Zealand Chinese writers, such as Alison Wong.

Where in the writing of Yang and Gu New Zealand appears as an exotic land in which the writer is isolated or displaced, the subsequent history of Sinophone New Zealand has stressed the building of a literary community. In 1994, the year following Xie Ye's and Gu Cheng's deaths, Huang Wukun with Lam Song (Lin Shuang) and others established the New Zealand Chinese Writers Association (*Niuxilan Huawen zuojia xiehui*), which since this time has run literary competitions and other community literary activities (though not without some internal disagreement, which led the organization to split in 2004 and to the dissolution of the original association by its founder Huang Wukun in 2006).[31] Lam Song's extensive writings and community activities in Auckland illustrate the institutional development of Sinophone New Zealand literature. She has played a prominent role in raising the profile of Sinophone New Zealand literature and culture abroad and has also worked as a cultural mediator and translator, presenting her work in Chinese and in English.[32] Her published books include Chinese translations of Māori legends and explanations of Māori traditions as well as a book that ranges from an account of the formation of the New Zealand Chinese Writers Association to poems in praise of New Zealand's Southern Alps.[33]

In the South Island, the New Zealand Chinese Writers Association of Christchurch led by Annie Shih (Shi Li'an) established New Zealand's first Sinophone literary periodical *Cang cheng wen cai huikan*, which was published in eight issues between 1998 and 2004. Through the journal, Shih, like Lam, took on the role of a cultural mediator in New Zealand society. As a member of the Anglophone-dominated New Zealand Society of Authors, Shih worked to promote exchange between Anglophone and Sinophone New Zealand writers, organizing Chinese sessions of the annual Christchurch festival Books and Beyond, in which, thanks to Shih, Sinophone writers were involved for the first time in 2000. She also published Sinophone translations of prominent Anglophone New Zealand writers in issues of the journal and in Taiwan, where she maintains strong literary linkages.[34]

Cang cheng wen cai huikan also included extensive original Sinophone New Zealand writing. Some of this involved fairly clichéd descriptions of New Zealand's scenery combined with traditional poetic forms, such as a seven-character *ci* style poem that described New Zealand from Auckland to its "gleaming snow-white mountain tops" (*baise shantou liang ai'ai*).[35] Yet here too there are moments where writers register the uneasy relationship of language to place that is a hallmark of both Anglophone and Sinophone New Zealand literature. For example, a two-line piece by Dong Shi adopts phrasing that recalls Gu Cheng's famous two-line poem "A Generation" (*Yidairen*), but replaces Gu's "dark night" and "dark eyes" with the "sea" and a "small boat"—a shift that registers the move from China to New Zealand in a similar way to Yang.[36] (In Yang's New Zealand and Australian work, the sea forms a leitmotif and a counterpoint to the "earth" of the Chinese tradition and of his earlier writing in China.) The journal also includes critical essays and reflections on Sinophone culture and literature in New Zealand, such as Lam Song's "Overseas Chinese Writers' Identity and Mission," in which Lam hails the twenty-first century as the "century of immigrant literature" and points to the importance of overseas Chinese writers in this context.[37] Lam's poetry appears in the same issue and explores questions of immigration and travel through an airport setting, continuing the theme of uncertain location.

The last issue of the journal features a poem entitled "Mt. Eden" (*Yidian shan*).[38] The title refers to one of Auckland's most prominent and centrally located volcanoes, an element of the Auckland landscape that also captured Yang Lian's imagination over a decade earlier. Language's relation to location is stressed by the superimposition of the text of the poem onto the image of mountain and through the poem's play on the name of the volcano.

Wounds, scabs, visceral imagery of blood and death fill the poem. Yet this depiction of the volcano transforms at its close into "green grass and cattle and sheep" surrounded by "birdsong and the fragrance of flowers," so that the poem ends with the "eternal Eve." This Christian redemption contrasts with Yang Lian's much less comforting depiction of climbing the same volcano. In Yang's "City of One Person," the volcano threatens to shatter the apparent tranquility, underscoring the protagonist's uncertain position. Despite— or indeed because of—their dissimilarity, such shared Sinophone literary responses to a prominent Auckland landmark suggest an engagement with place that belies—even as it marks—the unsettled ground of Sinophone New Zealand literature.

Some one hundred and thirty years after gold miners composed poems for an Australian-run competition adjudicated by mainland Chinese experts, much the same pattern of cultural relations is still in evident in a recent book published after the visit to Auckland of the prominent TV personality and popularizer of Chinese literary and cultural history Yi Zhongtian. The book comprises interviews and speeches from Yi's visit and the winning entries from a literary competition run by the Sinophone New Zealand press Mykiwi in collaboration with Mainland China's *Renmin wenxue* and the Auckland Chinese-language Culture and Book Festival.[39] Even as these Sinophone New Zealand publishers and book festivals mark the coming of age of Sinophone New Zealand literature, they also illustrate the ongoing desire to look to the Chinese tradition and cultural arbiters within China for legitimation. Still, much has changed since the mid-1990s, when Sinophone New Zealand print culture could still be described as "utilitarian," owing to "the struggle the community has undergone to survive in this country."[40] In 2011, print and electronic media cater to a much broader range of interests, reflecting a strong and growing community. Mykiwi, for example, operates as an agent for publishing in China as well as publishing its own books and a magazine. Equally important in establishing a literary community is *Ao Niu wang*, which, amongst an extensive range of news and information, provides reviews of Sinophone books published in Australia and New Zealand.[41] As an Australasian Web site, it points to the integration of Sinophone New Zealand and Australian literary communities in a way that again recalls much earlier nineteenth-century precedents.

The last two decades have led to the development of the necessary conditions for a vibrant Sinophone New Zealand literary tradition. Yet this has occurred at the very moment when such localized literary structures are being called into question by new information technologies and by the mobility of peoples, especially those highly educated speakers of Chinese most likely to contribute to a new literary tradition. New Zealand Sinophone litera-ture exists in and through this tension. Twenty years ago, two of mainland China's most important writers wrote work that was obsessively located in New Zealand and yet equally stressed utopian escape and dislocation. Today, Sinophone New Zealand writers continue to confront the tension between a transnational Chinese literary community and a localized Sinophone tradi-tion. In this tension, we can locate the problem—and the possibility—of a Sinophone New Zealand literature.

Notes

1. Brian Moloughney, Tony Ballantyne, and David Hood, "After Gold: Reconstructing Chinese Communities, 1896–1913," in *Asia in the Making of New Zealand*, ed. Henry Johnson and Brian Moloughney (Auckland: Auckland University Press, 2006), 62–63; Manying Ip, "Chinese," *Te Ara: The Encyclopedia of New Zealand*, http://www.teara.govt.nz/en/chinese. The key primary source for information on nineteenth-century Chinese New Zealand settlers is the missioner Alexander Don's roll, published in a facsimile edition as volume four of James Ng, *Windows on a Chinese Past* (Dunedin: Otago Heritage Books, 1993–1999). An electronic version of the roll is available online at http://www.otago.ac.nz/historyarthistory/don/don.php.

2. Cited in Ng, *Windows*, 2: 52.

3. Moloughney, Ballantyne, and Hood, 74–75.

4. On New Zealand Anglophone print culture as part of the "webs of empire," see Tony Ballantyne, "Race and the Webs of Empire: Aryanism from India to the Pacific," *Journal of Colonialism and Colonial History* 2, no. 3 (2001), http://muse.jhu.edu/journals/ journal_of_colonialism_and_colonial_history/v002/2.3ballantyne.html.

5. On the paper's role in the construction of an imagined Chinese community in Sydney, see Mei-Fen Kuo, "The *Chinese Australian Herald* and the Shaping of a Modern 'Imagined' Chinese Community in 1890s Colonial Sydney," *Chinese Southern Diaspora Studies* 2 (2008): 34–53 (on the poetry competition, see page 38). On Chinese New Zealanders' participation in the competition, see Ng, *Windows*, 2:66.

6. "Ben dao xinwen: *Minsheng bao* kaimu zhi sheng, "*Minsheng Bao* (Man Sing Times) July 21, 1921: 15. A digital facsimile of this and other early Sinophone New Zealand periodicals are available online at the Auckland Library Chinese Journals Project, http://www.nzchine-sejournals.org.nz.

7. James Ng and Nigel Murphy, "Chinese," in *Book and Print in New Zealand: A Guide to Print Culture in New Zealand*, ed. Penny Griffith, Ross Harvey, and Keith Maslen (Wellington: Victoria University Press, 1997), available at the *New Zealand Electronic Text Centre*, http://www.nzetc.org/tm/scholarly/tei-GriBook-_div3-N13B6B.html. For an insider's history of the Federation and its journal, see Joe Y. Sing, *A Brief History of the Overseas Chinese in New Zealand* (Wellington: Niuxilan shuang xing chubanshe, 1996).

8. Facsimile editions of all issues of the journal are available at the Auckland Library Chinese Journals Project.

9. While Fong's 1950s study of Chinese New Zealanders adopts a somewhat patronizing tone in asserting that "very few of the present Chinese in New Zealand know enough about [Chinese philosophy, literature, and art], or are able to interpret them to the dominant society," the study did accurately identify the growing lack of education in Chinese language and culture among the younger generation. See Fong, *The Chinese in New Zealand* (Hong Kong: Hong Kong University Press, 1959), 122.

10. On this wave of educated Chinese immigrants, their maintenance of connections with China, and their international impact, especially in the Australasian context, see, for example, Kam Louie, "Returnee Scholars: Ouyang Yu, the Displaced Poet and the Sea Turtle," *New Zealand Journal of Asian Studies* 8.1 (2006): 1–16. See also Manying Ip, ed., *Re-Examining Chinese Transnationalism in Australia-New Zealand* (Canberra: Centre for the Study of the Chinese Southern Diaspora, Australian National University, 2001).

11. Jacob Edmond and Hilary Chung, "Yang Lian, Auckland, and the Poetics of Exile," in *Unreal City: A Chinese Poet in Auckland,* by Yang Lian (Auckland: Auckland University Press, 2006), 4–5. The account there of this history is based on my personal collection of primary documents and on the video of the event held in the University of Auckland library.

12. Jacob Edmond, "The *Flâneur* in Exile," *Comparative Literature* 62, no. 4 (Fall 2010): 395.

13. For this cycle and the chronology of its composition, see Gu Cheng, *Gu Cheng shi quanji*, ed. Gu Xiang, vol. 2 (Nanjing: Jiangsu wen yi, 2010).

14. Gu, "Hui jia," in *Gu Cheng shi*, 865–866.

15. Utopian depictions of New Zealand are a commonplace of Anglophone New Zealand culture from the fairytale rural utopia conjured up by settler advertisements in the nineteenth century, through Samuel Butler's *Erewhon*, and the later notion of New Zealand as a utopian social "laboratory," to what Patrick Evans describes as the "paradise or slaughterhouse" binary in Anglophone New Zealand literature. Samuel Butler, *Erewhon: Or, Over the Range* (London: Jonathan Cape, 1921[1872]); Herbert Asquith, qtd. in Keith Sinclair, *William Pember Reeves: New Zealand Fabian* (Oxford: Clarendon, 1965), 212; Patrick Evans, "Paradise or Slaughterhouse: Some Aspects of New Zealand Proletarian Fiction," *Islands* 8, no. 1 (1980): 71–85. On this topic, see also Jacob Edmond, "No Place like Home: Encounters Between New Zealand and Russian Poetries," *Landfall* 213 (2007): 73–80.

16. Anne-Marie Brady, "Dead in Exile: The Life and Death of Gu Cheng and Xie Ye," *China Information* 11, no. 4 (1997): 128.

17. Quoted in Henry Zhao, "The Poetics of Death," in *Essays, Interviews, Recollections and Unpublished Material of Gu Cheng, 20th-Century Chinese Poet,* ed. Li Xia (Lewiston: Edwin Mellen, 1999), 12.

18. Tang Xiaodu, "The Death of Gu Cheng," in *Essays, Interviews, Recollections and Unpublished Material of Gu Cheng, 20th-Century Chinese Poet,* ed. Li Xia (Lewiston: Edwin Mellen, 1999), 47. Even when critics such as Tang Xiaodu point out this fantasy, they perpetuate it. Tang writes of Gu and Xie that "they lived chiefly in an out-of-the-way village among local Maoris" (46). This description of untouched tribal life is entirely at odds with the reality of Waiheke Island and of Māoridom's active engagement with the Anglo-European modernity over the past two centuries.

19. Brady, "Dead in Exile," 129. See, for example, Gu's reference to Waiheke Island as "my island, my home" in Gu Cheng and Lei Mi, *Ying'er: The Kingdom of Daughters*, trans. Li Xia (Dortmund: Projekt Verlag, 1995), 103.

20. Brady notes that Gu Cheng "did not understand New Zealand society and made no attempt to do so" but also that he was "exhilarated by the difference of life in New Zealand and the strangeness of its different culture." Brady, "Dead in Exile," 136.

21. Yang Lian, "Gelafudun qiao" (Grafton Bridge), *Xiandai Han shi* 1 (Spring 1991): 3–4.

22. Yang Lian, *Guihua—Zhili de kongjian: Yang Lian zuopin 1982–1997: sanwen—wenlun juan* (Shanghai: Shanghai wenyi chuban she, 1998), 21–26.

23. "Zhuixun zuowei liuwang yuanxing de shi" [In search of poetry as the prototype of exile], *Yang Lian and Yo Yo*, http://yanglian.net/yanglian/pensee/pen_wenlun_02.html.

24. Yang Lian, *Guihua*, 27–32; *Dahai tingzhi zhi chu: Yang Lian zuopin 1982–1997: shige juan* (Shanghai: Shanghai wenyi, 1998), 337–40. For more on Yang's unsettling of location in his New Zealand work, see Edmond, "Flâneur in Exile."

25. Alex Calder, "Unsettling Settlement: Poetry and Nationalism in Aotearoa/New Zealand," *REAL: Yearbook of Research in English and American Literature* 14 (1998): 165–181; *Cinema of Unease: A Personal Journey by Sam Neill* (Wellington Top Shelf Productions, 1995), DVD.

26. Yang, *Dahai*, 335–393.

27. For more on these poems and New Zealand connections, see Edmond and Chung, "Yang Lian," 12–14.

28. Cosima Bruno argues that Yang's New Zealand writings are "so strictly personal that they say very little about Auckland," though she acknowledges that "through translation, these poems appear woven into both the New Zealand and Chinese poetic traditions." Cosima Bruno, review of *Unreal City*, by Yang Lian, *The China Quarterly* 187 (2006): 811. More forcefully, Yiyan Wang argues that it is a "far-fetched suggestion that Yang Lian's work in Auckland can be considered as New Zealand poetry." Yiyan Wang, review of *Unreal City*, by Yang Lian, *Pacific Affairs* 79. 3 (2006): 514.

29. Harry Ricketts, "Asian Connections," in *99 Ways into New Zealand Poetry*, by Paula Green and Harry Ricketts (Auckland: Vintage; Random House, 2010), 486.

30. Yang Lian, Jacob Edmond, and Tze Ming Mok. "Whispers." *Borderline* spec. issue of *Landfall* 211 (2006): 64–72.

31. The founding of the association is documented in Lam Song, *Zhan chi Aokelan: Yi ge Xianggang jiao shi de yi min gu shi* (Hong Kong: Dangdai wenyi, 2001), 260–61. On the split and dissolution, see Huang Wukun, "Tuichu Niuxilan Huawen zuojia xiehui de shengming" at http://news.180.co.nz/2006829/stuff_news_20062793912120.html.

32. Lam Song's profile as a Sinophone New Zealand writer in the Chinese-speaking world and her frequent participation in international events for Sinophone writers are attested to in Lin Chenghuang, "Mu'ai, ernü xin zhong de yongheng fengbei: du Xinxilan Hua wen zuojia Lin Shuang 'Muqin song' yi shi," *Shijie Huawen wenxue yanjiu wanzhan*, http://www.fgu.edu.tw/~wclrc/drafts/China/lin-cheng-huang/lin-cheng-huang_01.htm.

33. Lam Song, *Niuxilan de yuan zhu min: Maoli zu shen hua, chuan tong ji li shi* (Taipei: Shi jie Hua wen zuo jia, 1998); Lam Song, *Zhan chi Aokelan*.

34. For example, see Stevan Eldred-Grigg, "Niuxilan de wenxue shi," trans. Shi Li'an, *Ming dao wen yi* 308 (November 2001): 46–53.

35. Wang Qingfeng, "Keju Niuxilan you gan fu shi," *Cang cheng wen cai huikan* 2 (1998): 17.

36. Dong Shi, "Xiao chuan" (Small boat), *Cang cheng wen cai huikan* 3 (1999): 22.

37. Lam Song, "Haiwai Huaren zuojia de wenhua shenfen yu shiming," *Cang cheng wen cai huikan* 6 (2001): 5–7.

38. Hong Huang, "Yidian shan," *Cang cheng wen cai huikan* 8 (2004): 41.

39. Yi Zhongtian, *Bai yun huang he: Yi Zhongtian Xinxilan yanjiang quan jilu* (Auckland: Mykiwi, 2010).

40. Ng and Murphy, "Chinese."

41. *Ao Niu wang*, http://www.ausnz.net.

23

Beneath Two Red Banners

Lao She as a Manchu Writer in Modern China

CARLES PRADO-FONTS

If there is a color with particular significance in twentieth-century China, this must be red—as the emblem and metaphor for a whole range of discourses and practices associated with Communist China. For Lao She (1899–1966), however, red also had another substantial meaning—as his family belonged to the Manchu Plain Red Banner (*zheng hongqi*). This chapter addresses the explicit and implicit impact of ethnicity in the trajectory of this writer of Manchu origin who was later canonized as one of the most important figures in modern Chinese literature.

Although there is not much biographical information on Lao She, the usual outlines in literary histories tend to shape a quite common, by now already well-known narrative, which can be summarized as follows.[1] Lao She was born in 1899, and only one year later his father was killed in the foreign armies' attack on Beijing during the Boxer Rebellion.[2] In his childhood, he lived in a segregated area in Northwest Beijing (what was called the Tartar City) that until 1911 was restricted to Manchu population only. After attending Beijing Normal School, he quickly earned several positions in the educational administration, which he rejected to remain a teacher. In the summer of 1924, he accepted a five-year appointment as lecturer in Chinese at the School of Oriental Studies in London—which it is suggested (but unclear) was offered to him due to his embrace of Christianity around that time. Lao She published his first novels in China while living in London. On his way back to China in 1929, he spent six months in Singapore. Already back in China, he held different teaching jobs that he combined with literary creation and finally decided to become a professional writer. His status in the literary field did not rise until the publication of *Camel Xiangzi* in 1937. Literary reputation and political neutrality made him elected chairman of the All China Association of Writers and Artists Against Aggression (*Zhonghua quanguo wenyijie kangdi xiehui*) in 1938. In 1946, he was invited by the U.S. State Department to tour the United States, where he remained until 1949. After the Communist victory, he decided to return to the newly established People's Republic. In the following decades, he held several official positions.[3] He died during the Cultural Revolution, under circumstances still unclear.

Within this rather straight biographical path, Lao She's work embeds tensions, contradictions, and ambivalences that have also captured the attention of several scholars: Fredric Jameson has analyzed the opposition between precapitalism and emergent capitalism in Lao She's work; Edward Gunn, the tension between literary style and socially progressive ideology; David Wang, the interplay between melodrama and farce as distinctive aspects of realism; Lydia Liu, the dialectic between language and modes of narration under the framework of translingual practices; Margaret Hillenbrand, the ambivalence toward nationalism; Kam Louie, the confrontation of class, gender, ethnicity, and race in the construction of a new Chinese masculinity; Rey Chow, the problematic construction of identity politics through material objects; Thomas Moran, the anxiety between moral indignation and reluctant nihilism; and Alexander Huang, the distinctive stress in relation to cosmopolitanism.[4]

What is striking is that most of these analyses examine such tensions, contradictions and ambivalences in Lao She's works without questioning his biographical trajectory and, especially, the *problematique* derived from his ethnic identity. Of course, scholars include more or less impressionistic references to Lao She's Manchu origins, such as "the significance of the depiction of the Cantonese compatriots is even more trenchant as Lao She himself was of Manchurian descent,"[5] or "Lao She, who was Manchurian rather than Han Chinese (. . .) could not but be sensitized to this very fraught, indeed ironic, complex of ethnic and national identification in modern China."[6] But the actual relevance of Lao She's ethnic identity—as well as the real impact of his stay abroad at a crucial formative moment in his career—have not been fully stretched. It is perhaps necessary to reverse the argument and turn the corollary into a more fundamental source. After all, Lao She's double peripheral condition (as a Manchu writer in China and as a Chinese citizen who lived in London for five years) inevitably generated the construction of a particular subjectivity and a specific positionality, key elements that significantly originate—rather than simply confirm—the multiple political tensions and contradictions in Lao She's works.

Recent contributions from New Qing historians consolidate even more the reasons that call for a reexamination of Lao She's case.[7] It could even be suggested that Lao She's (scarce) views on his own trajectory should not be taken at face value, since—just in the same way as the tensions, contradictions, and ambivalences mentioned before—they were embedded in a determinant framework of ethnic and identity politics.

New Qing historians have provided an alternative narrative to the construction of China's social, political, and intellectual modernity during the last stages of the Qing empire and the early twentieth century. Their contributions pay attention to the ethnic, social, and cultural relations between Manchus and Han Chinese, which are circumscribed by historical circumstances such as the following. After 1911, the banner system still remained without significant changes for a few years and Manchu people in the banner garrisons still received stipends and payments of grain during the 1910s. It was in the early 1920s when Manchus had to start making a living on their own, although it was difficult for them to adjust to the new reality: many of them were not willing to work, debts and gambling had become widespread, and indolence led to starvation in some cases. Thus, "although the de jure segregation of Manchus and Han ended with the revolution, de facto segregation continued."[8] This became progressively more visible as ethnic tensions were more noticeable in all spheres of society.

When the banner system was officially cancelled in 1924, ethnicity continued to be an unresolved issue and a social problem. Many Manchu citizens (Lao She among them) tried to pass as Han by strategies of a different nature: hiding their origins and altering their classification, changing the way they dressed, adopting Han-style surnames, abandoning hereditary settlements, binding girls' feet, or, simply, trying to find work among the Han. They strived to avoid trouble and blend unnoticed into the Han majority. As Rhoads concludes, "only by turning their back on their heritage, so a number of Manchus thought, could they make their way in early Republican China." The cost was "widespread discrimination, the erosion of their sense of self, and their seemingly imminent assimilation by the majority Han population."[9]

At the same time, these ethnic and social tensions were further complicated by the fact that China's political and intellectual reform came to be articulated upon the dichotomy between (Han) Chinese and Manchus, while also remaining in a problematic tension with the West (which has probably received more scholarly attention). The whole discourse of China's quest for modernity in the 1920s in general, as well as the May Fourth Movement in particular, stepped on and rearticulated the Manchu issue. Political change, institutional rupture, social alternatives, national independence, and, in sum, the yearning for modernization in all aspects of society were framed in an explicitly or implicitly oppositional way against the Manchu dynasty and, by extension, against people of Manchu ethnicity.

Decades later, after the tensions of the early Republic and the assimilationist policy undertaken by the Nationalists, the Communist government seemed to pursue a more pluralistic stance with some specific affirmative actions that, in fact, do nothing but denote that tensions and segregation were still prevalent. The fact that, for instance, the government was impelled to prohibit the use of derogative terms applied to Manchus in 1956 is clear evidence of it.[10]

As a consequence, the fate for Manchus in modern China was, as Pamela Crossley argues, none other than "a perpetually incomplete existence in a society that had no ready mechanism for the acknowledgment and acceptance of an inner difference that has no outward sign."[11] And, just as this ends up explaining the "eccentricity" and "crankiness" of the Manchu individuals examined in Crossley's book, it could also be applicable to better understand Lao She's alienation and the peripheral position from which he wrote—a position that explains the tensions, contradictions, and ambivalences summarized previously. In other words, within the "sharp dichotomy between their public and private identities,"[12] which was developed by most Manchus in the 1920s, 1930s, and beyond, there are gaps and discontinuities that are meaningful, as well as silences that speak implicitly.

It seems only natural, then, that Lao She's narrative production requires a reexamination that gives central attention to the implications of his Manchu condition and its problematic relation with dominant discourses in China. This Sinophone angle is even more significant if we take into account Lao She's stay in London, where his alienated experience was also constituted by an ethnic (racist) component—although this time, interestingly, as a "Chinese" living in the West. All this sets a complex triangular pattern of relations that needs to be addressed when considering Lao She's career and works. I will highlight here just a few issues derived from all of this.

First, a Sinophone perspective evidences a major continuity in Lao She's experience of alienation at different periods of his life: at home during his early years in Beijing, abroad in London, as well as after his return to China in 1930. In each of his works Lao She will try to adjust to and negotiate with this constant predicament in a different way—something that explains the extraordinary shifts in form and style of his works (especially the early ones), which would otherwise be difficult to explain. After having written *The Philosophy of Lao Zhang* (*Lao Zhang zhexue*, 1926), *Zhao Ziyue* (*Zhao Ziyue*, 1927) and *The Two Mas* (*Erma*, 1929) in London, Lao She's return to China seems to coincide with an intense period of literary experimentation that testifies that the evolution from his "English" novels toward *Camel Xiangzi* was not regular nor smooth at all: *Xiaopo's Birthday* (*Xiaopo de shengri*, 1930), written in Singapore, is a children's story; *Cat Country* (*Maocheng ji*, 1932) is a work of science fiction with a Swiftian flavor; and *Divorce* (*Lihun*, 1933) is a return to the Beijing satire. As a set, all these early novels written either in London or during and right after his return to China show a persistence in formal experimentation that stands in sharp contrast with the naturalism of *Camel Xiangzi* (*Luotuo Xiangzi*).

In addition, this early period puts into doubt the presumed teleological progression or "natural course" in Lao She's fiction[13] and calls for a more critical understanding of his work that reassesses his production by looking more sensitively at historical factors.[14] Traditionally seen by scholars as a major writer of modern Chinese realism,[15] and mostly known (and canonized) for his depictions of lower classes, Lao She's career has been typically understood as a refinement toward the publication in 1937 of what has generally been considered his masterpiece, *Camel Xiangzi*. This perception of literary progression tends to go hand in hand with a gradual political engagement.[16] But paying attention to his Sinophone condition shows how Lao She's position in modern Chinese literary history is the result of a certain hermeneutic violence applied to a trajectory that is actually more intricate.

Finally, this specific positionality provided Lao She with the relevant critical detachment or "out-of-place-ness" that has already been remarked on by many scholars.[17] Such a distance allowed Lao She's characteristic display of ambivalence when dealing with issues of class, ethnicity, nationalism, or cosmopolitanism in his fiction.

A reexamination of Lao She's fiction would demand a close reading of his works that situates them within this specific ethnic *problematique* and Lao She's positionality at the time of their writing.[18] Alternatively, it can also be done on a smaller scale by looking at Lao She's trajectory retroactively from *Beneath the Red Banner* (*Zheng hongqi xia*)—paradoxically Lao She's last (and unfinished) work.[19] Written in 1961–1962 and published (unfinished, with only eleven chapters) thirteen years after Lao She's death, in 1979, at a time when the official stance vis-à-vis ethnicity had changed, *Beneath the Red Banner* recuperates the Manchu world of the early twentieth century. Whereas Lao She had hidden his Manchu origins for the most part of his career and tried to blend into the Han Chinese majority, his Manchu identity reemerged at several stages after 1954. While holding different offices, for instance, he became—under his real Manchu name, Shu (Sumuru) Qingchun—a representative of the Manchus as a delegate in the National People's Congress. It is in this context that Lao She finally started writing about Manchu society in a more explicit way—very briefly in *Teahouse* (*Chaguan*, 1957) and more at length in his last and incomplete novel.

Beneath the Red Banner opens with six descriptive chapters that could be taken as a costumbrist outline of the lives of Manchu families in Beijing during the last years of the Qing empire. Narrated in a first-person voice, the birth of the narrator is the starting point of an excursion through the lives of his relatives, neighbors, and friends, which form their own scattered subplots. It is interesting to note how the first chapters are intensely descriptive—almost in an anthropological sense. Details illustrating the habits and customs of Manchu origin abound, such as "traditionally, Manchus respected the women on the paternal side of the family" (23); or "Butter was always used in making Manchu cakes, and my ancestors' diet probably included cow's milk, mare's milk and even butter and cream cheese" (122). The weight of these asides is such that the autobiographical tone presumably conferred by the first-person narrator becomes weak and the structure turns rather loose—as if it was formally difficult for Lao She to reconcile the intimacy of a remembrance that had been in the shadows with the responsibility he assumes as a social and cultural representative of the Manchu people. In other words, this seems to be an uneasy attempt for him to explicitly recuperate his own origin and translate it into the literary terrain, from which it had been hidden (Lao She had timidly attempted something similar in *Teahouse*, where two of the characters are Manchu). The two meanings of *representation* ("to depict" and "to speak on behalf of"), then, seem to fatally collapse.

What is significant in this dilemma of representation is that it is entangled in Lao She's complex positionality over the years. Therefore, while he makes the effort to recuperate a Manchu world that never got erased from his mind, at the same time he is enunciating this recuperation from a dominant Han Chinese perspective. It is not unusual, then, to find mentions of Manchu hedonism, for instance: "It appeared that they were living in some exquisite, explicit, and yet slightly muddled dream" (33), which is anchored in a Han position that justifies the fall of the Qing: "I was born just in time to witness the flickering candles of the funeral rites of the Qing Dynasty" (31). Seen retrospectively, the hesitations (weak turns in the plot or major uncertainties held by the characters) that in early novels such as *The Two Mas*, *Xiaopo's Birthday*, or *Cat Country* were used to habilitate a critical perspective (while often at the expense of turning the narrative structure weak and loose), three decades later in *Beneath the Red Banner* reappear this time as timid anthropological glimpses that, again, obstruct a neat unfolding of the argument.

Still, the kinds of hesitations of the old days are also present at the level of the plot in Lao She's last work. The actual detonator for the action does not appear until Chapter 7. Cousin Fuhai stands in an ethical dilemma: he sees the need to get involved in political revolution against both the foreign powers and the Manchu government, but he remains trapped by his condition of Manchu Bannerman:

> Cousin Fuhai was a genuine Manchu Bannerman, in full possession of the riding and shooting skills which had been refined over the course of two hundred years. But he had also assimilated many different Han, Mongolian and Moslem customs. He was accomplished with both the pen and the sword. Culturally he combined the best Manchu and Han attainments . . . (49–51; depiction continues for a couple of pages)

Fuhai's hybrid nature contrasts with Shicheng's character, a young Han Chinese who is vehemently committed to revolution. Through a radical attitude he wants to convince Fuhai to join the revolutionary movement: "The foreigners take all their cues from their Chinese flunkies, and the officials do whatever the foreigners say. (. . .) What I hate most is those flunkies. They've sold out!" (128). Later, in the last three chapters (of the remaining manuscript) cousin Fuhai will experience the social injustices that another Chinese character, Big Duo, has caused under the approval of foreigners such as Reverend Bull. The development of the novel seems clear enough to infer that Lao She wanted to create an inevitable encounter between cousin Fuhai's political awakening and the clash of the Boxer Uprising. But the novel was left unfinished and never gets to that potential climax. Yet, if the remaining manuscript makes it easy to anticipate such a development of the plot, it is much harder to speculate what the ending would be and what Lao She—in the 1960s, once he had recuperated the Manchu issue—had in mind for this particular finale.

In any case, the plot lays out some ethical dilemmas and contrasting binaries (like Shicheng/Fuhai, or Big Duo/Reverend Bull), which are probably the most accomplished aspect of the manuscript, even if they never get explored in full. Bannermanship, for instance, is a trap for Fuhai, who sees the injustices around him and would like to take action but is unable to do it because of his ethnic and social position: "I am a Bannerman soldier. Shouldn't I be supporting the imperial government? Or should I be supporting Shicheng? He felt tied up in knots" (133). The novel wants to lead toward the resolution of this dilemma and, perhaps, take it from the personal domain to a broader social and historical dimension. Yet the way this is developed, the frame in which it is set, and the perspective from which it is told, suggest that the weight of both Lao She's own past and present was still an element of struggle for him in this project.

Similarly, the identification between Lao She and the poor is also problematized. The novel proposes class to be a common interethnic condition.

Yet later ethnic hierarchies enhance the *problematique* of class. This gives a four-sided society as a result: Manchu Bannermen soldiers (poor), Manchu officers (rich and corrupted), Han Chinese (poor and humiliated), and foreigners (exploiters) (85). In Lao She's account, each category is initially quite hermetic, but he is interestingly committed to making them interact and mingle out of this lack of hybridity, while keeping this juxtaposition necessary in order to make the plot develop dialectically toward the Boxer incident at the end. In any case, the way class and ethnicity are associated is an implicit recognition of the boundaries and differences remaining at the foundation of social interaction of the time.

It is finally worth mentioning that, as the narration moves away from the anthropological account, Lao She's style turns more at ease, with humor and satire surfacing and even becoming central at certain moments—when focusing on Reverend Bull and the sardonic depiction of Westerners, for instance (146, 154). This, again, shows how the narrative development of *Beneath the Red Banner* is not cohesive—not only because the novel is left unfinished and probably unrevised (although Lao She was known for not revising much), but especially because we perceive his inability (or discomfort) to deal with all these differences and find the appropriate orientation for his critical angle.

Beneath the Red Banner enlightens some aspects of Lao She's trajectory and works that need to be reexamined. Why, for instance, did he decide to write about his Manchu origin at such a late stage in his life? Obviously, the favorable historical context in the 1960s allowed him—even pushed him—to do so. But, in any case, *Beneath the Red Banner* as a project tells us about the permanence of the Manchu issue in Lao She's mind until that time. Resurfacing at such a late period in his career, it stands as clear evidence that the Manchu *problematique* was always there before, even if it had been silenced, evaded, or implicitly negotiated in different ways at different moments.

Moreover, the plot of *Beneath the Red Banner*, even if unfinished, seems to progress more or less steadily toward the outbreak of the Boxer Rebellion, something that dilutes the (apparently) autobiographical tone set at the beginning. Why, then, did Lao She choose to include so many anthropological references to Manchu culture and society? There seems to be an attempt to integrate these personal remembrances into a broader understanding of the Boxer Rebellion in particular, and, probably, of history in general. If throughout the main part of his career Lao She had overlapped class and ethnicity under the guise of his public concern for the former (and subsequent elusion of the latter), he seems now to clarify that class and ethnicity, while sharing concerns, have actually different specificities indeed. Thus, the content of *Beneath the Red Banner* also offers a more critical view of Lao She on his own history, trajectory and works.

Finally, the formal construction of the novel reveals a naturalist project for historical interpretation. Autobiography and plot work accordingly, as memories are selected and shaped, clearly remembered, and apologetically forgotten. The chronological distance at the time of writing allows Lao She to construct a plot that wants to add complexity (stressing the ethnic issue) but that, at the same time, is clearly oriented toward the explanation of the Boxer Rebellion beyond a nationalist rhetoric that reveals itself too simplistically. In the postface, Hu Jieqing, Lao She's widow, notes: "Lao She intended to tell his readers how the Qing Dynasty was rotten to the core; how the Manchus were divided into two opposing camps; how the people rose in rebellion against the reactionaries; and how China became a unified country with a promising future" (213). This might be right. Yet a Sinophone reading of *Beneath the Red Banner* also suggests that, in spite of the inevitable and historical inscription of Lao She in a nationalist paradigm, there were more aspects (and red banners) at stake—which, in fact, justify the perplexed narrator's wondering: "To this day I do not understand this segment of my past" (13). The form of *Beneath the Red Banner* attempts precisely to offer a multiangled view on history that is even more valuable than the effort by Lao She to publicly recuperate his own ethnicity.

Notes

1. This biographical outline is based mainly on Ranbir Vohra, *Lao She and the Chinese Revolution* (Cambridge, Mass.: East Asian Research Center, Harvard University, 1974). Also, for a full biographical account with a detailed relation of schools and jobs attended, see Paul Bady, introduction to *Lao niu po che: Essai autocritique sur le roman et l'humour*, by Lao She, trans. Paul Bady (Paris: Presses Universitaires de France, 1974), ix–xci.

2. There is some controversy about Lao She's exact date of birth, as well as the exact location, whether it was Beijing or Shandong. See Vohra, *Lao She and the Chinese Revolution*, 167 fn. 1. Hu Jieqing, Lao She's widow, declared that his birth "was around seven o'clock in the evening of the twenty-third day of the twelfth month of the lunar calendar in 1898." Hu Jieqing, postface to *Beneath the Red Banner*, by Lao She, trans. Don Cohn (Beijing: Panda Books, 1982), 214. In the Western calendar, this would be February 3, 1899.

3. Vohra mentions the following official positions held by Lao She in the 1950s and 1960s: "People's Representative from Peking City to the National People's Congress; Member of the Chinese People's Political Consultative Conference; Member of the Peking City People's Council; Vice-Chairman of the Federation of Writers and Artists; Chairman of the Peking Writers Union; and Deputy Director of the Peking Russia-China Friendship Association. He was also connected with the organization set up to propagate the standard dialect, with the Federation of Afro-Asian Writers, and the Committee for Looking After Foreign Guests." Vohra, *Lao She and the Chinese Revolution*, 148–149. It is interesting to note that the first position quoted herein was specifically as representative of the Manchus.

4. Fredric Jameson, "Literary Innovation and Modes of Production: A Commentary," *Modern Chinese Literature* 1, no. 1 (1984): 67–72; Edward Gunn, *Rewriting Chinese: Style and Innovation in Twentieth-Century Chinese Prose* (Stanford, Calif.: Stanford University Press, 1991); David Wang, *Fictional Realism in Twentieth-Century China: Mao Dun, Lao She, Shen Congwen* (New York: Columbia University Press, 1992); Lydia Liu, *Translingual Practice: Literature, National Culture and Translated Modernity, 1900–1937* (Stanford, Calif.: Stanford University Press, 1995); Margaret Hillenbrand, "Ambivalent Attitudes to Nationalism in the Prewar Fiction of Lao She," *Archiv Orientalni* 65 (1997): 365–385; Kam Louie, "Constructing Chinese Masculinity for the Modern World: With Particular Reference to Lao She's *The Two Mas*," *The China Quarterly* 164 (2000): 1062–1078; Rey Chow, "Fateful Attachments: On Collecting, Fidelity, and Lao She," *Critical Inquiry* 28, no. 1 (2001): 286–304; Thomas Moran, "The Reluctant Nihilism of Lao She's *Camel Xiangzi*," in *The Columbia Companion to Modern East Asian Literatures*, ed. Joshua Mostow (New York: Columbia University Press, 2003), 4452–4457; Alexander Huang, "Cosmopolitanism and Its Discontents: The Dialectics Between the Global and the Local in Lao She's Fiction," *Modern Language Quarterly* 69, no. 1 (March 2008): 97–118.

5. Louie, "Constructing Chinese Masculinity for the Modern World," 1074.

6. Chow, "Fateful Attachments," 294.

7. These include Pamela Kyle Crossley, *Orphan Warriors: Three Manchu Generations and the End of the Qing World* (Princeton: Princeton University Press, 1991); Edward Rhoads, *Manchus and Han: Ethnic Relations and Political Power in Late Qing and Early Republican China, 1861– 1928* (Seattle: University of Washington Press, 2000); Pamela Kyle Crossley, *A Translucent Mirror: History and Identity in Qing Imperial Ideology* (Berkeley and Los Angeles: University of California Press, 2002); Mark Elliott, *The Manchu Way: The Eight Banners and Ethnic Identity in Late Imperial China* (Stanford, Calif.: Stanford University Press, 2001). For a shorter and contextualizing piece, see Evelyn S. Rawski, "Presidential Address: Reenvisioning the Qing: The Significance of the Qing Period in Chinese History," *Journal of Asian Studies* 55, no. 4 (1996): 829–850. For a summary of some of the main contributions in New Qing History, see Joanna Waley-Cohen, "The New Qing History," *Radical History Review* 88 (2004): 193–206.

8. Rhoads, *Manchus and Han*, 263.

9. Ibid., 270.

10. Ibid., 280.

11. Crossley, *Orphan Warriors*, 228.

12. Ibid., 216.

13. Bady, introduction, xl.

14. Lao She allegedly wrote another novel, *Daming Lake*, in 1932 that was unpublished.

15. In spite of this, Lao She was obliterated for quite a while both in the PRC and in Taiwan. During the Cultural Revolution, he was accused of (and hounded to death for) being an imperialist, and his works were banned in the PRC. See Paul Bady, "On Lao She's 'Suicide,'" in *Two Writers and the Cultural Revolution*, ed. George Kao (Hong Kong: Chinese University Press, 1980), 5–20. In Taiwan his works were never sold either. In the mid-1970s, there was a revived interest in his figure in Hong Kong. He was later rehabilitated in China.

16. Tang Tao, ed., *History of Modern Chinese Literature* (Beijing: Foreign Languages Press, 1998), 254–275.

17. William Lyell, introduction to *Cat Country. A Satirical Novel of China in the 1930s*, by Lao She, trans. William Lyell (Columbus: Ohio State University Press, 1970), xviii.

18. Carlos Prado-Fonts, "*In Alien Nation: Returned Writers in Modern China*" (PhD diss., University of California, Los Angeles, 2011).

19. Lao She, *Zheng hongqi xia*. All subsequent references to this novel will be made in the body of the text. The literal translation of the title should be "Beneath the Plain Red Banner."

24

Found in Translation

Gao Xingjian's Multimedial Sinophone

ANDREA BACHNER

Well into his second novel *One Man's Bible* (1999), the Sino-French writer Gao Xingjian has his protagonist utter the following reflections on literature and identity:

> Can literature and art communicate? It is, in fact, pointless discussing this, but there are people who do believe that this is impossible. And can Chinese literature communicate? Communicate with whom, the West? Or communicate with the Chinese on the Mainland, or with the Chinese living abroad? And what is Chinese literature? Does literature have national boundaries? And do Chinese writers belong to a specific location? Do people living on the Mainland, Hong Kong, Taiwan, and the Chinese-Americans all count as Chinese people? This again, brings in politics, so let's talk just about litera-ture. But what is literature? [...] You're tired of the debate over literature and politics. China is already so remote from you; moreover, you were expelled from the country long ago, and do not need to bear that country's label. You simply write in the Chinese language, and that's all.[1]

These musings, as well as the autobiographical novel itself that alternates between the experiences of a "he" during the Cultural Revolution and the efforts of a "you," a writer and playwright like Gao, to narrate "his" past, resume in condensed form much of the complex situation from which Gao Xingjian himself speaks, writes, and creates. Born in 1940 in China, having lived through the Cultural Revolution, Gao Xingjian fled literary censorship and political persecution in 1987 and has been living in France ever since. His oeuvre, begun in the People's Republic of China (PRC) in the form of translations from the French, a controversial book on Modernist aesthetics, short narratives, plays, and the draft of the novel *Soul Mountain*, has since expanded to include a second novel, more narrative, plays, as well as ink paintings and an experimental film, *Silhouettes/Shadows*, and was awarded the Nobel Prize for literature in 2000.

As the first Nobel Prize to be given to a literary work written in Chinese, it triggered an international debate around issues of literature and national identity politics—the very ideological framework from which Gao wants to extricate himself as far as possible.[2] For the Chinese authorities the decision of the committee to bestow this highest of literary honors upon a dissident writer in French exile equaled a provocation since, in the eyes of the Chinese State that banned Gao's whole work after his play *Escape* (1990), thematizing the 1989 Tiananmen Incident in which state forces violently suppressed a movement for more democratic rights, the author fails to represent Chinese culture. Gao's case is revealing of a paradox inherent in the central role of the Nobel Prize as a measure of literary excellence: whenever a country beyond the North-Atlantic universal[3] seeks recognition of its specific cultural identity by way of this prestigious literary prize, it will always be judged from a Eurocentric perspective that can only (mis)read the other cultural material in translation.[4] Of course, an identity politics that limits every individual cultural expression to one representative of a state or nation is itself highly problematic. Consequently, Gao distances himself and his work from the burden of cultural authenticity and national representation, even though, as his mouthpiece in *One Man's Bible* shows, literature cannot completely escape from politics. Instead of bearing a "country's label," the only culturally specific description his literary alter ego accepts is a linguistic one: "You simply write in the Chinese language, and that's all." No longer defined by nationality, ethnicity, or location, Gao has turned from a Chinese writer into a Sinophone one. To call somebody a "Sinophone" writer can certainly act as an antidote against identity politics, especially to counter the hold that national ideology has on literature. To designate a writer's work as "Sinophone" writing, however, makes it necessary to reconsider what "writing" means, especially given the emphasis on the phonic, not the graphic, of the term *Sinophone*. This becomes particularly important since Sinitic languages, unlike most other languages, are conventionally written in an only partially phonetic script, the Sinograph. In what follows, I will focus on the multimediality of Gao's work in particular and present possible impulses for thinking the "Sinophone" in relation to questions of mediality.

In a lecture given in 1996, "The Modern Chinese Language and Literary Creation," Gao lays out his vision of writing in the medium of the standard Chinese language. His talk focuses on a Sinophone understanding of the Chinese language *avant la lettre*, since he highlights the phonic dimension of his work, both for his plays—where language becomes audible in performance—and for his narrative. In a process of creation that seeks a return to the musicality of Chinese, partially lost in the Western-oriented language reform since the beginning of the twentieth century, the "vibrant sounds in ordinary speech" become the "soul" of writing.[5] Hence Gao's interest in musical form, for instance in the structure of his play *Weekend Quartet* (1995), or the libretto Gao wrote for the opera *Snow in August* (2002).

This emphasis on the phonic, as Gao formulates it, has several repercussions. It seems to enact a turn away from the graphic level of language and toward sound, since Gao understands sound as predating the recording device of writing. It aims at the recreation of a Sinophone expression freed from the influence of Western syntax, even though the modern Chinese language, in Gao's understanding, is inevitably an outcome of historical processes of translation. Even as Gao admits inspiration from the vibrant vocabulary of regional Chinese languages, he aims for a universally understandable Mandarin. Gao's Sinophone ideal also plays itself out on the phonic level that is a virtual projection of his process of writing and sounding out to the virtual voicing of an imagined (Chinese) reader. Musicality seems to rely on a standard pronunciation, since the speaker of another Sinophone language would not actualize the characters phonetically in the same way. Consequently, Gao's Sinophone vision is complicated, since shot through with various inherent processes of translation that exceed the author's control. The standard Chinese language, reshaped partly according to Western models in its phase of modernization, is already a hybrid; different Chinese readers perform the musicality of the written language differently.

The deceptively simple move from identity to language is fraught with problems as well as potential that Gao's case elucidates particularly well. Unlike other successful Chinese writers in France who have opted to write in French, such as writer and director Dai Sijie of *Balzac and the Chinese Seamstress* fame, or the poet and novelist Shan Sa (Ya Nini), Gao continues to write in the Sinitic script—with some more recent notable exceptions, such as the play *The Searcher of Death* (*Le quêteur de la mort*) written in French. Apart from a lively reception in Hong Kong, Taiwan, and the Sinophone world at large, it is most often in translation that his literary work meets its reader's eye. Circulation in translation is the lot not only of those who write in small languages, such as Catalan or Hungarian, but also of those with a vast number of speakers but little visibility on the international (mostly Anglo-centric) literary market.[6] Of course, the Nobel Prize boosts any writer's marketability, and explains why Gao's work has passed the hurdle of translation so well on an international market in which the need to translate from a small or difficult language often makes publishers discount a book for publication.

But for a reader who encounters Gao's work in translation, to call him a Sinophone writer seems to mean even less than the ethnically and linguistically imprecise label "Chinese," since the presence of the Sinitic language gets lost in translation. An absence that is merely visible in the translator's credits ("translated from the Chinese"), it becomes corollary information that allows a reader to create an extratextual image of the author—based partly on the content of Gao's works whenever they are set in China or thematize Chinese culture—as a Han Chinese who writes in the Sinitic script. In translation, disconnected from the linguistic politics and aesthetic strategies that can only be expressed in a specific language, the term *Sinophone* seems to lose its meaning, reducing linguistic specificity to another instance of identity politics external to the work itself but intrinsic to the perception and marketing of its author.

In what follows, I would like to show that the opposite is actually true. Of course, in translation the direct medial and aesthetic force of the Sinophone is lost. But what is found is an indirect return to a kind of Sinophone expression that signifies beyond the Chinese original. Gao's work is so compelling as Sinophone writing, since, even though it cannot escape the elision of linguistic and signifying specificity in translation, it supplements this erasure by continuously stressing the translational nature of artistic creation and reception itself. This does not mean that his work resists translation in that it can only be read in the original—that would itself be a misguided myth of authenticity. Nor does it mean that Gao's work is written with a view to translation, producing a "cozy ethnicity" for consumption in the global market, as Stephen Owen claims of the work of the Chinese poet Bei Dao in a controversial essay.[7] Rather, translation itself is active in Gao's oeuvre long before a translator sets to work.

What I mean by translation is not merely the process of rendering a given text in another language but something more fundamental to the use of language as such, visible whenever signification reaches its limits. In Gao's creative work, translation emerges as an essential necessity as well as impossibility, since language is neither an instrument of a successful intersubjective communication nor a means of unequivocally designating the world of phenomena. A creative universe in which meaning remains cryptic, in which language—both spoken and written—is constantly pushed to its limits, foregrounds language and signification as a question, as it activates translation as a constant strategy of the text, as well as of the reader in the process of making sense. In Gao's case, this does not merely comprise written or spoken language but branches out into a wider, multimedial realm in which meaning is only present once we readers have gone through the painstaking process of translation between media, between different levels of meaning, as well as between different languages. In the face of Gao's rich, varied work, in what follows, I am by no means trying to give a comprehensive overview, but rather discuss specific moments that illustrate the translational nature of Gao's multimedial Sinophone.

One example in which spoken language enters into a process of translation as it is pushed to its limits appears in Gao Xingjian's 1986 play *The Other Shore*, which, as most of his earlier works, shows a decided influence of modernist and absurd theater. After a group of characters reach the other shore after a perilous crossing, they have to relearn language from a female character whom they encounter there. The process of language acquisition proceeds from the referent—the woman points to a hand, a foot—to the production of the correct sound that signifies it. As with children, the travelers have to unlearn a multiplicity of phonic possibilities and single out, as well as produce, the adequate sound:

> 女人 （舉起手）這，是手。
> （眾人含混的聲音在喉嚨裏滾動。）
> 女人　這是手。
> 眾人　（依然含混地）Zh . . . . . . Zhai . . . . . . Zhei . . . . . . Sh . . . . . .
> She . . . . . . Shao . . . . . .
> Shou . . . . . .
> 女人　手——
> 眾人　手 . . . . . . 收 . . . . . . 獸 . . . . . . 手 . . . . . .

> Woman *(Raises her hand.)* Look here, this is a hand.
> *(The Crowd utter muddled sounds from their throat.)*
> Woman This is a hand.
> Crowd (Still mumbling.) The . . . The . . . This . . . ee . . . ha . . . han . . . hand.
> Woman Hand –
> Crowd Hand – band – sand – hand –[8]

In the script, the first phrase is transcribed in alphabetic letters, and then, once the sound has been narrowed down to "shou," in Sinitic characters that can only be sounded with their specific tones. In other words, to notate sound less specifically, without indicating tone, the script of *The Other Shore* has recourse to another phonetic notation tool, one not more, but less precise, namely the alphabetic script. Of course, this translation at play within the script, as a notation at the margins of the Sinophone, becomes invisible, yet audible, in the actual performance and disappears in the translation into languages with phonetic scripts. What does not disappear, however, is the emphasis on the translational quality of linguistic expression as such. If Sinophone specificity—in the form of the tones—is lost in translation, it is first intentionally lost, then found again, in the Chinese text. What continues to be operative however, is the tension between sound and articulated language.

This scene is one of many that specifically highlight the translational tension of Gao's plays that becomes a constant presence throughout his theatrical work and is underlined in the stage indications that Gao provides in his scripts. For instance, in the suggestions for staging *The Other Shore*, the playwright highlights the interplay of spoken language and voiced, inarticulate sound:

> The play's performance strives to expand and not to reduce the expressiveness of language in drama. The language in a play is voiced language, but it is not limited to beautifully written dialogue. In this play, all the sounds uttered by the actor in the prescribed circumstances are also voiced language. If an actor has learned to communicate using fragmented language which features unfinished sentences, disjointed phonetic elements, and ungrammatical constructions, he will be better able to make the unspoken words in the script come to life as voiced language.[9]

In general Gao underscores all dimensions of theatrical performance that exceed linguistic signification as well as mimetic representation: inarticulate sounds, gestures, and movement.

While all these form the very fabric of theater, Gao's plays invest in them especially strongly. Born in the Western-inspired modern Chinese tradition of "spoken drama" (*huaju*), Gao's theater also "translates" (back) into "sound drama" or action drama," thus recuperating, by different means, other Chinese forms of theatrical performance that rely on singing and music, on acrobatic action and symbolic movement, as well as speech.[10] As Gao draws from different culturally coded performance traditions, he insists on pushing the envelope of the mediality of theatrical art.

To stress expressive possibilities beyond the linguistic might account for the lack of resistance that the theatrical text (as performance) opposes to translation. Much as the stereotype of film's supposedly universal (since visual) language, theater, especially whenever it stresses sound and action, might be read as partly independent of linguistic and cultural specificity.

This might have some truth to it, but only when we elide the fact that aural and visual events resemble language in that they rely on a set of conventions in order to be "read." By constantly stressing the margins of signification, the difficulty of constructing meaning, Gao's work is not interested in a smooth erasure of translation, as a turn to a less linguistically oriented theater might suggest at first. Rather, Gao constantly highlights translation as a general, multifaceted process that both encompasses and exceeds the movements between different languages and cultures.

Another scenario emerges in the medium of written language, for instance in Gao's first novel, *Soul Mountain*. As Gao explains in "The Modern Chinese Language and Literary Creation" discussed previously, unlike the polyphonic, multimedial realm of theater, the novel remains tied to the sequence of written language, even though its author means it to be voiced. This is not least because of the dialogic form the novel displays for a large part, consisting in a multiplicity of voices marked by personal pronouns rather than character names.[11] But the example I want to highlight here focuses on the graphic aspect of writing. Split into the two personal pronouns *I* and *you*, the protagonist of Gao's *Soul Mountain* tours remote parts of China— as did the novel's author—in an attempt to escape persecution during the "Campaign Against Spiritual Pollution." Visiting natural reserves and regions where ethnic minorities dwell, eager to witness rituals and folk art that the Cultural Revolution had suppressed, his flight is not only a search for the mysterious Soul Mountain of the title but also an attempt at escaping traumatic history.[12] And yet, history inevitably catches up with him. Wherever he goes, history has already left its mark.[13] An especially dense array of historical inscriptions awaits the protagonist in Chapter 71 of *Soul Mountain*, as he reaches Shaoxing. Here, a tablet commemorating Lu Xun's famous character Ah Q, a monument for the pre-republican revolutionary martyr Qiu Jin, poet Xu Wei's residence, and the tomb of Emperor Yu are juxtaposed: the historical, the mythical, and the fictional placed together to form a palimpsest of different time periods. Against this history, first written in blood, and then immortalized in stone, Gao's protagonist pits another kind of history, one that privileges individual interpretation over and above the structurally integrating sweep of history. It comes in the guise of a reflection on and theory of history on the basis of decrypting—in this case of the unreadable inscription in the tomb of Emperor Yu:

In Yu's tomb there are now artefacts for reference but the experts still cannot decipher the tadpole-like script on the stone epitaph opposite the main hall. I look at it from various angles, ruminate for a long time, and suddenly it occurs to me that it can be read in this way: history is a riddle,

It can also be read as: history is lies
and it can also be read as: history is nonsense
[...]
and furthermore: history is history
and: history is absolutely nothing
even: history is sad sighs
Oh history oh history oh history oh history
Actually history can be read any way and this is a major discovery![14]

The protagonist's fantasizing about a radically different understanding of history becomes possible through a virtual process of translation. The tad-pole-script, a supposedly archaic Chinese script that can no longer be read, forms the basis on which Gao's "I" can invent meaning. Instead of demand-ing a faithful rendering, the very inaccessibility of the tomb inscription frees the creative energy of individual interpretation, leading the protagonist to reflect about the meaning of history: it is characterized as that which cannot be deciphered, likened to an inscription that has turned into empty signifiers of a sign system to which no one has access any longer. History is a riddle. Like an undecipherable series of traces, it suggests meaning, but ultimately means nothing. In its extreme, history thus becomes tautological ("history is history"), a marked absence of signification ("history is absolutely noth-ing"). In the end, it comes to signify two things that are beyond significa-tion proper: one that is beyond meaning, namely affect as expressed in the repeated exclamation "oh history"; and one that is above meaning, the meta-reflection on the manipulativity of history. This series of definitions of his-tory, a list that exhausts different possible readings and endorses none, thus proposes an encrypting, rather than a decrypting of history. Ultimately, his-tory becomes both unreadable—in the sense that it does not really form a coherent, meaningful whole—and immensely readable—a textual produc-tion by and through the reader, of history.

In this scene, translation is presented as a necessary, yet impossible pro-cess. The presence of a Chinese writing system that remains opaque to a Chinese reader (the novel's protagonist) enables a process not so much of deciphering, as of confabulation. This does not mean that translation is futile, but rather that it is essential to any attempt at constructing meaning, even if the emerging sense remains unstable. Much as the protagonist follows impossible, contradictory directions on his journey to Soul Mountain, much as he "translates" the unreadable tomb inscription, the novel ends with the suspension of meaning. And yet, the inability to make sense is not merely a statement of impotence, but also one of possibility, of the chance to continue to engage creatively with the world and its texts in a process of translation:

"While pretending to understand, I still don't understand. The fact of the matter is I comprehend nothing, I understand nothing. This is how it is."[15]

Both examples show a similar process of "Sinophone" translation in the original text, as well as in translation, across different media, rooted both in the phonic and graphic facets of signification. Gao is less interested in highlighting one medium than in pushing artistic creation to and beyond its linguistic limits. What is at stake is not a return to a pure (Chinese) language, but opening up linguistic expressions to the medial realms that border on it, such as sound, visuality, and performance. In the essay in which Gao opens written and spoken language to sound, he also adumbrates the turn from writing, especially in the form of calligraphy, to visual aesthetics. This applies to Gao's painting that, using the traditional medium of ink and paper, but often infused with an effect of depth and perspective more akin to a European tradition, is largely abstract.[16] It also emerges from Gao's first sally into the world of film. His first film, *Silhouette/Shadow*, a cinematic poem, experiments with an unusual combination of text, sound, and image, in which each medium comes into its own as an individual voice in a multimedial canon. One of his collaborators, Alain Melka, applies Gao's editing technique to his multimedial work as a whole:

> Gao's idea of film editing results from the clash between the three independent elements. The amount of discord between them determines the degree of intensity and the desired effect of tension. This tension is expressed in terms of plasticity: from one shot to another, from fiction to painting, or theatre to opera, Gao plays and experiments with lines, colorimetry, rhythms and movements.[17]

The film *Silhouette/Shadow* documents different facets of Gao's oeuvre, as well as mirroring its multimedial appeal. In different ways, a similar multimediality is active in his narrative and theatrical work, as the previous examples show. Most of his individual texts are microcosms that showcase the richness of Gao's creative work as a process of creation in which language is pushed to its limits, along the axes of sound, visuality, and performance. This process elides translation on the one hand, since it branches out into realms that, at first sight, do not need to be translated, since they are independent of linguistic conventions, even though they are not divorced from cultural contexts of apperception. On the other hand, the display of and play between different medial possibilities can themselves be read as processes of translations. The Sinophone in Gao's work is located on a continuum that comprises specific phonic and graphic expressions, but reaches beyond this into linguistically independent, yet not universally intelligible realms of meaning.

Paradoxically, Gao's Sinophone is found in translation, since the tendency of language to reach beyond the Sinophone can also act as a marker of translation. Consequently, the Sinophone is neither totally erased, nor essentialized, thus rendering translation as such impossible. What does Gao's work teach us about the Sinophone? That we should read its *phone* as marker of mediality, expressive of, though not limited to the oral and aural; and its *sino* as marker of linguistic specificity, that is always in excess of itself. As texts that reflect upon signification in different aesthetic, cultural, and medial contexts, Gao's works circumvent identity politics, but not without transporting a profound message concerning linguistic and aesthetic politics.

Notes

1. *One Man's Bible*, trans. Mabel Lee (New York: Harper, 2002), 296.

2. Gao repeatedly stresses the individual voice of the writer, as well as the universal, transnational nature of literature, for instance in his Nobel lecture of 2000: "Literature transcends national boundaries—and through translation it transcends languages, as well as specific social costumes and interhuman relationships created by geographical location and history—to make profound revelations about the universality of human nature." *The Case for Literature*, trans. Mabel Lee (New Haven and London: Yale University Press, 2007), 36.

3. Michel-Rolph Trouillot, "The Otherwise Modern: Caribbean Lessons from the Savage Slot," in *Critically Modern*, ed. B. M. Knauft (Bloomington: Indiana University Press, 2002), 220.

4. A lot has been written about the Nobel Prize controversy concerning Gao, see, for instance, Pascale Casanova's discussion in *The World Republic of Letters*, trans. M. B. DeBevoise (Cambridge, Mass. and London: Harvard University Press, 2004), 151–153 or Kwok-kan Tam's introduction to *Soul of Chaos: Critical Perspectives on Gao Xingjian*, ed. id. (Hong Kong: The Chinese University Press, 2001), 1–20.

5. *The Case for Literature*, 109.

6. See Pascale Casanova's discussion of translation and the literary market in *The World Republic of Letters*, especially the chapter "The Tragedy of Translated Men," 254–302.

7. Stephen Owen, "The Anxiety of Global Influence," *New Republic* (November 19, 1990): 28–32.

8. *Selected Plays by Gao Xingjian* (Hong Kong: Mingbao Publishing, 2001), 13; *The Other Shore: Plays by Gao Xingjian*, trans. Gilbert C. F. Fong (Hong Kong: The Chinese University Press, 1999), 8 for the English translation.

9. Ibid., 44.

10. As Chen Xiaomei points out in her essay, "A *Wildman* Between Two Cultures: Some Paradigmatic Remarks on 'Influence Studies'" *Comparative Literature Studies* 29:4 (1992): 397–416, the tradition of spoken drama in China is a mixed one: even though a "Western" import, modern Western drama has been inspired by non-Western theatrical traditions, such as Japanese Noh drama or Chinese Beijing Opera. Some of Gao's plays, such as *Wildman* (1985), *The Nether City* (1987), and *The Classic of Mountains and Seas* (1992) take up

mythical and folkloric material from different Chinese cultures. Important book-length studies of Gao's theater discuss the different cultural influences on his work, Sy Ren Quah's *Gao Xingjian and Transcultural Chinese Theater* (Honolulu: University of Hawai'i Press, 2004) and Henry (Yiheng) Zhao's *Towards a Modern Zen Theatre: Gao Xingjian and Chinese Theatre Experimentalism* (London: University of London, 2000).

11. For a discussion of Gao's technique of using personal pronouns as protagonists, see Mabel Lee, "Pronouns as Protagonists: On Gao Xingjian's Theories of Narration," *Soul of Chaos*, 235–256.

12. Several critics dwell on Gao's penchant for primitivism, see Jeffrey C. Kinkley, "Gao Xingjian in the 'Chinese' Perspective of Qu Yuan and Shen Congwen," *Modern Chinese Literature and Culture* 14, no. 2 (Fall 2002): 130–162 and Sy Ren Quah's *Gao Xingjian and Transcultural Chinese Theater*, 72–76.

13. For a discussion of *Soul Mountain*'s inscribed landscapes, see Thomas Moran, "Lost in the Woods: Nature in Soul Mountain," *Modern Chinese Literature and Culture* 14, no. 2 (Fall 2002): 207–236.

14. *Soul Mountain*, trans. Mabel Lee (New York: Harper Collins, 2001), 450–451.

15. Ibid., 506.

16. In an interview with Denis Bourgeois, Gao first asserts the difference of painting as a movement beyond signification in comparison to literature, then gives a much more multimedial account in which both types of artistic creation are located on a medial continuum in which sound and image intersect; see *Au plus près du reel* (Paris: éditions de l'Aube, 1997), 47–53. For a discussion of Gao's painting, see Michel Draguet, *Gao Xingjian: le goût de l'encre* (Paris: Hazan, 2002). In *Gao Xingjian's Idea of Theatre: From the Word to the Image* (Leiden, Boston: Brill, 2008), Izabella Labedzka thematizes the multimedial inspirations for Gao's theater (see 103–120).

17. Fiona Sze-Lorrain ed., *Silhouette/Shadow: The Cinematic Art of Gao Xingjian* (Paris: Contours, 2007), 42.

25

Generational Effects in Racialization

Representations of African Americans in
Sinophone Chinese American Literature

SAU-LING C. WONG

In studies of racialization in the United States, the effects of the immigrant experience on the process, hence the differences between foreign- and American-born-generation constructions of another ethnic group, have seldom been considered. As a bilingual scholar conversant with both Anglophone and Sinophone Chinese American literature, I have been struck by how immigrant-generation writers in Chinese represent African American characters in a negative light rarely seen in Anglophone works. Furthermore, the negative portrayals draw upon many of the racist stereotypes prevalent in the American cultural tradition—the very ones denounced and combatted by the Asian American movement of the 1960s and 1970s dominated by English-monolingual, American-born activists.[1] This chapter considers generational effects on racialization as seen in two related but contrasting bodies of work.[2]

African American characters are rare in both Anglophone and Sinophone Chinese American literature, but even so their presence is revealing. Some Anglophone writers active during or influenced by the Asian American "cultural nationalist" period in the 1960s and 1970s have created black characters who are protectors and inspirers of the U.S-born Chinese characters. In Maxine Hong Kingston's autobiographical *The Woman Warrior* (1976), an unnamed black girl protects the protagonist from bullies as she walks from school to her Stockton Chinatown home. In Ruthanne Lum McCunn's historical fiction *Thousand Pieces of Gold* (1981), a black man tells Lalu Nathoy about the freeing of slaves and thus inspires her to fight for her own freedom.

In Gus Lee's 1991 autobiography *China Boy*, the black boy Toussaint teaches street fighting to the protagonist so that he can survive in the rough San Francisco neighborhood to which his immigrant father, in reduced circumstances, has moved the family. And in Gish Jen's 1996 novel *Mona in the Promised Land*, Naomi, the accomplished and militant Harvard roommate of Callie, teaches both Callie and her sister Mona the tenets of the Black Power movement, causing Callie to turn into a politically conscious "Asian American," much to the consternation of her conservative immigrant parents.[3]

It is a historical fact that the Asian American movement indeed based its concept of "Yellow Power" on the "Black Power" model. Among the American-born Chinese activists and writers who spearheaded the movement, blacks were often admired for their outspokenness and radicalism. Frank Chin is well known for advocating an emulative form of "Negroization of the Chinese" (see following)—he considers assimilated Chinese Americans to be Uncle Toms while holding up defiant, aggressive blacks as masculine role models for Asian American men.[4] In recent years, scholarship in (or influenced by) the comparative ethnic studies tradition has increasingly focused on Asian-black cultural interactions.[5]

The belief in yellow-black solidarity that animated cultural nationalism has deep historical roots. Yellows (in this discussion, limited to Chinese Americans) and blacks share a long history of shared exploitation and discrimination at the hands of whites—a common fate epitomized by the "Negroization of the Chinese" first identified by historian Dan Caldwell in 1971.[6] Both groups have a history of traumatic, forcible removal and dispersal: the Middle Passage for black slaves, and the "selling of pigs" for Chinese laborers.[7] In the building of the American nation, yellows in the West and blacks in the South were both exploited for their labor, regarded as subhuman by whites, and targeted for violence and discrimination.[8]

While a small number of Sinophone Chinese American works express a sense of yellow-black solidarity,[9] more commonly, when African American characters appear in Sinophone Chinese American writing by the first generation, they are dehumanized to the point of caricature. Across the decades, from the short fiction of pro-Communist, working-class writers of New York Chinatown in the late 1940s, through the voluminous works of *liuxuesheng wenxue* ("foreign-student literature" or "study-abroad literature") produced by intellectuals of Taiwanese origin in the 1960s through the 1980s, to the immigrant writers from the People's Republic of China since the 1980s, especially working-class producers of *caogen wenxue* ("grassroots literature"), a common racial code operates that uses "blackness" to define and enhance "Chineseness." Black characters may be used to signal the lower limits of the Chinese immigrants' social fall, to serve as stepping stones for their upward climb, to salve their damaged ethnic pride, or to reinforce their sense of moral superiority. Blacks become the screen onto which Chinese immigrants project their disavowed desires, in a process that is heavily gendered and sexualized and typically classed as well.

The derogation of black characters in Sinophone Chinese American literature is partly a reflection of the American racial order. Immigrants often arrive with already-formed racist notions about blacks, from American media images spread abroad. At the same time, as noted by Claire Kim in her theory of "racial triangulation," the positioning of a racialized group is defined not only in a vertical hierarchy of status from the "superior" to the "inferior" but also in a horizontal array of belongingness from "foreigner" to "insider."[10] While Asian Americans may be placed higher than African Americans on the vertical axis, the former's history of putatively voluntary immigration marks them as more foreign than the latter with its history of indisputably "American" slavery. Immigrants are especially vulnerable to the charge of alienness. Given such unstable positioning, depending on shifts in historical conditions, and influenced by mainstream society's fluctuating ideological demands to play yellows against blacks in moments of crisis, a sense of yellow-black divergence rather than yellow-black solidarity is readily invoked by Chinese immigrants to ward off the threat of status loss. African Americans become a crucial boundary marker for Chinese immigrant identity in America's multiracial society, and the presence of blacks serves to index the strategies of identity negotiation deployed by some first-generation writers on behalf of their Chinese immigrant characters.

A few examples will suffice to illustrate this process at work. First, I will examine two stories by Cong Su, a writer from Taiwan active in the 1960s and 1970s. In a story tellingly entitled "The Chinese" (*Zhongguoren*, completed in 1978), we have a variation of an extremely common theme: "the foreign student (*liuxuesheng*) sells his/her soul." In a love triangle, the female *liuxuesheng* Shen Meng dumps her historian boyfriend, Wen Chaofeng, in the American South and marries a successful and assimilated computer scientist in New York City. An aborted attempt to revive the relationship and elope with Shen Meng leaves Wen dejected and pacing the streets near the train station. He runs into a working-class Chinese immigrant, an illegal alien named Ding Changgui, who at that point is battling two black muggers. Ding beats them back. His indomitable fighting spirit inspires Wen to put his past behind him and learn to be a real Chinese (*zhongguoren*) in his heart.

In this scene, Ding is made to represent the ideal, unadulterated Chinese, one who has not sold out like Shen Meng, or even Wen himself, a middle-class intellectual tormented by questions of assimilation. Ding's *zhongguoren* identity is built up from an intricately interwoven set of gender, class, and racial attributes. For example, the Chinese character for the surname, *Ding*, is already thoroughly gendered in traditional Chinese culture, denoting a full-grown male individual in the reckoning of family membership, community strength, and so forth. *Changgui*, which can be read as short for *changming fugui* ("long life and wealth"), is the sort of unsophisticated, earthy name favored by peasants expressing unabashed wishes for physical and material well-being. This confers upon Ding a sort of grassroots, unmediated, and unintellectualized national identity tied to the vast Chinese earth itself. Not only is Ding's immigrant Chinese identity couched in terms of native Chinese tradition, but it is constructed at the expense of the two black characters—the muggers. In contrast to the way they are reduced to brute physicality in mainstream stereotypes, the muggers are described as short and scrawny like "toy soldiers" and like "flies around a piece of watermelon."[11] Ding is the dignified, hardworking Chinese while the black men are shameless, lazy petty thieves and wannabe thugs. Ding calls them "bastards," "black Puerto Rican devils," and "two monkeys."[12] These vicious insults echo the epithets hurled at early Chinese immigrants by whites. Yet not only does the name-calling not diminish Ding in Wen's eyes, but it stirs Wen's blood with nationalism until Ding gradually "grows taller, grows larger" in front of his eyes. Ding is now like "an enduring, unmovable little mountain," and Wen is on the verge of tears.[13]

In another of Cong Su's short stories called "This Half of My Life" (*Zan zhe banbeizi*), we learn that Ding has been involved in a marriage of expediency, a "green card marriage." Having jumped ship in New York, Ding has no way to stay in the United States except by undergoing marriage for a fee with a black woman who has citizenship, then divorcing her after getting his green card or permanent residency. However, the author creates an unmistakable impression that Ding is forced by circumstances to resort to this charade and is free from blame for cultural betrayal. The demeaning manner in which the woman and her male companion are described evokes the worst of mainstream American stereotypes of the black body, which is dehumanized and fragmented into a collection of exaggerated physical attributes, especially sexual characteristics. The entrance of the "bride" and his companion is depicted in farcical terms:

> The meatball is a middle-aged woman in her 40s or 50s, her barrel-shaped body wrapped in red: red sweater, red pants, big boobs, big ass. . . . Her entire body is like an overcooked piece of tofu, puffy and swollen. On her shiny black face are a pair of staring eyes rolled up with too much white showing, an upturned nose, and beneath it a huge mouth, the lips like two crushed sausages painted blood-red. The full head of bristle-like hair is dyed a burnt yellow.[14]

Cong Su represents Ding's racist reaction as a positive sentiment, a sign of Chinese integrity or backbone (*guqi*). Thus a voluntary business transaction, in which both parties should be equal, and equally responsible, partners, is portrayed as featuring a victimizer and a victim. Ding's disavowed desire to partake of the goodies of America by getting a green card is projected as vicious greed on the part of the black woman. The economic circumstances informing Cong Su's story might have suggested a sense of yellow-black solidarity, with poor, limited-English-speaking Chinese immigrants occupying the same urban space as Puerto Ricans racialized as black, and both groups being forced to cooperate for economic survival. Instead, Cong Su has turned to racist representations of blacks as a means of maintaining a sense of a viable, admirable male Chinese diasporic identity in the face of adversity.

Finally, I turn to a recent short story called "Strange Encounters in a Mansion" (*Haozhai qiyuan*) by a writer from the People's Republic of China (PRC), Lao Nan, published in 1997, to show the extent to which Sinophone writers from diverse origins and different time periods share the same racial code while constructing Chinese diasporic identity. In this fantasy of the Chinese immigrant's economic, cultural, and moral vindication, Ma Lang, a fifty-eight-year-old male immigrant from southern China and a Russian major in college, has trouble getting a job in San Francisco. He finally finds a housekeeper position in a fancy mansion. The aristocratic, half-Chinese and half-Kazakh, and bibliophilic mistress favors him for his educated background. This provokes the jealousy of the original housekeeper, a black woman named Diana, who feels displaced and threatened. To this end, she tries to engineer a falling out between Ma Lang and the mistress, but to no avail. Diana is eventually expelled, and the mistress asks Ma's wife to replace Diana, as well as refer more Chinese workers to her.

In this recent story, as in Cong Su's earlier ones, African Americans are called upon to help define the Chinese immigrant's diasporic Chinese identity, at the expense of the dignity of the blacks themselves. Although the mistress is herself a relative newcomer to American society and has some Chinese blood, her half-whiteness, aristocratic upbringing, and immense wealth allow her to be constructed as white, or at least as a stand-in for the white society within Ma's reach. Serving her then becomes a symbol of acceptance by the powerful class; steady employment means securing a clearly defined "place" in American society, and the yellow and the black end up in naked economic competition. Diana is conscious of her unstable positioning in the racial triangle; her advantage on the foreigner/insider dimension (note she is the "original" housekeeper) may be canceled out by Ma's advantage along the superiority/inferiority axis (more education, more refined aesthetic sensibility, closer cultural affinities with the employer). Hence her resentment and desperate machinations. Through the economic outcome of the story (his triumph includes seeing Diana fired, securing Ma's housekeeper job; and getting Ma's wife and friends employed, in other words, becoming a sort of foreman), Lao Nan vindicates Ma's "superiority," which is also presented as a matter of cultural assets and, in the last analysis, of moral fiber.

In order to highlight the contrast between the upright Chinese man and the ignoble black woman, Lao Nan employs every trick in the racial imagery book, applying to Diana the same demeaning, fragmenting, animalizing images that Cong Su had used two decades earlier:

> The woman was very fat. If not for the big, round eyes and thick, black lips as well as the two rows of snow-white teeth, one would have thought a black bear was standing there. Ma Lang had never seen people with this skin color. The moment they met, he sensed a repulsive stench coming from her.[15]

Beast-like in appearance, Diana is also beast-like in her lack of morals. She schemes to get Ma into trouble with the boss (which then backfires on herself). What is more, she is grossly oversexed—another white stereotype of blacks that the Chinese immigrant writer uncritically inherits. One night, while Ma is suffering from insomnia, he senses Diana breaking into his bedroom wearing a diaphanous nightgown ("thin as a cicada's wings," as the Sinophone expression goes):

> Ma was about to open his eyes when he felt Diana leaning down to plant a kiss on his cheek. Then she started caressing and gently squeezing his private parts. . . . Diana held on tightly to the Chinese man as to a prey, as if she feared it would escape.[16]

When Ma resists, Diana threatens: "If you don't do as I say, I will scream that you're trying to rape me!"[17]

In this reversal of a common sexual drama—a man trying to rape a woman and threatening to tell on her—Lao Nan has assembled another wish-fulfillment fantasy to preserve the masculinity (hence the Chineseness) of the immigrant man. In mainstream American culture, Asian men have long been the victims of symbolic castration, and middle-aged, lightly assimilated recent immigrant men are especially dismissed as objects of sexual desire.[18] Lao Nan's "black woman attempting to rape yellow man" scenario rehabilitates the immigrant man's sexual desirability. At the same time, because the desire originates from a black woman, Ma Lang is free to refuse her—indeed, is obligated to refuse her—and thus preserve his moral superiority as a Chinese intellectual.[19]

Black Americans are thus an integral, albeit frequently obscured, component in the mechanisms of Chinese diasporic identity construction. An examination of the meaning of the black presence in the fiction by and about yellow immigrants compels us to reconsider such common but potentially essentialist terms as "Chinese identity," "Chineseness," and even "Chinese culture." Using a more materialist perspective, and locating Chinese immigrants squarely in the multiracial environment of the United States, I will analyze the process of simultaneous construction of the identity of yellows and blacks (typically with the whites implicated, even if not named), as well as the complex gender, sexuality, and class dimensions in the identity negotiations of Chinese immigrants.

While yellow-black antagonism is certainly not limited to the first generation, immigrants have been more susceptible to what Barry Sautman has identified as "theories of East Asian intellectual and behavioral superiority and discourse of 'race differences,'"[20] and with the increasing prominence of the foreign-born in the Chinese American population (as much as 72 percent, according to the 2000 U.S. Census),[21] whatever ethnocentric tendencies attributable to discourses of superiority could only be magnified. The model minority image, which arose in response to the agitations by people of color in the 1960s, has been eagerly embraced by many Chinese immigrants. There is also the perception of "demotion" from the majority to a minority—only one among many minorities, and not even the largest or most respected one. However hard life has been before immigration, Chinese subjects (at least Han ones) could still consider themselves part of the "natural" population of the nation; once in the United States, however, the immigrants are "lumped together," willy-nilly, with other groups of color. This coming down in the world is especially and acutely felt by those belonging to the elite in China before emigration. As the protagonist in Gish Jen's novel *Mona in the Promised Land* says of her immigrant parents: "They say they were never a minority when they were in China, why should they be a minority now?"[22] This is a sentiment that many Chinese immigrants subscribe to and that is occasionally reflected in Sinophone Chinese American writing. The kind of respect or admiration for blacks expressed by writers like Frank Chin or Gus Lee might strike these immigrants as utterly incomprehensible.

Given all this, then, Chinese immigrants must be understood as existing not simply in an amorphous or homogenous "American society" or "American culture" but in an internally diverse social environment comprised of differentially racialized groups. According to Claire Jean Kim's theoretical model of "racial triangulation," the positioning of a racialized group is defined not only in a vertical hierarchy of status from the "superior" to the "inferior," but also in a horizontal array of belongingness from "foreigner" to "insider."

On the vertical axis of a graph, yellows would be positioned below whites and above blacks. However, the history of putatively voluntary immigration marks them as more foreign than blacks, who, because of their history of forced slavery, cannot be seen as other than an integral part of American society. Thus, on the horizontal axis, yellows would be located to the left (the "foreigner" end) while whites and blacks are on their right.

This kind of multidimensional complexity provides maneuvering room for the ideological needs of white society. When the dominant group needs to divert attention from its responsibility for racial injustice, yellows are lauded for their industry, discipline, and contentment with the status quo, and other "model minority" attributes, thereby turning the sociostructural problems of blacks into private, personal failures. In other words, the superiority/inferiority dimension is invoked. On the other hand, when yellows need to be curtailed, the foreigner/insider dimension comes into play. Yellows are represented as the Yellow Peril—culturally unassimilable and ideologically suspect perpetual foreigners, whose claims to Americanness (and any of its attendant privileges) are much more recent and shaky than those of blacks, and therefore deserving of the latter's enmity. The points on the racial triangle are thus not fixed but highly unstable, creating a lot of space for a racialized subject's identity negotiations.

What is remarkable about the two sets of stories analyzed herein is that, despite vast differences in authorship, setting, and characters, the same racial lexicon is drawn upon, and the same racialization maneuvers are made, in order to subtend the protagonist's diasporic Chinese identity. The same dehumanization of black characters is deployed to underwrite the protagonist's idealized Chinese diasporic identity in gendered and sexualized terms. This suggests an enduring role for race as an experiential substrate as well as an interpretive medium.

Notes

This chapter is adapted and translated from my "The Yellow and the Black: Chinese and Blacks in the Works of Chinese Writers in America" (*Huang yu hei: meiguo huawen zuojia bijia de huaren yu heiren*) in a special issue on Sinophone American literature (*Meiguo Huawen wenxue*), ed. Te-hsing Shan, *Zhongwai wenxue* [Chung Wai literary monthly] 34, no. 4 (2005): 15–54. The original includes close readings of a number of short stories from the 1940s to the 1990s. From the original acknowledgments, I wish to reiterate my gratitude to Te-hsing Shan for the invitation to contribute in Chinese; Iyko Day for her tireless and expert research assistance; and Sylvia Chan for bringing to my attention Claire Jean Kim's theory of racial triangulation.

1. For the limited purposes of this essay, "first-generation" and "Sinophone" are used more or less interchangeably, as are "U.S.-born generation" and "Anglophone." However, there are a significant number of immigrant writers who publish in English. I am not aware of American-born Chinese writers publishing in Chinese. My usage of "Sinophone" here is strictly descriptive to distinguish Chinese American works written in the Sinitic script from those written in English. It differs from Shu-mei Shih's much broader and theoretically substantive usage of the term in the introduction to this volume.

2. A note on terminology: Whenever *racial* or *race* is used in this essay, the assumption is that the term does not refer to a biologically defined population but to a socially constructed identity. Thus, for example, Puerto Ricans are referred to as "black" without qualification when an author describes them as "black." All terms used to refer to a racialized group are necessarily suffused with history and evoke different connotations. Labels like *Negro, Colored, Black* (capitalized), *black* (lower case) *African American* (without hyphen), *African-American* (with hyphen), and so forth, each has its adherents and detractors. For the limited purposes of this essay, I use *African American* and *black* more or less interchangeably.

3. Maxine Hong Kingston, *The Woman Warrior: Memoir of a Girlhood Among Ghosts* (New York: Knopf, 1976); Ruthanne Lum McCunn, *Thousand Pieces of Gold: A Biographical Novel* (San Francisco: Design Enterprises of San Francisco, 1981); Gus Lee, *China Boy* (New York: Dutton, 1991); and Gish Jen, *Mona in the Promised Land* (New York: Knopf, 1996).

4. See Frank Chin, "Confessions of a Chinatown Cowboy," *Bulletin of Concerned Asian Scholars* (Fall 1972): 58–70; and "Back-Talk," in *Counterpoint: Perspectives on Asian America,* ed. Emma Gee (Los Angeles: University of California Press, 1976), 556–557.

5. This is a burgeoning area of research. A number of scholars using ethnic studies methodology have traced Asian-black connections, including Daniel Y. Kim, *Writing Manhood in Black and Yellow: Ralph Ellison, Frank Chin, and the Literary Politics of Identity* (Stanford, Calif.: Stanford University Press, 2005); James Kyung-Jin Lee, *Urban Triage: Race and the Fictions of Multiculturalism* (Minneapolis: University of Minnesota Press, 2004); Julia Hyoun Joo Lee, "Almost American: Narratives of Inclusion in Asian American and African American Literatures, 1896–1937" (PhD diss., University of California, Los Angeles, 2005); and LeiLani Nishime, "'I'm Blackanese': Buddy-Cop Films, *Rush Hour*, and Asian American and African American Cross-Racial Identification," in *Asian North American Identities: Beyond the Hyphen*, ed. Eleanor Rose Ty and Donald C. Goellnicht (Bloomington: Indiana University Press, 2004), 43–60.

6. Dan Caldwell, "The Negroization of the Chinese Stereotype in California," *Southern California Quarterly* 53, no. 2 (June 1971): 123–131.

7. The "selling of pigs" (*mai zhuzai*) is a slang term referring to the so-called "coolie trade," which often involved kidnapping, trickery, and abusive treatment. "Coolies" were shipped in vessels under inhumane conditions reminiscent of those on slave ships.

8. This is, of course, a highly simplified account. A study like Jung's illustrates the immense complexities in racialization and other matters in a given yellow-black connection.

9. For example, see Xiang Cha's "New Year's Banquet" (*Chunyan*) and Bai Fei's "An Afternoon in Late Autumn" (*Yige shenqiu de xiawu*), both of which are short stories from a short-lived literary magazine entitled *The Bud* (*Xinmiao*), which was published in New York's Chinatown in the late 1940s.

10. Claire Jean Kim, "The Racial Triangulation of Asian Americans," *Politics and Society* 27, no. 1 (March 1999): 105–138.

11. Cong Su, *Zhongguoren* [The Chinese] (Taipei: Shibao wenhua, 1978), 232–233.

12. Ibid., 232–238.

13. Ibid., 237.

14. Cong Su, "This Half of My Life" (*Zan zhe ban beizi*), in *Haiwai huaren zuojia xiaoshuo xuan* [Selected short stories by overseas Chinese writers] (Hong Kong: Sanlian shudian Xianggang fendian, 1983), 416.

15. Lao Nan, *Haozhai qiyuan* [Strange encounters in a mansion] (Shenyang: Shenyang chubanshi, 1997), 220.

16. Ibid., 232.

17. Ibid.

18. Early male Chinese immigrants were portrayed as sexual perverts who lured innocent white women into opium dens and laundries in order to violate them (Ronald T. Takaki, *Iron Cages: Race and Culture in 19th Century America*, rev. ed. [New York: Oxford University Press, 2000], 217; Tomas Almaguer, *Racial Faultlines: The Historical Origins of White Supremacy in California* [Berkeley: University of California Press, 1994], 160). That these images are not of "desexualization" or "emasculation" does not, however, mean that Chinese men were considered socially approved objects of sexual desire.

19. Xiao-huang Yin suggests a different ideological valence and function for Chinese immigrant men's sexual liaisons with white women depicted in Sinophone Chinese American literature. See Xiao-huang Yin, *Chinese American Literature since the 1850s* (Urbana: University of Illinois Press, 2000), 165–166.

20. Barry Sautman, "Theories of East Asian Intellectual and Behavioral Superiority and Discourses of 'Race Differences,'" *positions: east asia cultures critique* 4, no. 3 (1996): 519–567.

21. Yu Xie and Kimberly A. Goyette, *A Demographic Portrait of Asian Americans* (New York: Russell Sage Foundation / Washington, D.C.: Population Reference Bureau, 2004).

22. Gish Jen, *Mona in the Promised Land*, 52.

26

At the Threshold of the Gold Mountain

Reading Angel Island Poetry

TE-HSING SHAN

The ambivalence of hope and despair, longing and suffering expressed by the detainees on an island—the *Angel* Island, a place crowded with *fan, man, yi, hu,* or barbarians, dominated by *baigui* ("white devils")—finds its way into many Sinophone poems. The poems' vicarious presence on the walls of buildings on Angel Island first fell into oblivion before it was made known to the public years later. Among all Sinophone literary productions, Angel Island poetry is possibly the most peculiar one. These poems were originally written by immigrants from China who were detained at the Angel Island Immigration Station just outside of San Francisco during the period 1910 to 1940, when the majority of 175,000 immigrants used this site as their port of entry into the United States.

First written down and then carved on the wooden walls by the immigrants on their way to the United States (*meiguo* or, literally, "Beautiful Country") or back to China (*zhongguo* or, literally, "Middle Kingdom"), these poems escaped public memory after the immigration station was destroyed in a fire and was forced to close down in 1940. It was not until 1970 that these poems first came to the notice of park ranger Alexander Weiss. Notwithstanding, Weiss's discovery received no attention from his superiors. Through the concerted effort of the Asian American community, however, this building was preserved in 1976 as a living monument in the history of the Asian American immigrants. As a result, these poems have become the textual evidence of one of the saddest chapters in the history of American immigration.

In fact, Chinese immigration to the United States has a history spanning more than two centuries. Sucheng Chan designates four distinctive periods: "years of free immigration from 1849 to 1882; an age of exclusion from 1882 to 1943; a period of limited entry under special legislation from 1943 to 1965; and an era of renewed immigration from 1965 to the present."[1] Seen from this scheme, the Island poems produced between 1910 and 1940 fall exactly into the second period of exclusion.[2] Institutional acts such as the Chinese Exclusion Laws in 1882, the antimiscegenation laws, and the modeling of Angel Island after Ellis Island as a filtering center primarily for the Chinese immigrants were indeed the American government's response to the pervasive anti-Chinese sentiments. Some of the testimonies of the Chinese immigrants showed that they were aware of this unequal treatment due to the weakness of their motherland. Some Japanese immigrants could go ashore to San Francisco very quickly, while their Chinese counterparts had to stay on Angel Island from several days and up to three years.[3] The number of detainees was between 230 and 350,[4] and sometimes up to 700.[5] A few of them tried to escape and even committed suicide. Moreover, the discriminatory treatment left an indelible mark on the psyche of the Chinese American immigrants passing through Angel Island.

Although those immigrants expressed themselves by writing and carving on the wooden walls of the detention camp, it was not until the publication of these poems in an English-Chinese bilingual format in 1980 that those unique literary expressions became available to a much wider audience and further testified to the inner world of the suffering detainees.[6] This collection was done collaboratively by three descendants of those who passed through the Angel Island immigration station. In addition to laboriously trying to recover the original Chinese texts as best as they could, the historian Him Mark Lai provided historical information and annotations of literary and cultural allusions; the poetess Genny Lim polished the poetical texts; and the librarian and historian Judy Yung conducted the interviews. Such efforts, coupled with the inclusion of twenty-two old photos, make this volume a highly graphic work, standing as a powerful testament to the conditions at the time.

In terms of the poetic forms, the Island poems mostly adopt the popular traditional Chinese poetic forms of *wuyan jueju* (five-character quatrain), *wuyan lüshi* (five-character regulated verse), *qiyan jueju* (seven-character quatrain), and *qiyan lüshi* (seven-character regulated verse). As the editors and translators note:

All of the poems [totaling 135] are written in the classical style. Of these, about half [73] are written with four lines per poem and seven characters per line. About a fifth [30] have eight lines per poem and seven characters per line. The remainder consist of verses with six or more than eight lines and five or seven characters per line. There are also a few poems with lines of four characters each, as well as several couplets and one long composition written in the *pianwen* style (a euphuistic style utilizing parallel-constructed couplets with antithetical meanings), published in a San Francisco Chinese newspaper.[7]

The Angel Island poems are, as such, Sinophone texts produced by those who went to the United States, hoping for better life. Yet they were detained at the threshold of the gold mountain. In comparison with literary productions by other Sinophone writers, these poems were originally written not with an intention to get published but as a way to express the sense of fear, frustration, and anger of those who were suspended between their homeland in China and their dreamland in the United States. So far as the literary merits are concerned, these poems do not meet the criteria normally required of the Chinese literati. However, they did catch a specific juncture in Chinese and American history—and Chinese American history, for sure—and provide vivid and heart-wringing textual evidence to the collective fate of those immigrants.

Taken as a whole, these poems are significant in several aspects. First, since they were written and carved on the walls of the immigration camp, especially "the hall leading to the basketball court, because the wood there was softer,"[8] the very materiality of these literary expressions bespeaks the dire situation of these Chinese detainees and their desire to address it directly. Second, ironically enough, these Sinophone texts obtain a more comprehensive representation and reach a much wider circulation through a bilingual text only after half a century or so. Third, these sad, angry, and bitter poems by the Chinese immigrants who had some training in classical Chinese literature seek to express the deep feelings of anticipation and frustration, as well as resentment toward discrimination and maltreatment at the very threshold of San Francisco (*jiujinshan* or, literally, "Old Gold Mountain"). Fourth, the very anonymity of these poems, while creating a sense of collectivity among the detainees, reflects their fear that this vent of anger, the feeling of uncertainty about their own fate, and the strong sense of injustice might put them in an unfavorable and even perilous situation as they wait for the decision of the immigration officials. Fifth, the fact that all of these poems are written by men shows clear signs of the traditional Chinese patriarchy that invested education on the male and regarded that "So far as women are concerned, possessing no talent is itself a virtue."[9] Sixth, though without identifiable authorship, these poems are dialogical in nature not only because these anonymous writers deal with similar themes—some even echo each other as in an established convention of classical Chinese poetry—but also because through the literary and historical allusions in the poems, these poets come to envision themselves as in a similar situation with ancient Chinese heroes who persevered in hard times and were finally able to bring fame and fortune to themselves and their posterity—even to avenge themselves against their malefactors. Seventh, these poems collectively speak about the immigrant experience in a particular historical moment in Chinese, Asian, and American history, and, as important founding texts of Chinese American history/literature, offer an alternative to American (literary) history.[10] Last, but not least, these bilingual revisions and reinscriptions of the bygone days are oriented not only toward the past (as the epitaph of the collection suggests: "Dedicated to the Pioneers/Who Passed Through Angel Island" or *jingyang qianxian* [literally, "Paying homage to former sages"]) and the present, but also toward the future, as the editors say, "making this collection available to posterity."[11]

In addition to their materiality, one of the most conspicuous characteristics of these literary productions is their in-between status that can be interpreted at least in two ways. On the one hand, in terms of history and geography, these anonymous authors over a period of three decades were detained on Angel Island and literally suspended between China and the United States on their way to the Gold Mountain. On the other hand, in terms of language and literature, neither the original Sinophone texts nor their bilingual representations catch much attention of the English- and Chinese-speaking worlds or the respective critical circles. If a literary anthology somehow symbolizes the canon, the fact that Island poetry was denied entry to the canon is similar to the Chinese immigrants' being denied entry to the country.[12]

As a result of the occasional loose construction, empty words, forced imagery, violation of rhythm, cadence, and rhyme scheme, or even incompleteness, these poems cannot claim to meet the formal requirements of classical Chinese poetry and to fulfill the "literary" standard of the language in which they were written. Nor can the free-verse rendition of these poems, with their "exotic" allusions, boast high aesthetic value according to the criteria of English poetry. Similar to the immigrant authors of *Songs of Gold Mountain*, these writers on the walls are "unrecognized by the literary establishments in either China or the United States."[13] However, it is exactly this in-between status and conjunctional position, linguistically and culturally speaking, that characterize their historical specificity and lay claim to the Asian American sensibility or, to be more precise, Sinophone sensibility.[14]

Since the Island poems have been made widely available through the bilingual volume, it is almost impossible to discuss them as Sinophone texts without referring to their bilingual representation. Judging from the rich literary and historical materials of the Island poems, and the way of representation (the introduction and interviews are in English) in the volume, we may say that the target audience is primarily Anglophone, while the ideal reader is an Anglophone-Sinophone bilingual reader with some knowledge of Cantonese and pidgin English. The editors separate the collection into two major parts: the first part consists of sixty-nine poems that are subdivided into five groups ("The Voyage," "The Detainment," "The Weak Shall Conquer," "About Westerners," and "Deportees, Transients"); and the second part consists of sixty-six poems.[15] However, the richness and diversity of these poems defy such a facile categorization. One of the pervading themes is the recounting of the motivation or driving force behind this massive emigration of people from China: the weakness of the nation and the poverty of the family. Here, the national, the communal, the familial, and the personal intertwine. Themes include primarily: the economic pressure that forces the breadwinner to separate from his beloved ones and leave his home country for the Gold Mountain; the risks on the high seas; the suffering and maltreatment due to discriminatory acts; the high anticipation and heart-breaking frustration; the anxiety of being suspended and having no idea of one's own fate; the sorrow for the weakness of the nation, and so forth. All these are set in a historically and geographically specific juncture between China and the United States.

Whereas these themes permeate the whole collection, I will focus on three culturally specific aspects in these poems: the allusions to Chinese historical figures, the attitudes toward the Westerners, and a parody of a famous Chinese paired prose, "Muwu Ming" ("Inscription About a Wooden Building" [A33]). The names of the historical figures these poems refer to are many, and span over a period of hundreds or even thousands of years. All these figures—only one female (Xishi [B28]) and one Westerner (Napoleon [A60])—bear resemblance to the detainees. Among them, Taozhugong (Lord Taozhu [A11, A43]), probably *the* first famous man of fortune in Chinese history, serves as a symbol of success and thus the motivation behind the immigration. In these poems, Taozhugong appears as the only person with untainted success. All other historical figures suffer and bide their time one way or another. Among the twenty or so figures, I will discuss six who are mentioned most frequently and/or are of special historical and cultural significance: Wu Yuan (A18, B33, B39), King Wen (A20, A57, A59), Su Wu (A30, A57, B33), Ruan Ji (A30, A43, A62), Zu Di (A40, A69, B16), and Confucius (A28, B34).[16] Since these poems are composed anonymously and oftentimes echo one another, these references to historical figures obtain a certain degree of collectivity.

What characterizes these six persons is the theme of misfortune and confinement, and some of them also share the theme of revenge. Take King Wen, for example. As the annotation explains:

> King Wen (ca. 12th century, B.C.), founder of the Zhou state, was held captive at Youli because the last Shang king, Zhou (1154–1122 B.C., different Chinese character from the preceding), regarded him as a potential threat to Shang rule. His son, King Wu (1134–1115 B.C.) later did defeat the Shang and establish the Zhou dynasty (1122–249 B.C.).[17]

This legendary Chinese cultural hero (as the name *Wen* denotes "culture") was a man of humility, gentleness, and talents. He was able to serve the tyrannical and then overwhelmingly powerful Shang king without openly offending him so as to get killed. In his confinement, he annotated *I Ching* (*The Book of Changes*). After his release, he was still able to serve the tyrant and, in the meantime, attracted men of talent from all directions. It is on this firm foundation that his son King Wu (literally, "King of Martial Prowess") came to defeat the former ruler and enemy. Confucius, another annotator of *I Ching*, was among one of the earliest admirers of King Wen. Here the theme of confinement and suffering from a hegemonic power is more than obvious, whereas the theme of productivity, perseverance, and revenge is also implied. Confucius, the archetypal Chinese teacher and philosopher, is the one that generations of Chinese scholars have aspired to and identified with. The invocation of Confucius, who once suffered from confinement and starvation, surely gives comfort to these writers on the walls of the detention camp.

The allusions to Ruan Ji (210–263 c.e.) are also interesting. In Poem A30, one line reads: "When Ruan Ji reached the end of the road, he shed futile tears."[18] Two other poems also refer to this aspect of the scholar who is famous for enjoying "drinking and visiting mountains and streams." As the annotation indicates, "[o]ften when he reached the end of the road, he would cry bitterly before turning back."[19] It is this sense of loss and being-at-the-end-of-the-road that appeals to the detainees who could only shed idle tears. Yet, this passivity is merely one aspect of the complex feelings of the immigrants.

The same poem also alludes to Su Wu (140–60 b.c.e.), an envoy of the Western Han Dynasty to "Xiongnu, a nomadic people north of the Chinese empire."[20] Detained by the barbarian tribe for nineteen years, Su remained loyal to his emperor and was finally able to return to his home country with honors. This theme of prolonged exile and unflagging loyalty shows both the immigrants' innermost feelings on Angel Island and suggests the similarity between countries past and present, between Xiongnu and the United States. A hint of nationalism is to be detected in this allusion.

This theme of nationalism is further combined with the theme of barbarism/culture, Other/China in the allusions to Zu Di. As a general, Zu Di and his comrades were always obsessed with the idea of driving away the barbaric enemy who took possession of their territory. The allusions to Wu Yuan carried home the theme of revenge. The only survivor of his family, Wu Yuan, "who endured and hid" in a miserable life abroad, was "able to redress his grievance" (B39) by "[digging] up the corpse of the former king and whip[ping] it 300 times."[21] In other words, the allusions to Zu Di and Wu Yuan, with their aspiration for national recovery and revenge, express the fierce and aggressive side of their feelings. The previous discussion shows that most of these historical figures are remarkable for a special kind of heroism: although suffering from confinement, exile, homesickness, discrimination, and frustration, they are able to persevere and wait for a time to fulfill their wishes and even to take revenge themselves.

Written by Chinese males, these poems make rare references to female historical figures and foreigners. However, when female figures are referred to, references are made by way of pun. The line with reference to Xishi (B28), one of the four most beautiful women in Chinese history, reads, "Xishi always lives in golden houses."[22] In their annotations, the translators shrewdly observe that "Xishi is used here as an oblique reference to Westerners or Americans, since 'Xi' is the character for 'West' and Xishi is a beauty or 'mei-ren,' also the term for 'American.'"[23] Nonetheless, here Xishi is mentioned in contrast to the writer because immediately after the preceding line the poem reads, "Only the dirt walls and bamboo matted window are left for me."[24]

The allusion to Napoleon is intriguing in several ways. First, he is invoked to give comfort to the detainees, for "[e]xperiencing a little ordeal is not hardship. /Napoleon was once a prisoner on an island."[25] In this case, Napoleon seems to serve the same function as the Chinese historical figures mentioned before, though the very allusion to him might reveal some misreading of Napoleon's life history on the part of the writer.

What is of special interest is the pun produced via this cross-linguistic transaction. To fit into the metrical scheme, the Chinese translation/transliteration of "Napoleon," instead of being a three-character *napolun*, takes the form of *polun*. Judging from the fact that Angel Island can be simply transliterated as *ailun* (throughout the collection and even the English and Chinese titles of the book), it is not unreasonable to interpret *polun* along the theme of revenge by understanding *po* literally as "break" or "destroy" and *lun* as a short form of "Island."[26]

This interpretation of *polun* as a pun, hinting at "breaking Island" or "destroying Island," not only goes with the revenge theme that permeates many poems but also gains support from another play upon words. In the seven-character quatrain A46, as the editors are insightful to point out, "the first character of each line [*ai lun dai chan*] forms a sentence, 'Island awaits leveling.'"[27] We may therefore play upon this pun: It takes a *polun* (Napoleon) to *polun* (destroy [Angel] Island).

Some of the misfortune of the historical figures discussed herein is due to their contact with another powerful, foreign, and unjust presence. For instance, Su Wu's suffering came from the barbarian tribe's refusal to abide by the diplomatic protocols. This enmity toward non-Chinese peoples is also evident in many of the poems. With her long-standing sense of cultural superiority, China has had different names for the surrounding "barbarian" tribes in four directions: *dongyi* (Eastern barbarians), *xirong* (Western barbarians), *nanman* (Southern barbarians), and *beidi* (Northern barbarians). Even today, the Chinese name of China is unequivocally "Middle Kingdom" or "the Center of the Earth," suggesting that other countries are geographically and thus culturally marginal and peripheral. In some historical moments, however, China suffered from weakness and invasions from outside. Therefore, it is not unusual that this sense of cultural pride is sometimes mingled with an awareness of military and economic weakness.

This peculiar situation is evidenced by another poem. Although the detained poet is at the mercy of the immigrant official, he still treats the latter as a barbarian: "When I am idle, I have this wild dream / That I have gained the western barbarian's consent to enter America."[28] In this collection, the bad names applied to the Westerners/Americans are numerous: *fannu* ("barbarian" A7, A48, B55), *manyi* ("barbarian" A52), *hu* ("barbarian" A57, B34, B44), *gui* ("devils" B49, B50), *wuqing baigui* ("heartless white devils" B4), *langyi* ("savage [literally "wolf-like"] doctors" B51).

Some of these poets, especially those destined to be deported back to China, did not hesitate to pour their hatred against the "barbarians": "I am now being deported back to my country. / Some day when we become rich and strong, we will annihilate this barbaric nation" (B39); "The day my compatriots become prosperous and return to China, / They should once more outfit battleships to punish America" (B40); "Some day after China rises and changes, / She will be adept at using bombs to obliterate America" (B41); "The day our nation becomes strong, / I swear we will cut off the barbarians' heads" (B44); and "If there comes a day when China will be united, / I will surely cut out the heart and bowels of the western barbarian" (B46). Since Japan invaded China and dealt another blow to the already bad rural economy, these Japanese *wonu* ("dwarves") were also to be "annihilated" (B43). This peculiar combination of a strong sense of cultural superiority and an acute awareness of military and economic inferiority can be clearly seen from the way these poets refer to the Other. As a matter of fact, written in classical

Chinese poetic forms and without the poets' real names, these poems are more in the nature of verbal vent than real threat.

The feelings of the detainees are sometimes expressed in a subtle and even somewhat humorous way, as the following writing illustrates. As a parody of a famous piece of paired prose "Loushi Ming" ("Inscription About a Humble House," written by Liu Yuxi [772–842 C.E.]), the following "Muwu Ming" ("Inscription About a Wooden Building") imitates verbatim the sentence structure, rhythm, and rhymes of Liu's prose, yet it twists the theme in a completely opposite direction and depicts the plight of those living in the wooden building on Angel Island:

INSCRIPTION ABOUT A WOODEN BUILDING

A building does not have to be tall; if it has windows, it will be bright.
Island is not far, Angel Island.
Alas, this wooden building disrupts my travelling schedule.
Paint on the four walls are green,
And green is the grass which surrounds.
It is noisy because of the many country folk,
And there are watchmen guarding during the night.
To exert influence, one can use a square-holed elder brother [money].
There are children who disturb the ears,
But there are no incoherent sounds that cause fatigue.
I gaze to the south at the hospital,
And look to the west at the army camp.
This author says, "What happiness is there in this?"[29]

Whereas the original celebrates the carefree, pleasant, pastoral, and humble life of a man whose sense of satisfaction is communicated through a tender and humorous inscription about his shabby yet happy house, the parody mourns the difficult situation of those living in the wooden building on Angel Island. Consequently, playful as this parody might appear, the contrast between the humble house in an ancient idyllic China and the wooden building in a far-away country opposite the Pacific Ocean under the rule of barbarians is sharp indeed. So doing, the poet subtly inscribes the heart-rending predicament of the Chinese immigrants on this woeful Island. As Stan Yogi points out, "the island has come to symbolize the hardships endured by these early Chinese immigrants, who often underwent intense interrogations before being allowed into the U.S."[30]

Bearing witness to "the canonical Chinese American experience of the period,"[31] Angel Island has thus become not only a site of memory, but also a site of resistance where meanings can be constantly invested and contested, especially from the subject position of Chinese Americans. As a work of reclamation and verbal commemoration, *Island* with its bicultural profundity and historical complexity reinscribes and circulates the poems penned down or carved by the Chinese immigrants on the walls of the detention camp. This very act of reinscription, highlighting its peculiar materiality and textuality, characterizes a specific historicity in Chinese-American encounter, and, from this particular position, expresses a unique Chinese-American experience and sensibility. No longer insignificant to both Chinese and American literature, these Sinophone poems have moved from the margins of two literary traditions to their intersection.[32]

Notes

This chapter is an adaptation of my previously published chapter "Carved on the Walls: The Archaeology and Canonization of the Angel Island Chinese Poems," in *American Babel: Literatures of the United States from Abnaki to Zuni*, ed. Marc Shell (Cambridge: Harvard UP, 2002), 369–385.

1. Sucheng Chan, *Asian Americans: An Interpretive History* (Boston: Twayne, 1991), viii.

2. On the other hand, the selection of these poems falls into "The Modern Period: 1910–1945" in the *Heath Anthology of American Literature* (1990) edited by Paul Lauter. The fact that 1910 marks both the establishment of Angel Island as an immigrant station and the beginning of the modern period in American literature is purely coincidental. What is more significant to the Chinese mentality or national spirit is the Chinese revolution in 1911 that established the first republic in Asia. Moreover, for Chinese immigrants to the United States, 1943 was the year when the U.S. Congress repealed the Chinese Exclusion Laws, whereas 1945 marks the end of World War II when China finally obtained an equal status in the international community after decades of unequal treaties with many foreign countries, including the United States. For a discussion of the Angel Island poems and the literary productions of Anglo-American High Modernism, see Steven G. Yao's discussion in "Transplantation and Modernity: The Chinese/American Poems of Angel Island," in *Sinographies: Writing China*, ed. Eric Hayot, Haun Saussy, and Steven G. Yao (Minneapolis: University of Minnesota Press, 2008), 300–329.

3. Him Mark Lai, Genny Lim, and Judy Yung (eds.), *Island: Poetry and History of Chinese Immigrants on Angel Island, 1910–1940* (Seattle: University of Washington Press, 1991), 73, 96, 97.

4. Ibid., 16.

5. Ibid., 77.

6. Prior to the publication of this collection of poems, interviews, and photos, L. Ling-chi Wang published ninety-five poems from the Yee version in *Asian American Review* in 1976. L. Ling-chi Wang, "The Yee Version of Poems from the Chinese Immigration Station," *Asian American Review* (1976): 117–126.

7. Lai, et al., *Island*, 25.

8. Ibid., 136.

9. Ibid., 25.

10. Whereas Chan's *Asian Americans: An Interpretive History* offers a historical context of Asian American immigrants, Elaine H. Kim's *Asian American Literature: An Introduction to the Writings and Their Social Context* discusses this particular type of American literature from the perspective of its social context. And Xiao-huang Yin's *Chinese American Literature Since the 1850s* focuses mainly on the sociohistorical context of Chinese American literature for over a century. Xiao-huang Yin, *Chinese American Literature since the 1850s* (Urbana and Chicago: University of Illinois Press, 2000). Also see Chan's chapter on "The Chinese Diaspora" in *This Bitter-Sweet Soil* and Lynn Pan's *Sons of the Yellow Emperor: A History of the Chinese Diaspora* for an understanding of the background and situation of the massive Chinese immigration over the centuries. Sucheng Chan, "The Chinese Diaspora," in *This Bitter-sweet Soil: The Chinese in California Agriculture, 1860–1910* (Berkeley: University of California Press, 1986), 7–31. Lynn Pan, *Sons of the Yellow Emperor: A History of the Chinese Diaspora* (New York: Kodansha International, 1994).

11. Lai, *Island: Poetry and History of Chinese Immigrants on Angel Island, 1910–1940*) 6. One of the two anonymous reviewers of an earlier Chinese version of this paper supplements the following observations: (1) the explicit expression of the theme of revenge breaks the stereotype that the Chinese immigrants were passive, silent, and uncomplaining, and (2) the rich allusions in these poems also shatter the stereotype that earlier immigrants from China were illiterate.

12. I want to thank Doris Sommer for this analogy.

13. Sau-ling Cynthia Wong, "The Politics and Poetics of Folksong Reading: Literary Portrayals of Life Under Exclusion," in *Entry Denied: Exclusion and the Chinese Community in America, 1882–1943*, ed. Sucheng Chan (Philadelphia: Temple University Press, 1991), 247.

14. Lai, et al., *Island*, 28. Paul Lauter, et al. (eds.), *The Heath Anthology of American Literature*, 2 vols. (Lexington, Mass.: D. C. Heath, 1994), 1756.

15. In his letter to me, Him Mark Lai remarks, "So far as I can remember, originally we chose only dozens of representative poems of higher literary quality and intended to publish a small anthology. Later on, we accepted friends' suggestions and added historical background and oral histories so as to enrich the content. Finally, we realized that since this kind of book did not attract publishers' interest and since we had already devoted so much energy, we might as well incorporate other poems as appendix for the readers' reference. But I also agree [with you] that since we have published all poems, it seems to stand to reason if we merge these two parts." For the sake of convenience, in the following discussion each poem will be referred to as belonging to Part A or B, followed by its number in each part. Him Mark Lai, Letter to the author (May 9, 1995).

16. A list of other figures is as follows: Wang Can (A26), Yu Xin (A26), Han Yu (A45, A57), Yan Gaoqing (A40), Guangxu (A47), Han Xin (A59), Goujian (A59), Jiang Taigong (A59), Polun ("Napoleon," A60), Xiang Yu (A61), Li Ling (A62), Xishi (B28), Nan Jiyun (B33), Li Guang (B48), and Feng Tan (B48). Suffice it to say that most of these persons encounter similar fates with the other persons discussed later. The succinct annotations given by the editors/translators are of tremendous help not only to the English readers but also to the modern

Chinese readers who are no longer so familiar with their literary and historical traditions. It should also be noted that those poems with allusions generally are more compact and erudite and have a better literary quality according to the standard of classical Chinese poetry. And the seven-character regulated version A59 with four allusions in four consecutive lines (ll. 3–6) is one of the most allusion-laden poems whose last line urges revenge: "With extreme misfortune comes the composure to await an opportunity for revenge." Lai, et al., *Island*, 124.

17. Ibid., 56.

18. Ibid., 66.

19. Ibid.

20. Ibid.

21. Ibid., 56.

22. Ibid., 156.

23. Ibid., 169. In her analysis of *Songs of Gold Mountain*, "a two-volume anthology of anonymously composed folk songs published in San Francisco's Chinatown in 1911 and 1915," Wong makes a similar observation: "[t]he title ['Even Heroes Find it Difficult to Get Past Beautiful Women/The Beautiful Nation'] plays on the phrases *meiren* ('beautiful women') and *meiguo* ('America,' with *mei* representing the second syllable of the English name; *meiguo* can be rendered literally as 'beautiful country')." Wong, "The Politics and Poetics of Folksong Reading," 265.

24. Lai, *Island: Poetry and History of Chinese Immigrants on Angel Island, 1910-1940*, 156.

25. Ibid., 124.

26. Ibid., 71.

27. Ibid., 94.

28. Ibid., 157.

29. Ibid., 70.

30. Stan Yogi, "Review of Island," *MELUS* 17, no. 2 (1991–1992): 77.

31. Wong, "The Politics and Poetics of Folksong Reading," 48.

32. For a more detailed discussion, see my introduction to the *Chung-Wai Literary Monthly* special issue on Sinophone literature in the United States, entitled "From the Margins to the Intersection." Shan Te-hsing, "Cong Bianyuan dao Jiaoji" (From the margins to the intersection), in *Zhongwai wenxue* [Chung-Wai literary monthly] 34, no. 4 (2005): 5–14.

The Chinese Immigrant as a Global Figure in Lin Yutang's Novels

SHUANG SHEN

In *Looking Beyond* (1955), a story that takes place on an imaginary island where a group of idealistic thinkers have established an alternative society as a refuge from World War III, Laos, the social engineer of this colony, happens to be the descendant of a Chinese grandfather who "had trekked across Siberia and seeped like water in every nook and cranny of the world . . . without the shadow of a consulate's protection."[1] With the other side of his bloodline descending from the Greeks, Laos represents, from the perspective of the writer Lin Yutang, an almost perfect combination of Hellenistic and Confucian ideals. Laos loves nature and the arts. He proposes that the government should use its taxes to support musicians and artists, not to sustain a cumbersome bureaucratic structure or pay extra salary to public servants. He has a knack for abstract and philosophical thinking, but he does not reject the worldly wisdom of Chinese statesmanship and has even tried to translate a Chinese essay entitled "Keys to Success and Political Advancement." In essence, his wisdom represents an ideal version of hybridity and cosmopolitanism just as his bloodline embodies a different kind of mixedness.

The story in the novel is supposed to take place after transnational organizations such as the United Nations have been proven ineffective by the eruption of a new round of world wars. The writer Lin Yutang himself had some experience of working for UNESCO and was disillusioned by the United Nations' cumbersome bureaucratic structure. Although *Looking Beyond* is not a global novel in the sense that it does not propose an alternative set of political ideas that are supposed to replace the conceptual framework of the United Nations, both its main character and the writer Lin Yutang embody globalism to a large extent. Although Laos is a descendant of immigrants, he does not fit with the profile of a "typical" immigrant because he has easily transcended the framework of nation-state. The story of *Looking Beyond* is unanchored in any singular nation-state; similarly it is hard to situate Lin Yutang and his writings within the domain of a singular national literature. To a certain extent that is one reason that Lin has been received with ambivalence, or not completely understood even if he is positively received, by both Asianists and Asian Americanists.

How do we evaluate Lin's transnationality from a critical perspective? It seems that while some existing approaches to Lin Yutang and his works from very different perspectives in Asian or Asian American studies attempt to anchor the writer within the context of a particular nation-state, thereby to a certain extent usefully reestablishing the often repressed missing link between the author's works and their contexts, some key questions with regard to the logic of Chinese globalism remain unanswered. For instance, what enabled Lin Yutang to gain such great success in a transnational context in the first place? Arguments about successful transnational writers catering to existing stereotypes of a particular culture tend to present a flattened picture of transnational circulation and assume that some cultural misconceptions travel in an unhindered free manner. In fact, all cultural travels require the mediation of cultural forms and technology. In "Technologies of Public Forms: Circulation, Transfiguration, and Recognition," Dilip Parameshwar Gaonkar and Elizabeth Povinelli identify the great potential of approaching global relations from the perspective of translation, yet they also point out the limitations of contemporary translation theories for focusing too much on meaning and failing to take into account the materiality of the culture in circulation. They propose a focus on "transfiguration," the study of "the demanding environments of 'things' and their movement."[2] Following this provocative suggestion, I would argue that the Chinese immigrant in Lin's writings, as we have seen in *Looking Beyond*, can be considered as a figure of "transfiguration" in the sense that on the one hand, the durability of this figure indicates some form of imagined connection between China and the West as defined by Lin Yutang; on the other hand, the changing form and shifting meaning of this figure show his adjustment to the various "demanding environments" with which Lin as the immigrant himself negotiated. Thus, the immigrant is at the center of Lin's globalism closely related to his views on modernity and international relations.

First, I want to preface my discussion of the Chinese immigrant as a global figure by engaging with some existing disciplinary discourses that have tried to examine the works of this writer. Although at an earlier moment of Asian American studies non-American born writers such as Lin Yutang were excluded from Asian American literary history, recent developments in Asian American studies have done a great deal to recover the heterogeneity of earlier Asian American literary history. However, heterogeneity understood from the North American perspective is hardly sufficient for the consideration of the flow of people, culture, and capital that does not revolve around North America as the center or destination.[3] More specifically, in the case of Lin Yutang, Chinese immigrants as historical and cultural figures are related to his conceptualizations of cultural and racial hybridization in relation to Chinese modernity. Asian American perspectives may produce some nuanced readings of a few of Lin's works, but Asian Americanist perspectives cannot account for the continuity/discontinuity in Lin's self-definition and writings. Lin has multiple writerly personae that on the one hand sometimes fuse into each other, and on the other hand may indicate the lack of consistency in the self of Lin as a writer. His writerly identities as an essayist, a novelist, a translator, a scholar of philosophical ideas and traditions, and a cultural and political polemicist often fuse with each other in a singular work, creating intertextuality and generic ambiguity in his writings. How do we account for this kind of generic ambiguity in the context of the transnationalism embodied by Lin himself and his works?

In an article on Wong Chin Foo, a Chinese American writer from the 1870s to 1890s whose writings published in American magazines encompassed a great variety of voices, subjects, and political positions, Hsuan Hsu comments:

> Was Wong's versatility a product of the pressures of freelancing, or an attempt to reach as many readers as possible with writing that consistently emphasized the rationality, legibility, and humanity of the supposedly inscrutable Chinese? . . . The short, scattered, but remarkably crafted articles that Wong left behind give the impression of a talented writer without a definitive genre, a consistent voice, or a unified audience— a writer forced by circumstances into a versatile but uneven practice of transcultural *bricolage*.[4]

The multiple, discontinuous, and unstable self of an immigrant writer may not be an isolated phenomenon. Even though Lin eventually had a much bigger literary output than Wong Chin Foo, the changed relationship with his English-language audience might be the reason behind his constant shift of genre. As an essayist and polemicist, Lin's Chinese writings were popular in the 1920s and 1930s precisely because as articles written primarily for periodicals, these writings had a particular kind of timeliness that facilitated immediate communication between the writer and the reader. Yet as Lin immigrated to the United States, it seems that the performative quality of his politics began to diminish as the interaction between the speaker in his essays and the audience gradually diminished. This change was simultaneously accompanied by a shift of genre from the essay to the book, particularly ethnography and the novel. Fredric Jameson has famously observed that Third World literature can be read as national allegories since the public and the private are so much more intricately interrelated in the Third World than in the First World.[5] However, in making this assertion, Jameson ignores how different forms of "the public" may condition and mediate the role of a particular public intellectual. It is a curious question why Lin Yutang never wrote a novel in the Sinitic script or while he was in China. Several of his novels written in English are historical epics that weave fictional occurrences with real life characters and incidents. How well genres travel and to what extent different reading communities interpret and understand various generic conventions are questions that can only be answered by situating the author in a broader comparative context.

As a new approach that recently emerged from Chinese studies, Sinophone studies may be able to address some complex issues with regard to Chinese globalism particularly if Sinophone perspectives can be supplemented with local analysis of the social conditions that frame Sinophone practices. The term *Sinophone* takes the global circulation and use of Sinitic languages as its scope of analysis but pays particular attention to the internal variation and power differentiation among different Sinitic languages and the identity in association with each variation. Although it is a language-based category, Sinophone practices are closely connected with the history of dispersion and migration of Chinese people around the world, their social positions in the nation-states of their settlement, and transformations in immigrant communities over time.[6] In short, the Sinophone is a category of movement, one that studies the transnational circulation of culture against other types of transnational movement, such as capital, people, and ideology.

Examining Lin Yutang's writings in terms of Sinophone articulations runs into some difficulty—the obvious fact that most of Lin's writings first appeared in English, and that he was already writing in English before he left China. In fact, this aspect of Lin's bilingual practice actually poses a challenge to scholars who study Sinophone articulations, for it reminds us that the environment in which Sinophone practice is situated is often impure, and language choices and practices are deeply embedded in the specific social conditions of particular localities. Adopting locally anchored perspectives to the examination of the global circulation of Sinitic languages is crucial for Sinophone studies, and it is a fundamental feature that distinguishes Sinophone studies from Chinese studies as an area studies discipline. To study a Sinitic-language cultural production as a "Sinophone articulation" is supposed to draw our attention to the constructedness of this linguistic choice rather than assuming that the use of the Sinitic script automatically denotes a certain kind of cultural genealogy.[7]

Considering Lin Yutang's Anglophone writings in the category of the Sinophone articulation is not a self-contradictory move; it is meant to foreground an Anglophone-Sinophone encounter and highlight the mixedness of a particular languagescape, especially on its periphery. The particular form of mixedness and bilingualism was contextualized by the specific place of semicolonial Shanghai, as I argue in my other work on Anglophone periodicals.[8] In the place of encounter between Anglophone and Sinophone articulations, composing bilingually in both English and Chinese for Chinese intellectuals such as Lin meant participation in the making of Chinese national culture. This kind of translational politics was not necessarily reproducible in times and places beyond that particular moment; therefore, even though Lin engaged in back-and-forth translation between the two languages consistently throughout his life, the meaning of this translation changed as he moved from one context to another. One particularly important difference between Sinophone studies and Chinese studies, particularly in issues related to bilingualism, is the recognition that both English and Chinese are not monolithic languages, and that center and periphery can be evoked in different ways at different moments during immigrants' movement across the world. Even though Lin has historically been celebrated as a cross-cultural icon particularly in Sinophone regions, this kind of celebration often ignores the conditions of marginality to which he and his writings are often subject and seek to overcome.

An implicit argument I make in my work on Anglophone periodicals in semicolonial Shanghai is that translation should be viewed as a separate historical practice with a somewhat independent genealogy that intersects but does not completely overlap with the formation of national culture. It has been customary for too long for Chinese studies scholars to approach translation from a utilitarian perspective or simply treat it as background, subordinate or secondary to cultures composed in the native language. This reinforces a kind of language- and region-based cultural centrism in the Chinese context. By proposing that translation should be considered as having a separate genealogy, I am trying to emphasize that it is important to rethink national culture by considering intercultural contact at transnational and international scales.

The Chinese immigrant in Lin's writings is not one but several figures; in fact, the mutation from one to another is indicative of the changing notions of the self in the process of migration. The heroic immigrant in Lin's later writings actually overlaps with the enlightened intellectual who returns home from the West in his earlier writings, and hybridity as an ideal personality and a cultural program is embodied by both figures. Lin gives a clear description of this figure for the first time in the prologue of his first Anglophone book, *My Country and My People*. There he defines the position of the speaker as the "true" interpreter of "China," distinguished from both Western sinologists and traditional Chinese experts by his bilingual and bicultural competence. This speaker bases his competence on his hybridity, which is also the source of his identity conflict. The "true" interpreter is divided between "reason" and "heart," the objective "critical appraisal" of China and an unconditional "real appreciation" toward China, his sense of "shame" and "pride,"

> a conflict of loyalties belonging to different poles, a loyalty to old China . . . and a loyalty to open-eyed wisdom. . . . sometimes his clan-pride gets the better of him, and between proper pride and mere reactionism there is only a thin margin, and sometimes his instinct of shame gets the better of him, and between a sincere desire for reform and a mere shallow modernity . . . there is also only a very thin margin. To escape that is indeed a delicate task.[9]

It is fairly clear that this hybrid speaker refers to someone who has had the same educational background as Lin himself: an enlightened intellectual who returned home from the West. This hybrid person was not a loner in the modern Chinese context. A quick review of the history of the Chinese-language magazines that Lin launched in the early 1930s, such as *The Analects Fortnightly* (*Lunyu banyuekan*), *This Human World* (*Renjian shi*), and *Cosmic Wind* (*Yuzhou feng*), tells us that Lin was surrounded and supported by a group of friends including the philosopher Quan Zenggu, the sociologist Pan Guangdan, and the writer Lao She, all of whom had received varying degrees of Western training and had bilingual abilities. In the 1930s when *My Country and My People* was written, such a hybrid figure was embedded in the domestic cultural arena, and there was a political edge to some of their activities. As Charles Laughlin tells us in *The Literature of Leisure and Chinese Modernity*, the core writers of *The Analects Fortnightly* loved to practice what Laughlin calls "creative transliteration" in the essays and the cartoons published in the magazine to achieve a humorous effect.[10] Many of these writings and drawings were satirical toward the Nationalist government. The Mandarin word *youmo* is in itself a transliteration from the English word *humor*. *The Analects* group's practice of mixing Chinese and English sounds brings to mind the pidgin "Bamboo Rhyme" poems published in *Shanghai Times* (*Shen bao*), one of the first modern newspapers in China.

The fact that Lin Yutang refused to give a clear definition to the term *humor* but relied on the intuitive understanding of the reader shows the extent to which he was interactive with the domestic Chinese-language readership and based his politics on creating a performative connection with this readership. The persona assumed by Lin in his Sinophone essays is similar to that of a trickster figure, always ready to deliver some tongue-in-cheek remark on contemporary politics, society, and culture, without losing his cool composure. Therefore, contrary to Lin's own pronouncements and the criticism of the leftist faction of the cultural circle, to say that Lin's essays are apolitical could not be further from the truth. The fact is Lin tended to be evasive about doctrines or principles and relied on a context-bound performance to explicate his political positions.

In addition to writing about China, the growing importance in Lin's novels of the heroic Chinese immigrant situated in various diasporic locations signals a new conceptualization of the hybrid self and a new moment of self-reflection. The Chinatown in Lin's novel *Chinatown Family* (1948) gives an American anchor to the construction of the hybrid self as well as his ideas about cultural amalgamation.[11] There are many scenes of hybridization and cross-cultural education in this novel, which is set in New York's Chinatown in the 1940s. The oldest son of the Fong family is married to an Italian wife, who manages to preserve her Italian identity in everyday life while living with her Chinese in-laws. The two memorable characters, Old Tuck and young Tom, represent two generations of Chinese immigrants who have established roots in the United States without forgetting their homeland or traditional culture. Tom especially is a perfect product of cross-cultural education. He uses Walt Whitman's poem as a textbook to teach English to his Chinese girlfriend. Of all his novels, Lin's *Chinatown Family* is most frequently discussed from Asian American perspectives because it resembles most closely the classic genre of Asian American literature—the ethnic *Bildungsroman*, but in fact, taking advantage of the historical moment of World War II when the United States considered China as an ally, Lin treats pro-Chinese nationalism in the diasporic community in the United States as a convenient platform to elaborate on his ideas of cultural hybridization. Colleen Lye has argued that there is internal variation within the genre of the Asian American *Buildungsroman*. Books by Chinese American writers such as Lin Yutang, for instance, emphasize respect for the older generation and traditional culture while first-generation Japanese American writer Matsumoto's *A Brother Is a Stranger* holds a critical view toward Japanese

culture.[12] It needs to be added to this comment that as much as Lin emphasizes cultural heritage in this novel, his discourse on Chinese culture is not
traditional and cannot be reduced to Confucianism alone; it is actually
the product of an extremely eclectic body of philosophical thoughts reinterpreted from a modern perspective. It is the eclecticism and mixedness
inherent in Chinese culture, particularly the openness associated with
Taoism, that Lin thinks is the source of strength for immigrant characters
such as Old Tuck and Tom from *Chinatown Family* and the Greek descen-
dent of Chinese immigrants, Laos.

In *Chinatown Family*, Lin borrows but at the same time gives a twist to
the typical American story of upward mobility and the "American dream"
by emphasizing not material success but thirst for knowledge and pursuit
of some kind of enlightened way of life. That's why in *Chinatown Family*,
Tom's older brother, Fred, who is a salesman and financially successful, is
chastised and punished for his materialistic desires. On the opposite end
of the spectrum, both Old Tuck and Tom have wide-eyed curiosity toward
the writings of the American founding fathers and various schools of Chinese philosophy including Confucianism and Taoism. To characterize these
characters simply as "American heroes" does not quite take into account
Lin's criticism toward American modernity. They are in fact Lin's cultural
heroes deliberately created to embody and illustrate his cultural ideals formulated in a trans-Pacific context based on his reflections on both Chinese
and American societies.

At the same time, these main characters should not be taken as "Chinese
heroes," either. Although politically Lin became increasingly sympathetic
toward the Nationalist regime that settled in Taiwan, his cultural values actually should not be reduced to an undifferentiated notion of "Chineseness,"
nor should they be equated with the state ideology of the Nationalist regime.
Rather, they were an individualistic concoction of both Eastern and Western
cultures created deliberately for the diasporic context. As argued by Shu-mei
Shih in her recent book *Visuality and Identity: Sinophone Articulations Across
the Pacific*, "Chineseness" cannot be taken as a singular catch-all phrase to
describe the identity formation of the Chinese in the diaspora. Shu-mei Shih
defines the term *Sinophone* in her book in the following way:

> What it [Ang Lee's film *Crouching Tiger, Hidden Dragon*] engenders and
> validates . . . is the heteroglossia of what I call the Sinophone: a network
> of places of cultural production outside China and on the margins of
> China and Chineseness, where a historical process of heterogenizing and
> localizing of continental Chinese culture has been taking place for several
> centuries.[13]

Although Lin's writings are Anglophone, his views on Chinese cultural identity are in the realm of Sinophone articulations rather than simply expressions of "Chineseness."

Interestingly, in Lin's postwar writings, the displacement of the hybrid individual vis-à-vis a concrete social setting is emphasized, and this shows that a politics of place or location is at play in Lin's construction of cultural discourses. In *Looking Beyond*, for instance, Laos lives in a state of self-imposed exile where his great wisdom and abundant knowledge are no longer useful to the old world where he used to live. In fact, *Looking Beyond* structurally resembles the self-enclosed world of the island depicted in the novel. Generically, it is not clear whether this book should still be considered as a novel, since it contains so much more talk than action, and the reader seldom gets a chance to see Laos's great ideas about world government put into practice. Rather than opening up the narrative to some provocative connection between the fictional and the real, this generic mixedness actually registers a disconnection from the real world. The many lengthy passages in which Laos explicates his ideas make this book read like a book of political commentary that ironically has lost touch with the twists and turns of political currents. This lack of a concrete self-placement in the real world mirrors Lin's increasing alienation from American society and foreshadows his return to Asia.

Lin's interest in the global history of Chinese immigration is further explored in another novel, *Juniper Loa* (1963), which is set in Singapore in the 1920s.[14] In his real life, Lin had a brief sojourn in Singapore in the mid-1950s, when he accepted the position of president of soon-to-be-founded Nanyang University only to turn it down less than a year later. Nanyang University was funded by overseas Chinese Tan Lark Sye, and its aim was to provide an environment of Sinophone education for descendents of Chinese immigrants in Nanyang, the "South Seas." Because of all these connections with the history of Chinese immigration in Southeast Asia, it would make sense on the one hand for Chinese versions of this novel and *Chinatown Family* to be labeled as "overseas literature" (*Haiwai wenxue*), a category referring to books about or by immigrants or "overseas Chinese," if these books were marketed in the Sinophone regions. On the other hand, however, the term *overseas* hardly does justice to the complex routes of travel of Lin Yutang or the implicit comparative perspective he used to depict the Chinese family in Singapore versus that in New York. Lin Yutang is clearly aware of the differentiation between such localities as the United States and Singapore vis-à-vis China. Unlike in *Chinatown Family* where the specific regional origins of the immigrant family is de-emphasized, *Juniper Loa* not only gives us clear descriptions of their native place of origin—Changchow and Kulangsu of Fujian Province—but also incorporates English transliteration of regional dialects, both Cantonese and Fukienese, into the narrative. The main characters' name, Silok, sounds very similar to the Cantonese word meaning "the skinny one," and the female name Hamsun is rather close to the Cantonese word meaning "salt water girl," referring to sing-song girls and prostitutes serving foreign sailors. This implies that in addition to East versus West or China versus the United States, a third perspective comes into play in Lin's representation of the Chinese family in Singapore.

If in *Chinatown Family* and *Looking Beyond* race falls into the background, in Singapore, the racialization of characters, events, and the city tends to be intensified to such an extent that it becomes the only lens through which to understand Singapore or the lives of Chinese immigrants there. Silok, a young lawyer educated at the University of Malaya and working for a British firm, is attracted to Hamsun, a Eurasian woman born to a Chinese prostitute and a Portuguese sailor. Silok knows their romance would not be accepted into the family. As he says to Hamsun:

> My uncle is a stubborn man. Stubborn and very, very Chinese. He is as supercilious about his being a Chinese as an Englishman is proud of being English. He has always wanted to fix me up with a Chinese girl . . . I have made up my mind. It's either you, or nobody else.[15]

Yet Silok's interracial romance with Hamsun is short lived, not because of the disapproval from Silok's family but due to the racial determinism that controls the outcome of the characters. After a few romantic escapades behind Silok's back, Hamsun finds out that she still favors European over Chinese men and eventually finds a home for herself by marrying a Portuguese captain. Silok, on the other hand, has also returned to his racial family and reunites with his first lover, who has been brought to Singapore from Fukien. This outcome mirrors the social condition of Singapore, which from Lin's perspective is a place of many races and cultures without much intermingling or communication:

> It was like that in Singapore. There were people of all ethnic groups: Chinese, by far the majority, Malays, who were in their own country, and Hindus, Tamils, Parses and Europeans. The East and the West met for business but have never merged. The races had not integrated into a homogeneous community with common customs and beliefs.[16]

Contrary to the openness of Chinese culture and its wonderful eclecticism and potential for hybridization that Lin celebrates in almost every book before *Juniper Loa*, here we get a picture of "Chineseness" as an essentially

closed identity category that cannot accept any outsiders. Lin's representation of Singapore actually brings to mind his earlier depictions of Shanghai
in the English essays he wrote for the column "The Little Critic" in *China
Critic*. In those essays, Shanghai's hybrid culture is a tableau of bad taste and
rampant materialism associated with semicolonialism. It is a place that awaits
the rescue of a nationalist revolution.

What makes the "openness" of one Chinese immigrant family in one
context turn into "closedness" in another context? What are the conditions
of "openness" to begin with? While concocting a seemingly consistent discourse on Chinese culture and identity that would apply to different diasporic
communities in the world, Lin's transnational writings figuring the Chinese
immigrant repeatedly bring up the question of location. Shu-mei Shih has
questioned the dominant framework used to study the Chinese diaspora in
the following way:

> [T]he fact of the Sinophone peoples' dispersion through all continents
> and over such a long historical span leads one to question the viability of
> the umbrella concept of the Chinese diaspora where the criteria of deter-
> mination is Chineseness, or, to put it more precisely, different degrees of
> Chineseness.[17]

From Shih's point of view, this inability to go beyond Chineseness as an organizing principle has stopped the critic from fully accounting for the social
condition in which Chinese immigrants live in particular locations of Chinese diaspora. In the case of the creative writer Lin Yutang, his exclusive
focus on ethnicity has made him unable to see that other forms of difference,
for instance class, could also be at play in this story about interracial love. In
addition, his views on gender and family have consistently placed women in
the domestic sphere and equate femininity with certain notion of the idealized Chinese family. It is interesting to see how difference in terms of location opens up the homogenous discourse on culture and identity; whereas
in both in *Looking Beyond* and *Chinatown Family* ethnic difference is camou-
flaged by some form of cross-cultural education or hybridization, in *Juniper
Loa*, there is no transcendence over racial difference.

Paradigmatically, Sinophone perspectives address the so-often-ignored
interdisciplinary space between U.S. ethnic studies and area studies by challenging Chineseness as a holistic category. Ironically, Asian American studies'
critique of nationalism does not manage to open up more space for discussion of "Chineseness" as diverse, heterogeneous, and multiple categories. On
the other hand, the writings of Lin Yutang demonstrate that even for someone who played an important role in the U.S.-China relationship and cultural

exchange during World War II, it would be simplistic to argue that his discourses on Chinese culture solely revolved around these two powers—the United States and China. In fact, the Nationalist government's retreat from mainland China in the 1940s was already a threshold moment that forced Lin Yutang to choose between two political powers both associated with different conceptualizations of "Chineseness." His brief sojourn in Singapore further embedded him more deeply in the history of the global migration of the Chinese, which has always been multiply connected with Communist as well as anti-Communist forces and ideologies, the power relations within specific Southeast Asian nation-states, and other global players such as the United States.

Notes

1. Lin Yutang, *Looking Beyond* (New York: Prentice Hall, 1955), 50.

2. Dilip Parameshwar Gaonkar and Elizabeth Povinelli, "Technologies of Public Forms: Circulation, Transfiguration, and Recognition," *Public Culture*, 15, no. 3 (Fall 2003): 395.

3. For a recent discussion on recovering the heterogeneity of early Asian American history, consult a special issue of *Genre* on "Asian American Subgenres, 1853–1945," 39, no. 4 (Winter 2006).

4. Hsuan L. Hsu, "Wong Chin Foo's Periodical Writing and Chinese Exclusion," *Genre*, Special issue on "Asian American Subgenres, 1853–1945," 39, no. 4 (Winter 2006): 85.

5. Fredric Jameson, "Third-World Literature in the Era of Multinational Capitalism," *Social Text* 15 (Autumn 1986), 65–88.

6. For a definition of "Sinophone," see Shu-mei Shih's discussion in *Visuality and Identity: Sinophone Articulations Across the Pacific* (Berkeley: University of California Press, 2007), 23–39.

7. I take this point from Shu-mei Shih's *Visuality and Identity*.

8. See Shuang Shen, *Cosmopolitan Publics: Anglophone Print Culture in Semi-Colonial Shanghai* (New Brunswick: Rutgers University Press, 2009).

9. Lin Yutang. *My Country and My People* (London: Heinemann, 1939), 13.

10. Charles A. Laughlin, *The Literature of Leisure and Chinese Modernity* (Honolulu: University of Hawai'i Press, 2007).

11. Lin Yutang, *Chinatown Family* (New York: John Day, 1948).

12. See Colleen Lye, "The Sino-Japanese Conflict of Asian American Literature," *Genre* 39, no. 4 (Winter, 2006): 43–64.

13. Shih, *Visuality and Identity*, 4.

14. Lin Yutang, *Juniper Loa* (Taipei: Mei Ya Publications, 1975).

15. Ibid., 69.

16. Ibid.

17. Shih, *Visuality and Identity*, 27.

Latin America and the Caribbean in a Sinophone Studies Reader?

IGNACIO LÓPEZ-CALVO

This chapter is largely about writers who write in Spanish, not in the Sinitic script. Only one of the texts mentioned here was originally written in the Sinitic script: *The Cuba Commission Report*. Sinophone writing from Latin America and the Caribbean (including texts written or published in China by Chinese nationals who migrated to Latin America for some time) still needs to be discovered, researched, and translated. By looking at Chinese Latin American literature written in Spanish, however, we get a glimpse of the kinds of issues Sino-Latin American writers deal with in general. This chapter is a short introduction to these topics. Of course, many other writers of Asian descent could have been included in this study, but I will only consider some of the most representative names.

The millenary cultural heritage brought by the Chinese diaspora has contributed greatly not only to the region's literature, cuisine, art, language, and music, but also to its aspirations of independence (in the case of Cuba). Yet, in contrast with the relatively recent efforts by literary and cultural critics to incorporate the cultural production by people of pre-Colombian and African descent into Latin American and Caribbean studies, that of people of Asian descent continues to be, for the most part, neglected. Only in recent years have a few critics begun to acknowledge its importance, thus disrupting the official black-and-white or indigenous-and-white discourse of the nation. In any case, if, as Honoré de Balzac stated, the novel is the private history of nations, the fiction by Latin American writers of Chinese descent offers alternative ways to narrate the nation and to construct or imagine national identities.

Cuba

As is the case with the other Latin American and Caribbean countries, the Chinese experience in Cuba has been narrated, for the most part, by non-Chinese authors. Although several of them, including Severo Sarduy, Cabrera Infante, and Zoé Valdés, share the presence of Chinese ancestors in their ethnic background, the fact that they do not identify themselves as Chinese Cubans but as Cuban or Cuban American is a reason for caution or even skepticism when dealing with their representation of the Chinese. At any rate, by the last decades of the nineteenth century, the Chinese presence is reflected in Cuban cultural production, often with Sinophobic overtones. One of the most important texts written in the Sinitic script in Latin America and the Caribbean is the testimonial *The Cuba Commission Report: A Hidden History of the Chinese in Cuba* (1877). Although translated into English in 1876, it was not widely available until the last edition of 1993. Considering that, to this day, there is no translation of this document into Spanish, the complicity with the Cuban reader that might be expected from a *testimonio* never took place. Yet its primary objective was achieved since it did elicit empathy and a reaction from the Chinese government. As Denise Helly has explained, in May 1873, after the imperial viceroy in Canton (Kwangtung) had been hampering the recruitment of Chinese workers in this region for years, two agents of Cuban companies decided to complain to the emperor.[1] Subsequently, representatives of the Russian, British, French, and German embassies, who had been called to assist in the litigation, proposed to launch an investigation of the treatment received by Chinese emigrants in Cuba. After an inquiry that lasted six weeks, the findings of the Imperial Commissioner Ch'en Lan Pin (aided by A. MacPherson, commissioner of customs of Hankow, and A. Huber, commissioner of customs of Tientsin) not only provided Chinese laborers in Cuba with a voice, but also officially ended the coolie trade with the signing of a treaty between China and Spain in November 1877. In addition, four Chinese consuls were named to different towns in Cuba to grant protection to Chinese citizens.

Anyone reading the hundreds of testimonies recorded in this document would have little doubt that most coolies became de facto slaves from the moment they were deceived or kidnapped. Despite the efforts of Cuban officials and planters to conceal the truth, the replies supplied in 1873 by the Chinese laborers draw an appalling picture of their ordeals. From these testimonies of suffering collected in Cuban depots, prisons, plantations, jails, and sugar warehouses, we learn about numerous demoralizing and dehumanizing patterns of abuse. According to *The Cuba Commission Report*, eight out of ten coolies claimed to have been deceived or abducted. In sugar plantations, they rested about four hours a day, and the insufficient and inappropriate food they received was denounced by some as yet another form of humiliation. Once their contracts expired, Chinese workers in Cuba were often coerced into renewing them; if they refused, they were sent to the depots to do unpaid hard labor. Overall, the 1,176 depositions and 85 petitions recorded by the commission, supported by 1,665 signatures, indicate that the coolies worked in conditions of slavery. Marginalized, dispossessed, and sometimes vilified, Chinese subjects find in testimonials such as the *The Cuba Commission Report* a vehicle for the reconstruction of their collective history. Simultaneously, these counter-narratives—albeit often mediated by the political agenda of the interviewer(s)—become sites for resistance and identity construction.

As happened with *The Report*, behind purportedly autobiographical accounts such as Chuffat Latour's *Apunte histórico de los chinos en Cuba* (Historical notes about the Chinese in Cuba; 1927), lies a political struggle for representation and empowerment that responds to a collective project. At times marked by vacillation and contradiction, particularly when referring to political and ethnic affiliations, these texts ultimately represent an alternative way to narrate the nation. Chinese Cubans like Antonio Chuffat Latour and Regino Pedroso devote their efforts to a representation of difference based on the premise that the Chinese community "belongs" within the realm of the Cuban nation (something that is common in Chinese Latin American writing). In their zealous attempt to assimilate themselves and their community to mainstream society, however, they depict Cuba as the land of Western progress and freedom, while relegating China to the usual images of backwardness, oppression, and passivity—that is, the same images created by Western powers to justify their intervention and resulting colonization.

In *Apunte histórico de los chinos en Cuba*, Chuffat Latour challenges Creole dominance and demands the acceptance of Chinese culture in Cuba by using all the available rhetorical devices to lead his ethnic group far from the image of the strange Other. His text constitutes a sort of symbolic victory over oblivion: a Chinese mulatto subject, refusing to become a passive object of a non-Chinese anthropological study, writes in the language of the former oppressors (he admits to have studied Spanish to formulate a manifesto of Chinese diasporic thought). *Apunte histórico* is, therefore, an invaluable document of self-representation and self-empowerment by a Cuban of Afro-Chinese descent. Oddly, Chuffat Latour positions himself both as a representative of the Chinese community in Cuba (a native informant), and as someone who distances himself from them and speaks about them from "the outside." He refers to the Chinese in the third-person plural and often compares them with "us," the Cubans. While Chuffat Latour speaks for the disenfranchised Chinese "colony" and is proud of his Chinese descent, he considers himself fully integrated into Cuban society and allies himself with the Creoles to whom he targets his study. In a sense, he represents the colonial "mimic man" who reinforces colonial authority while he "talks back" (or writes back) to it. His conciliatory tone responds to a strategic positioning with a twofold goal: to "charm the oppressor," as Fanon puts it, and to express his disappointment in Cuba's failure to recognize the key role of the Chinese in the building of the nation.

Chuffat Latour displays a wide range of attributes commonly associated with the colonized mind and the sub-oppressor (to use Paulo Freire's term). Although he was also of African extraction, he often contrasts the assimilation of the Chinese to "the refinement of the white race" and their efforts to "civilize themselves"[2] with what he sees as the failures of black Africans in Cuba.[3] Yet he still tries to balance his stance by lamenting the marginalization of blacks and even quoting a poem written in Cantonese by Kan Shin Kon, the first editor of the Chinese Cuban newspaper *La voz del pueblo*, in which the enslavement of Africans is condemned:

> Black face, silver tooth/They mistreat him as if he were not a person/ Awake from lethargy/I long for your liberty/Break your chains/I long for your happiness/Fly like a bird/Death to the tyrant/Long live democracy/ Freedom, freedom/I desire it.[4]

Ultimately, his main rationale to have the Chinese community accepted as an inextricable part of the Cuban nation and, therefore, to validate its essential Cubanness is the disinterested patriotism of the Chinese combatants and the "peaceful Chinese" who helped *mambí* troops free the island from Spanish occupation. For this reason, in the fourth paragraph of his prologue, immediately after affirming the veracity of everything that follows, he declares his intention to record the testimonies of Chinese men who fought for Cuba's freedom.

Regarding Sino-Cuban self-representation through poetry, Regino Pedroso (1898–1983) asserts his ethnic pride through a process of Sinicization of his own poetry. Writing during the heyday of the *Negrista* poetic movement in Cuba, Pedroso follows the ethnic trend and chooses to rediscover his Chinese heritage through his poems and essays. In the prologue to *Nosotros* (We, 1933), Pedroso states that he belongs to "the human race" and that his pigmentation is "black-yellow. (With no other mixture)." He also explains that his race, "Ethiopic-Asian," is conceived as inferior by "bourgeois ideology." As part of his avowed goal of writing socially committed poetry, Pedroso mentions both his personal Chinese heritage and the injustice of the coolie trade in several poems in *Nosotros*. Lacking a first-hand experience in Chinese culture, he finds a basis for the re-creation of the Chinese world in the hackneyed and idealized Western stereotypes of Chinese exoticism. Intertwined within these lines that overflow with social commitment, is the view that the Chinese past is a negative set of oppressive and passive traditions. At the same time that he embraces his ethnic roots, he has obviously internalized the colonial discourse to the point where he tries by all means to distance himself from China and from the "embarrassing" past of his ancestors. On the other hand, the present becomes the threshold to a bright future of freedom and hope offered, from the poet's perspective, by Cuba.[5]

In contrast to the socially committed direction of previous works, in his collection of "Chinese poems" *El ciruelo de Yuan Pei Fu* (Yuan Pei Fu's plum tree, 1955), Pedroso concentrates on the re-creation of the exotic world of his ancestors from a philosophical and nostalgic perspective. In it, the poet decides to Sinicize his identity by "inventing" a Chinese ancestor: the multifaceted Yuan Pei Fu lived as a wandering apostle, preaching to his disciples, and performing miracles; however, he ended up becoming a rich mandarin in the court and leading a life of "Asian luxury." In all, Pedroso, like so many of his contemporaries, resorts to the Orientalist envisioning of China as a place where the subjects starve while the emperors squander riches and time on jewels, feasts, and orgies.[6]

Peru

The first important Tusán (second-generation Sino-Peruvian) author is the librarian, social activist, poet, and idealist philosopher Pedro Salvino Zulen (Zun Leng, 1889–1925). Zulen was born to a humble family in Lima: his father was a shopkeeper from Guangdong and his mother was a *mestiza* from Lima. He studied at the University of San Marcos in Lima (he also studied for a few months in 1916 at Harvard), and published two philosophical studies: *La filosofía de lo inexpresable* (The philosophy of the ineffable, 1920) and his doctoral dissertation, *Del neohegelianismo al neorealismo* (From neo-hegelianism to neo-realism, 1924). A collection of his poems from the 1920s was published posthumously, *El olmo incierto de la nevada* (The uncertain elm of the snowfall, 1930).[7] Some of his poems were collected by Dora Mayer de Zulen in *La poesía de Zulen: In Memoriam* (Zulen's poetry: In memoriam, 1927). Although Zulen did not consider himself a poet, it is interesting to note that some of his poems, including "Pampsiquismo" (Panpsichicism) and "Ocaso de ensueño" (Dreamy twilight), run parallel to his philosophy. He also reflected some of his experiences with spiritualism in poems such as "Vahído." By the same token, while his search for and love of wisdom is reflected in "Mis libros" (My books) and "En el vallezuelo . . ." (In the little valley), he echoes his ethical concerns in "El carácter y la moralidad" (Character and morality). Finally, he also wrote love poems, such as "Romántica," "Soñaba" (I dreamt), and "Gladys."

A contemporary of Pedro Zulen, the Sino-Peruvian A. Kuan Veng published several short stories in the newspaper *El Correo* as well as the collection of stories *Mey Shut, poemas en prosa* (1924). Although the subtitle of the book is "Poems in Prose," the texts are not poems but parables, moralizing short stories, and impressions. Several of Kuan Veng's texts, such as "Idealidad" (Idealism), "El mar" (The sea) and "Nocturno" (Nocturnal), have philosophical overtones. The narrator also shows his Confucian filial piety or *xiao* in "Plegaria" (Prayer), "Madre mía" (Dear Mother), and "Voces maternales. Sé sencillo" (Maternal voices: Be unassuming). In this last story, his ethical advice echoes his mother's words: one must be unassuming, modest, and pure like a lotus; one must not be arrogant (one of the precepts in the *Tao Te Ching*)or obsessed with money. The author continues with his moralizing, again in Taoist terms, in "Amor ideal" (Ideal love) and "Simbólico," where he exhorts his readers to avoid loving someone only for his or her money or beauty, as these are mutable and instable. A few of these texts are set in an idealized China and describe old traditions like the moon festival. Finally, in "El primer beso" (The first kiss), Kuan Veng exhibits a certain degree of double consciousness, as his characters are described from a Western point of view: "Her artistically slanted eyes looked tenderly at me."[8]

Moving on to contemporary authors, perhaps the most international Sino-Peruvian author is Julio Villanueva Chang (1967–). He was born in Lima, where he still lives, and he studied education at the University of San Marcos. Villanueva Chang has published the anthologies *Mariposas y murciélagos: crónicas y perfiles* (Butterflies and bats: Chronicles and profiles, 1999) and *Elogios Criminales* (Criminal praise, 2008). Villanueva Chang is widely considered one of the best *cronistas* (chroniclers). In *Mariposas y murciélagos*, he provides intriguing chronicles of daily life in Peru and profiles of interesting people, including a man who is probably the oldest professional model in the world, an Afro-Peruvian traffic officer, Gabriel García Márquez's dentist, a fisherman who became a millionaire, a man who walked the entire coast of Peru in ninety days, and the story of a German woman who is an expert in butterflies and bats (hence the title of the collection) and was the only survivor of an airplane accident in the Peruvian jungle in 1971. In one of his most engaging *crónicas*, "Viaje al centro de la noche" (Travel to the center of the night), Villanueva Chang describes the underworld of alcoholics and prostitutes that one can discover at night in downtown Lima. With his typical sarcasm, Villanueva Chang concludes: "If, as in the olden times, Lima's streets were baptized according to the predominant trades in them—Shopkeepers, Sword Makers, Merchants—, today Cailloma Avenue would be *Prostitutes*, and Quilca, the popular *Drunks* Street."[9] Revised versions of two of these texts were published again, along with five more profiles and chronicles, in the collection *Elogios criminales*.[10]

Another important Sino-Peruvian author is Siu Kam-Wen (his given name was Xiao Jin-Rong, 1951–). He was born in 1951 in Zhongshan, in the Chinese province of Guangdong, migrated to Peru at the age of nine, and now lives in Hawaii.[11] Although as a young, aspiring writer, Siu Kam-Wen began writing in the Sinitic script (Spanish is only his third language, after the Lungtu dialect of Southern China and Cantonese), he later chose to write in Spanish in order to reach a larger audience. He has published the collections of short stories *El tramo final* and *La primera espada del imperio* (1988), which were later reprinted, along with the collection *Ilusionismo*, in the volume *Cuentos completos* (Complete short stories, 2004). In the same year, he published the novels *La estatua en el jardín* (The statue in the garden) and *Viaje a Ítaca* (which the author himself translated in 1993 from an earlier English version titled "A Journey to Ithaca"). *La vida no es una tómbola* (2007; also translated by Siu Kam-Wen as *This Sort of Life* in 2008) and *El furor de mis ardores* (2008) are his last novels.

Siu Kam Wen only focuses on the tragic odyssey of the "coolies" in one of his short stories, "En alta mar" (On the high seas), included in *El tramo final*; the rest of his works that deal with the Sino-Peruvian experience take place in the 1960s or later and focus on the second wave of entrepreneurs from Hong Kong and their descendants. As we see in his works, the impressive economic success of the Chinese community in Peru has not come without side effects: self-exploitation and the harsh life of storekeepers mark the life of many youngsters. Although some of his publications do not deal with Chinese issues, in several of his short stories and novels he explores conflicts of personal and national identity, particularly regarding the relationships (including racism and reverse racism) among the *Wa Kiu* (*huaqiao* in Mandarin; overseas Chinese nationals or first-generation Chinese immigrants, both Hakka and Cantonese), the *Tusáns* (Chinese born in Peru), the *Sén-háks* (recent arrivals or new immigrants), and the *Kuei* (literally "devil"; foreigner, non-Chinese). Many of his texts reflect, with autobiographical overtones, the claustrophobic world of child exploitation, generational gaps, and the life of Chinese store owners. Siu Kam-Wen's works are one of the few testimonies of life in Lima's Chinatown from a Sino-Peruvian perspective. Ultimately, although some of his writings are marked by the nostalgia perhaps expected from an expatriate writer, one can also perceive a certain tone of reproach and resentment against a country that forced him into a third migration.

In Peru, there are also several Sino-Peruvian poets. One of them is Julia Wong Kcomt, who was born in 1965 in Chepén (La Libertad) and currently lives in New York.[12] She has published five collections of poems: *Historia de una gorda* (1994), *Los últimos blues de Buddha* (2002), *Iguazú* (2004), *Ladrón de codornices* (2005), and *Un salmón ciego* (2008). The exploration of her Sino-Peruvian identity appears in some of the lines in different poems in *Historia de una gorda*: "my surname"; "I don't need to be called Julia/I can show a stamp"; "I have dreamt about an enormous ship cruising the Pacific/ (My grandfather died without his coolie queue and in a violet habit)"; "Sleep, little Chinese girl"; "Because of my very black skin/And a spare hole in my ribs/That does not match Western aesthetics."[13] Wong Kcomt's second collection, *Los últimos blues de Buddha* (Buddha's last blues), continues to express sexual desire and to evoke maternity (frustrated or not) as well as different cities and countries. Pride in her Chinese identity is again suggested in poems like "Ritual del té" (Tea ritual), "Hijos de sabandija" (Children of a bug), and "Mentiras" (Lies). Likewise, in "Quiero (poema de colores)" (I want [poem of colors]) she describes herself as yellow. Yet her main sources of inspiration are still her need for company and love, the absence of a loved man, and transitory love affairs with tourists or men she has met in her travels and who will soon forget about her.

In other poems, her prosaic verses mention China directly, as we see in "Cuando atardece en China" (When the sun sets in China), where the poetic voice talks to a loved person who made her strong, just like this country made her strong as well. On occasion, she makes generalizations about Chinese women: "Are you calling me/Me?/Are you talking to me?/A Chinese woman is always plagued with doubt,"[14] she argues in "Un milagro en Chérrepe" (A miracle in Chérrepe).[15] Some lines in "Harnero" (Sieve) even denote essentialist overtones: "Because one has to understand Chinese,/ To understand why the tiger's stripes/Are painted by rich men."[16] Yet the sieve mentioned in the title makes reference to cultural differences; she may look like the other people in Chengdu, China, but she certainly feels different. The poetic voice even admits feeling guilty for not identifying with China. Later, she confesses that, in fact, she does not want to be the same. Likewise, in "Llueve en Shanghai" (It rains in Shanghai) she rejects this city, which she considers dirty. Yet in "Inmemorial China" (Immemorial China) the poetic voice seems to feel nostalgia for an ancestral China that she never knew, perhaps for invented memories about Chinese ancestors. Wong Kcomt has also published a short novel entitled *Bocetos para un cuadro de familia* (Sketches for a family portrait, 2008), which is divided into short, interrelated accounts. With this book, she joins Siu Kam-Wen in the narrative representation of Peru from a Sino-Peruvian perspective. The novel deals with the life of a family of Chinese immigrants in Chepén, Peru, who stop farming to become shopkeepers. Eventually, the children migrate to the city or abroad.

Another Sino-Peruvian poet is Sui-Yun (a pseudonym for Katie Wong Loo), who was born in the Amazonian city of Iquitos in 1955 to Chinese parents who migrated before the Chinese Revolution.[17] She devotes her first collection of poems, *Cresciente* (Waxing moon), to the moon. In this collection, which includes poems in both English and Spanish, and was published in California in 1977, all elements in nature, and particularly the moon and the sun, work in unison to express the poet's feelings of love and harmony through an extended pathetic fallacy. The nostalgic memory of the Amazonian landscapes and animals of her native land also provide inspiration for metaphysical thoughts. In other poems, they inspire philosophical thoughts close to Chinese philosophy, such as the yin and yang, the Taoist concept of the balance of opposites in the world: "The primitive from the civilized / The humble from the aristocrat / The positive from the negative / All these coordinate in the making of One whole."[18] Therefore, the ultimate answers are to be found in the magical powers of nature and in its unity.

In 1983, Sui-Yun published a second collection of poems in Lima (this time all the poems are only in Spanish, albeit with sporadic lines in French and English), whose title *Rosa fálica* (Phallic rose) seems to suggest that she has continued to search the yin-yang equilibrium between opposites (woman and man in this case) that we see in the previous book. Now, the prevalent topics are eroticism and love, which become the fundamental path to harmony. In contrast with Wong Kcomt's poetry, the only reference to her Chinese ethnic background to be found is in the line "And the memory of Chinese lanterns"[19] of an untitled poem in this last collection. Sui-Yun has also published the collection *Soy un animal con el misterio de un ángel* (1999) in Lima, and *Cantos para el mendigo y el rey* (2000), in Wiesbaden, Germany, as a bilingual edition.

The final author from Peru that I will mention is Mario Wong (Lima, 1967–). Wong has published the collection of poems *La estación putrefacta* (1985), the novel *El testamento de la tormenta* (1997), and the collection of short stories *Moi, je vis à San Miguel, mais je meurs pour Amalia* (2002).[20] With thirty characters roaming the streets of Lima and Piura in Peru, Paris, and an unspecified American city, many of the scenes in *El testamento de la tormenta* take place in the Wony, a Sino-Peruvian *chifa* restaurant and bar where the *"poètes maudits"* of the Kloaka movement meet to drink and discuss literature and politics. The nightmarish urban atmosphere—somewhat reminiscent of Julio Villanueva Chang's *crónica* "Viaje al centro de la noche"—is described sometimes through a frenzied, poetic cascade of existential thoughts and metaphors and other times through the coarse language of the protagonists, who navigate a world of alcohol, drugs, and nihilism. Wong portrays the violent 1980s in Peru as a hellish hallucination. Eight years of Sendero Luminoso (Shining Path)'s terrorism, combined with the official violence of the government, end up flooding Peruvian society with fear, torture, and senseless massacres. Self-reflective and surrealist writing becomes a way to look for answers and to exorcize inner evils. And when this tactic fails, his romantic passion for a woman called Amalia Morales, who has moved elsewhere, fills his thoughts. These two leitmotifs are at the core of the novel, around which several other episodes of fear, torture, violence, destruction, and self-destruction through alcohol and drug abuse take place. It is, as the title indicates, a testimony of a stormy time in Peru as well as in the life of the protagonist.[21]

Panama

Another Latin American country with a long tradition of Chinese immigration is Panama. One of the most prolific and well-known Sino-Panamanian authors is Eustorgio A. Chong Ruiz.[22] In *Techumbres, guijarros y pueblo*, short stories such as "El rapto" (Thekidnapping), "El machete," "Longoroneros," and "Kyrie Eleison" describe a small-town atmosphere of violent machismo in which boyfriends and parents feel compelled to defend their honor once someone else takes their women. In this last short story, the unnamed protagonist reminisces, while considering suicide, about his childhood, his father's death, and his bravery on January 9, 1964, when Panamanians marched into the Panama Canal Zone after U.S. students only raised the American flag. Although he mentions several times the socialist concept of the new man, the narrator has lost his faith in all ideologies.[23] This same concept of the new man reappears in the socially conscious play *Después del manglar* (After the mangrove swamp), where Chong Ruiz condemns the abuses committed against the lower classes in the countryside. He tells the story of a hamlet in a mangrove swamp close to the ocean, whose inhabitants end up being displaced by the "owner," Efigenio, even though they had legal papers bought from him. The play ends with the protagonist and his girlfriend, Gisela, who happens to be the landowner's daughter, leading the exodus in hopes of creating the new man some day and somewhere else.[24]

Even more prolific is Carlos Francisco Changmarín (he blends his two surnames, Chang and Marín, to express his mixed Chinese and *Criollo* heritage; 1922–), who was born in Los Leones, Santiago. His works often deal with nature, revolution, social justice, land ownership in the countryside, class struggle (his Chinese-Panamanian father's wealthy family always resented the latter's marriage to a peasant *Criolla*), or the recent history of Panama (including the U.S. invasion and the construction of the Panama Canal, in which he worked in his youth).[25] *Punto 'e llanto* is, for the most part, a collection of intimate love poems with a popular tone and atmosphere. However, some of them deviate from the norm. We find, for example, "Por las lomas negras" (On the black hills), which describes an inebriated black man who rapes and kills a young girl, and then flees when he hears her father's voice and dogs. In a poem reminiscent of César Vallejo's solidarity with human suffering, "Llanto del interiorano acabangado" (Weeping of the melancholic provincial man), he feels empathy for the underprivileged. In turn, in "El hijo que quiero tener" (The son I want to have), the poetic voice defends *mestizos* by explaining that although he had always wanted to have a white boy, he now has changed his mind. As we see in the last stanza, the poetic voice professes a sort of reverse racism nuanced by a questionable identification of *mestizaje* with gratuitous violence. The poem never clarifies what has made him so ashamed of his white son as to reject nothing else than his ethnicity.[26]

Nicaragua

Moving on to another Central American country, perhaps the most well-known Sino-Nicaraguan poet is Juan Chow. He was born in Managua in 1956.[27] Chow's first book, *Oficio del caos*, includes surrealist poems with long, often prosaic, verses and lists of oneiric and hallucinatory images. Poems such as "En defensa de Georgette Vallejo" imagine Latin American poets such as Rubén Darío, Vicente Huidobro, or César Vallejo in the bars and cafés of Paris. In other poems, these literary references give way to the reflection on the tragic civil war in his native Nicaragua, as we see in "Epigrama de un asesinado a su novia también asesinada" (Epigram of an assassinated man to his girlfriend, also assassinated) and "Reflexiones de un dios acabado" (Reflections of a finished God).[28]

Mexico

Óscar Wong is a Sino-Mexican poet, fiction writer, essayist, literary critic, and journalist. He was born in Tonalá, Chiapas, in 1948, and now lives in Mexico City. He serves as subsecretary of culture and recreation of the government of the State of Chiapas. In a speech he read during an event in Mexico City that commemorated his thirty years as a poet, Wong expressed his pride of being of Chinese descent: "It is true that I feel grateful to life for my lineage, for my dynastic origins, especially because I had a father that saw the world, not with the coarse and even rude optic of Westerners, but with the millenary wisdom of Chinese ancestors, with the diligence and discipline that forge universes and discover the infinite multiplicity of the ten thousand things that integrate the Cosmos."[29] He praises his father in poem: "My father was an incredulous wise man."[30] In *Poética de lo sagrado. El lenguaje de Adán* (Poetics of the sacred: The language of Adam, 2006), Wong describes the poet as a sort of priest who interprets the secret of existence. The "sacred" in the title of the book reveals—against the grain of current literary theory, we must say—poetic inspiration as a divine puff and the poet as a mystic or enlightened person.[31]

This peculiar way to understand poetry is reflected in his collections of poems. For example, in *Enardecida luz* (Flushed light), which is divided into seven different sections, we find poems, such as the one that opens the collection, or "En las fauces de lo oscuro" (In the jaws of darkness), "Sobre la ira estoy" (I am over the wrath), "Encabritado corazón" (Reared up heart), and "Ahora muerdo la lengua" (Now I bite my tongue), where a self-deprecating poetic voice turned into a sort of deity threatens all those who deride him and expresses his wrath and angry despair. Toward the last sections of the poem, however, the poetic voice has found harmony in the beauty of women and love, as we see in "Como una gota" (Like a drop), "Rumor del sol" (Rumor of the sun), "Tras la piel titubeante del otoño" (After the hesitating skin of autumn), and other poems.[32] In another collection, *Razones de la voz* (Reasons of the voice), Wong includes erotic poems such as "Espuma melacólica," "Piedra que germina," and "Ceremonial para Leticia," combining them with pantheistic chants to nature like "Resaca devorando el arrecife" (Undertow devouring the reef). Other poems establish an intertextual dialogue with Jaime Sabines, Octavio Paz, Remedios Varo, and other Mexican writers and artists. But perhaps the most intriguing and successful poems are those in which Wong explores metaphysical realities, such as "La noche yace aquí" (The night lies here) or "Herida brutal de los sentidos" (Brutal wound of the senses).[33]

Conclusion

Finding themes and topics that are common to the writings of all these Sino-Latin American authors is not an easy task since the sociopolitical circumstances that surround them are obviously extremely variegated. Therefore, any generalization runs the risk of falling into essentialism, reductionism, or homogenization of a clearly diverse corpus of works. At any rate, it is clear that, in many cases, texts dealing with Chinese Latin American and Caribbean characters and topics tend to explore the migrants' reasons for leaving

China and the different degrees of suffering, assimilation, or social agency enjoyed in the adopted country. They also reflect their uninterrupted contact with the sending communities. As previously mentioned, despite the large number of authors listed here, the story of the Chinese diaspora in the Americas and the Caribbean basin has been narrated, for the most part, by non-Chinese authors. But regardless of their ethnicity, many of these writers focus on the cultural differences as well as on the hybridity, liminality, and transculturation that characterize daily life in the Chinese and Sino-Latin American communities (or "colonies" as they are called in the region). These works also reveal the inevitable mixture of Sinitic and Latin American cultures, despite the Chinese immigrants' reputation, throughout Latin America, for preferring isolation from mainstream society. In other cases, however, the same authors that contest the stereotype highlight this very insularity in their works. For example, Siu Kam-Wen seems to feel a sort of claustrophobia in the demanding world of Chinese shopkeepers and in the traditionalism of strict kinship norms, while at the same time representing numerous cases of hybridity, particularly in autobiographical passages. These feelings, along with sociopolitical adversities, have made remigration another important literary topic. With each of these migrations, and with the passing of time, feelings of nostalgia may also find their way into the writing. Besides migrations and remigrations, some of these books reflect the tradition of returning to mainland China, Taiwan, Hong Kong, or Macao to look for a young wife.

Perhaps one of the most important overarching leitmotifs in Sino-Latin American cultural production is the presentation of the Chinese communities as an integral part of the nation. In fact, a narrative of "belonging" is often the latent or overt theme of the work. The justification may vary: from the participation of the Chinese in the wars of independence (as is the case the *chinos mambises* in Cuba) to the partial or complete unfamiliarity with Chinese cultures and languages, many other reasons are cited. As previously stated, the Chinese presence in national literatures as both characters and authors challenges the constructed dualism of the black/white or indigenous/*Criollo* discourse. In contrast, in other cases, texts offer a diasporic version of national identity, which shields itself from Eurocentric hegemony or "*Criollo*-centric" narratives of the nation. Another crucial overarching leitmotif is the realization that, with the freedom and social agency sometimes provided by flexible transnationalism, mobility and deterritorialization, often comes a great deal of marginalization, uprootedness, suffering, and victimhood (including imprisonment); indentured servitude, slavery, xenophobia, and Sinophobia are also recurrent topics in these works. While multiple displacements may allow Chinese subjects to flee repressive regimes and social customs, they can also make them fall into equality oppressive and dictatorial regimes.

Notes

Part of the information included in this chapter was published in my book *Imaging the Chinese in Cuban Literature and Culture* (Gainesville: University Press of Florida, 2008) and in the article "Sino-Peruvian identity and community as prison: Siu Kam Wen's rendering of self-exploitation and other survival strategies," *Afro-Hispanic Review* 27, no. 1 (Spring 2008): 73–90.

1. Denise Helly, Introduction, *The Cuba Commission Report: A Hidden History of the Chinese in Cuba*, ed. Denise Helly (Baltimore: Johns Hopkins University Press, 1993), 14.

2. Antonio Chuffat Latour, *Apunte histórico de los chinos en Cuba* (Havana: Molina, 1927), 16. All the translations in this chapter are mine.

3. "El refinamiento de la raza blanca" and "Civilizarse" (Ibid., 15–16).

4. "Hat Min Gan Ga/Toy pok ton un hay yan/Sen mai mon / Go sion ni chi yau/Tun lin/ Go sion ni fac tak/Chiok Fi/Shi Chung Chay/Chan sen pen tan/Chi yau-Chi yau/Go shion" (Ibid., 89).

5. Regino Pedroso, *Nosotros* (Havana: Letras Cubanas, 1984).

6. Regino Pedroso, *El ciruelo de Yuan Pei Fu. Poemas Chinos* (Havana: P. Fernández y compañía, 1955).

7. Pedro Zulen, *El olmo incierto de la nevada* (Lima: n.p., 1930). This collection included poems from previous books such as *CLAT Whitman en las bacanales, El poema sin nombre, El poema de una lágrima, Así habló una azucena,* and *El errante.* Zulen is also known as a pro-indigenous activist.

8. "Sus ojos artísticamente rasgados me miraban tiernamente" (A. Kuan Veng, *Mey Shut, poemas en prosa* [Lima: Lux, 1924], n.p.).

9. "Si como antaño las calles de Lima se bautizaran según los oficios que predominara en ellas—Bodegueros, Espaderos, Mercaderes—, el jirón Cailloma sería hoy *Prostitutas,* y Quilca, la popular calle *Borrachos*" (Julio Villanueva Chang, *Mariposas y murciélagos: crónicas y perfiles* [Lima: Universidad Peruana de Ciencias Aplicadas (UPC)], 1999, 122).

10. Julio Villanueva Chang, *Elogios Criminales* (Mexico: Random House Mondadori, 2008).

11. Siu Kam-Wen had to migrate to the United States when he realized that without a Peruvian passport, he would never find a job in Lima. The problem was that, as he explains, they would not give him a passport if he did not have a job.

12. The daughter of Chinese immigrants, Julia Wong Kcomt studied law and political sciences at the University of Lima and humanities and social sciences at the Catholic University of Peru. She has also studied at different universities in Germany and Macau, China. Since 2006, she has organized a festival of Peruvian-Argentine poetry in Buenos Aires.

13. "mi apellido"; "no preciso llamarme Julia/puedo enseñar un sello"; "he soñado un barco enorme cruzando el Pacífico/(mi abuelo murió sin su trenza de culí y con hábito morado)"; "duerme chinita"; "por mi piel negrísima/y un agujero sobrante en las costillas/que no concuerdan con la estética occidental" (Julia Wong Kcomt, *Historia de una gorda* [Trujillo, Peru: Libertad, 1994]).

14. "Me llamas/(¿a mí,/Te refieres a mí?/Una mujer china siempre está plagada de dudas" (Julia Wong Kcomt, *Los últimos blues de Buddha* [Lima: Noevas Editoras, 2002], 10–13).

15. "Como gruesa de lápices/amarrada con cintas brillantes/así somos las mujeres/así somos las mujeres chinas." Likewise, in "Harnero" (Sieve) she states, "Like a bundle of pencils/ Tied with shiny tape/That's how we, women, are/That's how we, Chinese women, are" (Ibid., 6–9).

16. "Porque hay que entender chino,/para saber por qué las rayas del tigre/están pintadas por hombres ricos" (Ibid., 23–24).

17. Sui-Yun was recently invited to represent both China and Peru during the Giornata Mondiale della Poesia (World day of poetry), which took place in Frascati, Italy. She lives between Peru and Europe and, in consonance with one of the main themes in her poetry, she devotes part of her time to ecological preservation.

18. Sui-Yun (Katie Wong Loo), *Cresciente* (California: n.p., 1977), 8–11.

19. "y el recuerdo de faroles chinos" (Sui-Yun [Katie Wong Loo], *Rosa fálica* [Lima: Loto, 1983], 3).

20. Mario Wong was born in Lima to a Chinese father and a *Criolla* mother, studied economics at the University of San Marcos, and has lived in Paris since 1989. He collaborates with the Mexican magazine *Archipiélago* and with the Peruvian journals such as *Maestra Vida* and *Ciberayllu*. He also participated in the anthology *Cuentos Migratorios, 14 escritores latino-americanos en París* (2000).

21. Mario Wong, *El testamento de la tormenta* (Madrid: Huerga Fierro Editores, 1997).

22. Born in Los Santos in 1934, Chong Ruiz received a bachelor of arts in philosophy and history from the University of Panama, a diploma in social sciences from the Universidad Nacional de Honduras, and another diploma in cinematography from the Cinematographic Institute in California. He has published several collections of short stories, often dealing with life in the countryside: *Con los pies en la tierra* (1958), *Del mar y de la selva* (1962), *A la luz del fogón* (1963), *Techumbres, guijarros y pueblo* (1964), *Otra vez, pueblo* (1966), *Canción del hombre en la ventana* (1980), *Diario de una noche de camino* (1987), *Y entonces, tú* (1991), and *El cazador de alforja* (2001). He has also published a collection of poems entitled *Poemas*, the plays *Detrás de la noche* (1966), *Después del manglar* (1973), and *Yaya* (1981), and the study *Los chinos en la sociedad panameña* (1993).

23. Eustorgio A. Chong Ruiz, *Techumbres, guijarros y pueblo* . . . (Panama: Ediciones del Ministerio de Educación. Dirección Nacional de Cultura, 1964).

24. Eustorgio A. Chong Ruiz, *Después del manglar* (Panama City: Incude, 1973).

25. He has published the following collections of short stories: *Faragual y otros cuentos* (1960), *La mansión de la bruma, Cuentos de la cárcel* (1965), *Nochebuena mala* (1995), *Las mentiras encantadas* (1997), and *Cuentos para matar el estrés* (2002). He has also published two historical novels: *En este pueblo no mataban a nadie* (1992) and *El guerrillero transparente* (1982). He has published the following collections of poems: *Romance de la niña perdida* (n.d), *Punto 'e llanto* (1942), *Poemas corporales* (1956), *Socabón. Décimas para cantar* (1959), *Dos poemas* (1963), *Versos del pueblo. Décimas* (1972), *Versos para entrar al canal* (1979), *Crónica de siete nombres memorables* (1980), *Las tonadas y los cuentos de la cigarra* (1987), *El gallo de las horas* (1993), *Cantadera. 130 décimas para cantar* (1995). Changmarín has also tried to deliver his social message through children's literature, publishing the novels *El cholito que llegó a general* (1978) and the semiautobiographical *Las gracias y las desgracias de Chico Perico* (2005), and the collections of poems *Versos de muchachita* (1974), *Las tonadas y los*

cuentos de la cigarra (1975), and *La muñeca de Tusa* (2001). He has published five essays about poetry and international politics: *Base social de la décima en Panamá* (1965), *Algunas áreas folclóricas de Veraguas* (1975), *Panamá 1903-1970* (1979), *Victoriano Lorenzo, primera víctima del canal norteamericano* (1980), *Vigencia de la décima en Panamá, en itinerario de una nación 1903–2003* (2003).

26. Carlos Francisco Changmarín, *Punto ´e llanto y Arcoiris en doce colores o Poema de un pueblo* (Panamá: Imprenta nacional, 1948). Among other Sino-Panamanian writers worth mentioning are the following: César Young Núñez, Carlos Fong, Elida Wong Miranda, Gloria Youmg, Luis Wong Vega, José Chen Barria, Berta Alicia Chen P., Lucía Kusial Singh, Arnoldo Díaz Wong, Carlos Wong, José Young, Camilo Siu, Lucy Cristina Chau, Moisés Chong, and Dagoberto Chung.

27. Juan Chow has worked as a journalist for the journal *Barricada*. His first collection of poems, *Oficios del caos* (1986; reedited as *Oficios del caos y otras versiones*, 2005), was influenced by surrealism and daily rationalism. His other collections of poems are *La inteligencia del alacrán y otros boleros* (2001), *Retórica del seductor* (2001), and *El amor razonado* (2004). Chow has also published the book of criticism *La paja en el ojo 1995–2002* (2003). His playful and ironic poetry has been compared to that of the Salvadoran poet and revolutionary Roque Dalton (1935–1975).

28. Juan Chow, *Oficio del caos* (Managua: Unión de Escritores de Nicaragua, Asociación Sandinista de Trabajadores de la Cultura, 1986).

29. "En verdad que me siento agradecido con la vida por mi linaje, por mis orígenes dinásticos, sobre todo porque tuve un padre que veía al mundo no con la óptica burda y hasta grosera del occidental, sino con la milenaria sabiduría de los ancestros chinos, con la constancia y disciplina que forjan universos y descubren la infinita multiplicidad de las diez mil cosas que integran al Cosmos" (n.p.).

30. He has published the collection of short stories *La edad de las mariposas* (1990) and the collections of poems: *Si te das al viento* (1978), *Fragmentaciones* (1979), *En un lugar del mundo* (1981), *Cántiga para la hermana Esther* (1982), *He brotado raíces* (1982), *Vuelta al camino* (collective book) (1983), *No creo que las rosas cambien* (1986), *El conjuro del druida* (1992), *Enardecida luz* (1992), *Vocación de espuma* (1993), *A pesar de los escombros* (1994), *Ritual de ausencias* (1994), *Espejo a la deriva* (1996), *Cantares del escriba* (1999), *Espuma negra* (2000), *Razones de la voz* (2000), *Piedra que germina* (2001), *Fulgor de la desdicha* (2002), and *Rubor de la ceniza* (2002). Wong has also edited several anthologies and has published the following essays and collections of essays: *Eso que llamamos poesía* (1974), *Una indagación sobre el hombre. Muerte sin fin, de José Gorostiza* (1982), *La salvación y la ira* (1986), *Entre las musas y Apolo. Presencia y realidad de la poesía mexicana* (1992), *Hacia lo eterno mínimo. Otra lectura de* Muerte sin fin (1995), *La pugna sagrada. Comunicación y poesía* (1997), *El secreto del verso* (2001), *Jaime Sabines. Entre lo tierno y lo trágico* (2005), and *Poética de lo sagrado. El lenguaje de Adán* (2006).

31. Óscar Wong, *Poética de lo sagrado. El lenguaje de Adán* (Mexico: Coyoacán, 2006).

32. Óscar Wong, *Enardecida luz* (Mexico: Universidad Nacional Autónoma de México, 1992).

33. Óscar Wong, *Razones de la voz* (Mexico: Práctica Mortal, 2002).

Glossary of
Sinitic Terms, Names, and Titles

Abracadabra (*Wuyan*) 巫言

"An Afternoon in Late Autumn" (*Yige shenqiu de xiawu*) 一個深秋的下午

Again the Palm Trees (*Youjian zonglü*) 又見棕櫚

Ahronglong Sakinu 亞榮隆·撒可努

Ai Wu 艾蕪

ailun 埃崙

ailun daichan 埃崙待剷

aiguo 愛國

aijia 愛家

aixiang 愛鄉

Alai (A legs) 阿來

The Analects Fortnightly (*Lunyu banyuekan*) 論語半月刊

Ang, Ien 洪美恩

"Another Embodiment" (*Ling yige huasheng*) 另一個化生身

Ao Niu wang 澳紐網

Atayal Footprints (*Taiya jiaozong*) 泰雅腳蹤

Atayal's Chi-chia Bay Creek (*Taiyaren de qijiawan xi*) 泰雅人的七家灣溪

Auvini Kadresengan 奧威尼·卡露斯

Awakening Foundation Press (*Funü xinzhi zazhishe*) 婦女新知雜誌社

Baba 峇峇

Baba and Nyonya (*Baba yu Niangre*) 峇峇與娘惹

Bada shanren 八大山人

Badai 巴代

Bai Fei 百非

baokuo zaiwai 包括在外

baolie 暴烈

baoliu 保留

The Bard's Dream (*Liulang geshou de meng*) 流浪歌手的夢

Barren Island (*Kudao*) 苦島

Beautiful Building (*Meili daxia*) 美麗大廈

Beautiful Ears of Rice (*Meili de daosui*) 美麗的稻穗

Bei Dao 北島

beidi 北狄

beishang 悲傷

"The Beloved" (*Ai de jiejing*) 愛的結晶

Beneath the Red Banner (*Zheng hongqi xia*) 正紅旗下

bensheng 本省

Beyond the Myriad Mountains Flows the River (*Qianshan wai shui changliu*) 千山外水長流

bitan 筆談

Black (Hei) 黑

Black Smoke (Heiyan) 黑煙

Black Wings (Heise de chibang)
　黑色的 翅膀

"Bloody Sacrifice with Color Make-up"
　(*Caizhuang xieji*) 彩妝血祭

Blossoms in Yunqiao (Yunqiao feixu)
　雲橋飛絮

"Board the Boat Here" (*Zai zheli shang
　chuan*) 在這裡上船

Books and the City (Shu yu chengshi)
　書與城市

Boyi 伯夷

"Break up"*Juelie*) 決裂

Brown Mountain and Moon Shadow
　(*Shanzong yueying*) 山棕月影

Bu qu 不屈

"Buddhist Pilgrimage" (*Chaofo*) 朝佛

The Bud (Xinmiao) 新苗

"Buds" (*Lei*) 蕾

Bukun Ismahasan Islituan 卜袞·伊斯 瑪哈
　單·伊斯立端

The Butcher's Wife (Shafu) 殺夫

"Caifeng's Wish" (*Caifeng de xinyuan*)
　彩鳳的心願

Call of the Oriole (*Chunying yinshe*)
　春鶯吟社

Camel Xiangzi (Luotuo xiangzi) 駱駝祥子

"Camellia" (*Shanchahua*) 山茶花

Cang cheng wen cai huikan 蒼城文採會刊

cangsheng 蒼生

cao 操

cao ni ma 操你媽

caoni ma 草泥馬

caogen wenxue 草根文學

caozuo 操作

Cat Country (Maocheng ji) 貓城記

Chan Tah Wei (Chen Dawei) 陳大為

Chang, Eileen (Zhang Ailing) 張愛玲

Chang Hsi-kuo (Zhang Xiguo) 張系國

Chang Kuei-hsing (Zhang Guixing)
　張貴興

Chang Ta-chun (Zhang Dachun) 張大春

changming fugui 長命富貴

Chao Foon (Jiaofeng) 蕉風

Chen, Chien-chung 陳建忠

Chen Fangming 陳芳明

Chen Huoquan 陳火泉

Ch'en Jo-hsi (Chen Ruoxi) 陳若曦

Chen Kuan-hsing (Chen Guangxing)
　陳光興

Chen Kuiyuan 陳奎元

Chen Lianqing 陳煉青

Chen Pingyuan 陳平原

Chen Ye 陳燁

Chen Ying-chen (Chen Yingzhen) 陳映真

Chen Yingxiong (Kowan Talall) 陳英雄

Chen Yonghua 陳永華

Cheng Chou-yu (Zheng Chouyu) 鄭愁予

chengshi wu gushi 城市無故事

Cheung Yin (Zhang Yan) 張彥

Chi Pang-yuan (Qi Bangyuan) 齊邦媛

Chiang Wei-wen (Jiang Weiwen) 蔣為文

Chien Yung-hsiang (Qian Yongxiang)
　錢永祥

Chinatown Family (Tangren jie) 唐人街

"The Chinese" (*Zhongguoren*) 中國人

Chinese Australian Herald (Guangyi hua bao)
　廣益華報

Chongzhen 崇禎

Choong Yee Voon (Zhong Yiwen)
　鍾怡雯

Chow, Rey 周蕾

Chu T'ien-hsin (Zhu Tianxin) 朱天心

Chu T'ien-wen (Zhu Tianwen) 朱天文

*Chung-Wai Literary Monthly (Zhongwai
　wenxue)* 中外文學

"The Circular Day" (*Yuanxing rizi*)
　圓形日子

"City" (*Cheng*) 城

*City at the End of Time (Xingxiang
　Xianggang)* 形象香港

"City of One Person" (*Yi ge ren de
　chengshi*) 一個人的城市

The Clan of the Sun (Taiyang buluo)
　太陽部落

The Classic of Mountains and Seas
(Shanhai jing zhuan) 山海經傳
Coconut Groves (Yelin) 椰林
"Collecting Bones" (Shigu) 拾骨
Cold Sea, Deep Passion (Leng hai qing shen)
冷海情深
Cong Su 叢甦
Cosmic Wind (Yuzhou Feng) 宇宙風
Credit News (Zhengxin xinwen) 徵信新聞
The Crocodile's Journal (Eyu shouji)
鱷魚手記
Crying Camels (Kuqi de luotuo)
哭泣的駱駝
The Cuba Commission Report (Guba
Huagong kougong ce) 古巴華工口供冊

da shengyin 大聲音
Dadelavn Ibau 達德拉凡·伊苞
Dai Sijie 戴思傑
Daming Lake (Daming hu) 大明湖
"Death in Chicago" (Zhijiage zhisi)
芝加哥之死
Deekwan the Witch (Diguan) 笛鸛
Deng Xiaoping 鄧小平
Desert Island (Huangdao) 荒島
"Devilish Woman" (Monü) 魔女
Ding Ling 丁凌
Ding Yun 丁雲
Divine Land (Shenzhou) 神州
Divorce (Lihun) 離婚
Dong Shi 冬石
Dong Shuming 董恕明
dongyi 東夷
dongyin shishe 東吟詩社
Don't be Angry, Dear A'ki (Qin'ai de A'ki qing
buyao shengqi) 親愛的
A'Ki 請不要生氣
"The Door" (Men) 門
"The Dragon" (Long) 龍
Dream of the Red Chamber (Hong lou meng)
紅樓夢
Drinking Once in a Long Time (Jiujiu jiu yi ci)
久久酒一次
Dung Kai-cheung (Dong Qizhang) 董啟章

East and Beyond (Dongfang zhi dong)
東方之東
"Eclipse" (Rishi) 日蝕
"The Eradication of 'The City'" (Xiaomie
chengshi) 消滅城市
Escape (Taowang) 逃亡

Fang Beifang 方北方
Fang Tian 方天
Fang Xuejia 房學嘉
fangong huaixiang 反共懷鄉
fangzhu 放逐
fannu 番奴
fei zhuliu 非主流
"The Fertile Town Chalk Circle" (Feitu zhen
huilan ji) 肥土鎮灰闌記
"Fin-de-siècle Splendor" (Shijimo de huali)
世紀末的華麗
Flying Carpet (Fei zhan) 飛氈
Fragrant Rice (Daoxiang) 稻香
"Freedom and Roti" (Ziyou yu mianbao)
自由與麵包
"From the Margins to the Intersection"
(Cong bianyuan dao jiaoji)
從邊緣到交集
Fu Chengde 傅承得
"Fungus of the Earth" (Diqiu zhimei)
地球之黴

ga 假
gaichi bungaku 外地文學
gaige kaifang 改革開放
gali 假黎
"A Gali Woman" (Jialipo) 假黎婆
gan 幹
Gao Xingjian 高行健
Ge Yang 格央
"Gecko" (Bihu) 壁虎
Gela Grows Up (Gela zhangda) 格拉長大
"A Generation" (Yidairen) 一代人
A God Without Gender (Wu xingbie de shen)
無性別的神
"Going Back" (Guisu) 歸宿
gongsuo 公所

Goodbye, Eagles (Laoying, zaijian)
老鷹，再見
Goodbye Snow Country (Xueguo zaijian)
雪國再見
"Grafton Bridge" (Gelafudun qiao)
格拉 夫頓喬
"A Group of Unemployed Persons"
(Yiqun shiye de ren) 一群失業的人
Gu Cheng 顧城
Gu Yanwu 顧炎武
gui 鬼
guixiu wenxue 閨秀文學
Guo Lianghui 郭良惠
Guo Moruo 郭沫若
Guo Qiusheng 郭秋生
guochi 國恥
guojia 國家
Guoyu 國語
guqi 骨氣
Gu yuezu 古越族

Ha Gong 哈公
Ha Jin 哈金
Haidong Blues (Haidongqing) 海東青
haijin 海禁
haiwai huaren 海外華人
haiwai huawen wenxue 海外華文文學
haiwai wenxue 海外文學
Hakka 客家
Hamada Hayao 濱田隼雄
Han 漢
Han Shaogong 韓少功
Han Shuli 韓書力
Hanban 漢辦
Hand Scrolls (Shoujuan) 手卷
Hanyu 漢語
Hanzang yuxi 漢藏語系
He Furen 何福仁
"Head and Body" (Shou yu ti)
首與體
"Her Tragic Death" (Kelian ta sile)
可憐她死了

Herds of Elephants (Qun xiang) 群象
Heritage: Walking out of Accusation
(Chuancheng: zouchu kongsu)
傳承: 走出控訴
High Mountain Youth (Gaoshan qing)
高山青
A History of Taiwan's New Literature (Taiwan
xin wenxue shi) 台灣新文學史
Ho Sok Fong (He Shufang) 賀淑芳
"Hometown" (Guxiang) 故鄉
Hometown of Taiwanese Cherries
(Shanyinghua de guxiang)
山櫻花的故鄉
Hong Huang 洪荒
Hong Quan 洪泉
"Hong Kong" (Xianggang) 香港
"How Couldn't We Promote Nativist
Literature?" (Zenyang bu tichang xiangtu
wenxue) 怎樣不提倡鄉土文 學
Hsia Yu (Xia Yu) 夏宇
Hsiao Li-hung (Xiao Lihong) 蕭麗紅
Hsu Fu-kuan (Xu Fuguan) 徐復觀
hu 胡
Hu Jieqing 胡絜青
Hu Jintao 胡錦濤
Hu Lancheng 胡蘭成
Hu Yaobang 胡耀邦
Hua 華
huaju 話劇
Huang Baotao 黃寶桃
Huang Fengzi 黃鳳姿
Huang, Hsinya 黃心雅
Huang Mei-e 黃美娥
Huang Seng 黃僧
Huang Shaohong 黃紹竑
Huang Shihui 黃石輝
huang wen ye zi 荒文野字
Huang Wukun 黃戊昆
Huang Yai 黃崖
Huang Zongxi 黃宗羲
huaqiao 華僑
huaqiao wenxue 華僑文學

huaren 華人
Huawen 華文
Huawen guoji 華文國際
Huawen wenxue 華文文學
huaxia 華夏
Huayi 華裔
Huayu 華語
Huayu wenxue 華語文學
Huayu yuxi wenxue 華語語系文學
Huayu yuxi yanjiu 華語語系研究
Huazong shijie huawen wenxue jiang
    花蹤世界華文文學獎
huiguan 會館
huigui zuguo 回歸祖國
"The Hunt" (Shoulie) 狩獵
Hunters' Culture (Lieren wenhua)
    獵人文化

"In Remembrance of My Buddies from the
    Military Compound" (Xiang wo juancun
    de xiongdimen) 想我眷村的兄弟們
"Inscription About a Humble House"
    (Loushi ming) 陋室銘
"Inscription About a Wooden Building"
    (Muwu ming) 木屋銘
It Ta-os (Gen Ah-sheng) 根阿盛

Ji Qiguang 季麒光
jia 家
Jian Zhen 簡媜
Jiang Guangci 蔣光慈
Jiang Risheng 江日昇
jiaoxin 交心
Jiarong 嘉絨
jiaxiang 家鄉
jiazu 家族
The Jiling Chronicles (Jiling chunqiu)
    吉陵春秋
jingyang qianxian 景仰前賢
jiujinshan 舊金山
juancun wenxue 眷村文學
jueju 絕句

Juniper Loa (Lai Boying) 賴柏英
Junma 駿馬
junzhu 君主

kan 看
kangzhan wenxue 抗戰文學
Kawanakajima (Chuanzhongdao) 川中島
King Ban Hui (Gong Wanhui) 龔萬輝
King Wen (Wen Gong) 文公
kōmin bungaku 皇民文學
kōminka 皇民化
"Kowloon" (Jiulong) 九龍
Koxinga (Guoxingye) 國姓爺
kuaigan 快感
kuei (gui) 鬼
Kung Peng-cheng (Gong Pengcheng)
    龔鵬程
Kuo Pao Kun (Guo Baokun) 郭寶崑
Kuomintang (KMT) 國民黨

Labyrinthine Garden (Miyuan) 迷園
Lai He 賴和
Lai, Him Mark 麥禮謙
Lam Song (Lin Shuang) 林爽
langyi 狼醫
Lao Nan 老南
Lao She 老舍
The Last Hunter (Zuihou de lieren)
    最後的獵人
"A La-tzu Woman" (Lazi fu) 拉子婦
Lau Siu-kai 劉兆佳
Lazy Corpse Ma (Lanshi Ma) 懶屍嬤
Leaving Tongfang (Likai tongfang)
    離開同方
Lee, Leo Ou-fan 李歐梵
Lee Tian Poh (Li Tianbao) 李天葆
Legends and Stories of Baka Mountains
    (Bakashan chuanshuo yu gushi)
    巴卡山傳說與故事
Lei Hsiang (Lei Xiang) 雷驤
Leung Ping-kwan (P. K. Leung) 梁秉鈞
Leung Po-shan (Liang Baoshan) 梁寶珊

Li Ang 李昂

Li Hongzhang 李鴻章

Li Rui 李銳

Li Xiangen 李仙根

Li Xiangping 黎湘萍

Li Yitao 李逸濤

Li Yong-song 李永松

Li Yung-p'ing (Li Yongping) 李永平

Li Zishu 黎紫書

Liang Fang 梁放

Liang Meng Kwang (Liang Mingguang)
梁明廣

Liang Qichao 梁啟超

Liao Hui-ying 廖輝英

lienü 烈女

Lienütu 烈女圖

"Life" (Rensheng) 人生

Liglav Awu 利格拉樂·阿(女)烏

Lim Chin Chown (Lin Xingqian)
林幸謙

Lim Kien Ket (Lin Jianguo) 林建國

Lim Pow Leng (Lin Baoling) 林寶玲

Lin Haiyin 林海音

Lin, Pei-Yin 林姵吟

Lin Yutang 林語堂

Ling Zuo 凌佐

Lion's Roar (Shi sheng) 獅聲

Lishan Plantation (Lishan nongchang)
笠山農場

Literary Review (Bungaku hyōron)
文學評論

Literary Weekly (Wenyi zhoukan)
文藝週刊

Literature Quarterly (Wenxue jikan)
文學季刊

Liu Binyan 劉賓雁

Liu Daren 劉大任

Liu Na'ou 劉吶鷗

Liu Xiaofeng 劉曉峰

Liu Youhong 劉友紅

Liu Yuxi 劉禹錫

liufang 流放

liuwang 流亡

liuxuesheng 留學生

liuxuesheng wenxue 留學生文學

liuyi 流蟻

Lo Yi-chin (Luo Yijun) 駱以軍

The Lock of the Heart (Xinsuo) 心鎖

Looi Yook Tho (Lu Yutao) 呂育陶

Looking Beyond (Qi dao) 奇島

Looking for the Lost Arrow (Xunzhao shiluo
de jianshi) 尋找失落的箭矢

Love and Revolution (Xingdao tianya)
行道天涯

"A Love Story Before Dawn" (Tianliang qian
de lian'ai gushi) 天亮前的戀愛故事

Lu Cheng-hui (Lü Zhenghui) 呂正惠

Lu Chun-yu 呂淳鈺

Lu Heruo 呂赫若

Lu Xun 魯迅

Lung Ying-tsung (Long Yingzong)
龍瑛宗

Luo Xianglin 羅香林

luodi shenggen 落地生根

luoye guigen 落葉歸根

lüshi 律詩

Lyiking Yuma 麗依京·尤瑪

Ma Hua 馬華

Ma Hua wenxue 馬華文學

Ma Hua wenyi dutexing 馬華文藝獨特性

Ma Lihua 馬麗華

Ma Yuan 馬原

mai zhuzai 賣豬仔

Malan's Autobiography (Malan zizhuan)
馬蘭自傳

Mama Looking for Her Cat (Xunzhao
xiaomao de mama) 尋找小貓的媽媽

Man Sing Times (Minsheng bao) 民聲報

manyi 蠻夷

Mao Xiang 冒襄

"Marvels of a Floating City" (Fu cheng zhiyi)
浮城誌異

Masao Aki 馬紹·阿紀

"A Measuring Stick" (Yi gan chengzai) 一
桿稱仔

Medrön (Meizhuo) 梅卓

meiguo 美國

Meixingzhe 媚行者
Memories of Peking (Chengnan jiushi) 城南舊事
Meng Yao 孟瑤
menglong 朦朧
Miao Xiu 苗秀
Minnan 閩南
Minnan yu 閩南語
minzu tuanjie 民族團結
Mo Yan 莫言
Modern Literature (Xiandai wenxue) 現代文學
Mok, Tze Ming 莫志明
Monanen Malialiaves 莫那能
Monkey Cup (Hou bei) 猴杯
The Moon Clan (Yueqiu xingshi) 月球姓氏
Morning Star (Chenxing) 晨星
Mother Fish (Mu yu) 母魚
Mountain-Sea Culture (Shanhai wenhua) 山海文化
Mountains of Sadness (Beiqing de shanlin) 悲情的山林
Moy Sook Chin (Mei Shuzhen) 梅淑貞
"Mt. Eden" (Yidian shan) 伊甸山
Mu Shiying 穆時英
Mu Yan 木焱
Muddiness (Hunzhuo) 渾濁
Muddy River (Nihe) 泥河
Mulberry and Peach: Two Women of China (Sangqing yu taohong) 桑青與桃紅
Musha (Wushe) 霧社
"My Brother, A Runaway Soldier" (Taobing erge) 逃兵二哥
My City (Wo cheng) 我城
My Country and My People 吾國吾民
My Cousin Lianyi (Lianyi biaomei) 漣漪表妹
Mykiwi 瑪克威
Mysterious Disappearance (Shenmi de xiaoshi) 神秘的消失
Mythology of Eight-Generation Bay (Badaiwan de shenhua) 八代灣的神話

na 拿
nanman 南蠻
Nanyang 南洋
Nanyang secai wenxue 南洋色彩文學
Nanyang Siang Pau (Nanyang shangbao) 南洋商報
Nanyang University 南洋大學
Nanyang Weekly (Nanyang zhoubao) 南洋週報
napolun 拿破崙
Native Sons (Yuanxiang ren) 原鄉人
Neizheng bu 內政部
Nequo Sokluman 乜寇·索克魯曼
The Nether City (Ming cheng) 冥城
"Never Mention It Again" (Bie zai tiqi) 別再提起
New Taiwan Citizen (Taiwan xinminbao) 台灣新民報
New Taiwan Sinophone Daily (Hanwen Taiwan riri xinbao) 漢文台灣日日新報
"New Year's Banquet" (Chunyan) 春宴
The New Zealand Chinese Growers Monthly (Qiao nong yuekan) 僑農月刊
"Newspaper Boy" (Shimbun haitatsufu) 新聞配達伕
Ng, Kim Chew 黃錦樹
Ngawa Alai (Aba Alai) 阿垻阿來
Nieh, Hualing (Nie Hualing) 聶華苓
Niezi 孽子
"A Night in Hong Kong" (Xianggang de yi ye) 香港的一夜
"A Night Without Stars" (Meiyou xingguang de ye) 沒有星光的夜
"Nineteen Days of the New Party" (Xindang shijiu ri) 新黨十九日
Nishikawa Mitsuru 西川滿
Niuxilan Huawen zuojia xiehui 紐西蘭華文作家協會
Notes of a Desolate Man (Huangren shouji) 荒人手記
Notes of a Doctor on Orchid Island (Lanyu xingyi ji) 蘭嶼行醫記
Notes on Tibet (Xizang biji) 西藏筆記
nü'er guo 女兒國

The Old Capital (Gudu) 古都
Oleanders (Jiazhutao) 夾竹桃
One Man's Bible (Yige ren de shengjing) 一
　　個人的聖經
Orphan of Asia (Ajia no koji or Yaxiya de
　　gu'er) 亞細亞的孤兒
The Other Shore (Bi an) 彼岸
Outside the Window (Chuangwai) 窗外
Ouyang Zi 歐陽子
"The Ox Carriage" (Gyūsha) 牛車

Pai, Hsien-yung (Bai Xianyong) 白先勇
Paiz Mukunana 白茲·牟固那那
Pak Yiu (Bai Yao) 白垚
Pan Guangdan 潘光旦
Pan Renmu 潘人木
Pan Yutong 潘雨桐
Pema Tseden (Wanma Caidan) 萬瑪才旦
The Philosophy of Lao Zhang (Lao Zhang
　　zhexue) 老張的哲學
pianwen 駢文
Ping Lu 平路
polun 破崙
The Postcolonial Chronicles (Houzhimin zhi)
　　後殖民誌
Post-Loyalist Writings (Hou yimin xiezuo)
　　後遺民寫作
"A Prematurely Withered Bud" (Caodiao de
　　beilei) 早凋的蓓蕾
Pu Chung-cheng (Basuya) 浦忠成
Putonghua 普通話

qi 棄
Qi Jun 琦君
Qian Qianyi 錢謙益
Qian Xuantong 錢玄同
qiao 瞧
qiaomin wenxue 僑民文學
qiaomin zuojia 僑民作家
qiaosheng 僑生
Qideng Sheng 七等生
Qiong Yao 瓊瑤
Qiu Miaojin 邱妙津
Qiu Shizhen 丘士珍

qiyan jueju 七言絕句
qiyan lüshi 七言律詩
Quan Zenggu 全增嘏
Quan Zuwang 全祖望

Rahic Talif 拉黑子·達立夫
Rain (Yu) 雨
The Rainforest Trilogy (Yulin sanbuqu)
　　雨林三部曲
Rape Seeds (Youma caizi) 油麻菜籽
Recollections of Qing River (Menghui Qinghe)
　　夢回青河
Record from Tamkang (Danjiang ji) 淡江記
Records of Waters and Lands (Lianhai shuitu
　　zhi) 連海水土志
Red Poppies (Chen'ai luoding, lit. "the dust
　　settles") 塵埃落定
"Remaining Snow" (Canxue) 殘雪
Remains of Life (Yusheng) 餘生
Renmin wenxue 人民文學
renzhongxue 人種學
Reticence, Muteness, Humility (Chenmo, anya,
　　weixiao) 沉默·暗啞·微小
"Revisiting Nativist Literature" (Zaitan
　　xiangtu wenxue) 再談鄉土文學
Rimui Aki 裡慕伊·阿紀
River Elegy (He shang) 河殤
"The Road" (Michi) 道
Rou Shi 柔石
Ruan Ji 阮籍

Sahara Stories (Sahala de gushi)
　　撒哈拉的故事
Saisai (Xi Xi) 西西
San Mao 三毛
Sanliujiu xiaobao 三六九小報
sansan jikan 三三集刊
Science Fiction World (Kehuan shijie)
　　科幻世界
"Season of Blossoms" (Huakai shijie)
　　花開時節
Sebo (Gsal po) 色波
Seen Mun Kong (Xian Wenguang) 冼文光
Sen Kim Soon (Xin Yinsong) 辛吟松

Sén-háks (xinke) 新客

"Sense of Sight, or Island No. 5" (Shijue, huo dao zhi wu) 視覺, 或島之五

The Seven-Generation Affectionate Bonds Between Taiwan and China (Qishi yinyuan zhi Taiwan-Zhongguo qingren) 七世姻緣之台灣-中國情人

Sha Qin 沙禽

Shan, Te-hsing 單德興

shandi ren 山地人

shandi wenxue 山地文學

Shang Wanjun 商晚筠

Shanghai Baby (Shanghai bao bei) 上海寶貝

Shanghai Times (Shen bao) 申報

Shao Ting 邵挺

shehua 奢華

Shen Guangwen 沈光文

Shen, Shuang 沈雙

shetou 舌頭

shi 士

Shi Shuqing 施淑青

Shi Tao 石濤

Shi Zhecun 施蟄存

Shiernüse 十二女色

Shih, Annie (Shi Li'an) 石莉安

Shih, Shu-mei 史書美

shijie huawen wenxue 世界華文文學

Shiqu de jinlingzi 失去的金鈴子

shitou 石頭

shizu 世族

Shu (Sumuru) Qingchun 舒慶春

shuangchong guoji 雙重國籍

shumianyu 書面語

Shuqi 叔齊

Silent Island (Chenmo zhi dao) 沉默之島

Silhouette/Shadow (Ceying huo yingzi) 側影或影子

Sin Chew Daily (Xingzhou ribao) 星洲日報

Sin Kok Min Jit Pao (Xin guomin ribao) 新國民日報

Sin Kok Min Magazine (Xin guomin zazhi) 新國民雜誌

Sinophone Malaysian Literature and Chineseness (Ma Hua wenxue yu Zhongguoxing) 馬華文學與中國性

Siren Song (Sailian zhi ge) 賽蓮之歌

Sirius (Tianlangxing) 天狼星

Siyapenjipeaya 夏本奇伯愛雅

"Small Boat" (Xiao chuan) 小船

Song Tze-lai (Song Zelai) 宋澤萊

Song Tzyy Herng (Song Ziheng) 宋子衡

Soul Mountain (Ling shan) 靈山

The Sound of a Flute in the Mountains (Shanye disheng) 山野笛聲

"Southern Barbarian" (Nan man) 南蠻

"A Space of One's Own" (Ziji de tiankong) 自己的天空

Spring Dreams Over White Water Lake (Baishuihu chunmeng) 白水湖春夢

"The Story of Blood" (Xie de gushi) 血的故事

"The Story of Fertile Town" (Feitu zhen de gushi) 肥土鎮的故事

Straits Gazette (Lat Pau) 叻報

"Strange Encounters in a Mansion" (Haozhai qiyuan) 豪宅奇緣

Student Weekly (Xuesheng zhoubao) 學生週報

A Study of the Origins of Hakka (Kejia yuanliu kao) 客家源流考

Su Tong 蘇童

Su Weizhen 蘇偉貞

Su Wu 蘇武

Su Xiaokang 蘇曉康

Su Xuelin 蘇雪林

Sun Ta-chuan (Sun Dachuan, Paelabang Danapan) 孫大川

suzhi 素質

Syman Rapongan 夏曼·藍波安

Szeto, Mirana May 司徒薇

Taiban Sasala 台邦·撒沙勒

Taidong Hotel (Taidong lüguan) 泰東旅館

Taiwan Battlefront (Taiwan zhanxian) 台灣戰線

Taiwan Cultural Association (*Taiwan bunka kyōkai* or *Taiwan wenhua xiehui*) 台灣文化協會

Taiwan huawen yundong 台灣話文運動

Taiwan Indigenous (*Taiwanyuan*) 台灣原

"Taiwan Miracle" (*Taiwan qiji*) 台灣奇跡

Taiwan Southern (*Taiwan nanshe*) 台灣南社

Taiwan Trilogy (*Taiwan sanbuqu*) 台灣三部曲

Taiwansheng funü xiezuo xiehui 台灣省婦女寫作協會

Taiyu 台語

Tale of Two Strangers (*Yixiang ren*) 異鄉人

tan 毯

Tan Chee Hon (Chen Zhihong) 陳志鴻

Tan Cheng Sin (Chen Zhengxin) 陳政欣

Tan, E.K. 陳榮強

Tan Lark Sye (Chen Liushi) 陳六使

Tan Swie Hian (Chen Ruixian) 陳瑞獻

Tang ren 唐人

Taozhugong (Lord Taozhu) 陶朱公

Tashi Dawa (Zhaxi Dawa) 扎西達娃

Teahouse (*Chaguan*) 茶館

Tee, Kim Tong 張錦忠

Testament of Montmartre (*Mengmate yishu*) 蒙馬特遺書

"This Half of My Life" (*Zan zhe banbeizi*) 咱這半輩子

This Human World (*Renjian shi*) 人間世

This Love, This Life (*Jinsheng yuan*) 今生緣

A Thousand Moons on a Thousand Rivers (*Qianjiang youshui qianjiang yue*) 千江有水千江月

ti 提

tianzi 天子

Tibet: A Soul Knotted on a Leather Rope (*Xizang, ji zai pisheng jieshang de hun*) 西藏，系在皮繩結上的魂

Tibet Daily (*Xizang ribao*) 西藏日報

Tibet: The Mysterious Years (*Xizang: yinmi suiyue*) 西藏：隱秘歲月

Tibetan Literature (*Xizang wenxue*) 西藏文學

Tie Kang 鐵抗

Tionghua (*Zhonghua*) 中華

Tong Zhen 童真

tongbao 同胞

Tonku Saveg (*Donggu shafei*) 東谷沙飛

Topas Tamapima 拓拔斯·塔瑪匹瑪

Traces of Dreams in Foreign Lands (*Yuwai menghen*) 域外夢痕

Tsai, Chien-hsin 蔡建鑫

Tu, Wei-ming 杜維明

tun yu jing meng 豚語鯨夢

Tusán (*tusheng*) 土生

The Two Mas (*Erma*) 二馬

Unfinished (*Wei liao*) 未了

Unforgettable Reminiscences (*Yi nanwang*) 意難忘

Unitas Publisher (*Lianhe wenxue*) 聯合文學

Unofficial Record of Taiwan (*Taiwan waiji*) 台灣外記

"Vase" (*Huaping*) 花瓶

"Volunteer Soldiers" (*Shiganhei*) 志願兵

waisheng 外省

waishengren 外省人

Walis Loqang 娃利斯·羅干

Walis Norgan 瓦歷斯·諾幹

Wan Kok Seng (Wen Xiangying) 溫祥英

Wang Anyi 王安憶

Wang, David Der-wei 王德威

Wang, Gungwu 王賡武

Wang, Ling-chi 王靈智

Wang Meng'ou 王夢鷗

Wang Wen-hsing (Wang Wenxing) 王文興

Wang Chen-ho (Wang Zhenhe) 王禎和

wangdi 王帝

wanku 紈綺

"The Weaker, Are Your Names Women?" (*Ruozhe, nide mingzi shi nüren*) 弱者，妳的名字是女人？

Wee Juan Hiong (Huang Yuanxiong) 黃遠雄

Wei Hui 衛慧

Wei Jiangong 魏建功

Wei Yun 韋暈

weihu 維護

Weiliang's Love (*Weiliang de ai*) 唯良 的愛

Weise (Özer) 唯色

wen 文

Wen Renping 溫任平

Wen Rui'an 溫瑞安

Wen Yiduo 聞一多

Weng Nao 翁鬧

wenzi lianjinshu 文字煉金術

"The Western Toy" (*Yang wanju*) 洋玩具

When Will You Return? (*Heri jun zailai*) 何日君再來

Who Will Wear the Beautiful Clothes I Weaved? (*Shei lai chuan wo zhide meili yishang*) 誰來穿我織的美麗衣裳

Wild Boar, Flying Squirrel, Sakinu (*Shanzhu, feishu, sakenu*) 山豬·飛鼠·撒可努

Wildman (*Ye ren*) 野人

Wind Walker (*Zou feng de ren*) 走風的人

wing mut see (*yongwu shi*) 詠物詩

"Winter Garden" (*Dongri huayuan*) 冬日花園

Wish to Marry an Aboriginal Man (*Yuan jia shandi lang*) 願嫁山地郎

"The Woman in the Wilderness" (*Chuanguo huangye de nüren*) 穿過荒野的女人

Wong Chin Foo 王清福

Wong, Sau-ling Cynthia 黃秀玲

wonu 倭奴

Wu Chin-fa (Wu Jinfa) 吳錦發

Wu He 舞鶴

Wu Tianshang 吳天賞

Wu Yongfu 巫永福

Wu Yousheng 伍友笙

Wu Yuan 伍員

Wu Zhihui 吳稚暉

Wu Zhuoliu 吳濁流

wugen de yidai 無根的一代

wuqing baigui 無情白鬼

Wurenbao 伍人報

wuyan jueju 五言絕句

wuyan lüshi 五言律詩

xiagang 下崗

xiang 象

xiang 鄉

Xiang Cha 湘槎

xiangcun 鄉村

xiangxia 鄉下

xiangyue 鄉約

xianqi liangmu 賢妻良母

xiao 孝

Xiao Hei 小黑

Xiao Man 小曼

Xiao Sa 蕭颯

Xiaopo's Birthday (*Xiaopo de shengri*) 小坡的生日

xiaoshun 孝順

xiaozhong 效忠

Xie Bingying 謝冰瑩

Xie Ye 謝燁

xin wenxue yundong 新文學運動

xinxing wenxue 新興文學

Xiongnu 匈奴

xirong 西戎

Xishi 西施

Xu Jie 許傑

Xu Mingliang 徐明亮

xue 雪

xuetong zhuyi 血統主義

xueyuan 血緣

xungen 尋根

xungen wenzu 尋根問祖

Ya See (Ye Si) 也斯

The Yami Who Fished Rain Shoes (*Diao dao yuxie de Yameiren*) 釣到雨鞋的雅美人

yan 言

Yan Fu 殷夫

Yang Kui 楊逵

Yang Lian 楊煉

Yang Mu 楊牧

Yang Qianhe 楊千鶴
Yang Ru 楊如
Yang Shoumo 楊守默
Yang Shouyu 楊守愚
Yang Yunping 楊雲萍
Yang Zhen 央珍
yangnü 養女
yangwen 楊文
Ye Hong 葉虹
Ye Tao 葉陶
Yeh Shih-tao (Ye Shitao) 葉石濤
yi 遺
Yi Jiao 一礁
Yi Zhongtian 易中天
Yidam Tsering (Yidan Cairang)
　　依丹才讓
Yik Khuan Pao (Yiqun bao) 益群報
yi-min 遺民
Yin Xiaohuang 尹曉煌
Ying'er 英兒
yinyu 隱語
Yo Yo 友友
You Chuan 游川
youmo 幽默
Youth's Park (Qingnian yuandi) 青年園地
Yu Mowo 于沫我
Yuan Jen (Yuan Ren) 遠人
Yuan Qiongqiong 袁瓊瓊
Yuanjing 遠景
yuanzhumin wenxue 原住民文學
Yubas Naogih 游霸士·撓給赫
Yue Hengjun 樂衡軍
Yuh Kwang-chung (Yu Guangzhong)
　　余光中
Yuh Li-hua (Yu Lihua) 於梨華

Zeng Aidi 曾艾狄
Zeng Shengti 曾聖提
Zeng Xinyi 曾心儀
zhan 氈
zhancao chugen 斬草除根
zhandou wenyi 戰斗文藝
Zhang Dai 張岱

Zhang Henshui 張恨水
Zhang Huangyan 張煌言
Zhang Jinyan 張金燕
Zhang Niansheng 張念生
Zhang Shuhan 張漱涵
Zhang Shunai 張叔耐
Zhang Wenhuan 張文環
Zhang Wojun 張我軍
Zhang Xiaofeng 張曉風
Zhao Ziyue (Zhao Ziyue) 趙子曰
Zhejiang 浙江
Zhen Keshuang 鄭克塽
Zheng Chenggong 鄭成功
Zheng He (Cheng Ho) 鄭和
zheng hongqi 正紅旗
Zhexianji 謫仙記
zhi 蛭
zhifu guanrong 致富光榮
zhong 忠
Zhong Lihe 鍾理和
Zhong Taimei 鍾台妹
Zhong Lihe quanji 鍾理和全集
zhongguo 中國
Zhongguo wenxue 中國文學
Zhongguo wenyi xiehui 中國文藝協會
Zhongguohua 中國話
Zhongguoren 中國人
Zhonghua quanguo wenyijie kangdi Xiehui
　　中華全國文藝界抗敵協會
Zhonghua wenyi jiangjin weiyuanhui
　　中華文藝獎金委員會
zhongxin 忠心
Zhongyuan zhongxin zhuyi 中原中心主　義
zhongzhen 忠貞
Zhou Jinpo 周金波
Zhou Rong 周容
Zhu Da 朱耷
Zhu Shunshui 朱舜水
zongzu 宗族
Zu Di 祖逖
Zuori zhinu 昨日之怒
zuoyi wenxue 左翼文學
zuyu wenxue 族语文学

Contributors

IEN ANG is professor of cultural studies and the founding director of the Center for Cultural Research at the University of Western Sydney, Australia. Ang is also a fellow of the Australian Academy of the Humanities, and author of several noted books: *Living Room Wars: Rethinking Media Audiences in a Postmodern World* (2002), *On Not Speaking Chinese* (2001), and *Alter/Asians: Asian Identities in Art, Media, and Popular Culture* (2000).

ANDREA BACHNER is assistant professor of comparative literature and Chinese studies at the Pennsylvania State University. Her research explores comparative intersections between Sinophone, Latin American, and European cultural productions in dialogue with theories of interculturality, sexuality, and mediality. Her first book, *Beyond Signology: Alterity, Mediality, and the Sinograph* (under review), analyzes how the Chinese script has been imagined in recent decades in literature and film, visual and performance art, design, and architecture, both within Chinese cultural contexts and in different parts of the "West."

BRIAN BERNARDS is assistant professor of East Asian languages and cultures at the University of Southern California, where he specializes in modern Chinese and Southeast Asian literature and cinema and postcolonial studies. His current manuscript project examines the colonial and postcolonial formation of Nanyang, the "South Seas," as a transnational and translingual literary trope in the modern literatures of China, Taiwan, Malaysia, Singapore, and Thailand.

IGNACIO LOPEZ-CALVO is professor of Latin American literature and chair of the Graduate Group of World Cultures at UC Merced. His forthcoming *Social Spatializations and Anxieties in Latino Los Angeles's Cultural Production* focuses on the evolution of the imaging of Los Angeles as depicted in Chicano and Latina cultural production from varied theoretical perspectives. His current research examines the cultural production of settlers from China and Japan in Peru and their contribution to the formation of Peruvian national identity.

CHIEN-CHUNG CHEN is associate professor of Taiwan literature at the National Tsing-Hua University in Taiwan. His fields of research are: Taiwan literature since the colonial period, postcolonial theory, and contemporary Chinese literature. He has published widely on Taiwan and Chinese literatures. Some of his recent publications include: "Urban Modernity and New Literary Sensation (2009), "Mystic Revelation and the Return of Nativist Ethics" (2008), "Historical Narrative and Aesthetic Ideology" (2007), *A Cursed Literature: On Taiwan Literature, 1945–1949* (2007), and *Writers from Colonial Taiwan: Modernity, Localness, and Coloniality* (2004).

REY CHOW is Anne Firor Scott Professor of Literature at Duke University. A leading scholar concerned with the legacies of deconstructionist theory as well as the politics of language as a postcolonial phenomenon, Chow has authored several field-defining works on Chinese cinema, diaspora, and literature: *Sentimental Fabulations, Contemporary Chinese Films* (2007), *The Protestant Ethnic and the Spirit of Capitalism* (2002), *Ethics after Idealism* (1998), *Primitive Passions* (1995), *Writing Diaspora* (1993), and *Woman and Chinese Modernity* (1991).

JACOB EDMOND is a senior lecturer in the Department of English at the University of Otago, New Zealand. His expertise includes literary theory, literature and politics, and comparative literature. Some of his recent publications are "The Flâneur in Exile" (2010), "The Borderline Poetics of Tze Ming Mok" (2008), and "No Place like Home" (2007).

HSINYA HUANG is a professor in the Department of Foreign Languages and Literature at the National Sun Yat-Sen University in Taiwan. She is the author of "Modernity and Taiwan Aboriginal Literature" (2006), "Writing Fever, Writing Trauma" (2005), and *(De)Colonizing the Body: Disease, Empire, and (Alter)Native Medicine in Contemporary Native American Women's Writings* (2004).

HA JIN is a Chinese American writer and winner of the National Book Award and the PEN/Faulkner Award. He is the author of many works of Anglophone fiction: *A Good Fall* (2009), *A Free Life* (2007), *The Crazed* (2002), and *Waiting* (1999). Ha Jin currently teaches at Boston University.

LEO OU-FAN LEE is a renowned scholar and cultural critic. He has previously taught at Princeton University, UCLA, and Harvard University. Lee is the author of *The Romantic Generation of Modern Chinese Writers* (1973), *Voices from the Iron House* (1987), and *Shanghai Modern* (1999). His most recent publication is *City Between Worlds*, a book about Hong Kong, its colonial history as well as its postcolonial development.

PEI-YIN LIN teaches modern Chinese and Taiwan literature at Cambridge University. Her recent publications include "European Research into the Humanities in Taiwan" (2011), "An Overview of Research on Taiwan Literature in Anglo-American Academia" (2011), and "Negotiating 'Civilization': Popular Fiction from Taiwan in the 1930s."

KIM CHEW NG is an award-winning Sinophone writer from Malaysia, currently teaching at Jinan University in Taiwan. He has authored both scholarly and fictional works. Ng's most recent book on Sinophone literature and literary criticism is *Wen yu hun yu ti* [Soul, literature, and body] (2006) and his most recent nonacademic work is *Tu yu huo: Tanah Melayu* [Earth and fire: Malay land] (2005).

CARLES PRADO-FONTS is associate professor in the Department of Arts and Humanities and the director of the East Asian studies program at the Universitat Oberta de Catalunya. His research examines the tensions between the global system and contemporary Chinese and Sinophone literatures in relation to Orientalism. He has published widely in English and Chinese.

CARLOS ROJAS is associate professor of Chinese cultural studies and women's studies at Duke. His research focuses on issues of gender and visuality, corporeality and infection, nationalism, and diaspora studies. He is the author of *The Naked Gaze: Reflections on Chinese Modernity* and *The Great Wall: A Cultural History*, both published by Harvard University. He is the cotranslator, with Eileen Cheng-yin Chow, of Yu Hua's two-volume novel, *Brothers* (Pantheon, 2009). Among his current projects, he is translating Yan Lianke's novel *Shouhuo* (Grove/Atlantic Press), coediting (with Eileen Chow) the *Oxford Handbook of Chinese Cinemas* (Oxford University Press), and completing a book manuscript on Chinese discourses of corporeality and infection throughout the twentieth century.

PATRICIA SCHIAFFINI teaches at Southwestern University. She has published many articles on Sinophone Tibetan literature and Chinese literature. Her book (coedited with Lauran Hartley) *Modern Tibetan Literature and Social Change* examines the formation of modern Sinophone Tibetan literature through works of Tibetan writers living in China and abroad. She is also the president and founder of the nonprofit organization Tibetan Arts and Literature Initiative (http://www.talitibet.org), which supports projects that promote Tibetan culture and language in Tibetan areas within the People's Republic of China.

TE-HSING SHAN is a distinguished research fellow and director of the Institute of European and American Studies in Academia Sinica in Taiwan. His research areas include American literary history, Asian American literature, cultural studies, and translation studies. He has published numerous journal articles, and edited and written books on Asian American writers and important thinkers such as Edward Said. Two of his most recent monographs are: *Dialogues and Interchanges: Interviews with Contemporary Writers and Critics* (2001) and *In the Company of the Wise: Conversations with Asian American Writers and Critics* (2009).

SHUANG SHEN is assistant professor of comparative literature and Chinese at the Pennsylvania State University. Her fields of research and specialization include modern and contemporary Chinese Literature, Sinophone Literature, Asian American Literature, and postcolonial literature and theory. She is the author of *Cosmopolitan Publics: Anglophone Print Culture in Semi-Colonial Shanghai.*

SHU-MEI SHIH is professor of Asian languages and cultures and Asian American studies at UCLA. Her research fields include modern and contemporary Chinese literature, Sinophone literature, Asian American literature, critical theory, and translational studies. She has published numerous articles in noted journals such as *PMLA, Journal of Asian Studies, differences, positions, Signs, Postcolonial Studies,* and *New Formations.* She is also author of *The Lure of the Modern: Writing Modernism in Semicolonial China, 1917–1937* (2001) and *Visuality and Identity: Sinophone Articulations Across the Pacific* (2007). She currently codirects UCLA's Mellon Postdoctoral Fellowship Program in the Humanities with Françoise Lionnet. The Mellon project examines minor and minority cultures from comparative perspectives, and its project title is "Cultures in Transnational Perspective."

MIRANA MAY SZETO is assistant professor of comparative literature at the University of Hong Kong. She is completing two projects: *The Radical Itch: Cultural Politics and Its Discontents* and *Decolonizing Neoliberalism: Urban Cultural Politics in Post-1997 Hong Kong*. Her current research is on Hong Kong cultural policy and politics. Her research areas are postcolonial and feminist theory, literature and film, as well as cultural studies on China, Hong Kong, and Taiwan.

E. K. TAN is assistant professor of comparative literary and cultural studies at the State University of New York, Stony Brook. His areas of interest include Sinophone literature and film, modern and contemporary Chinese literature, Southeast Asian studies, and film theory. He has several publications in Chinese and English, and is currently completing a manuscript tentatively entitled *Translational Identity: Articulations of Chineseness in Narratives of the Nanyang Diaspora*.

KIM TONG TEE is associate professor of English and American literatures at National Sun Yat-Sen University in Taiwan. He is the author of two books in Chinese: *About Sinophone Malaysian Literature* (2009) and *South Seas Discourse: Sinophone Malaysian Literature and Cultural Attributes* (2003). He has also published several journal articles in both Chinese and English and several edited volumes.

CHIEN-HSIN TSAI is assistant professor of modern Chinese literary and cultural studies at the University of Texas at Austin. He has published essays on writers from colonial Taiwan and contemporary Chinese literature in both Chinese and English. He is the author of *Of Classics and Men: Lian Heng and the Writing of History and Poetry in Taiwan at the Turn of the Twentieth Century* (2012). He is completing a manuscript tentatively entitled *A Passage to China: Postloyalism and Writers from Colonial Taiwan, 1895–1945*. His current project is fictional autoimmunity in China since the early twentieth century.

WEI-MING TU is professor of philosophy and dean of the Institute for Advanced Humanistic Studies at Peking University, and professor and senior fellow of the Asia Center at Harvard University. He has written and edited many books in English and has published numerous articles in both Chinese and English. Select publications include: *Way, Learning, and Politics: Essays on the Confucian Intellectual* (1993); *Neo-Confucian Thought in Action: Wang Yang-ming's Youth* (1994); *China in Transformation* (1994; editor); *The Living Tree: Changing Meaning of Being Chinese Today* (1994; editor).

DAVID DER-WEI WANG is Edward C. Henderson Professor of Chinese Literature at Harvard University and director of CCK Foundation Inter-University Center for Sinological Studies. His areas of specialization include modern and contemporary Chinese literature, Sinophone literature, late Qing fiction and drama, and comparative literary theory. He is the author of *Fictional Realism in 20th Century China: Mao Dun, Lao She, Shen Congwen* (1992), *Fin-de-Siècle Splendor: Repressed Modernities of Late Qing Fiction, 1849–1911* (1997), *The Monster That Is History: Violence, History, and Fictional Writing in 20th Century China* (2004); and some of his books in Chinese include *The Making of the Modern; The Making of a Literature* (1997); *Methods of Imagining China* (1998);

After Heteroglossia: Reviews of Contemporary Chinese Fiction (2001); *Into the Millennium: 20 Contemporary Chinese Fiction Writers* (2002).

GUNGWU WANG is university professor and chairman of the East Asian Institute at the National University of Singapore. He is a leading scholar in the field of Chinese politics, nationalism, as well as migration and studies of overseas Sinophone communities. Some of his publications include *The Chinese Overseas: From Earthbound China to the Quest for Autonomy* (2000); *Don't Leave Home: Migration and the Chinese* (2001); *War, Trade, Science and Governance* (2003).

LING-CHI WANG is professor emeritus of ethnic studies at UC Berkeley. He is a founder of Chinese for Affirmative Action and the recipient of the Association for Asian American Studies Lifetime Achievement Award. He cofounded the International Society for the Study of Chinese Overseas (ISSCO) in 1992, which has since sponsored conferences at sites around the world where Chinese diaspora communities are located. He has many publications on race, migration, citizenship, and identity politics.

SAU-LING WONG is professor emerita of Ethnic Studies at UC Berkeley. Her fields of specialization are Anglophone and Sinophone Chinese American literatures, immigrant writing and film, transnational reception studies, and canon formation. She is the author of *AsianAmerica.net: Ethnicity, Nationalism, and Cyberspace* (with Rachel Lee, 2003); *A Resource Guide to Asian American Literature* (with Stephen H. Sumida, 2001); *Reading Asian American Literature: From Necessity to Extravagance* (1993).

Index

in, 397–408; in English, 22–23, 35, 117–124, 375–376, 397–408; overview, 184–185; representations of African Americans in, 375–382; Sinophone, 35

Chinese Americans, dilemmas of place and practice, 135–136, 140–141

Chinese American studies: assimilationist and loyalty paradigms, 171–175; overview, 128–129, 170–171; structure of dual domination, 175–180

Chinese Among Others (Kuhn), 5

Chinese cosmopolitanism, 65–66, 160–161, 167–168

Chinese Cuban authors, 411–413

Chinese culture. *See* cultural China

Chinese diaspora: Chinese American studies, 170–180; cultural China concept, 60–67, 127, 148–149, 151–154; and definition of Chineseness, 58–61; diasporic identities, 65–66; dilemmas of place and practice, 126; doubly diasporic condition of Sinophone Malaysian writers, 336; as having end date, 37; as misconceived category, 25–30; overseas Chinese concept, 133–135; Peranakan Chinese, 67; post-loyalism in Taiwan, 103–104; sentiments identifying Chinese persons, 67–69; in Sinophone studies, 3–6. *See also specific countries by name*

Chinese émigré writings in Taiwan, 21–22

Chinese historical figures, in Angel Island poetry, 389–392

Chinese immigrant as global figure, 397–408

Chinese language. *See* Cantonese; Mandarin; *specific entries beginning with Sinophone*

Chinese Latin American literature, 409–421

Chinese literature, 34, 49–52

Chinese Malayan writers, 304–313

Chinese nationals (*Zhongguoren*), 6

Chineseness: cultural spectrum of, 29; discrepant perspectives on, 125–129; discrimination against "inauthentic" Chinese, 55n12; essence of, 82–83; question of, and cultural China concept, 145–147; Sinophone hospitality and, 275–276; in Sinophone studies, 17–24; in study of Chinese diaspora, 26–30; Wandering Chinese, 127–128, 158–168; in works by Lin Yutang, 404–405

—as theoretical problem: "Chinese" literature, 49–52; ethnic supplement and logic of the wound, 43–47; language issue, 47–49; reimagining field, 53

—cultural China: challenge, 147–148; diaspora, 151–154; discourse, 148–151; overview, 126–127, 145; prospects, 154–155; question of Chineseness, 60–65, 145–147

—dilemmas of place and practice: Hong Kong, 137–139; identifying Chinese, 131–132; overseas Chinese, 132–134; places and practices, 134–136; San Francisco, 140–141; Shanghai, 136–137; Singapore, 139–140; toward modern Chineseness, 141–142

—saying no to: cultural China concept, 60–65; diasporic identities, 65–66; overview, 57–60; Peranakan Chinese, 67; sentiments identifying Chinese persons, 67–69

Chinese New Zealanders, 339–349

Chinese people: perceptions of Sinophone Tibetan writers, 288; in Tibetan literature, 282–285

Chinese Singaporeans. *See* Singapore

Chinese variant of Mandarin, 74–89; analyzing Sinophone, 74–79; state of language in Malaysia and Singapore, 84–86; written script and cultural identity, 79–83

—Taiwanese versus mainland language: duality/metafictionality, 87; emphasis on colloquial speech/technique, 86; grammar of spoken dialogue, 87–89; technique versus culture, 86–87

Chong Ruiz, Eustorgio A., 418

Chow, Juan, 419

Chow, Rey, 19

Chuffat Latour, Antonio, 411–412

Chu Tien-hsin, 105–106, 110

citizenship, dual literary, 121

civilization-state, China as, 150

Clan of the Sun, The (*Taiyang buluo*), Medrön, 287

class, as theme in *Beneath the Red Banner*, 359–360

Clifford, James, 65

codification of ethnicity, 48

collective level, loyalty paradigm, 173–174

colloquial speech, Taiwanese versus mainland language, 86, 87–88

colonialism: continental, 2–3, 11–12; European, 1–2; in history of Sinophone, 30–31; Hong Kong, 207–212, 219–223; serial, 4, 31; settler, 3–6, 12–13, 185–186; in Sinophone literature, 35–36; South Seas postcolonial discourse, 325–335

colonial modernity, Taiwan, 227–229, 234–236

colonial rule of Taiwan. *See* Taiwan

common culture, Singaporean. *See* multiracialism in Singapore

commonplace: Hong Kong, 212–214; in poems of Leung Ping-kwan, 219

communal level, loyalty paradigm, 173–174

communication, as theme in *Mama Looking for Her Cat*, 319–321

community: Chinese New Zealand, 340–342; Sinophone, 37–38

"Comparison of the Language in Mainland versus Taiwan Fiction, A" (Wang Anyi), 86–89

compartmentalization, of ethnic communities in Singapore, 317–319

competitions, literary, by Chinese New Zealanders, 340

complete language, 84

comprador style, 79–80

Confucius, mention of in Angel Island poetry, 390

Cong Su, 377–379

Conrad, Joseph, 120, 121

consensus model, 166–167

consumption, in poems of Leung Ping-kwan, 218

"Contemplating an Open Culture: Transcending Multiracialism" (Kuo Pao Kun), 321–323

continental colonialism, 2–3, 11–12

controversial topics, in literature by women writers in Taiwan, 258

controversy surrounding Ha Jin, 122–123

coolie trade, 383n7, 410–411

core area, Chinese, 145–146

cosmopolitanism, Chinese, 65–66, 160–161, 167–168

counter-colonialism, rainforest imaginary, 331–335

creolization: in Malaysia, 20–21; plantation, 331; of Sinitic languages, 32; Sinophone literature, 186–187

Cresciente (Waxing moon), Sui-Yun, 417

critical modernity, Taiwan, 231–232

critical position, Sinophone concept as allowing for, 38–39

Crocodile's Journal, The (*Eyu shouji*), Qiu Miaojin, 264

cross-cultural education, in *Chinatown Family*, 403

Cuba, 410–413

Cuba Commission Report, The, 410–411

cultural China: challenge, 147–148; diaspora, 151–154; discourse, 148–151; overview, 126–127, 145; prospects, 154–155; question of Chineseness, 60–67, 145–147

Cultural Enlightenment Movement, Taiwan, 231

cultural essentialism, 45–46, 58–59

cultural identity: of Singapore, 317–319, 321–323; of Sinophone Malaysians in Taiwan, 312; written script and, 79–83

culturalist sentiment, and concept of Chineseness, 67–68

cultural level, loyalty paradigm, 173–174

cultural literacy, and Sinophone Malaysian literature, 77–78

cultural nationalism, 375–376

cultural orphans, Singaporeans as, 318

cultural pluralism, 167–168

cultural production, Sinophone as places of: Chinese diaspora as misconceived category, 25–30; general discussion, 37–40; overview, 25; Sinophone, defined, 30–37

cultural return of Sinophone Malaysians in Taiwan, 312

cultural spectrum of Chineseness, 29

cultural studies, Chinese, 53

Cultural Tibet, 300

cultural workers, in Tibet, 282–283

culture: and differentialist racism, 46; open, in Singapore, 321–323; Taiwanese versus mainland language, 86–87

Dai Sijie, 122

death, in writing of Lo Yi-chin, 111

decentering the center, diasporic paradigm, 60–67

decoding, linguistic, as theme in "The Hunt" story, 298

deconstruction, 213–214

demotion, perception of by immigrants, 381

derogation of black characters in Chinese American literature, 375–382

Derrida, Jacques, 55n15, 102

Desert Island (*Huangdao*) supplement, 306

de-Sinicization, 153

desire, in writing of Lo Yi-chin, 111

Después del manglar (After the mangrove swamp), Chong Ruiz, 418

detective fiction, in colonial Taiwan, 237

determinism, ethnic, 66

"Devilish Woman" (*Monü*), Ouyang Zi, 258

diaspora, Chinese: Chinese American studies, 170–180; cultural China concept, 60–67, 127, 148–149, 151–154; and definition of Chineseness, 58–61; diasporic identities, 65–66; dilemmas of place and practice, 126;

doubly diasporic condition of Sinophone Malaysian writers, 336; as having end date, 37; as misconceived category, 25–30; overseas Chinese concept, 133–135; Peranakan Chinese, 67; post-loyalism in Taiwan, 103–104; sentiments identifying Chinese persons, 67–69; in Sinophone studies, 3–6. *See also specific countries by name*

diaspora, Jewish, 151

differentialist racism, 46, 52

direct colonial rule, 327

dirty feminism, 198

discrimination: against "inauthentic" Chinese, 55n12; towards Chinese in West, 44–45

discursive construct, Chineseness as, 60

disenchantment, in colonial Taiwanese fiction, 230

dissident political activities in Chinese America, suppression of by Taiwanese government, 182n6

diversity. *See* multiracialism in Singapore

Dong Shi, 347

Dorjé Tsering Chenaktsang (Jangbu), 289, 292n8, 295n45

doubleness of Sinophone New Zealand literature, 340–341

double peripheral condition, of Lao She, 354

Double-Three Club, 260–261

doubly colonial conditions, Sinophone Malaysian literature in Taiwan, 336

doubly diasporic conditions, Sinophone Malaysian literature in Taiwan, 336

Drinking Once in a Long Time (Sun Ta-chuan), 252–253

dual domination, structure of, 128–129, 175–180

duality, Taiwanese versus mainland language, 87

dual literary citizenship, 121

Dung Kai-cheung (Dong Qizhang), 203n11

early Republican China, Manchus in, 355–356

East Asia, 147–148

ecology, in Taiwanese indigenous literature, 249

economic success, of Hong Kong, 207–212, 214

El ciruelo de Yuan Pei Fu (Yuan Pei Fu's plum tree), Pedroso, 413

El testamento de la tormenta (Wong), 417–418

Emergent Literature movement, 305–306

emigration: from China, 4–6, 13–14; of professionals, 153–154; voluntary exile, 158–168. *See also* immigrants

émigré writings in Taiwan, 21–22, 256

empire, China as, 1–3. *See also* Qing empire

Enardecida luz (Flushed light), Óscar Wong, 420

English language: in Chinese American literature, 22–23, 35, 117–124, 375–376, 397–408; in Chinese New Zealand literature, 342, 346–347; in Hong Kong, 215; as lingua franca in Singapore, 316–318; in *Mama Looking for Her Cat*, 319–321; translation of Sinophone Tibetan literature to, 295n45; in works by Lin Yutang, 397–408

enlightenment, through Sinophone Malaysian realism, 76

enlightenment fiction, Taiwan, 229–231

environmentality, in Taiwanese indigenous literature, 249

eremitism, 158

essay (popular) writing, by women writers in Taiwan, 261

essence of "Chineseness", 82–83

essentialism, cultural, 45–46, 58–59

ethical burden, loyalism as, 98

ethnically hybrid Tibetan writers, 288–289

ethnic Chinese, 26, 133–134

ethnic determinism, 66

ethnicity: codification and management of, 48; generational effects in racialization, 375–382; Lao She as Manchu writer in modern China, 353–361; as theoretical problem, 46–47; in works by Alai, 296–303. *See also* Chineseness; multiracialism in Singapore

ethnic labeling, categorizing intellectual subject matter through, 44

ethnic studies, 6–7, 178

ethnic supplement, 43–47

ethnocentrism, 26

European empires, 1–2

exclusion: of Chinese Americans, 172–173; of Chinese immigrants from America, 386; racial, structure of dual domination, 176–180; of Sinophone peoples, 28

exclusionary approach, Sinophone as, 20

exile: perceptions of Sinophone Tibetan writers by Tibetans in, 289; as theme in Angel Island poetry, 390; voluntary, 158–168, 311–312; Wandering Chinese, 127–128, 158–168

"Exiled to English" essay (Ha Jin), 22–23

extraterritorial domination, structure of dual domination, 176–180

failure, in writing, 119–120
faith, in cultural identity, 82–83
Fang Tian, 309
Far Away (*Yuanfang*), Lo Yi-chin, 110
"Fate of Language, The" (Wang Anyi), 84–86
female writers: literary "goddesses" of 1990s in Tibet, 285–287; Taiwanese, and gendered experience of modernity, 238–239; Taiwanese indigenous, 251; Tibetan, 285–287. *See also specific writers by name*
—of Sinophone literature in Taiwan: breaching limits of anti-communist framework, 256–257; multifarious literary activism, 260–261; overview, 255–256; pluralism, identity politics, and post-national writing since 1980s, 261–264; thematic/formal innovations and popular romances, 257–259
femininity: analogy between Hong Kong and, 208–210; as theme in "The Hunt" story, 299
feminism: dirty, 198; in works by women writers in Taiwan, 261
"Fertile Town Chalk Circle, The" (Saisai), 204n13
fiction: process of translation in, 370–372
—Taiwanese, under Japanese colonial rule: colonial modernity and literary modernity, 227–229; enlightenment fiction, 229–231; modernity in popular narratives, 236–237; proletarian fiction, 231–232; with themes of *kōminka* or imperialization, 234–236; urban fiction and literary new sensationism, 232–234; women writers, 238–239
"Fin-de-siècle Splendor" (*Shijimo de huali*), Zhu Tianxin, 263
first-generation Chinese Americans, and generational effects in racialization, 375–382
"Flame Tree, The" (Leung Ping-kwan), 217–218
Flâneuse, The (*Manyou zhe*), Chu Tien-hsin, 105–106
Flying Carpet (Saisai), 194, 196
folk culture, in colonial Taiwanese fiction, 230–231
forced modernization of Taiwan by Japan, 228
foreigner status, racial triangulation, 381–382
foreign language education, and cultural identity, 79–80
formal innovations, Sinophone literature by female writers in Taiwan, 257–259
formalists, 90n6
formal level, loyalty paradigm, 173–174
form of literary genre, in Sinophone Malaysian literature, 77

fragmented self, 311
Francophone Caribbean: overview, 326; plantation thinking, 326–331; rainforest imaginary, 331–333
Francophone Quebec, 31
Francophonie, 36–37
French Polynesia, Chinese in, 134
Freud, 208–209
"Fungus of the Earth" (*Diqiu zhi mei*), Zhong Lihe, 274

"Gali Woman, A" (Zhong Lihe), 270–271
Gaonkar, Dilip Parameshwar, 398
Gao Xingjian, 364–373
gendered experience of modernity, Taiwan, 238–239
Gendün Chömpel, 282
generational continuity, in Taiwanese indigenous literature, 249–250
generational effects in racialization, 375–382
Generation of 1968, Malaysia, 309–311
genre: form of literary, in Sinophone Malaysian literature, 77; shifts in in works by Lin Yutang, 399–400
geopolitical concept, China as, 145–146
geopolitical realism, 44
Ge Yang, 286
Glissant, édouard: overview, 326; plantation thinking, 326–331; rainforest imaginary, 331–333
global figure, Chinese immigrant as, 397–408
government: Chinese, in structure of dual domination, 175–180; focus on retaining Chinese cultural identity, 171; language policy of, in Singapore, 315–319; Taiwanese, suppression of dissident political activities in Chinese America by, 182n6
grammar of spoken dialogue, Taiwanese versus mainland language, 87–89
Greater China, 71n8
Gu Cheng, 342–344
guests. *See* Sinophone hospitality
Guo Lianghui, 258
Guo Qiusheng, 232
Guoyu. See Mandarin
Gypsies, Romani, 196–197

Ha Gong, 211
Haidong Blues (*Haidong qing*), Li Yung-ping, 108–109

minority writers, 284, 288–289, 296–303. *See also specific writers by name*

minor literature, 12, 14

miscommunication, as theme in *Mama Looking for Her Cat*, 319–321

misfortune, as theme in Angel Island poetry, 390

model minority, 381, 382

"Modern Chinese Language and Literary Creation, The" (Gao Xingjian), 366

modern Chineseness: dilemmas of place and practice, 141–142; Shanghai as model of, 136–137

modern Chinese studies, 47

modernism: of female writers in Taiwan, 259, 260; overview, 90n6; in Sinophone Malaysian literature, 309–311; written script and cultural identity, 81

modernity: Chineseness and, 61–62, 147–148; of Hong Kong, 138; loyalism and, 97–98; of Singapore, 139–140

—in colonial Taiwan: ambiguous, 232–234; anti-traditional and liberated, 229–231; colonial and literary, 227–229; gendered experience of, 238–239; nationalism and colonial modernity, 234–236; nativist and critical, 231–232; in popular narratives, 236–237

modern literature, emergence of in Tibet, 282–283

Mok, Tze Ming, 346

Mongolian literature, Sinophone, 35–36

Monkey Cup (Hou bei), Chang Kuei-hsing, 327–331, 332–336

monolingualism, 10–11

Moon Clan, The (Yueqiu xingshi), Lo Yi-chin, 110

mortality, as theme in "The Hunt" story, 299

"Mt. Eden" (*Yidian shan*), 347–348

mourning, as loyalist posture, 98

Mukden, Zhong Lihe's life in, 274–276

Mulberry Green and Peach Red (Two Women of China), Hualing Nieh, 161–162

multidisciplinary, Sinophone studies as, 8–9

multifarious literary activism, female writers in Taiwan, 260–261

multilingualism: of American literature, 184; Sinophone literature, 186–187; and Sinophone Malaysian literature, 76–77; South Seas postcolonial discourse, 325–335

multimedial Sinophone, 364–373

multiple modernities of colonial Taiwan: ambiguous, 232–234; anti-traditional and liberated, 229–231; colonial and literary,

227–229; gendered experience of, 238–239; nationalism and colonial modernity, 234–236; nativist and critical, 231–232; in popular narratives, 236–237

multiracialism in Singapore: contesting, in *Mama Looking for Her Cat*, 319–321; language policies, 315–319; open culture, 321–323; overview, 315

murder suicide, of Gu Cheng, 344

Musha (Wushe), Taiwan, 107–108

musicality of language, 366

"Muwu Ming" ("Inscription About a Wooden Building"), 393

My City (Saisai), burning of, 195

My Country and My People (Lin Yutang), 402

Mykiwi, 348

Nabokov, Vladimir, 120, 121

Nanyang (Southeast Asia): Chinese in, 152–153; Han settlers in, 5–6; Peranakan Chinese in, 67. *See also specific countries by name*

Nanyang Emergent Literature movement, 305–306

Nanyang literature: local color literature, 306; nationalized, 306–307

Nanyang local color literature, 306

Napoleon, mention of in Angel Island poetry, 391–392

national characteristics, 40n1

national culture, and translation, 401

national identity politics, 365

nationalism: Chinese, 2–3, 174; cultural, 375–376; and loyalism in Taiwan, 101, 104; in Sinophone Malaysian literature, 307–309; Taiwan, 234–236; as theme in Angel Island poetry, 390–391; in works by Alai, 296–303; in works by women writers in Tibet, 286

Nationalist (KMT) regime, in Taiwan, 100–101

nationalized Nanyang literature, 306–307

national language: issues related to, 21; Mandarin as, 47–49; production of, 9–11

national literature model, 301

national unification phrase, in "The Hunt" story, 296–300

nativism, Taiwanese, 228–229, 243, 260

nativist modernity, Taiwan, 231–232

natural course in Lao She's fiction, 357

nature: in rainforest imaginary, 331–335; in Taiwanese indigenous literature, 249

Negroization of the Chinese, 376

"Never Mention It Again" (Ho Sok Fong), 39–40

New Culture Movement, 82

Philippines, Chinese in, 152–153
phonetic script, vernacular Sinitic script as, 76–77
phonic, focus on in works by Gao Xingjian, 365–373
photographer, poet as, 217
Ping Lu, 80–81, 263
place: Sinophone concept as based on, 36–37,
      58–59; in Sinophone New Zealand literature,
      343–348; in works by Lin Yutang, 405–407
—and Chineseness: Hong Kong, 137–139;
      identifying Chinese, 131–132; overseas
      Chinese, 132–134; overview, 126; places and
      practices, 134–136; San Francisco, 140–141;
      Shanghai, 136–137; Singapore, 139–140;
      toward modern Chineseness, 141–142
—of cultural production, Sinophone as: Chinese
      diaspora as misconceived category, 25–30;
      general discussion, 37–40; overview, 25;
      Sinophone, defined, 30–37
plantation system, 326–331
plasticity of Sinitic languages, 11
plays, of Gao Xingjian, 368–370
pluralism: cultural, 167–168; Sinophone literature
      by female writers in Taiwan, 261–264
Poetics of Relation (*Poétique de la relation*),
      Glissant, 326–327, 331–332
poetry: Angel Island, 385–394; Sino-Mexican,
      419–420; Sino-Nicaraguan, 419; Sino-
      Panamanian, 419; Sino-Peruvian, 416–417.
      See also specific authors by name
political connotations of loyalty, 174
politics: Chinese New Zealanders, 341; and
      economic success of Hong Kong, 207–208;
      identity, in Sinophone literature by female
      writers in Taiwan, 261–264; and loyalism
      in Taiwan, 101, 104; national identity, 365;
      rhizomatic, of Hong Kong writers, 191–202;
      in works by Lin Yutang, 402–403
polyphonic, Sinophone as, 9–10
polyscriptic, Sinophone as, 10
popular (essay) writing, by women writers in
      Taiwan, 261
popular audiences, Sinophone Malaysian realism, 76
popular narratives, modernity in Taiwanese,
      236–237
popular romances by female writers in Taiwan,
      257–259
port city, Hong Kong as, 212–214
Po-shan, Anthony Leung, 195
position, wars of, 4
positionality of Lao She, 357–359
Postcolonial Chronicles (Wong Bik-wan), 192–193

postcolonial discourse, South Seas: overview,
      325–326; plantation thinking, 326–331;
      rainforest imaginary, 331–335
postcolonial Sinophone communities, 31
post-loyalism: cessation of Taiwan to Japan,
      97–100; general discussion, 101–105; history
      of, 95–97; literary examples, 105–113; "new
      loyalists", 100–101; overview, 93–95
post-national writing by female writers in Taiwan,
      261–264
post-Tiananmen exodus of Chinese intellectuals,
      163–166
post-totalitarian systems, 167
Povinelli, Elizabeth, 398
practice, and Chineseness: Hong Kong, 137–139;
      identifying Chinese, 131–132; "overseas
      Chinese", 132–134; overview, 126; places and
      practices, 134–136; San Francisco, 140–141;
      Shanghai, 136–137; Singapore, 139–140;
      toward modern Chineseness, 141–142
prejudice: against "inauthentic" Chinese, 55n12;
      towards Chinese in West, 44–45
preservation movement, Hong Kong, 193–194
professionals, emigration of, 153–154
progression, literary, in Lao She's fiction, 357
proletarian literature: Malaysian, 305–306;
      Taiwan, 231–232
public policy, assimilationist and loyalty
      paradigms, 172–175
Punto ´e llanto (Changmarín), 419
Putonghua. See Mandarin
Pye, Lucian, 150

Qing empire: continental colonialism, 11–12; as
      empire, 1–3; loyalism in early Qing period,
      94–96; loyalism in late, 98–99; New Qing
      historians, and life of Lao She, 355
Qiong Yao, 259
Qiu Miaojin, 264, 269n38
Qiu Shizhen, 307
Quebec, Francophone, 31
Queen's Pier, Hong Kong, 194
queer writing, by women writers in Taiwan, 264

race, and concept of Chineseness, 68–70. *See also*
      multiracialism in Singapore
racial exclusion, structure of dual domination,
      176–180
racialization, generational effects in, 375–382
racialized concept of Chinese, 26–29, 133
racial triangulation, 377, 381–382

racism: differentialist, 46, 52; towards Chinese Americans, 172–173

radical women, in writing of Wong Bik-wan, 197–199

rainforest imaginary, South Seas postcolonial discourse, 331–335

"Rainforest Trilogy" (*Yulin sanbuqu*), Chang Kuei-hsing, 326

rape analogies, Hong Kong, 209–211

Razones de la voz (Reasons of the voice), Óscar Wong, 420

realism, 90n5; in colonial Taiwanese fiction, 229–230; linguistic, in Sinophone Malaysian literature, 75–76; magical, 284–285, 291; in Sinophone Malaysian literature, 309, 311; in works by women writers in Tibet, 286

reality, representation of in Sinophone Malayan literature, 76

Red Poppies (*Chen'ai luoding*), Alai, 288, 297

reductionist concept, race as, 69–70

reformist works, by women writers in Taiwan, 260

Remains of Life (*Yu sheng*), Wu He, 243–244

remigration of Chinese, 153–154

reportage fiction, in colonial Taiwan, 237

representation, in *Beneath the Red Banner*, 358

Republic of China. *See* Taiwan

resistance: to extraterritorial domination of Chinese government, 176; Sinophone subaltern, in Hong Kong literature, 197–199

returns, of Sinophone Malaysian writers, 335–336

revenge, as theme in Angel Island poetry, 391

revolutionary literature, Malaysian, 305–306

rhizomatic politics of Hong Kong writers: Sinophone rhizomatic nomadology, 199–202; Sinophone subaltern resistance, 197–199; Sinophone subaltern transnationalism, 193–197; vertical articulation, 191–193

"Road, The" (Chen Huoquan), 234

romances, popular, by female writers in Taiwan, 257–259

Romani Gypsies, 196–197

rootless generation, 159–160, 259

roots, relationship between routes and, 38

Rosa fálica (Phallic rose), Sui-Yun, 417

routes, relationship between roots and, 38

Ruan Ji, mention of in Angel Island poetry, 390

Saisai (Xi Xi): overview, 203n4; Sinophone subaltern transnationalism, 193–196; vertical articulation, 191–193

San Francisco: dilemmas of place and practice, 135–136, 140–141; modern Chineseness, 141–142

Sanliujiu xiaobao tabloid, 237

San Mao, 261

Saussy, Haun, 50

script, Sinitic: cultural literacy, 77–78; form of literary genre, 77; linguistic intuition, 78–79; linguistic realism, 75–76; multilingual environment, 76–77; overview, 10; in Sinophone Malaysian literature, 304–305; state of language in Malaysia and Singapore, 84–86; in Taiwanese indigenous literature, 245–246; Taiwanese versus mainland language, 86–89; written script and cultural identity, 79–83

"search for roots" (*xungen*) movement, 128, 163–168

"Season of Blossoms" (*Huakai shijie*), Yang Qianhe, 239

Sebo (Gsal po/Xu Mingliang), 283–285

segregation of Manchus and Han, 355–356

Sekikanki (Nishikawa Mitsuru), 235–236

self-exile, 158–168, 311–312

self-writing, 264

sensationism, literary new, 232–234

serial colonialism, in Taiwan, 4, 31

settlement of Han Chinese, 4–6

settler colonialism, 3–6, 12–13, 185–186, 327

Seven-Generation Affectionate Bonds Between Taiwan and China, The (*Qishi yinyuan zhi Taiwan-Zhongguo qingren*), Li Ang, 262

sexuality: analogy between Hong Kong and feminine, 208–210; and generational effects in racialization, 380; in works by women writers in Taiwan, 263–264

Sexual Life in Ancient China (Van Gulik), 52

shandi wenxue (mountainscape literature), 244, 245

Shandongnese, 32

Shanghai: dilemmas of place and practice, 135–137; and Hong Kong, 192–193

Shang people, loyalism of, 94

Shen Guangwen, 95–96

Shih, Annie (Shi Li'an), 347

Shih, Shu-mei, 17, 19–20, 404, 407

Shils, Edward, 166–167

Shi Shuqing, 259, 269n33

Sichuan province, 300

Silent Island (*Chenmo zhi dao*), Su Weizhen, 262–263

Silhouette/Shadow film (Gao Xingjian), 372

socialist ideas, in colonial Taiwanese fiction, 231–232

social nature of vernacular script, 77–78

social-realist style, in Sinophone Malaysian literature, 309, 311

sojourners' literature, 308

Sojourning Chinese literature, 305

solidarity, yellow-black, 376

Soul Mountain (Gao Xingjian), 370–372

South, language in. *See* Mandarin; *specific regions or countries by name*

Southeast Asia (Nanyang): Chinese in, 152–153; Han settlers in, 5–6; Peranakan Chinese in, 67. *See also specific countries by name*

"Southern Barbarian" (Saisai), 203n12

South Korea, Shandongnese in, 32

South Seas postcolonial discourse: overview, 325–326; plantation thinking, 326–331; rainforest imaginary, 331–335

Spanish, Chinese Latin American literature in, 409–421

spoken language: grammar of, Taiwanese versus mainland language, 87–89; in process of translation, 368–369

stability, fixation on, 220

standard language: Mandarin as, 47–49; production of, 9–11

Standard Mandarin. *See* Mandarin

standard script, Sinitic languages, 10. *See also* Sinitic script

state-sponsored migration and settlement of Han Chinese, 4

stereotypes, racist, 375–382

"Story of Blood, The" (*Xie de gushi*), Lin Haiyin, 257

"Story of Qi, The" (*Qi de gushi*), Lo Yi-chin, 112–113

"Strange Encounters in a Mansion" (*Haozhai qiyuan*), Lao Nan, 379–380

structure of dual domination, 128–129, 175–180

students studying abroad, 159

stylistic experiments, in works by women writers in Taiwan, 262–263

subaltern, in Hong Kong literature: charming ascetic, 199–202; resistance, 197–199; transnationalism, 193–197

subjectivity, rainforest imaginary, 331–332

success, in writing, 119–120

suffering, as theme in Angel Island poetry, 390

suicide of Gu Cheng, 344

Sui-Yun (Katie Wong Loo), 417

Sung Tze-lai, 92n25

Sun Ta-chuan, 248, 252–253

superiority, perception of by immigrants, 381–382

"Surviving History—the Past, Present, and Future of the Indigenes" (Sun Ta-chuan), 248

Su Weizhen, 262–263

Su Wu, mention of in Angel Island poetry, 390

Syaman Rapongan, 248–250

symbolic universes, cultural China concept, 148–154

Tahiti, Chinese in, 134

Taidong Hotel (*Taidong lüguan*), Zhong Lihe, 274–276

Taiwan: Chinese émigré writings in, 21–22; cultural China concept, 148–151; efforts to suppress dissident political activities in Chinese America, 182n6; history of serial colonialism, 31; loyalty paradigm, 171–175; overseas Chinese concept, 132–133; settler colonialism in, 4, 6, 12–13; Sinophone hospitality, 270–272, 272–274, 274–277, 277–279; Sinophone indigenous literature of, 188, 242–253, 268n29; Sinophone literature by female writers in, 255–256, 256–257, 257–259, 260–261, 261–264; Sinophone literature from, 187–188; Sinophone Malaysian writers in, 311–313, 325–337

—fiction under Japanese colonial rule: colonial modernity and literary modernity, 227–229; enlightenment fiction, 229–231; modernity in popular narratives, 236–237; overview, 187; proletarian fiction, 231–232; with themes of *kōminka* or imperialization, 234–236; urban fiction and literary new sensationism, 232–234; women writers, 238–239

—post-loyalism in: cessation of Taiwan to Japan, 97–100; general discussion, 101–105; history of, 95; literary examples, 105–113; "new loyalists", 100–101; overview, 93–95

Taiwanese language, 86–89, 266n5

Tan Swie Hian, 310

Tao tribe, Taiwan, 248–250

TAR (Tibet Autonomous Region): overview, 292n3; Sinophone literature outside of, 287–288; Sinophone literature within, 283–287

Tashi Dawa (Zhaxi Dawa/Zhang Niansheng), 283–285, 289

technique: versus culture, Taiwanese versus mainland language, 86–87; emphasis on, Taiwanese versus mainland language, 86, 89

GPSR Authorized Representative: Easy Access System Europe, Mustamäe tee
50, 10621 Tallinn, Estonia, gpsr.requests@easproject.com